The New Century Handbook of

GREEK MYTHOLOGY AND LEGEND

The New Century Handbook of

GREEK MYTHOLOGY AND LEGEND

edited by

Catherine B. Avery

APPLETON-CENTURY-CROFTS
Educational Division
MEREDITH CORPORATION
NEW YORK

Selected from *The New Century Classical Handbook,*
edited by Catherine B. Avery
Copyright © 1962 by
APPLETON-CENTURY-CROFTS, INC.

72   73   74   75   76/10   9   8   7   6   5   4   3   2   1 ,

Library of Congress Catalog Card Number:
75-183796

PRINTED IN THE UNITED STATES OF AMERICA
390-66946-6

The New Century Handbook of

GREEK MYTHOLOGY AND LEGEND

Preface

The Greeks described the creation, wonder, and terror of their world in a collection of marvelously inventive stories. The stories — the myths — explained the inexplicable, often through the creation of a theogony of capricious, wilful, omnipotent Olympian gods and other immortals who gloried in the exercise of their powers, and used them to interfere with the lives of men and with each other. Many of the myths have to do with the ways of the gods. Others deal with the vagaries of mankind, which the Greeks thoroughly understood (no one has had a really new idea of the variations of which the human personality is capable since). Certain themes recur in the myths; among them, that a swift and certain fate overtakes the man of arrogant pride, as it does also men who defy, resist, or question the gods; that one should beware the rash promise or vow; and that personal honor in all its aspects is to be sought above all else. The ideas expressed in the Greek myths and legends have influenced western thought for over two thousand years.

Poets and mythographers preserved and embroidered the myths and legends. Homer, for example, gives us a great epic on a legendary war — legendary because there was a basis in fact for his epic on the Trojan War. In his long poem he makes reference to myths (pure creations of the imagination) that would have been familiar to those who heard the verses of his epic sung. The poets and mythographers, however, did not always agree on the details of the stories they preserved. Homer does not mention the horrors in the story of the family of Atreus, from whom two of his chieftains, Agamemnon and Menelaus, sprang. Pindar is shocked by the version of the story of Pelops that would have had the gods feasting on human flesh, and wrote his own version. The poets interpreted the age-old myths to suit their needs and did not seem to feel that such interpretations invalidated the old ideas. The mythographers scrupulously recorded all the variations of which they were aware.

In 1962 Appleton-Century-Crofts published *The New Century Classical Handbook*. That book of 1162 pages includes entries on a wide variety of subjects, including mythology. In the belief that a smaller book, devoted to mythological and legendary figures alone, would be useful as well as instructive and entertaining, the entries on the following pages have been selected from the larger book. Arranged in alphabetical order, each entry in *The New Century Handbook of Greek Mythology and Legend* deals with a separate mythological or legendary figure. Articles signed with the initials JJ were prepared by the late Jotham Johnson, Head of the Department of Classics, New York University, who served as Editorial Consultant for *The New Century Classical Handbook*. Those signed with the initials AH and PM were prepared by Professors Abraham Holtz and Philip Mayerson of New York University.

For the ancient Greeks, the activities of the immortals and of the characters in their stories were as real as yesterday. That is the way they have been presented in *The New Century Handbook of Greek Mythology and Legend*.

Catherine B. Avery

—A—

Abantes (a̯-ban′tēz). According to Homer *(Iliad)*, a warlike tribe of Euboea, who allied themselves with the Greeks in the Trojan War. They were fierce fighters, and it was their custom to shave the hair from the fore parts of their heads to prevent their enemies from grasping the forelock in close combat. Theseus emulated their practice. The Abantes are also named in legend as a people of Epirus among whom the Colchians, frustrated in their attempt to capture Jason and Medea, settled rather than return to Colchis and face the wrath of Aeëtes.

Abaris (ab′a̯-ris). [Called *the Hyperborean.*] Mythical Greek sage, assigned by Pindar to the 6th century B.C., by Eusebius to the 7th. According to these writers and to Herodotus, Apollo gave him a magic arrow on which he traveled and which he gave to Pythagoras in exchange for instruction in the latter's philosophy. He was believed to have worked miraculous cures, and was widely invoked by the ancient Greeks in oracles and charms.

Abas (ä′ba̯s). A legendary companion of Diomedes. He accompanied Diomedes on his voyage to Italy after the Trojan War. Aphrodite continued to persecute Diomedes because he had wounded her during the war. She sent storms at sea and war on land to harass him. Abas and others were transformed into birds by Aphrodite because a companion, Acmon, defied her to prevent Diomedes' company from reaching sanctuary in Italy.

Academus (ak-a̯-dē′mus). A legendary Arcadian who had moved to Athens. When the Dioscuri came to Attica in

fat, fāte, fär, fåll, a̯sk, fãre; net, mē, hėr; pin, pīne; not, nōte, möve, nôr; up, lūte, pu̇ll; oi, oil; ou out; (lightened) ẹlect, agọny, ūnite; (obscured) erra̯nt, arde̯nt, acto̯r; ch, chip; g, go; th, thin; ᴛʜ, then; y, you; (variable) ḏ as d or j, ṣ as s or sh, ṭ as t or ch, ẓ as z or zh.

search of their sister Helen who had been kidnaped by Theseus, Academus is said to have revealed to them her hiding place in Aphidna. As a reward for his services on this occasion the Spartans ever after treated him with great honor and courtesy. After his death, when the Spartans warred on Athens they spared his estate on the Cephissus River. The estate of Academus with its pleasant garden came to be used as a meeting place for philosophers and became known as the Academia or Academy.

Achaeus (a̧-kē'us). Legendary son of Xuthus and Creusa. He fled with his father from Athens to Aegialus in the Peloponnesus. Two of the sons of Achaeus married two daughters of Danaus, settled in Argos and Lacedaemon and their descendants became known as Achaeans. They later invaded Aegialus, took over the region and named it Achaea. Achaeus left Aegialus and went to Thessaly where he won back his father's lands, and named the region Achaea and the people Achaeans for himself. Thus there were two groups in Greece known as Achaeans, those in Achaea in the Peloponnesus, and those in Thessaly in the region of Phthia. The name *Achaean* was also sometimes applied as a collective name for all the Greeks.

Achelous (ak-ȩ-lō'us). The river-god of the Achelous River in NW Greece which formed part of the boundary between Aetolia and Acarnania. He was the oldest of the 3000 sons of Oceanus and Tethys, and as such was worshiped throughout Greece and in the colonies. His name in religious rites became synonymous for any stream, and sacrifices to Achelous were always prescribed along with the prophecies given out by the oracle of Dodona. He had the power to assume three forms: that of a man with a bull's head, that of a speckled serpent, and that of a bull. Achelous was one of many who courted Deianira, supposed daughter of Oeneus of Calydon. When Heracles also came wooing her, all her other suitors left the field to him and Achelous. Achelous claimed her on the ground that he was a deity. Heracles boasted that he could give her Zeus for a father-in-law. To this Achelous retorted that if it were so, which he doubted, then Alcmene, Heracles' mother, was an adulteress. Heracles, enraged at this slur on his mother's honor, proposed that he and Achelous wrestle for the hand of Deianira, the winner to become her husband. Achelous wrestled first in his form as a bull-headed man, and Heracles succeeded in throwing Achelous. The river-god, finding himself pinned by the mighty Heracles, transformed himself into a serpent. But Heracles laughed, told him he had strangled serpents in his cradle, and grasped Achelous firmly in his fists. Achelous now assumed the shape of a bull. Heracles seized him by the horns and hurled him to the ground, thus defeating him in all his forms. One of Achelous' horns was broken off in his fall and, according to some, naiads took it and filled it with fruits. It became the Cornucopia (Horn of Plenty), and was always miraculously filled. To cover the spot where the horn had been Achelous ever after wore a wreath of river reeds. Achelous was said to have been the father of Pirene, who was transformed into a fountain. He was also said by some to have been the father, by the muse Terpsichore, of the Sirens. He fell in love with Perimele, daughter of Hippodamas, and ravished her. Her father hurled her into the sea but Achelous caught her and held her up. He prayed that she might be given a resting place or that she herself would be changed into such a place. She was transformed into an island, one of the Echinades islands which lie at the mouth of the Achelous River. Achelous purified Alcmaeon for the murder of his mother and gave his daughter Callirrhoë to Alcmaeon for a wife.

Acheron (ak′e̩-ron). In Greek mythology, one of the five rivers surrounding Hades, the river of woe. The souls of the dead had to bathe in it or cross it. Later it became synonymous with the lower world in general.

Achilles (a̩-kil′ēz). In Greek legend, a son of Peleus (for this reason he was also called Pelides) and the sea-goddess Thetis. He was the grandson of Aeacus (for this reason he was also known as Aeacides), and thus a descendant of Zeus. He was the youngest of seven sons born to Peleus and Thetis. His mother, wishing to immortalize her sons, one by one placed his older brothers in the flames to destroy their mortal parts and sent the immortal remains to Olympus. When Achilles was born she anointed him with ambrosia by day and placed him in the fire at night to burn away his mortal parts. Peleus interrupted her as she was performing this ritual and cried out in terror. She dropped her infant and fled back to the sea in anger. Some say Achilles' entire body had been made invulnerable by the ministrations of his

(obscured) errant, ardent, actor; ch, chip; g, go; th, thin; ᵮH, then; y, you; (variable) d̩ as d or j, s̩ as s or sh, t̩ as t or ch, z̩ as z or zͪh.

mother, except for one ankle-bone which had been scorched but not burned. Peleus replaced the ankle-bone with one taken from the giant Damysus. Others say Thetis rendered her son invulnerable by dipping him in the Styx. The ankle by which she held him in the water was his only vulnerable spot. When Thetis disappeared into the sea, Peleus entrusted his infant son to the care of Chiron, the centaur. The kindly centaur reared him on Mount Pelion, feeding him on the entrails of bears and lions to give him courage and, some say, on honey and the marrow of fawns to give him swiftness of foot. He learned to ride, hunt, play on the lyre, and to master the arts of healing. He was taught how to sing by the muse Calliope. He was so swift of foot and had such courage that at the age of six he overtook and subdued wild animals and dragged them back to Chiron's cave. Although Thetis had left the house of Peleus she did not lose interest in her son, of whom it had been predicted that he would be greater than his father. (It was because of this prophecy that Zeus gave up his pursuit of Thetis and married her to Peleus.) She was a sea-goddess and had the gift of prophecy. When the Greeks massed to sail to Troy to recover Helen, Thetis knew that if Achilles accompanied them he would gain glory and die young. She sent him to the court of Lycomedes on the island of Scyrus to save him from this fate. There he was dressed as a girl and lived among the women, and there he fathered Neoptolemus on Deidamia, the daughter of Lycomedes.

The Greeks were informed by a seer that they could not overcome the Trojans without the aid of Achilles. Odysseus, Nestor, and Ajax (as some say), the cousin and friend of Achilles, therefore went to Scyrus to fetch him. Some say Odysseus brought jewels, girdles, and other things of interest to ladies. Lycomedes welcomed these envoys but disclaimed all knowledge of Achilles. Odysseus, ever ready with a scheme, asked permission to make gifts to the ladies of the court. He displayed his rich gifts, among which were included a shield and a spear. As the ladies hovered over the treasures, a loud trumpet blast was heard. One of the maidens instantly seized the shield and spear, and prepared to rush into battle. Others say Odysseus came to Scyrus disguised as a merchant and that among his wares he included a few weapons. Achilles revealed himself by lovingly han-

fat, fāte, fär, fåll, àsk, fâre; net, mē, hėr; pin, pīne; not, nōte, möve, nôr; up, lūte, pùll; oi, oil; ou out; (lightened) ĕlect, agŏny, ūnite;

dling the weapons. In either case, Achilles revealed himself to the triumphant Odysseus and promised to lead his Myrmidons against Troy. But others say these are just tales to exalt the ingenuity of Odysseus. According to their accounts, Achilles readily agreed to march against Troy when Nestor and Odysseus came to his father's court in Phthia. Peleus armed him with an ashen spear and golden armor, and gave him immortal horses, and sent him off with Phoenix, his trusted friend and tutor. Patroclus, his beloved friend, and his Myrmidon warriors also accompanied him.

Achilles was the handsomest, the swiftest, the strongest, and the bravest of the Greeks who went to Troy. The mere sight of him struck terror into the hearts of his enemies. Accompanied by Patroclus, Phoenix, and the Myrmidons, he sailed from Aulis with the other Greeks. Under the impression that it was the Troad, they attacked the coasts of Asia Minor. Achilles and Patroclus attacked Mysia. Telephus, king of Mysia, bravely drove the Greeks back but in pursuing them he tripped over a vine and was wounded by Achilles' spear. After the Greeks left Asia Minor, their fleet was scattered by a storm and they returned separately to their homelands. Achilles went back to Scyrus and married Deidamia. At the second gathering at Aulis, the Greeks were windbound. Calchas the seer said that only the sacrifice of Iphigenia, Agamemnon's daughter, would appease Artemis and secure favorable winds. In order to secure the presence of Iphigenia, Agamemnon told his wife Clytemnestra that Iphigenia was to be married to Achilles. Achilles was furious when he learned that his name had been used to bring Iphigenia to Aulis so that she could be sacrificed. He offered to defend her, but Iphigenia readily consented to be sacrificed and, the rites having been performed, favorable winds sprang up and the Greeks put to sea again. They sailed to the island of Tenedos near the Troad. Achilles had been warned by his mother that if he killed a son of Apollo, he would die by Apollo's hand, and he took Mnemon, a servant, with him to remind him not to attack the sons of Apollo. When the Greeks neared Tenedos, King Tenes, said to be a son of Apollo, refused them permission to land and hurled huge stones at their ships. Achilles impulsively leaped into the sea, swam ashore, and killed Tenes. Too late he remembered his mother's warning and then killed Mne-

(obscured) errᶏnt, ardᶒnt, actǫr; ch, chip; g, go; th, thin; ŦH, then; y, you;
(variable) ḏ as d or j, ş as s or sh, ṯ as t or ch, ᶎ as z or zh.

mon for failing to remind him of it. But some say Achilles
killed Tenes because of a quarrel that arose over Tenes'
sister Hemithea. An embassy which the Greeks sent to Troy
from Tenedos to demand the restoration of Helen was unsuccessful. They now sailed past the headland of Sigeum
and beached their ships before Troy. There was a prophecy
that the first to land at Troy would be the first to die. For
this reason Achilles did not leap ashore immediately; some
say he was the second and some say the last to land. When
he did reach shore, he was attacked by Cycnus, a son of
Poseidon who had been rendered invulnerable to sword,
spear, and arrow. Cycnus had killed many Greeks before he
confronted Achilles. Achilles hurled his spear at him only to
see it bounce harmlessly aside. His sword also being ineffec-
tive, Achilles battered Cycnus about the head with his shield
until he fell, whereupon Achilles strangled him with the
straps of his own helmet. But some say Achilles killed Cycnus on Tenedos by crushing his head with a stone. It is said
that after landing at Troy, he found Troilus, said by some
to be a son of Apollo. He was in the sanctuary of Thymbraean Apollo, which was in neutral territory, when Achilles
came upon him and killed him. He captured Lycaon, son of
Priam, and sold him as a slave. But Lycaon was ransomed
and returned to Troy where, 12 days later, he again fell into
the hands of Achilles, who killed him. He made a raid on the
cattle of Aeneas. Until this time Aeneas had been neutral in
the struggle, but because of this raid, in which he barely
escaped capture, Aeneas went over to the side of the Trojans. In raids which Achilles made in Asia Minor and the
Troad, he seized and sacked 11 inland cities and 12 seacoast
towns, among them: Lesbos, Phocaea, Colophon, Smyrna,
Clazomenae, Cyme, Aegialus, Tenos, Adramyttium, Side,
Endium, Linnaeum, Colone, Hypoplacian, Thebes, Lyrnessus, Antandrus, and others. To Agamemnon, as commander
of the expedition, he handed over the lion's share of the
booty from these conquests. For himself, he kept Briseis,
wife of Mynes of Lyrnessus whom he had slain and whose
kingdom he had destroyed. Briseis was the cause of the
famous quarrel between Achilles and Agamemnon. The latter, on being forced to relinquish his captive Chryseis to
placate Apollo, demanded Briseis from Achilles in her place.
As Agamemnon was the commander Achilles had no choice

fat, fāte, fär, fâll, àsk, fāre; net, mē, hèr; pin, pīne; not, nōte, mŏve,
nôr; up, lūte, pŭll; oi, oil; ou out; (lightened) ĕlect, agǫny, ūnite;

but to obey and yield Briseis whom he had come to love dearly. But to punish Agamemnon and the Greeks, Achilles withdrew from the fighting, taking Patroclus and his Myrmidons with him. He persuaded his mother to ask Zeus to make the Greeks suffer at the hands of the Trojans, to atone for the arrogance of Agamemnon and the injuries inflicted by him. Agamemnon soon regretted his rash action in arousing the ire of Achilles. As the Greeks were battered by the Trojans, he sent an embassy to Achilles to try to persuade him to return to the war. The ambassadors offered to restore Briseis, to give Achilles any one of several rich cities, and also one of the daughters of Agamemnon for his wife. Achilles rejected their offers, saying that all Agamemnon's proffered gifts he could acquire, but the soul of a man is never won by pillage or capture. Agamemnon, Achilles said, could not soothe his injured spirit with bribes. He threatened to take his ships and his men and go home; he remembered his mother's prophecy that if he fought at Troy he would gain everlasting fame but would die young. On the other hand if he returned to his homeland he would enjoy a long life, but one without glory. The disasters which overtook the Greeks when they no longer had the irresistible aid of Achilles, the death of Patroclus, and Achilles' return to the battle, are described in the *Iliad.* After Achilles had avenged the death of Patroclus by slaying Hector, whose body he shamefully mistreated until it was ransomed by Priam, he buried Patroclus and remained in his tent, mourning his loss with his dear friend and cousin, Telamonian Ajax. Ajax heard the clamor of battle as it increased to a roar and roused Achilles. They sped to the battle and found that Penthesilea the Amazon had come to the aid of the Trojans, boasting that she would kill Achilles. Fighting with glorious valor, she had driven the Greeks back to their ships. Achilles sought her out and, mocking her for her daring, he slew her. He removed the helmet from his fallen foe and saw her young face, lovely as a sunrise even in death. Instantly he fell in love with her beauty and was pierced with wild regret for her death. Thersites, the ugliest man of the Greek expedition, sneered at him for his tears over his dead enemy. Achilles flew at him in a rage and killed him. Odysseus took Achilles to the island of Lesbos where, after he had sacrificed to Apollo, Artemis, and Leto, he was purified for the

(obscured) errạnt, ardẹnt, actọr; ch, chip; g, go; th, thin; ᵺн, then; y, you; (variable) ḍ as d or j, ş as s or sh, ṭ as t or ch, ẓ as z or zh.

murder. Memnon, the son of Eos, next came to aid the
Trojans. He and Achilles met in combat. Each boasted of his
immortal forbears; each swore to kill the other. But Memnon's fate, clad in black, came to his side, and after a glorious struggle, Achilles slew him. Hector, dying before the
Scaean gate, had prophesied that Achilles would die at the
hands of a god and a hero. Other omens, oracles, and
prophecies made it plain that Achilles would not survive the
war. Apollo meant to avenge the deaths of Troilus and
Tenes. Poseidon resolved to avenge the death of his son
Cycnus. Achilles' hour had now come. Paris directed an
arrow at him as he fought before the Scaean gate and
pierced his ankle, his only vulnerable spot. Some say Apollo
guided the arrow of Paris, and some say the god shot it
himself, disguised as Paris. Achilles drew the arrow out of
his foot and flung it from him; it was instantly sped back to
Apollo. Achilles wrathfully demanded to know who shot
him. Glaring and warlike to the last moment, he grasped his
spear, hurled it, and slew one more Trojan before he expired. Telamonian Ajax lifted his body and protected it,
though besieged on all sides by the Trojans. All day the
battle raged for possession of Achilles' body, but Ajax stood
firm, and succeeded in carrying it back to the ships. Then
Zeus sent a great storm to end the fight. However, others say
Achilles died in quite another way. They say he saw Polyxena, daughter of Priam, as she stood on the walls of Troy
casting down rings and bracelets to make up the ransom for
Hector's body, and that Achilles fell in love with her. He
secretly entered into negotiations with Priam, who promised
to give him Polyxena if he would persuade the Greeks to
raise the siege of Troy. When Achilles went alone and unarmed to the sanctuary of Thymbraean Apollo to confirm
the negotiations, he was treacherously slain by Deïphobus.
Or, as some say, Paris shot him from ambush when Achilles
went to the sanctuary to ratify the treaty of marriage with
Polyxena. On the death of Achilles, Thetis rose with a great
cry from the sea. Accompanied by her Nereids, she came to
mourn her son. The Muses also grieved. Thetis commanded
the Greeks, grievously wounded by his loss, to hold funeral
games in his honor, and to award his armor, which Hephaestus had made for him at her request, to the bravest of the
Greeks. His ashes, along with those of his beloved friends

fat, fāte, fär, fåll, ȧsk, fāre; net, mē, hėr; pin, pīne; not, nōte, möve,
nôr; up, lūte, pûll; oi, oil; ou out; (lightened) ẹlect, agǫny, ūnite;

Patroclus and Antilochus, were placed in a golden urn fashioned by Hephaestus, and buried on the headland of Sigeum. Thetis took his spirit to Leuce, an island off the mouths of the Ister which was given to Achilles by Poseidon. There, according to some accounts, he married Helen and lived happily. Travelers who sailed near the island said they could hear the voices of Achilles and his friends across the water as they recited the verses of Homer which extolled their own exploits, accompanying themselves on the lyre as they sang. But some say Achilles married Medea and went to live in the Isles of the Blest. Homer, however, says he went to Tartarus, and when Odysseus visited the Underworld on his way home from Troy, he saw Achilles striding unhappily about the Fields of Asphodel, bitterly lamenting his fate, and declaring that he would far rather be a live slave than a dead hero. The women of Elis honored Achilles with funeral rites at the opening of the Olympic Festival, and the Thessalians sacrificed to him annually. He was honored and worshiped at many places, the most revered of his shrines being his tomb on the Hellespont.

Acis   (ā'sis). In classical legend, a beautiful Sicilian youth, the son of Faunus and the sea-nymph Symaethis. He was beloved by Galatea and was slain by the Cyclops Polyhemus, his unsuccessful rival. Galatea transformed the blood of his crushed body into a river which bore his name.

Acrisius   (a̱-kris'i-us). In classical legend, a son of Abas and Aglaia, and the great-grandson of Danaus. He was the twin of Proetus with whom he struggled in his mother's womb and with whom he was destined to struggle all his life. Their father, king of Argos, left his kingdom to his twin sons with instructions that they should rule alternately. But Acrisius refused to give up the throne when it was Proetus' turn to rule, and drove him out of the kingdom. Proetus fled to Iobates in Lycia. He later returned with reinforcements supplied him by Iobates and waged war on Acrisius. The battle was indecisive and the brothers decided to divide the kingdom between them: Acrisius took Argos and Proetus became ruler of Tiryns. Acrisius' wife Aganippe, or as some say, Eurydice, bore him a daughter, Danaë. Acrisius, who wanted a son, consulted an oracle and was told that he would have no sons and that he would meet his death at the hands of Danaë's son. To prevent the fulfillment of the

(obscured) errạnt, ardẹnt, actọr; ch, chip; g, go; th, thin; ₮H, then; y, you;
(variable) ḍ as d or j, ṣ as s or sh, ṭ as t or ch, z̧ as z or zh.

oracle, Acrisius confined Danaë in a prison with bronze doors. Zeus, however, came to Danaë in a shower of gold and she bore him a son, Perseus. Acrisius, on learning of this, doubted the paternity of his grandson; nevertheless, he wanted to destroy him. Reluctant to kill his own daughter and her son, he locked them in a chest and set them adrift on the sea. The chest was washed ashore on Seriphus, and Danaë and Perseus were saved. Perseus grew to manhood and carried out his mission to secure the head of Medusa. Acrisius learned of his exploits and, mindful of the oracle, fled from Argos to Larissa. Perseus, unaware that his grandfather was there, also went to Larissa to take part in funeral games. In the discus-throwing contest his discus was carried out of its course by the wind or by fate. It struck and killed Acrisius who was standing as a spectator, unaware of the fact that his grandson was one of the contestants. Thus the oracle concerning the death of Acrisius was fulfilled. He was buried in the temple of Athena on the acropolis of Larissa.

ACTAEON BEING TORN TO PIECES BY HIS HOUNDS
Red-figured Greek crater, Pan Painter, 475–450 B.C.
Museum of Fine Arts, Boston

Actaeon (ak-tē′on). In mythology, a son of Aristaeus and Autonoë, daughter of Cadmus. He lived in Orchomenus.

fat, fāte, fär, fâll, àsk, fâre; net, mē, hèr; pin, pīne; not, nōte, möve, nôr; up, lūte, pùll; oi, oil; ou out; (lightened) ĕlect, agŏny, ūnite;

Weary one day from hunting, he sought rest in a grove which, unknown to him, was sacred to Artemis. As he wandered through the grove he inadvertently came on the spring where Artemis and her nymphs were bathing. To punish him because, through no fault of his, he had seen the goddess in her bath, Artemis splashed water in his face and transformed him into a stag. In his new form Actaeon fled. His own hounds, which some say were the Telchines that had fled from Rhodes, picked up the scent of the stag and gave chase. Overtaking him at last, they tore their former master to pieces.

Actis (ak'tis). In mythology, one of the six sons of Rhode and Helius. Banished from Rhodes for killing his brother, he went to Egypt and founded the city of Heliopolis. There, inspired by Helius, he taught the Egyptians astrology. The Colossus of Rhodes was built in his honor.

Admetus (ad-mē'tus). A legendary king of Pherae in Thessaly. He was a son of Pheres. He joined in the Calydonian Hunt and was also a member of the expedition of the Argonauts. When he returned from that expedition, Apollo was sent to labor for him for one year as a punishment for killing the Cyclopes. Apollo served him well and was his good friend. He helped Admetus to yoke a lion and a boar to a chariot, a condition which Pelias set for the suitors of his daughter, Alcestis, and thus Admetus won Alcestis for his bride. Admetus forgot to sacrifice to Artemis on the wedding day and in anger the goddess punished him. Apollo interceded and won her forgiveness, and also won a promise from Artemis that when Death came for Admetus he could win a reprieve on condition that some one else could be found to take his place. Too soon, Hermes came to take Admetus to the Underworld. Apollo made the Fates drunk so that they did not immediately snip the thread of his life. This gave Admetus time to search for a substitute. He asked his father and mother but, though very aged, they loved life and neither would give it up for Admetus. Only Alcestis, his devoted wife, was willing to cut short her life that Admetus might prolong his: she went with Hermes to the Underworld in his place. Admetus, grieving at her loss, let her go.

Adonis (ạ-don'is, ạ-dō'nis). In mythology, a son of Myrrha and Cinyras, her own father. Cinyras had not realized that the young girl with whom he was consorting was his own daughter. When he learned the truth, he was horrified and

(obscured) errạnt, ardẹnt, actọr; ch, chip; g, go; th, thin; ₮ʜ, then; y, you;
(variable) ḍ as d or j, ṣ as s or sh, ṭ as t or ch, ẓ as z or zh.

sought to kill her. She fled and was transformed into a myrrh tree. When it was time for her child to be born the birth goddess Lucina split the trunk of the tree and Adonis tumbled out. He was cared for by nymphs and grew to be a young man of surpassing beauty. According to another account, Aphrodite, repenting that she had caused Myrrha to fall in love with her father, saved the infant Adonis when he was born from the trunk of the tree and hid him in a chest which she gave to Persephone to guard, with admonitions not to look inside the chest. Persephone disobeyed her command and was so struck by the beauty of the child in the chest that she brought him up herself, and refused to give him up when Aphrodite demanded him. The muse Calliope, who was called on to judge the dispute between Aphrodite and Persephone, decided that Adonis, now a handsome youth and the lover of both, should spend a third of the year with Aphrodite, a third with Persephone, and should have a third for himself. But Aphrodite, with the aid of the magic girdle of love, persuaded him to spend most of his time with her thus violating the terms of the decision. She bore him a son Golgos and a daughter Beroë. Although she cautioned Adonis to avoid ferocious beasts when he followed his favorite pastime of hunting, he could not resist the thrill of the chase. His hunting dogs raised a wild boar from its lair and Adonis eagerly gave chase. He shot at the boar but his arrow only wounded and maddened the animal. It turned savagely on Adonis and tore him to pieces. A blood-red flower sprang from the drops of his blood that fell to the earth, the anemone, which flourishes briefly. Its handsome blossom grows swiftly to beauty and as rapidly dies, even as Adonis died in the full bloom of youth. Some say it was Ares in the shape of a boar who destroyed him, because he was jealous of Aphrodite's love for him. Aphrodite was heartbroken at the death of her youthful lover. She appealed to Zeus and persuaded him to allow Adonis to spend the summer months of the year with her. The rest of the time his shade lingers in the Underworld. Adonis has been considered by some scholars to have been originally an oriental deity of nature, typifying the withering of nature in winter and its revival in summer. By way of Asia Minor his cult came first to Greece, then passed to Egypt, and thence finally was brought to Rome. The yearly festival of Adonis in the spring

---

fat, fāte, fär, fåll, àsk, fāre; net, mē, hėr; pin, pīne; not, nōte, möve, nôr; up, lūte, púll; oi, oil; ou out; (lightened) ęlect, agǫny, ūnite;

was a special favorite with women. In the Old Testament reference is made to the weeping of the women over Tammuz, the Babylonian equivalent of Adonis (Ezek. viii. 14), a name which may be a form of the Semitic *'adon,* "lord."

Adrastea (ad-ras-tē'a) or **Adrastia** (ad-ras-tī'a). A Cretan nymph, daughter of Melisseus, to whom Rhea entrusted the infant Zeus to be reared in the Dictaean grotto. According to some accounts, Zeus rewarded her by giving her the horn of the goat Amalthea, which thereafter was filled with whatever food or drink its possessor desired, and became known as the "Cornucopia" or "Horn of Plenty."

Adrastus (a-dras'tus). [Also: *Adrastos.*] A mythical grandson of Bias. He was a king of Argos. His two daughters Aegia and Deïpyle had so many powerful suitors that Adrastus hesitated to choose among them for fear the disappointed suitors would become his enemies. He consulted the oracle at Delphi and was told to yoke a boar and a lion that fought in his palace. Shortly thereafter Tydeus, son of Oeneus of Calydon, and Polynices, son of Oedipus of Thebes, came to Argos. When these two exiles began to quarrel in his palace Adrastus remembered the oracle, for the emblem of Calydon is a boar, and the emblem of Thebes is a lion. (Some say Tydeus was clad in a boar's hide and Polynices in a lion's skin.) He pacified their quarrel and gave his daughter Aegia to Polynices and his daughter Deïpyle to Tydeus. Polynices had been refused the throne of Thebes when it was his turn to rule, by his brother Eteocles. Tydeus had been banished from Calydon for a murder. Adrastus promised to restore them both to their lands. He called his chieftains together for a march against Thebes to restore Polynices. The Seven against Thebes who assembled were Adrastus, Capaneus, Hippomedon, Parthenopaeus, Amphiaraus, Polynices, and Tydeus. Amphiaraus, brother-in-law of Adrastus, was unwilling to go. He was a seer and foresaw disaster. But some years previously he had quarreled with Adrastus and driven him to Sicyon. Their quarrel was later resolved and Amphiaraus married Eriphyle, the sister of Adrastus, who made them both promise that in any future dispute they would abide by her decision. In this case, bribed by Polynices, she decided that Amphiaraus should be one of the expedition. Amphiaraus yielded to her decision though he knew it would cause his death. In the war against Thebes, the Seven met

(obscured) errant, ardent, actor; ch, chip; g, go; th, thin; ŦH, then; y, you;
(variable) ḍ as d or j, ṣ as s or sh, ṭ as t or ch, ẓ as z or zh.

with disaster, as Amphiaraus had foreseen. Every one of the champions was killed except Adrastus who escaped on the winged horse Arion, which had been given to him by Heracles. Some years later the sons of the Seven against Thebes, known as the Epigoni, again attacked Thebes to avenge their fathers. Aegialeus, the son of Adrastus, was among the Epigoni and was killed in the attack. When Adrastus learned of his death he died of grief. But some say Adrastus accompanied the Epigoni to Thebes and died of grief over his son's death at Megara, on his way home from the successful attack. He was worshiped as a hero at Athens, Sicyon, and Megara.

Aeaea (ē-ē′a̠). A name applied to two homes of the enchantress Circe. One was an alder-fringed island at the head of the Adriatic Sea near the mouth of the Po River. It is described as gloomy and heavily wooded, but on the other hand was sometimes called the Island of the Dawn. The other was identified with a promontory or small rocky island (in ancient times an island, now connected to the mainland) off the west coast of Italy near Terracina. Jason and Medea went to Aeaea to be purified by Circe of the slaying of Apsyrtus on their way to Iolcus from Colchis. Odysseus also visited Circe in her island home of Aeaea and remained with her a year. The name Aeaea was sometimes applied to the enchantress herself.

Aeacus (ē′a̠-kus). A mythological son of Zeus and Aegina, the daughter of the river-god Asopus. He was born on the island of Oenone, or Oenopia, whither Zeus had taken Aegina when he carried her from her father's land. Aeacus became king of the island and renamed it Aegina in his mother's honor. By his wife Endeïs, the daughter of Sciron, Aeacus was the father of Peleus and Telamon. By the sea-nymph Psamathe he was the father of Phocus. Phocus was his father's favorite and caused such jealousy on the part of his brothers that, with the encouragement of their mother, they murdered him. Telamon and Peleus fled but Telamon sent word to his father from Salamis that he was innocent, and asked permission to plead his case. Aeacus refused to let him land on the island. Telamon was forced to plead his case from a mole which he secretly constructed in the harbor. But Aeacus was unmoved by his plea and refused to permit Telamon to return. Some say that Aegina was an un-

fat, fāte, fär, fåll, ȧsk, fãre; net, mē, hėr; pin, pīne; not, nōte, möve, nôr; up, lūte, pṳll; oi, oil; ou out; (lightened) e̠lect, agǫny, ṵnite;

populated island, and that Zeus transformed ants into men
who became subjects of Aeacus, and that this was the origin
of the famous Myrmidons. But others tell a different story:
Hera, when she learned that Aeacus was the child of Zeus
by one of her rivals, and that an island had been named for
this rival, was infuriated as usual. She vowed to punish the
inhabitants of the island. In pursuit of this vow she sent a
plague of serpents to infest the rivers and springs of the
land. She caused the hot south wind to blow across the
island for four months, thus parching the fields and ruining
the crops. The springs and fountains were poisoned by the
serpents; men and beasts died of drinking the waters. In the
towns men sickened and died. The people prayed for relief
to Zeus, but the animals prepared for the altars collapsed
and died before they could be sacrificed. Men became desperate under the dire pestilence, and a wave of crime and
impiety broke out. Soon nearly all the inhabitants were
dead. Aeacus continually prayed to Zeus for relief. One day
his prayer was answered by a shattering thunderclap. He
prayed that if he were really the son of Zeus, his father would
either repopulate his land or let him die. Pointing to a
nearby oak tree that had grown from the acorn of a sacred
Dodonian oak, Aeacus asked Zeus to send him as many men
as there were in the army of ants busily carrying grain up the
trunk of the tree. When Aeacus made this request the oak
trembled and the leaves rustled although there was no wind.
In the night Aeacus dreamed that a shower of ants fell to the
ground from the oak tree and were transformed into men.
Next morning his son Telamon called to him that an army
of men, all of the same age and size, had arrived. Aeacus
recognized them from his dream as ants that had been transformed by Zeus into men in answer to his prayer. He called
them Myrmidons, "ants," and they were ever after marked
by the thrifty, energetic qualities of the ants from which they
had sprung. At the same time, the plague of serpents was
lifted, the south wind stopped blowing, and a heavy rain fell
on the parched land. Aeacus divided his lands among his
new people and gave thanks to Zeus.

According to some accounts, Apollo and Poseidon enlisted the aid of Aeacus when they built the wall of Troy, for
they knew that unless a mortal assisted in the building of the
wall it would be impregnable and the inhabitants within it

could defy the gods. After they had finished building the
wall, three serpents slithered up and tried to scale it. Two
fell back and died. The third, making his attack on the part
of the wall built by Aeacus, was successful. Apollo prophesied that the wall would be breached and the city destroyed
by the descendants of Aeacus; as indeed it was, by Telamon
and later by Ajax.

Aeacus was renowned as a pious and wise man and as the
powerful ruler of a strong country. He was often appealed
to in disputes, as when Sciron and Nisus quarreled over
Megara. Aeacus was asked to decide; his judgment was that
Nisus should be king but that Sciron should command the
army. He was considered so powerful that many Spartans
and Athenians wished to fight in his army. When the Athenians caused the death of Androgeus, son of Minos of Crete,
Minos waged war on Athens and sought Aeacus as his ally.
But Aeacus announced that he was closely allied to Athens
and offered the Athenians his aid instead. He had made it
nearly impossible for any power to attack his island by surrounding it with a sunken wall of rocks, and though Minos
threatened, he did not dare attack. In the war that followed,
all Greece was afflicted by a drought; or as some say, by
earthquakes and famine. The oracle at Delphi, appealed to
by the Greeks, advised them to ask Aeacus to pray to Zeus
for relief. Aeacus heeded their request. He ascended Mount
Panhellenius, the highest peak of the island. As he stretched
out his hands to Zeus a loud thunderclap was heard, a cloud
settled on the mountain top, rain began to fall, and the
drought was broken. The earthquakes ceased in all of
Greece except Attica, which had to make amends to Minos
in another manner. In gratitude, Aeacus built a sanctuary to
Zeus on the mountain, which could be seen from the shores
of the mainland. Ever after, a cloud hovering over the peak
of Mount Panhellenius was a sign of rain. But some say the
drought that afflicted Greece and which Aeacus caused to be
broken with his prayers to Zeus had come because Pelops,
in a war against Stymphalus, king of Arcadia, treacherously
slew Stymphalus during a truce in which he pretended
friendship, and scattered his mangled limbs.

Aeacus, greatly honored during his lifetime, was equally
honored after death. Zeus made him one of the three judges
in Tartarus. It is said that he makes decisions concerning the

fat, fāte, fär, fåll, åsk, fãre; net, mē, hėr; pin, pīne; not, nōte, mŏve,
nôr; up, lūte, pŭll; oi, oil; ou out; (lightened) ĕlect, agŏny, ūnite;

souls that come from Europe; and also that he is the keeper
of the keys of Tartarus.

Aëdon (ā-ē′dọn). In legend, a daughter of Pandareus of
Ephesus. According to Homer she was the wife of Zethus,
king of Thebes, and the mother of Itylus. Inspired by envy
of Niobe, the wife of Amphion, who had seven sons and
seven daughters, she formed the design of killing Niobe's
eldest son, but by mistake destroyed her own son Itylus. To
relieve her grief she was changed by Zeus into a nightingale,
and her song became one long lament for her lost son.
According to another account which closely follows the
story of Procne in some respects, Aëdon was the wife of
Polytechnus. She and her husband so gloried in their happiness that she boasted they were a happier couple than Zeus
and Hera. To punish her arrogance Hera sent Eris to cause
strife between them, and Eris caused Aëdon to arrange a
contest between herself and her husband: that whoever
completed specified tasks first should be presented with a
slave by the other. Aëdon won the contest. Polytechnus
angrily went to Pandareus in Ephesus and carried off Chelidon, the sister of Aëdon, under the pretext that he was
taking her on a visit to her sister, and on the journey he
ravished her. He bound her to secrecy and gave her, disguised, as a slave to Aëdon. Aëdon learned that this was her
sister and conspired with her to punish Polytechnus. Together the sisters slew Itylus, the son of Aëdon and Polytechnus, dismembered his body, cooked it, and gave it to his
father to eat. When he had eaten, the nature of his meal was
revealed to Polytechnus. He sought to kill the sisters, but as
he pursued them, the gods transformed them into birds.
Aëdon became a nightingale, Chelidon a swallow, and Polytechnus a pelican.

Aeëtes (ē-ē′tēz). In classical myth, a son of Helius and Persa,
and the brother of Circe, Pasiphaë, and Perses. He was king
of Aea in Colchis at the far end of the Euxine Sea. By the
nymph Asterodia he was the father of Chalciope. His second
wife was Idyia, who bore him Medea and a son Apsyrtus.
Phrixus, son of Athamas, landed on his shores when he fled
from Orchomenus on the ram with the Golden Fleece.
Aeëtes welcomed him hospitably, despite the reputation of
the Colchians for hostility to strangers, and gave him his
daughter Chalciope for a wife. The ram, according to its

(obscured) errạnt, ardẹnt, actọr; ch, chip; g, go; th, thin; ŦH, then; y, you;
(variable) ḍ as d or j, ṣ as s or sh, ṭ as t or ch, ẓ as z or zh.

own instructions, was sacrificed to Zeus. Its fleece was hung in a grove sacred to Ares in Colchis and was guarded by a dragon that never slept. Phrixus died after fathering several sons and his ghost was said to haunt Pelias, king of Iolcus, demanding that the fleece be restored to Hellas. For this reason, and also to get rid of him, Pelias sent Jason to Colchis to fetch the Golden Fleece. When Aeëtes learned the reason for Jason's arrival on his shores, he was enraged. Only the laws of hospitality prevented him from slaying Jason at once. He thought also that his grandsons, whom Jason had rescued at sea and brought with him to Colchis, were plotting to seize his throne with Jason's help. He schemed to bring about the death of Jason without actually being involved in it himself. He said he would give Jason the fleece if he could do what Aeëtes himself had done: yoke two fire-breathing bulls, plow a field, and sow in it the dragon's teeth which had been given to Aeëtes by Athena. With Medea's help Jason successfully performed this feat. Then, being warned by Medea of her father's intention to betray him, Jason fled, taking Medea with him. Aeëtes pursued the Argonauts with a great fleet but he was delayed, according to some accounts because he stopped to gather up the pieces of Apsyrtus' body which Medea had cut up and flung into the sea. Others say Apsyrtus did not go with the Argonauts but pursued them and was betrayed and slain by Jason. Aeëtes never did overtake the fleeing Argonauts and all his attempts to secure the return of Medea ended in failure. However, some years later when his throne was seized by his brother Perses, Medea returned to Colchis, killed Perses, and restored her father to his throne.

Aegaeon (ē-jē′ǫn). See *Briareus.*

Aegeus (ē′jē-us, -jös). In mythology, a son of Pandion the Younger, king of Athens, and Pylia. His brothers were Pallas, Nisus, and Lycus. But some say Aegeus was an adopted son of Pandion and therefore was not a true descendant of Erechtheus. Pandion had been driven from Athens but after his death his sons marched against Athens, drove out their enemies and divided Attica into four parts. Aegeus, being the oldest, became king of Athens. Pallas claimed that Aegeus was not a true son of Pandion. He and his 50 sons were ever plotting to unseat Aegeus as king, and another brother, Lycus, became so threatening that Aegeus exiled

fat, fāte, fär, fâll, àsk, fāre; net, mē, hèr; pin, pīne; not, nōte, möve, nôr; up, lūte, pùll; oi, oil; ou out; (lightened) ēlect, agǫny, ūnite;

him. Aegeus married twice, but neither of his wives bore him
a child. He visited the oracle at Delphi to inquire what he
should do to procure an heir. The oracle answered that he
should not untie the neck of the bulging wine-skin until he
came to the highest point of Athens or he would die of grief.
Aegeus did not understand the meaning of this pronouncement. On his return from Delphi he stopped in Corinth.
There he saw Medea, the sorceress Jason had brought back
from Colchis, and promised her that if she ever needed help
he would provide it for her. In return Medea promised to get
him an heir by her magic. Aegeus visited his friend Pittheus
in Troezen and told him of the oracle's warning. Pittheus,
affected from afar by Medea's magic, entertained him lavishly, pressed wine on him, and when he was drunk sent his
daughter Aethra in to lie with him. The next day Aegeus told
Aethra if she should bear a son, she was to raise him in secret
in Troezen, and when he grew up she was to send him to
Athens if he could recover a sword and sandals that Aegeus
now hid under a huge rock. Aegeus departed for Athens to
celebrate the Athenian Festival. Some say that at these
games Androgeus, son of Minos of Crete, won all the contests and that the Athenians were furious with jealousy. To
get rid of Androgeus, Aegeus sent him to capture the Marathonian Bull, a fierce animal brought from Crete by Heracles. Androgeus was killed in his attempt to subdue the bull.
But others say he was killed when he was ambushed by
jealous Athenians, or that Aegeus ordered him ambushed
and slain because he feared that Androgeus might persuade
Minos to help the sons of Pallas who were plotting to seize
the throne from Aegeus. Minos, king of Crete, waged war on
Athens to avenge his son's death. He could not defeat the
Athenians and prayed the gods to punish them. The gods
sent famine and pestilence against Athens, and lifted these
scourges only when the Athenians agreed to give Minos any
amends he might demand. He demanded a tribute of seven
youths and seven maidens to be sent to Crete every nine
years to be devoured by the Minotaur.

    In the meantime, Medea had fled from Corinth to Athens
and reminded Aegeus of his promise to help her. He not
only gave her asylum; he married her. She bore him a son,
and Aegeus, not knowing that Aethra had already borne his
son Theseus, thought this child, Medeus, was the heir that

(obscured) errạnt, ardẹnt, actọr; ch, chip; g, go; th, thin; ᴛʜ, then; y, you;
(variable) ḍ as d or j, ṣ as s or sh, ṭ as t or ch, ẓ as z or zh.

Medea had promised him. But Theseus, now grown to young manhood, took up the tokens Aegeus had hidden under the rock and, after many adventures, arrived in Athens. Medea, through her arts, instantly realized this was Aegeus' first-born and warned Aegeus that the young stranger was a threat to his kingdom. She induced Aegeus to hand him a cup of poisoned wine. But just as Theseus raised it to his lips, Aegeus noted the hilt of the young man's sword, recognized it as his own, and realized that this was his son whom he had never seen. He dashed the cup from his hand and welcomed his son with delight. Medea was obliged to flee from Athens for her plots, but Aegeus provided an escort for her and her son. Shortly after, the time for sending tribute to Minos arrived. In spite of the pleas of Aegeus, Theseus resolved to go as part of the tribute. He promised to return, however, and told his father that on the return journey he would substitute, for the black sail the ship customarily carried, a white sail to show that he had vanquished the Minotaur.

Theseus, however, forgot to change the sail on the return journey. Aegeus mounted to the top of the Acropolis, to a point where the little temple of Athena Nike later stood. Each day he scanned the horizon for a sail. When at last he saw the black sail from afar, he read in it a message of his son's death and hurled himself from the Acropolis, to his death in the vale below. The Latin writers say Aegeus hurled himself into the sea which henceforth bore his name. Theseus, returning safely, buried him and erected a shrine in his honor.

Aegicores   (ē-ji-kô′rēz). According to tradition, one of the four sons of Ion. One of the four ancient tribes of Athens was named for him. His brothers were Argades, Geleon, and Hoples.

Aegipan   (ē′ji-pan). In Greek Mythology, a name sometimes used for the goatish god Pan. In some forms of the myth he is identified with Pan. He is variously called the son of Zeus and Aega, Pan's wife, and also the father of Pan. On one occasion together with Hermes he restored to Zeus the sinews taken from him by the giant Typhon.

Aegis   (ē′jis). The wondrous and terrifying breastplate of Zeus and Athena, sometimes loaned to Apollo. In the center of the breastplate was the head of the Gorgon Medusa, and in

fat, fāte, fär, fåll, åsk, fâre; net, mē, hèr; pin, pīne; not, nōte, möve, nôr; up, lūte, pŭll; oi, oil; ou out; (lightened) ĕlect, agŏny, ūnite;

Homeric legend it is often spoken of as being encircled with flames.

Aegisthus (ē-jis′thus). In Greek legend, the son of Thyestes and Pelopia, his own daughter. As an infant he was exposed by his mother to die but was rescued by shepherds and brought up by Atreus, whom Pelopia had married, as his own son. When very young, he was ordered by Atreus to kill Thyestes as he slept, unaware that the latter was his true father. Thyestes escaped the blow and, recognizing the sword which Aegisthus had aimed at him as the one he had lost the night he ravished Pelopia, he asked Aegisthus where he had gotten it. When Aegisthus told him his mother had given it to him, Thyestes realized that this was indeed his son. He sent Aegisthus to fetch his mother, and when she came and learned that she was the mother of Aegisthus by her own father, she plunged the sword into her breast in horror. Thyestes next commanded Aegisthus to kill Atreus, king of Mycenae. Thyestes then became king and ruled until he was forced into exile by Atreus' son Agamemnon. Aegisthus fled from Mycenae at the same time but returned while Agamemnon and Menelaus were away at the Trojan War. To get revenge on the house of Atreus, because Atreus had served Aegisthus' brothers to Thyestes in a ghastly banquet and because Agamemnon had become king of Mycenae, he became Clytemnestra's paramour and plotted with her to kill her husband Agamemnon. When the latter returned from Troy he was welcomed by both Aegisthus and Clytemnestra, according to their plot. They prepared a banquet for him, and as he emerged from his bath, ready to enjoy the feast, he was struck down. According to some accounts it was Aegisthus who split his skull with a two-headed ax. According to other accounts Clytemnestra stabbed her husband. In the *Odyssey* Zeus complained of the wickedness of men citing Aegisthus' wickedness in wooing Clytemnestra and killing Agamemnon, in spite of the fact that he had been especially warned by Hermes not to do so. Clytemnestra and Aegisthus ruled in Mycenae for seven years after the death of Agamemnon. Clytemnestra was the real ruler while Aegisthus, on the whole a cowardly sort, lived in fear that her son Orestes would return to Mycenae, from which he had been sent before his father's death, and slay him. In the eighth year after the murder of Agamemnon Orestes did

(obscured) errant, ardent, actor; ch, chip; g, go; th, thin; ŦH, then; y, you;
(variable) ḍ as d or j, ş as s or sh, ţ as t or ch, ẓ as z or zh.

return and killed both Aegisthus and Clytemnestra, thus fulfilling the command of the oracle of Delphi and avenging his father's murder.

Aegyptus (ē-jip′tus). In classical myth, a son of Belus, king in Egypt, and Anchinoë, and the twin of Danaus. He became ruler of Arabia and conquered the land which, according to some accounts, he later named Egypt after himself. By various women he was the father of 50 sons, whom he wished to marry to the 50 daughters of his brother Danaus. Danaus refused his consent to the marriages and fled. Aegyptus sent his sons in pursuit of the Danaids with orders not to return without them. In Argos, whither Danaus and his daughters had fled, they ultimately compelled Danaus to give them his daughters, but all save one of the sons of Aegyptus were murdered on the wedding night. Aegyptus followed his sons to Argos, but when he learned of their murders he fled. He died and was buried in the Peloponnesus.

Aeneas (ē-nē′as). In classical myth, the son of Anchises and the goddess Aphrodite. Some say he was brought up for the first years of his life by the nymphs of Mount Ida in the Troad. Others say Alcathous, his sister's husband, reared him. Anchises, king of the Dardanians, was crippled by a thunderbolt from Zeus because he boasted of having lain with a goddess. Unable to rule his kingdom, he was succeeded by Aeneas. Some say Aeneas accompanied Paris when the latter went on his voyage to Sparta and abducted Helen. He did not immediately offer his aid when Troy was attacked by the Greeks to recover her. Some say he was on cool terms with his relative, King Priam of Troy, either because Priam did not accord him the honor Aeneas thought fitting, or because Priam feared fulfillment of the prophecy that Aeneas would rule the Trojans. However, in the ninth year of the war against Troy, when Achilles was raiding the surrounding country and sacking the cities in it, he made a raid on the cattle of Aeneas during which Aeneas barely escaped with his life. Thenceforth Aeneas allied himself and his Dardanians with the Trojans, and fought with great valor and skill. He was honored by the Trojans for his piety and his spirit. The gods protected him in battle because he was destined to found a new home for the Trojan race in Italy. In the course of the war, Diomedes flung a huge boulder at Aeneas and felled him, but Aphrodite swooped down to rescue her son. When she too was wounded by Diomedes, Apollo rescued Aeneas and bore him off to Pergamus where Leto healed him. He then returned to the battle and slew many of the enemy. At the attack on the Greek fortifications protecting their ships Aeneas was in the vanguard. Later, as the Trojans were being driven back in the struggle for the body of Patroclus, Apollo appeared to him in the guise of a herald and encouraged him to inspire the Trojans to new efforts. Again, encouraged by Apollo, he was the first to go out to meet Achilles, although his courage failed him at first as he remembered how Achilles had driven him from Mount Ida and Lyrnessus when he sacked that town. But Apollo filled him with bravery and he pressed forward against Achilles. His spear, however, could not pierce Achilles' magic armor, and Aeneas found himself in deadly peril. To save him, Poseidon sent a mist to dim Achilles' eyes, then he spirited Aeneas away. Poseidon, who in all other respects favored the Greeks against the Trojans, saved Aeneas to preserve the line of Dardanus, from whom he had sprung, and because he pitied Aeneas, who was fighting another man's war. He promised Aeneas that no other Achaean would take his life and that he would live to fulfil his destiny. Aeneas rescued the body of the Lycian Glaucus when he was slain by Telamonian Ajax, and then was himself wounded by Ajax in the struggle for possession of Achilles' body. He withdrew into the city to nurse his wound. Later, Aeneas scorned the proposal of Polydamas to withdraw to the city and there to fight from the safety of its towers. He preferred, he said, death in the open, fighting bravely, to death like a trapped animal. As leader of the Trojans, Hector being dead, again and again Aeneas returned to the attack, aided by the gods. He slew many Greeks in engagements in which Penthesilea, Memnon, and Eurypylus, each of whom had come to help the Trojans, were killed. When Neoptolemus came to the aid of the Greeks, Thetis, out of respect for Aphrodite, prevented him from coming face to face with Aeneas. When Athena aided the Argives and they drove the Trojans back, Aphrodite snatched Aeneas away in a mist. But the bitter struggle was hopeless, and at last Zeus, though grieving, abandoned Troy to its long delayed fate. Various accounts are given of the fate of Aeneas in the sack of Troy. Some say he was captured by Neoptolemus, carried

(obscured) err*a*nt, ard*e*nt, act*o*r; ch, chip; g, go; th, thin; ᵻʜ, then; y, you; (variable) ḍ as d or j, ş as s or sh, ṭ as t or ch, ẓ as z or zh.

off to Greece as the most valuable of the spoils of the war and ultimately ransomed by the Dardanians. Others say he was spared by the Greeks because he had favored the return of Helen to Menelaus, and that he reigned, as did his descendants, in the Troad. Still others say he defended Troy bravely until the last then, seeing that the cause was hopeless, retired with the aid of Aphrodite to Mount Ida, taking his father, his son, the sacred images of Troy and a few followers with him. Later he went to Pellene (Pallene) in Thrace and died there, or in Orchomenus. The Romans say that after he retired to Mount Ida with his father, son, wife, and the sacred images (for they say Diomedes stole only a copy of the Palladium from the citadel of Troy), he fled from the Troad at the command of the gods and set out to found a new home for the Trojans in Italy. Having fulfilled his destiny, he fell in battle and was taken to heaven. His adventures in pursuing his destiny are described in Vergil's *Aeneid*. In Homer, Aeneas is the greatest of the Trojans after Hector, a favorite of the gods, and a brave, reasonable, and pious man, whose piety and courage are leavened with a few human and endearing weaknesses. In the *Aeneid* the character of Aeneas suffers a great change; from a man of admirable but believably human traits, he becomes a symbol of the divinity which the Romans considered fitting in the founder of their nation. In the *Aeneid,* "pious Aeneas" is often insufferably conscious of his divine mission.

Aeolus (ē′ọ̄-lus, ẹ̄-ō′lus). In mythology, a son of Hellen and the nymph Orseïs, and a grandson of Deucalion and Pyrrha. He was the brother of Dorus and Xuthus, and succeeded his father as king of Magnesia in Thessaly. By Thea, a daughter of Chiron whom he seduced, he was the father of Arne and grandfather of the twins Aeolus and Boeotus; the former became keeper of the winds. He bequeathed part of his kingdom to his grandson Boeotus who became the ancestor of the Boeotians. By his wife Enarete, Aeolus had seven sons: Athamas, Cretheus, Deion, Magnes, Perieres, Salmoneus, and Sisyphus, and five daughters: Alcyone, Calyce, Canace, Pisidice, and Perimedes.

Aeolus. In mythology, a son of Poseidon and Arne, daughter of Aeolus, king of Magnesia in Thessaly. He and his twin brother, Boeotus, were exposed to die on Mount Pelion at the order of their mother's foster father. They were saved by a shepherd and handed over to Theano, the childless wife of Metapontus, king of Icaria. She presented them to her husband as her own children. Metapontus was delighted with them, thinking they were his own sons. Even when his wife later bore twins of her own, he preferred Aeolus and Boeotus. Grown, the twins frustrated a plot arranged by Theano in which they were to be killed by their foster brothers. Instead Aeolus and Boeotus killed Theano's sons with the aid of their father, Poseidon. They then fled. Poseidon came to them and revealed that he was their father and told them to free their mother, who had been imprisoned since their birth by her foster father. They freed Arne, who married Metapontus, Theano having killed herself, but after a time Metapontus put her aside in favor of a new wife. Aeolus and Boeotus took their mother's part and killed the new wife, after which they fled. Aeolus and some companions sailed to the Tyrrhenian Sea and there they established a kingdom on an island, usually thought to be one of the Aeoliae Insulae (Lipari Islands). He was on friendly terms with the gods and was entrusted with the task of guarding and controlling the winds. These were locked behind the sheer cliffs of the island. When he wanted to release any of the winds, he pierced the side of the cliff with his spear and the wind streamed through the opening. To shut off the wind he simply stopped the hole. Aeolus and his wife, whom some call Enarete, had six sons and six daughters. They all lived in great happiness and prosperity on their island until Aeolus discovered that his six sons and daughters had formed incestuous unions, unaware that such marriages were frowned upon by the gods. He broke up these combinations by requesting some of his sons to emigrate. Odysseus visited Aeolus on his wanderings at the end of the Trojan War, and was royally entertained. Aeolus gave him a skin in which all the winds were confined to help him on his journey home. The ship was in sight of Ithaca when his comrades, while Odysseus slept, thinking that the skin Aeolus had given him contained a rich treasure, opened it to take their share. All the winds flew out and raised a great storm. Odysseus was blown to sea again. He revisited Aeolus and told him what had happened. But Aeolus would not help him again, on the ground that a man who had such bad luck must be hated by the gods, and therefore there was

(obscured) errạnt, ardẹnt, actọr; ch, chip; g, go; th, thin; ᴛʜ, then; y, you;
(variable) ḍ as d or j, ṣ as s or sh, ṭ as t or ch, ẓ as z or zh.

nothing he could do to help such a man. (In the *Aeneid*, at Juno's behest, Aeolus sent winds to raise a storm at sea in an attempt to destroy Aeneas and his ships but the plan was thwarted by Neptune.) Aeolus fulfilled his duties as guardian of the winds so capably that Zeus did not permit him to die, but placed him on a throne in the Cave of the Winds where he continues to perform his duties faithfully.

Aesacus (ē′sạ-kus). In classical myth, one of the 50 sons of Priam, king of Troy. His mother was Arisbe, the daughter of Merops the seer. After the birth of Aesacus Priam gave Arisbe to Hyrtacus for a wife, and Priam married Hecuba. From his grandfather Aesacus learned the art of prophecy. Hecuba, about to bear Paris, dreamed that she produced flames and fiery serpents, and awoke in terror under the impression that Troy was in flames. Aesacus interpreted the dream to mean that the child she was about to bear would bring ruin to the city and must be destroyed. The day Paris was actually born Aesacus again prophesied, saying that the son born to the royal house of Troy that day must be done away with. But Priam and Hecuba did not apply the prophecy to their own child, but to another princeling of Troy who was also born that day. Aesacus withdrew to the country where he fell desperately in love with Asterope, or Hesperie, a daughter of the river-god Cebren. She did not return his love immediately and fled from his ardent embraces. As he pursued her she stepped on a serpent, was bitten by it, and died. Aesacus, in a torment of remorse and grief, sought to kill himself by leaping into the sea but Thetis transformed him into a bird, and he continues to dive savagely into the sea in an attempt to destroy himself.

Aesculapius (es-kụ-lā′pi-us). See *Asclepius.*

Aeson (ē′sọn). In Greek legend, a son of Tyro and Cretheus, founder and king of Iolcus. He was the half-brother of Pelias and Neleus, Tyro's twin sons by Poseidon. After the death of Cretheus, Pelias seized the throne of Iolcus and kept Aeson, the rightful heir, a prisoner. Aeson had a son by his wife who is variously known as Perimede, Amphinome, Alcimede, and Polymede. The child, who was first named Diomedes but is known as Jason, was brought up by Chiron the centaur on Mount Pelion. Aeson was still a virtual prisoner of Pelias when Jason arrived in Iolcus and claimed the throne. After Jason had departed on the quest for the

fat, fāte, fär, fâll, ȧsk, fãre; net, mē, hėr; pin, pīne; not, nōte, möve, nôr; up, lūte, pụll; oi, oil; ou out; (lightened) ẹlect, agọny, ụnite;

Golden Fleece, Pelias believed that he would not return. He threatened to kill Aeson but allowed him to commit suicide by drinking bull's blood, which only the immortals could imbibe and survive. But some say Aeson did not commit suicide, that he still lived, an aged and broken man, when Jason returned from Colchis; and that Medea restored his youth with her magic arts learned from Hecate.

Aethalides (ē-thal'i-dēz). In Greek legend, a son of Hermes by Eupolemeia, daughter of Myrmidon. He was born near the Amphrysus River in Thessaly. He joined Jason in the quest for the Golden Fleece, and served as herald of the Argonauts. Aethalides was given two remarkable gifts by his father: the ability to live either in the Underworld or on earth, and an infallible memory. Since he could remember everything, even in the Underworld, his soul remembered, even after death, that it had migrated from Aethalides to Euphorbus, to one Hermotimus, and then to the philosopher and mathematician Pythagoras.

Aether (ē'thėr). In Greek mythology, the son of Chaos and Darkness, and the brother of Night, Day, and Erebus; in the Orphic hymns, the soul of the world and source of life; later, the expanse of heaven or abode of the gods.

Aetna (et'nä). A nymph of Sicily. Some say she was a daughter of Uranus and Gaea; others say Briareus was her father. In a dispute between Hephaestus and Demeter for control of Sicily, Aetna, according to some accounts, was the arbitrator. By Zeus or by Hephaestus she was the mother of the Palici. The volcanic mountain in Sicily was named for her. Some say that Hephaestus had one of his forges under this mountain, and that it was in this forge that the Cyclopes made the thunderbolts for Zeus. The mountain also figures in the stories of Enceladus the Giant, who was buried under it after he had been charred by the lightning of Zeus. They say that when Enceladus turns over to ease his aching sides, all Sicily quakes and rumbles. Typhon, the hideous monster who warred against Zeus and was defeated by him, is also buried under Mount Aetna. On the slope of the mountain, Hiero, tyrant of Syracuse, founded a city which he named Aetna (c476 B.C.).

Aetolus (ē'tō̞-lus). In mythology, one of the sons of Endymion. He competed with his brothers for the throne of Elis, his father's kingdom, but lost. In the course of funeral

(obscured) errᶐnt, ardᶒnt, actᶐr; ch, chip; g, go; th, thin; ꞮH, then; y, you;
(variable) ḍ as d or j, ṣ as s or sh, ṭ as t or ch, ẓ as z or zh.

games for Azan, son of Arcas, the first ever held in Greece according to some accounts, he accidentally killed Apis, the son of Phoroneus. He was banished and crossed the Gulf of Corinth to the land of the Curetes. There he killed his hosts, Dorus, Laodocus, and Polypoetes, the sons of Apollo and Phthia, and made himself ruler. He named the land Aetolia after himself. He married Pronoë, a daughter of Phorbas, who bore him two sons. Two cities he founded in Aetolia were named Pleuron and Calydon after these two sons.

Agamedes (ag-a̯-mē′dēz). In mythology, a son of Erginus the Argonaut. He was the brother of Trophonius. The brothers were born in their father's old age, after he had taken the advice of an oracle and married a young wife. They were famous builders. With his brother Agamedes built the temple of Apollo at Delphi and the brothers were guardian spirits of its threshold until they were replaced by Neoptolemus. They also built a treasury for King Hyrieus of Boeotia. In it they so placed a stone that it could be removed from the outside and thus they were able to rob the treasury at will. According to some accounts, Hyrieus arranged a trap and caught Agamedes stealing in this manner. Trophonius cut off his brother's head in order to save himself. The gods were angry with Trophonius and swallowed him up in the earth in a grove at Lebadia. The oracle of Trophonius at Lebadia thereafter became famous, and suppliants there, before entering the pit where the oracle gave answers, ate of a ram that had been sacrificed to the shade of Agamedes. According to other accounts, as a reward for building the temple of Apollo at Delphi the god granted them seven days of pleasure, at the end of that time they received their reward: they went peacefully to sleep and died.

Agamemnon (ag-a̯-mem′non). In Greek mythology, the son of Atreus and Aërope and the brother of Menelaus and Anaxibia. Following the murder of their father by Aegisthus, Agamemnon and Menelaus remained at the court of Oeneus, a king in Aetolia, until they were restored to their own kingdom by Tyndareus, king of Sparta. Agamemnon became king of Mycenae and, making war on Tantalus, king of Pisa, slew him and his infant, and compelled his widow to marry him. She was Clytemnestra, a daughter of Tyndareus, and she bore Agamemnon Orestes, Electra (sometimes known as Laodice), Iphigenia (sometimes known as

Iphianassa), and Chrysothemis. When Paris abducted Helen, Menelaus reminded the Grecian princes who had been her suitors of their oath to assist whomever she married in case any ill came to him as a result of the marriage. A great expedition was organized to go to Troy and recapture Helen. Agamemnon, brave but vain and eager for glory, yearned to be made leader of the expedition, although he pretended with a great show of humility that he did not seek the honor. As he had planned, however, he was chosen captain of the Greek armies which gathered to go to Troy. The Greek fleet, assembled at Aulis, was prevented from sailing by violent storms or, according to another account, by a calm. Calchas the seer said that the storms were caused by the anger of Artemis, because Agamemnon had killed a stag, one of her creatures. Only the sacrifice of Agamemnon's daughter would appease the goddess and quiet the storms. Urged on by Menelaus, Agamemnon sent a message to Clytemnestra, telling her to send their daughter Iphigenia to Aulis to be married to Achilles. This scheme had been hatched by Odysseus to make sure that Clytemnestra would send Iphigenia. Agamemnon regretted his decision to sacrifice his own child and would have changed his order, in spite of his overwhelming desire to be the leader of the glorious expedition, but he was persuaded that events had moved too fast: the armies knew of Calchas' interpretations and demanded the sacrifice so that they could proceed. Menelaus taunted him with seeking power and glory but being unwilling to take the responsibilities that went with them if personal sacrifice was involved. When Iphigenia arrived, unexpectedly accompanied by Clytemnestra, the sacrifice was performed, despite the latter's pleas and Agamemnon's own misgivings. The fleet then sailed.

For nearly ten years the Greeks raided the allies of Troy and the cities of the Troad. In the tenth year they attacked the city itself, but were beset by a plague of arrows sent by Apollo. Calchas informed Agamemnon that Apollo was angry because Agamemnon had taken Chryseis, daughter of a priest of Apollo, as a captive and refused to return her to her father who had offered a rich ransom for her. Agamemnon agreed to give her up, but demanded Briseis, a captive who had been awarded to Achilles, in her place. This aroused the famous wrath of Achilles and caused that hero to withdraw

(obscured) err**a**nt, ard**e**nt, act**o**r; ch, chip; g, go; th, thin; ŦH, then; y, you; (variable) **d̠** as d or j, **s̠** as s or sh, **t̠** as t or ch, **z̠** as z or zh.

from the war, and so it was that Agamemnon's arrogance and hasty temper brought great losses and near disaster to the Greeks. Brave, rash, and vain, Agamemnon wanted the glory of leadership but did not know how to exercise it. He therefore constantly sought advice from Nestor who encouraged him to remain and fight when, discouraged, he would have given up and sailed for home. Also he continually turned to Odysseus who was ever ready with some scheme to save the situation. In the last year of the war Agamemnon volunteered to fight Hector in single combat but was eliminated by the drawing of lots. As the battle went against the Greeks he regretted his arrogance toward Achilles and tried to lure him back into the struggle with the offer of rich rewards. Achilles refused, and Agamemnon threw himself into the fighting until he was compelled by a wound to withdraw. After the death of Patroclus he admitted his fault to Achilles, saying he was spurred on by Ate, the goddess of mischief, and returned Briseis, untouched, to her former master. When Achilles later was killed, Agamemnon, possibly jealous of Telamonian Ajax' glorious fame, voted to award the armor of Achilles to Odysseus, whereupon Ajax, divinely inspired with madness by Athena, committed suicide. It was only the persuasive intervention of Odysseus that prevented him from denying honorable burial to Ajax. It was Odysseus again who persuaded him to order Astyanax, young son of Hector, to be hurled from the towers of Troy when that city had fallen, lest at a later date he gather the Trojans and again make war on the Greeks. Agamemnon took Cassandra, daughter of Priam and Hecuba, as his captive from Troy and began preparations to return to Greece. Once again weather prevented the sailing and Calchas informed him that the spirit of Achilles demanded the sacrifice of Polyxena, youngest daughter of Priam and Hecuba, on his funeral pyre. He ordered the sacrifice and commanded that her body be returned to her mother for burial. However, when he went to Hecuba to learn why she had not claimed the body, she appealed to him at least to permit her to avenge herself on Polymnestor, a former ally of Troy who had murdered the young son of Priam and Hecuba left in his care for safe-keeping. He agreed to let her take whatever vengeance a captive woman could, but would give her no assistance. The Greeks then sailed for home.

Agamemnon was one of the few Greek leaders who arrived
home directly. When he landed, Clytemnestra, who had
learned of his approach by an elaborate system of beacon
fires, welcomed him so extravagantly that he was uneasy but
yielded to her efforts to treat him almost as a god. She
invited him and his captive Cassandra, who seemed to be in
a frenzy and was raving of bloody baths, into the palace for
purification rites. As he stepped out of the ceremonial bath,
Clytemnestra wrapped him in a robe that immobilized him
and, according to Aeschylus, stabbed him three times, and
then killed Cassandra. According to Homer, it was Aegisthus, her paramour, who actually killed Agamemnon. After
the murders, with wild elation, Clytemnestra told the
stunned subjects of Agamemnon that she had taken vengeance on her husband for the sacrifice of her daughter and
for bringing back Cassandra as a rival wife.

Agave (ạ-gā′vẹ). In Greek mythology, a daughter of Cadmus
and Harmonia. She was the wife of Echion, one of the
"Sown Men" of Thebes, and was the mother of Pentheus.
When Dionysus made his appearance in Thebes, Pentheus
denied the divinity of the god and sought to suppress his
worship. Agave, who had been driven mad by Dionysus
because she too denied his godhead, joined her sisters and
other Theban women who were participating in the revels
of Dionysus on Mount Cithaeron. There Pentheus, also inspired with madness by Dionysus as a punishment for his
doubts, went to spy on the women. They seized him and,
frenzied with wine and religious ecstasy, tore him to pieces.
Agave herself, under the impression that she was subduing
a lion, wrenched his head from his mangled body and bore
it impaled on her thyrsus to the palace at Thebes. When she
was restored to her senses, she was horrified and lamented
the death of her son. Dionysus appeared to her and told her
this was her punishment for her unbelief and sentenced her
to exile from Thebes. She went to Illyria, as did her mother
and father, and there married the king. When she later
learned that her father had become commander of a force
of Encheleans in Illyria, she murdered her new husband and
turned his kingdom over to her father.

Agraulos (ā-grô′lus). In Greek mythology, the wife of Cecrops, the first king of Attica, and the mother of Agraulos
the Younger, Herse, and Pandrosos. Athena entrusted her

(obscured) errạnt, ardẹnt, actọr; ch, chip; g, go; th, thin; ŦH, then; y, you;
(variable) ḍ as d or j, ṣ as s or sh, ṭ as t or ch, ẓ as z or zh.

with a casket to guard, with orders not to look inside it. One day, overcome by curiosity, Agraulos and her daughters opened the casket and beheld in it the infant Erichthonius whose body ended in a serpent's tail. Agraulos and her daughters were so terrified they leaped to their deaths from the Acropolis. But some say Agraulos leaped from the Acropolis during an attack on Athens in response to an oracle which said the city would be saved by such a sacrifice. There was a sanctuary of Agraulos on the Acropolis, where young Athenian warriors took an oath "to regard wheat, barley, the vine, and the olive as the natural boundaries of Attica" and to defend those boundaries with their lives.

Agraulos the Younger. In Greek mythology, a daughter of Cecrops, king of Athens, and Agraulos. She demanded much gold from Hermes in return for furthering his cause with her sister Herse. Having offended Athena, Agraulos was made to fall in love with Hermes, and in an attempt to bar him from seeing Herse she was turned to stone. Some say Agraulos was a daughter of Alcippe by Ares. See **Herse.** (AH)

Aidos (ī'dos). In Greek mythology, the personification of Conscience, or the shame that is caused by conscience. Her altar was on the Acropolis at Athens, near the temple of Athena, whose nurse she was said to have been. Aidos was thought to be a deity that ranged the earth, and did not live among the immortal gods in Olympus. At the theater of Dionysus a seat was reserved for the priestess of Aidos.

Ajax (ā'jaks), **Telamonian** or **Great.** In Greek legend, a son of Telamon of Salamis and Periboea. Before he was born, Heracles visited his parents in Salamis. Observing that Periboea was about to produce a child, he prayed to Zeus that she would bear a son whose skin was as tough as a lion's and whose courage would match it. Zeus sent an eagle to show that his prayer was heard. When Ajax was born, Heracles covered him with his own lion's skin, and made him invulnerable except in the neck and armpit that had not been covered by the skin. Ajax became king of Megara, and was a suitor of Helen. Like her other suitors, he took an oath to defend the man she chose as her husband if that man should ever suffer ill on account of his marriage. To carry out his oath, he joined Achilles, his beloved cousin, and the other Greek captains who sailed to Troy to recover Helen when she was carried off by Paris. Next to Achilles he was the

fat, fāte, fär, fȧll, ȧsk, fãre; net, mē, hèr; pin, pīne; not, nōte, mȯve, nôr; up, lūte, pu̇ll; oi, oil; ou out; (lightened) ĕlect, agọny, ūnite;

handsomest and the bravest of the Greeks. He also stood
head and shoulders above them in stature. In the tenth year
of the Trojan War he accepted Hector's challenge to the
Greeks to engage in single combat. They fought all day and
when the contest ended with neither gaining the advantage
the heroes exchanged gifts, each praising the other's prowess. Hector gave Ajax his sword and Ajax gave Hector his
gleaming belt. In the war Ajax fought side by side with his
half-brother Teucer who was a skilled bowman. Teucer
dodged out from the shelter of Ajax' shield to shoot his
deadly arrows. Among his many deeds in the Trojan War he
acted as one of the envoys who went to Scyrus to fetch
Achilles to the war; later he was one of the ambassadors who
went to Achilles' tent to try to persuade him to return to the
war after his quarrel with Agamemnon; with Menelaus he
rescued Odysseus when the latter was cut off and surrounded by the Trojans; with the Lesser Ajax he held off the
enemy from the Greek ships; he defended the body of Patroclus and fought off the Trojans until it could be rescued by
his comrades. When Penthesilea the Amazon came to the
aid of the Trojans after the death of Hector, she furiously
drove the Greeks back. Ajax, mourning with Achilles over
the death of Patroclus, heard the clamor and roused
Achilles. They immediately joined the fray. Penthesilea
sprang at them like a leopard. She hurled her lance at Ajax
but it glanced off harmlessly, as fate had decreed that no
enemy's blade would taste his blood. He drove the Trojans
back and left Achilles to deal with Penthesilea. Together,
Ajax and Achilles seemed irresistible, but Ajax' courage and
skill were his undoing. As he left his home his father admon-
ished him to go forth and win, but to win with the gods on
his side. Ajax boasted that any fool could win with the help
of the gods; he would gain honor and glory by himself. He
refused to acknowledge Agamemnon as his commander on
the grounds that he had come to Troy of his own free will,
in fulfillment of his oath, and was not subject to anyone. In
battle he rejected the aid of Athena and advised her to go
and help those who needed it, for the line would not break
where he was in command. The gods did not forget. After
the death of Achilles, his mother Thetis commanded that
her son's arms be given to the mightiest of the Argives. Only
Odysseus and Ajax dared claim them, although it was Ajax

(obscured) errant, ardent, actor; ch, chip; g, go; th, thin; ᴛʜ, then; y, you;
(variable) ḑ as d or j, ş as s or sh, ţ as t or ch, ʐ as z or zh.

who had borne the body of dead Achilles back to his comrades through the very ranks of the enemy. Ajax suggested that Idomeneus, Nestor, and Agamemnon should choose which of them had earned the arms. Nestor grieved; for he said that whoever was not selected would be lost to the Greeks. He suggested that they let the captive Trojans decide who had done them the most harm—Ajax or Odysseus. Ajax was insulted. He accused Odysseus of cowardice, reminding him that he had tried to escape coming to Troy in the first place. He scornfully pointed out that Odysseus had his ships in the center of the line where they would be protected, whereas Ajax had his own ships guarding the flank of the line. He challenged Odysseus to a duel to decide who should have the arms. Odysseus replied that strength was not wisdom, and that his wisdom had meant more to the Greeks than the strength of Ajax. The Trojan captives agreed with Odysseus that his cunning had harmed them more than Ajax' valor, and the armor was awarded to Odysseus. Ajax was infuriated, feeling that the armor was rightly his. Moreover, Odysseus was his ancient enemy and he scorned him as an intriguer who fought with words, not with weapons. Crazed with jealousy, he resolved to kill the Greeks who had been responsible for the award. Athena maddened him, so that through one long night he slaughtered innocent cattle under the impression that they were his Greek enemies. He seized a ram and hung it up in his tent and tortured it, thinking that it was Odysseus. Then in the midst of his frenzy Athena restored his sanity. He was appalled and humiliated to learn that he, the bravest of the Greeks, had so disgraced himself by the slaughter of animals. Too late he recognized that he was being punished for his pride. Bidding goodby to his captive wife Tecmessa, who loved him dearly, and to their young son Eurysaces, he went off alone to wash himself clean in the salt sea and to pray to the gods. Finally he fixed his sword, which Hector had given him, in the foreign sands of Troy and hurled himself upon its point. From his blood was said to have sprung up a purple flower bearing on its leaves the letters *ai,* which were the first letters of his name in Greek, and also an exclamation of woe: *alas!* According to some accounts, Menelaus tried to prevent his heartbroken brother Teucer from giving honorable burial to his corpse, and Agamemnon agreed with him, but they were persuaded by Odysseus, who now acknowledged the great contributions and courage of his old enemy, and who even offered to help Teucer with the funeral rites. But others say Agamemnon grieved over the loss of Ajax, and that Odysseus did too, saying that he would never haven taken the arms of Achilles if he had known how much they meant to Ajax. It is also said that Ajax' body was not burned as was the custom for warriors who fell in battle, but that he was buried on the headland of Cape Rhoeteum. The arms of Achilles were later given to Neoptolemus, Achilles' son. On the way home from Troy they were lost in the sea during a great storm. Thetis found them and, as recompense to Great Ajax in death, she caused them to be washed ashore on his tomb. Ajax was worshiped as a hero by the Athenians. Each year young men sailed from Athens to Salamis to sacrifice to him.

Ajax the Lesser, or *Oilean Ajax.* In Greek legend, a son of Oileus and Eriopis. He was a captain of Locrians who went with the Greeks to Troy, and although he was small and wore only a linen corselet, he surpassed all the Greeks in skill as a lancer. Also, next to Achilles he was the fleetest runner of the Greeks. As did others, he accepted Hector's challenge to single combat but was eliminated by the drawing of lots. Poseidon, in the guise of Calchas, came to encourage the Greeks after Hector had driven them back to their ships, and put divine strength into the two Ajaxes to stand firm. Ajax, a runner himself, could tell by the legs and ankles that it was not Calchas and realized it was a god who aided them. He fought savagely and, being so swift, slew more Trojans in that fight than any of the other Greeks. He cut off the head of Imbrius and hurled it into the Trojan camp, and when the Trojans at length breached the fortifications he and Telamonian Ajax held them off from the ships. After the fall of Troy the Greeks sacked the city. Ajax found Cassandra in the temple of Athena and dragged her away from the sacred image as his concubine. However, Agamemnon wanted Cassandra. To get her, Odysseus spread the tale that Ajax had committed sacrilege in Athena's shrine. This aroused the wrath of all the Greeks and Cassandra was taken away from him. On the way home from Troy Ajax' ship was wrecked on the Gyraean rocks. Ajax saved himself by climbing onto the rocks but, according to some accounts, was slain by a thunderbolt hurled by Athena to punish him for violating her shrine, in spite of the fact that he had expiated this crime. According to other accounts, it was Poseidon who sundered the rocks with his trident and drowned him. Thus did the gods easily change sides to bring disaster to those they had formerly aided. The spirit of Ajax went to the island of Leuce where it consorted with the spirits of Achilles and Helen. Thetis rescued his body and buried it on the island of Myconus, and for many years thereafter his countrymen annually launched a ship with black sails and burnt it in his honor.

Alcestis (al-ses'tis). A legendary daughter of Pelias, king of Iolcus. According to some accounts, she refused to take part with her sisters in the spurious rites Medea proposed to prolong her father's life, but which resulted in his death. These accounts say that Jason then gave her as wife to Admetus, king of Pherae. Others say that Admetus won her by yoking a boar and a lion to a chariot and successfully driving them. In any event, she was the wife of Admetus, who had been promised by Artemis that when Death came for him, he would be spared if he could find a substitute to go in his place. When the time came all too soon, no one was willing to go in place of Admetus except his devoted wife Alcestis. She gave her life that Admetus might be spared. But she did not remain long in the Underworld. On learning of her sacrifice Admetus' friend Heracles went to the Underworld, wrestled with Death to secure her release, and restored her to Admetus. The story of Alcestis' nobility and unselfishness, contrasted with Admetus' willingness to give up what he most loved in order to live a little longer, is told by Euripides in his drama *Alcestis*.

Alcimedon (al-sim'e-don). A legendary Arcadian hero whose daughter Phialo was ravished by Heracles. When she bore a son, Alcimedon banished them from his mountain cave, bound and gagged Phialo, and left her and her baby on the mountain to die. Her child's cries were heard by a jay which, mimicking the infant's cries, flew off to Heracles. Thus he was led to the spot where Phialo and her child were lying and he rescued them.

Alcinous (al-sin'ō-us). In Homeric legend (*Odyssey*), a king of the Phaeacians. He was the husband of Arete and the father of Nausicaä. Odysseus managed to get ashore on the island

fat, fāte, fär, fâll, åsk, fåre; net, mē, hėr; pin, pīne; not, nōte, möve, nôr; up, lūte, pûll; oi, oil; ou out; (lightened) ẹlect, agǫny, ụnite;

kingdom of Alcinous after the raft on which he had sailed from Calypso's island broke up in a storm. Encountering Nausicaä on the shore, Odysseus prevailed upon her to conduct him to her father's court. Alcinous, encouraged by his wife, welcomed him as a stranger and promised to provide a ship to take him home. In the course of a feast Odysseus was called on to tell his name and history, and many of the adventures which he had experienced since leaving Troy are told for the first time during his stay with the Phaeacians. When Alcinous learned who he was, he wanted to keep Odysseus as a son-in-law, but refused to hold him against his will. He gave him many gifts and sent him in one of the Phaeacians' ships to Ithaca. In later legend it is said that Jason and Medea landed on the island of the Phaeacians in their flight from Colchis. Here the Colchians overtook them and claimed Medea. But Alcinous, advised by his wife, refused to surrender Medea if she was married to Jason. A marriage was hurriedly arranged and some of the disappointed Colchians, fearing to return to Colchis without Medea, settled among the Phaeacians.

Alcis (al'sis). According to some accounts, a daughter of Antipoenus of Thebes, a descendant of the Sparti. When Heracles decided to resist Erginus, king of the Minyans who was attacking Thebes, an oracle foretold victory if a descendant of the Sparti voluntarily died for Thebes. Alcis and her sister Androclea gladly killed themselves for the good of their country, and were afterward worshiped as heroines in the temple of Artemis in Thebes.

Alcmaeon (alk-mē'on). In Greek legend, a son of Amphiaraus the seer and Eriphyle. Ten years after the disastrous expedition of the Seven against Thebes, in which Amphiaraus disappeared into the earth, the Epigoni (sons of the original Seven) proposed to make war on Thebes and avenge their fathers. They learned from an oracle that the expedition would be successful if Alcmaeon commanded it. According to some accounts, before Amphiaraus had departed on the first expedition, he had left orders commanding his sons to kill their mother Eriphyle and to march on Thebes when they grew up. Because he had not yet punished his mother, Alcmaeon was reluctant to lead the new expedition. Others say he thought it was unwise and disputed with his brother Amphilochus about the matter, and that they agreed to submit the question to their mother for a decision. She, bribed by Polynices' son Thersander, advised them to make war on Thebes. The expedition was successful, but Alcmaeon overheard Thersander boasting that he had brought about the success by bribing Eriphyle, as his father had bribed her before the first expedition. Alcmaeon was furious when he learned of this second bribe that might have caused his death as the first bribe had caused his father's. He consulted the oracle at Delphi and interpreted the answer to mean that he should kill his mother. This he did with the help, some say, of Amphilochus. As she was dying Eriphyle uttered a curse, praying that no land should offer shelter to her murderers. Alcmaeon, pursued by the Furies, first fled to his grandfather Oicles in Arcadia then went to Phegeus, king of Psophis. He took with him the necklace and robe with which his mother had been bribed. Phegeus purified him and gave to him in marriage his daughter Arsinoë. Alcmaeon gave the fatal necklace and robe to his new wife. But Eriphyle's curse was operating and he was hounded by the Furies. The land of Psophis became barren. An oracle advised him to go to the river-god Achelous. Achelous purified him and gave him his daughter Callirrhoë in marriage. Alcmaeon colonized the land that had been deposited as silt by the Achelous river; this land, not having been formed at the time of his mother's curse, was free to receive him and here he lived peacefully for some years. Callirrhoë bore him two sons, Acarnan and Amphoterus. Some time later Callirrhoë coveted the ill-omened necklace and robe of Eriphyle and commanded Alcmaeon to fetch them for her. He went to Phegeus and told him an oracle had instructed him to take the necklace and robe to Delphi and he would be cured of his madness. Phegeus, with Arsinoë's consent, gave him the robe and necklace but on learning that Alcmaeon had taken another wife for whom he sought the robe and necklace, Phegeus commanded his sons to kill Alcmaeon and take the robe and necklace to Delphi where they could bring no further disasters. The sons of Phegeus carried out their father's orders. Alcmaeon was killed. The robe and necklace were taken to Delphi where, according to Pausanias, they remained until the 4th century B.C. when they were stolen. According to Euripides, when Alcmaeon and the Epigoni took Thebes, Alcmaeon took Manto, a daughter of the seer

Tiresias, and became the father of a son Amphilochus and a daughter Tisiphone by her. He later sent Manto to Delphi as part of the booty from Thebes and gave his two children to be brought up by Creon, king of Corinth. Tisiphone grew to be so beautiful that Creon's wife, jealous of her beauty, sold her as a slave. The purchaser, unaware of her identity, was Alcmaeon.

Alcmene (alk-mē′nē). In Greek mythology, a daughter of Electryon and the mother of Heracles. Her father promised her to Amphitryon but she would not allow the marriage to be consummated until the deaths of her eight brothers had been avenged. While Amphitryon was away fighting the Taphians for this purpose, Zeus visited Alcmene. He had decided to make her the mother of a mighty hero, and because he knew she was chaste he came to her disguised as her husband. Alcmene was the last mortal woman Zeus embraced. He told her that her brothers had been avenged and spent with her one night, which he caused to be prolonged to three times the usual length. Amphitryon returned the next day but Alcmene, having entertained Zeus in the belief that he was her husband, did not welcome the returned warrior with great enthusiasm. In due time she bore twin sons, Heracles and Iphicles. Heracles, who she learned from the seer Tiresias was the child of Zeus, she abandoned out of fear of Hera, but he was restored to her by Athena. Iphicles was the child of Amphitryon. Alcmene outlived her famous son and was the protectress of his children. She accompanied them to Athens, the only Greek city willing to defy Eurystheus' order to banish them, and when he made war on Athens and was defeated, Alcmene ordered his death. After the death of Amphitryon Alcmene married Rhadamanthys, who had fled from Crete to Greece, and lived with him at Ocalea. She died at a great age and a tomb at Haliartus was said to be the tomb of Alcmene and Rhadamanthys. But some say she died in Thebes, where she was worshiped as a goddess. These claim that when Alcmene died Zeus sent Hermes to steal her body from the coffin. Hermes substituted a stone for the body of Alcmene and carried her off to the Elysian Fields and it was there that she married Rhadamanthys. The Heraclidae, carrying the coffin in the funeral procession, were astonished at its great weight. After some discussion they set the coffin down, opened it, and found the stone Hermes had put inside. This they set up in a sacred grove at Thebes where there was later a shrine of Alcmene. But still others say she died in Megara where there was also a shrine of Alcmene.

Alcon (al'kon). In Greek legend, a skilled archer who accompanied Heracles on his mission to obtain the cattle of Geryon. He could shoot through rings on the helmets of soldiers standing in file, and could split arrows that were impaled on spear points. He was the father of Phalerus the Argonaut and once killed with an arrow, without harming the boy, a serpent that had coiled around his son's body.

Alcyone (al-sī'ọ̄-nē). In Greek mythology, a daughter of Aeolus and the wife of Ceyx. After her husband's death she was changed into a kingfisher *(alcyon);* it was said that her father causes the winds to cease for seven days at the beginning of the winter solstice and seven days after it, so that the seas will be calm while the kingfishers nest. See *Ceyx.*

Aletes (ạ-lē'tēz). In Greek legend, a son of Hippotes, and a descendant of Heracles. After the Heraclidae invaded the Peloponnesus, he learned that he could win the city of Corinth only if he was given a clod of earth. Later when he asked a Corinthian peasant for bread he was given a lump of earth instead. Outside the city walls he met the daughters of the king of Corinth. On his promise to marry the youngest daughter, he persuaded her to open the gates of the city so that he could conquer it. Thus 30 years after the invasion of the Peloponnesus by the Heraclidae, he took possession of Corinth. When he was waging war against Athens he was informed by an oracle that he would take the city if its king remained unharmed. Codrus, king of Athens at the time, also learned of the oracle and some say that he killed himself, or took measures that led to his death, in order to fulfill the oracle and save his country.

Alethia (al-ē-thī'ạ). In Greek mythology, the personification of Truth. She was supposedly a daughter of Zeus. Her Roman counterpart was called Veritas.

Alexander (al-eg-zan'dèr). Another name for Paris, son of Priam and Hecuba, brother of Hector, and abductor of Helen.

Alexandra (al-eg-zan'drạ). Another name for *Cassandra.*

Alkmene (alk-mē'nē). See *Alcmene.*

---

fat, fāte, fär, fåll, åsk, fāre; net, mē, hèr; pin, pīne; not, nōte, möve, nôr; up, lūte, pùll; oi, oil; ou out; (lightened) ẹlect, agọny, ụnite;

Aloidae (al-ọ̄-ī'dē). Ephialtes and Otus, the sons of Poseidon and Iphimedia or Canace. In Greek mythology they were called the Aloidae, "sons of Aloeus," because he was their mother's husband and their foster father. The handsome children grew at an astonishing rate each year, and by the time they were nine years old they felt equal to waging war on the gods. They seized Ares in Thrace, bound him and imprisoned him in a bronze vessel. After 13 months Ares was freed by the cunning of Hermes. They then piled Mount Pelion on Mount Ossa and attacked Olympus itself. Poseidon persuaded them to cease their attack on Olympus in return for the promise of Zeus not to punish them for their arrogance. This armistice was easier to arrange because of a prophecy that no other men or gods could kill the Aloidae. They next decided to carry off two goddesses. Otus chose to abduct Hera and Ephialtes desired Artemis. They first sought Artemis, but that goddess, on the advice of Apollo, fled over the sea to Naxos. Like all the sons of Poseidon, the Aloidae could skim over the sea and they followed her. She disappeared in a wood on the island and a white hind appeared in her place. The brothers separated to pursue it and approached it from opposite sides of the wood. Unaware that his brother was on the other side of the hind, each hurled his spear at the same time and, as the hind vanished, the spear of each went unerringly into the heart of the other. Thus the prophecy that no other men or gods could kill them was fulfilled, and Artemis had her revenge on them for daring to desire a goddess by causing the devoted brothers to kill each other. The Aloidae were the first mortals to worship the Muses; they were also paid the honors due to heroes by the people of Naxos. Their bodies were carried back to Boeotia for burial but their souls descended to Tartarus and were tied to posts with ropes of writhing serpents.

Alpheus (al-fē'us, al'fẹ-us). River-god of the Alpheus River in Elis. On one occasion Arethusa, one of the chaste companions of Artemis, was bathing in his waters, and was terrified to feel an embracing movement about her. She leaped to the bank and fled. Alpheus pursued her and she called on Artemis for help. Artemis took her away to Ortygia near Syracuse, rent the earth and transformed Arethusa into a fountain that flowed from the chasm. Alpheus dived under the sea and made his way to Ortygia, and there mingled his waters with those of the fountain of Arethusa. It was said that a flower thrown into the Alpheus River in Greece would ultimately turn up in the fountain of Arethusa at Ortygia, having followed the route under the sea that was taken by Alpheus. On another occasion Alpheus went to Letrini where Artemis was holding revels with her companions with the intention of seizing the goddess. But Artemis suspected him and disguised herself and her maidens with white clay. Alpheus was unable to distinguish the goddess and was compelled to retire, as the maidens laughed at his disappointment.

Althaea (al-thē′a). In Greek legend, a daughter of Thestius. She was said to be the wife of Oeneus, king of Calydon in Aetolia, and the mother of Meleager, Tydeus, and Deianira. According to some accounts, Meleager was her son by Ares and Deianira was her daughter by Dionysus. Shortly after Meleager's birth the Fates prophesied that he would live only as long as a brand at that time burning in the fire was unconsumed. She seized the brand, quenched it and hid it away, thus saving his life. When, following the hunt for the Calydonian Boar, Meleager killed her brothers, Althaea recovered the partly burned brand and hurled it into the flames, thus causing Meleager's death. In despair at the violation of her maternal feelings she then hanged herself.

Amalthea (am-al-thē′a). In Greek mythology, a goat-nymph who provided milk for the infant Zeus when he was reared by nymphs in a cave in Crete. According to some accounts, Zeus borrowed one of her horns and gave it to the nymphs. This horn, the "Cornucopia," had the property of being filled with whatever food or drink its possessor required. In gratitude to Amalthea, Zeus set her image among the stars as the constellation Capricorn.

Amazons (am′a-zonz). In Greek legend, a race of warrior women supposed to have dwelt near the Thermodon River on the coast of the Euxine Sea, and in the Caucasus Mountains. They are represented as forming a state from which men were excluded. They were governed by a queen. Girl children had their right breasts cut off (the name Amazon has been said by some to mean "breastless") so as not to interfere with the bow arm. Male children were slain in infancy. The Amazons devoted themselves to war and hunt-

fat, fāte, fär, fåll, åsk, fāre; net, mē, hėr; pin, pīne; not, nōte, möve, nôr; up, lūte, půll; oi, oil; ou out; (lightened) ĕlect, agŏny, ūnite;

ing. Bellerophon fought them. Heracles, as one of his labors
for Eurystheus, went to their country to fetch the girdle of
the Amazon queen Hippolyte. By a misunderstanding inspired by Hera he made war on the Amazons, who had been
inclined to be friendly, killed many and took some prisoners.
According to Herodotus the Amazons who were being
shipped back to Greece rose up and massacred the Greek
crews. Unfamiliar with the ways of ships, they then were
carried by the winds to the shores of Lake Maeotis. Here
they went ashore, fell among the Scythians and seized their
horses. After some time, these Amazons mingled with the
Scythians and formed a new race. The new race, ancestors
of the Sauromatae according to Herodotus, moved to lands
north of the Tanais River and settled there. The women
continued to hunt and make war and it was one of their laws
that no girl should marry until she had killed a man in battle.
During the reign of Theseus, the Amazons remaining about
the Thermodon River marched to Athens and attacked it.
Some say this was done because Theseus had accompanied
Heracles on his raid and had carried off the Amazon Antiope, who became the mother of his son Hippolytus. The
Amazons were defeated by the Athenians and were driven
off. In the Trojan War the Amazons under their queen Penthesilea came to the aid of the Trojans. They were defeated
by the Greeks and Penthesilea was slain by Achilles. Plutarch
reports of the Amazons that they annually met with the
Albanians on the banks of the Thermodon River for two
months, after which they withdrew again to their own country and lived without the company of men. The wars between the Amazons and Greeks were a favorite subject with
Greek painters and sculptors. Many friezes of temples, vase
paintings, and metopes were devoted to this subject.

Ambrosia (am-brō′ẓiạ). Literally, "immortality." A celestial
substance, commonly represented as the food of the gods,
sometimes as their drink, and also as a richly perfumed
unguent. When eaten by mortals it conferred immortality on
them. It was also supposed to preserve against decay and
corruption. In the *Iliad* the bodies of Hector, Patroclus, and
Sarpedon were preserved and made whole by applications
of ambrosia by the gods.

Ammon (am′ọn). The Greek and Roman conception of the
Egyptian sun-god, Amon (Amon-Re), Amen (Amen-Ra).

(obscured) errạnt, ardẹnt, actọr; ch, chip; g, go; th, thin; ᴛʜ, then; y, you;
(variable) ḍ as d or j, ş as s or sh, ṭ as t or ch, ẓ as z or zh.

The Greeks called him Zeus-Ammon to identify him with
Zeus. The Romans called him Jupiter-Ammon. According to
the Greeks, when Typhon attacked the gods Zeus transformed himself into a ram and fled to Egypt. Later, when
Heracles was in Libya in quest of the Apples of the Hesperides, he visited the oracle of Ammon and demanded to see
Zeus. The god did not wish to show himself but when Heracles persisted, Zeus killed a ram, flayed it, and cut off its
head. The god then held the ram's head before him, covered
himself with the ram's fleece and in this guise he presented
himself to Heracles. It is for this reason, according to
Herodotus, that the Egyptians show their images of Zeus-
Ammon with the face and horns of a ram, and it is for this
reason that rams are held sacred by the Thebans of Egypt
and are not sacrificed except on the one day of the year when
the festival of Zeus-Ammon is celebrated. On this day they
kill one ram and flay it. They cover the image of Zeus with
the fleece and then present to the fleece-covered statue of
Zeus an image of Heracles, after which they mourn the ram
and bury it in a sacred spot. The oracle of Zeus-Ammon in
Libya (situated at what is now the Oasis of Siwa in NW
Egypt) was greatly venerated and was consulted by seekers
from all over the ancient world. Laomedon, king of Troy,
sent to the oracle of Ammon to learn how he could rid his
land of the plague and sea monster that Apollo and Poseidon had sent against his land because he did not pay them
as he had promised for their help in building the walls of
Troy. The oracle told him to sacrifice his daughter Hesione
to the monster. Cepheus, father of Andromeda, consulted
the oracle to learn how he could be delivered from a monster that was ravaging his land and received similar advice.
Croesus, king of Lydia, consulted the oracle of Ammon
among others, when he was considering a war against Cyrus
and the Persians. This oracle was founded, according to
some accounts, in obedience to the command of a black
dove that flew from the temple of Egyptian Thebes to this
place, and ordered the inhabitants to establish an oracle of
Zeus. Remains of the ancient temple of Zeus-Ammon on the
site are still to be seen. The Spartans, who consulted the
oracle of Ammon more frequently than the other Greeks,
had their own sanctuary and oracle of Ammon in Sparta.
Ampelos (am'pe-los). A beautiful satyr who fell and was killed

when plucking grapes from a vine that grew up an elm tree. He was a favorite of Dionysus, who placed him among the stars. A genus of singing birds that haunt vines, among them the Carolina waxwing, was named for him.

Amphiaraus (am″fi-ạ-rā′us). In Greek legend, an Argive seer and hero; he was the son of Oicles and was married to Eriphyle, sister of Adrastus, king of Argos. He took part in the Calydonian Hunt and accompanied Jason as an Argonaut on the voyage to Colchis to secure the Golden Fleece. When Adrastus proposed to march against Thebes to restore his son-in-law Polynices to the throne, he asked Amphiaraus to accompany him on the expedition as one of the leaders. Amphiaraus, who foresaw that all except Adrastus would perish, was reluctant to go and tried to discourage the others. His wife Eriphyle, however, had once settled a quarrel between him and Adrastus and had extracted a promise from each that they would abide by her decision in any future difference of opinion. Polynices now bribed her to compel Amphiaraus to march with Adrastus. She reminded him of his promise and he consented to go, but he left orders with his sons, Alcmaeon and Amphilochus, to kill their mother and march against Thebes when they grew up. Amphiaraus saw an omen of disaster in the death of the child Opheltes at Nemea who was killed by a serpent while his nurse showed the Argives where they could get water. At the assault on Thebes all the champions were killed except Adrastus. Amphiaraus fled in his chariot. Before Periclymenus, who was pursuing him, could cast his spear into his back, Zeus cleft the earth with his thunderbolt and Amphiaraus, his chariot, and his charioteer vanished into the chasm. The spot where he disappeared into the earth was shown not far from Thebes on the road to Potniae. Zeus made Amphiaraus, the one upright man in a lawless company, immortal. He was deified and worshiped as a divine, oracular hero at various places. He had a temple at Oropus in Attica and a famous oracle of Amphiaraus there was noted for the interpretation of dreams. Some say Amphiaraus, by means of an oracle, proposed to the Thebans that they make a choice: either to take him as their prophet or as their helper in war. The Thebans decided to take him as their helper in war. For this reason it was unlawful for the Thebans to consult him as an oracle; it was therefore forbidden

(obscured) errạnt, ardẹnt, actọr; ch, chip; g, go; th, thin; ŦH, then; y, you; (variable) ḍ as d or j, ṣ as s or sh, ṭ as t or ch, ẓ as z or zh.

to them to sleep in his temple and receive his prophecies in dreams.

Amphictyon (am-fik'ti-ọn). According to some accounts, a son of Deucalion and Pyrrha, but others say he sprang from the soil. He rose against Cranaus, king of Attica, and seized the throne. He entertained Dionysus and is said to have been the first man to mix water with wine, a wise precaution for preventing disputes at the meetings of the Amphictyonic Council. After a reign of 12 years Amphictyon in his turn was driven from the throne by Erichthonius, the earthborn son of the spilled seed of Hephaestus.

Amphidamas (am-fid'ạ-mạs). In Greek legend, a son of Aleus. He and his brother Cepheus left their home in Tegea in Arcadia and joined the Argonauts on the quest for the Golden Fleece. When the Argonauts approached the island of Ares they were afraid to land because of the birds of Ares that dropped iron feathers and attacked with bronze bills and claws. Amphidamas suggested that the Argonauts should cover their heads with their shields and clash their weapons together to frighten the birds away. This ruse was successful and the Argonauts landed on the island of Ares as they had been advised to do by Phineus.

Amphilochus (am-fil'ọ-kus). In Greek legend, a son of Amphiaraus and Eriphyle, and the brother of Alcmaeon. Like his father, he was a seer. Some say he accompanied the Epigoni on their expedition against Thebes and that he helped Alcmaeon kill Eriphyle when they learned that she, by being bribed, had caused the death of their father by urging him to go as one of the original Seven Against Thebes. He accompanied the Greeks to Troy and after the war he traveled overland with Calchas and Podalirius to Colophon where they met the seer Mopsus, and where Calchas died. Amphilochus did not return to Argos immediately but remained in Cilicia where he founded the city of Mallus with Mopsus. After some time he departed for Argos, leaving Mopsus as ruler of Mallus, but later he returned from Argos and sought to resume his former role as joint ruler of Mallus. He and Mopsus quarreled bitterly when Mopsus refused to share the powers. They attempted to resolve their quarrel in a duel, in the course of which they killed each other. After their bodies had been consumed to ashes on funeral pyres, the ghosts of Amphilochus and Mopsus became intimate friends. An oracle was established in their names which came to be regarded as most infallible. Questions were written on wax tablets and the answers were revealed in dreams.

Amphinomus (am-fin'ō-mus). In Homeric legend *(Odyssey)*, a son of Nisus of Dulichium. Of all the suitors of Penelope he was the most pleasing to her, and according to some accounts, was the father by Penelope of Pan. In general, he was kinder and more sympathetic than Penelope's other suitors. He protested against the plan of Antinous to ambush and kill Telemachus as he returned from Sparta. Because he was a good man, Odysseus, when he returned to Ithaca disguised as a beggar, advised Amphinomus to leave Ithaca. He warned him that death awaited the wooers. But Amphinomus did not follow this advice. He remained and was slain by Telemachus during the slaughter of the suitors.

Amphion (am-fī'on, am'fi-ǫn). In Greek mythology, a son of Antiope and Zeus and twin brother of Zethus. The twins were exposed on Mount Cithaeron to die when they were born but were found and raised by a herdsman. As young men they slew Dirce, who had mistreated their mother, by causing her to be dragged to death by a bull. They made themselves masters of Thebes and built part of the city. Amphion, a gifted musician, played so beautifully on the lyre which Hermes had given him, while the walls were being constructed, that the stones slid into place by themselves. He married Niobe and became the father of seven sons and seven daughters. When his children were slain by Artemis and Apollo because of Niobe's boasting, Amphion, in grief, killed himself. According to other accounts Amphion was killed by Apollo and was punished in the Underworld for attacking the priests of Delphi in revenge for the slaying of his children by Apollo.

Amphitrite (am-fi-trī'tē). In early mythology, the personification of the sea; the goddess who sends the waves and governs the inhabitants of the sea. In later mythology she is a Nereid, the daughter of Nereus and Doris. Some say Poseidon saw her dancing on the island of Naxos and carried her off to be his wife. Others say she fled to Atlas from his advances. He sent Delphinus as an ambassador to plead his cause, and this he did so successfully that Amphitrite consented to marry Poseidon. She bore him Triton, Rhode, and

(obscured) errạnt, ardẹnt, actǫr; ch, chip; g, go; th, thin; ₮H, then; y, you; (variable) ḍ as d or j, ş as s or sh, ţ as t or ch, ẕ as z or zh.

Benthesicyme. She was jealous of her many rivals for Poseidon's affections. She punished Scylla, a daughter of Phorcys whom Poseidon loved, by changing her into a hideous monster with six heads and twelve feet. Amphitrite is represented with a net about her hair and with crab claws on the top of her head. As queen of the sea she rides over the waves in a chariot made of shells and drawn by Tritons or dolphins, or sometimes she simply rides on the backs of the creatures of her domain. The Romans identified Amphitrite with their Salacia.

Amphitryon (am-fit′ri-ọn). In Greek legend, a descendant of Perseus. When Electryon, king of Mycenae, warred against the Taphians and the Teleboans because they had made a raid on his cattle and killed his eight sons, he left Amphitryon to rule in his place, and promised him his daughter Alcmene if he ruled well. Amphitryon learned that the Eleans had Electryon's cattle and bought them back. On learning that he was expected to pay for his own cattle Electryon was furious, and charged Amphitryon with incompetence. In the course of the dispute, Amphitryon hurled a club at one of the cattle and accidentally struck and killed Electryon. He was then banished from Mycenae and went with Alcmene to Thebes. However, she would not allow the marriage to be consummated until the murder of her eight brothers by the Taphians was avenged. Amphitryon was permitted by Creon, king of Thebes, to raise an army for that purpose on condition that he catch a ravaging fox, the Teumessian vixen, which by a decree of fate could not be caught. Amphitryon borrowed Laelaps, a dog which fate had decreed should catch whatever animal it might pursue, and went after the fox. Under these conditions the gods resolved the problem posed by these two animals by turning them both into stone. Amphitryon now attacked the Taphians but could not overcome them so long as the chief Pterelaus, who was rendered immortal by one golden hair, continued to live. Comaetho, daughter of Pterelaus, cut off this hair for love of Amphitryon, and Pterelaus perished. Amphitryon was successful, but he killed Comaetho for her betrayal of her father. While Amphitryon was away at the war Zeus, disguised as her husband, embraced Alcmene, telling her the deaths of her brothers had been avenged. When Amphitryon returned, he learned from a seer that

fat, fāte, fär, fåll, åsk, fãre; net, mē, hėr; pin, pīne; not, nōte, mŏve, nôr; up, lūte, pùll; oi, oil; ou out; (lightened) ẹlect, agọny, ūnite;

Alcmene had been loved by a god. Later twin sons, Heracles and Iphicles, were born a day apart, to Alcmene. According to some accounts, Amphitryon put two harmless serpents into the children's cradle while they were yet babes in order to find out which child was his. Heracles seized the serpents in his bare hands and strangled them gleefully. Iphicles screamed, and Amphitryon knew this was his son. But others say it was Hera who sent the serpents in order to destroy Heracles. In the war between Thebes and Erginus, leader of the Minyans, Amphitryon was killed and was buried in Thebes.

Amymone (a-mi-mō'nē). In Greek mythology, one of the 50 daughters of Danaus. Danaus instructed his daughters to appease Poseidon who had dried up the streams of Argolis in anger. Amymone, while searching for water, disturbed a satyr, who attempted to ravish her. She called for help. Poseidon appeared and hurled his trident at the satyr, but the satyr avoided the blow and fled. The trident was implanted in the rock. Poseidon fell in love with Amymone and embraced her. When he learned that she was searching for water, he caused a spring to gush from the rock where the three prongs of his trident had struck it. This spring, known as the fountain of Amymone, became the source of the Lerna River and never dries up, even in midsummer when the other streams of Argolis are dry. The Hydra of Lerna, child of Echidna, was born under a plane tree near this fountain of Amymone. Amymone bore Nauplius, the famous navigator, by Poseidon.

Anaxarete (an″ak-sar'ȩ̄-tē). In Greek mythology, a Grecian princess who was beloved by Iphis, a man of humble birth. He sent messages of love to her and adorned the doorposts of her house with garlands and wreaths of flowers. Anaxarete mocked him and scorned his love. In despair, Iphis resolved to place one final testimonial of his love on the doors of her house. He fixed a noose to the lintel and hanged himself. His funeral procession passed by Anaxarete's house, and as she watched it without compassion, the gods turned her to stone. The stone statue was placed in a temple in Salamis as a warning to hard-hearted maidens who mocked their lovers.

Ancaeus (an-sē'us). In Greek legend, a son of Poseidon. He left his palace in Tegea and joined the Argonauts on the voyage in quest of the Golden Fleece. From his father he had great skill in navigation, and after the death of Tiphys in the land of the Mariandyni, Ancaeus became the helmsman of the *Argo*. He guided the ship to the Phasis River in Colchis and acted as steersman on the voyage of return from Colchis. After the many perils of the voyage Ancaeus returned safely to his home in Tegea. He had been told by a seer that he would not survive to taste wine from recently planted grape vines. On his return the vines had flourished, grapes had been harvested, and wine pressed. Ancaeus, about to set a cup of the wine to his lips, reminded the seer of his old prophecy and accused him of being a false prophet. The seer replied that "there is many a slip between the cup and the lip." At that instant a tumult arose over a wild boar that had been discovered in the vineyard. Ancaeus set down the cup, the wine untasted, and rushed off to slay the boar but the animal charged him and gored him to death.

Anchises (an-kī'sēz, ang-). In mythology, a son of Capys and Themiste, and a descendant of Dardanus and Ilus, founders of the Trojan race. While he was tending his flocks Aphrodite came to him, disguised as the daughter of a Phrygian king. The goddess, who became the mother of Aeneas by Anchises, later revealed her true identity to him, and made him vow that he would never reveal it. However, Anchises, having overindulged in wine, boasted that he had lain with a goddess. For this he was struck by a shaft of lightning and crippled in his limbs. After the fall of Troy he expressed his determination to remain and end his days in the city. He said he was old and useless and did not wish to flee with his son Aeneas. He was persuaded to go by a sign—a curl of flame settled on his young grandson's hair but didn't burn it—and a falling star confirmed the favorable omen. Carrying the gods of Troy, he rode out of the city on Aeneas' shoulders. When the oracle of Delos told the Trojans to seek out their mother country, Anchises took this to mean Crete, but a dream informed Aeneas that the oracle meant Italy, whither they then journeyed. Anchises died, according to Vergil, in Drepanum in Sicily, after having been a bulwark of advice and counsel to Aeneas. Even after his death he continued to aid his son. When the Trojan women, despairing that their journeying never ceased, burnt the ships in Italy, Anchises' shade appeared to Aeneas and advised him to leave those who were weary of wandering where they were, and to proceed to carry out his destiny with those who still had a love of glory. He also told Aeneas that he must visit him in Hades to find out what the future held. In accordance with these instructions, Aeneas entered the Underworld near Cumae. Anchises welcomed him and pointed out the souls in the Underworld that were waiting to be reborn and to win honor in Rome. He also gave Aeneas a very wide look at the future history of the empire he was destined to found.

Androgeus (an-droj'ē-us). In Greek legend, a son of Minos, king of Crete, and Pasiphaë. On a visit to Athens he defeated all competitors in the Panathenean games. According to some accounts, King Aegeus, to get rid of him, then sent him on a mission to kill the Marathonian Bull, which Heracles had brought back from Crete as one of his labors. It was now roaming the plains of Marathon, destroying men and cattle. Androgeus found the bull, but was killed by it. Others say that King Aegeus, fearing Androgeus would support a rebellion against him, had Androgeus ambushed and though he fought valiantly he was killed. In revenge for his son's death, Minos waged war on the Athenians, and compelled them to send a tribute of seven maidens and seven youths to Crete every nine years. These youths and maidens were given to the Minotaur.

Andromache (an-drom'a-kē). In Greek legend, a daughter of Eëtion, king of Thebes in Cilicia. She was the wife of Hector and the mother of Astyanax. In the tenth year of the Trojan War when the city was besieged by the Greeks, she tried to persuade Hector not to engage in the battle on the plain. Since her father and her seven brothers had been killed by Achilles when he took Thebes, and her mother, though ransomed, had died, she told Hector that he was father, mother, and brother to her as well as husband. She warned him that his courage would be his undoing as the Greeks would certainly make him their prime target. She asked him to take pity on her and on their infant son and to remain within the walls of the city. With great compassion and nobility of spirit Hector refused her request to keep apart from the battle. Weeping, Andromache returned to the palace as Hector put on his war helmet and set out for the battlefield. She never again saw him alive. When his body was ransomed and returned to Troy she clasped dead Hector's head in her arms and mourned, grieving bitterly that he had not been able to give her any word in farewell. With Hector dead she foresaw doom for herself, her son, and for Troy. Penthesilea the Amazon came to the aid of Troy and boasted that she would kill Achilles. Andromache doubted her good sense in speaking so recklessly of the man who had killed Hector. After the fall of Troy, Astyanax was taken from Andromache's arms and hurled to his death from the towers of the city. Andromache was taken as the captive and concubine of Neoptolemus. He took her to Thessaly and she bore him sons: Molossus, Pergamus, and Pielus. For ten years Neoptolemus treated her with kindness. At the end of that time he married Hermione, the daughter of Helen and Menelaus, but he did not abandon Andromache and her children. However Hermione, who remained childless, jealously persecuted Andromache and with the help of her father would have slain her and her sons during Neoptolemus' absence. Peleus arrived in time to save Andromache and her children. Neoptolemus, who was slain at Delphi, bequeathed Andromache to Helenus. She married him and accompanied him to Epirus where he built a miniature Troy at Buthrotum. There Aeneas, on his way to Italy, found her as she was performing rites for Hector. She had never stopped mourning for him and told Aeneas that the women who died at Troy were fortunate; they had been spared the life of slavery and humiliation which had been her fate. Following the death of Helenus Andromache returned to Asia with her son Pergamus.

Andromeda   (an-drom′ē-dạ). In Greek legend, the daughter of Cepheus, king of Joppa in Ethiopia, and Cassiopea. She was betrothed to Phineus, the brother of Cepheus according to some accounts. Her mother boasted that she and her daughter were more beautiful than the Nereids of the sea. This boast angered Poseidon. He sent a savage sea monster to devastate the land as a punishment for the foolish arrogance of Cassiopea. Cepheus, on appealing to the oracle of Ammon, was told that only the sacrifice of Andromeda to the monster would appease Poseidon and cause him to relieve the country of the depredations of the beast he had sent. Cepheus had no choice; he chained Andromeda, naked except for her jewels, to a rocky cliff at the edge of the sea. Phineus felt unable to take any steps to save her. Perseus,

fat, fāte, fär, fåll, ȧsk, fāre; net, mē, hèr; pin, pīne; not, nōte, mȯve, nôr; up, lūte, pùll; oi, oil; ou out; (lightened) ēlect, agǫny, ūnite;

returning with the head of Medusa, flew over the shores of Ethiopia and saw the beautiful maiden chained to a rock. Instantly he fell in love with her and flew down to learn the reason for her unhappy state. He learned the story from Cepheus and promised to slay the monster if Cepheus would reward him with Andromeda's hand in marriage. Cepheus willingly promised. When the monster emerged from the sea Perseus cut off its head with one stroke and freed his bride. The marks made by her chains on the rocks were visible for generations afterwards. At the wedding festivities for Perseus and Andromeda, Phineus and a company of his followers burst in and asserted that he was betrothed to Andromeda and she could not marry Perseus. Andromeda insisted that her father's promise be fulfilled. Cepheus weakened, now that all danger was past. Phineus attacked Perseus, but he exhibited the head of Medusa and turned them all to stone. Andromeda departed for Greece with Perseus. She bore him six sons and a daughter, and during their life together she enjoyed the knowledge, unusual for the wife of a Greek hero, that her lord was constant in his affection for her. After she died Athena placed her image among the stars.

Antaeus   (an-tē′us). In Greek mythology, a Libyan giant and wrestler, son of Poseidon, god of the sea, and Gaea, the earth. He was invincible so long as he remained in contact with his mother. He compelled strangers in his country to wrestle with him, and built a house to Poseidon of their skulls. Heracles discovered the source of his strength, and, lifting him into the air, crushed him.

Antenor   (an-tē′nor). In Greek legend, a Trojan, husband of the priestess Theano. As one of Priam's counselors he advised the Trojans, after the duel between Hector and Ajax in the tenth year of the war, to return Helen and all her possessions to Menelaus. His advice was disregarded. In the closing days of the war he was sent to negotiate peace with Agamemnon but instead, according to some accounts, because of his hatred of Deïphobus, son of Priam, he plotted with Agamemnon to help Odysseus enter the city secretly and steal the Palladium, the sacred image of Athena which protected the city as long as it remained within the walls. When Troy was taken by the device of the Wooden Horse, Menelaus hung a leopard's skin over the door of Antenor's house as a sign that it should not be plundered in the sack of the city. Antenor, Theano, and his remaining sons, slipped through the Greek lines and crossed over to Thrace. At length he sailed up the Illyrian Gulf and founded a city at the head of the Adriatic which was called "New Troy." Its inhabitants were afterward known as Venetians. Antenor is also said to have founded Padua, shortly before the arrival of Aeneas in Latium.

Anteros (an'tẻr-os). In Greek mythology, a son of Aphrodite and Ares, and brother of Eros. He was sometimes represented as the avenger of unrequited affection and sometimes as the symbol of mutual love and tenderness.

Anticlea (an-ti-klē'ạ). A daughter of Autolycus. She was the wife of Laertes the Argive but was seduced by Sisyphus and some say Sisyphus was the father of her son Odysseus, although Laertes passed as his father. Odysseus, who had not known of her death, met her shade when he visited the Underworld to consult the seer Tiresias on his way home from Troy. Although she assured him that Penelope was faithful to him she discreetly refrained from telling him of the number of suitors who were besieging Penelope. She told Odysseus that his father had retired to the country and was grieving for him, and that she had died, not from illness or a shaft from the gods, but because of her longing for his return from Troy.

Anticlus (an'ti-klus). In Greek legend, one of the Greeks who entered Troy in the Wooden Horse. Helen, inspired by Aphrodite to see if the Wooden Horse was a trap, imitated the voices of the Greeks' wives and called to the Greek heroes by name. When Anticlus heard what he thought was his wife's voice, he tried to answer but Odysseus choked him so that he could not give them away, and Anticlus perished in one of the hollow legs of the horse.

Antigone (an-tig'ọ-nē). In Greek legend, a daughter of Oedipus by his mother Jocasta. She was the sister of Eteocles, Polynices, and Ismene. According to some accounts, she faithfully accompanied Oedipus as he fled through Greece pursued by the Furies because he had killed his father and sired children by his own mother. They came at last to Colonus in Attica where Oedipus died and there, with the aid of Theseus, Antigone buried him. She returned to Thebes where her brother Eteocles was now on the throne.

By agreement with Polynices, Eteocles was to rule for a year and then yield to Polynices for a year. However, at the end of his term Eteocles refused to give up the throne. Polynices enlisted the aid of Adrastus, king of Argos. The latter, accompanied by the Argive chieftains who made up the Seven against Thebes, marched with Polynices against Thebes and waged an ill-fated war to restore Polynices to the throne. In the battle Eteocles and Polynices met in single combat and slew each other. Creon, uncle of Antigone, now became king. He ordered funeral honors for Eteocles, the valiant defender of the city, but gave orders that the body of Polynices should be cast outside the walls to become the prey of scavenger birds because he had treacherously attacked his own city. Antigone, moved by the claims of blood loyalty, resolved to bury Polynices in defiance of Creon. She attempted to enlist her sister's aid in the project but Ismene dared not risk rousing Creon's anger. Antigone succeeded in giving Polynices the minimum rites of burial by sprinkling dust over his body. Some say that she heaped a burial mound over his body or burned it on a pyre. When Creon learned that his order had been defied he demanded death for the person who had disobeyed him, and was not deterred even when he learned that the culprit was his own niece. He ordered her to be buried alive. Some say Antigone was entombed alive in a cave, or in the family tomb, and hanged herself, and that Haemon, the son of Creon, to whom she was betrothed, slew himself on her tomb. Others say that Creon handed Antigone over to Haemon with orders to destroy her. Haemon pretended to carry out his father's order but he secretly married Antigone and sent her away to live among his shepherds. She bore him a son. Years later the son returned to Thebes to take part in funeral games. Creon recognized him as a son of Antigone by the birthmark which all the descendants of the Sparti bore on their bodies. He charged Haemon with having disobeyed his orders, and in spite of the pleas of Heracles for clemency, ordered punishment for Antigone and Haemon. Haemon, to forestall Creon's vengeance, killed Antigone and then slew himself.

Antilochus (an-til′ō-kus). In Greek legend, a son of Nestor, who had been exposed by his mother to die on Mount Ida but was nursed by a bitch until found and saved. He had been left at home as too young to accompany his father

(obscured) errạnt, ardẹnt, actọr; ch, chip; g, go; th, thin; ᵺH, then; y, you; (variable) ḍ as d or j, ş as s or sh, ţ as t or ch, ẓ as z or zh.

when the latter sailed off to the Trojan War. A few years later he followed the Greeks to Troy and appealed to Achilles to soften his father's wrath because he had defied him and joined the fighting. He became a great friend of Achilles. Though he was one of the youngest Greeks at Troy the handsome lad was a brave fighter. He slew many Trojans and on occasion was protected by Poseidon from the spears of the enemy. Because of his friendship with Achilles and his fleetness of foot he was sent to tell Achilles of the death of Patroclus. At Troy one of Nestor's horses was pierced by an arrow. The other horse became frenzied. As Antilochus hurried to his father's assistance, Memnon the Ethiopian killed him. Achilles avenged the death of his friend Antilochus as he did that of Patroclus. The three friends were buried in the same mound, and were seen by Odysseus walking together over the asphodel meadows of the lower world.

Antinous (an-tin′ō̇-us). In the *Odyssey*, the most arrogant of the suitors of Penelope during Odysseus' long absence. He complained to her son Telemachus that Penelope would not make up her mind which of her suitors to choose, and he accused her of guile in weaving a web, supposedly a shroud for her father-in-law, which she unraveled each night. Antinous assured Telemachus that the wooers would camp on him until she chose a husband. He was enraged when he learned that Telemachus had gotten a ship and set out for Pylus for news of his father, and resolved to ambush and kill Telemachus on his way home. He was most abusive when Odysseus returned to his own house disguised as a beggar, and he was the first one Odysseus killed.

Antiope (an-tī′ō̇-pē). In Greek mythology, the daughter of Nycteus of Thebes. She was seduced by Zeus in the form of a satyr and fled from her father's wrath to the king of Sicyon. Her father secured a promise from his brother Lycus to help him capture and punish Antiope and she was brought back from Sicyon by force, her father having died. The twin sons she bore to Zeus, Amphion and Zethus, were left on Mount Cithaeron to die, but were saved by a herdsman. Antiope was cruelly treated by Lycus and his wife Dirce. She fled to the hut where her sons, now grown up, were living. Dirce pursued and told the twins to put the runaway to death by tying her by the hair to the horns of a wild bull. As they were about to do so the herdsman informed them that Antiope

fat, fāte, fär, fâll, ȧsk, fãre; net, mē, hėr; pin, pīne; not, nōte, mȯve, nôr; up, lūte, pu̇ll; oi, oil; ou out; (lightened) ḝlect, agǫny, ūnite;

was their mother. Thereupon they seized Dirce and put her
to death in the manner she had suggested for Antiope. According to other accounts, Antiope was the daughter of the
river-god Asopus and was married to Lycus who divorced
her to marry Dirce. In both accounts she was persecuted by
Dirce and avenged by her Zeus-fathered sons.

Antiope. In Greek mythology, an Amazon queen, sister of
Hippolyte. She became Theseus' captive and bore a son,
Hippolytus, to him. In the war which the Amazons and Scythians waged against Athens she fought loyally at Theseus'
side against her own countrywomen. According to some
accounts she was killed in the battle. Others say Theseus
killed her when she tried to prevent his marriage to Phaedra.

Aornis (ā-ôr′nis). In Greek mythology, one of the five tribu-
taries of the river Styx in the Underworld. The others were
Acheron, Phlegethon, Cocytus, and Lethe.

Aphrodite (af-rō̹-dī′tē). One of the 12 Olympian deities, goddess of love and beauty who ruled the hearts of gods and
men and symbolized the irresistible generative powers of
nature operating on land, in the sea, and in the air. Only
Artemis, Athena, and Hestia among the goddesses were
successful in denying the power of the great goddess of love.
All others, including Zeus himself, were under her sway.
Conscious of her power to give beauty and love, Aphrodite
punishes those who fail to honor her or who attempt to deny
her, and willingly aids those who honor and seek her.

Some say that Aphrodite was the daughter of Zeus and the
Titaness Dione. But others say that when Cronus emasculated his father Uranus with a sickle and flung his dismembered parts into the sea, foam gathered about them; and
from this sea foam Aphrodite rose and was borne to land on
a sea-shell, whence her epithets Aphrogeneia *(Foam-born)*,
and Anadyomene *(Risen from the Sea)*. She first stepped
ashore on the island of Cythera, and then went to Paphos on
Cyprus. Paphos was the most ancient seat of her worship,
and every spring the priestess of her temple renewed herself
by bathing in the sea. From these two islands, Aphrodite has
the names Cytherea and Cypris. Wherever she treads, according to the ancient Greeks, flowers spring up, and doves
and sparrows murmur in the air about her. She possesses a
magic girdle which imparts surpassing grace and charm to
whomever wears it and compels all who behold it to fall in

love with the wearer. Some say Eros and Himeros *(God o Longing)*, her constant companions, along with the Horae and the Charites, were born with her.

She was given in marriage by Zeus to the lame god He phaestus, to whom she was notoriously unfaithful, especially with the magnificent war god Ares. To Ares she bore Phobus *(Fear)*, Deimos *(Terror)*, and Harmonia, who married Cad mus, and some say Eros and Anteros *(Unrequited Love)* were also her children by Ares. Helius, who saw everything in his circuit across the heavens, reported to Hephaestus that Aphrodite was entertaining Ares in his absence. Hephaestus laid a trap for them. He pretended that he was going to Lemnos but secretly spied on them. He found Aphrodite and Ares together and cast a great bronze net he had forged over them, from which they could not escape. He then called the gods to witness their disgrace and his own dishonor. He demanded that the gifts he had given Zeus on his marriage to Aphrodite be returned as a condition for releasing the lovers from the net. Zeus was disgusted by the public spec tacle Hephaestus had made of his private affairs and refused to return the marriage gifts. Poseidon, who was in love with Aphrodite, guaranteed that Ares would pay the equivalent of the marriage gifts to Hephaestus in return for his freedom from the net, and if Ares failed to do so Poseidon promised that he himself would pay Hephaestus and take Aphrodite as his wife. Ares was freed, but never did pay, as he claimed that since Zeus had refused he could do the same. Aphrodite renewed herself by bathing in the sea. Afterward she re warded Poseidon for his good offices and bore him two sons, Rhodus and Herophilus. Hermes, who had expressed his admiration for her as she struggled in Hephaestus' bronze net, received her favors. She bore him Hermaphroditus who had the features of both sexes. But Eos, who seduced her lover Ares, she punished. She caused Eos to have a fatal weakness for young and beautiful mortal boys. In the end Hephaestus took Aphrodite back as his wife on her own terms, as he was madly in love with her. In later myth she is the wife of Ares. She subsequently bore the fertility god Priapus to Dionysus.

By her power to rule the hearts of gods as well as men Aphrodite many times caused Zeus to fall in love with mortal maidens. To make her understand what it was like to love

a mortal, Zeus caused her to fall in love with Anchises, son
of Capys. She went to the herdsman's hut of Anchises, on
the "cloud-kissing" peaks of Mount Ida near Troy, and appeared to him when he came in from tending his flocks.
Anchises was stunned by her loveliness, and instantly took
her for a goddess. But she told him she was a mortal, the
daughter of the Phrygian King Otreus, and that she had
been brought to Mount Ida by Hermes to become Anchises'
wife. Anchises was enchanted and at once embraced her.
Afterward he fell into a deep sleep. As he slept Aphrodite
donned her immortal robes, and then woke him, and revealed to him that he had embraced a goddess. Anchises was

APHRODITE RIDING ON A GOOSE
Attic cup, white ground, Pistoxenus Painter, 500–475 B.C.
British Museum

terrified, for he knew what terrible punishments were visited
on mortals who embraced gods. However, Aphrodite reas-
sured him. She said she would bear him a son who would be
named Aeneas, "the Terrible," because of the terrible pain
she suffered in loving a mortal. This son would be brought
up by the nymphs of Mount Ida for five years. At the end of

that time he would return to Anchises, who must say that he was the son of a mountain nymph. Aphrodite promised Anchises a long and prosperous life on condition that he never mention that he had lain with a goddess. Anchises readily agreed but later, either bemused by wine or for some other reason, he revealed that he had embraced Aphrodite. Instantly Zeus struck him with lightning, and though he was saved through the intervention of Aphrodite his strong straight body was permanently crippled. Some say that before this happened, Aphrodite bore him not only Aeneas but another son Lyrus who died childless.

For all her grace and charm, Aphrodite is an exacting goddess. Smyrna, daughter of Cinyras, scorned her power or, as some say, Smyrna incurred her wrath because her mother boasted that Smyrna was more beautiful than Aphrodite. Aphrodite caused her to fall in love with her own father, to meet him in darkness so that he didn't know what maiden he was embracing, and to conceive a son by him. When Cinyras learned that the maiden who visited him was his own daughter he was horrified, and sought to kill her. Smyrna fled, and Aphrodite transformed her into a myrrh tree. From the trunk of the tree Smyrna's son Adonis was born. Aphrodite rescued him and gave him to Persephone to rear. Persephone fell in love with him as he grew to be a handsome youth, and refused to give him up to Aphrodite. The muse Calliope was called on to judge the case. She divided the year into three parts—Adonis was to spend one third of it with Persephone, one third with Aphrodite, and the last third by himself. In the end, Aphrodite persuaded him, by means of her magic girdle, to give her the third he was supposed to have by himself. Some say that Aphrodite grieves so during the time Adonis spends with Persephone that she withdraws her generative powers, and vegetation withers, and this is the winter. At her joy over his return she causes the earth to flower in the spring. Some say, however, that Aphrodite was so enraged by Calliope's decision that it was she who caused the Thracian maenads to go mad and tear Calliope's son Orpheus to pieces. The muse Clio, who mocked her love for Adonis, she caused to fall in love with Pierus and to bear him a son who some say was Hyacinthus. Again, Aphrodite inflicted a most terrible punishment on Hippolytus, son of Theseus, because he scorned her powers

fat, fāte, fär, fâll, àsk, fãre; net, mē, hėr; pin, pīne; not, nōte, möve, nôr; up, lūte, pùll; oi, oil; ou out; (lightened) ẹlect, agǫny, ūnite;

and denied her due honor. She caused his stepmother Phaedra to fall in love with him and brought about the catastrophe which cost the lives of Phaedra and Hippolytus. Aphrodite aided Melanion (or as some name him, Hippomenes) to win Atalanta by giving him three golden apples. But some say the pair forgot her help in their happiness and were transformed into beasts as a punishment. It was Aphrodite who caused the men of Lemnos to prefer their captive women to their own wives, because the Lemnian women denied her power. This led to the slaughter of all the males of Lemnos by the women to avenge the insults the men had directed toward them.

But for Theseus, who took Aphrodite as his guide on the advice of the Delphic oracle when he set out on his mission to Crete, she caused Ariadne to fall in love with him and to make possible his escape from the labyrinth of the Minotaur and from Crete. And at the request of Hera and Athena, she furnished a love charm to insure that Medea's passion for Jason would endure and that she would help him in his trial at Colchis and to secure the Golden Fleece. This love charm consisted of a wryneck (a fish-eating bird) stretched to a fire-wheel, and was considered by the Greeks to be a potent love charm. To Paris, who awarded her the Apple of Discord (prize of beauty thrown among the wedding guests at the marriage of Peleus and Thetis), she promised the most beautiful woman in the world. She helped him to win Helen, although she was the wife of Menelaus, and carry her off to Troy. This interference by Aphrodite led to the Trojan War, disastrous for Troy. In the course of the war Aphrodite aided the Trojans, saved Paris when he was about to be slain by Menelaus in a duel, and rescued her son Aeneas when he was wounded by Diomedes. Diomedes also wounded the goddess, who fled to Olympus to be cured by her mother Dione. Hera and Athena scorned her when she arrived in Olympus, but Zeus smiled and advised her to "busy herself with the gladsome duties of wedlock" and leave war to the gods and goddesses who were suited to it. Dione comforted her, healed the wound, and promised that Diomedes would be punished for his temerity in attacking an immortal. At the sack of Troy some say it was Aphrodite who interposed and prevented Aeneas from killing Helen, and some say that it was she who caused love to surge anew in the heart of

Menelaus when he saw Helen again, so that instead of killing her, as he had said he would do, he forgave her and lovingly carried her off to his tent.

When the Argonauts sailed by the island of the Sirens on their way home from Colchis, Orpheus played so sweetly that their music was unheard except by Butes who leaped into the sea, maddened by the strains of the Sirens. Aphrodite rescued him and bore him to Lilybaeum in Sicily where she bore him a son, Eryx.

The myrtle, rose, apple, and poppy were sacred to Aphrodite, as were the dove, sparrow, swan, swallow, hare, goat, and ram. Incense and flowers were offered to her in sacrifice. The principal seats of her worship were at Amathus, Idalion, and Paphos on the island of Cyprus, in the latter of which was the most ancient temple of Aphrodite in the Greek world; on the island of Cythera; at Cnidus, where her temple held the famous statue of her by Praxiteles; at Mount Ida in the Troad; Cos; Abydos; Athens; Thespiae; Megara; Sparta; Sicyon; and Corinth; and at Eryx in Sicily.

Many epithets signified her varied aspects. She was Aphrodite Acrae (*Of the Height*), Doritis (*Bountiful*), and Epistrophia (*She who turns men to love*). Having sprung from the sea, she was regarded as a goddess of the sea who protected sailors and navigation and was named Euploia (*Fair Voyage*), Limenia (*Of the Harbor*), and Pontia (*Of the Deep Sea*); when Zeus and Typhon struggled and all the gods were forced to flee, Aphrodite escaped by transforming herself into a fish, a symbol of the fertility of the sea. She was a goddess who gave victory and was worshiped in Sparta as Area (*Warlike*), possibly because of her connection with Ares. Hypermnestra, daughter of Danaus, dedicated an image to Aphrodite Bringer of Victory, after she was acquitted by the Argives for defying her father and refusing to murder her husband. When Theseus, some time after his safe return from Crete, federated the demes of Attica he instituted the worship of Federal Aphrodite and Persuasion, another aspect of the goddess. Most of all she was the goddess of love. As goddess of the physical love that unites men and women there was a sanctuary of Aphrodite Migonitis (*Uniter*) opposite the island of Cranaë, raised by Paris to commemorate his first embrace of Helen. In Memphis in Egypt, whither some say Paris and Helen were blown by storms on the way

fat, fãte, fär, fâll, ȧsk, fãre; net, mē, hėr; pin, pīne; not, nōte, mȯve, nôr; up, lūte, pu̇ll; oi, oil; ou out; (lightened) ẹlect, agǫny, ūnite;

to Troy, there was a temple of Aphrodite the Stranger, said to have been dedicated by Helen herself. Theseus raised a sanctuary of Aphrodite Nymphaea *(Bridal)* when he abducted the youthful Helen and made her his wife. She was Aphrodite Melaenis *(Black)*, some say because men invoke her at night for love-making, but others say it was because of her role as goddess of the Underworld, in which role she was also called Scotia *(Dark One)*, Androphonos *(Man-slayer)*, and Epitymbria *(Of the Tombs)*. As a goddess of marriage and family life she was Aphrodite Pandemos *(Common to All)*. This aspect was perverted in the time of Solon, so that Aphrodite Pandemos came to be a goddess of prostitution, with temple prostitutes. As a goddess of the spiritual love of mankind she was worshiped widely as Aphrodite Urania *(Heavenly)*, and had many temples. In this aspect she was also goddess of the heavens and the winds and many of her temples were on elevated headlands, as at Eryx in Sicily. As a goddess of the heavens she was also Pasiphaë *(Shining on all)* and Asteria *(Starry)*. At Thebes the ancient temple originally contained three wooden images made from the figureheads of the ships that brought Cadmus to Greece, that were dedicated by Harmonia. The images represented Aphrodite Urania *(Heavenly)* of the pure love of mankind, Aphrodite Pandemos *(Common)*, to represent the goddess of the family and community life for all the people, and Aphrodite Apostrophia *(Rejecter)*, the goddess who helps men to reject unlawful passion and sinful acts. Tyndareus dedicated an image of Aphrodite Morpho *(Shapely)*, representing the goddess veiled and with fetters on her ankles. Some say this represented the bonds of faithfulness and modesty in marriage. Under the special circumstances surrounding the daughters of Tyndareus, however, it could have been an ironic reminder to the goddess.

Some say that Aphrodite was originally the Assyrian goddess Ishtar, and that her worship was brought to Paphos in Cyprus by the Phoenicians of Ascalon, who called her Astarte, and from whose ancient temple the Paphians copied their temple. And they say that the Phoenician traders who came to Cythera taught worship of her to the Cytheraeans. Among the Syrians, a goddess similar to her was called Derceto. The Babylonians worshiped Mylitta and the Arabians Alilat, who were equivalent to Aphrodite in some respects. Whatever the origin of her worship, the Greeks evolved the worship of Aphrodite, in all its aspects, into a purely Greek conception. The Romans, who claimed Aphrodite as their ancestress through her son Aeneas, worshiped her as Venus. Aphrodite was one of the favorite subjects in art. Of her representations in classical art the most famous are the replica of her statue of Cnidus by Praxiteles, the original statues of Melos in the Louvre, of Capua at Naples, the Medicean at Florence, and the Capitoline at Rome.

Apollo   (a̱-pol'ō). "Lord of the Silver Bow," one of the great Olympian gods. He was the god of music, poetry, and the dance, and in classical times came to be regarded also as god of the plastic arts and of science and philosophy, the god of the intellect and the enemy of barbarism. He was the protector of flocks and herds, the patron of the founding of towns and colonies who helped build the walls of Troy and Megara, and to whose oracle all went before setting out to found colonies. He was the god of healing, Alexicacus (*Averter of Evil*), who was called on to dispel plagues and heal sickness; and he was the god of prophecy. Above all, he was the god of light: of the physical light that dispels darkness, of the light of spring and summer that puts the winter to flight, and of the spiritual and moral light that dispels the darkness of ignorance from men's minds and evil from their hearts. The worship of Apollo was one of the most potent of the forces that brought Greek civilization to full flower.

When Leto was about to bear her children by Zeus she fled throughout the world. No place would receive her, for jealous Hera had decreed that Leto could not bear her children in any place where the sun shone. At last she came to the tiny floating island of Delos. Delos gladly received Leto, but feared that her future son, "the Archer-king," would scorn the modest island and would thrust it under the sea. Leto swore an oath that her son would build his first temple there, and would honor it above all other places, whereupon Delos welcomed her warmly. Some say Leto first bore Artemis on the neighboring island of Ortygia, and that when she was born Artemis helped her mother across to Delos where her twin was to be born. Even here Hera's jealousy afflicted her for she kept Ilithyia, the goddess who helps women in childbirth, on Mount Olympus by guile. Leto's labor lasted nine days and nights. Then the goddesses—Dione, Rhea,

fat, fāte, fär, fâll, a̱sk, fāre; net, mē, hėr; pin, pīne; not, nōte, mŏve; nôr; up, lūte, pu̇ll; oi, oil; ou out; (lightened) ĕlect, agŏny, ūnite;

Themis, Amphitrite—who were all present, sent Iris to
Olympus to fetch Ilithyia. That goddess, informed of the
circumstances, hurried to Delos at once. Leto knelt on the
ground, clasped a palm tree in the shadow of Mount Cyn-
thus, and gave birth to Apollo. The goddesses washed him
and clothed him. Themis fed him on nectar and ambrosia.
He was born on the seventh of the month, and ever after the
number seven was sacred to him, and sacrifices were made
to him on the seventh of every month. The palm tree
beneath which he was born was one of the sights of antiquity
from the time of Homer to the time of Pliny. Other places
in the Greek world claimed to be his birthplace, as the grove
of Ortygia in Ephesus, Tegyra in Boeotia, and Zoster in
Attica, but Delos in generally honored as the birthplace of
Apollo, and it was there that his universal sovereignty began. After his birth the island was covered with golden flowers in its joy, and as a reward for its kindness to Leto it was
anchored in the sea and ceased to float about. Four days
after he was born Apollo sundered the golden bands of his
swaddling clothes, leaped up, and proclaimed that he would
in future announce the will of Zeus to men. Some say at this
time he called for bow and arrows, which Hephaestus at
once gave him, and declared them and the lyre sacred to
him. And some say that when he was four years old he built
an altar at Delos entirely composed of the horns of goats
shot by his sister Artemis. In search of a place to found his
oracle he left Olympus, where clad in royal raiment he had
given a concert to the delighted gods, and passed through
Pieria to Euboea. He then crossed the Euripus and went by
Teumessus and the site where the city of Thebes would one
day stand, passed Onchestus, crossed the Cephissus River
on the border of Phocis, and so arrived at Haliartus. There
he thought to found his oracle, but the fountain nymph,
Telphusa, advised him not to found an oracle in her domain
because she did not want to share the honors with him, and
suggested that he go on to Crisa (Delphi). There he slew
with his arrows the dragon that guarded the spring. Some
say this dragon had, at Hera's orders, pursued Leto across
the world before her children were born, and it was for this
reason that Apollo killed it. Others say the dragon was slain
because it tried to prevent Apollo from approaching the
chasm of an ancient oracle. In any event, the world was rid

of a murderous pest and the place where the creature's body was left to rot was named Pythos, "the place of the rotting," and Apollo acquired the epithet Pythian. But some say the dragon was named Python, and this was the reason for Apollo's epithet, and the reason why his priestesses at Delphi were called Pythonesses. He laid the foundations for his temple, for which Trophonius and Agamedes paved the floor with marble and scores of laborers raised the structure, and founded his oracle. But some say there was formerly an oracle of Gaea there, and then one of Themis, and that it was from the latter that Apollo took the oracle. And some say Apollo was compelled to go to Tempe to do penance and to be purified for the slaughter of the dragon, which they say was Hera's earthborn child or was the guardian of an ancient oracle. The killing of the dragon and the purification of Apollo were memorialized every eighth year (for he was in Tempe seven years atoning for the murder) in a festival at Delphi, and the Pythian Games held at this time were instituted to propitiate the dead dragon. Because he had endured penance and purification himself, Apollo could purify others, and in this function the worship of Apollo encouraged the substitution of law and penance for blood vengeance. After slaying the dragon Apollo remembered that Telphusa had advised him to come to this spot but had not warned him of the serpent. To punish her, he sealed up her fountain in Haliartus with a huge stone. On the spot he erected an altar, and thereafter Apollo was worshiped and Telphusa was forgotten. Having built his temple near Crisa (at Delphi) Apollo pondered how he should choose priests to serve in it. He gazed far out to sea and beheld a Cretan vessel on its way to Alphaean Pylus. Instantly he changed himself into a dolphin, swam out to the vessel and leaped aboard. The Cretan crew tried to hurl the dolphin into the sea, but he shook the ship so that they were afraid and dared not even man the tiller. Under Apollo's unseen guidance the ship sailed around the Peloponnesus to the Gulf of Crisa (an inlet in the Gulf of Corinth) where a strong wind blew it ashore. Apollo went to his shrine and lit an altar fire, as all the people acclaimed him. He returned to the Cretan ship and invited the crew to stow their tackle and come ashore for food and rest. The captain replied that he did not know what land they were in, that his vessel had been brought

fat, fāte, fär, fâll, ȧsk, fãre; net, mē, hėr; pin, pīne; not, nōte, möve, nôr; up, lūte, p·ull; oi, oil; ou out; (lightened) ẹlect, agǫny, ūnite;

there by a god, and that he wished to go home. Apollo revealed himself as a god and announced that they would never return to Crete, but would become his priests and be the most honored among men. He instructed them to build an altar there by the sea and to worship him as the Delphian god, because he had first appeared to them as a dolphin. As Delphian Apollo, or Apollo Delphinius, he was the patron of sailors and ports, and at Athens was worshiped as the patron of the founding of colonies. Jason sacrificed a yoke of oxen to Apollo Embasius *(Apollo of Embarkations)*, before setting out on his journey to Colchis. And as a god of sailors and sailing he was worshiped as Apollo Ecbasion *(Apollo of Disembarkations)*, who assures successful landings. Diomedes raised a temple of Apollo Epibaterius *(Seafaring)*, in gratitude for his having weathered the storms that scattered the Greeks at sea on their way home from Troy.

Apollo, "Lord of the Silver Bow," received his bow and arrows from Hephaestus, who forged them for him, and used them to punish the wicked and arrogant. He slew Tityus, the monstrous son of Zeus and Elara, because he attacked Leto as she was going to Delphi. Again, for the greater honor of his mother, he and his sister Artemis killed the children of arrogant Niobe who had boasted that she was at least equal to Leto who had only two children. It was Apollo who sent the plague of arrows on the Greeks encamped before Troy, because Agamemnon haughtily denied the plea of Apollo's priest Chryse to accept ransom for his daughter Chryseis. In the battle with the Giants, Apollo shot Ephialtes in the left eye, and Heracles dispatched him by shooting him in the right eye. Apollo was a helpful god, as when he appeared to the Argonauts, caught in a black and raging storm on their way home from Colchis, and by a flash of light revealed an island where they could find haven. The Argonauts built an altar to Radiant Apollo, and named the island Anaphe *(Revealed,* or *Unexpected)*. As Apollo Parnopius *(Locust-god)* he lifted a plague of locusts that infested Attica. He was also Acesius *(Healer)*, Patroüs *(Paternal)*, Archegetes *(Founder)*, Prostaterius *(Protecting)*, and Boëdromius *(Rescuer)*. In the Trojan War he rescued Hector many times, and abandoned him to death only at the command of Fate.

Under the leadership of Hera, Apollo took part in the

conspiracy of the gods to bind Zeus. Zeus was freed by the intervention of Thetis. To punish Apollo, Zeus ordered him to work with Poseidon to build the walls of Troy for Laomedon. (But some say the gods labored on the walls to prove the wickedness of Laomedon; and some say Apollo served as the herdsman of Laomedon.) When the walls were completed Laomedon not only refused to pay as he had promised, but threatened to cut off the ears of the gods and sell them as slaves. Apollo sent a pestilence to afflict Troy, and Poseidon sent a sea monster. Both afflictions were removed when Heracles came and killed the monster. In the Trojan War Apollo aided the city whose walls he had helped to build. When the gods who actively participated in the conflict fell to quarreling and attacking each other, Apollo refused to quarrel with Poseidon although the latter taunted him for aiding the descendants of the man who had tricked them over the building of the walls. In this case it was beneath his dignity to fight. On another occasion he showed his willingness to take vigorous action to protect his property. Heracles came to the shrine at Delphi to inquire how he could cure himself of a sickness. The priestess refused to give him an answer. Enraged, Heracles seized the tripod and said he would found his own oracle. Apollo sprang to the defense of his priestess and wrestled with Heracles. Zeus parted them with a thunderbolt and compelled them to make friends, and the two went off together and founded the town of Gythium.

Apollo had many loves. He was the father of Linus by the muse Calliope, according to some accounts. Some say he was the father of the Corybantes by the muse Thalia. By Phthia he was the father of Dorus, Laodocus, and Polypoetes who were killed by Aetolus, who took their land and named it Aetolia after himself. Aria bore him Miletus who afterward fled from Crete to Caria and founded the city of Miletus. His son Amphissus by the nymph Dryope founded the city of Oeta and raised a temple of Apollo there. Anius, king of Delos and Apollo's priest there, was his son by Rhoeo. Some say that Hector and Troilus, reputed sons of Priam, were Apollo's children. By Creusa he was the father of Ion, founder of the Ionian race. Again, it is said that Apollo was the father of Tenes, king of Tenedos. When the Greeks landed on Tenedos on their way to Troy Achilles killed

Tenes. It had been foretold that if Achilles killed a son of Apollo he would die by Apollo's hand. According to some accounts, when Achilles fell at the Scaean Gate of Troy the arrow that killed him, though shot by Paris, was guided by Apollo, and was wafted back to Apollo when Achilles pulled it from his ankle. Others say Achilles was killed in the sanctuary of Thymbraean Apollo in the Troad. On one occasion Apollo saw the huntress Cyrene struggling with a boar, fell in love with her, and asked Chiron the centaur if he should woo Cyrene. Chiron said Apollo would take Cyrene to a luxuriant land and that she would bear him a son. Apollo carried her off to Libya, where she bore him Aristaeus and Idmon the seer. Another of his loves was Coronis. She was unfaithful to him while she was carrying his child and the news was brought to the god by a white raven he had set to guard her. Apollo turned the raven's feathers black for bringing him the news (which he already knew by divination), instead of pecking out the eyes of Coronis' lover. He went to Coronis and caused her death. But as she was lying on the pyre he regretted his harsh act; he commanded Hermes to snatch the unborn child from her womb, and sent it to Chiron to be reared. This son was Asclepius who inherited his father's skill in healing and was so successful in his art that he raised men from the dead. Some say Zeus feared he would teach his skill to others; others say Hades complained to Zeus that owing to the ministrations of Asclepius the population of his realm was decreasing, and Zeus struck Asclepius dead with his thunderbolt. In anger at the loss of his son, Apollo killed the Cyclopes who had forged the thunderbolt of Zeus. Zeus would have banished him to Tartarus, but yielded to the pleas of Leto to spare her son and sentenced Apollo to serve Admetus, king of Pherae, for a year. While in his service as a herdsman Apollo caused all his flocks to bear twins. He also helped Admetus to win Alcestis for a bride by yoking a boar and a lion to a chariot for a race, one of the conditions her successful suitor must fulfill. Admetus forgot to honor Artemis properly at his marriage ceremonies, and in anger Artemis declared he must die. Apollo went to the Fates, who control the span of life, got them drunk, and exacted a promise from them that they would spare Admetus' life, but only on condition that someone who loved him would consent to die in his place. When he had completed his term of penance by serving Admetus, Apollo never again defied Zeus, but learned to control himself and became a force for moderation in all things.

Apollo did not enjoy unvarying success in his love affairs. Idas, the only mortal who dared to struggle with him, vied with him for the affections of Marpessa. Marpessa, given the choice by Zeus, chose Idas, for she feared that as she aged she might lose the love of the god and would have a better chance of happiness with Idas, who would grow old and lose his beauty even as she would. Apollo pursued the nymph Daphne, daughter of the river-god Peneus in Thessaly. Leucippus was his rival in this case, and disguised himself as a girl that he might be in the company of the chaste nymph. Apollo learned of his ruse by divination and revealed the disguise when he advised the nymphs to bathe naked. He now sought Daphne but she fled, and when she was about to be overtaken prayed to her father to so transform her beauty that Apollo would cease his pursuit. Her prayer was answered: as Apollo was about to clasp her to him she was changed into a laurel tree. Even transformed, Apollo still loved her and made the laurel (or bay) his sacred tree and gave it never-fading leaves. Wreaths of laurel crowned the victors at the Pythian Games, and leaves of laurel were chewed by the priestesses of Apollo to inspire them with prophetic powers. Another of Apollo's loves was Hyacinthus. Thamyris the musician and Zephyrus (West Wind) were Apollo's rivals. Thamyris was deprived by the Muses of his sight and of his gift for song because he had boasted of his art. Zephyrus, a jealous rival, came one day when Apollo was teaching Hyancinthus how to throw the quoit, seized the quoit in a gust of wind and hurled it back with such force that it struck Hyacinthus on the head and killed him. Others say that Hyacinthus was killed when the quoit ricocheted from the ground and struck him on the forehead.

Apollo was the god of prophecy and divination, an attribute which some say he had received as a gift from Zeus, and others say he learned from Pan. In his role as seer he passed on to men the will of Zeus, but men did not always interpret his prophecies correctly; for that reason he was called Loxias (*Crooked,* or *Ambiguous*). Some hold this epithet to mean Interpreter. Many famous seers claimed to have received their powers from Apollo. He taught the art of divination to

fat, fāte, fär, fåll, åsk, fāre; net, mē, hėr; pin, pīne; not, nōte, mŏve, nôr; up, lūte, pùll; oi, oil; ou out; (lightened) ĕlect, agǫny, ūnite;

Melampus, Helenus, Epimenides, and the Cumaean Sibyl;
and Idmon, the Argive Argonaut, and Mopsus, son of
Manto, inherited the gift as Apollo's sons. He could give the
gift to others. When he fell in love with Cassandra he gave
her the gift of prophecy in return for the promise of her
favors. She refused to honor her promise, however, and
since the god would not take back what he had given he
turned her gift into a curse by decreeing that, although she
would make true prophecies, no one would believe her.

APOLLO
Red-figured Greek psykter, Pan Painter, c490 B.C.
Munich

Apollo was the god of flocks and herds. One day some of
his cattle were missing from their pasture in Pieria. By his
powers of divination, or as some say, by watching the flight
of a long-winged bird, he knew that Hermes, a new-born
infant, had stolen the cattle. He went to the cave on Cyllene
where Hermes was lying in his cradle and accused him of the
theft. Hermes protested his innocence of a crime that would
be, he claimed, impossible for one of his tender age. Nevertheless, Apollo took him off to appear before Zeus, and
Hermes was compelled to admit the theft and led Apollo to
where he had set them to graze. Arrived at the spot, Hermes
played on the lyre which he had just invented, and so
charmed Apollo that he agreed to give up the cattle to

(obscured) errạnt, ardẹnt, actọr; ch, chip; g, go; th, thin; �ꞁH, then; y, you;
(variable) ḍ as d or j, ṣ as s or sh, ṭ as t or ch, ẕ as z or zh.

Hermes in exchange for the lyre. Hermes gave it to him, and immediately invented a shepherd's pipe, made of reeds, on which he played so artfully while the cattle grazed that Apollo demanded the new instrument also, and offered Hermes the golden wand he used when herding cattle in exchange for it. Hermes agreed to give him the pipe if Apollo would throw in the art of divining as well as the wand. As protector of flocks, Apollo was Lycius *(Wolf-god)* who destroys the wolves that prey on flocks.

As the god of music, poetry, and the dance, he influenced the Muses to leave their frenzies on Mount Helicon and join him in stately dances, and so earned the epithet Musagetes *(Leader of the Muses)*. As god of music he brooked no rivals. Marsyas challenged him to a musical contest, contending that his instrument, the flute, was superior to Apollo's lyre, and was defeated in the contest of which the Muses were the judges. To punish him for his presumption Apollo flayed him and hung up his skin on a pine tree. On another occasion, he took part in a contest with Pan. Midas, the Phrygian king, and Tmolus, the mountain god, acted as judges. Tmolus awarded the prize to Apollo, but Midas stubbornly clung to his opinion that Pan was the better player. Apollo caused asses' ears to grow from Midas' head, as being worthy ears for one who was such a donkey as to prefer the music of Pan to that of Apollo.

Apollo had many epithets. He was Phoebus *(Bright,* or *Pure god)*, and the "Fardarter." In his role as a god of agriculture he was "Ruler of the Seasons," and was accompanied by the Horae. As "Rearer of Boys" he fostered young men and was patron of their athletic training grounds, and to him they sacrificed the first clippings of their hair. He was Apollo Smintheus *(Mouse-god)*, an epithet which may have applied to his role as god of healing, for mice were associated with disease and its cure, and white mice were kept in Apollo's temples to protect against plague and against plagues of mice. He was Apollo Agyieus *(God of Streets)*, who let in the good and kept out evil, and whose symbol, a pillar with a pointed top, stood before the doorways of houses and was honored with offerings of wreaths and ribbons. He was also Agraeus *(Hunter)*, Platanistius *(God of the Plane-tree Grove)*, Theoxenius *(Strangers' God)*, Spodius *(God of Ashes*—of victims), and Moeragetes *(Guide of the Fates)*. The Spartans wor-

fat, fāte, fär, fâll, ȧsk, fāre; net, mē, hėr; pin, pīne; not, nōte, möve, nôr; up, lūte, pull; oi, oil; ou out; (lightened) ēlect, agǫny, ūnite;

shiped him as Apollo Carneus and held a splendid festival for him in August, the Carnea. In addition to the epithets celebrating a particular role or incident concerning him, he had numerous epithets which associated him with places, as Apollo Actius *(of Actium)*, Apollo Acritas *(of Acritas)*, Apollo Ismenius *(of Ismenium)*.

Some among the ancients considered Apollo to be a god of the Hyperboreans, who were all priests of Apollo and who lived in a land of perpetual light and happiness far to the North. The center of their cult was at Delos, and to it the Hyperboreans sent offerings wrapped in wheaten straw. Although most anciently he was a Dorian or a non-Greek deity, his worship became panhellenic. In later times he came to be identified with and worshiped as the Sun. Among the Greek colonists of Asia Minor the golden cicada was his emblem as the Sun-god. But earlier Apollo and the Sun-god, Helius, had been regarded as two separate deities. His most sacred oracles were at Delphi, the most influential oracle of the ancient world, and at Tempe. Other oracles were at the Lyceum and on the Acropolis at Argos; at Ismenium in Boeotia, where oracles were derived from the inspection of entrails by priests; at Clarus near Colophon, where the priests drank the waters of a secret well and gave the oracles in verse; at Telmessus in Asia Minor, where the oracles were revealed in dreams; and in many other places.

The attributes of Apollo were the bow, the lyre, and the tripod. Sacred to him were the laurel, commemorating Daphne, and the palm tree, under which he had been born. The wolf, swan, hawk, raven, snake, mouse, and grasshopper were also sacred to him. His festivals were the *Delphinia,* held at Athens in April to celebrate the end of winter storms and the opening of the seas to navigation; the *Thargelia,* held in the spring as a fertility rite; in midsummer the Athenians offered him sacrifices of hecatombs, so that the hot sun would not destroy their crops. At this time the Spartans held the *Hyacinthia.* In the autumn when the crops were harvested first fruits were offered to Apollo at the *Pyanepsia.* In addition there were the *Carnea, Daphnephoria, Delia, Stepteria, Apollonia,* and *Pythia.*

By the Romans, who derived all their ideas of Apollo from the Greeks, he was worshiped primarily as a god of healing. They raised a temple to him in 430 B.C., in obedience to an

(obscured) errạnt, ardẹnt, actọr; ch, chip; g, go; th, thin; ᴛн, then; y, you;
(variable) ḍ as d or j, ṣ as s or sh, ṭ as t or ch, ẓ as z or zh.

oracular command and in order to arrest a plague. A second temple was erected in 350 B.C. Augustus greatly furthered the worship of Apollo. He dedicated a portion of the spoils of his victory at Actium to him, reconstructed and beautified the temple of Apollo Actius, and instituted the Actian Games. He also built a new temple at Rome.

Apollo was one of the favorite subjects in ancient art, and was represented in the full majesty of youthful manhood, usually unclothed or only lightly draped, and usually characterized by the bow and arrows, the lyre, the oracular tripod, the serpent, or the dolphin.

Apple of Discord. A golden apple, inscribed "To the Fairest," thrown into an assembly of the gods (at the marriage of Thetis and Peleus) by Eris, goddess of Discord, who had not been invited to the feast. Aphrodite, Hera, and Athena claimed it, and its award to Aphrodite by Paris of Troy, selected by Zeus as judge, so inflamed the jealousy of Hera and her hatred toward all the Trojan race that she did not cease her machinations till Troy was destroyed.

Apples of the Hesperides (hes-per′i-dēz). According to mythology, Mother Earth gave Hera, as a wedding gift when she married Zeus, a tree which bore golden apples. Hera planted the tree in her own orchard. Some say the orchard was located in the land of the Hyperboreans, some say it lay on the slopes of Mount Atlas in Mauretania, others say it was in a region beyond the western ocean, or on two islands near Ethiopia. Atlas was the gardener in the orchard, and the tree was guarded by his daughters, the Hesperides, and by Ladon, a never-sleeping dragon. As his eleventh labor for Eurystheus, Heracles fetched the Golden Apples. He took them to Eurystheus, but as the apples were sacred Eurystheus returned them to Heracles who then gave them to Athena. She restored them to the orchard of the Hesperides.

Arachne (ạ-rak′nē). In Greek legend, a maiden of Colophon in Lydia. She was so skilled in spinning and weaving that her reputation spread throughout Lydia. Admirers of her work suggested that she must have been taught by Athena. Arachne scorned the suggestion and boasted that she could compete with Athena. The goddess, jealous of Arachne's fame in an art that was considered peculiarly her own,

fat, fāte, fär, fâll, ȧsk, fãre; net, mē, hėr; pin, pīne; not, nōte, möve, nôr; up, lūte, pu̇ll; oi, oil; ou out; (lightened) ẹlect, agǫny, ūnite;

learned of her boast and appeared to her disguised as an old woman. She advised Arachne that it was unwise to vie with the gods, that it was enough to excel all mortals. Arachne repeated her boast and demanded that Athena come to her in person and meet her challenge. Athena then revealed herself and agreed to a contest which was begun at once. Athena's work portrayed the Olympian gods in all their majesty. Arachne wove into her work scenes of the more scandalous love affairs of the gods, but so delicately and beautifully that no flaw could be found in her work. It was evident that the goddess had not surpassed the maiden, and in a frenzy of jealousy Athena destroyed her rival's work, then touched the girl on her forehead and made her conscious of her presumption and impiety. Arachne hanged herself from a rafter, and as she was hanging there Athena condemned her to hang on a thread and spin eternally by transforming her into a spider.

Arcas (är′kạs). In Greek mythology, a son of the nymph Callisto and Zeus. His mother was transformed into a bear through the jealousy of Hera, and Arcas was brought up by Maia in Arcadia. When, as a youth, he was hunting wild beasts in the forest, he came face to face with his mother in her guise as a bear. She recognized him and approached him, but he did not know her and would have killed her as the wild animal he thought she was. Zeus lifted her to the heavens in a whirlwind and set her among the stars as the constellation of the Great Bear. A common account also has Arcas translated to the heavens as the Little Bear. Arcas succeeded his uncle, Nyctimus, son of Lycaon, on the throne of the land that was then known as Pelasgia. He changed its name to Arcadia after himself, and is said to be the ancestor of the Arcadians. Some say that Arcas was taught how to cultivate crops by Triptolemus, and that he in turn taught the arts of agriculture to the Arcadians and also taught them how to bake bread and the crafts of spinning and weaving. Some say Arcas had two sons—Elatus and Aphidas—and that their mother was either Meganira or the nymph Chrysopelia. Others say the dryad Erato bore him three sons— Azan, Aphidas, and Elatus. Azan became ruler of Azania in Arcadia; Aphidas became ruler of Tegea; Elatus inherited the region of Mount Cyllene. Arcas was buried on Mount

Maenalus in Arcadia, but his bones were removed and placed near an altar of Hera at Mantinea in obedience to the following command of an oracle:

"Maenalia is storm-swept, where lies

Arcas, from whom all Arcadians are named,

In a place where meet three, four, even five roads;

Thither I bid you go, and with kind heart

Take up Arcas and bring him back to your lovely city.

There make Arcas a precinct and sacrifices."

The place of his grave was called the Altars of the Sun. The image of Arcas was translated to the heavens, where it was known as Arcturus. Located behind the Great Bear, Arcturus is the guardian or watcher of the Great Bear, his mother.

Arce (är′sē). In Greek mythology, a daughter of Thaumas, and the sister of Iris and the Harpies. Because she aided the Titans in their war against Zeus, he took away the wings of Arce, after the Titans had been defeated and banished, and gave them to Thetis as a wedding present when she married Peleus. Some say Thetis gave the wings to her son Achilles, and this accounted for his fleetness. After Zeus had taken away her wings he banished Arce to Tartarus.

Archelaus (är-kẹ-lā′us). In Greek legend, a son of Temenus and a descendant of Heracles. When he arrived at the kingdom of Cisseus in Macedonia after fleeing from his brothers in Argos, he was promised the throne and the hand of Cisseus' daughter if he overcame the enemies of Cisseus. Archelaus was successful but instead of fulfilling his promise Cisseus plotted to kill him. However, a slave warned him of the pit of hot coals Cisseus had concealed in his path, and Archelaus hurled Cisseus into it and fled. Archelaus is the traditional founder of the Macedonian royal house.

Archias (är′ki-ạs). According to Greek tradition, a descendant of Heracles. He lived in Corinth. Some say he went with a companion to visit the oracle at Delphi. The priestess asked him to choose between wealth and health. Archias chose wealth, and his companion, Myscellus, chose health. In later times Archias went to Sicily and founded Syracuse (734 B.C.), which became noted for its wealth. Myscellus went with a colony to Croton, which became noted for its physicians.

Ares (ār′ēz). One of the 12 Olympian gods. He was the hated and feared god of war who engaged in bloody strife for love

fat, fāte, fär, fâll, ȧsk, fãre; net, mē, hėr; pin, pīne; not, nōte, möve, nôr; up, lūte, pull; oi, oil; ou out; (lightened) ẹlect, agọny, ṵnite;

of combat itself. He flung himself impetuously into battle, accompanied by his sister Eris *(Strife)*, and other deities of relentless battle. Of all their gods, for whom the Greeks showed on the one hand reverence and on the other interested affection and curiosity, Ares alone won no sympathetic attention. As a symbol of an evil that exists, and the sorrow and suffering it causes, Ares was acknowledged but not loved.

Ares was the son of Zeus and Hera, both of whom disliked him, and Zeus often hinted that it was from his mother that Ares got his quarrelsome temper. The only one of the gods who appreciated Ares was Hades, for by his activities the population of Hades' realm was greatly increased. The various myths attached to Ares indicate that the Greeks were pleased to think their war god sometimes got a taste of his own medicine, and that he was by no means invulnerable. The Aloidae, giant sons of Iphimedia and Poseidon, captured Ares before they made war on the gods and shut him up in a bronze vessel. There he languished for 13 months before he was released through the intervention of Hermes. In the war of Heracles against Pylus, Athena aided Heracles, while Ares—along with Hera, Poseidon, and Hades—aided the Pylians. With Athena's aid Heracles wounded Ares twice and compelled him to withdraw. In the fight between Heracles and Cycnus, son of Ares, Ares sided with his son and was again wounded by Heracles. In this instance Athena led him away to Olympus to be healed.

Homer tells that Aphrodite, married to the lame god Hephaestus, fell in love with the straight and handsome Ares, and entertained him frequently in her husband's absence. Hephaestus, informed by Helius of his wife's unfaithfulness, laid a trap for the lovers. He made a brazen net of mesh so fine as to be invisible and as strong as it was fine. This he draped on the bed where Ares and Aphrodite were accustomed to disport themselves. He told Aphrodite that he was going on a journey to his favorite haunt, the island of Lemnos. As soon as he had gone Ares came joyfully to his house and embraced Aphrodite. The net fell on the lovers and bound them fast. Hephaestus, again informed by Helius, returned and published their disgrace by calling the gods to witness how Aphrodite had dishonored him. He vowed he would not release the lovers until Zeus repaid him the rich marriage gifts he had made when he was given Aphrodite's hand. Ares promised to repay him, and Poseidon offered his guarantee that if Ares failed to keep his promise he would assume the debt. Aphrodite and Ares were freed. Ares went off to Thrace, his favorite dwelling place because of its war-like people and savage country. Aphrodite went to the isle of Cyprus and was purified by the nymphs. This, however, was not the end of the affair. Eos seduced Ares, and Aphrodite, out of jealousy, punished Eos. And when Aphrodite fell in love with Adonis, Ares, some say, disguised himself as a wild boar, one of his sacred animals, and killed Adonis. To Ares, Aphrodite bore Harmonia, later the wife of Cadmus, and Eros, Anteros, Deimos, and Phobos. He had many other children, among them: Oxylus, whose mother was Protogonia, daughter of Calydon; Demonice bore him Evenus, Molus, Pylus, and Thestius; some say he was the father of Althaea's son Meleager; Ascalaphus and Ialmenus, the Argonauts, were his sons; Cyrene bore him Diomedes of Thrace, master of the man-eating mares; Pyrene bore him that Cycnus who fought with Heracles on the Echedorus River in Macedonia and was only saved by the intervention of Zeus; Pelopia bore him another Cycnus, who also fought with Heracles, at Pagasae, and was slain; Phlegyas, who became a king in Boeotian Orchomenus, was his son; Tereus of Thrace, the seducer of Philomela, claimed Ares as his father; and some say he was the father of Atalanta's son Parthenopaeus. Among his daughters were the Amazon Penthesilea, and Alcippe, for whose sake Ares slew Halirrhothius. For this killing he was tried, the first ever to stand trial for murder, on the Hill of Ares, afterwards known as the Areopagus and sacred to him. He was acquitted on the ground that he was protecting his daughter's honor. Ares gave arms and swift horses to Oenomaus who, some say, was his son. He gave the belt to the Amazon Hippolyte, which led to her death when Heracles came to fetch it as one of his labors for Eurystheus. Some say the dragon that guarded the spring at Thebes, slain by Cadmus, was a son of Ares. To atone for its murder Cadmus was compelled to serve Ares for a great year, that is, for eight years. The descendants of Cadmus also felt the wrath of Ares on account of the slaying of the dragon. In the war of the Seven against Thebes, Menoeceus, son of Creon, voluntarily sacrificed himself to Ares on the advice of an oracle, to appease him

fat, fāte, fär, fåll, åsk, fâre; net, mē, hėr; pin, pīne; not, nōte, mȯve, nôr; up, lūte, py̆ll; oi, oil; ou out; (lightened) ĕlect, agŏny, ŭnite;

and to give victory to Thebes. Another dragon guarded the
Golden Fleece that hung in a grove sacred to Ares in Col-
chis. Colchian was one of his epithets, from his temple in
Colchis.

Wherever conflict broke out, there Ares delighted to be.
Some say it was Ares, with his sister Eris, who caused the
wars between the Lapiths and the centaurs, because Pirithous, king of the Lapiths, had not invited them to his marriage to Hippodamia. In the Trojan War Ares helped the
Trojans at the request of Aphrodite, and by so doing he
roused his mother's (Hera's) anger against himself. But
whereas he was a strong and violent fighter, he was not
skilled in strategy. Athena twice worsted him in battle. She
inspired Diomedes with immortal courage and encouraged
him to attack Ares himself. She seized the spear Ares had
hurled at Diomedes and deflected it, but the lance Diomedes
threw, guided by her hand, found its target. Wounded, Ares
withdrew to Olympus to be healed, and complained to Zeus
about Athena. Zeus sternly advised him not to come whining
to Olympus, and addressed him as the most hateful to him
of all the gods of Olympus, because all his joy was in strife
and battle. Zeus also mentioned the untamed temper of
Ares' mother, and observed that it might be by her will that
Ares had been wounded. However, since Ares was his own
son, Zeus commanded that he be healed. If he had not
happened to be his son, Zeus assured him that he would
long ago have banished him to Tartarus. Later in the war
Ares came face to face with Athena and accused her of
encouraging Diomedes to attack him and of guiding his
lance. He rushed at her, vowing vengeance. As he lunged
with his spear she took up a huge boulder, flung it at him
and flattened him. Ares' bright hair lay in the dust. Athena
stood over him and laughed at his boasts and his foolish
belief that his strength could overcome her skill.

Ares was worshiped by the Spartans, and had sanctuaries
under the name Enyalius in several places, but unlike the
other Olympians, he had no cities, with the exception of
Thebes, where he was especially worshiped. The Spartans
called him "Theritas," and the oldest sanctuary of Ares in
Laconia was that of Ares Theritas on the road from Therapne to Amyclae. In the sanctuary was an image said to
have been brought back from Colchis by the Dioscuri. Ac-

cording to Pausanias, the name Theritas came from a Colchian nurse of Ares, called Thero. But, Pausanias adds, his opinion is that the name comes from a word meaning "wild beast," because it is necessary to cast aside all the qualities of gentleness and humanity when one engages in battle. The Spartans sacrificed dogs to Ares under his title of Enyalius. Near Tegea on Mount Cresius is a sanctuary of Ares Aphneius. The story is that Ares embraced Aërope, a daughter of Cepheus, and that she died in giving birth to a child. However, the child clung to its mother, even though she was dead, and through the will of Ares sucked great quantities of milk from her breasts. For this reason Ares was named Aphneius *(Abundant)*. At Tegea also, he was worshiped as Gynaecothoenas, because when the women of Tegea armed themselves and drove out the Spartans who had attacked them under Charillus, the women offered sacrifice to Ares for their victory on their own account. They gave the men no share in the meat of the victims, and named Ares Gynaecothoenas *(He who entertains women)*.

The attributes of Ares are the spear and the blazing torch. Sacred to him were the vulture, the dog, and the boar. Priests of Ares marched in front of the armies and hurled the blazing torches at the enemy as a signal for battle to begin. In art Ares is represented as a muscular, handsome man, sometimes bearded and wearing armor, sometimes cleanshaven and wearing only the helmet. He is often shown also in company with Aphrodite and their son Eros. In the decipherment of the bronze-age tablets in the Linear B script appears the name *Enyalios,* which later appears as an epithet or alternate name of Ares, indicating that Ares had been equated with a Mycenaean divinity.

Arete (a̯-rē′tē). In Greek mythology, the personification of courage, or the manly virtues.

Arethusa (ar-ē̯-thū′sa̯). In mythology, a nymph of Elis, or Achaea, and a companion and follower of Artemis. Her remarkable beauty was only a nuisance to her as she preferred the pleasures of the chase. One time when she sought refreshment after a hot day of hunting she came to the bank of a cool stream, slipped off her robes, and splashed in the waters. As she was bathing she heard a curious murmuring in the river and, frightened, leaped out onto the bank. The river-god Alpheus, in whose waters she had bathed, fell in love with her and sought to embrace her. In terror she ran naked over fields and mountains, though he cried out to her with loving words. At last she knew her strength was failing and that the river-god would overtake her. She called on Artemis to save her. The goddess responded at once. She wrapped Arethusa in a mist and swept her off to Ortygia, an island in the harbor of Syracuse in Sicily. There the goddess split open the ground and Arethusa, transformed into a fountain, gushed forth from the chasm. Alpheus plunged into the ground of Elis and, passing under the sea, came at last to Ortygia and mingled his waters with those of the fountain of Arethusa. It was said that a flower dropped into the Alpheus in Greece ultimately floated to the surface of the waters of the fountain of Arethusa in Sicily, having traveled under the sea along the path taken by Alpheus when he pursued Arethusa. Various springs in ancient Greece also bore the name Arethusa.

Argades (är′gạ-dēz). According to tradition, one of the four sons of Ion. One of the four ancient tribes of Athens was named for him. His brothers were Aegicores, Geleon, and Hoples.

Argo (är′gō). The name of the famous fifty-oared ship in which the Argonauts sailed with Jason to Colchis to fetch the Golden Fleece. It was built by Argus, son of Arestor, and supposedly named after him. Its prow contained a beam, supplied by Athena, from a sacred talking oak of Dodona, which occasionally gave advice to the Argonauts on their journey. According to ancient writers the *Argo* was the first ship that ever sailed the sea.

Argonauts (är′gō-nôts). The Greek heroes and demigods who sailed with Jason on the *Argo* to fetch the Golden Fleece from Colchis. Various writers have drawn up varying lists of Argonauts, until finally the roster, which originally may have included only Minyans from Iolcus, Orchomenus, and Pylus, came to include representatives from all over Greece. Thus, every part of Greece shared in the expedition (which may have had an historical basis in an early trade venture), and therefore shared the glory and any future advantages which might derive from it. Following is the list of Argonauts given by Apollonius Rhodius in his *Argonautica:*

Acastus, son of King Pelias of Iolcus
Admetus, prince of Pherae, son of Pheres

Aethalides, son of Hermes
Amphidamas, son of Aleus, from Arcadia
Amphion, son of Hyperasius, from Pellene
Ancaeus, son of Lycurgus, from Arcadia
Ancaeus, a steersman, son of Poseidon, from Tegea
Areus, a son of Bias
Argus, builder of the *Argo*
Asterion, son of Cometes
Asterius, brother of Amphion
Augeas, son of Helius, from Elis
Butes, son of Teleon, from Athens
Canthus, son of Canethus, from Euboea
Calais, winged son of Boreas and Orithyia
Castor, one of the Dioscuri, from Sparta
Cepheus, son of Aleus, from Arcadia
Clytius, son of Eurytus, from Oechalia
Coronus, son of Caenus, a Lapith from Thessaly
Echion, herald of the Argonauts, son of Hermes
Erginus, son of Poseidon, from Orchomenus
Eribotes, son of Teleon, from Athens
Erytus, brother of Echion, from Alope
Euphemus, son of Poseidon, from Taenarus
Eurydamas, son of Ctimenus, a Dolopian
Eurytion, son of Irus
Heracles, son of Zeus, from Tiryns
Hylas, squire of Heracles
Idas, son of Aphareus, from Arene
Idmon, a seer, son of Apollo, from Argos
Iphiclus, son of Thestius, from Aetolia
Iphiclus, son of Phylacus, from Phylace
Iphitus, brother of Clytius
Iphitus, son of Naubolus, from Phocis
Jason, son of Aeson, captain of the expedition
Laocoön, uncle of Meleager
Leodocus, brother of Areus
Lynceus, brother of Idas
Meleager, son of Oeneus, from Calydon
Menoetius, son of Actor
Mopsus, son of Ampycus, a Lapith
Nauplius, son of Clytonaeus, from Argos
Oileus, father of Ajax the Lesser, from Locris
Orpheus, the musician and poet, from Thrace

Palaemonius, lame son of Hephaestus, from Aetolia
Peleus, father of Achilles, from Phthia
Periclymenus, son of Nestor, from Pylus
Phalerus, archer from Athens
Phlias, from Araethyrea
Polydeuces, one of the Dioscuri, from Sparta
Polyphemus, son of Elatus, from Arcadia
Taenarus, son of Poseidon
Talaus, brother of Areus
Telamon, father of Great Ajax, from Salamis
Tiphys, the steersman, son of Hagnias, from Boeotia
Zetes, winged brother of Calais

Others listed as members of the Argonauts by other writers include:

Actor, son of Deion, from Phocis
Amphiaraus, the seer, from Argos
Ascalaphus, son of Ares, from Orchomenus
Atalanta, the virgin huntress, from Calydon
Caeneus, the Lapith, father of Coronus
Euryalus, son of Mecisteus, one of the Epigoni
Iphitus, from Mycenae
Laertes, son of Acrisius, from Argos
Melampus, son of Poseidon, from Pylos
Peneleus, son of Hippalcimus, from Boeotia
Phanus, son of Dionysus, from Crete
Poeas, father of Philoctetes, from Thessaly
Staphylus, brother of Phanus.

Argus (är′gus). In Greek mythology, a son of Niobe and Zeus. He reigned in the Peloponnesus and named it Argos after himself. His great grandson, the son of Agenor, who bore the same name and was called Argus Panoptes *(All-seeing)*, had a hundred eyes placed all over his body. No matter how many of his eyes were resting, two were always awake. He killed a bull that was ravaging Arcadia and wore its hide. He came upon the monster Echidna while she was sleeping and killed her. It was Argus Panoptes to whom Hera had given the task of guarding Io, after the latter had been transformed into a heifer by Zeus to protect himself from the jealousy of Hera. Argus guarded Io night and day. At length Zeus sent Hermes to rescue her. Hermes beguiled Argus with many stories and songs, accompanying himself on the syrinx, until at last every one of Argus' hundred eyes fell asleep. Hermes touched them with his magic sleep-inducing wand, lest they open suddenly, and then cut off Argus' head. Hera placed the hundred eyes of Argus in the tail of the bird sacred to her, the peacock, where they make a brilliant display and perpetuate the memory of Argus.

Argus.   He built the *Argo* for Jason, according to tradition, and sailed in her on the quest for the Golden Fleece. His parentage and nationality are variously given.

Argus.   In the *Odyssey,* Odysseus' hound. He recognized Odysseus when he returned to his home after an absence of twenty years, wagged his tail once, and died.

Ariadne   (ar-i-ad′nē). In Greek mythology, a daughter of Minos, king of Crete, and Pasiphaë. She was the sister of Acacallis, Androgeus, Catreus, Glaucus, and Phaedra. When Theseus came to Crete as one of the 14 Athenian youths and maidens who were sent as tribute to Crete every nine years to be thrown to the Minotaur, Ariadne fell in love with him. She offered to help him overcome the Minotaur and to find his way out of the Labyrinth if he would promise to take her back to Athens and marry her. Theseus agreed. Ariadne gave him a ball of golden thread which she had obtained from Daedalus, the builder of the Labyrinth in which the Minotaur was housed. According to some accounts, she held the end of the thread, but others says Theseus was instructed to fasten the end of it to the doorpost of the Labyrinth. As he penetrated the Labyrinth Theseus unwound the ball of thread. Instructed by Ariadne, he seized the Minotaur by the hair and, as some say, killed him with a sword given to him by Ariadne, and sacrificed him to Poseidon. He then found his way out of the Labyrinth by rewinding the golden thread until he came again to the entrance. Ariadne who was awaiting him led the Athenians to the ships which had been made ready, and all escaped. On the island of Naxos, where they stopped, Ariadne fell asleep. When she awoke Theseus and the Athenians had sailed away. Some say that Dionysus appeared to Theseus in a dream and warned him to leave Ariadne, and this was what caused him to forget his promise. In any case, while Ariadne wept alone and demanded vengeance on Theseus, Dionysus came to her. He fell in love with her and married her immediately. Later he set the golden marriage crown, made by Hephaestus, among the stars. Zeus made Ariadne immortal. She bore Dionysus

fat, fāte, fär, fâll, ȧsk, fãre; net, mē, hėr; pin, pīne; not, nōte, mŏve; nôr; up, lūte, pull; oi, oil; ou out; (lightened) ĕlect, agŏny, ŭnite;

many children, including Oenopion, Thoas, Staphylus, Latromis, Euanthes, and Tauropolus. But some say Dionysus did not marry Ariadne. On the contrary, he asked Artemis to slay her because she had profaned his shrine with Theseus. And others say that Ariadne was put ashore at her own request and that the fleet of Theseus was blown away in a violent storm, and when Theseus returned he found Ariadne had died. Ariadne was given divine honors. Festivals were held for her at Naxos, in which women first wailed to commemorate her abandonment by Theseus, and then reveled to celebrate her marriage to Dionysus. In the palace at Crete there was an elaborate mosaic floor, said to have been laid out by Daedalus, which was made for Ariadne to dance upon.

Arimaspians   (ar-i-mas′pi-ạnz). In classical mythology, a one-eyed people of Scythia. They were at war with the Griffins whose gold they sought.

Arion   (ạ-rī′ọn). A reputed son of Poseidon and the nymph Oneaea, but more likely the son of Cycleus, of Methymna in Lesbos. He was a skilled musician from Lesbos (fl. 628–625 B.C.). He journeyed from Corinth to Taenarus in Sicily and there won such great riches for his playing on the lyre that it is said the sailors on the ship bearing him home decided to kill him and steal his treasure. He asked to be allowed to sing one song before death, and sang so beautifully that dolphins gathered around the ship to listen. On finishing his song he leaped into the sea. A dolphin bore him up on its back and speedily took him to Corinth, arriving there before the ship. When the sailors were questioned about Arion when they came to Corinth, they said he was still in Sicily. On being confronted with him in person they acknowledged their guilt and were put to death. Apollo is said to have placed an image of Arion and his lyre among the stars. According to legend, Arion invented the dithyramb, a choral song in honor of Dionysus, and taught it to Corinthian choruses.

Arion.   In Greek legend, a fabulous horse. It was said to be the offspring of Poseidon by Demeter (or, in other accounts, Gaea or a Harpy) who to escape him had metamorphosed herself into a mare. It was successively owned by Copreus, Oncus, Heracles, and Adrastus. It possessed marvelous powers of speech, and its right feet were those of a man.

(obscured) errạnt, ardẹnt, actọr; ch, chip; g, go; th, thin; ᵺ, then; y, you;
(variable) ḍ as d or j, ṣ as s or sh, ṭ as t or ch, ẕ as z or zh.

Aristaeus (ar-is-tē′us). In Greek mythology, a son of Apollo and Cyrene. He was born in Cyrene, whither his mother had been brought by Apollo, and was reared by nymphs who taught him how to make cheese, to build beehives, and to raise the cultivated olive. From Libya he went to Boeotia, where Apollo took him to Chiron's cave in order that he might be instructed in the Mysteries. The Muses taught him the arts of healing and of prophecy and when he had grown to manhood they married him to Autonoë, by whom he became the father of Actaeon and Macris, the nymph who cared for the infant Dionysus. Instructed by the Delphic oracle to visit Ceos, he immediately sailed to that island and found it suffering from a plague. This plague was caused by the Dog Star because the murderers of that Icarius who was the first to make wine were hiding among the Ceans and had not been punished. Aristaeus lifted the plague by raising altars to Zeus, on which he offered sacrifices, and by finding and slaying the murderers of Icarius. Ever after this Zeus caused the cooling summer winds to blow on Greece and the islands for forty days following the rising of the Dog Star. The islanders annually offered sacrifices to appease the Dog Star, and gave divine honors to Aristaeus in gratitude for relief from the plague. From Ceos Aristaeus went to Arcadia. In the valley of the Peneus River near Tempe he came on Eurydice, wife of Orpheus. He attempted to ravish her and she fled. In so doing she stepped on a serpent and died of its bite. Shortly afterward, all of Aristaeus' bees died. He appealed to the naiads of the Peneus River and they advised him to consult the sea-god Proteus. He caught Proteus as he slept on the island of Pharos; seized the god and held him fast through all the changes he underwent in an effort to escape from Aristaeus' clasp. At last Proteus resumed his own form and told Aristaeus his bees had died because he had caused the death of Eurydice. Aristaeus now appealed to his mother. She told him to raise altars to the dryads, companions of Eurydice, and to offer sacrifices of bulls and heifers, and to leave the animals' carcasses at the altars. After nine days Aristaeus returned; a swarm of bees rose from the decaying carcasses. He captured the swarm and put it into a hive. Later Aristaeus sailed to Sardinia and taught all he had learned from the nymphs and Muses to the inhabitants there, as he had done wherever he went. He also visited Sicily and Thrace and taught the arts of agriculture there. He founded the city of Aristaeum in Thrace and finally disappeared. As the deity who presides over hunting and herds and the domestic arts of beekeeping, wine-making, and olive-growing, he was worshiped in Thessaly, Boeotia, and various other parts of Greece, as well as in the islands, in Cyrene, Thrace, Sicily, and Sardinia.

Arne (är′nē). In Greek mythology, a daughter of Thea (daughter of Chiron the centaur), and Aeolus, king of Magnesia in Thessaly. Her mother was transformed into a mare by Poseidon before Arne was born, and Arne's first appearance into the world was as a foal which bore the name Melanippe. She was then transformed into an infant girl by Poseidon, and was given by Aeolus, who renamed her Arne, to Desmontes to bring up. When she grew up she was seduced by Poseidon. Desmontes, on discovering that she was about to bear a child, blinded and imprisoned her. She bore twin sons, Aeolus, who became guardian of the winds, and Boeotus, ancestor of the Boeotians. Desmontes ordered the twins exposed on Mount Pelion but they were saved by shepherds. They were given to Theano, the childless wife of Metapontus, king of Icaria, who presented them to her husband as her own children. Metapontus was delighted with them, thinking they were his own children. Later Theano bore twins of her own but Metapontus still preferred Aeolus and Boeotus. Thenao now wanted to be rid of them. She advised her sons to attack them on a hunting expedition and kill them. But her scheme miscarried. Poseidon came to the aid of his sons and they killed Theano's children. Aeolus and Boeotus, on being informed by Poseidon that he was their father, were then ordered to kill Desmontes and to free their mother who was still languishing in prison. They did as commanded and were reunited with Arne whose sight was restored by Poseidon. When Metapontus learned the truth he married Arne and adopted her sons. Later he tired of her and put her aside to take a new wife. Aeolus and Boeotus took their mother's part and slew the new queen. They then fled. Arne and Boeotus went to Thessaly, to the home of her father Aeolus. He gave Boeotus part of his kingdom, which Boeotus renamed Arne in honor of his mother.

Arne. In Greek mythology, a princess of the island of Siphnus. Minos, desiring to win her friendship for his war against the Athenians, bribed her with gifts of gold and secured her aid. To punish her greed she was changed into a magpie, ever attracted by the glitter of bright things.

Arsinoë (är-sin′ō̧-ē). In Greek mythology, a daughter of Phegeus, king of Psophis. Phegeus gave her in marriage to Alcmaeon, who had fled to his court to be purified. Alcmaeon gave her the necklace and peplus of Harmonia, which he had brought with him and which caused disaster to whomever possessed them. Alcmaeon, pursued by the Erinyes for the murder of his mother, went to the river-god Achelous for purification. On his return to Psophis he asked Arsinoë to surrender the necklace and peplus to him. This she willingly did, unaware that during his absence he had married the daughter of Achelous and wished to give the necklace and peplus to her. When Phegeus learned the truth he had Alcmaeon killed. Arsinoë would not listen to the truth about Alcmaeon and prayed that her father and brothers would die before the next new moon to punish them for having widowed her. Her father locked her in a chest and gave her to the king of Nemea for a slave. But her prayer was answered, her father and brothers were dead within a month.

Artemis (är′tẹ-mis). One of the 12 Olympian gods, the daughter of Zeus and Leto, and the twin sister of Apollo. As with Apollo, the worship of Artemis was supposed to have come from the Hyperboreans, for which reason she was known as Hyperborean Artemis. Armed like Apollo with a silver bow, she was a mighty hunter, a "Rainer of Arrows," who sent them to punish the wicked and impious, and who could also heal and reward. Sudden death occurring in women was attributed to the arrows of Artemis. She did not share with Apollo the gift of prophecy, nor had she any connection with the arts. She was the virgin huntress, devoted to the chase, the goddess of streets and the founding of towns, the protectress of all young animals, and the goddess of flocks. As Apollo was a god of light, sometimes identified with the sun, so Artemis was also a goddess of light and was identified with the moon, particularly with Selene and Hecate.

Leto was compelled to wander through the earth searching for a place to bear her children, because jealous Hera had decreed that no place where the sun shone could receive her rival. At last she came to the tiny island of Ortygia. There she bore Artemis, and because she was born without pain Artemis became the goddess invoked by women in childbirth, and was sometimes known as Ilithyia, the birth-goddess. As soon as she was born Artemis helped her mother across the narrow strait to the neighboring and

ARTEMIS
Red-figured Greek crater, Pan Painter, 475–450 B.C.
Museum of Fine Arts, Boston

slightly larger floating island of Delos, which offered to receive Leto in spite of Hera's threats. On Delos Artemis acted as midwife and helped her mother to bear Apollo, her twin. But some say Artemis was born on Delos itself, and some say she was born in the Ortygian grove at Ephesus. While she was yet a child, her father Zeus took her on his knee and

asked what gifts she desired of him. At once, Artemis asked
for the gift of eternal virginity. This was granted her, and she
became one of the three goddesses whose heart could not
be moved by the power of Aphrodite (the others were
Athena and Hestia). She also asked for bow and arrows like
her brother's, for 60 ocean nymphs to be her companions,
and 20 river nymphs from Crete to look after her hunting
gear and her hounds. Besides, she wanted all the mountains
of the world and just one city, for she expected to spend
most of her time hunting on the mountains. Zeus promised
her all she asked and more, and made her goddess of roads
and harbors. Artemis went off to the realm of Oceanus and
to Crete, where she chose her companions. Then she went
to visit the Cyclopes, at the invitation of Hephaestus.
Brontes, who had been told to make whatever she asked,
took her on his knee, but she did not care for his fondling,
and tore a handful of hair out of his chest to express her
annoyance. At the time of her visit the Cyclopes were at
work on a silver trough for Poseidon. Artemis imperiously
told them to interrupt the work and make her a silver bow
and a quiver of arrows, and promised to give them the first
thing she shot with them as a reward. The Cyclopes did as
she bid. Armed with her bow, Artemis went to Arcadia.
There she met Pan, who gave her hounds for the chase. Next
she captured alive two pairs of golden-horned, bronze
hoofed stags and harnessed them to a golden chariot. In this
she set off for Thrace to try out her weapons. Her first two
arrows struck trees; her third slew a wild beast; and her
fourth was used to punish a city of unjust men.

Artemis jealously guarded the honor of her mother and
her brother. She helped Apollo kill Tityus when he attacked
Leto as she was on her way to Delphi. She killed the daughters of Niobe, who had boasted of her many sons and daughters, taunted Leto because she had only two children, and
recommended to the Thebans that they worship her instead
of Leto. Some say that she slew Coronis the Lapith with her
arrows when Apollo complained to her that Coronis had
been unfaithful to him. But others say she helped Coronis
when she was bearing Apollo's son Asclepius. Artemis sent
heavy punishments on those who failed to give her due
honor. Oeneus of Calydon forgot her when he was sacrificing first fruits to the gods. Helius informed Artemis of this

---

oversight, and she sent a monstrous boar to ravage Calydon, the realm of Oeneus. Meleager, the son of Oeneus, called together a group of heroes and the boar was at length slain, but Meleager quarreled with his uncles and finally killed them and brought about his own death. Artemis turned all but two of his wildly grieving sisters into guinea-hens. Admetus also offended her by neglecting her at his marriage rites. When he went to the marriage chamber he found it filled with writhing serpents. Apollo, who was serving as bondman of Admetus at the time, told him how to appease Artemis. Atreus, son of Pelops, promised to sacrifice the best of his flocks to Artemis. Hermes, who wanted to punish the Pelopidae because Pelops had murdered his son Myrtilus, schemed with Pan, and put a lamb with golden fleece and a horn of gold into the flocks that Pelops had left to his sons Atreus and Thyestes. Atreus claimed the lamb with golden fleece, and did indeed kill it and offer the flesh to Artemis but he took the skin, stuffed it, and hid it in a chest. But some say it was Artemis herself who put the lamb with golden fleece among the flocks of Atreus, to test him. By withholding the golden fleece from the sacrifice he incurred her wrath, and she punished his family, especially his son Agamemnon. Broteas, son of Tantalus, was a great hunter. He failed to honor Artemis and, some say, she drove him mad; he cast himself on a pyre and so perished. On the other hand, she rewarded those who honored her. Hippolytus, son of Theseus, worshiped Artemis above all, and even denied the power of Aphrodite. Aphrodite caused his death, not because he honored Artemis, but because he denied her, the goddess of love. Artemis begged Asclepius to restore Hippolytus. He did so with a magic herb, and Artemis wrapped him in a cloud and carried him off to Italy. There in her sacred grove of Aricia she changed his name to Virbius and gave him the nymph Egeria for a wife.

Artemis, the chaste goddess, resisted all would-be lovers. Otus, one of the Aloidae, sought to embrace her. With his brother Ephialtes he pursued her to the island of Naxos. As the brothers were about to discover her, Artemis transformed herself into a hind. The brothers separated to attack from opposite sides. With the hind between them, each hurled his spear, but Artemis disappeared, and the spears so forcefully hurled sped on; each brother was pierced by the other's spear. Some say that Orion, returning from the East with his sight restored after Oenopion had blinded him, met Artemis as he sought Oenopion for revenge. She persuaded him, as a mighty hunter, to give up the idea of revenge and go hunting with her. Apollo, fearing that Orion might melt the heart of his virgin sister, caused a great scorpion to attack him. Orion fought the monster with his arrows and his sword, but could not kill him. He fled into the sea to escape the scorpion and swam off toward Delos. Apollo now approached Artemis. He pointed to the speck on the sea made by Orion's head as he swam rapidly away and challenged her to hit it with one of her arrows. Artemis took aim, shot at the speck, and killed Orion. When she learned that she had killed Orion she begged Asclepius to restore him to life, but Asclepius was killed by the thunderbolt of Zeus before he could do so. Artemis then set Orion's image among the stars, with the image of the scorpion ever in pursuit. But some say Artemis herself sent the scorpion against Orion, either because he had attempted to violate her, or pursued one of her maidens who had come from the Hyperboreans, or because he challenged her to a match at quoits, and that Orion died of the scorpion's bite. Unfortunate Actaeon, who accidentally happened to pass a fountain where the goddess and her companions were refreshing themselves, stopped to watch the goddess in her bath. When he was discovered Artemis transformed him into a stag and he was pursued and torn to pieces by his own hounds. Artemis escaped the amorous advances of the river-god Alpheus at Letrini in Elis by daubing her own face and the faces of her companions with white clay. For this she was given the epithet Alphaea (*Whitish*). When Alpheus came in search of her he could not tell which was the goddess and was forced to withdraw disappointed. And Artemis punished those of her companions who forgot their vows of chastity. When she noticed that Callisto, loved by Zeus, was about to have a child, she transformed her into a bear and set her companions to hunt her, but Zeus saved Callisto by translating her to the heavens. Others say it was not Artemis who transformed Callisto into a bear, but Zeus, to save her from Hera, and that Artemis and her maidens were tricked by Hera into pursuing the bear.

Artemis loved all animals, but the hind was her favorite.

fat, fāte, fär, fâll, àsk, fãre; net, mē, hèr; pin, pīne; not, nōte, möve, nôr; up, lūte, pùll; oi, oil; ou out; (lightened) ĕlect, agǫny, ūnite;

She transformed the Pleiad Taÿgete into a hind to help her escape the embraces of Zeus. Afterward, Taÿgete dedicated a hind with golden horns and bronze hoofs to Artemis in gratitude. Inscribed on the hind was the legend, "Taÿgete dedicated me to Artemis." But others say this hind, called the Cerynian hind because it roamed the Cerynian Hill, was one of five hinds with bronze hoofs and horns of gold that Artemis had seen as a child. She captured four of them and harnessed them to her chariot, but the fifth escaped. Heracles was ordered by Eurystheus to catch the Cerynian hind as one of his labors. Because it was sacred to Artemis he was reluctant to harm it. He pursued it for a year, and at last transfixed the forelegs of the creature with one arrow and captured it alive. Artemis reproached him for having harmed her sacred hind, but forgave him when he explained the necessity under which he was operating, and allowed him to carry it off to Eurystheus at Mycenae.

Some say that Artemis visited her anger at Atreus on his son Agamemnon because Atreus failed to sacrifice the golden-fleeced lamb to her as he had promised. Others say that she punished Agamemnon because he killed a hare that was about to bear young, or because he killed a stag and boasted that "Artemis herself could not have done better." As the Greek fleet was gathered at Aulis in preparation for the voyage to Troy, it was windbound. Calchas the seer said Artemis was angry, and would not send favorable winds until Agamemnon had sacrificed his daughter Iphigenia to her. Agamemnon secured the presence of Iphigenia at Aulis by a trick, and made ready to sacrifice her. As she bared her throat to receive the knife, Artemis spirited her away and left a hind in her place. She took Iphigenia to her temple in Tauris and made her a priestess there, while the goddess went off and, like Apollo, helped the Trojans in the war. In the temple of Artemis at Tauris was an ancient wooden image of the goddess that had fallen from heaven. Strangers who were forced by storms to land on the coast were sacrificed to the Taurian Artemis, who was also called Artemis Tauropolus, Artemis Dictynna, Hecate, and Trivia. Certain preparatory rites were performed on the victim. He was then clubbed to death and his head severed from his body. The head was nailed to a cross and the decapitated body was cast into the sea from the cliff on which the temple of Taurian

(obscured) errant, ardent, actor; ch, chip; g, go; th, thin; ŦH, then; y, you;
(variable) ḍ as d or j, ş as s or sh, ţ as t or ch, z̧ as z or zh.

Artemis stood. If the victim was of noble blood he was killed with a sword by the priestess herself, and his corpse was burned in a sacred flame that rose from Tartarus. While Iphigenia was serving as priestess, Orestes, her brother, came, in obedience to an oracle, to fetch the image and take it back to Greece. Like other strangers, he was about to be sacrificed, but Iphigenia recognized him and with her help he escaped, taking her with him, and returned to Brauron, near Athens, with the image. Some say the goddess made Iphigenia immortal, and that she was sometimes known by the name Iphigenia herself. A temple of Artemis was raised at Brauron, and Iphigenia was its first priestess. At the temple, in obedience to instructions from Athena, the rites included pricking the throat of a man with a knife just enough to draw blood, in commemoration of the narrow escape of Orestes at Tauris. Brauronian Artemis was worshiped at Athens and Sparta, and stags and goats were sacrificed to her. An oracle said the altar of the Taurian image of Artemis should be stained with blood, as was the marble altar at Tauris, and at first human sacrifices were offered to her. In the time of Spartan Lycurgus this practice was changed. Young boys were scourged in the temple while the priestess held the image of the goddess. If the scourgers did not lay on heavily enough the image grew so heavy the priestess could scarcely hold it. When the scourgers laid on with more vigor the image became light. An image of Brauronian Artemis, made by Phidias, was in her sanctuary on the Acropolis at Athens. Some say the ancient wooden image of Taurian Artemis was at Brauron, and that it was taken by Xerxes in the Persian War and given to the Syrians, who still claimed it was in their possession in the 2nd century A.D., but the Lydians and the Cappadocians each also claimed that they had the image. And others say Orestes took it to the sacred grove of Artemis at Aricia, in Italy, and that the Romans later returned it to Sparta. But the Spartans, who claimed they had the true image, said the Taurian image was lost. After centuries it was found in a thicket of willows at Limnaeum in Laconia by two noble Spartans who subsequently went mad. Because the image was held upright by willow fronds that twined around it, Artemis has the epithet Orthia (*Upright*) and Lygodesma (*Willow-bound*). This image at Limnaeum, the Spartans say, is the true image.

When Zeus asked Artemis what gifts she would like from him she asked for as many names as her brother Apollo. In addition to the epithets already mentioned, she was Agrotera *(Huntress)*, Coryphaea *(Of the Peak)*, Limnaea and Limnatis *(Of the Lake)*, Daphnaea *(Of the Laurel)*, Lyceia or Lycea *(Wolfish)*, Aeginaea *(Goat-goddess)*, Caryatis *(Of the Walnut-tree)*, Cedreatis *(Of the Cedar)* from an image of the goddess set in a cedar tree, and Eurippa *(Horse-finder)* from a sanctuary raised by Odysseus in Arcadia where he found his mares for which he had been searching throughout Greece. She was Hiereia *(Priestess)*, Pyronia *(Fire-goddess)*, Peitho *(Persuasion)*, Selasphorus and Phosphorus *(Light-bearer)*, Ariste *(Best)*, Calliste *(Fairest)*, and Paedotrophus *(Nurse of Children)*. Artemis Savior was worshiped in many places. In Megara there was an ancient sanctuary of Artemis Savior erected by grateful Megarians because the goddess helped them to defeat a force of Persians during the Persian War. The Persians lost their way in the hills at night. Thinking the enemy was nearby they shot off a volley of arrows. The arrows struck rocks, which Artemis caused to groan. Under the impression that they were killing Greeks, the Persians fired all their arrows, and the next day when the Megarians attacked them had no ammunition with which to defend themselves and were slain. Theseus raised a temple of Artemis Savior at Troezen in gratitude for her help in overcoming the Minotaur; and the people of Boeae in Laconia worshiped Artemis Savior because she helped them to find a site for their city. At Condylea, in Arcadia, she was worshiped as Condyleatis and as the Strangled Lady because some children playing near the sanctuary found a rope and tied it around the neck of the image, and said the goddess was being strangled. The Calydonians worshiped her as Laphria. At Patrae an annual feast was held, called Laphria. A circle of green logs was set up around the altar. A procession marched to the temple. The maiden priestess rode in a car drawn by a deer at the end of the procession. The next day, great numbers of live wild beasts were hurled on the fire that was lighted within the circle of green logs. Some say Artemis got the epithet Laphria from a Calydonian man named Laphrius. Others say the name was given her because her wrath weighed more lightly *(elaphroteron)* on the Calydonians and Oeneus as time passed. In Arcadia she was

(obscured) errant, ardent, actor; ch, chip; g, go; th, thin; ᴛʜ, then; y, you;
(variable) ḍ as d or j, ṣ as s or sh, ṭ as t or ch, ẓ as z or zh.

also Hemerasia *(She who Soothes)* because at her sanctuary Melampus cured the daughters of Proetus of their madness. At Pyrrhicus in Laconia she was worshiped as Astrateia because she stayed the advance of the Amazons there.

The worship of Artemis was universal in Greece, Delos, Crete, Sicily, and southern Italy, and was especially strong in Arcadia, where she had many temples and sanctuaries, and throughout the Peloponnesus. In Thrace, Artemis was Tauropolus, to whom human sacrifices were made, and who drove men mad. Later, the Thracians sacrificed dogs to her. In Greek Asia she was widely worshiped. At Ephesus, where the Amazons were said to have introduced her worship, she was a fertility goddess. In the magnificent temple of Artemis there, was an image of Artemis Polymastus *(Many-breasted)*, which had many breasts and bore a mural crown on the head. The symbol of Artemis Polymastus at Ephesus was a bee. Chaste Artemis, the huntress who roamed the mountains and streams and in whose care were all animals, led her nymphs in the groves and received sacrifices on woodland altars. She was known as Arcadian Artemis. Artemis of Ephesus, known as Ephesian Artemis, was an Asiatic deity adopted and adapted by the Greeks who settled in Asia Minor. The laurel and the fir tree were sacred to Artemis, as were the hind, the bear, the dog and the boar. Her attributes were the bow and quiver, torch, javelin, and crescent. In art she is represented as a young woman of noble and severe beauty, tall and majestic, and generally bearing bow and quiver as the huntress or mountain goddess, and often accompanied by a hind or a dog. She was identified by the Romans with their Diana, an original Italian divinity.

Asclepius (as-klē′pi-us). In Greek mythology, a son of Coronis and Apollo. Apollo caused Coronis' death, before Asclepius was born, because he found she had been unfaithful to him. As her body lay on the funeral pyre he was overcome with remorse and resolved at least to save his son. He sent Hermes to snatch the unborn child from his mother's womb. Hermes took the infant to Chiron the centaur, who brought him up and taught him the arts of healing and hunting. Asclepius was much more interested in the medical arts than in sport, and soon outstripped his master. Aided also by instruction from Apollo, he became a skilled surgeon and

fat, fāte, fär, fȧll, ȧsk, fãre; net, mē, hėr; pin, pīne; not, nōte, mȯve, nôr; up, lūte, pṳll; oi, oil; ou out; (lightened) ẹlect, agǫny, ūnite;

highly successful in prescribing drugs. Some say Athena gave him two phials of the blood of Medusa when her head was cut off by Perseus. The blood that was drawn from the left side was used to restore the dead to life; that from the right side he used to destroy life. But others say Athena divided the blood drawn from Medusa between herself and Asclepius. She used her share for destructive ends; Asclepius used his share for healing. Asclepius was the father of Podalirius and Machaon, the physicians who accompanied the Greeks to Troy, and of Hygea. Asclepius is said to have used the blood of Medusa, or an herb known only to him, to restore Lycurgus, Capaneus, Tyndareus, Glaucus, Orion, and Hippolytus to life. Hades complained to Zeus, some say, that Asclepius was taking away his subjects by restoring them to life, and Zeus killed him with his thunderbolt. Others say Asclepius accepted a bribe in defiance of divine law, and restored the dead to life, and was slain by the thunderbolt of Zeus. Apollo, infuriated at the slaying of his son, killed the Cyclopes, because they had forged the thunderbolt of Zeus. To punish him, Zeus ordered him to serve Admetus of Pherae for a year without pay. Some say Asclepius was later restored to life himself, thus fulfilling a prophecy that he would fulfill his destiny twice. His image was set among the stars. Asclepius was worshiped throughout Greece as a hero and god of healing for centuries. One of his most famous shrines was at Epidaurus. In his temple there several serpents were kept, for serpents, annually renewing themselves by shedding their skins, were connected in some mysterious way with the art of healing. Asclepius was always shown with a serpent, usually carrying a staff about which a serpent was coiled. The cock was commonly sacrificed to him. Patients who went to the healing shrine at Epidaurus slept in the temple, presided over by an image of Sleep or Dreams, and their cures were related to them in dreams. A great festival in honor of Asclepius was held every five years at Epidaurus. There were temples and shrines to Asclepius throughout Greece. At Pergamum, founded by a colony from Epidaurus, there was another famous shrine, as there was also at Tricca in Thessaly, whose inhabitants claimed that their town was the birthplace of the healing god. After 293 B.C. Asclepius was worshiped in

Rome, under the name Aesculapius. He had been brought to Rome in the form of a serpent; his shrine was on the Tiber island.

Asopus (a̱-sō'pus). The god of the Sicyonian river of the same name. By his wife Metope, the daughter of Ladon, he was the father of two sons, Pelasgus and Ismenus, and 12 (or some say, 20) daughters—Corcyra, Salamis, Aegina, Pirene, Cleone, Thebe, Tanagra, Thespeia, Asopis, Sinope, Ornia, and Chalcis. His beautiful daughters were harassed by the attentions of various gods who carried them off and ravished them. Sinope was carried off by Apollo, according to some accounts, and bore him a son, but later shrewdly frustrated the attentions of Zeus. Corcyra and Salamis were abducted by Poseidon. Thebe disappeared with Zeus. When Aegina too disappeared Asopus lost pa̱tience with the gods and determined to recover her. He learned that Sisyphus of Corinth had information concerning her whereabouts, but Sisyphus never gave away anything for nothing. It was necessary for Asopus to bribe him by giving Corinth the never-failing Pirene Fountain, to tell what he knew. Sisyphus then divulged that Zeus had carried off Aegina. Asopus pursued Zeus and overtook him in a forest. Zeus, who was carrying no thunderbolts at the time, fled and changed himself into a huge stone to escape the wrath of Asopus. When Asopus had passed by, Zeus resumed his shape, returned to Olympus, and from there hurled thunderbolts at Asopus. He wounded Asopus and lamed him. It is for this reason that the Asopus River flows sluggishly, and the thunderbolts hurled by Zeus at Asopus are said to account for the lumps of burned coal that are sometimes found in the river bed.

Asphodel Fields (as'fō-del.) Named by Homer as the meadow of the dead, where the shades of heroes wandered disconsolately. In Greek mythology the asphodel was the peculiar plant of the dead, its pale blossoms covering the meadows of Hades; perhaps because in Greek lands it is a very common weed, plentiful in barren and desert places and about tombs.

Asteria (a̱-stē'ri-a̱). In Greek mythology, a daughter of the Titans Coeus and Phoebe, and the mother, by Perses, of Hecate. Pursued by Zeus, she assumed the form of a quail and leaped into the sea to escape him. She was then transformed into an island, Ortygia, which floated in the sea. Later, when her sister, Leto, sought refuge to bear her chil-

dren, the tiny island received her gladly; four pillars rose
from the sea floor to anchor it, and the modest island, thereafter called Delos, became famed as the birthplace of Leto's
children, Apollo and Artemis.

Astraea or **Astrea**   (as-trē′ạ). In classical mythology, the goddess of justice.

Astraeus   (as-trē′us). In Greek mythology, a son of the Titan
Crius and Eurybia, and the brother of the Titans Pallas and
Perses. He was the father of the winds and the stars by Eos,
the goddess of Dawn.

Astyanax   (as-tī′ạ-naks). In Greek legend, the son of Hector
and Andromache. At the fall of Troy Odysseus advised Agamemnon to kill Astyanax lest, when he was grown up, he
assemble the Trojans and make war on the Greeks. In consequence of this advice and a prophecy by Calchas, Astyanax
was taken from his mother's arms and hurled from the towers of Troy. Astyanax was also known as Scamandrius.

Atalanta   (at-ạ-lan′tạ) or **Atalante**   (-tē). In Greek legend, the
supposed daughter of Iasius of Arcadia, but some say Zeus
was her father. Iasius had hoped for a son. In his disappointment over the birth of a daughter he exposed the child on
a mountain to die. Artemis became her protector and sent
a she-bear to nurse the infant until she was found by a band
of hunters. They rescued her and brought her up. Once
later, when Atalanta was fainting from thirst she called on
Artemis for help, and struck the earth with the point of her
spear. Artemis caused a stream of water to gush forth. Atalanta was warned by the oracle at Delphi against marriage,
but the oracle added that she would marry and that she
would not enjoy her marriage. She therefore shunned the
society of men and devoted herself to hunting, as did the
virgin goddess Artemis. She became a skilled and fearless
hunter, and once killed two centaurs who pursued her in the
forest. According to some accounts, she accompanied the
Argonauts in the quest for the Golden Fleece, but others say
that Jason refused her request to be admitted as a member
of his company on the ground that the presence of one
woman among so many men would cause trouble. When she
heard of the great company that Meleager of Calydon was
assembling to hunt the Calydonian Boar she eagerly went to
join the group. Meleager saw her lovely face, fell in love with
her charm, which was boyish and feminine at the same time,
and welcomed her as a member of the hunt. But the great

(obscured) errạnt, ardẹnt, actọr; ch, chip; g, go; th, thin; ᵺн, then; y, you;
(variable) ḏ as d or j, ṣ as s or sh, ṭ as t or ch, ẕ as z or zh.

heroes who had come at Meleager's call objected strongly to the presence of a woman in their midst, and some threatened to withdraw. Meleager announced that they must accept Atalanta or he would abandon the project of the hunt entirely. They reluctantly agreed to accept her. When the boar was raised from its lair many of the noble hunters sprang to attack it, but none succeeded in wounding it. On the contrary, the boar killed some of the hunters and drove others to cover. Atalanta was the first to draw blood by striking it in the head with one of her arrows. Ancaeus, who scoffed at Atalanta because she hadn't killed the boar, boasted that he would show her how to hunt, but as he went to the attack the boar charged him and disembowelled him with its tusks. Meleager administered the final blow to the boar after it had been wounded by Atalanta. He awarded the boar's hide and tusks to her because she had drawn first blood. To honor a woman in this way was a humiliation in the eyes of some of the hunters. Meleager's uncles protested the award. They said either Meleager, who had killed the boar, should have the hide, or it should be awarded to one of them, as those most to be honored among those present. Their anger in this matter led to their own and Meleager's deaths. Some say that Atalanta bore a son to Meleager in secret and that she exposed the child, Parthenopaeus, on a mountain to die, and afterward pretended that she was a virgin. After her success in the Calydonian Hunt Atalanta returned to her father's house and was delightedly received. He wished her to marry, as he hoped for grandsons. Atalanta, mindful of the warning of the oracle, agreed to marry, but set up certain conditions which her future husband must first meet. Relying on her swiftness of foot, she said any suitor for her hand must run against her in a race. If he won she would marry him; if he lost she would kill him. In spite of the harsh conditions there were many suitors, and many lost the race and their lives. Hippomenes came to watch the contest. He was astonished that any man would be so foolish as to take such a risk, thought no woman alive was worth it. But when he saw Atalanta's beauty he changed his mind. He fell in love with her and decided to race for her hand himself. When he made known his intentions Atalanta looked at him and her heart softened. She did not want him to die, and hoped he would win. Before the race began Hippomenes

fat, fāte, fär, fåll, àsk, fâre; net, mē, hèr; pin, pīne; not, nōte, möve, nôr; up, lūte, pùll; oi, oil; ou out; (lightened) ēlect, agǫny, ūnite;

appealed to Aphrodite for help, because, he said, it was
Aphrodite who had caused him to fall in love with Atalanta
and take such a mad risk. Aphrodite answered his prayer by
giving him three golden apples and instructions for the use he
should make of them. As the race started the runners
were even for a time but soon Atalanta fleetly drew ahead.
Hippomenes cast one of the golden apples in front of her.
On seeing it Atalanta hesitated, then bent and picked it up.
This gave Hippomenes a chance to draw ahead. When she
again overtook him and widened the space between them he
used a second apple, and toward the end of the course it was
necessary for him to use the third. With their help he was
able to beat Atalanta and win her for his bride. As Atalanta
had already fallen in love with him before the race everyone
was delighted. But in their happiness they forgot to show
their gratitude to Aphrodite. That goddess, in anger because they had so quickly forgotten her and also to punish
Atalanta for denying the power of love for so long, caused
them to profane the temple of Cybele with their love-making. Cybele avenged the outrage to her shrine by transforming them into lions and yoking them to her car. Sometimes
Atalanta is called the daughter of Schoeneus of Boeotia, and
her husband is variously named as Melanion; and some
think the Atalanta of Arcadia and the Atalanta of Boeotia
were two different maidens who had almost identical histo-
ries.

Ate (ā′tē). A daughter of Zeus (according to Homer) or of
Eris (according to Hesiod). She was the goddess of mischief,
who ensnared the feet of mortals and caused them to act
rashly and unreasonably. It was Ate who so blinded Zeus to
his own interests on the day when he was awaiting the birth
of his hero son Heracles, that he promised Hera that the first
son born that day would be lord over all those who dwelt
around him. Hera then delayed the birth of Heracles until
after Eurystheus, grandson of Perseus, was born, in consequence of which Heracles had to serve Eurystheus. For causing this mischief Zeus clutched Ate by the hair and flung her
out of heaven. Agamemnon blamed his rash act in taking
Briseis from Achilles on Ate, naming her the goddess who
strikes men with blindness and makes them stumble and fall.

Athamas (ath′a-mas). In Greek mythology, a son of Aeolus
and Enarete, and the brother of Sisyphus and Salmoneus.

He was a king of Orchomenus in Boeotia. At Hera's command he married Nephele, a cloud in the shape of a woman, and by her had two sons, Phrixus and Leucon, and one daughter, Helle. Tiring of his phantom wife, he abandoned Nephele in favor of Ino, the daughter of Cadmus, and had two sons by her, Melicertes and Learchus. Ino, to get rid of his heirs by Nephele, duped him into believing that a famine which was devastating the land could be lifted by the sacrifice of Phrixus. As Athamas prepared to carry out the sacrifice a winged ram with golden fleece, sent by Hermes, arrived at the altar and carried Phrixus and his sister Helle away on its back. Nephele complained to Hera because she had been replaced by Ino. The goddess resolved to punish Athamas, both because of his treatment of Nephele and because Ino had sheltered Dionysus, the son of Zeus and Semele. Hera laid a divine frenzy on Athamas, in which he killed his son Learchus and would have killed Ino too, but with the aid of Dionysus she escaped, carrying Melicertes in her arms. Athamas' remaining son Leucon died. Since he was banished from Boeotia for his crimes, Athamas consulted the oracle at Delphi to learn where he should go. He was told that he should settle where wild beasts provided his dinner. He wandered into Thessaly and there came upon wolves mauling sheep that they had just killed. The wolves fled at the approach of Athamas and his companions. The slain sheep provided Athamas and his friends with a hearty meal and, in accordance with the instructions of the oracle, he founded a city, Alos, on the site. In Thessaly he married again and raised a new family.

Athena (a̧-thē′na̧) or *Athene* (-nē). [Also: *Pallas Athena.*] One of the 12 Olympians. Although she was worshiped throughout Greece, her cult was especially strong in Attica, where she was a national divinity, and where her worship was gloriously memorialized in the Parthenon, the Temple of the Maiden Goddess on the Acropolis at Athens. The worship of Athena is essentially an expression of developing ethical and social principles. She is a goddess of war who fights in righteous causes. Like Zeus, she wields the thunderbolt and the lightning. She personifies the clear upper air as well as mental clearness and acuteness, embodying the spirit of truth and divine wisdom; she wears the aegis, symbolizing the dark storm-cloud, and is armed with the resistless spear (the shaft of lightning). She participates with skill and wisdom in wars to defend the state, but does not fight, like Ares, with uncontrolled ferocity for sheer love of strife. Her activities in war restore order, and thus she is a goddess of peace. She upholds law and order, encourages the arts by which the state is strengthened, and has invented so many aids to mankind that she is called the *Contriver*. Athena is also the goddess who taught and encourages the household arts of spinning, weaving, and cooking. She is the protectress of the young, the patroness of agriculture, of construction of all kinds, of healing, and of music. She is especially devoted to the interests of mankind for, some say, when Prometheus fashioned men of clay and water it was Athena who breathed life into them.

Some say Athena was born beside the lake Tritonis in Libya, and that Poseidon was her father. By the temple of Hephaestus at Athens was a blue-eyed statue of Athena, signalizing her relationship to Poseidon with blue eyes like his. But she quarreled with Poseidon and appealed to Zeus, who then adopted her as his daughter. Others say she was reared by the river-god Triton, and that his daughter Pallas was her dear companion. They often played at war games together, and one day Athena accidentally struck and killed her. In memory of her grief, Athena placed the name of her playmate before her own, and was henceforth known as Pallas Athena. She made a wooden image of Pallas, wrapped it in her aegis, and set it up and honored it. This image, the Palladium, afterwards dropped, or was hurled, from heaven. It fell into the Troad and was found by Ilus, who made a temple in which he set it up, and it became the sacred image that protected Ilium (Troy) as long as it remained in the citadel. Others say the winged giant Pallas was the father of Athena, and that he attempted to violate her and she killed him. She flayed him, they say, and used his skin for her aegis, and attached his wings to her own feet. The generally accepted account is that Zeus fell in love with the Titaness Metis, called by some his first wife, and embraced her. An oracle of Gaea predicted that Metis would bear a girl child, and if she should have another child it would be a son who would destroy Zeus, as he had destroyed his father Cronus. On learning of this oracle Zeus swallowed Metis. Some months later as he walked beside Lake Tritonis in Libya he

(obscured) errạnt, ardẹnt, actọr; ch, chip; g, go; th, thin; ₮ʜ, then; y, you;
(variable) ḍ as d or j, ṣ as s or sh, ṭ as t or ch, ẓ as z or zh.

was smitten with a violent headache and roared with pain. Hermes recognized the cause of his anguish and called Hephaestus, or as some say, Prometheus, who took up an axe and smote Zeus on the forehead. Out of his cloven skull Athena leaped, fully armed. She became the favorite of her father Zeus, and sat at his right hand, giving him counsel. Oaths taken in her name, along with those of Zeus and Apollo, were most sacred. Some say her epithet *Tritogeneia* means "Triton-born," and was given to her because she was born near Lake Tritonis. Because of the connection with Triton in the varying accounts of her birth, any place that had a lake or a river named Triton claimed to be her birthplace. The oldest seat of her worship in Greece was on the Triton River that flows into Lake Copaïs, in Boeotia, for it was here that the river-god was said to have reared her. But some say she came to Greece from Libya by way of Crete, and that Alalcomeneus, the first man, brought her up near Lake Copaïs, for which reason she had the epithet *Alalcomeneis*.

As a goddess of war Athena was called Area *(Warlike)*. She took part in the war between the gods and the giants, but first she prudently sought out Heracles, for an oracle had foretold that the gods could not defeat the giants without his help. She found him and helped him to find the magic herb that would make him invulnerable, then conveyed him to the battle, where she advised him how to kill Alcyoneus. Because she drove a chariot—which she invented—in the struggle with the giants, she was given the name Hippia *(Horse-goddess)*. She pursued Enceladus and flattened him with a rock so that he became the island of Sicily, and some say the Pallas whose skin she used for her aegis was a giant she killed in this war. Athena contended with Hera and Aphrodite for the prize of beauty, thrown among the wedding guests at the marriage of Peleus and Thetis by Eris. She promised Paris, who was given the task of awarding the prize, victory in all his battles, but when he gave the prize to Aphrodite she became an implacable enemy of Paris and the Trojans. In the Trojan War her services were always on the side of the Greeks. She so inspired Diomedes with valor that he wounded Aphrodite and then, with Athena riding beside him in his chariot and guiding his spear, he wounded Ares. When Diomedes was wounded by Pandarus, Athena

fat, fāte, fär, fâll, ȧsk, fãre; net, mē, hėr; pin, pīne; not, nōte, möve, nôr; up, lūte, pull; oi, oil; ou out; (lightened) ēlect, agŏny, ūnite;

cleared the mist from his eyes and filled him with new courage. In gratitude for her help, Diomedes dedicated a sanctuary to Athena Oxyderces *(Bright-eyed)* at Corinth when he returned from the Trojan War. She was a protector of Achilles. When Hector stood alone before the walls of Troy Athena assumed the guise of his brother, Deïphobus, and stood beside him and tricked him into remaining to face Achilles and death. It was Athena, some say, who inspired the stratagem of the Wooden Horse and helped Epeus to build it. On the side of the Horse was an inscription that dedicated it to Athena. After the capture and sack of Troy, Locrian Ajax (Ajax the Lesser) seized Cassandra as she clung to the image of Athena in the sanctuary whither she had fled for refuge. In tearing Cassandra from the sanctuary he bore off the image which she clasped with her. This brought the wrath of Athena on Ajax, and on the Greeks because they did not punish him. She caused the death of Ajax in a storm at sea on his way home, and for 1000 years afterward the Locrians were compelled to propitiate Athena by supplying two Locrian maidens to serve in her sanctuary at Troy. Odysseus was one of her favorites. He raised several sanctuaries to Athena Celeuthea *(Lady of the Road),* along the road in Laconia on which he had raced for the hand of Penelope. Athena caused Telamonian Ajax to go mad to save Odysseus from his wrath when the armor of Achilles was awarded to Odysseus instead of to him. Though she could not prevent Poseidon from harrying Odysseus on his voyage home from Troy, she took the opportunity, when Poseidon was absent, to appeal to Zeus to let Odysseus, already delayed ten years on his journey, return home. She helped Odysseus regain his own shores and instructed and aided him so that, with his son Telemachus, he slew the suitors who had been reveling in his halls at his expense and won back his wife and his kingdom. Agamemnon, who had made proper sacrifices to Athena before leaving Troy, had a speedy voyage home. Menelaus, angry at the gods for allowing the war to last so long, refused to sacrifice to the goddess, and was punished by being driven about the seas for seven years before he was permitted to return to Sparta.

In the reign of King Cecrops, Athena and Poseidon contended for control of Athens. Poseidon struck the rock of the Acropolis with his trident and a fountain of sea water gushed forth, and whenever the south wind blows the sound of waves can be heard in this fountain. Athena's gift to Athens was an olive tree, as Cecrops testified. (Both the well and the olive tree were later enclosed in the Erechtheum. When this temple was burned during the Persian War, 480 B.C., the olive tree was destroyed, but instantly a new shoot

ATHENA WITH HERACLES
Red-figured Greek cup, Duris, c480 B.C.
Munich

sprang forth from the burned trunk, and the tree was shown to the traveler Pausanias in the 2nd century A.D.). The gods, called on to decide which gift was of more benefit to the people of Athens, voted in favor of the olive tree and Athena. In a rage, Poseidon flooded the plain. Athena's town of Athenae was engulfed by the flood, whereupon she took Athens as her city and gave it her own name. On another occasion she contended with Poseidon for Troezen. By a decree of Zeus they were directed to share it, and the Troezenians raised a temple of Athena Sthenias *(Strong)* on their citadel.

Athena was one of three goddesses (the others were Artemis and Hestia), who did not yield to the power of love exerted by Aphrodite; she remained a virgin. Hephaestus, tricked by Poseidon into thinking she would welcome his advances, once tried to make love to her when she entered his forge. She repulsed him, and his spilled seed fell to the ground and fertilized Earth. When the child Erichthonius was born of this accidental union Earth refused to have anything to do with him. Athena took the child, half-man and half-serpent, put him in a chest and gave the chest to the daughters of Cecrops—Aglauros, Herse, and Pandrosos—with the admonition to take good care of it but not to look inside. Curiosity compelled the maidens, with their mother, to open the chest. When they saw the strange creature inside they were seized with fear, and leaped to their deaths, some say, from the Acropolis. A white crow brought the news to Athena as she was carrying a huge rock to fortify the Acropolis. She dropped the rock, which stayed where it fell and became Mount Lycabettus, and punished the crow for bringing her the distressing news by changing its feathers to black and forbidding crows to perch on the Acropolis in future. She took Erichthonius up into her aegis and reared him in the Erechtheum, the oldest temple on the Acropolis, and thereafter sacred serpents were kept in the temple in his honor. Erichthonius became king of Athens and instituted the Panathenaea in her honor. In another case, Athena rescued the heart of Zagreus, who had been torn to pieces by the Titans, enclosed it in a clay figure, and breathed life into it, making Zagreus immortal.

Athena Promachus *(Champion)* was the protector and defender of heroes and freely gave them her aid. Cadmus, desiring to sacrifice the cow that had led him into Boeotia to Athena, killed the dragon that guarded the sacred spring whither he had gone to fetch water for the sacrifice. Athena appeared to him and thanked him for the sacrifice. She told him to sow half the dragon's teeth and gave him the city of Thebes. She gave the other half of the dragon's teeth to Aeëtes of Colchis. She advised Danaus to build a ship and flee with his daughters from Egypt. He set up an image of Athena at Lindus, in Rhodes, in acknowledgment of her help. Afterward, on the order of Zeus, Athena and Hermes purified the daughters of Danaus for the murder of their husbands, and Danaus raised a sanctuary of Athena Saitis (*Sais,* the name of the Egyptian goddess identified with Athena) on the hilltop at Lerna where, some say, the heads of the murdered men were buried. Athena helped Perseus when he went to fetch the head of Medusa. She gave him a bright shield to use as a mirror when he cut off Medusa's head, and guided his hand as he did so. After he had put Medusa's head to good use Perseus gave it to Athena and she placed it in her aegis, or as some say, in the middle of her shield. Some say the Gorgon Medusa was transformed from a beautiful maiden into a hideous monster because she had vied with Athena in beauty. Others say she was transformed for committing impious acts with Poseidon in a sanctuary of Athena. Athena gave Cepheus of Tegea a lock of Medusa's hair to protect his city, and to Asclepius she gave some of Medusa's blood. Some say the blood that came from the right side of Medusa was used to bring death, and that from the left side was used for healing; and some say all the blood of Medusa that was given to Asclepius was used by him for healing and restoring life. She gave Erichthonius two drops of Medusa's blood, one to bring death and the other to cure, contained in vials, and fastened them with golden bands to his body. Bellerophon owed much to her for she bridled Pegasus, for which reason she was called Chalinitis *(Bridler),* and gave the winged horse to him. Brave Tydeus, father of Diomedes, was especially loved by Athena When he was wounded in the fighting of the Seven against Thebes, she hurried off to Zeus and fetched an herb that would make him immortal. She arrived with the magical herb just in time to see Tydeus gulp the brains of Melanippus from his dismembered head. This sight so disgusted her that she refrained from healing his wound and making him immortal, as she had intended to do, and let him die. Heracles was another of her favorites, and by one of her devices he was restored to his mother when he had been abandoned as an infant. She gave him a robe when the gods were arming him with gifts, gave him bronze castanets with which to frighten the Stymphalian birds, advised him how to attack the Lernaean Hydra, helped him fetch the Apples of the Hesperides (which were later returned to her as it was unlawful for mortals to keep them), and guided him to the Underworld to fetch Cerberus. Heracles raised a sanctuary of Athena Axiopoenus (*Just Requital*) in Laconia after he had avenged the death of Oeonus by slaying Hippocoön and his sons. In all his labors and trials Athena stood as his friend; twice she took his part in battles against the gods, and when he was immortalized she led him to the gods of Olympus. She was a friend to Jason and helped Argus build the *Argo* for the expedition for the Golden Fleece, and inserted in the keel a beam of oracular oak from the sacred grove at Dodona which gave Jason good advice on his journey.

As a patroness of law and order, Athena compelled the Erinyes to allow Orestes to come to trial before the Areopagus for the murder of his mother, and when the vote was even she cast her vote in favor of Orestes. This strengthened the Areopagus and substituted law and mercy for vengeance. In gratitude, Orestes dedicated an altar to Athena Area (*Warlike*). The Erinyes were much exercised at what they considered a perversion of their ancient privileges. They threatened to lay a blight on Athens if the verdict was not reversed but Athena persuaded them, with promises of gifts and honor from the Athenians for all time, to dwell peacefully in a grotto on the Acropolis. In return for honors and sacrifices from the Athenians the Erinyes promised favorable winds for Athena's ships, fertility for her land, and prosperous marriages for her people. The Erinyes, henceforth known as The Kindly Ones, were then led in a torchlight procession to their new home on the Acropolis, which became an oracular shrine and a place of sanctuary.

Athena is credited with having invented many things. She constructed the double flute of stag's bones, but when she played on it Hera and Aphrodite laughed, although she drew from it delightful music. One day she went to a quiet pool, and watching herself in its surface, she played on her flute. When she saw how distorted her face was, with her cheeks puffed out, she cast the flute from her and laid a curse on whoever should pick it up. It was found by Marsyas and caused his death. Some say she also invented the trumpet, and Hegeleos, son of Tyrsenus, raised a sanctuary of Athena Salpinx (*Trumpet*) in Argos. But others say it was Tyrsenus, son of Heracles and a Lydian woman, who invented the trumpet, and that Hegeleos taught the Dorians how to play it. Among her other inventions were earthenware pots, the plow, the ox-yoke, bridle, chariot, ship, and the science of numbers. She also made dice from knucklebones and usec them for divination.

On the whole, Athena was not a vindictive goddess. She did transform Arachne, who had the arrogance to challenge her to a weaving contest, into a spider. But when Tiresias the son of her dear companion Chariclo, happened to see her as she bathed in the Hippocrene Spring on Mount Heli con, he was blinded at the will of the gods for having seer what was unlawful. But some say Athena laid her hand over his eyes and blinded him. When Chariclo reproached he Athena could not restore his sight, because he had seer what was unlawful, but she gave him the gifts of prophecy and divination, and a long life.

Athena had many epithets. As Athena Polias *(Of the City* she had temples on the Acropolis at Athens, at Troezen, in Arcadia, and at Erythrae in Asia Minor. As Poliatas *(Keepe of the City)* she had a sanctuary at Tegea into which the pries entered but once a year, and as Poliuchus *(City-protecting)* she had a citadel in Sparta. The citadels at Athens, Argos Sparta, Epidaurus, Troezen, Pheneus, and Troy anc Smyrna, among others, were all sacred to her and illuminate her important role as a guardian and strengthener of cities As patroness of the useful and decorative arts she was Er gane *(Worker)*, a name first given to her by the Athenians There was a sanctuary of Athena Ergane on the citadel a Sparta, and an altar at Olympia in Elis. The descendants o Phidias, known as Burnishers or Cleansers because they hac the hereditary task of cleaning and polishing the great statu of Olympian Zeus, sacrificed to Athena Ergane before the began their work. The cock, a bird supposedly very ready t fight, was sacred to Athena Ergane. At Elis there was also a altar to Athena Leitis *(Goddess of Booty)*, and the Eleans wor shiped her as *Mother* in gratitude for the repopulation of Eli after the destruction of the population by Heracles. A tem ple of Athena Narcaea, raised by Narcaeus, son of Dionysu and Physcoa, also stood in Elis, as well as a temple of Athen; Cydonia. This last was said to have been founded by Clyme nus, a descendant of the Cretan Dactyl Heracles, who cam from Cydonia in Crete. Pelops sacrificed to Cydonia Athena before he began his race with Oenomaus for th hand of Hippodamia. As Paeonia *(Healer)* Athena had a image at Athens and an altar at Oropus, and as *Health* she

fat, fāte, fär, fâll, ȧsk, fāre; net, mē, hėr; pin, pīne; not, nōte, möve nôr; up, lūte, pùll; oi, oil; ou out; (lightened) ĕlect, agŏny, ūnite

had an image on the Acropolis at Athens. Amphitryon dedicated an image of Athena Zosteria *(Girder)* at Thebes because here he put on his armor when he went to fight against
Chalcedon and the Euboeans; Castor and Polydeuces raised
a temple of Athena Asia in Laconia, near Gythium, when
they returned from Colchis, in honor of the Colchian shrine
of Athena Asia. The temple of Athena Anemotis *(Of the
Winds)* was founded in Messenia after prayers to the goddess
had caused violent and unseasonable winds that were dam-
aging the country to cease. The sanctuary of Athena Alea in
Tegea was founded by Aleus, great-grandson of Zeus and
Callisto, and was respected throughout the Peloponnesus as
an inviolable place of sanctuary. The sanctuary of Athena
Itonia in Boeotia was named, some say, for Itonius, son of
Amphictyon. The bronze image in it was made by Agoracritus, a pupil of Phidias. In the sanctuary the Boeotians
gathered annually for their general assembly. One story
concerning the sanctuary is that Iodama, a priestess, entered
the sacred precinct at night and Athena appeared to her.
When Iodama saw the head of Medusa in Athena's aegis she
was turned to stone. Ever after, fire was put on the altar of
Iodama each day, with the thrice repeated chant that Iodama
lives and is asking for fire. But some say Athena was a daughter of Itonius, and that Iodama was her sister. There was
another sanctuary of Athena Itonia between Larisa and
Pherae. The Spartans dedicated a bronze image of Athena
on the citadel at Sparta; the bronze sanctuary in which it was
housed, and for which reason the image was called Athena
of the Bronze House, was begun by Tyndareus and was
finished early in the 6th century B.C. by the Spartan Gitiadas.
At other places there were images and sanctuaries of Athena
Promachorma *(Protector of the Anchorage)*, Pronaea *(Of the
Fore-temple)*, Pronoia *(Forethought)*, Xenia *(Hospitable)*,
Larisaea *(Of Larisa)*, Ophthalmitis *(Of the Eye)*, Cissaea *(Ivy-
goddess)*, Cyparissia *(Cypress-goddess)*, Coryphasia ·*(Of Cory-
phasium)*, Aeantis *(Ajacian)*, Aethyia *(Gannet)*, Agoraea *(Of
the Market-place)*, Apaturia *(Deceitful)*, and Hippolaitis *(Of
Hippola)*. As Athena Nike *(Victory)* she had a special temple
on the Acropolis at Athens, and was sometimes depicted
holding a figure of Victory in her outstretched hand. To the
Athenians she was especially Parthenos *(Virgin* or *Maiden)*,
and for her they built the Parthenon. Inside the temple the

gold and ivory image of Athena Parthenos, by Phidias, was
set up (438–7 B.C.). The face, hands, and feet were of ivory;
precious stones formed the pupils of the eyes. The robe was
of gold. The gold, which weighed 40 talents, could be
removed from the image, and because of this Phidias was
acquitted of a charge that he had stolen some of it, for when
it was weighed it was found that the 40 talents were all
accounted for. In the image the goddess wears her aegis. On
her left side is her shield, on the outside of which is depicted
in relief the battle of the Amazons and the Athenians. Into
this scene Phidias put a portrait of himself, a bald-headed
old man lifting a stone, and a portrait of Pericles, the face
of which is somewhat obscured by his arm raised to hurl his
spear. Because of these two portraits on an image of the
goddess Phidias was convicted of impiety. On the inside of
the shield the Battle of the Giants was shown. In her extended right hand Athena held an image of Victory wearing
a golden crown. In her left hand, beside the shield, was her
spear. Under the shield was a golden serpent, and on her
helmet was the Sphinx. The war between the Centaurs and
the Lapiths was depicted on her sandals, and the pedestal
showed the birth of Pandora. Also on the Acropolis was the
great bronze Athena Promachus *(Champion)* by Phidias,
made from the spoils taken by the Athenians at the Battle of
Marathon, and a third image, dedicated by the Lemnians
and thought by some to be the most beautiful, called Lemnian Athena. All of these works have perished; descriptions
from ancient writers and some copies of the Athena Parthenos are all that remain.

The chief festival of Athena was the great Panathenaea, at
which time a peplus embroidered by the Athenian women
was presented to the goddess, games and contests were
held, and the festival was terminated by a great procession
to the Acropolis. Other festivals of Athena were held at
various times of the year to mark the progress of the crops.
The sea-eagle, cock, serpent, and olive tree were sacred to
her, but above all she was identified with the owl, symbol of
wisdom. The coins of Athens bore the head of Athena on
one side, and her sacred owl on the other. As a goddess of
war she is represented in art with a helmet, shield, and
spear; as a goddess of peace and the useful arts she is some-

fat, fāte, fär, fâll, ȧsk, fāre; net, mē, hėr; pin, pīne; not, nōte, möve,
nôr; up, lūte, pṳll; oi, oil; ou out; (lightened) ḙlect, agǫny, ṳnite;

times represented without her helmet and holding a distaff. The Romans identified their Minerva with Athena.

Atlas (at′lạs). In Greek mythology, a Titan, the son of Iapetus and the nymph Clymene. His brothers were Prometheus, Epimetheus, and Menoetius, and he was the father of the Pleiades (by Pleione), of the Hyades (by Aethra), of the Hesperides (by Hesperis), and according to Homer, the father of Calypso. He lived in the western lands, beyond the stream of Ocean, in the land of the Hyperboreans, or some say in Mauretania, and was the proud gardener of the orchard where grew the tree with the golden apples which had been a wedding present to Hera. According to Hesiod he was condemned by Zeus for his part in the battle of the Titans, in which he was the leader, to stand at the western extremity of the earth near the habitation of the Hesperides, upholding the heavens with his shoulders and hands. His station was later said to be in the Atlas Mountains in Africa. Heracles, seeking the golden apples as one of his labors for Eurystheus, sought the aid of Atlas, but he hesitated to help him for he remembered a prophecy that one day a son of Zeus would rob him of the golden fruit. He told Heracles he feared Ladon, the hundred-headed serpent that guarded the apples. Heracles immediately shot Ladon with one of his arrows, and then offered to hold up the heavens if Atlas would pluck the apples for him. Atlas was so glad to get rid of his burden that he agreed, and while Heracles assumed the heavens he fetched the apples. He offered to take them to Eurystheus himself, but Heracles had no intention of holding up the heavens indefinitely, and cunningly agreed to this plan, if Atlas would just take back the heavens for a moment so that he could pad his shoulders, which were getting sore from the unaccustomed weight. Atlas amiably resumed the burden, and was then amazed and distressed as Heracles walked off, leaving him holding the heavens as before. Another story concerning Atlas is that Perseus, returning from slaying Medusa, visited him and asked for refreshments. Atlas remembered the prophecy about a son of Zeus and treated him inhospitably. Perseus punished him by showing him the head of Medusa and turned him to stone, and it is this huge bulk of stone which is now called the Atlas Mountains in Africa.

Atreus (ā'trē-us, -trŏs). In Greek legend, a son of Pelops and Hippodamia, and the brother of Thyestes, with whom he was fated ever to struggle. After the death of his half-brother, Chrysippus, in which he may have had a hand, he fled from Elis to Mycenae where he succeeded Eurystheus as king and wielded the sceptre, made by Hephaestus and given to him by Pelops. He first married Cleola, who died after giving birth to a son, Plisthenes. He then married Aërope and by her was the father of Agamemnon, Menelaus and Anaxibia. He had a horned lamb with golden fleece which he claimed authorized whoever possessed it to be king. It had been sent to him by Hermes who wanted to avenge the death of Myrtilus by Pelops. Hermes was sure that Atreus would not, as he had vowed to do, sacrifice the golden lamb along with the finest of his flocks, to Artemis. He did kill the lamb but had it stuffed and mounted and decreed that whoever possessed it was endowed with royal power. Thyestes, in a plot with Aërope who had fallen in love with him, stole the lamb and was acknowledged as king. Atreus then proposed that if he could cause the sun to reverse its path through the heavens—to go from West to East—Thyestes should acknowledge him as the rightful king. With the help of Zeus and Eris the sun did just this. Atreus became king again and Thyestes went into exile. This by no means ended the struggle between the brothers. Thyestes arranged the murder of Plisthenes and then, on being lured back to Mycenae, was served his own sons in a ghastly banquet of welcome given him by Atreus. After Thyestes had eaten, Atreus revealed that it was the flesh of his own children he had enjoyed. Thyestes laid a curse upon the House of Atreus and again went into exile. An oracle told Atreus to bring back Thyestes in order to end a famine that then wasted Mycenae. He sought him in Sicyon, where he met Pelopia and, unaware of her true parentage and that she was soon to bear a child, he married her, having cast Aërope into the sea because of her unfaithfulness with Thyestes. Pelopia bore Aegisthus, whom she exposed, but he was rescued and brought up by Atreus as his own son. In fact this was the child of Thyestes and his own daughter Pelopia, although she did not know that it was her father who had ravished her when she was sacrificing to Athene one night. After some years Atreus brought Thyestes back

fat, fāte, fär, fåll, ȧsk, fāre; net, mē, hėr; pin, pīne; not, nōte, mŏve;
nôr; up, lūte, pùll; oi, oil; ou out; (lightened) ēlect, agǫny, ūnite

to Mycenae, threw him in prison, and commanded Aegisthus, still a child, to kill him. Aegisthus tried to obey but was foiled by Thyestes, and by means of the sword which his mother had given him Thyestes identified him as his own son. Together they then killed Atreus.

tropos (at′rō̆-pos). In Greek mythology, that one of the three Fates who severs the thread of human life.

tys (ā′tis) or **Attis** (at′is). Mythical personage in the worship of the Phrygian goddess Cybele. Some say he was the son of the Lydian supreme god Manes. Others say Nana, daughter of the river-god Sangarius, ate the fruit of an almond tree and as a result bore Atys. He was a beautiful Phrygian youth beloved of Cybele. The goddess wished to make him a guardian of her temple to keep him for herself. She exacted a promise from him to remain faithful to her, and he swore to do so, saying, "If I lie, may the love for which I break faith be my last love." But Atys forgot his pledge. He fell in love with and embraced the nymph Sagaritis. Wild with rage and grief, Cybele hacked down the tree in which the nymph lived and so killed her. Atys was driven mad. He fled to the top of Mount Dindymus and there mutilated himself and dragged his head in the dust. He died at a pine tree, which received his spirit while from his blood sprang violets. A tomb was raised to him on Mount Dindymus, in the sanctuary of Cybele, and henceforward the priests of Cybele emasculated themselves and tossed their hair in feigned madness in commemoration of Atys. A festival of orgiastic character, lasting three days, was celebrated in his honor in the spring. A pine tree covered with violets was carried to the shrine of Cybele as a symbol of the departed Atys. Then, amidst tumultuous music and the wildest exhibition of grief, the mourners sought for Atys on the mountains. On the third day he was found, and the rejoicing which followed was as extravagant as the mourning which preceded. (A similar ceremony was observed by women and girls to commemorate the death and rebirth of Dionysus.) The myth may be considered as the counterpart of the Greek legend of Aphrodite and Adonis, which itself is reminiscent of the Semitic legend of Tammuz and Ishtar.

uge (ô′jē). In Greek mythology, a daughter of Aleus, king of Tegea, and Naera. Her father made her a priestess of Athena in an attempt to circumvent a prophecy that her son

bscured) errạnt, ardẹnt, actọr; ch, chip; g, go; th, thin; ŦH, then; y, you; ariable) ḍ as d or j, ṣ as s or sh, ṭ as t or ch, ẓ as z or zh.

would kill her mother's brothers. Heracles, who was bein[
entertained by Aleus, violated her nevertheless. When i[
became apparent that she was about to bear a child, Aleus
who mocked her plea that Heracles had ravished her, gav[
his daughter to Nauplius with instructions to drown her
Nauplius departed for the coast with her. On the way Aug[
felt that the time to give birth to her child had come. Sh[
went into a thicket on Mount Parthenius and gave birth t[
Telephus, whom she left to die on the mountain, but he wa[
rescued. Auge and Nauplius proceeded on their journey an[
Nauplius, who had no intention of killing Auge, sold her t[
some traders who took her to Mysia and sold her to Kin[
Teuthras. According to some accounts Teuthras marrie[
her, and many years later Telephus came to Mysia on the
advice of the oracle and was reunited with his mother. Othe[
accounts say that Auge was adopted as a daughter by Teu[
thras, and that when Telephus arrived, gave him his adopte[
daughter as a wife in return for Telephus' aid in a war. Bu[
on the wedding night the miraculous appearance of a ser[
pent caused their true relationship to be revealed.

Augeas (ô′jē-as, ô-jē′as) or *Augeias* (ô-jē′as). In Greek myth
ology, a son of Helius (or of Phorbas). He was a king of th[
Epeans in Elis, and one of the Argonauts. Augeas was th[
owner of a herd of 3000 oxen, including 12 white bull[
sacred to the sun. His cattle, by a gift of the gods, wer[
extremely fertile and never sickened and died of disease
They were kept in a stable that had not been cleaned in 3[
years. As one of his labors for Eurystheus, Heracles under[
took to clean the stables in one day, and Augeas agreed t[
pay him one-tenth of his herds if he fulfilled the task in th[
time stipulated. Phyleus, son of Augeas, was called as [
witness to the bargain. Heracles carried out his contract b[
diverting the rivers Alpheus and Peneus and washing then[
through the stables. Augeas refused to honor his agree
ment, on the ground that Heracles had been commanded t[
carry out this task by Eurystheus and furthermore, he ha[
been assisted by the river-gods. He banished Phyleus, wh[
upheld Heracles. Heracles ultimately had his revenge; h[
gathered a force and attacked and killed Augeas and hi[
other sons, and made Phyleus ruler of the kingdom.

Autolycus (ô-tol′i-kus). In Greek mythology, a son of Herme[
and Chione, and the twin half-brother of Philammon, whos[

father was Apollo. He was a famous thief and possessed the power, given him by his father, of making himself and the things that he stole invisible or of giving them new forms. He stole the cattle of Sisyphus but Sisyphus found them and seduced Anticlea, the daughter of Autolycus. Autolycus was the grandfather of Odysseus and gave him his name, which means the "angry one." He gave Odysseus rich gifts when the latter visited him as child, and it was during this visit that he received the scar from a gash of a boar, by which Odysseus was recognized when he returned to Ithaca ten years after the end of the Trojan War. Autolycus was the thief who stole the cattle of Eurytus of Oechalia and, after changing their color, sold them to Heracles.

B

acchus (bak′us). In classical mythology, a name of Dionysus, the son of Zeus and Semele. He was the god of wine, personifying both its good and its bad qualities. Bacchus was the current name of the god among the Romans. The orgiastic worship of Bacchus was especially characteristic of Boeotia, where his festivals were celebrated on the slopes of Mount Cithaeron, and extended to those of the neighboring Parnassus. In Attica the rural and somewhat savage cult of Bacchus underwent a metamorphosis, and reached its highest expression in the choragic literary contests, in which originated both tragedy and comedy, and for which were written most of the masterpieces of Greek literature. Bacchus was held to have taught the cultivation of the grape and the preparation of wine. It is thought that while the worship of Dionysus originated in Phrygia, the name *Bacchus* is Lydian in origin.

aphyra (bä′fi-rạ). According to Greek mythology, when the maenads who had torn Orpheus limb from limb attempted to wash away the blood that stained their hands in the waters of the Helicon River, the river, rather than be of any assistance to the murderers, plunged underground. In this way it avoided being an accessory in any way to the murderesses.

The river emerged from the ground several miles away an took the name Baphyra.

Baucis (bô'sis) and **Philemon** (fi-lē'mọn, fī-). Zeus, disguise as a mortal, once visited the earth with Hermes, accordin to a Greek myth. They went to many homes, seeking refresh ment and rest, but wherever they knocked, they were turne away. At last they came to a humble cottage in Phrygia. I was inhabited by an old couple, Baucis and Philemon, wh had spent their lives together in this dwelling. They we comed the strangers who knocked at their door, warml invited them in, and set about to make them comfortabl Baucis stirred up the fire and prepared vegetables while h husband set out the meat. Whatever of comforts they had i their home they offered to the strangers who had com When the meal was ready, Baucis and Philemon happil served their unknown guests. They set a jug of their loc wine on the table. As the meal progressed and the wine wa passed around, Baucis and Philemon observed that no ma ter how much wine was drunk, the jug remained filled. In th presence of this obvious miracle they were frightened. Zeu now revealed that he was a god and that his companion wa Hermes. He told Baucis and Philemon that they were th only ones in the area who had shown kindness to stranger Because of their surly attitude Zeus resolved to punish thos who had been unfriendly to the disguised gods, but h wished to spare Baucis and Philemon. He told them to clim the nearby mountain for safety. They did as the god con manded. When they reached the top of the mountain the looked back and saw that the land below was covered wit marshy water. Only their poor hovel was spared. It wa miraculously transformed into a golden-roofed, marbl temple. As they watched, pitying those who had lost the homes, Zeus spoke to them. He promised to give them wha ever boon they desired. After thinking it over, they told Zeu they would like to serve as priests in his temple for the re of their lives. When it came time to die, they asked that the might be allowed to die in the same instant, that neith would have to bear the grief of losing the other. Zeu granted their wish. For the remainder of their lives the goo and pious couple looked after the temple. One day, in the extreme old age, as they stood on the temple steps talkin of their life, each noted that the other was gradually becoming covered with leafy foliage. Bark grew up around their bodies. Before their faces were enclosed, they bade each other goodby and both were transformed into trees at once. Standing side by side, the two trees were later honored with floral wreaths as befitted those whom the gods loved and who had loved the gods.

Bellerophon   (bẹ-ler'ọ-fon). In Greek legend, a son of Glaucus and the grandson of Sisyphus. His name was originally Hipponous but was changed to Bellerophon after he killed Bellerus, a countryman. Following this death and the accidental killing of his brother, he left Corinth and went to Proetus, king of Tiryns. There Antia (Stheneboea in some accounts), the wife of Proetus, fell in love with him but he rejected her advances. Enraged, she told Proetus that Bellerophon had made love to her against her will and asked Proetus to kill him. Proetus was unwilling to take such drastic action against a guest. Instead he sent Bellerophon to Iobates, king of Lycia, who was Antia's father. With him he sent a letter, asking Iobates to kill the bearer for the insult to Antia. But Iobates also hesitated to act himself. He imposed a task on Bellerophon that he felt sure would bring about his death: to slay the Chimaera, a monster that shot flames from its lion's head, had the body of a goat and a slashing serpent's tail. Bellerophon was advised by a seer to catch the winged horse Pegasus to assist him in this task. Aided by Athena, who gave him a golden bridle, he found Pegasus drinking at a spring, slipped the bridle over his head and tamed Pegasus. He leaped on Pegasus' back and sped off to find the Chimaera. According to some accounts, he first attacked it with arrows as he soared above it, then when it was weakened and gasping he poured molten lead into its mouth and dispatched it. Iobates was amazed at Bellerophon's success in this venture and sent him off to fight the Solymi and the Amazons. The special advantage of flying over his enemies and attacking from above again gave him success. Iobates then sent Lycian warriors to lie in wait for Bellerophon and kill him, but he defeated them with the aid of a flood sent by Poseidon. This convinced Iobates that he was dealing with the offspring of a god and he gave up further attempts to have him killed. Instead he made him the heir of his

kingdom and gave him his daughter Philonoë in marriage
Three children were born of this marriage: Isander, Hippolochus, and Laodamia. But Bellerophon's successes went
to his head. He felt he was the equal of the gods and decided
to fly up to Olympus on Pegasus. Such arrogance offended
the gods. As he rose through the air on Pegasus' back, Zeus
sent a gadfly to sting Pegasus; the winged horse reared, and
Bellerophon fell to earth and was lamed and blinded by the
fall. Pegasus continued to Olympus. From that time on Bellerophon was hounded by the gods and became a miserable,
solitary wanderer until he died.

Biton and Cleobis (bī'tŏn; klē'ō̯-bis). In Greek legend, the
sons of Cydippe, priestess of Hera at Argos. During a festival, the priestess had to ride to the temple in a chariot, and,
as the oxen were not at hand, Biton and Cleobis dragged the
chariot 45 stadia to the temple. There they fell asleep; in
answer to a prayer of their mother to Hera to reward this
act of filial piety with the greatest boon possible for mortals, they were given painless and swift death in their
sleep. Herodotus makes Solon relate this story to Croesus.

Boeotus (bē-ō'tus). In Greek legend, a son of Arne and Poseidon, and the twin brother of that Aeolus who became guardian of the winds. The twins were exposed to die as infants
but were saved and brought up by Theano and Metapontus.
Theano had passed them off to her husband as her own
children. When she had sons of her own, she plotted to have
them kill Boeotus and Aeolus but they were killed instead.
They slew Desmontes, who had imprisoned and blinded
their mother, then they freed their mother, and caused
Theano to kill herself. Metapontus married Arne but later
cast her aside, whereupon the twins killed the new queen.
Boeotus fled to his grandfather Aeolus, and got from him
the part of his kingdom which he renamed Arne, the home
of the Boeotians.

Boreadae (bō̯-rē'a̯-dē). In Greek mythology, a name for the
descendants of Boreas. It was applied especially to Calais
and Zetes, his twin sons by Orithyia, the daughter of Erechtheus, king of Athens. These youths sailed with Jason in the
Argo on the expedition for the Golden Fleece. In the course
of the voyage the Argonauts landed in Thrace, and found

fat, fāte, fär, fâll, ȧsk, fāre; net, mē, hėr; pin, pīne; not, nōte, möve,
nôr; up, lūte, pṳll; oi, oil; ou out; (lightened) ḝlect, agǫny, ṳnite;

Phineus, a blind seer, who had been married to Cleopatra,
the sister of the Boreadae. Phineus promised to help the
Argonauts if they would free him from the visits of the
loathsome Harpies who polluted his food and kept him constantly on the verge of starvation. Calais and Zetes, who had
grown wings as they attained manhood, pursued the Harpies and caught them. They would have killed them but Iris
came as a messenger from the gods and warned them not
to kill "the hounds of Zeus." In return, Iris promised the
Boreadae that the Harpies would cease to harass Phineus.
Grateful for being freed from the pestilent Harpies, Phineus
gave the Argonauts much useful advice about their course
to Colchis. Earlier in the voyage, when the Argonauts had
landed in Mysia, Hylas, the squire of Heracles, had disappeared. Heracles searched frantically for him and delayed
his return to the *Argo.* Some of the Argonauts wished to
await the return of Heracles, but the Boreadae supported
Jason's decision to proceed without him. It was in revenge
for this that, long after the voyage of the *Argo,* Heracles
killed them on the island of Tenos as they were returning
from Pelias' funeral games. He buried them there and set up
two columns, one of which moved at the breath of the North
Wind.

Boreas (bō′rȩ̄-a̧s). In Greek mythology, the North Wind, the
son of Astraeus and Eos, or of Aeolus, and the brother of
Hesperus, Zephyrus, and Notus. He fell in love with
Orithyia, daughter of Erechtheus, king of Athens, and
wished to marry her. Her father delayed the marriage, and
Boreas abandoned his hitherto patient wooing, swooped
down to the banks of the Ilissus River where Orithyia was
playing, and carried her off in a gust of wind to his home in
Thrace. Their children were Cleopatra, Chione, and the
winged twins, Calais and Zetes. Enamored of the mares of
Erichthonius, Boreas changed himself into a black stallion
and produced 12 swift fillies by them that could run over
standing grain without bending it and over the waves of the
sea. A violent and stormy character, he was often appealed
to by the gods to torment mortals, or even demigods, who
were under the displeasure of the gods, as, for example,
Hera appealed to him to shipwreck Heracles on Cos. Because he had carried off Orithyia from the banks of the

Ilissus River at Athens and married her, the Athenians cam‹
to regard Boreas as kin to them. During the Persian Wa‹
when the Persian fleet lay at anchor off Chalcis in Euboea

BOREAS CARRYING OFF ORITHYIA
Red-figured Greek amphora.
Munich

an oracle came to the Athenians, instructing them to see‹
help from their son-in-law. They offered sacrifice to Borea‹
and Orithyia and prayed for their aid. A violent storm aros‹
and battered the Persian fleet. Four hundred Persian ship‹
and uncounted men and treasure were engulfed in the rag‹
ing storm. In gratitude to their son-in-law Boreas, th‹
Athenians erected a sanctuary to him on the bank of th‹

fat, fāte, fär, fâll, ȧsk, fãre; net, mē, hėr; pin, pīne; not, nōte, mȯv
nôr; up, lūte, pu̇ll; oi, oil; ou out; (lightened) e̤lect, ago̤ny, ūnit

Ilissus River. Boreas was identified by the Romans with their Aquilo.

Branchus (brang'kus). In Greek legend, the son of Apollo and a woman of Miletus. During his birth his mother had a vision that the sun was passing through her body. The priests interpreted this as a favorable omen. Apollo loved his son and gave him the gift of prophecy. Branchus founded an oracle at Didyma, near Miletus, which was highly regarded, especially by the Ionians and the Aeolians. The descendants of Branchus became priests of the oracle and were said to have built the temple of Apollo at the place that became known as Branchidae.

Briareus (brī-ār'e̱-us). In Greek mythology, the son of Uranus and Gaea and the brother of Gyges and Cottus. He was a sea giant who had one hundred arms. When Hera, Poseidon, and Athena confined Zeus in chains as he slept, Thetis, a sea-goddess, called on Briareus to free Zeus. The gods called him *Briareus* but men called him *Aegaeon*.

Briseis (brī-sē'is). In Homeric legend *(Iliad),* a daughter of Briseus and the wife of Mynes, king of Lyrnessus. On a raid on Lyrnessus, Achilles killed her husband and took her captive. She was awarded to him as part of the spoils from the raid and he loved her dearly. Agamemnon took her from Achilles when his own captive, Chryseis, was restored to her father at Apollo's demand. After the death of Patroclus, Agamemnon restored Briseis to Achilles, untouched, and she wept over dead Patroclus, who had always been so good and gentle to her.

Britomartis (brit-ō-mär'tis). A Cretan divinity of hunters and fishermen. The name probably means "Sweet Maiden." According to some accounts, she was a daughter of Leto. Minos pursued her and she fled from him and hid in the marshes. Later he pursued her over mountains and hills, and to save herself she flung herself into the sea. She was caught in fishermen's nets, which she is said to have invented, and saved. Artemis immortalized her and in Crete, where there are many temples to her, she was called Dictynna. In Greece she was identified with Artemis.

Brizo (brī'zō). A goddess worshiped by women and known

for prophecy through dreams. She was also a protectress of sailors. Her seat was the island of Delos.

Bronze Age. One of the Ages of Man described by Hesiod. It was the third of the five ages, each of which was less good than the last. In the Bronze Age men ate flesh. They armed themselves with weapons and delighted in warfare. Death carried them all off.

Broteas (brot'ē-as). In Greek mythology, a son of Tantalus and the brother of Pelops. He had a son Tantalus, named for his father (Thyestes is also named as the father of this Tantalus). He carved an image of the Mother of the gods in the living rock of Mount Sipylus, high above the plain, which is still visible. He refused to honor Artemis, boasting that even fire could not hurt him. In punishment for his arrogance, he was divinely inspired with madness, and cast himself into a fire and burned to death. But some say that Broteas was a son of Zeus and was blinded by Zeus for his wickedness. Others say that he was so ugly that in discouragement he killed himself.

Busiris (bū-sī'ris). According to Greek legend, a king of Egypt, who was the son of Poseidon and, as some say, Lysianassa, daughter of Epaphus. During his reign Egypt was afflicted with a famine that lasted nine years. Phrasius a learned seer of Cyprus, visited the land and told the Egyptians the famine would cease if they sacrificed one stranger each year on the altar of Zeus. Busiris adopted his advice and began by sacrificing Phrasius himself. When Heracles came to the land, after he had secured the apples of the Hesperides for Eurystheus, Busiris seized him and dragged him off to the altar to be sacrificed. At the altar Heracles burst his bonds and slew Busiris, his son Amphidamas, and all his followers, an event commemorated in several Greek vase-paintings.

Byblis (bib'lis). According to legend, a daughter of Miletus, and the twin sister of Caunus, with whom she fell in love. When she confessed her love, he fled in horror to Lycia. In despair Byblis searched for him through many lands, until she fell of exhaustion. As she lay weeping, the Lelegian nymphs changed her and her tears into a fountain that never fails, and over the spot there grew an ilex tree.

fat, fāte, fär, fâll, ȧsk, fãre; net, mē, hėr; pin, pīne; not, nōte, möve, nôr; up, lūte, pŭll; oi, oil; ou out; (lightened) ēlect, agǭny, ūnite

Cabiri (kạ-bī'rī). [Also: *Cabeiri, Kabeiri.*] In Greek mythology, certain beneficent deities of whom little is known.
They were worshiped in parts of Greece and in the islands
of Imbrus, Lemnos, and Samothrace. They are possibly of
Phrygian origin. Their rites were secret. The mysteries of
the Cabiri of Samothrace were regarded as inferior only to
the Eleusinian. Later they became associated with the Dioscuri and gave protection against mishaps, especially by sea.

Cadmus (kad'mus). In Greek mythology, a son of Agenor of
Phoenicia and Telephassa, and the brother of Cilix, Phoenix, and Europa. When Europa was carried off by Zeus, who
had taken the form of a bull on this occasion, Agenor commanded his sons to find her, and threatened them with exile
if they failed to do so. Cadmus, accompanied by his mother,
sailed to Rhodes. He dedicated a bronze tripod in the sanctuary of Athena at Lindus, in Rhodes. This tripod was inscribed with Phoenician letters, and thus it was that Cadmus
brought the alphabet into the Greek world. He also founded
a temple of Poseidon in Rhodes, in fulfillment of a vow made
during a storm at sea. He touched at the island of Thera and
founded a colony there. Still in search of Europa, he journeyed to Thrace. Telephassa died there and Cadmus buried
her. He next proceeded to Delphi to make inquiries of the
oracle as to how he could find his sister. The priestess told
him to give up his search. She instructed him to follow a
cow, and where it should lie down, there he must build a city.
Cadmus traveled through Phocis. He detached a heifer
which had white marks in the shape of a full moon on its
flanks from the herd of King Pelagon, and drove it through
Boeotia. At last the cow lay down on the site of the city which
later came to be known as Thebes. Cadmus wanted to sacrifice the cow to Athena at once. He sent his followers to a
nearby spring for water. This was a spring of Ares, and was
guarded by a fierce dragon that killed the companions of
Cadmus. Cadmus slew the dragon and, on the advice of

Athena, sowed part of its teeth. Instantly armed men sprang up from the soil; these were the Sparti, "sown" men. Cadmus flung stones into the midst of the Sparti and they, thinking they were being assaulted by some of their own number, fell to fighting among themselves and all except five were slain. The five survivors were Echion, Udaeus, Chthonius, Hyperenor, and Pelorus. They agreed to help Cadmus build his city, and became the ancestors of five of the leading families of Thebes. But Ares was angry with Cadmus for killing his dragon, and as a punishment compelled Cadmus to serve him for a Great Year, that is to say, for eight years, for such was the term of a "Great" or "Eternal" year. At the end of his term of service Athena made him king of Thebes, which at that time was known as Cadmea, and its inhabitants as Cadmeans. Zeus gave him Harmonia, the daughter of Aphrodite and Ares, for a wife, and all the gods attended the wedding. This was the first wedding of mortals which the gods honored with their presence.

Cadmus built the upper city of Thebes and reigned peacefully, but his descendants suffered grievously for his fault in killing the dragon of Ares. Harmonia bore Cadmus four daughters: Autonoë, Semele, Ino, and Agave, and one son, Polydorus. After some time, Cadmus gave up the throne in favor of his grandson, Pentheus, the son of Agave. In this time Dionysus came to Thebes. Pentheus doubted the divinity of the god and ordered the Thebans not to take part in the revels. Dionysus punished him by driving him mad and by causing his mother, who had also at first refused to believe that Dionysus was a god, to tear Pentheus to pieces while she was under a spell of divinely inspired madness. After this Cadmus and Harmonia fled, grief-stricken, from Thebes. They went to the land of the Encheleans, who were at war with their neighbors, the Illyrians. The Encheleans were informed by an oracle that they would defeat the Illyrians if Cadmus was their leader. They therefore made him their leader and defeated the Illyrians. Thus Cadmus became king of the Illyrians, and when a son was born to him in his old age, he named him Illyrius. In the end, Cadmus and Harmonia were turned into spotted serpents by Zeus, and finally went to the Elysian Fields.

Caduceus (ka̤-dū′sẹ̄-us). The rod or wand borne by Hermes, or Mercury, as an ensign of authority, quality, and office. It

---

fat, fāte, fär, fâll, ȧsk, fāre; net, mē, hèr; pin, pīne; not, nōte, mȯve, nôr; up, lūte, pṳll; oi, oil; ou out; (lightened) ẹlect, agọny, ụnite;

was originally merely the Greek herald's staff, a plain rod entwined with fillets of wool. Later the fillets were changed to serpents; and in the conventional representations familiar at the present day the caduceus is often winged. The caduceus is a symbol of peace and prosperity and in modern times figures as a symbol of commerce, Hermes being the god of commerce. It is also used as an emblem by physicians in this country. The rod represents power; the serpents represent wisdom; and the two wings, diligence and activity.

Caeneus (sē'nūs). In Greek legend, a Lapith, originally the girl Caenis, daughter of Elatus, who was violated by Poseidon. He promised to grant any wish she might make and fulfilled her request to be changed into a man. She became a warrior who was invulnerable to the sword or spear and was renamed Caeneus and later had a son, Coronus. Caeneus was so powerful the Lapiths made him their king. He took part in the quest for the Golden Fleece and in the Calydonian Hunt. In the battle with the centaurs which broke out at the marriage of Pirithous and Hippodamia, the centaurs tried in vain to slay Caeneus, who was killing centaurs unmercifully. At length they entombed him beneath huge tree trunks. His soul flew out in the form of a bird, and when the Lapiths sought his body to bury it, it was found transformed back to its original form as a girl.

Calais (kal'a̱-is). An Argonaut, the winged son of Boreas and Orithyia, and the twin of Zetes. See ***Boreadae.***

Calchas (kal'ka̱s). In Greek legend, a son of Thestor, a scion of Idmon, the seer who accompanied the Argonauts. He learned the art of divination from his father and became, according to Homer, the wisest of seers, "who knew all that has been, now is, or shall be in the future." His prophecies and interpretations of omens encouraged the Greeks to fight through the ten years of the Trojan War. He said Troy could not be taken without the help of Achilles; the Greeks accordingly sent for Achilles. When the Greeks first assembled at Aulis to sail against Troy, a crimson-backed serpent wound its way up a nearby plane tree, swallowed eight young sparrows in their nest and devoured their mother. The serpent, still coiled about the tree, then turned to stone. Calchas interpreted this to mean that the Greeks would fight nine years, in the tenth year would take Troy. In the second gathering at Aulis, after years of raiding the coasts of the

Troad because they did not know the course to follow to Troy, the Greeks were held windbound. Calchas advised Agamemnon that only the sacrifice of his daughter, Iphigenia, to Artemis would bring favorable winds. Iphigenia was sacrificed and the storm winds ceased. Calchas then confirmed that the course which had been given them by a Mysian was correct and the Greeks sailed once more. While they were encamped before Troy, they were harassed by a rain of arrows sent by Apollo. Calchas offered to tell the reason for this plague on condition that Achilles would protect him from Agamemnon's anger. Achilles agreed and Calchas explained that Apollo was sending the arrows to punish Agamemnon for refusing to accept the ransom offered by a priest of Apollo for his daughter, Chryseis, Agamemnon's captive. Agamemnon was indeed angry and accused Calchas of always prophesying evil for him. However, he restored Chryseis to her father and the rain of arrows ceased. Other predictions that Calchas made and that the Greeks acted on were: 1) that Troy, after the death of Achilles, could not be taken without the aid of Achilles son, Neoptolemus; 2) that the bows and arrows of Heracles at that time in the possession of Philoctetes, who had been abandoned by the Greeks in Lemnos, were necessary for the taking of Troy; 3) that only Helenus, a son of Priam, could tell them what protected Troy and therefore he should be captured; and 4) that Troy could not be taken by direct siege but must be captured by stratagem. This last led to the ruse of the Wooden Horse, and some say Calchas was one of those who entered the city in it. After the taking of Troy he told the Greeks to spare Aeneas because it was his destiny to found a new nation in Italy. He prophesied that Astyanax, young son of Hector, would grow up and raise an army which he would lead against the Greeks if he were spared. Astyanax was slain. He said that Polyxena, daughter of Priam, must be sacrificed on Achilles' tomb; otherwise Achilles' shade, wrathful that he had not been duly honored, would raise great storms and prevent the Greeks from returning home. When the Greeks left Troy, he was forewarned by his prophetic powers of the disasters that would overtake them at sea. He therefore went by land to Colophon. It had been prophesied that Calchas would die when

fat, fāte, fär, fåll, ȧsk, fâre; net, mē, hėr; pin, pīne; not, nōte, mŏve, nôr; up, lūte, pùll; oi, oil; ou out; (lightened) ẹlect, agǫny, ūnite;

he met a seer wiser than himself. In Colophon or Clarus, he met Mopsus, a son of Apollo and Manto. Calchas challenged him to give the number of figs growing on a tree nearby. Mopsus answered that there were 10,000 figs, plus one bushel, plus one fig left over. When the tree was stripped and the figs counted, Mopsus was found to be correct. He then challenged Calchas to say how many pigs a sow that was about to farrow would produce. Calchas looked at the sow and said there would be eight male piglets, born within nine days. Mopsus disagreed. There would be three piglets, he said, only one a male, and they would be born the next day at noon. Again Mopsus proved correct and Calchas, having met a seer wiser than himself, died of a broken heart and was buried at Notium. But some say he committed suicide on account of the injury done his pride.

Calliope (kạ-lī′ọ-pē). In Greek mythology, one of the nine daughters of Zeus and Mnemosyne. She is the chief of the Muses, the Muse of epic or heroic poetry, and her attributes are a scroll and stylus. Calliope was the mother of Orpheus by Oeagrus, a king in Thrace, and is sometimes said also to have been the mother of the poet Linus and of the Thracian Rhesus who went to the aid of Hector in the Trojan War. In a dispute between Aphrodite and Persephone over possession of Adonis, Calliope decided that Adonis' year should be divided into three parts: one third to be spent with Aphrodite, one third with Persephone, and one third by himself. See *Muses*.

Callisto (kạ-lis′tō). In Greek mythology, a daughter of Lycaon, a king of Arcadia who had been transformed into a wolf because of his wickedness. Zeus fell in love with Callisto and she bore him a son, Arcas. According to some accounts, Artemis was angry with Callisto, who had been one of her chaste companions, and transformed her into a bear. Others say it was Zeus who transformed her to save her from the wrath of Hera. When Arcas reached young manhood, he was hunting wild beasts in the forest, and seeing a bear, would have killed it, unaware that she was his mother. Zeus rescued Callisto by carrying her off in a whirlwind and translating her to the heavens, where she became the constellation Ursa Major (the Great Bear). Hera was jealous of the honor that had come to Callisto of being placed in the skies, and persuaded Poseidon to forbid Callisto ever to bathe in the sea. For this reason the Great Bear never sinks below the horizon.

Calydonian Boar. A huge, savage boar sent by Artemis to ravage the land of Calydon in Aetolia because Oeneus, the king had forgotten to sacrifice first fruits to her when he made offerings to the other gods and goddesses. The boar was wounded by Atalanta and killed by Meleager in a great hunt in which many of the legendary heroes of Greece participated.

Calypso (kạ-lip′sō). A nymph who was, according to some accounts, the daughter of Oceanus and Thetis; others say Nereus or Atlas was her father. She lived in a tree-shrouded cavern on the island of Ogygia. Odysseus drifted to her shores after losing all his ships and men as he attempted to return to Ithaca after the Trojan War. Calypso welcomed him warmly and offered him eternal youth and immortality if he would remain with her. As he had no means of leaving the island, he remained with her seven years and, some say, she bore him Latinus as well as the twins Nausithous and Nausinous. At the end of seven years Athena appealed to the gods on Olympus to allow Odysseus to return to his home. Zeus, taking advantage of the absence of Poseidon who was the enemy of Odysseus, commanded Hermes to go to Calypso and instruct her to provide Odysseus with whatever was needed for his journey. She bowed to the god's command, helped Odysseus to build a raft, furnished stores for his needs on the voyage, and sent him on his way, although she assured him that if he knew the troubles still in store for him, he would prefer to stay with her, notwithstanding the charms of his wife Penelope.

Capaneus (kap′ạ-nūs). In mythology, the son of Hipponous and the father of Sthenelus. He was an Argive chieftain, and marched against Thebes as one of the Seven against Thebes. As he climbed the wall of Thebes, he was struck by a thunderbolt because he had boasted that not Zeus himself could stop him. When his body was returned to his homeland for funeral honors, his wife Evadne, who had been watching from a rocky height, leaped down on to his funeral pyre and was consumed by the flames.

Capys (ka′pis). In legend, a Trojan who mistrusted the Wooden Horse when it was first seen outside the walls of

fat, fāte, fär, fâll, ȧsk, fāre; net, mē, hèr; pin, pīne; not, nōte, möve, nôr; up, lūte, pùll; oi, oil; ou out; (lightened) ẹlect, agǫny, ūnite;

Troy, and advised that it be cast into the sea. When the city fell he accompanied Aeneas on his flight from Troy, and eventually became the founder of the city of Capua.

Cassandra (kạ-san′drạ). In Greek legend, one of the 12 daughters of Priam, king of Troy. Her mother was Hecuba, and she was the twin of Helenus. According to some accounts, the children fell asleep in the temple while their parents were celebrating a festival of Apollo. Sacred serpents came and licked their ears as they slept, but on being discovered by Hecuba, who screamed in terror at the sight, the serpents glided away. However, because they had been ministered to by sacred serpents, from that time forth both children were endowed with the power of divination. Other accounts say that Apollo fell in love with Cassandra and promised to give her prophetic powers in return for her love. The god thereupon taught her the art of prophecy but Cassandra refused to carry out her end of the bargain. Apollo could not withdraw the gift he had given her, but in revenge he turned it into a curse by decreeing that although she would correctly foretell the future, no one would ever believe her. Her name has become synonymous for those prophets of doom whose warnings go unheeded until it is too late. The more accurately she predicted disaster, the more convinced her hearers were that she was mad. She predicted that if Paris carried out his intended voyage to Sparta he would bring ruin to Troy. Her father ignored her warnings and provided the fleet in which Paris subsequently abducted Helen. From the beginning of the Trojan War Cassandra incessantly prophesied that it would end in disaster. She was scorned and kept as a virtual prisoner so that the Trojans would not have to listen to her gloomy predictions. In appearance Cassandra, the fairest of Priam's daughters, was described as a rival of Aphrodite, and she had many suitors. Towards the end of the Trojan War, Priam promised her to Eurypylus, descendant of Heracles, in return for assistance in the defense of Troy, but he was killed. Cassandra protested violently against bringing into the city the Wooden Horse which had been left outside the walls of Troy by the Greeks. She said there were armed men in it and predicted that Troy would become dust, Priam and Polyxena would die, Hecuba would be metamorphosed into a dog, and she herself carried off into slavery. Priam rebuked

(obscured) errạnt, ardẹnt, actọr; ch, chip; g, go; th, thin; ᴛʜ, then; y, you; (variable) ḍ as d or j, ṣ as s or sh, ṭ as t or ch, ẓ as z or zh.

her for her raving and the Horse was dragged into the city. The Trojans wreathed it with garlands and offered sacrifices. The sacrificial fires poured forth blood-red smoke and then fizzled out. The statues of the gods wept. Cassandra correctly interpreted these omens of disaster but no one heeded her. In desperation she tried to set the Horse afire, but was prevented from doing so by her countrymen. In the sack of Troy she sought refuge at the altar of Athena. There, according to some accounts, Ajax the Lesser seized her and violated her. Others say no such thing happened, and that this was a malicious lie spread by Odysseus, and indeed, Cassandra did not claim that Ajax had injured her. In the awarding of captives Cassandra was taken by Agamemnon as his concubine and, according to some, subsequently bore him twin sons. Before she left Troy, she promised to destroy her most bitter foes by her alliance with Agamemnon. In a spell of what seemed to be madness, she declared that Agamemnon had lost what he loved most—his wife and his children—and declared that the Greeks fought and died in foreign lands, while the Trojans had the glory of dying in defense of their homeland. She predicted the death of Agamemnon, the long wanderings of Odysseus, and her own death, and then left her mother to go off as a captive to Greece. On his arrival in Argos Agamemnon was royally acclaimed by Clytemnestra. Cassandra remained mute until the reunited pair entered the palace for the feast which Clytemnestra said she had prepared for her returning husband. Then Cassandra broke into frenzied speech. She cried out at the smell of blood that came from the palace; she expressed horror at the frightful deeds kinsmen were committing on kinsmen. In this she was saying that Clytemnestra was murdering Agamemnon, as was, in fact, the case. But the citizens who had come to the palace to welcome Agamemnon home listened compassionately, convinced that her sufferings had unhinged her mind, and made no effort to go to Agamemnon's assistance. However, when she alluded to the ghastly feast which Thyestes, uncle of Agamemnon, had made on the flesh of his own sons, and recalled his curse, they were filled with foreboding and uneasy wonder that one from so far away should know the horrible history of the House of Atreus. Again she spoke of the death of Agamemnon and foretold that one (Orestes) would some

fat, fāte, fär, fåll, àsk, fãre; net, mē, hėr; pin, pīne; not, nōte, möve, nôr; up, lūte, půll; oi, oil; ou out; (lightened) ēlect, agǫny, ūnite;

day come to avenge him. Then, knowing her own death to be at hand, she appealed to the gods to make it swift and entered the palace. There Clytemnestra, who had just murdered Agamemnon, set upon Cassandra and killed her. In the mêlée which followed the murders, the sons of Cassandra and Agamemnon were slain. Cassandra was known sometimes as Alexandra. Her character, with its tragic element of impotent wisdom, has been variously introduced into later literature.

Cassiopea (kas″i-ọ-pē′ạ) or *Cassiepea* (kas″i-ẹ-) or *Cassiope* (kạ-sī′ọ-pē). In Greek legend, the wife of Cepheus, king of Joppa in Ethiopia, and the mother of Andromeda. Her boasts that she and her daughter were more beautiful than the Nereids angered Poseidon and he sent a sea monster to devastate the land. To appease Poseidon, Andromeda was offered to the monster in accordance with an oracle. She was saved by Perseus, however, and became his bride. Cassiopea was unwilling to have Perseus for a son-in-law, as she preferred Phineus, brother of Cepheus, in that role. At the wedding of Perseus and Andromeda she supported the cause of Phineus when he burst in on the festivities and attempted to seize Andromeda. Perseus turned Phineus and his other enemies, including Cepheus and Cassiopea, into stone by exhibiting the head of Medusa. Poseidon set the image of Cassiopea among the stars, but in such a way as to humiliate her, for at certain times of the year she appears hanging in the heavens upside down.

Castalides (kas-tal′i-dēz). A name for the Muses, derived from the fountain of Castalia on the slopes of Mount Parnassus, Greece, sacred to them.

Castor (kas′tọr). The twin brother of Polydeuces (Pollux). See *Dioscuri.*

Catreus (kā′trūs). In Greek legend, a son of Minos, king of Crete, and Pasiphaë. He was the father of three daughters, Aërope, who married Atreus and became the mother of Agamemnon and Menelaus, Clymene, who married Nauplius and became the mother of Palamedes and Oeax, and Apemosyne. He had one son, Althaemenes, whom he dearly loved. An oracle predicted that he would die at the hands of one of his own children. To avoid beng the instrument that would fulfill the oracle, Althaemenes and Apemosyne went into voluntary exile at Rhodes. Catreus, on discovering his daughter Aërope entertaining a lover, proposed to cast her into the sea. But as Catreus suspected both Aërope and Clymene of plotting against his life, he was instead persuaded to sell them as slaves to Nauplius on condition that they never return to Crete. Years later, Catreus went to Rhodes, seeking his beloved and pious son. He landed on Rhodes at night and in the darkness was mistaken for a pirate. Although he tried to explain who he was, the uproar drowned his voice. Althaemenes, rushing up and unaware of the stranger's identity, hurled a spear at him and killed him, thus fulfilling the oracle.

Cecrops (sē'krops). In Greek mythology, a son of Gaea. He was a man in his upper parts and a serpent in his lower parts. He is said to have been the first king of Attica and the land was sometimes called Cecropia in his honor. It was Cecrops who divided Attica into the 12 demes. He also built temples and established the worship of the gods, especially Athena and Zeus. He established the custom of monogamy and abolished human sacrifices. Some say he also gave the people their institutions of burial and writing. By his wife Agraulos (or Aglauros) he was the father of three daughters, Agraulos II (or Aglauros), Herse, and Pandrosos. During his reign Athena and Poseidon struggled for control of Athens. Poseidon struck the rock of the Acropolis with his trident and salt water gushed out and formed a deep well. This was his gift to the people. (Some say a horse came forth when he struck the rock.) But Athena gave the people the olive tree and Cecrops, who was to judge which gift was more valuable, according to some accounts, awarded the city to her. Others say the women, who outnumbered the men, voted to give Athena control of Athens. A second Cecrops was a son of Erechtheus, and was made king of Athens by his brother-in-law Xuthus, but his brothers quarreled over this decision and to save him Athena, disguised as a bird, carried him off under her wings to safety.

Centaurs (sen'tôrz). In mythology, the descendants of Ixion and Nephele, a cloud-born woman. They dwelt in Thessaly and were conceived of as being half man and half horse. In general, they were wild and savage, more like beasts than men but some of them, notably Chiron, had close associations with men as friends and teachers. The centaurs were

fat, fāte, fär, fåll, åsk, fãre; net, mē, hėr; pin, pīne; not, nōte, möve, nôr; up, lūte, pull; oi, oil; ou out; (lightened) ĕlect, agŏny, ūnite;

invited to the marriage of Pirithous, king of the Lapithae, and Hippodamia. There, inflamed by wine, they attacked the women, in particular, the bride. A fierce battle took place in which the Lapithae succeeded in driving off the centaurs. On another occasion the centaurs, again maddened by the fumes of wine, attacked Heracles as he visited Pholus, one of their number, in a cave near Mount Pholoë. Nephele sent a violent rain to help her descendants. The centaurs, being four-footed, had an advantage over Heracles in the slippery mud. Nevertheless, Heracles slew many of them and drove the rest away. In later times the centaurs were thought of as peaceful followers of Dionysus and Eros.

Cephalus (sef'a̱-lus). According to some accounts of the legend, a son of Hermes and Herse, daughter of Cecrops, king of Athens. Others say he was a son of Deion. He was married to Procris, daughter of Erechtheus, king of Athens, and loved her deeply. One day while he was hunting, Eos saw him and fell in love with him. She carried him off, offering her love. Cephalus rejected her advances, saying he had sworn undying fidelity to Procris. Eos, the dawn-goddess, scoffed at his pledge and mocked his belief that Procris was equally faithful. To prove her contention, she transformed him into a handsome youth with the name Pteleon, and sent him back to Procris. In this guise he approached his wife, who was grieving for her lost husband, and finally persuaded her with rich gifts and ardent protestations of love to weaken and yield to him. Immediately he revealed himself, denounced her for infidelity, and deserted her. Later he met a handsome youth, Pterelas, who was the owner of a hound, Laelaps, that could not fail to catch its quarry, and of a spear that could not fail to reach its target. He offered Pterelas a large sum for these two marvellous aids to hunting, but was told that Pterelas would only give them up for love. Cephalus then offered his love. At this Pterelas threw off his disguise and was revealed as Procris. The couple was reconciled and Cephalus enjoyed many successful hunts with his hound and spear, and recovered his devotion to Procris. But Procris, who had not forgotten his absence with Eos, was jealous and thought when she overheard him calling for a breeze to cool him that he was calling a lover. She followed him and hid in a thicket to watch him. Cephalus' keen eye detected a slight movement of the bushes in which she was hidden, and thinking it was caused by a wild beast, hurled his spear. It went straight to the mark and transfixed Procris. Afterward, Cephalus was banished from Athens for murder. He went to Thebes, and loaned his hound to Amphitryon, foster father of Heracles, to catch the Teumessian fox that was ravaging the countryside. Since the fox, by decree of the gods, could not be caught, and the hound must catch its quarry, both were turned to stone by Zeus. Cephalus also helped Amphitryon in his war against the Taphians and Teleboans. In return for his aid he was awarded the island which was named Cephallenia in his honor. But he never recovered from the death of Procris, and blamed himself for the disguise which he had assumed to test her, as well as for her death. He built a temple to Apollo on Cape Leucas and one day went there and, calling his wife's name, leaped into the sea.

Cer (sēr) or *Ker* (kēr). In Greek mythology, a goddess of violent death, according to some accounts, a daughter of Nyx, and the sister of the Moerae. There were several goddesses representing different sorts of death, and together they were called Ceres. They were described as hateful and dreaded because they carry man off to the hopeless halls of Hades. But it was thought that the Ceres were not entirely free agents; Zeus and the other gods could control them, and sometimes even men could do so. In battle the Ceres were accompanied by Eris, and wandered about in blood-stained garments, quarrelling among themselves over the wounded and the dead. Epidemic diseases were sometimes associated with them, and they came in time to be regarded as goddesses who punish men for their crimes. For this reason they came to be identified with the Erinyes.

Cerberus (sẻr′bẻr-us). In Greek mythology, the watchdog at the entrance to the Underworld, whose duty it was to devour the living who attempted to invade the infernal regions or the shades that attempted to escape from them. Orpheus, Aeneas, and Odysseus successfully passed Cerberus on visits to the Underworld. He was an offspring of Typhon and Echidna, and was usually represented as having three heads, a serpent's tail, and a mane of serpent's heads. As one of their burial customs, the Greeks buried with the corpse a honey cake with which the spirit was to quiet Cerberus so that it might pass the monster-dog on its way to Elysium;

fat, fāte, fär, fåll, åsk, fāre; net, mē, hẻr; pin, pīne; not, nōte, mŏve, nôr; up, lūte, pủll; oi, oil; ou out; (lightened) ẹlect, agǫny, ụnite;

thence the expression "a sop to Cerberus." The last labor of Heracles was to bring Cerberus up from the Underworld. Hades permitted him to do this if he could take Cerberus without weapons. Heracles grasped him firmly around the neck, disregarding the stings of the serpent's tail with which Cerberus lashed him, and choked him until he yielded. As Cerberus faced the light of earth for the first time, either at Troezen or at Heraclea on the Euxine Sea, foam fell from his jaws onto the ground. From the foam sprang the poisonous plant aconite, which, it was claimed, flourished ever after around Heraclea.

Cercopes (sėr-kō′pēz). A legendary race of men in Lydia. They are sometimes conceived of as mischievous gnomes, who attacked Heracles as he slept, when he was serving Queen Omphale, and stole his weapons. Awakened, Heracles was amused by their attempts. He gathered them up in his lion's skin and took them to Omphale. Others say that they were deceitful men who were changed into apes by Zeus, and that Heracles captured them and carried them, head down on a pole, to Omphale. The Pithecusae (Ape) islands of Ischia and Procida, off the coast of Naples, were named for them.

Ceres (sir′ēz, sē′rēz). In ancient Italian mythology, the goddess of grain and harvest, later identified by the Romans with the Greek Demeter. Her cult was quite old; one of the *flamens* (15 priests, each assigned to one god and his cult observance) was the *flamen Cerealis.*

Cerynean Hind (ser-i-nē′an). A fabled creature in Greek mythology, referred to in the legend of Heracles. With golden horns and hoofs of bronze, this creature, sacred to Artemis, was as fleet as the wind. Its capture was one of the 12 labors imposed upon Heracles. Some say he pursued it through Arcadia and finally transfixed its forefeet with one arrow as it stopped at the Ladon River to drink. He then carried it to Eurystheus. Others say that after a long pursuit, he drove it into a deep drift of snow in a northern region and thus captured it without injuring it.

Cestus (ses′tus). Aphrodite's magic girdle, which had the power of enhancing the beauty of any who wore it and of inspiring love in those who beheld the wearer of it. Hera borrowed the cestus from Aphrodite to charm Zeus, during the Trojan War, so that he would forget about helping the

Trojans in his aroused love for her, and thus give her fa
vored Greeks a chance to drive back the Trojans. The cestu
played an important role in many of the myths.

Ceto (sē'tō). In Greek mythology, a daughter of Gaea and
Pontus. By her brother Phorcys she was the mother of the
Graeae, the grayhaired sisters who share one eye and one
tooth between them, and of the Gorgons, winged sister
who dwelt in Libya. According to some accounts, Ceto and
Phorcys were also the parents of Echidna, an immortal mon
ster, half-maiden and half-serpent; the Hesperides, who
dwelt in the garden called by their name; and of Ladon,
many-headed monster who guarded the Apples of the
Hesperides.

Ceyx (sē'iks). In Greek mythology, a son of Phosphorus, the
Morning-Star. He was a king in Trachis who welcomed Her
acles when he went into exile there with his wife Deianira fo
an accidental murder, but was not strong enough later to
defy the order of Eurystheus to banish Heracles' children
Ceyx was celebrated for the tender love he bore his wif
Alcyone. On a journey to Clarus to consult the oracle c
Apollo, he was drowned at sea. His wife, who had pleade
to accompany him, was informed in a dream sent by Her
that her husband was dead. She went to the water's edge t
weep and discoverd her husband's body, which had bee
washed to his native shores. Alcyone grieved so over the los
of her husband that the gods in pity changed her and Cey
into kingfishers (alcyones), whose affection for each other i
the mating season is proverbial. The Halcyon Days, a perio
of 14 days when the sea is calm, are named for them. Ac
cording to another version of this myth, Ceyx and Alcyon
were so happy that they dared to compare themselves t
Zeus and Hera. Their arrogance so annoyed the gods tha
Zeus sent a storm which wrecked the ship in which Ceyx wa
sailing to consult the oracle, and he was drowned. Accord
ing to this verison also, the gods in pity for Alcyone's gri
changed the pair into kingfishers, or into a sea-mew (Cey
and a kingfisher (Alcyone).

Chaos (kā'os). In Greek mythology, the original formles
state of the universe; or, the diety presiding over it. Perhap
no other myth exhibits quite so much confusion and varie
as are found in the concepts of Chaos. The one thing con
mon to all versions was the idea of infinite space in whic

---

fat, fāte, fàr, fâll, àsk, fãre; net, mē, hèr; pin, pīne; not, nōte, mö
nôr; up, lūte, pùll; oi, oil; ou out; (lightened) ēlect, agǫny, ūni

matter existed without form and in complete darkness; to some of the ancient poets, this was Chaos, and alone existed, but others said that Earth and Eros were coeval with Chaos. In some cosmogonies, the first of all things was Chronos (Time), from whom proceeded Chaos and Aether (Light, or the upper air). But in another formulation, Chaos was the deity presiding over the formless mass with his wife Nyx (Night). Their son Erebus (Darkness) slew or dethroned Chaos and married his mother; from this union came Aether and Hemera (Day), who with the aid of their son Eros (Love) created Pontus (the Sea) and Gaea (the Earth). But in other accounts, Gaea proceeded directly from Chaos, and was the mother of Eros as well as of Tartarus (the Nether World).

Charites (kar'i-tēz). The Greek name for the Graces, goddesses of the beauty, brightness, and joy in nature and humanity. Some say they are the daughters of Helius and Aegle, a naiad. Others say they are the daughters of Zeus and Eurynome. Their most familiar names are Aglaia (Brilliance), Euphrosyne (Joy), and Thalia (the Bloom of Life). The Charites are associated with the Muses, with whom they dwell on Mount Olympus, as the inspiration for music, poetry, the arts of painting and sculpture, beauty and knowledge. They are also associated particularly with Aphrodite, Eros, and Dionysus. Their shrine at Orchomenus in Boeotia, where they were worshiped with Aphrodite and Dionysus, was said to be the oldest there. In it were ancient stone images, said to have fallen from heaven. In Athens, where only two graces, Auxo (Increase) and Hegemone (Queen), were recognized, the Athenian youths, on first receiving their shields and spears, swore by these goddesses to be loyal to their country. The Charites were worshiped in Athens, Sparta (where also only two were recognized), Messene, and elsewhere in Greece.

Charon (kār'on). In Greek mythology, a son of Erebus. He is the ferryman who transports the souls of the dead (but only of those who have been properly buried) across the river Styx to the Underworld. His fee is an obolus or other coin, and this is placed for him in the mouth of the dead at the time of burial. Few have passed Charon in defiance of the rules concerning proper burial. Orpheus so charmed him that he was ferried over; Heracles terrified him into taking him across; and Aeneas bribed him with the Golden Bough.

scured) errant, ardent, actor; ch, chip; g, go; th, thin; ᴛʜ, then; y, you; riable) ḍ as d or j, ṣ as s or sh, ṭ as t or ch, ẓ as z or zh.

There were, however, several back entrances to the Under
world, and by using these Charon and his fee could b
avoided.

Charybdis (ka̲-rib′dis). In Greek mythology, a monster, th
daughter of Gaea and Poseidon. Because of her greed Zeu
struck her with his thunderbolt and hurled her into the se
near Sicily. There, three times a day she gulps in the water
and spews them out again. Odysseus twice narrowly escape
death passing by Charybdis. In later times Charybdis wa
identified as a whirlpool in the Straits of Messina.

Chelone (ke-lō′nē). In Greek legend, a maiden who refused t
attend the wedding of Zeus and Hera. To punish he
Hermes cast her house into a river and transformed Chelon
into a turtle, which carries its house on its back.

CHIMAERA
Proto-Corinthian lecythus, 675–640 B.C.
Museum of Fine Arts, Boston

Chimaera (kī-mē′ra, ki-). In Greek mythology, a fire-breath
ing monster of divine origin. It had the head of a lion, th
body of a goat, and the tail of a serpent. It dwelt in Lycia an
was slain by Bellerophon. Hesiod says it was the offsprin
of Echidna and Typhon and described it as having thre
heads: a lion's, a goat's and a serpent's. It was supposed b
the ancients to represent a volcanic mountain of the sam
name in Lycia, the top of which was said to be the home c
lions, the middle that of goats, and the foot that of serpent

Chiron or *Cheiron* (kī′ron). In Greek mythology, a wise and just centaur, the friend and teacher of many of the heroes of Greece, and renowned for his powers of healing and prophecy as well as for his skill in hunting and music. In his gentle and beneficent qualities he was the direct opposite of his wild and unruly brothers. Some say Cronus consorting with Philyra on a tiny island which afterward bore her name, was surprised by Rhea. He transformed himself into a stallion. The child which Philyra subsequently bore was half-man and half-horse, the kindly centaur Chiron. Others say that Zeus was Chiron's father. But still others say that he was a descendant of Ixion, who fathered Centaurus on the cloud Nephele. Centaurus in his turn fathered the race of centaurs on mares and Chiron, the king of the centaurs, was one of these. Many instances are recorded of Chiron's kindness to and friendship for men. He saved Peleus when he was abandoned by Acastus and attacked by centaurs; he told Peleus

CHIRON
Black-figured Greek amphora.

how he could capture the sea-goddess Thetis by holding fast to her no matter what transformations she might assume to escape his embrace. Peleus, successful, was married to Thetis in Chiron's cave on Mount Pelion; Chiron gave him an ashen spear for a wedding gift, which was afterward used by

Achilles at Troy. When Thetis deserted Peleus, he gave h
infant son Achilles into Chiron's charge, and the centau
reared him. He taught Achilles to ride and hunt, and ir
structed him in the arts of healing. Later, he is said to hav
restored the sight of Phoenix, who became Achilles' tuto
and second father. He reared and instructed Jason and
some say, his son by Medea, Medeus. Others he nurture
were Asclepius, who excelled his teacher in the art of hea
ing, Castor and Polydeuces, and Actaeon. When the cer
taurs were driven away from Mount Pelion by the Lapith
Chiron went to Malea and dwelt in a cave there. Hither h
friend Heracles pursued the centaurs who had attacked hir
in Pholoë. By accident, one of Heracles' poisoned arrov
pierced Chiron's leg. Heracles immediately withdrew it b
nothing could heal the wound. Chiron suffered unbearabl
and could not be released from his sufferings by death as b
was immortal. Zeus, at the plea of Heracles, offered to r
lease Prometheus from his chains on the rock if he could fir
someone to take his place in Tartarus. Chiron offered h
immortality to Prometheus and went to Tartarus in h
stead, and won release from his sufferings at last. Zeus s
his image among the stars.

Chryseis (krī-sē′is). In Homeric legend *(Iliad)*, a daughter
Chryses, priest of Apollo on the island of Sminthus. Know
also as Astynome, she was taken captive by Achilles in th
Trojan War and was awarded to Agamemnon as his sha
of the spoils. Apollo sent a plague of arrows against th
Greeks because Agamemnon refused to accept a rich ra
som for her from her father, and to appease the god Ag
memnon sent her back to Chryses by Odysseus, althoug
she was perfectly willing to remain where she was, accordi
to later accounts. The return of Chryseis to her fath
caused the famous quarrel between Agamemnon an
Achilles, for to make up for her loss Agamemnon to
Achilles' captive, Briseis.

Chrysippus (krī-sip′us, kri-). In Greek legend, a bastard son
Pelops and the nymph Astyoche, a Danaid. Laius, king
Thebes, fell in love with the boy and carried him off
Thebes. Hera sent the Sphinx, a monster that devour
those who could not answer the riddle she propounded,
punish Thebes because its king had abducted Chrysippu

Hippodamia, wife of Pelops, killed Chrysippus, either alone or with the aid of her sons Atreus and Thyestes, because she feared that Pelops might leave his kingdom to him rather than to her own sons.

Chrysothemis (kri-soth′e̤-mis). According to Homer and Sophocles, a daughter of Agamemnon and Clytemnestra. In the *Iliad,* Agamemnon offered her or either of her two sisters to Achilles as part of a rich peace offering if Achilles would forget his quarrel with Agamemnon and take up his arms again to help the Greeks defeat the Trojans. When Agamemnon returned from Troy and was murdered by his wife and Aegisthus, Chrysothemis and her sister Electra remained in their mother's house. She shared Electra's hatred of Clytemnestra and Aegisthus, but felt that she was helpless to do anything about it and accepted her fate with resignation. She urged Electra to refrain from publicly accusing their mother and Aegisthus of being murderous adulterers and to make the best of her lot. She thought Electra's desire for vengeance for her father's death was mad and refused to help Electra kill Aegisthus on the ground that she was only a weak woman, who would rather be miserable and alive than heroic and dead.

Cicones (sik′o̤-nēz) or **Ciconians** (si-kō′ni-a̤nz). In Homer, a people of Thrace, dwelling on the shores of the Aegean near the Hebrus River. Orpheus settled among the Cicones, and it was the Ciconian women, either inspired with madness by Dionysus, or enraged because he scorned them, who set upon Orpheus, a priest of Apollo, and tore him limb from limb. According to some accounts, it was the practice thereafter for the Ciconian women to be tattooed as a warning against the murder of priests. Odysseus, on his way home after the Trojan War, landed on their shores and plundered their chief city of Ismarus. The Ciconians rallied their neighbors and made an attack on the forces of Odysseus who, in spite of his urgings for a speedy departure, lingered and enjoyed themselves over their wine. The Ciconians killed six men from each of Odysseus' ships before he was able to withdraw. A priest of the Ciconians, Maro, grateful that he and his family had been spared in the attack on the city, gave Odysseus several skins of a special wine which Odysseus later used to good advantage when he was confined by Polyphemus, the Cyclops. The Ciconians had been allies of Troy in the Trojan War, which was enough reason for Odysseus to plunder their city.

Cinyras (sin'ẹ-rạs). A mythical king of Cyprus. He was a descendant of Pygmalion and Galatea and established the worship of Aphrodite on the island of Cyprus. It was he who built the famous temple to the goddess there, and it was said that he was the first to use songs in connection with the worship of Aphrodite. For this reason he was noted as one of the earliest musicians. He promised, as one of Helen's former suitors, to send Agamemnon 50 ships to help the Greeks carry on war against Troy. In fact, he sent only one ship and 49 clay models manned with dolls. But he did send a magnificent corselet to Agamemnon, which the latter wore at the siege of Troy. The wife of Cinyras boasted that her daughter Myrrha, or Smyrna as she was sometimes called, was more beautiful than Aphrodite herself. Aphrodite instantly took vengeance on her for her arrogant boast by causing Myrrha to fall in love with her own father. With the aid of a doting nurse Myrrha was brought to her father either in disguise or while he was befuddled by wine. When, after several such meetings, he discovered that his lover was his own daughter, he was filled with horror and tried to kill her. She fled from his sword and was transformed into a myrrh tree, from the trunk of which sprang her child, Adonis, the fruit of her incestuous union with her father. Cinyras was so revolted by the situation that he committed suicide.

Circe (sẻr'sē). In Greek mythology, an enchantress learned in the use of herbs, charms, and spells. She was the daughter of Helius and Persa, and the sister of Aeëtes and Pasiphaë. As it was the custom in Colchis, where she at first dwelt, to bury only women, and as the Colchians did not follow the Greek way of burning bodies on pyres, Circe had a cemetery outside Aea in Colchis where the bodies of men, wrapped in ox-hides, were suspended from willow trees. There as they swayed in the breezes, the birds ate them. Some say that Circe was the daughter of Hecate and Aeëtes, that she was the sister of Medea, and that both sisters excelled in the black arts, but that Circe used her skill for evil purposes whereas Medea used hers for good. According to these accounts, Circe married a king of Scythia, but poisoned him after a time. She was so wicked and violent she was at last

---

fat, fāte, fär, fåll, åsk, fãre; net, mē, hẻr; pin, pīne; not, nōte, mȯve, nôr; up, lūte, půll; oi, oil; ou out; (lightened) ẹlect, agǫny, ūnite,

compelled to flee. Some say she went to Italy, and made her home on a promontory which bore her name, Circaeum. But others say she fled to the sea and established her home on an island ringed with alders. This island, which lies at the head of the Adriatic, near the mouth of the Padus, was known as Aeaea. Circe was noted for her cruel transformations. She fell in love with Picus, and when he spurned her advances, she transformed him into a woodpecker. Glaucus, the sea-god, appealed to her when his love was rejected by Scylla. Circe fell in love with him and suggested that he abandon his love for Scylla and transfer his affections to her. Glaucus refused, saying nothing could change his love for Scylla. Circe was enraged. She could not harm Glaucus, because he was immortal. Therefore she took her revenge on Scylla by transforming her into a hideous and dangerous sea-monster. But she had some loyalty for members of her family. When Jason and Medea visited her island on their way home from Colchis, she purified them of the murder of Apsyrtus by sprinkling the blood of a suckling pig over their hands. On his way home after the Trojan War Odysseus beached his ships on Circe's island. Though they were weary and thirsty, the Greeks hesitated to go ashore in a strange place after the disastrous experiences they had suffered in other unknown lands. By lot, 23 men under the leadership of Eurylochus were chosen to investigate the island. As they approached Circe's palace they were terrified by hordes of lions, wolves, bears, and other animals which came rushing to meet them. But the beasts licked their hands and fawned over them in a most unbeastly fashion. The envoys from Odysseus found Circe in her palace. She welcome them and invited them in. All entered save Eurylochus, who lurked outside to see what would happen. As he watched, he saw Circe give his companions a refreshing drink which they gulped greedily. She then lightly touched their heads and they were instantly turned into swine. Eurylochus fled back to the ship in terror and told all he had seen to Odysseus and begged him to sail with his remaining men at once. However, Odysseus determined to rescue his men. He set out alone for Circe's palace. On the way, Hermes met him and gave him a magic herb which would protect him from Circe's enchantments. He ate the herb, or some say, he merely sniffed it, and entered the palace. He too was graciously welcomed and given a potion to drink. But when she touched him to transform him, he drew his sword and threatened her. At this Circe fell at his feet and appealed for mercy. She retransformed his men from swine to men again, and also at Odysseus' command, transformed the wolves, bears, lions, and other animals back to men. She invited Odysseus and his companions to remain with her and entertained them royally. The Greeks stayed with her a year or more and Circe bore three sons to Odysseus—Agrius, Latinus, and Telegonus. Before Odysseus left Circe to return to Ithaca, she told him that he must go to Tartarus and find Tiresias the seer, who would tell him what to expect in the future. She gave him full directions for the voyage to Tartarus and instructed him what to do when he got there: he must fill a trench with the blood of a young ram and a black ewe; when the shades came to drink of the warm blood, he must keep all except Tiresias away. Tiresias, after drinking the blood, would tell him all he wanted to know. She then sent a fair wind and Odysseus sailed away. But when he was in Tartarus, he met the shade of one of his companions who had been killed on Circe's island and had not been properly buried. So after he had consulted Tiresias, he sailed back to Circe's land to bury the dead sailor. This time she gave him useful advice about how to pass the Sirens in safety and warned him not to harm the cattle of Helius. Some say that Odysseus, having learned from an oracle that his son would kill him, sent Telemachus into exile. He went to Circe's land and married the enchantress.

Cithaeron (si-thē'ron). In Greek legend, the brother of Helicon. He was a fierce and savage man, who murdered his father and attempted to kill his brother, but as he hurled Helicon from a rocky height, both fell and were dashed to death. The gods changed them both into mountains. Mount Cithaeron in Boeotia is a wild and rugged mountain, where children were often exposed to die, as was Oedipus. It was also a home of the Furies, and ferocious beasts had their lairs there. Even so, many of the children who were exposed on Mount Cithaeron were saved because of the number of shepherds and herdsmen who watched their flocks on its slopes. Mount Cithaeron was sacred to Zeus and to Dionysus, and its name figures in many Greek myths and

legends. According to another account, Cithaeron, a king of
Plataea, was loved by the Fury Tisiphone, but he scorned
her love and was bitten by one of the serpents of her snaky
locks. He died on the mountain and it thereafter bore his
name.

Cleobis (klē′ō-bis). See **Biton and Cleobis.**

Clio (klī′ō). One of the nine daughters of Zeus and Mnemosyne. She is the muse who sings of glorious actions; specifically, the muse of History. She is usually represented with
a scroll in her hand and a *scrinium* (case for manuscripts) by
her side, and sometimes with the trumpet of fame in her
hand. According to some accounts, as a punishment because
Clio had mocked Aphrodite for her attachment to Adonis,
Aphrodite caused her to fall in love with Pierus, to whom she
bore Hyacinthus. See **Muses.**

Clotho (klō′thō). In Greek mythology, that one of the three
Fates or Moerae who spins the thread of life.

Clymene (klim′ē-nē). In Greek legend, a daughter of Minyas,
king of Thessaly. She married Phylacus and bore him Iphiclus and Alcimede. Alcimede was the mother of Jason, according to some accounts, and her descent through
Clymene from Minyas accounts for the name Minyans which
was sometimes given to the Argonauts.

Clytemnestra or *Clytaemnestra* (klī-tem-nes′tra̯, klit-am-). In
Greek legend, a daughter of Tyndareus, king of Sparta, and
Leda. She was the sister of Helen, Castor, and Polydeuces.
Clytemnestra married Tantalus, son of Broteas, who was
king of Pisa. Clytemnestra had just borne him a son when
Agamemnon attacked Pisa, slew Tantalus and the infant at
Clytemnestra's breast, and forced her to marry him. Her
brothers would have avenged her but Agamemnon appealed to Tyndareus as a suppliant and was purified by him
for the murder of Tantalus, and allowed to keep Clytemnestra as his wife. She bore him a son, Orestes, and three
daughters: Electra (also known as Laodice), Iphigenia (also
known as Iphianassa), and Chrysothemis. When the Greeks
were massed at Aulis in preparation for the voyage to Troy
to recapture Helen, unfavorable winds prevented them from
sailing. Calchas the seer said Artemis had sent the winds
because she was angry at Agamemnon for killing one of her
sacred creatures. Only the sacrifice of Iphigenia to Artemis,
Calchas advised, would appease the goddess and cause her

to send favorable winds. Agamemnon sent for Iphigenia
with the message that she must come to Aulis to be married
to Achilles. Clytemnestra, radiant with joy at this excellent
match, accompanied Iphigenia to Aulis and there learned
the truth. No pleas of hers could sway Agamemnon from his
purpose of sacrificing Iphigenia, although he grieved to do
so and had, in fact, tried to stop the messenger who went for
her. But once she had arrived and the whole Greek army
knew of the oracle he was persuaded by Odysseus that as
commander of the 1000 ships assembled to sail to Troy he
had a responsibility to do whatever was necessary for the
conduct of the war. Thus Clytemnestra lost a second child
to her warlike husband's ambition. Aegisthus, a cousin and
an enemy of Agamemnon, had not joined the Greeks in the
war against Troy. He now came to Argos. Although he had
received special warnings from Zeus through his messenger
Hermes not to encroach on Agamemnon's household, he
now made elaborate plans to seduce Clytemnestra. He dis
patched the bard whom Agamemnon had left behind to spy
on Clytemnestra and went ahead with his plans. This was the
easier to do because Nauplius, to avenge the death of his son
Palamedes at the hands of the Greeks, had circulated rumor
among the wives of the Greek heroes that their husbands
had taken concubines in Troy whom they intended to bring
home as wives. Clytemnestra readily believed such a tale of
Agamemnon and, after some hesitation, yielded to the em
braces of Aegisthus. For his success in becoming her lover
Aegisthus offered rich gifts to the gods. To add to her many
and painful grievances, Clytemnestra now learned that Aga
memnon had taken Cassandra as his concubine. She and
Aegisthus plotted to murder them both when they should
come to Argos. She established an elaborate system of bea
con fires which would inform her of the end of the Trojan
War and of Agamemnon's progress towards Argos. A look
out watched from a tower for a year before the flash of fire
signalling the approach of Agamemnon blazed over the sea
Aegisthus went to Nauplia to meet him. When he arrived in
Mycenae, accompanied by Cassandra, Clytemnestra wel
comed him extravagantly. She insisted that so glorious
victor must walk on a purple carpet into the palace. Aga
memnon was reluctant to usurp a prerogative that was re
served for the gods but her appeals to his vanity induced him

to follow her wishes. As he stepped onto the purple he piously hoped no jealous god would take offense. Clytemnestra led him into the palace for the ritual bath before the great feast which she said had been prepared for him. As he was stepping out of the bath she flung a netlike robe, without sleeves or a neck, over his head, and while he was helplessly trussed in it she, according to some accounts, killed him. Others say Aegisthus slew him and Clytemnestra cut off his head with a double-edged ax. She then, with the same weapon, slew Cassandra. A struggle between the supporters of Aegisthus and the followers of Agamemnon ensued, from which Aegisthus emerged victorious. Clytemnestra proclaimed the day as a monthly festival. Her claim was that the murder of Agamemnon was abundantly justified because he had killed Iphigenia and because of his insult in bringing Cassandra to Argos. For the next seven years she was the actual ruler of Argos, although ostensibly Aegisthus ruled. In fact he lived in terror of vengeance the whole time and did as Clytemnestra told him to do. She bore him three children, among them Erigone and a second Helen. But Clytemnestra's life was by no means serene. Her daughter Electra constantly charged her with being a murderess and an adulteress, and haunted her with the threat of vengeance. Orestes, who had been spirited away at the time of Agamemnon's murder, would surely return, Electra said, and avenge his father's death. In addition to the goading by Electra, Clytemnestra was troubled by dreams which seemed to indicate the furious return of Orestes. Eight years after the death of Agamemnon she received a false message that Orestes was dead. Her soul was divided; as a mother she must grieve at the death of her son, but as the murderer of his father she knew the greatest relief that now Orestes would not come seeking vengeance. The message had been planted by Orestes himself. He was in the neighborhood when Clytemnestra received it. He may, according to some accounts, actually have given it to her himself in disguise. With the encouragement of Electra and the aid of his friend Pylades, he made himself known to his mother and, despite her pleas to be spared as the mother who had nursed him, he killed her and her lover Aegisthus. Whatever the estimate of Clytemnestra, whether as a strong and purposeful woman whose character was distorted by the wrongs she had suf-

fered, or as a monster who was a disgrace to womankind, sh
was a fearless, intelligent, and arresting character. She ar
ranged the plot to kill Agememnon and did not flinch wher
it came to carrying it out. She ruled Argos with never ai
apology for the manner in which she obtained her power

Clytië (klī'ti-ē or klish'i-ē) or **Clytia** (klish'i-ạ). In Greek myth
ology, a water-nymph so enamored of the sun-god Apoll
that every day she watched his course across the sky. Th
gods took pity on her unrequited love and metamorphose
her into a heliotrope, a flower whose face follows the cours
of the sun. Hence, the heliotrope has come to symboliz
unwavering love.

Cocytus (kō-sī'tus). In Greek mythology, one of the five river
surrounding Hades. Cocytus was the so-called Wailin
River. The other four were: the Styx (Hateful), Achero
(Woeful), Pyriphlegethon (Fiery), and Lethe (Forgetful).

Colaxaïs (kol-ak-sā'is). A son of Targitaus, who was said b
the Scythians to be a son of Zeus and a daughter of th
river-god Borysthenes, and the first inhabitant of Scythi
Colaxaïs was the youngest of the three sons of Targitau
While they were in the land four golden objects, a plov
yoke, battle-ax, and drinking cup, fell from the sky. Lipoxaï
the eldest of the three sons, ran to pick them up, but as h
approached they blazed with fire and he was driven bacl
Next Arpoxaïs, the second son, approached and the sam
thing happened. But when Colaxaïs went near them th
flames died out, he seized the golden objects and carrie
them away to his house. After this, the two older brothe
acknowledged Colaxaïs as the king of the land, and fror
him sprang the tribe of Scyths called the Royal Scythian
The Royal Scythians kept the sacred golden objects an
guarded them with the utmost care. At the annual festiva
at which great sacrifices were offered in their honor, if th
man guarding them fell asleep in the open air it was thougl
that he would not live the year out. Lipoxaïs was the found
of the Scythian tribe known as the Auchatae. The Catiari an
Traspians sprang from Arpoxaïs.

Comaetho (kom-ē'thō). In Greek tradition, a priestess c
Artemis in Patrae. She fell in love with Melanippus, but the
love was opposed by both their parents. In defiance of the
parents and religious custom, they profaned the sanctua
of Artemis by making love in it. Artemis sent a punishme
on all the inhabitants of Patrae, the land became barren an

---

fat, fāte, fär, fåll, åsk, fåre; net, mē, hėr; pin, pīne; not, nōte, möv
nôr; up, lūte, pùll; oi, oil; ou out; (lightened) ėlect, agǫny, ūni

strange sicknesses afflicted the people. Envoys were sent to appeal to the oracle at Delphi, to learn how the plagues could be lifted. The priestess told the envoys these evils came because of the impieties of Comaetho and Melanippus, and advised that in order to be free from them the Patraeans must sacrifice Comaetho and Melanippus to the goddess. Furthermore, each year they must crown a youth and a maiden with wreaths of ivy and grain and sacrifice them to Artemis Tridaria (*Threefold Assigner of Lots*). The practice of human sacrifice continued until Eurypylus arrived in the land, after the Trojan War, bearing a chest with the image of Dionysus. Thenceforth human beings were no longer sacrificed.

Corcyraean   (kôr-sī-rē′ạn) *Bull.* According to Greek tradition, a great bull on the island of Corcyra took up the custom of leaving the cows in the pasture and going down to the sea-shore, where he would stand and bellow at the sea. When the herdsmen one day followed him they saw the water in front of him swarming with fish. They reported this to the Corcyraeans, but when the fishermen tried to net the fish they were unable to do so. They sent an envoy to Delphi to inquire about this circumstance. The oracle instructed them to sacrifice the bull to Poseidon. They did so, and immediately they netted the fish. With a tithe of their catch the Corcyraeans dedicated offerings at Olympia and Delphi. To Delphi they sent a bronze image of a bull, and set it up beside the Sacred Way to Apollo's temple. The pedestal on which the image stood was seen by Pausanias.

Coroebus   (kọ-rē′bus). In Greek legend, an Argive hero who killed the monster Poena, sent by Apollo to punish Argos for the deaths of Psamathe and her son Linus. After the slaying of the monster Argos was ravaged by a plague. Coroebus went to Delphi and confessed that he had killed Poena and asked that the plague be lifted. The priestess instructed him to carry a tripod from the shrine at Delphi. Where the tripod fell from his hands, he was to build a temple to Apollo. Coroebus did as he was bid. The tripod fell from his hands at Mount Gerania, and there he built the temple. The tomb of Coroebus, upon which was represented Coroebus slaying Poena, was at Megara.

Coronis   (kọ-rō′nis). In Greek mythology, a daughter of Phlegyas, king of the Lapiths. She was beloved by Apollo, and during the absences of the god was guarded by his bird—

bscured) errạnt, ardẹnt, actọr; ch, chip; g, go; th, thin; ᴛʜ, then; y, you;
ariable) ḍ as d or j, ṣ as s or sh, ṭ as t or ch, ẓ as z or zh.

a raven with pure white feathers. During one of Apollo's absences Coronis fell in love with Ischys and was unfaithful to Apollo. The raven flew off to tell him, although, according to some accounts, the raven was warned by the crow, which had also once been white, not to be so anxious to be the bearer of bad news. On hearing the tale Apollo was enraged and turned the raven's snowy feathers black; some say because the raven had not driven off Ischys by pecking his eyes out; others say it was done because Apollo was so angry with the raven for bringing bad news. Either Apollo or his sister Artemis, to whom he had complained of Coronis' unfaithfulness, shot an arrow into the breast of Coronis. As she was dying Apollo repented of his anger, and in remorse tried to save her and his unborn child, but it was too late. He sorrowfully watched as her body was laid on the funeral pyre, then hastily called Hermes and asked him to snatch the unborn child free from its mother's womb. In this manner Asclepius, for so the child was named, was saved.

Coronis. According to some accounts, a daughter of Coroneus, king of Phocis. Poseidon pursued her and she appealed to Athena for help. Athena heard her prayers and transformed her into a white crow, so some say. Afterward, Coronis spied on the daughters of Cecrops, who disobeyed Athena's orders and looked inside the chest she had given them to guard. The chest contained the infant Erichthonius. Coronis flew off and told Athena of their disobedience. In anger at her talebearing, Athena forbade her to visit the Acropolis in future. But some say Athena turned Coronis feathers black as a punishment.

Corybantes (kor-i-ban′tēz). Priests of the Great Mother goddess in Phrygia, whose worship they celebrated by orgiastic dances. From the identification of Rhea with the Asiatic Great Mother, they are often equated with the Curetes, Rhea's satellite deities, since the priests were themselves representatives of these minor fertility gods. Some say the Corybantes were the children of Apollo and the Muse Thalia; others say they were the sons of Helius and Athena or of Zeus and the Muse Calliope, or of Cronus. Still others say their mother was Rhea, and that she took them to the Holy Isle of Samothrace, and that the name of their father was revealed only to those who were initiated into the Samothracian mysteries.

Cottus (kot'us). In Greek mythology, one of the Hecaton-chires, the 100-handed giants who were the children of Uranus and Gaea. His brothers were Gyges and Briareus.

Cranaus (kran'ā-us). In Greek mythology, an earth-born man of what came to be known as Attica. He succeeded Cecrops on the throne. Cranaus had a daughter Atthis who died a maid. In her honor he named his land (formerly called Cecropia after Cecrops) Attica, after this daughter. It is said that it was during his reign that the flood of Deucalion took place in Thessaly. Amphictyon, said by some to be a son of Deucalion, and by others to be earth-born, rose against Cranaus and expelled him from Attica.

Creon (krē'on). In Greek legend, a son of Menoeceus of Thebes and a brother of Jocasta, mother and wife of Oedipus. He was ruler of Thebes after the death of Laius but when Oedipus came to Thebes and freed it of a plague by killing the Sphinx, Creon gave him the throne and his sister, the widow of Laius, in marriage, as he had promised he would do for whoever rid Thebes of the Sphinx. Plague again struck Thebes, some years later, and ominous signs pointed to Oedipus as the reason for it. He accused Creon of treachery and of spreading lies about him. But Creon was his loyal friend and when Oedipus left Thebes, having by this time learned the true reason for the plague, he left his children in Creon's care. Creon ruled until Eteocles was old enough to take the throne. In the war of the Seven against Thebes it was prophesied that Thebes would be victorious if a royal prince voluntarily sacrificed himself to Ares. Menoeceus, son of Creon, killed himself before the walls. In the fighting Eteocles was killed, Creon took command and drove the Argives back, and Thebes was saved. He ordered a magnificent funeral for Eteocles, defender of the city, but forbade anyone, on pain of death, to bury Polynices, his other nephew who had inspired the attack on Thebes. Antigone, sister of Polynices, defied his order. She crept out of the city and buried her brother. When Creon learned of her defiance he ordered her to be buried alive. His son Haemon, to whom Antigone was betrothed, killed himself on her tomb. Theseus and the Athenians, some say, compelled Creon to yield the bodies of the other Argive dead and to restore them to their families for burial. To deny proper burial to the dead was the most wicked punishment that could be devised against an enemy, because the unburied had to wander for many years on the near side of the Styx before they could be ferried across to their final resting place in Hades. Creon ruled Thebes after the death of Eteocles until Laodamas, the son of Eteocles, grew up and assumed the throne.

Creon. In Greek legend, a king of Corinth, father of Creusa, or Glauce, the intended wife of Jason. He perished when he tried to save his daughter, who was burning from the poisoned robe Medea had sent her. Creon attempted to pull the robe from his daughter and was destroyed with her.

Cressid (kres′id) or **Cressida** (kres′i-dạ). Mythical daughter of the Trojan priest Calchas, whose supposed infidelities have made her name a byword for female faithlessness. The name represents the accusative case of *Chryseis* (q.v.) The story of Cressid is believed to have originated with Benoît de Sainte-Maure, a 12th-century trouvère, who called his character Briseida (she was thus identified with Homer's Briseis). Guido delle Colonne later reproduced the story in a popular Latin work, the *Historia Trojana.* The story was later taken up by Boccaccio, Chaucer, and Shakespeare. A modern version may be found in Christopher Morley's *The Trojan Horse* (1937). Shakespeare's *Troilus and Cressida* is probably the best-known version of the tale.

Cretan Bull, The. In Greek mythology, a magnificent fierce bull, given to Minos, king of Crete, by Poseidon. Minos refused to sacrifice it to Poseidon, as he had promised to do, and as a punishment Poseidon caused Minos' wife to fall in love with the bull and to become by the bull the mother of the Minotaur. Heracles captured the bull as one of his labors for Eurystheus, and rode on its back as it swam from Crete to Greece. The bull was turned loose in Greece and roamed the countryside until it came to Marathon, where it terrified the populace. It then became known as the Marathonian Bull, and was responsible for the death of Androgeus, son of Minos. Theseus finally slew the bull.

Creusa (krẹ-ö′sạ). In Greek mythology, a daughter of Erechtheus, king of Athens, and Praxithea. Apollo fell in love with her while she was still a very young girl and ravished her. Deserted by the god, whom she had called on for aid in vain, when her time came she bore Apollo a son in secret, and abandoned the child in the cave where he was born under the Acropolis. She was soon overcome by remorse and concern for her baby and returned to the cave to recover him but he had disappeared. Even the tapestried coverlet in which he was wrapped was gone, and there were no traces of blood to show that he had been devoured by animals. Creusa carried her sad and guilty secret alone. She later married Xuthus, the son of Hellen, who had fled to Athens from Thessaly and had helped Erechtheus in a war. The Athenians looked down on him as an alien, and thought it was just as well when some time had passed and no children were born to the couple. Xuthus longed for a son and went with Creusa to consult the oracle at Delphi. He was told that he should consider the first person he met on leaving the sanctuary as his son. Ion, a young and handsome priest of Apollo, was the first person he met and Xuthus joyously claimed him. Creusa, jealous because Xuthus had a son and she didn't know what had become of her child, and also incensed to think that Xuthus had a child by another woman, resolved to slay the youth. She offered him a cup of poisoned wine, but as he poured out part of it as a libation to the gods a dove sent by Apollo flew down, drank of the wine, and instantly expired. Creusa's plot against him being exposed, Ion pursued her to the altar where she fled and would have killed her, but the priestess of Apollo appeared. She told Creusa and Ion how he had been brought by Hermes as an infant from a cave to Delphi. When she showed the coverlet in which he had been wrapped Ion was overjoyed as he thought now he would be able to trace his mother. Creusa recognized the coverlet as one she had made herself and wrapped about her new-born child in the cave. She revealed to Ion that she was his mother and a reconciliation was effected. On instructions from the priestess Creusa did not tell Xuthus that Ion was her child. She allowed him to go on thinking that he was a gift to her husband from the oracle. Later she bore Xuthus two sons, Achaeus and Dorus.

Creusa. [Also: *Glauce.*] In Greek legend, daughter of Creon, king of Corinth. Jason the Argonaut, tiring of his wife Medea, fell in love with Creusa and planned to marry her. Medea sent Creusa as a wedding gown a magic robe which, when she put it on, burned her flesh and caused her to die in terrible convulsions.

Crocus (krō′kus). According to some accounts, a youth who loved the beautiful youth Smilax. Smilax did not return his love, and the gods changed the unhappy Crocus into a saffron plant. Others say that Crocus was transformed into a saffron plant by Hermes, his friend, who had accidentally killed him while they were playing a game of quoits.

Crommyonian (krom″i-ō′ni-ạn) *Sow*. In Greek legend, a savage sow that ravaged the countryside. It was killed by Theseus as he journeyed from Troezen to Athens. The sow was sometimes called Phaea after the woman who reared it. But some say this sow was a fierce female bandit called a sow because of her greed and her notorious habits.

Cronus (krō′nus) or **Cronos** (-nos). In Greek mythology, a Titan, the youngest son of Gaea and Uranus; he was the lord of the universe before the time of the Olympian gods. Gaea incited him to attack Uranus because he had imprisoned the Cyclopes, his sons, in Tartarus. She gave Cronus a sickle which had been forged by the Telchines. He used it to cut off his father's genitals and flung them and the sickle into the sea. Once Cronus and the Titans were victorious over Uranus they released their brothers from Tartarus and made Cronus the ruler. But Cronus again bound the Cyclopes and imprisoned them, along with the Hecatonchires, in Tartarus. The reign of Cronus was so peaceful and happy it was known as the Golden Age. Iron had not been beaten into swords and shields, thus there were no wars. There were no laws and no penalties, for men lived justly without them. The earth produced spontaneously, without any effort on man's part, and men ate what the earth of itself gave them. Cronus married his sister Rhea. She bore him Hestia, Demeter, Hera, Hades, and Poseidon. But as both Gaea and the dying Uranus had prophesied that he would be dethroned by one of his children he swallowed them as soon as they were born. When her sixth child was about to be born Rhea fled to Mount Lycaeus in Arcadia and there, where no shadow is cast, gave birth to Zeus. She gave her new-born son to Gaea for safe-keeping and wrapped a stone in swaddling clothes which she presented to Cronus. He instantly swallowed it. Zeus was raised by nymphs in Crete. When he was grown he consulted Metis, a daughter of Oceanus, and learned from her how to compel Cronus to disgorge his sisters and brothers. He gave Cronus a potion which caused him to heave up first the stone which had been substituted for Zeus, and then his children. Zeus and his brothers and sisters then waged war on Cronus and the Titans, who were led by Atlas. The war lasted ten years. Then Gaea advised Zeus to free the Cyclopes and Hecatonchires from their prison in Tartarus and enlist their aid. He acted upon her advice and with their help was victorious. Cronus and the Titans were hurled into Tartarus, according to some accounts, and the Hecatonchires were set to guard them. Others say they were banished and fled to the west, where Cronus established another Golden Age in Italy and became known as Saturn. In Hades Cronus rules over Elysium. By the Oceanid Philyra, with whom he consorted in the form of a horse, Cronus was the father of Chiron the centaur. After the defeat of Cronus the universe over which he had ruled was divided among his three sons; Zeus won the sky, Hades the underworld, and Poseidon the sea. The earth remained common to all.

Crotus   (krō′tus). According to some accounts, a son of Pan by Eupheme, nurse of the Muses. He lived on Helicon, the mountain sacred to the Muses, and grew up as their beloved companion. He was a skilled archer and, at his own request, was placed among the stars as the constellation Sagittarius. But some say Crotus was a centaur.

Crow.   The bird sacred to Apollo. Its feathers were originally snow white. According to one account, Apollo changed its feathers to black to punish the crow for bringing him the news that Coronis, the mother of Asclepius, was unfaithful to him. Apollo felt the crow would have done better to peck out the eyes of his rival. Others say it was Athena who changed the crow's feathers to deepest black, for bringing her the news that Agraulos and her daughters had leaped from the Acropolis to their deaths on discovering Erichthonius, the serpent child, in the casket Athena had given them to guard. Thenceforth crows were forbidden to visit the Acropolis.

Curetes   (kū-rē′tēz). In Greek mythology, attendants of Zeus, properly in Crete, who are often wrongly identified with the Corybantes, the Cabiri, and others. The Curetes were probably characters in a ceremony to Zeus the infant, and the myth explained their noisy dance. When Zeus was taken away and hidden from Cronus, who had swallowed his other children, the Curetes danced near him and, with the noise of spears and shields, drowned his infant cries so that his father might not hear them.

Cyane (sī'ạ-nē). In mythology, a nymph of Syracuse who was a companion of Persephone. She tried to prevent Hades from carrying Persephone to the Underworld. Unsuccessful in this, she wept so that she was transformed into a fountain. Since she had lost the power of speech she could not tell Demeter, frantically searching for her daughter, what had happened to Persephone but she washed Persephone's girdle, which had dropped off as she was carried away, to Demeter's feet when the goddess came to the rim of Cyane's fountain searching for her daughter. On the spot where this occurred, the people of Syracuse annually celebrated a festival, said to have been established by Heracles, in the rites of which a bull was cast into the fountain as a sacrifice.

Cybele (sib'ẹ-lē). [Also known as **Berecynthia, Cybebe, Dindymene,** and the **Great Idaean Mother.**] An oriental goddess of Phrygia and Lydia. She came to be identified by the Greeks with Rhea, the wife of Cronus and mother of the Olympian gods, and by the Romans with Ops, wife of Saturn. She was the "Great Mother of the Gods." Early seats of her worship were Mount Ida, Mount Sipylus, Cyzicus, and Sardis. As well as being the "Great Mother of the Gods" she was the great mother of Nature, a fertility goddess symbolizing the powers of reproduction and fruitfulness in man, plants, and animals. As the goddess who presided over the wild forests and fastnesses of mountains she was worshiped on the mountains, and was conceived as traversing them in a chariot drawn by lions. As the goddess and giver of the rich treasures hidden in the earth she was worshiped in caves and grottoes. She came to be regarded as the mother of the arts of civilization and the special protectress of cities. Her priests, called Corybantes and Galli, were emasculated to commemorate the emasculation of Atys, the beloved of Cybele, and dressed like women to achieve unity with the goddess. Her festivals were celebrated with wild dances and orgiastic excesses amid the resounding music of drums and cymbals. From Asia Minor her worship spread through Thrace and thence to Greece, where it was known in Boeotia in the 6th century B.C. During the Second Punic War her cult was brought to Rome in 205–204 B.C. and established in a temple on the Palatine in obedience to a Sibylline prophecy that said that a foreign enemy could be expelled if the Great Idaean Mother was brought to Rome. The *Megalesia,* and later also the *Taurobolia* and *Criobolia,* were celebrated in Rome in her honor. The oak, pine, and lion were sacred to her. Among her other attributes were the drum, cymbals, flute, and horn. She is usually represented enthroned between lions, with a turreted crown on her head and a small drum or cymbal, the instrument used in her rites, in her hand.

Cychreus (sī'krös). In Greek mythology, a son of Poseidon and Salamis, daughter of the river-god Asopus. His daughter was Glauce, who became the wife of Telamon. Cychreus was made king of Salamis, the Serpent Isle, for slaying a destructive serpent that was ravaging the island. Some say he kept a young serpent that caused as much damage until it was expelled by Eurylochus, after which it went to Eleusis and became an attendant of Demeter. Others say it was Cychreus himself, called the "serpent" because of his cruelty, who was banished and went to Eleusis to become an attendant of Demeter. Cychreus was one of the guardian heroes of Salamis. There he was buried, facing the west, and sacrifices were offered at his tomb. In the famous naval battle between the Greeks and Persians in the bay of Salamis in 480 B.C., Cychreus was said to have appeared in serpent form among the Greek ships.

Cyclopes (sī-klō'pēz) or **Cyclops** (sī'klops). In Greek mythology, three sons of Gaea and Uranus: Arges, Brontes, and Steropes. They were giants with but one eye, which was circular and in the middle of the forehead. They were great builders, said to have built the walls of Mycenae and other fortifications, and they were master smiths, said by some to have made Artemis' silver bow. Uranus hated his one-eyed sons and hid them away in Tartarus. They were freed temporarily by Cronus after he had overthrown Uranus, but then imprisoned again, along with their brothers the Hecatonchires. Zeus made war on his father Cronus for ten years. At the suggestion of Gaea, his grandmother, he freed the Cyclopes and enlisted their aid against Cronus. The Cyclopes gave Zeus the thunderbolt, forged a trident for Poseidon, and gave Hades a cap of darkness. With these weapons and with the help of the Hecatonchires, whom Zeus also freed, the Olympian gods defeated Cronus and divided up his universe. The Cyclopes dwelt in Thrace, Crete, and Lycia, and their descendants went to Sicily, or islands near Sicily, where Odysseus ran afoul of them on his way home from the Trojan War. Aeneas also landed on the island of the Cyclopes, on his way to Ialy, but hurriedly departed on learning on what land he had come ashore. Some say the Cyclopes, or their descendants, worked in Hephaestus' forge. Apollo, to avenge the death of his son Asclepius, killed by Zeus' thunderbolt, slew the Cyclopes. Their ghosts dwell under Aetna in Sicily, and cause it to rumble and roar, and sometimes to spout flames and red-hot boulders.

Cycnus (sik′nus). In Greek mythology, a son of Poseidon and Calyce. He was born in secret and exposed by his mother on the seashore. Swans that flew down to comfort him revealed his hiding place to some fishermen, who rescued him and cared for him. He became a king of Colonae in Phrygia and married Proclea, who bore him Tenes (but some say Tenes was the son of Apollo), and a daughter Hemithea. After the death of Proclea, Cycnus married Phylonome. She tried to seduce Tenes, and when he rejected her advances she falsely accused him to his father, and produced a witness that Tenes had tried to ravish her. Cycnus put his two children in a chest and cast them into the sea. The chest floated safely to an island which Tenes named Tenedos and of which he became ruler. Later Cycnus learned that Phylonome had lied. He buried her alive and sought Tenes to ask his forgiveness. Tenes angrily cut the cables of his ship when he put in at Tenedos, but later was reconciled to him, and Cycnus settled near his son on Tenedos. Cycnus was an ally of the Trojans in the Trojan War, and when the Greeks landed in the Troad he slew them in droves. Achilles rushed up to attack him, but as he was invulnerable neither spear nor sword could make any impression on his body. Achilles flung his spear at him in vain, although each time the spear struck Cycnus, and Achilles blunted his sword on Cycnus' invulnerable flesh. In a rage Achilles battered Cycnus' head with his shield and forced him back. As he retreated Cycnus stumbled over a stone and fell on his back. Achilles planted his knees on Cycnus' chest and strangled him with the straps of his own helmet, but when he went to strip the body of its armor he found the armor empty. Poseidon had transformed his son into a swan and in that form Cycnus flew off.

Cycnus. In Greek legend, a son of Ares and Pelopia. Some say this Cycnus was in the habit of cutting off the heads of passing strangers. He used the skulls thus acquired to build a temple to his father Ares. Others say he challenged all comers to a chariot duel with him. Apollo, enraged because Cycnus stole the cattle that were being sent to Delphi for sacrifice, encouraged Heracles to accept the challenge. Heracles armed himself with the armor the gods had given him and made ready to meet Cycnus. Iolaus, Heracles' charioteer, was to fight on his side, and Ares would support Cycnus. Athena, the patroness of Heracles, warned him that though he might kill Cycnus, he must not attack Ares, a god. She then mounted the war-car with him, to protect him. Both Heracles and Cycnus were hurled from their chariots by the shock when they collided at full speed. They then took up the battle on foot. Athena protected Heracles from the sword Ares was aiming at him, and Heracles killed Cycnus. Ares rushed to attack him and, forgetting Athena's warning, he defended himself and wounded Ares in the thigh. Since it was not fitting for Heracles to attack a god, Zeus sent a thunderbolt between them and broke up the fight. Athena led Ares away to Olympus to be cured. Heracles and Iolaus stripped Cycnus of his armor. Some say this duel took place in Itonus, a city of Phthiotis. Others say it was at the Peneus River, or at Pagasae in Thessaly. And some say Cycnus was buried near the Anaurus River in Thessaly, and that Apollo caused the river to rise and wash away the gravestone.

Cyllene (si-lē′nē). In Greek mythology, a nymph who nursed Hermes in a cave on Mount Cyllene in Arcadia. Silenus and the Satyrs, who had undertaken to find Apollo's stolen cattle for him for a reward, were attracted to the cave by strange musical sounds. Cyllene told them of the marvellous infant she was guarding, who grew like a god and who had constructed a musical instrument from a tortoise shell and some hides. Silenus and the Satyrs (*The Trackers*), suspected this infant of the theft of Apollo's cattle, especially when they learned from Cyllene that he had used hides in the construction of the instrument. She hotly rebuked them for their suspicions, citing Zeus and Maia, the honest parents of her charge.

Cyrene (sī-rē′nē). In Greek mythology, a daughter of Hypseus, king of the Lapiths, and Chlidanope, a naiad. She was an ardent huntress and the guardian of her father's flocks and herds near the Peneus River. Apollo watched her wrestle with a lion and fell in love with her. He carried her away to Libya, to the site on which the city of Cyrene was founded, and made her queen of a realm in which hunters and farmers prospered. She bore Aristaeus and Idmon the seer to Apollo. When they needed her advice her sons repaired to a spring where they knew she would be visiting her naiad relatives and consulted her. By Ares, Cyrene was the mother of Diomedes of Thrace, the owner of the man-eating mares.

Cyzicus (siz'i-kus). A legendary king of the Doliones in the country of Cyzicus. Jason and the Argonauts landed there on their way to Colchis on the expedition for the Golden Fleece and were hospitably received. When the Argonauts sailed away they were driven back by unfavorable winds and, landing again on the shores of Cyzicus in darkness, were mistaken for enemies. The Argonauts were unaware that the land to which they had been driven was Cyzicus and in the struggle which followed Jason killed Cyzicus, the king who had entertained him.

D

Dactyls (dak'tilz) or **Dactyli** (dak'ti-lī) or **Daktyloi** (-loi). In Greek and Roman mythology, supernatural and magical beings living on Mount Ida in Phrygia, the discoverers of iron and copper and of the art of working them. They were transferred, in the legends, to Mount Ida in Crete, where they were said to have been born of the nymph Anchiale, as she grasped the earth with both hands, in a cave on Mount Dicte. According to this version, and a similar one in which they were born as Rhea grasped the earth in giving birth to Zeus, there were ten Dactyls, five male and five female. The males were fabulous ironworkers in Crete. The females were experts in the art of making magic spells and dwelt in Samothrace. In Crete, the Dactyls were sometimes identified with the Curetes, Corybantes, and other mountain-dwelling semi-divine beings. Their number, originally three, was increased, in various accounts, to ten, and even to 100.

Daedalus   (ded′a̯-lus, dē′da̯-lus). A legendary Athenian; son of
Metion and grandson of Erechtheus. He was a marvelous
smith, having been taught by Athena, and was regarded as
the personification of all handicrafts and of art, and as such
was worshiped by artists' guilds in various places, especially
in Attica, and was a central figure in various myths. He was
said to have made various improvements in the fine arts,
including architecture, and to have invented many mechani-
cal appliances, as the ax, the awl, and the bevel. For the
murder of his nephew Talus, of whose inventive skill he was
jealous, he was banished or escaped to Crete, where he
constructed, to contain the monster Minotaur, the famous
Labyrinth, in which he and his son Icarus were confined for
a time. In one legend the reason given for his imprisonment
is that he built a cow disguise for Pasiphaë in order that the
bull sent by Poseidon might mount her. Escaping, he and
Icarus fled over the sea on wings of wax which they had
made. Icarus, ignoring his father's warnings, soared too
near the sun; his wings melted, and he fell into the sea
(which has since been called, after him, the Icarian Sea).
Daedalus circled over the waves where he fell, recovered his
son's body and took it to a nearby island, now called Icaria.
A partridge perched nearby and watched gleefully as he
buried Icarus there. It was his sister, Polycaste, who had
been transformed into a bird when she hanged herself in
grief at the death of her son Talus, and who was now
avenged by the sight of Daedalus, the murderer of Talus,
burying his own son. In some accounts Perdix ("partridge")
is given as the name of Polycaste's son. In his flight from
Minos, Daedalus went to Cumae and there built a golden-
roofed temple. On the doors of the temple he depicted the
story of Androgeus, of the Athenians and the tribute which
they paid because of his death, of Pasiphaë, the Minotaur,
Theseus, and Ariadne, but he had not the heart to engrave
the story of his son's death. From Cumae he went to Sicily
and settled in the realm of King Cocalus. Minos, in the
meanwhile, had set out in pursuit of him. As a scheme to
trap Daedalus, Minos announced that he would give a rich
reward to whoever could run a thread through a spiraled
triton shell. Cocalus, to whom Minos had given the shell,
passed it on to Daedalus. Daedalus attached a thread to an
ant. He then bored a hole at the apex of the shell and
confined the ant in the mouth of the shell. The scent of

honey smeared on the bored hole lured the ant into traversing the coiling chambers of the shell, drawing the thread with it, until it reached the honey at the other end. When Cocalus returned the shell, with the thread running through it, to Minos and demanded his reward, Minos knew that he had found Daedalus. He demanded his surrender. Cocalus, however, refused to give him up. Still seeking the return of Daedalus, Minos died in Sicily, either in a struggle for his recapture or by being scalded to death as he lay in his bath. Daedalus ultimately joined Iolaus, the nephew of Heracles, in the colonization of Sardinia, and ended his days in that island. Many archaic wooden images were, in ancient times, believed to be the work of Daedalus (and figures of the type are still called Daedalian).

Daemon or **Demon** (dē'mọn). In Greek mythology, a term which had two significances: 1) a supernatural agent or intelligence, lower in rank than a god; a spirit holding a middle place between gods and men, as the Corybantes, Curetes, Dactyls, Satyrs, and Sileni; 2) a ministering spirit, sometimes regarded as including the souls of deceased persons, which was generally considered by the Greeks to be a protective spirit.

Damarchus (dạ-mär'kus). An Arcadian of Parrhasia. According to legend, he was transformed into a wolf at the sacrifice of Lycaean Zeus. He kept this shape for nine years, at the end of which time, because he had eaten no men, he was restored to his shape as a man. Afterward he took part in the Olympic Games and won in the boxing match. His statue was set up at Olympia. Pausanias, who tells the story of his transformation into a wolf, doubts that the story is true. If it were, he says, it would surely have been inscribed on the pedestal of his image at Olympia.

Damastes (dạ-mas'tēz). See **Procrustes**.

Damia (dam'i-ạ). Spirit of fertility, worshiped in Epidaurus and Aegina. A famine struck Epidaurus and to learn how they might find relief, the Epidaurians consulted the oracle at Delphi. The priestess told them to set up images of Damia and Auxesia (Increase). To the question whether the images should be of stone or bronze, the priestess replied that they should be made of olive wood. Having no olive trees of their own, the Epidaurians sent to Athens for permission to cut trees there. The Athenians gave permission on condition

fat, fāte, fär, fâll, ȧsk, fãre; net, mē, hėr; pin, pīne; not, nōte, mŏve, nôr; up, lūte, pull; oi, oil; ou out; (lightened) ẹlect, agǫny, ụnite;

that the Epidaurians make annual offerings to Athena Polias *(Of the City)* and Erechtheus. The Epidaurians agreed; the images were made, and the Epidaurians made the annual offerings. Afterward the Aeginetans, subjects of Epidaurus, revolted, attacked Epidaurus and seized the images, which they took to Aegina and set up there. The Epidaurians now ceased their offerings to Athena and Erechtheus. The Athenians demanded offerings from the Aeginetans on the ground that they had the images. The Aeginetans refused, and also refused to give up the images to Athens. Enraged, the Athenians sailed against Aegina, made their way to the temple, and tried to seize the images. They could not move them. They bound them with ropes and tried to haul them from the temple. Instantly a great thunderclap was heard; all the crew of the Athenian ship were struck with madness and fell upon each other with such savagery that all save one were killed. He alone returned to Athens. This is the Athenian story. But the Aeginetans say that as the Athenians made to haul off the images, the statues fell to their knees, in which position they remained ever after. Meantime the Argives, forewarned by the Aeginetans, came and cut off the retreat of the Athenians. Both agree that only one Athenian escaped. He, when he returned, was set upon by the wives of those who had been killed. As each one asked where her husband was, she jabbed the unfortunate man with the pin of her brooch. In this manner the one who had escaped from Aegina was killed by the widows of his fellows. The Athenians were so shocked by this deed of the women that henceforth the Athenian women were compelled to adopt a style of dress which required no brooches.

Danaë (dan'ā-ē). In Greek mythology, a daughter of Acrisius, king of Argos, and Aganippe. Some say that Proetus, the twin brother of Acrisius, with whom he fought in the womb, seduced Danaë. He was discovered by Acrisius and this brought on a furious quarrel, in which the brothers took up arms against each other, and Proetus was compelled to flee. Later Acrisius, who wanted a son, consulted the oracle. He was told that he would have no sons and that the son of his daughter would cause his death. To prevent the fulfillment of the oracle, Acrisius imprisoned Danaë in a bronze underground chamber so that she should have no traffic with men. His precautions were in vain. Zeus visited Danaë in a shower of gold and embraced her. She subsequently bore him a son, Perseus. Acrisius refused to believe that the child was the son of Zeus and longed for his death. But he dared not risk the wrath of the gods and the avenging Furies by killing his own grandson. He shut Danaë and her child in a chest and cast it into the sea. The chest floated safely to the shores of the island of Seriphus. Dictys, a fisherman, found the chest, opened it, and took Danaë and her son to his house. There he and his wife sheltered them and there they remained as Perseus grew up. Polydectes, king of the island and brother of Dictys, fell in love with Danaë, but as Perseus, now grown to manhood, stood in his way, he got rid of Perseus, as he thought, by sending him to fetch the head of the Gorgon Medusa. During Perseus' absence Polydectes so harassed Danaë that she, with Dictys, went into hiding to escape him. When Perseus returned and learned that his mother and Dictys had fled to a temple for refuge from Polydectes he went to the palace, exhibited the head of Medusa, and turned Polydectes and his unfriendly court to stone.

Danaidae   (dạ-nā'i-dē). In Greek mythology, descendants of Zeus and Io, the 50 daughters whom Danaus sired on various women. Their mothers were naiads, hamadryads, princesses, and other mortals. Their uncle, Aegyptus, wished them to marry his 50 sons, but Danaus, fearing a plot and on consideration of an oracular pronouncement, fled with his daughters to the Peloponnesus. With them the Danaidae took the rites of Demeter, called by the Greeks the Thesmophoria, and taught these rites to the Pelasgians (Argives). Later, however, when the inhabitants of the Peloponnesus were harried by the Dorians, the observance of the rites ceased, except in Arcadia. The Danaidae also helped the Argives to find springs, and one of them, Amymone, secured a never-failing fountain from Poseidon which is the source of the Lerna River. Danaus made himself king of Argos, and presently the sons of Aegyptus came from over the sea in pursuit of his daughters. After a siege of the city Danaus yielded to their demands to make his daughters their wives, but in secret he gave each of his daughters a sharp pin and ordered them to kill their husbands on the wedding night. All except Hypermnestra obeyed their father. She, divinely inspired, spared her husband Lynceus. The Danaidae buried their husbands' heads at Lerna and their bodies below the walls of Argos. At the command of Zeus, Athena and Hermes purified the Danaidae of the murder of their husbands. Even so, they were punished in the Underworld for their crimes. They were ordered by the judges in Tartarus forever to fetch water in jars that leaked like sieves. After their purification, Danaus sought husbands for his daughters, and awarded them to various men who took part in a foot race, the winner to have first choice, the runner-up second choice, and so on. The descendants from these marriages were known as Danaans, or Danai, a name given in honor of Danaus and sometimes applied to all Argives, and used by Homer to apply to all the Greeks who fought at Troy. According to some accounts the Danaidae, sisters of Hypermnestra, were slain by her husband Lynceus to avenge the deaths of his brothers.

Danaus (dan'ā-us). In Greek mythology, a son of Belus, king of Egypt, and Anchinoë. He was the twin of Aegyptus. Danaus, who became ruler of Libya, was the father of 50 daughters by various nymphs and mortal women. After the death of Belus, Danaus and his brother quarreled about the inheritance. Aegyptus suggested that the 50 daughters of Danaus marry his 50 sons, and thus consolidate the family power. But Danaus, warned by an oracle that he would die at the hands of a son-in-law, fled with his daughters from Libya. With the aid of Athena he built a ship; according to some, it was the first ship ever built, but others say it was the first 50-oared ship. He put to sea with his daughters and sailed to Rhodes, where he raised a temple to Athena and dedicated an image to the goddess. Some say three of his daughters—Lindus, Camirus, and Ialysus—died in Rhodes and gave their names to three cities there. Danaus next sailed to the Peloponnesus. Landing near Argos he informed the Argives, or the Pelasgians as they were also called, that he had been chosen by the gods to be their king. The Argives, who already had a king, were not disposed to accept this dictum but decided to sleep on the question. During the night a wolf attacked the herds of the Argives and killed the best bull. The Argives took this as an omen warning them to accept Danaus willingly or risk violence. Their king, Gelanor, or as some name him, Pelasgus, stepped aside and Danaus became king. In gratitude for the omen Danaus built the temple of Lycian Apollo in Argos, for

(obscured) errạnt, ardẹnt, actọr; ch, chip; g, go; th, thin; ŦH, then; y, you;
(variable) ḍ as d or j, ş as s or sh, ţ as t or ch, ẕ as z or zh.

he thought the wolf was Apollo in disguise. Danaus became a powerful ruler. He built the Acropolis of Argos and later taught the inhabitants how to dig wells, for Poseidon, enraged that Inachus had awarded the land to Hera instead of to himself, had dried up all the springs. Aegyptus now sent his 50 sons in pursuit of the daughters of Danaus, and ordered them not to return without their brides. Danaus remained adamant in his refusal to let his daughters wed their cousins. The sons of Aegyptus besieged Argos, and since there were no fountains in the citadel, Danaus was compelled to capitulate. He agreed to the marriages of his daughters, but in secret he furnished each of them with a lethal rapier and ordered them to kill their bridegrooms on the wedding night. All of his daughters except Hypermnestra obeyed his command. The daughters of Danaus buried the heads of their husbands at Lerna. Now Danaus decided to choose other husbands for his daughters. He arranged a race for the suitors of his daughters and announced that the winner would have first choice of a wife, the runner-up second choice, and so on until all his remaining daughters had husbands. This race was run on a street in Argos and was afterward celebrated by the Argives in a contest commemorating it. There were not enough contestants in the first race, as many men were reluctant to wed known murderesses, but ultimately all the daughters were wed. Their descendants were known as Danaans, or Danai, after their ancestor Danaus. Danaus met his end at the hands of the one bridegroom who had been spared among the sons of Aegyptus. He was Lynceus, who after murdering his father-in-law, took the throne.

Daphne (daf'nē). In Greek mythology, a nymph, the daughter of the river-god Peneus, or, in other accounts, of Ladon, an Arcadian. She delighted to spend her days in the forest hunting, as did the virgin goddess Artemis, and rejected all suitors for her hand. Her father pleaded with her to take a husband and give him grandsons, but Daphne became so tearful at the prospect of marriage that Peneus did not insist. But Daphne was so beautiful that many fell in love with her. Apollo, wounded by one of the arrows of Eros because the god of love wished to punish him for mocking his skill with the bow and arrow, saw Daphne and fell in love with her. Leucippus, son of Oenomaus, also loved her. Leucippus,

---

fat, fāte, fär, fâll, ȧsk, fāre; net, mē, hėr; pin, pīne; not, nōte, möve, nôr; up, lūte, pull; oi, oil; ou out; (lightened) ẹlect, agǫny, ụnite;

seeing that he could make no progress with Daphne, disguised himself as a maiden and joined Daphne and the nymphs in their hunting expeditions in order to be near the object of his adoration. Apollo, jealous of Leucippus' proximity to Daphne, suggested that the nymphs bathe naked in the mountain stream, and thus Leucippus' disguise was betrayed, whereupon the nymphs tore him to pieces. Apollo then pursued Daphne when she was separated from her companions. She fled from him in terror, some say because Eros had shot her with the arrow that drives away love. The more Apollo called to her of his love, the faster she flew from him. Nearly at the end of her strength in her flight, she approached the Peneus River and called out to her father to save her from the embraces of Apollo. Her prayer was answered. As Apollo was about to clasp her in his arms, she was transformed into a laurel tree. He embraced the tree, still quivering from the chase, and declared that its leaves would always be green and that he would always bind them around his head in memory of his love for Daphne. From then on the laurel wreath replaced the oak wreath as the prize to the victors in Apollo's festival of the Pythian Games, and laurel became the symbol of victory.

aphnis (daf'nis). In mythology, a son of Hermes and a Sicilian nymph. He was exposed by his mother in a laurel grove, but was found and brought up by shepherds. Pan taught him to sing and play the flute, the Muses endowed him with a love of poetry, and he was the companion of Apollo and Artemis. He was a shepherd who tended his flocks in Sicily. A nymph, Nomia, fell in love with him, and made him swear to be faithful to her. One of her rivals, Chimaera, made him drunk and then seduced him. When Nomia heard of it she blinded him. Daphnis, who is said to have invented pastoral or bucolic poetry, mourned the loss of his sight in song and Hermes took pity on him and transformed him into stone and caused a spring, named Daphnis, to flow from the earth near his home in Sicily. Annual sacrifices were offered there in memory of Daphnis.

ardanus (där'da̲-nus). In Greek mythology, a son of Zeus and the Pleiad Electra, and the ancestor of the Trojans. He migrated from Arcadia to Phrygia and built a city near the foot of Mount Ida, which he named Dardania. He brought with him to the Troad the sacred images of the gods which

had formed part of his wife's dowry, and instituted their
worship into the region. According to an oracle, his city
would remain safe as long as the images remained in it. The
city which Dardanus founded later became part of Ilium, or
Troy. The children of Dardanus were Erichthonius, Ilus,
Deimas, Idaeus, and one daughter, Idaea.

Deianira (dē-yạ-nī'rạ). In Greek mythology, a supposed
daughter of Oeneus, king of Calydon, and Althaea, but actually Dionysus was her father. After the death of her brother
Meleager, Artemis changed his grieving sisters into guinea
hens, but Dionysus persuaded the goddess to let Deianira
and Gorge keep their human forms. Heracles, on a journey
to the Underworld to fetch Cerberus, promised Meleager
that he would marry Deianira on his return to earth. After
some years he went to Calydon and fought Achelous, the
river-god and an unwelcome suitor of Deianira, and won her
hand. She bore him Hyllus, Hodites, Glenus, possibly Ctesippus, and his only daughter, Macaria. On a journey from
Calydon to Trachis, Deianira and Heracles came to the
Evenus River. Here Nessus, a centaur, offered to ferry
Deianira across on his back. He did so and attempted to
ravish her. Heracles shot him with one of his poisoned arrows. Before he died Nessus secretly told Deianira to preserve his blood, that it would be a powerful love charm by
which she would hold Heracles if his interest ever strayed to
another woman. Deianira gathered up the blood and kept it.
When Heracles left to wage war on Eurytus of Oechalia he
told Deianira that he would return at the end of fifteen
months and pass the rest of his days peacefully or, at the end
of that time, he would be dead. He was successful in his war
against Eurytus, and sent Iole, daughter of Eurytus, back to
Deianira as his captive and his concubine. Deianira, although she had nothing but sympathy for the young and
beautiful captive, decided that the time had come to make
use of the love charm Nessus had given her. She rubbed it
on a robe which Heracles had sent his herald Lichas to fetch
so that he could wear it as he sacrificed to Zeus at Cenaeum
and gave the robe to Lichas. After the herald had left, she
noticed that a bit of wool with which she had anointed the
robe had fallen to the ground and had caused the ground
to smoulder. In fear she tried to recall Lichas but it was too
late. Heracles received the robe, put it on, and soon his body

was burning with the poison of the Hydra with which Heracles had coated the arrow that killed Nessus. When Deianira learned that Nessus had merely sought revenge by telling her of the love charm, and of the effect it had on Heracles, she hanged herself. Thus the poisoned robe killed Heracles long after Nessus had died, in accordance with a prophecy that no living man could kill him, but that he would fall at the hands of a dead enemy. Deianira was the innocent tool of that dead enemy, Nessus.

Deimos (dī′mos). Fear, or Terror, personified in the *Iliad,* and later regarded as a son of Ares.

Deïphobus (dē-if′ō-bus). In Greek legend, a son of Priam and Hecuba, and one of the great heroes of the Trojan War. He led a group at the siege of the Greek fortifications and slew many. He himself was wounded by Meriones. As Hector was fleeing around the walls of Troy before Achilles, Athena assumed the shape of Deïphobus and encouraged Hector to make a stand against Achilles. But when Hector hurled his spear in vain at Achilles, and turned to his supposed brother for another one, Deïphobus had disappeared, and Hector knew that the gods had forsaken him. After the death of Paris, Helen was given to Deïphobus because of his deeds in the war. He married her by force. When the Wooden Horse had been dragged inside the walls of Troy, Deïphobus accompanied Helen, who walked around it and imitated the voices of the wives of the Greeks in an attempt to find out whether there were actually Greeks hiding inside the horse. Menelaus and Odysseus prevented the Greeks inside from answering Helen's calls and convinced the Trojans that the Horse was indeed a divine gift. In the sack of Troy Deïphobus was slain, and his body terribly mutilated, either by Menelaus or Odysseus. According to the *Aeneid,* Aeneas met his shade in the Underworld and learned that he had been betrayed by Helen, who revealed his hiding place to Menelaus and Odysseus. Other accounts say that it was Helen herself who killed him, by stabbing him.

Dejaneira (dej-a-nī′ra). See **Deianira.**

Delphinus (del-fī′nus). In Greek mythology, an agent of Poseidon who followed Amphitrite to the Atlas Mountains, whither she had fled to escape the attentions of Poseidon. He pleaded Poseidon's cause so successfully that Amphitrite yielded and agreed to marry Poseidon. As a reward for his

services, Poseidon placed Delphinus among the stars, where
he was known in ancient times as the constellation Dolphir

Delphyne   (del-fī'nē). In Greek mythology, a monstrous earth
born serpent who guarded the oracle at Delphi and, accord
ing to some accounts, gave the site his name. Apollo sle
Delphyne at Delphi, and made the oracle his own from tha
time forth. The serpent is also known as *Python*.

Demeter   (dē-mē'tẽr). One of the great Olympian deities; th
golden-haired giver of the fruits and flowers of the earth
protectress of social order and of marriage, she was "Mothe
Earth," "the Good Goddess," and the great benefactress o
mankind. The gentle goddess of the fertility of the earth an
of man was called "the greatest help and cause of joy to th
undying gods and mortal men." In the Greek theogony sh
is one of the most important and revered of the gods, an
her mysteries are among the holiest of the Greek rites.

Demeter was the second child of Cronus and Rhea, an
like the first, Hestia, was swallowed by Cronus as soon as sh
was born. Zeus, with the aid of Metis, caused Cronus t
disgorge her, along with his sisters and brothers. In he
youth, some say, Demeter, during the wedding festivities o
Cadmus and Harmonia, lay with Iasion, son of Electra an
Zeus, in a thrice-plowed field and bore Plutus *(Wealth)* t
him. Some say the thrice-plowed field where Iasion love
Demeter was a fertile district in Crete. And some say Zeu
slew Iasion with a thunderbolt because he embraced th
goddess. But others say Iasion was slain by his brother Dai
danus. By her brother Zeus, Demeter was the mother o
Iacchus and Core *(The Maid)*, who is widely known as Perse
phone, and some say that it was she who bore Dionysus t
Zeus. The rape of Persephone by Hades is the heart of th
legend and worship of Demeter, symbolizing as it does th
death and rebirth, or disappearance and reappearance, o
the nourishing produce of the earth.

According to the myth, Hades saw Persephone an
desired her. (Some say it was Aphrodite, wishing to exten
her sway over Tartarus as well as over Earth and Sea, wh
caused her son Eros to shoot his arrows into the heart o
Hades and awaken love for Persephone in him.) With th
connivance of Zeus, who did not like to thwart his brothei
Hades planned to seize Persephone. One day as she wa
gathering flowers with her maidens, Persephone wandere

fat, fāte, fär, fâll, àsk, fãre; net, mē, hẽr; pin, pīne; not, nōte, möv
nôr; up, lūte, pùll; oi, oil; ou out; (lightened) ẽlect, agǫny, ūnit

away from them, enticed by a strange and beautiful flower, which some say was a kind of narcissus. As she bent to pluck the flower the earth parted; a great chariot drawn by black horses thundered forth, swept down on Persephone, and the black-clad charioteer swept her into his car. She cried out for help but her companions neither heard her nor saw the stranger who carried her off, for the chariot flew over the meadow and disappeared in a chasm that opened in the earth. The Sicilians say that the abduction took place near Enna, in Sicily. Others claim it was at Colonus in Attica, or at Hermion in Argolis, or at Pisa, Lerna, Pheneüs, Nysa, or Crete, but the priests of Demeter say it was at Eleusis. Demeter was heartbroken when she learned of the disappearance of her daughter. For nine days she searched frantically for her, carrying blazing torches through the night and stopping neither to eat nor to bathe. Of all those she questioned, gods and men, none would tell her the truth. On the ninth day she met Hecate, who said she had heard Persephone's cries, but when she rushed up to assist her, she had disappeared without a trace. Together, Demeter and Hecate went in search of Helius and questioned him on whether in his passage through the skies he had seen anything. Helius told Demeter that Hades had carried off Persephone with the consent of Zeus, and he advised Demeter not to grieve, for the ruler of Tartarus was not an unworthy son-in-law. But some say that Demeter, as she wandered about looking for Persephone, learned from the people of Hermion that it was Hades who had carried off her child, and the chasm through which he disappeared into the earth in their land was the same one by which Heracles dragged Cerberus to the upper air from Tartarus. And some say that the nymph Cyane, in Sicily, saw Hades as he prepared to steal Persephone, and that she attempted, without success, to stop him. Afterward, in grief, Cyane was transformed into a fountain, so that when Demeter came her way, she was unable to tell the goddess what had happened, but on the waters of her fountain she caused Persephone's girdle, dropped when she was caught up into Hades' chariot, to float. Demeter saw the girdle and knew that Persephone had passed that way. In any event, when Demeter learned that it was by the consent of the gods that Hades had abducted Persephone, she left Olympus and wandered all over the face of the earth to search for her. As she roamed through Arcadia, Poseidon saw her and pursued her. Demeter, weary and grief-stricken wished to elude Poseidon and his amorous intentions. She transformed herself into a mare and grazed with the mares of Oncus. But Poseidon would not be denied. He changed himself into a stallion and ravished her. From this union was born the marvelous horse, Arion, and a girl child whose name it was unlawful to utter, but some say this child's name was Despoena. Demeter was so infuriated by the outrage of Poseidon that the people of the region gave her the name Erinnys *(Fury)*, but afterward her rage subsided, and she cleansed herself by bathing in the Ladon River, whence her epithet Lusia *(Bather)*. In her temple at Thelpusa, in Arcadia, were two images, one for each of these names. The images had face, hands, and feet of marble, but the body was of wood. Also in Arcadia, Demeter went to the city of Pheneüs and was received kindly by the inhabitants. To reward them she gave them every kind of pulse except the bean, which was considered to be impure by the Pheneatians. Wherever she was treated kindly in her wanderings, Demeter rewarded the people, as she gave the fig tree to Phytalus who welcomed her when she stopped beside the Cephissus River on the Isthmus. The Argives say that when she came to Argos, Pelasgus received her, and that one Chrysanthis knowing of the rape of Persephone, told it to her. Disguised as a humble old woman she came to Eleusis. Some say it was in the reign of King Pandion of Athens that she came to Eleusis; others say it was when Erechtheus, son of Pandion was king that wheat was first sown by Triptolemus, and that the mysteries of Demeter were first celebrated by Eumolpus. On the road from Megara to Eleusis she sat down on a rock called *Laughless* because of her sorrow when she rested on it. Nearby was a well where the inhabitants came to draw water; some name this well Anthium *(Flowery)* and some name it Callichorum *(Well of Fair Dances)*. While the goddess rested here the four daughters of Celeus came to fetch water. They saw the sad old woman and spoke kindly to her and asked her what fortune had brought her to their land. Demeter told them she had escaped from pirates who had carried her away from her home in Crete and intended to sell her as a slave, and that she had made her way alone to this place seeking refuge. She asked the maidens if the knew a house where she might be welcome as a nurse or helper. The daughters of Celeus said there were many who would be glad to welcome her, but that they would like best to have her come to their father's house, and asked her to wait while they went and consulted with their mother. They soon returned and invited Demeter to go home with them. When she entered the doorway of Celeus' house, a heavenly radiance glowed about her. Metanira, wife of Celeus, was awed by the sight, and asked her to be seated, but Demeter would take only the lowliest stool, denying herself all comforts in her grief. The family of Celeus welcomed her warmly, but she seemed so sad that Iambe, the lame daughter of Celeus, made bawdy jokes and caused her to smile, and Baubo, nurse of the new-born son of the house, Demophoön, gave her barley water flavored with mint, and to make her laugh, Baubo groaned as if in labor, and suddenly produced Demeter's own son Iacchus from beneath her skirt. The child leaped into his mother's arms and kissed her. Because of the kindly efforts of these two to cheer Demeter in her grief, it became the custom to make broad jests at Demeter's feast of the Thesmophoria, and the cup of mint-flavored barley water was the cup offered to worshipers at the great mysteries of Eleusis. As Demeter drank, Abas, an older son of Celeus, mocked her because she drank so thirstily. Some say she threw the liquid in his face, in her anger, and transformed him into a spotted lizard, and some say that it was by a look alone that he was transformed into an animal that needs very little water and slithered away before his stricken mother's eyes. Demeter became the nurse of Demophoön, and because of the kindness of his parents, she decided to make the child immortal. Under her care he flourished like a god. By day she fed him ambrosia, and each night she plunged him into the fire to burn away his mortal parts. One night as she was engaged in this ritual, she was surprised by his mother, who cried out in fear and broke the spell. Some say Demeter dropped the child, revealed herself in all the glory of her godhead, and told Metanira and her astonished household who she was. Now, she said, she could not make Demophoön immortal, but because he had been nursed by a goddess, great honor would come to him. Others say that when she dropped the child, he was consumed in the fire, and to make up for the loss of this son, Demeter

promised to make his brother Triptolemus immortal. Som
say she chose to confer immortality on Triptolemus becaus
he had recognized her as a goddess, and had told her tha
some days before his brothers—Eumolpus and Eubuleus–
had seen the earth open, and into it a chariot bearing
blackclad figure clasping a maiden had disappeared. Thi
had happened as they were tending their father's swine an
cattle in the fields, and Eumolpus had made a song about th
event. It is because of this that the priests of Demeter say th
rape of Persephone took place at Eleusis. Demeter com
manded Celeus to raise a temple to her at Eleusis, an
instructed him and Eumolpus, as well as Triptolemus, in he
mysteries. (Later, when Heracles came to Eleusis, she estab
lished the Lesser Mysteries in his honor.) Then she sat in he
temple and mourned her lost daughter. At her command th
earth became barren; men plowed, but as fast as the plant
sprang from the soil they withered. Some say this continue
for a year, and then Zeus sent Iris to persuade her to retur
to Olympus, and to restore fertility to the earth, for he di
not wish mankind to die, nor to lose the rich sacrifices an
gifts men made to the gods of Olympus. But Demeter ig
nored his messenger because he had turned his head whil
Hades seized Persephone; and when the gods themselve
bearing gifts, came and tried to persuade her she sti
refused to return to Olympus, and declared the earth mus
remain barren until Persephone was restored to her. At las
Zeus sent Hermes to Hades with an order to him to restor
Persephone to her mother; and from Hades Hermes went t
Demeter to inform her that Persephone would be returne
on condition that she had not eaten anything while she wa
in Tartarus. When Hades received his message, he had n
choice but to let Persephone go, but he spoke regretfully t
her, and reminded her that it was no small thing to be hi
wife and a queen in Tartarus. Hermes came to fetch her; a
she set out Ascalaphus, a gardener in Tartarus, said that h
had seen her eat some seeds of a pomegranate, and there
fore, as she had eaten of the food of the dead, she mus
return to the world of the dead. Demeter was overjoye
when Persephone returned to her at Eleusis, but was im
mediately downcast when she learned of the pomegranat
seeds, and hurled a great stone on Ascalaphus for his tale
bearing. She refused to restore fruitfulness to the earth

fat, fāte, fär, fâll, ȧsk, fãre; net, mē, hėr; pin, pīne; not, nōte, mōve
nôr; up, lūte, pùll; oi, oil; ou out; (lightened) ḝlect, agǫny, ūnit

Persephone was compelled to return to the Underworld. In the end a compromise was worked out by Rhea; Persephone, having eaten some of the food of the dead in the form of the pomegranate seeds (some say she ate seven), must spend one third of the year in the kingdom of the dead; the rest of the time she could spend with her mother. On this basis, with Hecate watching to see that the agreement was faithfully carried out, the matter was settled, and Demeter returned to her home among the gods. But before she left Eleusis she gave Triptolemus the gift of wheat and a wooden plow, and taught him the arts of sowing and threshing on the Rharian Plain in a place that came to be known as the "Threshing Floor," and which annually ever after was plowed in commemoration of this event. Then, in a car drawn by winged dragons, she sent him all over the earth to teach men how to cultivate crops. The time that Persephone spends with her mother represents the time of the sowing, growing, and harvesting of crops; the time when she must reign as a queen in the kingdom of the dead is the period of barren and blasted fields. The great Eleusinian Mysteries, among the holiest rites celebrated by the Greeks, were established at Eleusis by Demeter herself. When Athens conquered Eleusis, the Athenians won the right to share in them, and Eleusinia were also established in the other Greek states, but those at Eleusis were always the most sacred. The mysteries are thought to have been a reënactment of the suffering and grief of Demeter over the loss of her daughter, and of her joy when Persephone was restored. By extension, the mysteries and their symbolism were an expression of the idea of the immortality of the soul. But the rites of the mysteries were a well-kept secret; only the initiated knew them and they never betrayed the secret.

Demeter is a kind and gentle goddess, the giver of good to man. She takes no part in war and strife, and seldom is aroused to wrath. Erysichthon, however, did feel her just anger. He cut down a tree, the home of a nymph, in her sacred grove. Demeter appeared to him, disguised as her own priestess, and remonstrated with him when she heard the cries of the nymph, but Erysichthon defied her and proceeded to cut down her sacred trees. To punish him, Demeter sent insatiable hunger to destroy him.

Eleusis and Athens were the most ancient seats of the

worship of Demeter, but she was worshiped througho
Greece; and Sicily, noted for its fertility, was said to be o
of her favorite haunts. Among her many names, Demet
was called Black Demeter, for the time, during the loss
Persephone, when she clothed herself in black and went in
seclusion in a cave in Phigalia in Arcadia. The Phigalians s
that after Poseidon, in the form of a stallion, ravished Dem
ter, disguised as a mare, she clothed herself in black and h
in this cave. The Phigalians later set up an image in the cav
it was a figure of a woman seated on a rock, but instead
a woman's head it had a horse's head, out of which gre
serpents and other beasts. In one of her hands the ima
held a dolphin, in the other, a dove. This was the ima
called "Mare-headed Demeter." She was known as "Cal
rea" because she instructed the Cabiri of Thebes in her rit
and entrusted a sacred thing into their keeping. Because
her connection with the kingdom of the dead through t
annual loss of Persephone she was called Chthonia *(Of t
Lower World),* and a festival of the same name was held ann
ally in her honor. She was widely known as Eleusinian De
eter and had many sanctuaries in this name. *
Thesmophorus *(Law-giver),* she was worshiped at the gre
festival of the Thesmophoria, and had many sanctuarie
She was also called Lernaea *(Of Lerna)* because, some sa
Hades disappeared into the earth with Persephone at Lern
Carpophorus *(Fruit-bearer)*; Malophorus *(Sheep-bearer* or *A
ple-bearer)*; Mycalessia *(Of Mycalessus),* after the city in B
eotia where her sanctuary was said to be opened ea
morning and closed each night by Heracles the Dact
Mysia, from Mysius, an Argive who entertained her; Pan
chaea *(All Achaea)* from her sanctuary in Aegium, in Achae
Pelasgis, because Pelasgus founded a sanctuary for her
Argos; Stiria or Stiritis *(Of Stiris)* from her sanctuary at t
place in Phocis; Thermasia *(Warmth)*; Thesmia *(Law-gi
dess)*; Chloë *(Green)*; and Anesidora *(Sender-up of Gifts).*

The festivals of Demeter, celebrated in conjunction wi
rites for her daughter Persephone, were the Gre
Eleusinian Mysteries and the Thesmophoria. Fruit, hone
the cow and the sow were offered to her. Her attributes we
the poppy, a flower that grows with the wheat and is also
symbol of sleep and death, and stalks of wheat. In art she w
sometimes also depicted with a basket of fruit and a pigle

or with a torch or a serpent. The Romans of the end of the Republic and of the empire assimilated to the Greek conception of Demeter the primitive Italic chthonian divinity Ceres.

miphon (dem'i-fon). According to legend, a king whose and was smitten by a pestilence. He was commanded by an oracle to sacrifice one noble maiden each year and the pestilence would be lifted. Annually thereafter one noble maiden's name was drawn by lot and she was sacrificed. At last one Mastusius, whose daughter was sacrificed, learned that the names of Demiphon's own daughters were never placed among the lots to be drawn. He invited Demiphon and his daughters to a banquet and had the daughters murdered. He then served Demiphon with a cup containing their blood. When Demiphon discovered the horrible deed, he caused Mastusius and the cup to be hurled into the sea.

modocus (dẹ-mod'ọ-kus.) In the *Odyssey,* a blind minstrel of Alcinous, king of the Phaeacians. It was said of him that the gods took away his sight but gave him in its place the great gift of song. During the stay of Odysseus at the court of Alcinous he delighted the guests by recounting the feats of the Greeks at Troy, but as he sang of the quarrel between Odysseus and Achilles, Odysseus, whose true identity was unknown to Alcinous, wept. At the request of Odysseus Demodocus sang of the Wooden Horse, and ended with singing of the amours of Aphrodite and Ares.

spoena (des-pē'nạ). The name, meaning "the Mistress," given by the Arcadians to the daughter of Demeter and Poseidon. This goddess may be identified with Persephone, who is usually described as the daughter of Zeus and Demeter. Pausanias indicates his unwillingness to identify "the Mistress," but mentions Persephone as "the Maid." *Despoena* appears also as an epithet of Aphrodite and Demeter. The Arcadians worshiped Despoena more than any other gods. In their sanctuary of the Mistress near Acacesium, there were altars to Demeter and Despoena, and an image of them. The images, along with the throne and pedestal for them, were carved from one block of stone. The Arcadians had dug this huge stone from the earth in obedience to a command given in a dream. Next to Demeter stood Artemis clad in a deer skin and accompanied by a hunting dog. Next to Despoena stood Anytus, a Titan who was thought to have reared her. The Arcadians made offerings of all kinds of cultivated fruits except the pomegranate. In the sacred grove behind the sanctuary an oak and an olive tree grew from the same root. Also in the precinct there was an altar of Poseidon Hippius, the father of Despoena.

Deucalion (dū-kā'li-ọn). In Greek mythology, a son of Prometheus and king of Phthia. Because of the wickedness of mankind Zeus determined to send a flood to destroy the evil race of man. Deucalion, who because of his piety was intended to found a new race, was warned by Prometheus of the impending destruction. He and his wife Pyrrha, the daughter of Epimetheus took refuge in a huge chest. Rather than set the earth afire with his thunderbolts, and risk destroying the heavens as well, Zeus enlisted the aid of Poseidon in his plan to destroy mankind. For nine days the rains fell, the winds blew, and the sea washed over the earth, inundating villages and farms and drowning all the inhabitants. At the end of that time the waters began to recede and the chest in which Deucalion and Pyrrha had ridden out the flood came to rest on Mount Parnassus. Now the water subsided, the winds ceased, and the earth was restored to its normal appearance, but as far as he could tell Deucalion and his wife were the only living creatures left in the land. Near the banks of the Cephissus River they found a temple still standing and entered it. Deucalion thanked the gods for saving him from the flood and prayed to Themis that the earth would be repeopled. Themis heard their prayers and instructed them, through an oracle, to leave the temple, veil their heads, loosen the girdles of their garments, and throw the bones of their mother behind them. Deucalion interpreted this to mean that their mother was the earth and that stones were her bones. They veiled their heads, loosened their garments, and picked up stones which they cast over their shoulders behind them. After a short time the stones were transformed: those which Deucalion had cast became men; those thrown by Pyrrha became women. Soon the land was repopulated, and animals, birds, and insects sprang up from the muddy earth which presently recovered its customary verdure. Thus a new and, it was to be hoped, better race of man populated the earth. Deucalion was the father of Orestheus, Amphictyon, and Hellen.

Diana (dī-an'ạ). Ancient Italian divinity, goddess of the moon, protectress of the female sex, later identified with the

Greek Artemis. Like Artemis she was goddess of the hunt and the woods, protectress of chastity, and patroness of childbirth. She was called Luna, as goddess of the moon; Hecate, as an infernal deity, invoked in magic rites; and Diana, as goddess of the chase.

ce (dī'sē) or ***Dike*** (dī'kē). In Greek mythology, one of the Horae, the personification of justice; daughter of Zeus and Themis *(Law)*, and sister of Irene *(Peace)* and Eunomia *(Order)*.

ctynna (dik-tin'a̯). A Cretan goddess, identified with Britomartis. She was the protectress of hunters and seafarers. In Sparta she was identified with Artemis; the Aeginetans worshiped her as Aphaea; but the Samians, who built her a temple at Cydonia, in Crete, worshiped her as Dictynna.

omedes (dī-ọ-mē'dēz). In Greek legend, the "high-souled" son of Tydeus and Deïpyle. He was a king in Argos and was one of the Epigoni—the sons of the Seven against Thebes—who successfully attacked Thebes and avenged their fathers. In fulfillment of the oath he had taken as an ardent suitor of Helen—to protect whomever she should choose as a husband—he rallied to Menelaus when Helen was carried off by Paris. In the war which followed he was one of Agamemnon's most loyal supporters. He went with Sthenelus and Euryalus to Troy as the commander of a great fleet of 80 ships carrying warriors from Argos, Tiryns, Hermione, Asine, Troezen, Eionae, Epidaurus, Aegina, and Mases. He was the darling of Athena, and next to Achilles was the mightiest of the Greek heroes. To his own reckless courage the goddess added unparalleled strength, marvelous skill at arms, and unfailing valor. He was fearless and at times held off the Trojans single-handed. When he was wounded by Pandarus, Athena saved his life and restored him. Later she guided the spear with which he killed Pandarus. He felled Aeneas with a huge stone and would have killed him, but Aphrodite came and saved her son. Undaunted by the interference of a goddess, Diomedes pursued her, wounded her, and drove her from the field. Athena now encouraged him to attack Ares. He caught the spear which Ares hurled at him and in his turn turned on Ares, wounded him and forced the god of war to quit the field. In addition to attacking the gods, he killed many Trojans. In the savage fighting he came face to face with Glaucus, the companion of the Lycian king

Sarpedon. As they squared off to fight, each boasted of h
ancestry and prowess, and thus it was that they discovere
that their grandfathers had been friends. They put dow
their weapons and swore an oath of friendship. To bind th
oath, they exchanged arms. In this Diomedes got by far th
better bargain. He gave Glaucus his bronze armor. Glauc
graciously, but foolishly, handed over his own armor of pu
gold. Several times when the war went against the Greek
Agamemnon proposed that they give up the struggle and g
home. This was a purely psychological gambit. Agamemno
knew he could count of the fearless Diomedes to rega
such a suggestion as a personal insult and to rally the Gree
to fight harder than ever. Diomedes was one of those wh
accepted Hector's challenge to a duel, but he was eliminate
in the drawing of the lots. He rescued Nestor from Hector
attack and was prevented from pursuing Hector only by th
thunderbolt of Zeus. He accused Agamemnon of cowardi
when the latter, believing the gods favored the Trojan
wanted to leave Troy, and volunteered to go with Odysse
as a spy on the Trojan camp. On this expedition they ca
tured and killed Dolon, a Trojan spy, raided the Troja
camp and slew Rhesus, a king of Thrace and an ally of Tro
captured his marvelous horses, and returned safely to th
Greek camp. This patrol with Odysseus was one of many. H
and Odysseus went to Lemnos to fetch Philoctetes, th
owner of the arrows of Heracles, when it was learned th
Troy could not be taken without them. Accompanied b
Phoenix, they next went to Scyrus and successfully pe
suaded Neoptolemus, son of Achilles, to join the Greeks
Troy. The last mission was to steal from the citadel of Tro
the Palladium, which guarded Troy as long as it remaine
in the city. In rags and tatters they made their way to th
walls of the city. Diomedes, according to some account
climbed on Odysseus' shoulders but refused to pull Ody
seus up after him. He scaled the wall and entered the ci
alone, found and stole the Palladium, and rejoined Ody
seus at the wall. As they were returning, Diomedes, who wa
carrying the Palladium ahead of Odysseus, caught a glint
moonlight reflected from Odysseus' naked sword. H
whirled around in time to see Odysseus with his swor
raised ready to strike him. Odysseus had planned to murde
Diomedes so that he could return alone and reap the glo

of having stolen the Palladium. Diomedes now laid about Odysseus' flanks and sides with the flat of his sword. Odysseus had no choice but to run before him, howling miserably from the whacks of Diomedes' sword, and in this undignified manner he was driven back into the Greek camp. From this incident arises the expression "Diomedes' complusion"—to do something because necessity leaves no choice. Some say Diomedes, cousin of Thersites, was the only one who mourned him when he was slain by Achilles for mocking the latter as he grieved over the death of Penthesilea. Diomedes in a rage seized Penthesilea's body by the foot, dragged it to the river, and hurled it in. Her body was rescued and restored to the Trojans for burial. He was one of those who entered Troy in the Wooden Horse, and after the sack of the city, was, according to some accounts, one of the few who had a prosperous voyage home to Greece. Others say Aphrodite caused him to be shipwrecked on the coasts of Lycia, and that he was saved from being sacrificed by the king only through the good offices of the king's daughter, who helped him to escape. Arrived in Argos he found that his wife, Aegiale, had been unfaithful to him, largely owing to false reports spread by Nauplius. She and her lover drove him out of his kingdom. He went to Corinth, and then to Calydon and restored his grandfather, Oeneus, to his throne. Ultimately he sailed to Italy and settled in Daunia. He married Euippe, daughter of King Daunus and founded many cities, among them Brundisium. The Latins asked his help in their war against Aeneas, who had also come to Italy. Diomedes cited the suffering the Greeks had endured during and after the Trojan War, and said he had had enough of fighting Trojans. As he refused to lend his aid to the Latins, he advised them, out of his own experience, to make peace with Aeneas and his Trojan followers. According to some accounts, Diomedes was murdered by King Daunus, who had become jealous of the wealth and power he had acquired in Italy, and he was secretly buried on the Diomedan Islands. Others say he was divinely spirited away, and that his followers were transformed into gentle birds which nest on these islands. The golden armor that he got from Glaucus was preserved by the priests of Athena in Apulia, and he was worshiped as a god in southern Italy and in the region around Venice.

Dione (dī-ō′nē). In early Greek mythology, the consort
Zeus; his feminine counterpart as sky-deity, supplanted
Hera. In later mythological genealogy, she is a female Tita
daughter of Oceanus and Tethys. In the *Iliad,* she is name
as the mother of Aphrodite, who comforted Aphrodite whe
the latter was attacked and wounded by Diomedes in th
Trojan War. Dione foretold the death of Diomedes for wa
ing war against immortals.

Dionysus (dī-ō-nī′sus). God of the vine, and youngest of th
Olympian gods. He was the son of Zeus and Semele, and th
only god to have a mortal for a parent. Zeus fell in love wi
Semele, a daughter of Cadmus, and the sister of Ino, Agav
and Autonoë. He visited her in mortal guise, although h
assured her that he was the god Zeus. A few months befo
it was time for her child to be born, Semele, inspired there
by jealous Hera who had taken the guise of Semele's nur
for the purpose, pleaded with Zeus to appear to her in th
same majesty he showed to Hera, and thus prove to her th
her lover was really a god. Zeus tried to persuade her to a
any other boon, but Semele insisted this was the only boo
she craved. Since he had sworn by the Styx, the most sacre
of oaths, that he would grant whatever she asked, Zeus a
peared to her in blazing majesty, armed with the awful thu
derbolts. Mortal Semele could not stand the divine fire an
was burned to ashes, but Zeus snatched her unborn chi
from her womb and sewed it up in his thigh. When the chi
reached maturity, he was born from the thigh of Zeus. B
cause he had been taken from his mother and also fro
Zeus, Dionysus was sometimes called the child of "the do
ble door," or given the epithet "Twice-born." But some sa
this epithet came from another circumstance. They say h
was born with a horn growing from his head, around whic
serpents twined, and that Hera commanded the Titans
seize him. This they did, although he transformed himse
into various shapes to escape, and tore him to pieces. H
grandmother Rhea gathered up the fragments of his bod
which the Titans had boiled in a cauldron, and restored hi
to life. (A similar story is told of Zagreus, with who
Dionysus is identified.) Others say, to save his son fro
Hera, who always sought to destroy her rival's child, Zen
gave him to the nymphs Philia, Coronis, and Clide, to re
on the isle of Naxos. Still others say Zeus gave him

Hermes, with orders to convey him to Ino and her husband
Athamas in Thebes. Ino disguised him as a girl and reared
him in secret. But Hera unmasked the secret and drove Ino

ZEUS DRAWING DIONYSUS FROM HIS THIGH IN THE PRESENCE
OF HERMES
Red-figured Attic lecythus, c450 B.C.
Museum of Fine Arts, Boston

and Athamas mad. Zeus saved Ino for her kindness to
Dionysus by transforming her into the sea-goddess Leucothea. To protect Dionysus from the wrath of Hera, Zeus now
transformed him into a kid and Hermes transported him to
the nymphs of Nysa, who cared for him. Some say these
nymphs were afterward placed among the stars as the
Hyades, to reward them, and that these stars rise in the rainy
season that makes the vine grow. Nysa has never been definitely located: Asia, Ethiopia, Libya, Egypt, and Mount Helicon in Greece, as well as other places where the vine is
cultivated, have all been named as the site which held the
cave of Nysa where Dionysus was nurtured. The name
Dionysus has been fancifully interpreted as a combination of
Zeus (Dio) and Nysa. Silenus became the tutor of the young
god, taught him the secrets of nature, and helped him to
discover wine, a two-sided gift to man, for it could be the
source of freedom and joyousness, or of weakness and brutality. The attributes of wine were also embodied in the god,
who could be merry and gentle or ruthless and powerful. He

bscured) errant, ardent, actor; ch, chip; g, go; th, thin; ᴛʜ, then; y, you;
ariable) ḍ as d or j, ṣ as s or sh, ṭ as t or ch, ẓ as z or zh.

traveled about the earth teaching men the mysteries of hi
worship and how to cultivate the vine. Those who welcome
him received the gift of the vine; those who resisted hir
were visited with terrible punishments. According to tradi
tion, Oeneus of Calydon was the first mortal to whom h
gave the vine, Icarius of Attica was the first mortal to dis
cover wine, and Amphictyon, who entertained Dionysu
was the first whom he taught to mix wine with water. In th
vineyards, masks of Dionysus were hung, which turned i
the wind and were supposed to make fruitful whatever vine
they looked upon. Dionysus grew to be a beautiful girlish
appearing young man, but Hera recognized him and drov
him mad. He began to wander about the world, accom
panied by Silenus, satyrs, nymphs, other woodland deities
and a band of female followers called maenads. In his ma
wanderings he went to Egypt, where he was warmly wel
comed and taught the cultivation of the vine. With the hel
of the Amazons he waged a successful war. Next he went o
toward India. He crossed the Euphrates River on a bridg
of ivy and vines. When he came to another broad river, Zeu
sent a tiger to carry him across, for which reason the rive
came to be called "Tigris." In India, where he taught th
arts of cultivation, many became his willing worshipers; eve
lions and panthers submitted to him and willingly drew hi
triumphal chariot. On his way back from India he passe
through Phrygia, where he was purified by Rhea of the mu
ders he had committed during his madness, and where h
learned the rites of initiation into her mysteries. She, som
say, gave him the costume for his ceremonies: a fawn ski
or panther skin draped about his body, a band of ivy or vin
leaves for his head, and a reed, the narthex, tipped with
pine cone and wreathed with ivy for his staff. This reed
turned-staff was the thyrsus. Dionysus adopted it rather tha
a wooden staff so that his followers, flushed with wine
would not hurt each other when they beat about with it. I
Phrygia he lost Silenus for a short time. Silenus was brough
before Midas, the king, and entertained him so delightfull
with his stories that it was with regret that Midas restore
him to Dionysus. In return for his courtesies to Silenu
Dionysus offered to grant Midas whatever he wished. Un
happily his greed got the better of him, and Midas wishe
for the golden touch. Dionysus was disappointed bu

granted the wish from which he ultimately freed him. From
Phrygia he went to Thrace. Lycurgus, king of the Edonians
on the Strymon River, did not welcome the wild new religion. He chased Dionysus with an oxgoad and captured his
followers. Dionysus fled to the sea and was given asylum by
the Nereid Thetis. Rhea freed the maenads and the gods
(Rhea or Zeus) drove Lycurgus mad, so that he killed his
own son Dryas, under the impression he was pruning a vine.
Thrace was afflicted by a plague, which was lifted only when
Lycurgus, guilty of the murder of his own kin, was torn to
pieces by wild horses. Some say that when he was in Thrace,
Dionysus found that Orpheus refused to honor him, and
preached other mysteries, and to punish him Dionysus inspired the maenads to attack Orpheus and tear him to
pieces. His dismembered head was flung into the Hebrus
River and floated, still singing, to the island of Lesbos. Afterward it was laid to rest in a cave sacred to Dionysus. But
others say this was not the case at all, that Dionysus did not
cause the death of Orpheus, for it was the latter who invented the mysteries of Dionysus. Still others say, concerning these mysteries, that they were brought from Egypt to
Greece by Melampus, who also introduced the ceremonies
and phallic procession with which the god was honored, and
these identify Dionysus with Egyptian Osiris. At the end of
three years, or in the third year after his departure, Dionysus
returned to Greece at the head of a great triumphal procession, in which Indian elephants were a feature. He freed
the cities of Boeotia, and founded Eleutherae, the "city of
freedom." When he came to his birthplace, Thebes, Pentheus, the king, who was the son of Agave and therefore a
cousin of Dionysus, looked with misgiving on the revels of
the followers of this new leader who claimed to be a god.
The Theban women immediately accepted him and flocked
to his revels on the mountain, but Pentheus denied his
divinity and ordered him and his followers seized. This Pentheus did in spite of the warnings of Cadmus and the seer
Tiresias, who warned him not to resist the gods. The walls
of the prison where Pentheus had jailed the companions of
Dionysus fell down of their own accord. Dionysus willingly
appeared before Pentheus and endeavored by persuasion to
secure his acceptance of the new god, but Pentheus would
not be persuaded and ordered him bound; the fetters in-

stantly fell from his limbs. Even these signs did not convince
Pentheus; he arrogantly refused to recognize the divinity of
the new god. Agave, his mother, had likewise refused to
believe that Semele's lover was a god. Dionysus caused her
and the women of Thebes to revel frenetically on Moun
Cithaeron in celebration of his rites. He now caused Pen
theus, who had refused every chance offered him to accep
and worship the new god, to go mad. In his madness he wen
to the mountain to spy on the women at their revels, wa
discovered by them, and was torn to pieces by his own
mother, who in her frenzy thought she had captured a young
lion. From Thebes Dionysus went to Argos. There all the
women except the daughters of King Proetus joined in hi
worship. To punish those who refused, Dionysus drove
them mad, and they fled wildly over the mountains. The
were ultimately cured of their madness by the seer Melam
pus. Wishing to go to Naxos, he hired a ship at Icaria and
set off. The ship was manned by Tyrrhenian pirates, and
they, observing the beauty of their young passenger and hi
rich robes, resolved to kidnap him and sell him for ransom
They changed the course of their ship and set out for Asia
When Dionysus accused them, they scorned him. Only one
member of the crew, the steersman, recognized him as a god
and warned his fellows, but they mocked him and ordered
him to steer for Asia. Suddenly the ship stood still as if on
rock; ivy grew up the mast, vine leaves covered the sails
wine streamed over the deck, and their passenger himsel
was transformed into a lion; or, as some say, lions and pan
thers were suddenly seen crouching at his feet. The pirate
were maddened with fright and leaped into the sea, where
they were transformed into dolphins. Only the steersman
who had recognized his godhead was spared, and at hi
request steered the ship to Naxos. Theseus had stopped on
Naxos with Ariadne on his way from Crete to Athens. There
Dionysus, according to some accounts, fell in love with
Ariadne. He appeared to Theseus in a dream and ordered
him to leave Ariadne and depart for Athens. While Ariadne
slept, Theseus obeyed his command. Dionysus woke her
with a kiss and bore her away to Drius in Thessaly. She bore
him Oenopion, Thoas, Staphylus, Latromis, Euanthes, and
Tauropolus. But others say Theseus, for reasons unknown
abandoned Ariadne on Naxos, and that Dionysus came

upon her weeping, fell in love with her, and married her. He loved her devotedly, and when she died he placed the gem-studded crown, made by Hephaestus, which he had given her as a wedding gift, among the stars as the *Corona Borealis,* or *Ariadne's Crown.* Dionysus was also said to have had a short-lived affair with Aphrodite, who bore him Priapus, and to have loved Carya, daughter of a king in Laconia, but she died suddenly and he transformed her into a walnut tree. At last, when he was universally recognized and worshiped as a god, Dionysus ascended to Olympus and took his place among the gods. As there were to be only Twelve Olympians, Hestia withdrew and gave her place to him. Once he had taken his place among the gods, he desired to fetch his mother from Hades. According to some accounts, he did not know the way, and asked a wayfarer to show him the path. The wayfarer agreed to do so in return for a reward. He led him to the Alcyonian Lake at Lerna, which was one of the entrances to Hades. Dionysus plunged into its bottomless depths and found his mother in the Underworld. He defied the lord of the Underworld to rescue her, or, as some say, he bribed Persephone with a gift of myrtle to free her, and returned with her to the upper air. When he returned, the wayfarer to whom he had promised a reward had died, but Dionysus honored his promise by placing the agreed sum on the dead man's grave. But some say he returned from Hades at a place near the bay of Troezen. The descent of Dionysus to Hades was annually celebrated with nocturnal rites on the bank of the Alcyonian Lake. A lamb was thrown into it as an offering to the guardian of Hades; trumpets were sounded with startling suddenness to summon Dionysus from the depths of the lake. When Dionysus took his mother to Olympus, he changed her name to Thyone so that the spirits who had been left behind in Hades would not know of her resurrection. The gods received her as the mother of a god and made her immortal.

Dionysus was the god of the vine, fertility, and of joyous life. He was the god of hospitality who brings joy to the feast and frees men from care. He was a god of peace, who brings men law and civilization. He was associated with Apollo and the Muses as a god of poets and musicians. He was honored with a special series of festivals, the *Oschophoria, Lesser Dionysia, Lenaea, Anthesteria,* and the *Greater Dionysia.* This last,

celebrated in Athens in the spring (March—April), when th
vine begins to sprout, and lasting for five days, was mos
splendid of all. During the celebration all the ordinary bus
ness of life stopped, prisoners were freed to take part, an
no one was imprisoned during its course. The festival wa
marked by the Thymelic contest (the Thymele was the alta
of Dionysus that stood in the center of the orchestra in th
Greek theaters). These were performances of the works c
poets given in open air theaters. Even to observe them wa
an act of worship. The works the poets and musicians wrot
for the Greater Dionysia were the foundation, and ult
mately, the whole magnificent structure of Greek drama
The dithyramb, the form used by the poets, was invented b
Arion of Corinth in honor of Dionysus. In honor c
Dionysus musicians were freed from paying taxes, and fror
the 4th century B.C. for 800 years thereafter, members of th
guild of the Artists of Dionysus were freed from militar
service. Dionysus was the god of joy and freedom, of vegeta
tion, of peace, and the arts of civilization, who was every
where worshiped with merry revels. He was also a god of th
earth. The death of the vine and vegetation with the comin
of winter was associated with the flight or the death of th
god. The renewal of the vine in the spring was associate
with his rebirth. Every third year festivals, celebrated b
women and girls only, were held in his honor. Some say th
festivals were held every third year because Dionysus wa
away on his travels this length of time before he returned t
Greece. Others say the interval marks the period which
Dionysus, as a son of Zeus and Persephone, spends in th
Underworld, at the end of which he is reborn. The tomb
from which he was resurrected was at Delphi. During th
festival the rites symbolized frantic grief over the death o
the god and wild joy over his resurrection. The women who
performed them were the maenads (also called bacchant
and Thyiades). The maenads celebrated his worship with
wild dances, clashing cymbals, drums, and piping flutes
They did not worship him in temples, but rather held thei
revels in the umblemished fastnesses of mountain and for
est, coursing through the wilderness with heads crowned
with ivy and swinging torches to light their revels. They tor
the flesh of sacrificial victims apart with their hands and at
it raw to commemorate the dismemberment of Dionysus b

the Titans. The wildest orgies took place in Thrace and Asiatic Greece, in which latter area the worship of Dionysus came to be associated with that of Cybele (Rhea), Atys, and Sabazius. In Greece itself, the revelers retired to Mount Parnassus near Delphi, and to Mount Cithaeron and Taÿgetus for their orgies, as well as to various other places in Boeotia, Argos and Laconia. Some say there was another Dionysus, a son of Zeus and Persephone, who was called Zagreus and Sabazius. As Sabazius he was very wise, and was the first to yoke oxen, for which reason he was sometimes represented wearing a horn. Celebrations for Sabazius, particularly in Thrace, were held at night to cloak the disgraceful conduct attending them. Dionysus was also identified with Iacchus, the brother or lover of Demeter, and was worshiped at the Eleusinian Mysteries with Demeter and Persephone.

Dionysus had many epithets. Among them were Lenaeus, because he taught men how to crush grapes in vats—*lenoi;* Mitrephorus *(Mitre-bearer,)* because he wore a band around his head to prevent, according to some accounts, the headache which sometimes followed over-indulgence in wine; Bromius, from the thunder which accompanied his birth; Pyrigenes, because he was born amid fire; Thriambus, because he was the first to celebrate a triumph on his return from India; and Lyaeus *(the Loosener)* because of the relaxing effect of wine. The vine, ivy, rose, laurel, and asphodel were sacred to him, as well as the lion, panther, lynx, tiger, dolphin, ox, and goat. In art he appeared sometimes as a mature, bearded man, but the more usual representation was as a slim youth of almost effeminate beauty, clad in the skin of a wild animal, and with his flowing locks crowned with a wreath of ivy or vine leaves. His attributes are the thyrsus and cup, or grapes, and often he is represented surrounded by satyrs, nymphs, maenads, Muses, or other members of his retinue.

Perhaps more than the other gods, except Demeter, Dionysus represented an enlightened symbolism on the part of the Greeks. The wine he gave to man was a power for good or ill, depending on the use to which it was put. His worship embraced wild and savage elements, as well as the most highly developed arts. The death and renewal of vegetation, symbolized by the death and resurrection of the god was an intimation of immortality.

Dioscuri (dī-os-kū′ri). In mythology, Castor and Polydeuces (Latin, Pollux), the twin sons of Leda, and the brothers of Helen and Clytemnestra. According to some accounts, Tyndareus of Sparta was the father of Leda's sons, and as such they were called *Tyndaridae*. Others say Tyndareus was the father of Polydeuces only, and Zeus was the father of Castor. Some maintain that Zeus was the father of both (*Dios-Kouroi* i.e. "Sons of Zeus"), but the generally accepted account is that Castor and his sister Clytemnestra were the children of Tyndareus, and Polydeuces and Helen were the offspring of Zeus. In any event, they were such noble, manly youths that they were named Dioscuri, "striplings of Zeus," and became Spartan heroes. Castor was renowned as a tamer of horses and won prizes at the Olympic Games. Some say he taught Heracles the arts of fencing, cavalry tactics, and strategy. Polydeuces was noted for his skill in boxing, and also won prizes at the Olympic Games, as well as at the funeral games for Pelias. The brothers were among the Argonauts who accompanied Jason to Colchis to recover the Golden Fleece. In the course of the journey Polydeuces overcame Amycus, king of the Bebryces, in a boxing match, and killed him. The Dioscuri also took part in the Calydonian Hunt. Among their other deeds, they helped Peleus devastate Iolcus and kill Cretheïs, the wife of Acastus who had falsely accused Peleus. When their sister Helen was carried off at an early age by Theseus and Pirithous, they went to Athens to rescue her. They conquered Athens, and, as Theseus was at this time in Hades with Pirithous, they set Menestheus on the throne of Athens, found Helen in Aphidnae where Theseus had hidden her with his mother, and carried her and the mother of Theseus back to Sparta. When, much later, Helen stood on the walls of Troy and pointed out to King Priam various Greek heroes who were besieging the city to recover her, she looked in vain for her valorous brothers, unaware that they had died and been deified since she had been carried off from Sparta by Paris. The Dioscuri were invited to attend the marriage of the twins, Idas and Lynceus, to Phoebe and Hilaira, the daughters of Leucippus. At the wedding they seized the prospective brides and carried them off and had children by them. Phoebe bore Mnesilus to Polydeuces; Hilaira bore Anogon to Castor. At some later date the Dioscuri and Idas and Lynceus were reconciled, and united their forces to make a cattle raid in Arcadia. When it came time to divide the spoils, Idas, who had been chosen by lot to fix on a method of division, cut one of the cows into four parts and decreed that whoever ate his part first should have half the stolen cattle, and that he who finished his part next should get the other half. Idas thereupon gobbled down his quarter and immediately set to work to help Lynceus finish his. Thus having disposed of their two quarters the quickest, Idas and Lynceus claimed all the cattle and drove them off to Messenia. Castor and Polydeuces later followed them into Messenia, and while Idas and Lynceus were away sacrificing they seized the cattle, took other booty, and waited in a hollow tree to waylay Idas and Lynceus on their return. But Lynceus, who had such sharp eyes he could see through the bole of a tree, warned Idas, and as they came toward the place of ambush Idas hurled his spear and killed Castor. Polydeuces attacked him, and though felled by a stone Idas cast at him, he succeeded in killing Lynceus. At this point Zeus intervened to save his son, and killed Idas with a thunderbolt. (But some say this fight between the two sets of twins broke out when the Dioscuri carried off the brides of Idas and Lynceus.) Polydeuces was heartbroken over the loss of his brother, and after he had set up a trophy to commemorate his victory over Lynceus, he prayed that he might die too. But as the son of Zeus, he was immortal. He asked to share his immortality with his brother. Zeus agreed. Thereafter Castor lived in the upper air one day, while Polydeuces was under the earth, and the next day they changed places, and so they alternated. Or, as some say, Polydeuces spent every other day with the gods in Olympus, the intervening day being spent with his brother in Hades. But according to the Spartans, Polydeuces, the immortal twin, was the Morning Star and Castor was the Evening Star; as one set, the other rose. And some say that Zeus set the images of the Dioscuri in the heavens as the Twins to honor their devotion to each other. According to a story told by Pausanias, the house where the Dioscuri lived still stood in Sparta long after their disappearance from the earth. Once the Dioscuri, pretending to be strangers, appeared there one night and asked to be allowed to sleep in their old room. The owner, although welcoming them, regretfully refused their request for that room, as it was occupied by his daughter. The next morning the girl and everything in the room had disappeared. All that remained were images of the Dioscuri and some sprigs of an herb. The Dioscuri were regarded as the saviors of shipwrecked sailors: sailors in danger, seeing the sign of their presence in a flame at the masthead, prayed to them, vowed the sacrifice of a white lamb, and the danger passed. They were renowned for their bravery and skill in arms, and were the patron gods of warlike youth, by whom they were honored as the composers of certain warlike dances and songs. They were also the protecting gods of the rites of hospitality. Their attribute is an egg-shaped cap crowned with a star. They were honored in Athens as gods, and at Sparta they were worshiped with Heracles and other heroes. The Spartans carried a symbol of the Dioscuri, consisting of two parallel beams connected by cross-pieces, when they went into battle. The Dioscuri were said to have hated the Messenians, because two Messenian youths, Gonippus and Panormus, impersonated them in the Second Messenian War. The Dioscuri sat in a wild pear tree during a battle, and when Aristomenes, a Messenian hero, was driving the Spartans back, the Dioscuri seized his shield. While he looked for his shield, the Spartans escaped. Again, with their sister Helen, they drove Aristomenes back when he attempted to make a night attack on Sparta. Their enmity to the Messenians lasted until the founding of the new city of Messene (369 B.C.), when the Messenians sacrificed to them and won their forgiveness. At the Battle of Aegospotami (405 B.C.), the Dioscuri were said to have hovered over the Spartan fleet and to have helped them to the decisive victory they won over the Athenians there which brought the Peloponnesian Wars to a close. After this victory the Spartans dedicated two golden stars at the shrine of Delphi to commemorate their divine companions in the battle. Shortly before the Battle of Leuctra (371 B.C.), the golden stars fell from their place at Delpi and disappeared. The Spartans met disastrous defeat at the hands of the Thebans in this battle, from which Sparta never recovered. The worship of the Dioscuri passed to Italy in early times, and they were especially honored in Rome and Tusculum. The original temple of Castor in Rome, in which the Senate sometimes sat, was erected in the Forum

---

fat, fāte, fär, fȧll, ȧsk, fãre; net, mē, hėr; pin, pīne; not, nōte, mӧve, nôr; up, lūte, pu̇ll; oi, oil; ou out; (lightened) ĕlect, agǫny, ūnite;

in their honor in 484 B.C., in gratitude for their assistance
at the battle of Lake Regillus that had taken place 12 years
earlier. An annual review of the Roman knights was held in
their honor on the 15th of July. Greeks and Romans also
worshiped them as gods of the sea; before the invention of
the compass, the twin stars Castor and Pollux were important aids to navigation.

Dirce (dėr'sē). In Greek mythology, the wife of Lycus, put to
death by Amphion and Zethus, sons of Antiope, in revenge
for her ill treatment of their mother. She was bound to the
horns of a bull and dragged to death. (Her execution is
represented in the famous sculpture group *The Farnese Bull*.)
Her body was thrown into a well on Mount Cithaeron thereafter known as the fountain of Dirce.

Dolon (dō'lon). In Homeric legend *(Iliad)*, a Trojan, the son
of Eumedes. On condition that he be given the immortal
horses of Achilles once they were captured, he volunteered
to go as a spy to the Greek camp in the tenth year of the
Trojan War. Clad in a wolf's skin, he set out on his mission,
but was captured by Diomedes and Odysseus, who had set
out to spy on the Trojan camp. He betrayed the positions
of the Trojans and their allies, and advised Diomedes and
Odysseus that Rhesus, leader of the Thracian allies, was
encamped at some distance from the main body of the Trojans. As soon as they had learned what they wanted from
Dolon, the two Greeks, ignoring his pleas, killed him and
proceeded to the Trojan camp.

Dorus (dō'rus). In Greek mythology, generally represented
as the youngest son of Hellen and Orseïs (but some say he
was the son of Creusa and Hellen's son Xuthus). He migrated from Thessaly to the region between Mount Ossa
and Mount Olympus. His followers, being compelled to
move from there, went to the Pindus mountains, and from
there to Dryopis. From Dryopis they crossed over into the
Peloponnesus and established the race of the Dorians.

Dryad (drī'ạd). A deity or nymph of the woods, or a nymph
supposed to live in trees or preside over woods. See *Hamadryad.*

Dryope (drī'ọ̄-pē). In mythology, sometimes named as a
nymph and sometimes as the sister of Iole, daughter of
Eurytus. As she played with hamadryads, Apollo appeared
among them disguised as a turtle. Dryope picked up the

(obscured) errạnt, ardẹnt, actọr; ch, chip; g, go; th, thin; ŦH, then; y, you;
(variable) ḍ as d or j, ṣ as s or sh, ṭ as t or ch, ẓ as z or zh.

turtle, which immediately changed into a snake and frightened the hamadryads away. Apollo then assumed his own form and ravished Dryope, who bore him a son, Amphissus. One day as she was carrying her infant son, she stopped to pick blossoms from a lotus tree for her child. Blood dropped from the blossoms and ran down the tree trunk, for Dryope had unfortunately chosen to pick flowers from a tree that was the home of the nymph Lotis. In terror Dryope tried to flee but her feet were rooted to the ground, her body became wooden, and as her husband, Andraemon, and her father came to look for her, bark grew up over her breast and neck. She had time only to plead with Andraemon to take care of her child before her face was forever enclosed in bark. In place of the nymph there stood a slender poplar tree.

Echidna (ē-kid′na̱). In Greek mythology, a monster, half beautiful maiden and half serpent. She was the daughter of Ceto and Phorcys (or of Chrysaor and Callirrhoë), and by Typhon was the mother of: two-headed Orthus, the hound of Geryon; Cerberus, the brazen-throated hound of Hades; the Hydra of Lerna; the fabulous Chimaera. By her own son Orthus she was the mother of the Theban Sphinx that was slain by Oedipus, and of the Nemean Lion, slain by Heracles. In addition, according to some accounts, she was the mother of Ladon, the vultures that gnawed Prometheus' vitals, and the sea monster Scylla. Echidna was slain while asleep by the many-eyed Argus.

Echion (ē-kī′on). In Greek mythology, one of the crop of armed men who sprang up when Cadmus sowed the dragon's teeth. He was one of the five who survived when the armed men warred among themselves, and later married Agave, daughter of Cadmus, and founded one of the five great families of Thebes. Pentheus was his son.

Echo (ek′ō). In mythology, a talkative wood nymph who at last lost the power to originate any conversation. This came about because Hera, suspicious of the many amorous adventures of her husband Zeus, was too often delayed in discovering him in his affairs by listening to the chatter of Echo. To punish Echo for protecting Zeus in this manner Hera took away her power of speech, leaving her only the ability to repeat the last words spoken to her. By Pan, Echo was the mother of Iynx. Later she fell in love with Narcissus and, being scorned by him, wasted away until nothing was left of her but her voice.

Eirene (ī-rē′nē). See **Irene,** goddess of peace.

Electra (ē-lek′trạ). In Greek legend, a daughter of Agamemnon and Clytemnestra, and the sister of Orestes, Iphigenia, and Chrysothemis. When Agamemnon returned victorious from Troy he was brutally murdered by Clytemnestra and her lover Aegisthus. Electra secretly gave the young Orestes into the charge of an aged tutor and commanded him to take the boy to Strophius in Phocis, where he would be safe from the evil designs of Aegisthus. Electra remained in Mycenae, kept in a state of virtual slavery by Clytemnestra and Aegisthus. However, her spirit was far from broken and she continually and publicly condemned her mother as an adulteress and a murderess. Electra had been betrothed to her cousin Castor, and after he died and was deified the leading princes of Greece sought her hand. But Aegisthus feared that she might bear a son who would avenge the murder of Agamemnon, and so rejected all her suitors. He wanted to have Electra slain but Clytemnestra heeded the prohibitions of the gods against the slaying of one's own kin and forbade him to do so. As she saw it was impossible to convince Electra that the murder of Agamemnon was justified, because of his sacrifice of Iphigenia at Aulis, she kept her in a state of misery, and according to some accounts, finally allowed Aegisthus to marry her to a peasant. But he, out of respect for his high-born bride, and out of fear of her brother, never consummated the marriage. Electra's one hope for release from her miserable state and for vengeance for her father's murder lay in the return of Orestes. She sent him frequent urgent reminders of his obligation and maintained her defiance of Clytemnestra and her scorn for Aegisthus by vociferously praying for the return of Orestes and with open expressions of her hope for vengeance. In the eighth year after the murder of Agamemnon Orestes se-

cretly returned to Mycenae with Pylades, a son of Strophius
and the faithful friend of Orestes. While his presence in
Mycenae was still unknown to Clytemnestra he made himself known to Electra and was joyously reunited with her.
Rapidly they made their plans. Orestes was troubled by
doubts concerning the deed he was planning, but Electra
spurred him on: a son must avenge his father or risk the
displeasure of the gods. She had been beside herself for
years with grief over her father's hateful death, humiliation
over her own state, and a burning desire for vengeance on
Clytemnestra and Aegisthus. When Orestes wavered she
stiffened his resolution. By pretending he was a messenger
with news of Orestes' death he secured entry into the palace
and killed his mother and Aegisthus. Electra ultimately married Pylades, after he had returned from Tauris with
Orestes, and bore him two sons, Medon and Strophius. She
died and was buried at Mycenae.

Electrides (ē-lek′tri-dēz). In Greek legend, the Amber Islands
(where the trees weep amber), situated at the mouth of the
fabulous river Eridanus (later identified with the Po River in
Italy).

Electryon (ē-lek′tri-on). In Greek mythology, the son of Perseus and Andromeda, and the grandfather of Heracles. He
was a king of Mycenae. He left Amphitryon to rule in his
place while he waged war against the Taphians, who had
slain eight of his sons during a raid in which they stole his
cattle, and promised his daughter Alcmene to Amphitryon
if he ruled well during his absence. When he returned he
found that Amphitryon had ransomed the cattle and expected him to pay the ransom. He refused. Amphitryon
angrily hurled a club at one of the cattle, but it struck Electryon instead and killed him.

Elysium (ē-liz′i-um, -lizh′um). [Also: *Elysian Fields.*] Abode of
the souls of the good and of heroes exempt from death, in
ancient classical mythology. It is described, particularly by
later poets, as a place of exceeding bliss, and contrasted with
Tartarus, an afterworld of torment. Some have thought it to
be in the center of the earth, some in the Islands of the Blest,
and some in the sun or mid-air. In the *Odyssey* it is a plain
at the end of the earth "where life is easiest to man. No snow
is there, nor yet great storm nor any rain."

Empusae (em-pū′sē). In Greek mythology, cannibal monsters
with the legs of asses and hoofs of brass. Sometimes called

the children of Hecate, at her direction, disguised as bitches, cows, or even as beautiful maidens, they were sent to frighten travelers. The Lamiae were reckoned among the Empusae who were believed eventually to devour their human lovers.

Enalus (ē'na̱-lus). According to legend, a young man who leaped into the sea because his sweetheart, Phineis, was chosen by lot to be hurled into the sea as a sacrifice to Amphitrite when colonists were first setting out for Lesbos. He was saved by a dolphin, who bore Enalus on his back to shore. The dophin's mate rescued Phineis.

Enceladus (en-sel'a̱-dus). In Greek mythology, one of the Giants, a son of Gaea and the blood of Uranus, who waged war on the gods. In the battle he was crushed flat by a huge stone flung at him by Athena as he fled. He now lies crushed under Aetna in Sicily. When he stirs the mountain shakes, and when he breathes it erupts.

Endymion (en-dim'i-o̱n). According to some accounts, he was a son of Zeus and the nymph Calyce; but some say he was a son of Aëthlius. He seized the throne of the region that was later known as Elis and made himself king. By his wife, whose name is variously given as Cromia, Asterodia, and Hyparippe, he was the father of three sons—Paeon, Epeus, and Aetolus—and a daughter, Eurycyda (or Eurydice). To choose a successor for his throne, he had his sons engage in a running race at Olympia. Epeus won, became king, and named the people of the land Epeans. Selene, the moon-goddess, came upon Endymion lying asleep in a cave, and fell in love with his beauty. She visited him nightly and bore him 50 daughters. Some say she asked Zeus to give him perpetual youth and eternal sleep. Others say that Endymion was a hunter on Mount Latmos in Caria, and that it was in a cave there that Selene found him, and that it was he himself who asked Zeus for immortality, eternal slumber, and undying youth. In all versions of his myth he is described as a youth of great beauty who kept his youth and his beauty in never-waking slumber. The Eleans (the name by which the Epeans came to be known) claimed that the tomb of Endymion was at Olympia in Elis, but others say he lies in eternal sleep in a cave on Mount Latmos in Caria, near Miletus.

Enyo (ē-nī′ō). In Greek mythology, a goddess of war, sacker of cities, and companion of Ares. The Romans identified her with Bellona, destroyer of cities.

Eos (ē′ọs). The "rosy-fingered" goddess of the dawn. Clad in a saffron-colored mantle she drives her golden chariot, drawn by two white horses, from the east to Olympus each day to announce to men and gods the coming of her brother Helius. She is the herald of the day. Eos is a daughter of the Titans Hyperion and Thia, and by Astraeus she is the mother of the winds and the stars, especially the morning star. It is said that Eos once seduced Ares, the lover of Aphrodite, and so enraged the latter that she caused Eos to yearn for the fresh and youthful beauty of mortals. This accounts for her many mortal lovers. When Orion, blinded, came to the east Eos fell in love with him and caused her brother Helius to restore his sight by touching his lids with his rays. Eos then carried him off to Delos with her. She bore a son, Phaëthon, to Cephalus, whom she had caused to doubt his wife Procris. Some say it was Eos who carried off Ganymede, and that Zeus took him from her to be his cupbearer. In return she asked Zeus to grant eternal life to Tithonous, another Trojan whom she had carried off. Zeus granted her plea and she bore Memnon and Emathion to Tithonous. In the Trojan War Memnon went to the aid of the Trojans. On the day he was fated to die Eos came reluctantly from the east. When death, at the hands of Achilles, overtook him that day, the children of Eos slipped down from heaven and rescued his body and carried it off. Eos threatened to withdraw her light from the earth. If Zeus loved Thetis and her son Achilles better than Eos and her son Memnon, let Thetis provide light to the world, she said. For some time darkness covered the earth, but the Horae came to Eos and led her to Zeus. At his command she resumed her daily course, but thenceforth she wept tears of dew each morning, in memory of Memnon.

Epeus (ep-ē′us). In legend, a son of Panopeus. Although he had the reputation of being a coward, and was, as a punishment to his father for breaking his oath, he accompanied the Greeks to the Trojan War. At the funeral games for Patroclus he won the boxing match, and again, at the funeral games for Achilles, he contended with Acamas, son of Theseus, in the boxing match. The match was stopped, as the contestants were evenly matched. Epeus, with the aid of Athena, built the Wooden Horse which led to the fall of Troy, and entered the city in it, although trembling with fear.

Epeus. According to legend, a son of Endymion. In a race arranged by his father against his brothers, he won and was awarded the throne of his land in the Peloponnesus. He named the people after himself, Epeans. He married Anax-iroë and had one daughter, Hyrmina, but no sons. During his reign, Pelops won the land of Pisa and neighboring Olympia after the death of Oenomaus, and separated it from the land of Epeus. The Eleans, the name by which the Epeans were later called, said that Pelops was the first in the Peloponnesus to erect a temple of Hermes. He did this to appease the god for the death of Myrtilus. Epeus was succeeded by his brother Aetolus, who was forced to flee from his country because he accidentally killed Apis at the funeral games for Azan. The kingdom fell to Eleus, son of Poseidon and the daughter of Endymion, who changed the name of the people to Eleans.

Ephialtes (ef-i-al′tēz). In Greek mythology, a son of Poseidon. He was the brother of Otus. See **Aloidae.** Ephialtes was also the name of the nightmare demon of ancient Greece.

Epicaste (ep-i-kas′tē). Name used in Homer for **Jocasta.**

Epigoni (ē-pig′ō-nī). The name given to the sons of the Seven against Thebes; it means "the After-born." Ten years after the disastrous rout of the Seven against Thebes by the Thebans, the Epigoni proposed to march against Thebes to avenge their fathers. An oracle foretold that they would be successful if Alcmaeon commanded the expedition. Alcmaeon was persuaded to do so and the expedition set out. The chieftains who made up the Epigoni were: Alcmaeon and Amphilochus, sons of Amphiaraus; Aegialeus, son of Adrastus; Diomedes, son of Tydeus; Promachus, son of Parthenopaeus; Sthenelus, son of Capaneus; Thersander, son of Polynices; and Euryalus, son of Mecisteus. The Thebans, under the command of Laodamas, son of Eteocles, met the Epigoni on the plain outside the walls of Thebes. Aegialeus was killed by Laodamas, but he in his turn was slain by Alcmaeon. The Thebans retired within the walls and were advised by Tiresias the seer to send a herald to negotiate

with the Epigoni and to flee the city, for, said Tiresia
Thebes would fall when Adrastus, the only survivor of th
original seven, died. And Adrastus would die of grief whe
he learned of the death of his son Aegialeus. The Thebar
followed Tiresias' advice and fled to the north and founde
Hestiaea in Thessaly. But some say they went to Illyr
where the descendants of Cadmus ruled. The Argives en
tered Thebes, pulled down the walls, and took much boot
some of which they sent to Apollo at Delphi in fulfillment c
a vow to give him the best fruits of their victory. Thersande
and his heirs became the rulers of Thebes. The successfi
war of the Epigoni took place before the expedition of th
Argonauts and before the Trojan War. It has been placed b
some in the 14th century B.C.

Epimetheus (ep-i-mē'thūs, –thȩ̄-us). In Greek mythology,
son of Iapetus, and the brother of Prometheus, Atlas, an
Menoetius. Some say Epimetheus, whose name mear
"Afterthought," was given the task of creating animals t
populate the world after it had been formed. He careless
gave the best gifts to the animals—fur to keep them warr
feathers to soar into the air, cunning, and courage. When
came to man all the protections had been used up, and b
sought the aid of Prometheus to find some means by whic
men could protect themselves. Prometheus made man t
stand erect and stole fire from heaven and gave it to mar
To counterbalance the gift of fire, Zeus commanded H¢
phaestus to make a maiden, Pandora. She was endowed wit
gifts by all the gods and taken by Hermes to Epimetheus ¿
a gift. Epimetheus forgot until it was too late Prometheu
warning never to accept a gift from Zeus. He married Pan
dora. Up to this time there had been only men in the worl
and they lived without evils or hardship. Pandora, in he
character and in the dowry she brought with her, inflicte
endless trouble and grief on men. Epimetheus and Pando
were the parents of Deucalion's wife Pyrrha.

Erato (er'a̧-tō). One of the nine daughters of Zeus an
Mnemosyne. She is the muse of lyric and amorous poetr
In art she is often represented with the lyre. See *Muses.*

Erebus (er'ȩ̄-bus). [Also: *Erebos.*] In Greek mythology, th
son of Chaos and some say, of Darkness, but others sa
Erebus was Darkness. He was the brother of Nyx (Nigh
and, according to some accounts, of Aether (Air) and Hem

fat, fāte, fär, fåll, ȧsk, fāre; net, mē, hėr; pin, pīne; not, nōte, möv
nôr; up, lūte, pu̇ll; oi, oil; ou out; (lightened) ȩ̄lect, agǭny, u̧nit

era (Day), but others say Aether and Hemera were his children. By his sister Nyx he was the father of the Fates and such personified evils as Doom, Death, Slumber, Dreams, Misery, Deceit, Eld *(the Destroyer)*, and Strife. In general, Erebus signified the unknown darkness.

rebus. [Also: **Erebos.**] In Greek mythology, a place or region, and a state or condition. As the first, it is that part or section of the Underworld through which the souls of the dead must pass in order to reach Hades. As the second, it is "darkness" itself, and, in particular, the darkness of the west.

rechtheus (ē-rek'thūs, –thḝ-us). A son of Pandion, the twin of Butes, and the brother of Procne and Philomela. He was a legendary king of Athens and a protegé of Athena, who gave him her shrine for a dwelling. By his wife Praxithea he had four sons: Cecrops, Metion, Orneus, and Pandorus, and seven daughters: Chthonia, Creusa, Orithyia, Otionia, Pandora, Procris, and Protogonia. During a war between the Athenians and the Eleusinians an oracle informed him that if he sacrificed his youngest daughter he would secure victory. She, Otionia, willingly gave her life for Athens. Protogonia and Pandora killed themselves also, as they had vowed that they would kill themselves if one of them died by violence. In the same war, Erechtheus slew Eumolpus, leader of the Eleusinians, who was his own great-grandson. Poseidon, father of Eumolpus, took immediate revenge, either by destroying Erechtheus with his trident, or by invoking Zeus, who felled Erechtheus with a thunderbolt.

rginus (er-jī'nus). According to some mythographers, a son of Clymenus, king of the Minyans in Orchomenus. Others say he was a son of Poseidon. In the course of the games for Poseidon at Onchestus, Clymenus was killed by a Theban. Erginus, who succeeded his father as king, forthwith attacked and conquered Thebes, and imposed a tribute of 100 head of cattle yearly for 20 years. Heracles met the heralds who were on their way to collect the cattle, and cut off their ears and noses, which he threaded on cords and hung around their necks. He then bound their hands behind their backs and sent them back to Erginus. Erginus again attacked the Thebans in retaliation for this outrage, but this time Heracles aided the Thebans. He routed Erginus, scattered his army, and forced the people of Orchomenus to pay dou-

ble the tribute which Erginus had been exacting from th
Thebans. Some say Erginus was killed in this battle. Othe
say he survived the defeat and later joined the Argonauts o
their journey to Colchis. In his old age he followed th
advice of an oracle and married a young wife who bore hi
the famous builders, Agamedes and Trophonius

Erichthonius (er-ik-thō'ni-us). In Greek mythology, a so
sprung from the seed of Hephaestus which fell on Gae
Gaea abandoned him and Athena took the infant, who wa
half human and half serpent, put him in a chest, and gav
him to the daughters of Cecrops, king of Athens, to guar
She gave them strict instructions not to open the ches
Ulitimately, of course, their curiosity got the better of ther
They opened the chest and when they saw the child with
serpent's tail for legs they were maddened with fear ar
leaped to their deaths from the Acropolis. A white cro
brought Athena the news of the death of Agraulos and he
two daughters. Athena was so saddened by the news sh
changed the crow's color from white to black and hencefor
banished crows from the Acropolis. She put Erichthonius
her aegis and reared him herself. Some say she gave him th
power to restore the dead to life by presenting him with tw
drops of the blood of the Gorgon Medusa. When he lat
became king of Athens he established the worship of Athe
there. He invented the four-horse chariot and later w
identified with the constellation Auriga on this account. Th
royal family of Athens claimed descent from Erichthoniu
as well as from Erechtheus, with whom he is sometim
confused.

Erigone (ē-rig'ō-nē). In Greek mythology, the daughter
Icarius of Athens. When her father was slain by peasant
made drunk by wine he had given them, his dog led her
his grave. Stricken with grief, she prepared to hang hers
from the pine tree under which the peasants had buried hi
She prayed that all Athenian daughters would suffer a dea
similar to hers until Icarius was avenged. When Atheni
maidens began to be found swinging from trees, an orac
explained that this came about in answer to Erigone
prayer. The Athenians found the peasants who had mu
dered Icarius and killed them, extinguishing the curse.

Erinyes (e-rin'i-ēz). Female divinities, avengers of iniquit
who live in Erebus and are older than Zeus and the Olymp

fat, fāte, fär, fâll, ȧsk, fãre; net, mē, hėr; pin, pīne; not, nōte, mö
nôr; up, lūte, pùll; oi, oil; ou out; (lightened) ẹlect, agǫny, ūni

ans. According to Hesiod, they are daughters of Gaea (Earth), sprung from the blood of Uranus when he was mutilated by his son Cronus. According to others, they are the children of Night and Darkness. The Erinyes are monstrous hags; coiling serpents stream from their dogs' heads, wings sprout from their black bodies, and in their hands they carry bronze scourges to attack their victims. They hunt down offenders, make them mad, and punish them in Tartarus. In later times the number of the Erinyes was limited to three: Alecto *(Unresting)*, Megaera *(Jealous)*, and Tisiphone *(Avenger)*. The Erinyes are not vindictive; their punishments are impartial and impersonal; crimes, or other offenses, must be avenged to satisfy the souls of the dead whose representatives they are and who have called on them for vengeance. Orestes, who slew his mother, is hounded by the Erinyes, even though his act was fully in consonance with what he was required to do: he had killed his mother to avenge his father. But the Erinyes, called on by Clytemnestra's soul, demanded payment for his crime. Athena, goddess of law and order as well as of wisdom, came to the defense of Orestes. She persuaded the Erinyes to let him stand trial before the Areopagus. In the trial the vote of the judges was evenly divided, whereupon Athena cast her vote in favor of Orestes and broke the tie. The Erinyes bitterly protested the trial and the verdict. If now, they said, a confessed murderer was to go free they would lose all authority as avenging deities. They threatened to put a blight on Athens if the verdict was not reversed. Athena cajoled them. She promised that the Athenians would honor them with offerings of first fruits and sacrifices. She invited them to take up their residence in a grotto on the Acropolis and receive their honors from the Athenians. In return for these honors the Erinyes were to promise prosperity for the land, ships, and marriages of the Athenians. The Erinyes accepted Athena's proposal, agreed to the promises she exacted from them, and were led away by torchlight procession to their new home in the grotto on the Acropolis, which henceforth became a shrine and a sanctuary. After this they were honored by the Athenians as the "Solemn Ones," their rites were performed in silence, and acquitted murderers sacrificed black victims to them. Other places in Greece had altars of the Solemn Ones. At Phyla, in Attica, sheep were

sacrificed to them, and libations of honey were poured. Her
flowers were worn at their processions instead of the myrtl
wreaths that symbolize the Underworld. The Erinyes ar
also called the Eumenides. Some say this name, meanin
"the Kind Ones," was given to them by Orestes, and som
say the name was given to them because it was considere
dangerous to mention them by the name Erinyes. And som
say only three of the Erinyes agreed to Athena's proposal t
cease hounding Orestes and make their home in the grott
on the Acropolis. They say that the other Erinyes, whos
number varies, continued to pursue Orestes, and it was nc
until he had gone to Tauris and fetched the image of Arte
mis there that he was freed from their scourging. The Rc
man name for the Erinyes was Furiae or Dirae.

Eriphyle (er-i-fī'lē). In Greek legend, the wife of the see
Amphiaraus and the sister of Adrastus, king of Argos. Sh
was the mother of Alcmaeon and Amphilochus. In a quarre
between Amphiaraus and Adrastus she intervened to pre
vent them from injuring each other, and made them eac
promise to abide by her decision in any future dispute whic
might arise between them. When Adrastus proposed t
march on Thebes to restore his son-in-law, Polynices, to th
throne, he asked the help of Amphiaraus in the expeditior
Amphiaraus refused, because he knew all would perish ex
cept Adrastus. Polynices learned of the agreement betwee
Adrastus and Amphiaraus to allow Eriphyle to settle an
disputes between them. He gave Eriphyle the necklace c
Harmonia which he had brought with him from Thebes an
begged her to compel Amphiaraus to accompany the expe
dition. Eriphyle accepted the bribe, although Amphiarau
had forbidden her to accept any presents from Polynice
and persuaded her husband to accompany Adrastus t
Thebes. As Amphiaraus had foreseen, the expedition ende
in disaster; only Adrastus survived it. Ten years later th
Epigoni, as the sons of the original Seven against Thebe
were called, proposed to march against Thebes to aveng
their fathers, and sought Alcmaeon as their leader. Al
maeon was reluctant to go. He argued the matter with h
brother Amphilochus and they agreed to let their moth
decide it. Once again Eriphyle was bribed, this time by The
sander, son of Polynices, who gave her the robe of Ha
monia, which had been given to Harmonia as a wedding gi

fat, fāte, fär, fåll, åsk, fāre; net, mē, hėr; pin, pīne; not, nōte, möv
nôr; up, lūte, pull; oi, oil; ou out; (lightened) ēlect, agǫny, ūnit

by Athena. She advised Alcmaeon to lead the new expedition. The Epigoni were successful and captured Thebes. On his return Alcmaeon learned that Eriphyle's acceptance of the bribe of the necklace had caused his father's death, and that her acceptance of the robe might have caused his own. He consulted the oracle of Delphi and then killed Eriphyle, some say with the help of Amphilochus. As she was dying, Eriphyle uttered a curse: she called on all the lands of Greece and Asia to deny a home to her murderers.

·is (ē'ris, er'is). [Latin: ***Discordia***.] According to some accounts, a daughter of Zeus and Hera, and the twin of Ares. Others say she was a daughter of Nyx. She is the goddess of discord who stirs up strife by spreading rumors and by inciting men to jealousy. The most famous example of how Eris roused jealousy concerns the Apple of Discord. In revenge for not having been invited to the nuptials of Peleus and Thetis, she threw among the guests a golden apple bearing the inscription "To the Fairest." A dispute arose among Aphrodite, Hera, and Athena concerning the apple, whereupon Zeus ordered Hermes to take the goddesses to Mount Gargarus, to the shepherd Paris, who should decide the dispute. He awarded the apple to Aphrodite, who in return assisted him in carrying off the beautiful Helen from Sparta, thus giving rise to the Trojan War.

·os (ē'ros, er'os). In Greek mythology, the god of love. Some say he was born from a silver egg laid by Nyx, that he set the world in motion, and was the first of the gods. According to Hesiod he is the offspring of Chaos, coeval with Earth and Tartarus, and the companion of Aphrodite; in later myths he is the youngest of the gods, son of Aphrodite and Ares, Hermes, or Zeus, represented as a beautiful winged boy, armed by Zeus with bow and arrows, or flaming torch. In the older view he was regarded as one of the creative powers of nature, the principle of union among the diverse elements of the world, more especially as the power of sensuous love, and also of devoted friendship. In the later legend he is characterized as a beautiful, wild, mischievous, irresponsible, and irresistible boy, who shoots his arrows of desire at random, without regard for former commitments or future welfare of those whose hearts he wantonly sets on fire. Although he was never given a place among the 12 Olympians, the gods had not the smallest compunction

about employing him to further their own ends. For exam
ple, he was bribed by Aphrodite, at the request of Hera an
Athena, to cause Medea to fall so madly in love with Jaso
that she betrayed her father and her country for his sak
Nor were the gods themselves immune to his arrows. He wa
worshiped at Thespiae in Boeotia, where a festival, the *Er
tidia* or *Erotia,* was celebrated every five years in his hono
His brother is Anteros, the god of mutual love or the aveng
ing god who punishes those who do not return love. Th
Romans identified Eros with Cupid or Amor, and the late
Greeks adopted the Roman concept of a plural Eros.

Erymanthian Boar (er-i-man′thi-ạn). In Greek legend, a sa
age boar that roamed the slopes of Mount Erymanthus an
ravaged the countryside. One of Heracles' labors for Eury
theus was to bring it alive to Mycenae. He drove it into
snow drift, captured it and carried it back to Mycenae slun
across his shoulders. The scene, when Eurystheus, in terro
of Heracles arriving with the still struggling boar, takes re
uge in a large *pithos* or storage jar, whose lid he raises cau
tiously to follow the course of events, amused Greek artis
and appears frequently in vase-painting and sculpture
metopes.

Erysichthon (er-i-sik′thon). In Greek mythology, a The
salonian who cut down the trees in a grove sacred to Deme
ter. According to some accounts, when his servants refuse
to obey his order to cut down the tallest tree, he seized th
ax and cut the tree himself. Some say the blood of th
hamadryad who inhabited the tree flowed out and that he
voice warned Erysichthon that Demeter would surely punis
him. Others say that Demeter herself, in the guise of th
priest of the grove, appeared and told him not to cut dow
the trees. In both cases he persisted in spite of warning
Demeter punished him by sending Famine to embrace hin
and from that time forward he could never eat enough t
satisfy his hunger. He sold everything he had to buy foo
Ultimately, he sold his daughter, Mestra. She, like some o
the sea-gods, had the power of changing her shape at wil
and as fast as she was sold she changed her form and re
turned to her father. She was then sold again, in this wa
providing an unending means of obtaining money for h
insatiable hunger. But Famine grew ever more ravenous an

at last Erysichthon turned upon his own body and devoured himself.

Eteocles (ē-tē′ō̧-klēz). In Greek legend, a son of Oedipus and Jocasta. When Oedipus learned that he had killed his own father and produced children by his own mother he blinded himself in despair. According to some accounts, his sons Eteocles and Polynices shut him away to hide the shame of their family; others say they banished him. Still others say his sons gave him a slave's portion of a sacrificial victim. For one of these reasons Oedipus laid a curse on his sons: that they should divide their inheritance by the sword. After Oedipus left Thebes, Eteocles and Polynices agreed to rule the kingdom by turns. Eteocles, being the elder, was first to rule. When his term was ended he refused to give up the throne, on the grounds of Polynices' violent character, and banished him. Polynices fled to Argos and enlisted the aid of Adrastus to lead an expedition against Thebes to recover the throne. This was the famous, ill-fated expedition of the Seven against Thebes. Eteocles mustered his forces within the city to meet the attack. He assigned one Theban chieftain to each of the seven gates of Thebes which were being attacked by the seven leaders of the enemy forces. When only three of the attacking Argives remained, the others having been killed, Eteocles and Polynices met in single combat to decide which should have the throne. They fought furiously and in the end slew each other, thus carrying out the curse which Oedipus had laid on his sons. The attackers then fled and Thebes was safe. Creon, uncle of Eteocles, succeeded to the throne. He commanded that Eteocles, as the valiant defender of the city, be given full funeral honors. But as for Polynices, who had treacherously attacked his home city, Creon commanded that his body be flung outside the walls to become the prey of scavenger birds.

Eubuleus (ū-bū′lȩ̄-us). In Greek mythology, a son of Trochilus, priest of Argos who fled to Eleusis. He was the brother of Triptolemus and, some say, of Eumolpus, a shepherd. Some say Eubuleus was an oracular swineherd (his name means "good counsel"). He was feeding his animals in the fields one day when suddenly the earth parted and engulfed one of his swine. Almost at once a chariot drawn by black horses appeared, and before it too disappeared into

bscured) errạnt, ardẹnt, actọr; ch, chip; g, go; th, thin; ᴛʜ, then; y, you; ariable) ḍ as d or j, ş as s or sh, ţ as t or ch, z̧ as z or zh.

the chasm, Eubuleus saw in the chariot a girl tightly clasped in the arms of a stranger. Eubuleus told Triptolemus of this sight, and he in turn gave the information to Demeter when she came searching for her lost daughter Persephone. In commemoration of the service of Eubuleus to Demeter live swine were hurled into a chasm in his honor at the festival of the Thesmophoria at Eleusis.

Eumenides (ū-men'i-dēz). Euphemistic name, meaning "the gracious (or kindly) ones," for the Erinyes in Greek mythology.

Eumolpus (ū-mol'pus). A priestly bard, reputed founder of the Eleusinian mysteries. According to the tale, he was the son of Chione, granddaughter of King Erechtheus of Athens, and Poseidon. In fear of her father's anger if he discovered she was the mother of a son, Chione cast her infant into the sea, but he was watched over by Poseidon and washed ashore in Libya. There he was brought up by Benthesicyme, a daughter of Poseidon and Amphitrite. She gave him one of her daughters in marriage when he grew up, but when he fell in love with another of her daughters she banished him to Thrace. There he plotted against the king Tegyrius, and, having been discovered, was compelled to flee to Eleusis. In Eleusis he became the first priest of the rites of Demeter and Dionysus, and initiated Heracles into the Mysteries of Demeter and Persephone. Being highly skilled on the lyre and flute—he won the flute contest at the funeral games for Pelias—he taught the musical arts to Heracles also. He is said to have written hymns and to have discovered the art of cultivating trees and vines. The upright life he led in Eleusis caused King Tegyrius to forgive him for his earlier conspiracy, and he made Eumolpus the heir to his throne. When war broke out between Eleusis and Athens, Eumolpus, who had by now inherited the throne of Thrace, led a band of Thracians against Athens and claimed the throne for himself as Poseidon's son. In the war the Athenians, under Ion, won and the Eleusinians, by the treaty of peace which was then concluded, became subject to Athens in all respects except that they retained control of the sacred Mysteries of Eleusis. Eumolpus was slain in battle by his great-grandfather Erechtheus, and was succeeded as priest of Demeter by his son. To avenge the slaying of Eumolpus Poseidon hurled his trident at Erechtheus and killed him, or

fat, fāte, fär, fâll, àsk, fāre; net, mē, hèr; pin, pīne; not, nōte, möve, nôr; up, lūte, pùll; oi, oil; ou out; (lightened) ělect, agǫny, ūnite

as some say, he appealed to Zeus to slay him with his thunderbolt. The family of the Eumolpidae were hereditary priests of Demeter at Eleusis.

Eumolpus. In Greek mythology, a flute-player of Colonae. He swore that Tenes, son of King Cycnus, had made improper advances to Phylonome, wife of Cycnus and stepmother of Tenes. The evidence he presented was a lie, and when later Cycnus learned that he had sworn falsely he ordered Eumolpus to be killed. Because of Eumolpus, no flute-player was ever allowed to set foot in the sacred precincts of the temple on the island of Tenedos.

Eunomia (ū-nō′mi-ą). One of the Horae, goddesses of the seasons and of nature. She was Order.

Euphemus (ū-fē′mus). In Greek legend, a son of Poseidon and Europa (daughter of Tityus). From his father he had the gift of being able to skim across the sea so swiftly his feet were hardly dampened. He was a member of the Calydonian Hunt and went from Taenarus to join Jason on the expedition of the *Argo* to Colchis. He released the dove which prepared the way for the *Argo* through the Symplegades (Clashing Rocks). When the Argonauts were driven to the Tritonian Lake in Libya, Euphemus persuaded Triton to help them back to the sea. Triton gave him a clod of earth as a guest-gift, and because of this the descendants of Euphemus gained sovereignty over Libya. Euphemus, either in obedience to a dream or on the advice of Medea, cast it into the sea and the island of Calliste (Thera), afterward the home of his son, rose from it.

Euphorbus (ū-fôr′bus). In Greek legend, a Trojan, the son of Panthous. According to some accounts it was he who killed Protesilaus, the first Greek to leap ashore at Troy. It was he, too, who was the first to wound Patroclus when he attacked the walls of Troy and was stunned by a blow from Apollo. Immediately afterward Hector delivered the death blow to Patroclus, and in the struggle for possession of his body Euphorbus was slain by Menelaus and stripped of his armor. Menelaus dedicated the shield of the brave Euphorbus in the temple of Hera, near Mycenae. Pythagoras, who expounded the theory of metempsychosis, professed to be animated by the soul of Euphorbus, who in his turn was animated by the soul of the Argonautic herald and son of Hermes, Aethalides.

Europa (ū-rō′pạ) or *Europe* (-pē). In Greek mythology, th daughter of Agenor, king of Tyre, and Telephassa. She wa the sister of Cadmus, Phoenix, Cilix, Thasus, and Phineus Zeus fell in love with her and sent Hermes to lure her to th seashore. Hermes did as he was bid, and one day as she wa playing with her maidens on the shore near Tyre, Zeu transformed himself into a white bull with golden horns an approached her. Europa was charmed by the creature' beauty, and, as he appeared gentle, decked his horns wit wreaths of flowers. When the bull knelt before her sh climbed on his back. Instantly Zeus plunged into the sea an carried the maiden on his back to Crete. There Europa bor three sons to Zeus: Minos, Rhadamanthys, and Sarpedor When Zeus left Europa she married Asterius, the king c Crete, and since he had no children, he adopted Europa' three sons and made them his heirs. But some say that it wa Greeks from Crete who raided the Phoenician shores an carried off the king's daughter, and that this was one of th causes of the ancient enmity between Greece and Asi which culminated in the Persian Wars.

Eurotas (ū-rō′tạs). In mythology, son of Myles and grandso of Lelex. He ascended the throne of Laconia after the grea flood, and drained the marshes caused by the flood by cor structing a trench to the sea. He named the river so forme after himself. Some say he had no son of his own and left hi kingdom to Lacedaemon, the son of Taÿgete and Zeus, an gave him his daughter Sparta for wife. And some say that i a war with the Athenians he was warned to wait until the fu of the moon to commence the battle. He ignored the warr ing and suffered a disastrous defeat. In humiliation at thi defeat he leaped into the river in Laconia, and according t some, this was why the river came to be known by his nam

Eurus (ū′rus). The east wind.

Euryclea (ū-ri-klē′ạ) or *Euryclia* (-klī′ạ). According to Home (*Odyssey*), a daughter of Ops. She was the nurse and atten dant of Telemachus, son of Odysseus, and helped him se cretly to prepare for his voyage to Pylus in quest of news c his father. She promised not to tell his mother until he wa well on his way. When Odysseus returned to Ithaca, dis guised as a beggar, Euryclea, who had also been his nurse thought the beggar bore a strong resemblance to Odysseu

She was ordered by Penelope to wash the beggar's feet, and as she did so she recognized an old scar on his leg and knew that the beggar was in fact Odysseus. At his hissed command —and especially in view of the fact that his hands were clasping her throat—she did not reveal his identity. Later, when he had destroyed the suitors, she told him which of his serving women and men had been loyal to him during his long absence.

Eurydice (ū-rid′-i-sē). In Greek mythology, the beloved wife of Orpheus. Aristaeus attacked her and as she fled from him she stepped on a snake, was bitten by it, and died. The bees of Aristaeus died as a punishment to him. Orpheus, over-whelmed with grief at the loss of Eurydice, descended to Tartarus in an effort to bring her back. This was granted on a condition that Orpheus lead the way, and not look back at her until they reached daylight. They had almost reached safety when in his anxiety Orpheus looked back and Eurydice's shade was snatched away forever. Some say he was ultimately reunited with her in Tartarus and that they could be seen strolling hand in hand in the Elysian Fields. See *Orpheus.*

Eurylochus (ū-ril′ō-kus). In the *Odyssey,* one of the compan-ions of Odysseus on the voyage home from Troy. He led the group who went to Circe's palace but, suspecting a trick, he did not enter it with the others. As a result of his prudence he was able to return to Odysseus and inform him that his men had been turned into swine by Circe. Later in the voy-age when Odysseus and his companions were stranded on the island of the Sun (Trinacria), Eurylochus persuaded the men, during an absence of Odysseus, to disobey his com-mands and to kill and eat the cattle of the Sun—which they had been expressly warned not to do by Circe and Odysseus. Eurylochus' argument for disregarding the warnings was that they might as well die as a result of the anger of a god as from starvation. They ate the cattle and they were later all destroyed, except Odysseus, in a great storm.

Eurynome (ū-rin′ō-mē). In Greek mythology, a daughter of Oceanus or of Chaos. She and Ophion, whom she created from the wind, were the first rulers on Olympus according to some accounts, but she yielded her power to Rhea (Oph-ion yielded his to Cronus), and fell into the sea. She was the mother by Zeus of the three Graces, or Charites. Homer names Eurynome one of the ocean nymphs who helped Thetis to save Hephaestus when Hera hurled him out of heaven.

Eurypylus   (ū-rip′i-lus.) In Greek legend, a son of Telephus and Astyoche, and the nephew of Priam. His mother, bribed with a golden vine, sent him to Troy near the end of the war in command of a group of Mysians. He fought valiantly, slaying, according to some accounts, the Greek surgeon Machaon, and being at last slain himself by Neoptolemus, son of Achilles.

Eurypylus.   In Greek legend, a son of Euaemon, and a leader of the Thessalians at Troy. As a former suitor of Helen he fought valiantly at Troy, and was one of several to accept Hector's challenge to single combat, but was eliminated in the drawing of lots. He went to the aid of Telamonian Ajax when the latter, stunned and wounded, was compelled to withdraw from the fighting. In defending Ajax he slew Apisaon, and was himself wounded by Paris as he bent to strip Apisaon of his armor. Patroclus tended his wound, and was convinced by Eurypylus that he should join the Greeks and fight against the Trojans even if Achilles still refused to aid his beleaguered countrymen. After the war Eurypylus received a chest as his part of the spoils of victory. Some say Aeneas abandoned the chest when he fled from Troy; others say Cassandra left it to be a curse to whatever Greek found it. Inside it was an image of Dionysus, made by Hephaestus and given to Dardanus by Zeus. When Eurypylus opened the chest he was driven mad by the image. In an interval of sanity he went to Delphi to inquire concerning his malady. The priestess told him to find a people making a strange sacrifice and to settle there. Eventually he came to Aroë, later a part of Patrae, where he found the people sacrificing a youth and a maiden to Artemis, to propitiate the goddess for the crime of Comaetho and Melanippus, who had polluted her shrine. Eurypylus understood that this was the strange sacrifice indicated by the priestess. The people of the town recognized him as a leader an oracle had said would come to them and made him their king. Henceforward Eurypylus recovered his sanity and the people of Patrae ceased to make human sacrifices. The tomb of

Eurypylus is in Patrae, and ever after the people of the city sacrificed to him as a hero at the festival of Dionysus, and the city flourished.

Eurystheus (ū-ris'thē-us). In Greek mythology, a son of Nicippe and Sthenelus, king of Mycenae, and a descendant of Perseus. Thanks to Hera's activities in delaying the birth of Heracles and causing Eurystheus to be born two months ahead of time, he profited by Zeus' vow that the first child born to the house of Perseus would become ruler of Argos and the descendants of Perseus. Zeus could not withdraw his vow, and Eurystheus became king, but Hera agreed that after Heracles had performed whatever labors Eurystheus should demand of him, he would become immortal. It was thus that Eurystheus became the master of Heracles. When Heracles had carried out twelve great labors he returned to Mycenae, but Eurystheus, who was absolutely terrified of him, banished him from Argos, claiming he was a threat to the throne. When Heracles had been taken to live among the gods, Eurystheus banished his children from all Hellas, lest they grow up and seize his throne. Only Athens dared defy Eurystheus and offer protection to the Heraclidae. In the war which followed Eurystheus was captured by Hyllus, Heracles' son, and killed. According to some accounts, Hyllus cut off his head and Alcmene, mother of Heracles, gouged out his eyes. Others say the Athenians would have spared Eurystheus, but yielded to Alcmene's demand for his death.

Eurytus (ū'ri-tus). In Greek legend, the son of Melaneus of Thessaly. He was a king of Oechalia, and a famous archer who had been taught by Apollo, and who in his turn had taught Heracles. He promised his daughter, Iole, to whoever could defeat him in an archery contest. Heracles easily won the contest, but Eurytus, fearing a recurrence of Heracles' madness, refused to give him his daughter and banished him from his palace. Heracles thereupon raised an army and marched against him. He slew Eurytus and some of his sons, and took Iole captive. Eurytus' bow finally fell into the hands of Odysseus, who used it to kill Penelope's suitors. In another account, Eurytus challenged Apollo to an archery contest and the god, angered by his presumption, caused his early death.

Euterpe (ū-tèr'pē). One of the nine daughters of Zeus and
Mnemosyne. She is the muse of music, a divinity of joy and
pleasure, the patroness of flute-players. She invented the
double flute, and favored rather the wild and simple melo
dies of primitive peoples than the more finished art of music
and was associated more with Dionysus than with Apollo
She is usually represented as a maiden crowned with flow
ers, having a flute in her hand, or with various musical in
struments about her. According to some accounts she wa
the mother of the Thracian Rhesus by the river-god of th
Strymon River. See *Muses.*

Evadne (ē-vad'nē). In Greek legend, the wife of Capaneus, a
Argive chieftain who was one of the Seven against Thebe
and perished there. When his body was recovered from
Thebes by Theseus and the Athenians it was placed on
funeral pyre for funeral honors. Evadne leaped into th
flames, as she preferred death with one she loved to life b
herself.

Evenus (ē-vē'nus). In Greek mythology, a son of Ares, an
father, by Alcippe, of Marpessa. He wanted his daughter t
remain a virgin and therefore challenged all her suitors t
a chariot race with him, with the understanding that the firs
one to defeat him would win Marpessa. Whoever raced an
lost had his head cut off and nailed to the walls of Evenus
palace. When Idas defeated him, with the help of winge
horses provided by his father Poseidon, Evenus killed hi
horses and flung himself into the river which from that tim
on bore his name.

Expedition of the Seven against Thebes. See *Seven again.
Thebes, Expedition of the.*

F

Flood. In Greek mythology, the means which Zeus employe
to destroy the wicked men of the Age of Iron. According t
most accounts, only Deucalion, the son of Prometheus, an
his wife Pyrrha were spared to create a new race of me
Other accounts say that Megarus, a son of Zeus, was warne

by cranes and fled to Mount Gerania, which was not covered
by the flood; also Cerambus was saved. The latter was
changed into a beetle by nymphs and flew off to Mount
Parnassus.

G

aea (jē'a). [Also: *Gaia, Ge.*] In Greek mythology, the goddess of the earth. Some say she was the child of Air and Day.
Others say she was sprung directly from Chaos. She was the
mother of Uranus (the sky-god), Pontus (a sea-god), and the
mountains. She bore Uranus in her sleep and by him became
the mother of the Hecatonchires, the Cyclopes, the Titans,
and the Titanesses. Because Uranus hid the Cyclopes in
Tartarus, Gaea plotted against him. She gave Cronus, one
of the Titans, the sickle with which he cut off Uranus' genitals when all the Titans except Oceanus attacked their father. Drops of blood from this mutilation fell on Gaea and
she bore the Erinyes and the Melic nymphs. Gaea prophesied that Cronus, who had deposed his father, would be
dethroned himself by one of his children. When Cronus was
later attacked by his son Zeus, Gaea advised Zeus to release
the Cyclopes, who had again been imprisoned in Tartarus
by Cronus. By her son Pontus, Gaea was the mother of
Nereus, Phorcys, Thaumas, Eurybia, and Ceto. After the
defeat of the Giants by Zeus, Gaea, enraged, lay with Tartarus and brought forth the monster Typhon. She is also
said by some to have been the mother of Ladon, the dragon
that guarded the golden apples of the Hesperides; of
Antaeus, a king in Libya who was killed by Heracles; of
Charybdis, the sea monster; of the 24 Giants born at Phlegra
in Attica; and of the earth-born serpent-kings Erechtheus
and Cecrops. Gaea was invoked as a witness to oaths. She
was worshiped with the sacrifice of a black lamb and her
priestesses drank bull's blood, considered to be deadly poison to ordinary mortals. She was honored as the mother of
all, who nourishes her children and gives them rich bless-

ings. She was also regarded as an Underworld deity wh
reclaims her children in the end. Her cults were very nume
ous. The earliest oracle at Olympia was hers, as was also th
first oracle at Delphi. Some say Apollo stole the latter fro
her, but others say she gave it to the Titaness Phoebe ar
it was from her that Apollo got it. The Romans identifie
Gaea with their Tellus.

Gaia (gā′a̤). See *Gaea.*

Galatea (gal-a̤tē′a̤). In mythology, a sea-nymph, the daught
of Nereus and Doris, who frolicked on the shores of Sici
near Mount Aetna. She was loved by Polyphemus, the on
eyed Cyclops, who pursued her constantly, singing of h
love for her and of the gifts he could offer her. But Galat
loved the handsome and youthful son of Faunus and a se
nymph. He was Acis, and she gave him the love Polyphem
so ardently desired. One day as Polyphemus was playir
love songs about Galatea on his shepherd's pipe, he chanc
upon her, lying in the arms of Acis. In a rage he attacke
them. Galatea plunged into the sea to escape, momentari
abandoning her lover, and Polyphemus hurled a huge stor
at Acis and crushed him. Galatea, returning in search
Acis, caused the rock which covered him to crack open, ar
from the cleft the blood of Acis flowed out and was tran
formed into the river which bears his name.

Galatea. In mythology, a beautiful ivory statue, made by th
sculptor Pygmalion, son of Belus, who lived on the island
Cyprus. He fell in love with his work of art and asked Aphr
dite, at a festival in honor of the goddess, to give him a wi
like the statue. Flames leaped up from the altar to show th
the goddess had heard his plea, and when he returned hon
and kissed the statue it came to life. As the wife of Pygm
lion, Galatea bore Paphus and Metharme.

Galatea. In Greek legend, Cretan mother of a daught
(called Leucippus) who brought the girl up disguised
boy's garments in order to deceive her husband who ha
ordered that the child be killed at birth if it were a gi
Eventually Galatea and Leucippus took refuge in the temp
of Leto. Galatea prayed that her daughter might be chang
into a boy, and the transformation took place. This sam
story is told by Ovid, in the *Metamorphoses,* of Telethu
whose daughter Iphis was transformed by the help of Io
a young man.

aleus (gā′lē-us). In mythology, a lizard, the son of Apollo. The Galeotae, soothsayers of Sicily, declared that Galeus was their ancestor.

alinthias (ga-lin′thi-as), or *Galanthis* (-this), or *Galen* (gā′len). In Greek mythology, a faithful handmaid of Heracles' mother Alcmene. Hera conspired with Ilithyia and the Moerae to delay the birth of Heracles for nine days and nights, the Moerae sitting outside the door with knees crossed and hands clasped in sympathetic magic. Galinthias, to help Alcmene end her long labor, mendaciously announced to the waiting goddesses that the birth had taken place. At this news they jumped up, uncrossing their legs and unclenching their hands, thus breaking the spell, and Heracles was born. Galinthias laughed at the goddesses she had tricked and Ilithyia seized her by the hair and changed her into a weasel and, according to some accounts, because she had lied about the birth of Heracles, she was condemned to bear her young through her mouth. Later Hecate pitied her and made her one of her handmaidens, and Heracles erected a shrine for her at Thebes.

allus (gal′us). In mythology, a priest of Cybele who emasculated himself in the service of Cybele. From then on it was the usage that these priests should be eunuchs. Their worship consisted essentially of wild and boisterous rites and the name was associated with that of the river Gallus, in Phrygia, whose waters were fabled to make those who drank them mad.

anymeda (gan-i-mē′da). Another name for Hebe, handmaiden of the gods. See *Hebe*.

anymede (gan′i-mēd) or *Ganymedes* (gan-i-mē′dēz). In Greek mythology, a beautiful Trojan youth, the son of Tros and Callirrhoë. He was transferred to Olympus (according to Homer, by the gods; according to others, by the eagle of Zeus, or by Zeus himself in the form of an eagle, or by Eos, goddess of the dawn, from whom he was taken by Zeus), to become the cup-bearer of the gods, and became immortal. To compensate his father for the loss of his son, Zeus gave Tros a golden vine and two immortal horses which could run like the wind over water or standing grain. Ganymede supplanted Hebe in her function as cup-bearer, his presence in Olympus thus annoying Hera and giving the goddess another reason for hating the Trojans. Ganymede was late regarded as the genius of water, especially of the Nile, an he is represented in the Zodiac by the constellatio Aquarius. In Latin the name appears as Catamitus, whenc the English term catamite.

Garden of the Hesperides. A legendary garden owned by Atla on Mount Atlas, either in Mauretania, in the land of th Hyperboreans, or on an island beyond the stream of ocean In this garden grew the tree with the golden apples, gift t Hera from Mother Earth. It was guarded by the Hesperide daughters of Atlas, hence the name.

Gargaphia (gär-gā′fi-a̱), **Vale of.** In Greek mythology, the va where Actaeon was torn to pieces by his own hounds, afte being transformed into a stag in punishment for having see Artemis bathing. It was used by Jonson as the scene o *Cynthia's Revels.*

Gasterocheires (gas″tẻr-o̱-kī′rēz). In Greek mythology, seve gigantic Cyclopes, who went with Proetus from Lycia, whe Proetus and his brother Acrisius divided the kingdom be tween them, and built the massive walls of Tiryns.

Ge (jē). See **Gaea.**

Geleon (jel′e̱-on). According to Greek tradition, one of th four sons of Ion. One of the four ancient tribes of Athen was named for him. His brothers were Aegicores, Argade and Hoples.

Genetyllis (jen-e̱-til′is). [Also: **Gennaides.**] In Greek myth ology, a goddess, protectress of births, a companion o Aphrodite. The name is also used as an epithet of Aphrodi and of Artemis. In the plural, Genetyllides, it is applied t a body of divinities presiding over childbirth, and attache to the train of Aphrodite.

Geryon (jē′ri-o̱n, ger′i-o̱n) or **Geryones** (jē-rī′o̱-nēz). In Gree mythology, a monster with three heads or three bodies an powerful wings, dwelling in the island of Erythea in the fa west; son of Chrysaor and Callirrhoë. He possessed a larg herd of red cattle guarded by Eurytion (his shepherd) an the two-headed dog Orthus. To carry away these cattle wa the tenth labor of Heracles, which he successfully pe formed, after killing the shepherd, the dog, and Geryo himself. According to a later account, Chrysaor was a re nowned king in Iberia, the father of three brave sons wh were symbolized in the three-headed Geryon. When Her cles went there to steal the cattle the three sons headed three forces against him. Heracles separated them and killed Chrysaor's three sons.

iants, Gigantes (ji-gan′tēz). In Greek mythology, an earth-born race which sprang from the blood of Uranus when he was mutilated by his son Cronus. From the drops of blood which fell on Phlegra in Attica, 24 sons were born to Gaea (Earth). They had the bodies of serpents and the heads of men. Gaea, and their own rage because Zeus had banished the Titans to Tartarus, inspired them to wage war on the gods. Armed with tree trunks and rocks, they attacked Olympus. The war was frightful. Hera prophesied that only a mortal, wearing a lion's skin and protected by a magic herb, would be able to slay the Giants. Zeus sent Athena to Heracles. While Eos, Helius, and Selene, as commanded by Zeus, ceased to pour their light on the world, Athena helped Heracles find the herb and brought him to the battle. The gods succeeded in wounding many of the Giants but only Heracles could deliver the death blow. Those Giants who were not killed on Olympus fled to Arcadia, near Trapezus, and there, attacked and wounded by the gods, were finished off by Heracles. According to ancient accounts the ground in the region still smoldered from the thunderbolts Zeus hurled at the Giants, and plowmen often turned up huge bones in their fields. Other accounts say the final stand of the Giants took place on the Phlegraean Plain, which borders the Bay of Naples near Cumae in Italy, and that they are buried under mountains there, where they rumble and explode from time to time as volcanos.

laucia (glô′shạ). In Greek legend, a daughter of the Trojan river-god Scamander. When Heracles attacked Troy and sacked it Deimachus, one of his companions who had been Glaucia's lover, was killed. She sought protection and Heracles took her back to Hellas with him. She bore Deimachus' son, whom she named Scamander. Heracles later made him a king in Boeotia, where he renamed the Inachus River Scamander, after himself.

laucus (glô′kus). In Greek legend, a son of Hippolochus and grandson of Bellerophon. He was a captain of the Lycians, allies of Troy in the Trojan War, a valiant hero, and the close friend and cousin of Sarpedon. He met Diomedes face to face in combat, and in response to Diomedes' chal-

bscured) errạnt, ardẹnt, actọr; ch, chip; g, go; th, thin; ₮ʜ, then; y, you;
ịriable) ḍ as d or j, ṣ as s or sh, ṭ as t or ch, ẓ as z or zh.

lenge, said that as a grandson of Bellerophon he would fight
anyone. On learning of his ancestry Diomedes planted his
spear in the ground. He recalled that his own grandfather
Oeneus, was a close friend of Bellerophon, and declared
that the grandsons should continue the friendship. As an
expression of the ancient friendship he gave his bronze ar
mor to Glaucus. Glaucus, whose wits were addled by Zeus
gave his pure gold armor to Diomedes in return—the classic
example of getting the worst of a bargain—and they parted
friends. Glaucus accompanied Sarpedon at the siege of the
fortifications surrounding the Greek ships and was wounded
by Teucer. Later, although wounded, he called on Apollo to
help him rescue Sarpedon's body, as his friend had asked
with his last breath. Apollo heard his prayer and cured his
wound. Glaucus then rallied the Trojans and with them
defended Sarpedon's body until it was borne away by
Apollo. Later, when fighting for possession of Achilles
body, Glaucus was slain by Telamonian Ajax. His body was
rescued by Aeneas and taken to Troy, from whence it was
borne to Lycia by Apollo, for funeral rites.

Glaucus. A fabled fisherman of Boeotia, one of the Ar
gonauts. According to some accounts, he was a son of Posei
don, or of Anthedon, who saw a dead fish that was laid on
a certain grass come back to life again. Glaucus ate some of
the grass and, leaping into the sea, was transformed into a
sea-god and became an attendant of Poseidon. Among many
others, he loved the sea-nymph Scylla. Circe, or perhaps it
was Amphitrite, who also loved Glaucus, changed Scylla into
a hideous sea-monster out of jealousy that she had won
Glaucus' love. Glaucus had the gift of prophecy, and is
represented in the *Aeneid* as the father of Deïphobe, a priest
ess of Apollo and Trivia at Cumae—the Cumaean Sibyl.

Glaucus. In Greek legend, a son of Minos, king of Crete, and
Pasiphaë. While still a child he disappeared one day and
could not be found. His parents at last consulted the oracl
at Delphi and were told that whoever could give the best
comparison concerning a heifer that changed its color three
times a day would find that lost child. Polyidus, an Argiv
descendant of the seer Melampus, compared the changing
colors of the heifer—from white to red to black—with
ripening mulberry, which follows the same color changes
Minos thereupon ordered him to find Glaucus and he a

---

fat, fāte, fär, fâll, ȧsk, fāre; net, mē, hėr; pin, pīne; not, nōte, mȯv
nôr; up, lūte, pu̇ll; oi, oil; ou out; (lightened) ẹlect, agǫny, ūnit

length did find him, drowned in a vat of honey. Minos then told him that since he had found the child he must now restore him to life, and locked him in a tomb with the dead child. As Polyidus, in despair, sat in the tomb, he saw a snake crawl into the crypt and approach the body of Glaucus. Polyidus killed it with his sword. Presently the serpent's mate crawled up and deposited a magic herb on the dead snake, whereupon the dead snake slowly came to life. Polyidus seized the herb and laid it on the body of Glaucus, where it had the same miraculous results. He and the restored Glaucus were released from the tomb and Minos, in his joy at finding his son alive, gave Polyidus rich gifts and asked him to teach the art of divination to Glaucus. Polyidus did as he was commanded, but just before he sailed from Crete to return home to Argos, he asked Glaucus to spit into his open mouth. Glaucus did so and immediately forgot all Polyidus had told him about divination. Apparently spitting into the mouth of the teacher was the time-tested way to make the pupil forget what his master had taught him.

laucus.   In Greek legend, a son of Sisyphus and Merope. He lived near Thebes and was the father of Bellerophon. Glaucus refused to let his mares breed, on the theory that they were better racing horses if they did not breed, and so offended Aphrodite. She punished him by feeding his mares on a magic herb, hippomanes, which drove them mad. When Glaucus harnessed them to his chariot for the race at the funeral games for Pelias, they became frenzied, overthrew the chariot, and plunged Glaucus to the ground. They then tore their master to pieces and devoured his flesh.

olden Age.   According to Hesiod's account of the Creation, this was the period of the first race of men, who lived during the reign of Cronus. There were no women in the Golden Age. Men lived like gods. They knew neither sorrow nor toil, old age nor sickness. It was a period of patriarchal simplicity, when the earth yielded its fruits spontaneously and spring was eternal. When it was time for men to leave the earth, Death came gently and led them off in a peaceful sleep.

olden Apples of the Hesperides.   In Greek mythology, Gaea presented Hera with the tree which bore the golden apples as a wedding gift. The tree was planted in a garden in the remote West, on Mount Atlas in Mauretania, or in the land of the Hyperboreans, or perhaps on an island beyond the

stream of Ocean. It was guarded by the Hesperides, daughters of Atlas, or of Hesperus, the evening star or the personification of the West or of sunset, and by the 100-headed
sleepless dragon Ladon. As one of his labors, Heracle
fetched the golden apples to Eurystheus, but as it was unlaw
ful for a mortal to possess the apples they were restored t
the garden through the good offices of Athena. In one ver
sion Heracles prevails upon the giant Atlas, who holds th
sky on his shoulders, to wade out across Ocean and fetch th
apples for him while Heracles holds the sky in his stead. Thi
incident is an occasional subject of Greek art, as on one o
the metopes of the temple of Zeus at Olympia.

Golden Fleece, The. The fleece of pure gold taken from th
winged ram which Hermes sent to snatch Phrixus and Hell
away from the altar as they were about to be sacrificed. Th
ram flew with them to Colchis but as they crossed the Helles
pont Helle fell into the sea which has since borne her name
Phrixus arrived safely in Colchis and sacrificed the ram, a
instructed, to Zeus. The Fleece was hung up in Colchis an
guarded by a dragon. It was recovered from King Aeëtes b
the Argonautic expedition under Jason, with the help o
Medea, the daughter of King Aeëtes. Modern travelers hav
reported that in the Caucasus gold dust is obtained by stak
ing fleeces in the river gravels, which after some weeks ar
lifted out, dried and burned, leaving as residue the gol
which had clung to the wool, and suggesting a possibl
origin for the oriental phase of the legend.

Good Fame or **Good Repute.** Goddess, usually identified wit
Artemis. There was an altar and an image of the goddess o
Good Repute in the market-place of every town in Boeoti
and Locris. An image of her was also in the market-place a
Corinth.

Gorgons (gôr'gọnz). In Greek mythology, three daughters o
Ceto and Phorcys (whence they are called Phorcides) dwell
ing in the Western Ocean near Night and the Hesperides (i
later mythology, in Libya). They had originally been beauti
ful maidens but were transformed into such horrible winge
monsters, with coiling serpents for hair, brazen claws, an
staring eyes, that all who looked upon them were turned t
stone. Their names were Stheno, Euryale, and Medusa
Medusa, the only one of the three who was mortal, was slai
by Perseus.

orgophone (gôr-gof′ō-nē). In Greek legend, the daughter of Perseus and Andromeda. She married Perieres, king of Messenia and son of Aeolus, and had two sons: Aphareus and Leucippus. When Perieres died she married Oebalus, king of Sparta, and bore him two sons: Tyndareus and Icarius. According to some accounts, she was the first widow to remarry, as it was the custom up to then for women to commit suicide on the death of their husbands.

ortys (gôr′tis). In Greek legend, a son of Stymphalus. He was said to be the founder of the city of Gortys, in Arcadia, on the river of the same name. Also; a son of Tegeates of Arcadia. Some say this Gortys migrated voluntarily to Crete, and there founded the Cretan city of Gortyna; but the Cretans say Gortyna was founded by their own Gortys, son of Rhadamanthys.

raeae (grē′ē). [Also: *Graiae*.] In Greek mythology, three daughters of Ceto and Phorcys. They were sea-goddesses, old from birth, having been born with gray hair. They had but one eye and one tooth between the three of them which they passed back and forth. They were the protectors of the Gorgons, and inhabited a plain in the farthest reaches of Libya, where the light of neither the sun nor the moon ever shone. Perseus visited them to learn where the Gorgon Medusa could be found, and compelled them to give him the information he sought by seizing their only eye and tooth. Their names were Dino, Enyo, and Pemphredo.

aiae (grā′e, grī′ē). See *Graeae*.

eat Mother. In ancient mythologies, the goddess of birth and fertility: an almost worldwide concept. Cybele is the Great Mother of ancient Anatolia whose cult spread throughout the whole Mediterranean region. Ishtar was the ancient Babylonian and Assyrian Great Mother; the Sumerian Great Mother was Nana; the Phoenician was Astarte; the Egyptian was Isis. Anahita was the Great Mother of ancient Iranian religion. The Greeks identified Cybele with their Rhea, and later her cult became fused with those of Artemis and Aphrodite. The Romans identified her with Ops and Bona Dea, and later with Venus. The North American Indians also have their mother goddesses, Earth Mothers, Corn Mothers, and others, who are all nature and fertility deities. The ancient Peruvians had the concept; Pa-

chamama was their great Mother Earth. Various other Sou
American Indians also conceive of a great chief deity who
they regard as the common mother of all things. The co
cept is widespread in primitive African Negro religior
Surinam Negroes worship a Gro Mama, or Great Mothe

Griffins (grif'inz). In Greek mythology, fabulous monste
sometimes called "the Hounds of Zeus." They were said
have been generated between the lion and the eagle, and
combine the head, front, and wings of an eagle with t
body and hindquarters of a lion. Their duty was to guard t
mines of gold and the river of gold which flowed in t
region of the Hyperboreans from the one-eyed Arimasp
who were always trying to steal it. The figure of the grif
is seen on ancient coins, and is borne in coat-armor. It is al
a frequent motive in architectural decoration.

Gyges (jī'jēz) or *Gyes* (jī'ēz). In Greek mythology, one of t
Hecatonchires, the 100-handed giants who were the ch
dren of Uranus and Gaea. His brothers were Cottus a
Briareus.

H

Hades (hā'dēz). One of the 12 Olympian gods, he was t
lord of the Underworld, feared alike by mortals and go
as ruler of the dead and for his terrible justice. No soari
temples rose in the bright air of Greece in his honor, n
were festivals celebrated to glorify him. When mortals call
on him they struck the earth with their hands and invok
him with oaths and curses. He reigned in a splendid pala
and, besides his function of governing the shades of t
dead, he was the giver to mortals of all treasures deriv
from the earth and was given the name Pluto *(Wealt*
Hermes conducted the shades of the dead to his kingdo
and from there they never escaped. Hades took pride in
growth of his kingdom, and once complained to Zeus abo
Asclepius, who was raising the dead, that if he were allow
to continue this practice the population of the Underwo
would not increase as it should.

Hades was the son of Cronus and Rhea. Like his sisters before him he was swallowed by Cronus as soon as he was born, and later was disgorged with them when Zeus, aided by Metis, tricked Cronus. In the war between Zeus and Cronus, Hades was given a cap of invisibility by the Cyclopes. (The cap symbolized the invisible world of which he was the ruler; the name Hades happens also to mean "the Unseen.") Wearing it, he crept into the presence of Cronus and stole his weapons. When Cronus was defeated, Hades, Zeus, and Poseidon drew lots from a helmet to see what regions of the universe each would control. By the lots Zeus was assigned to the heavens, Poseidon to the sea, and Hades to the Underworld. The earth was to remain open to all. Hades descended to his kingdom and seldom appeared thereafter on earth.

Some say that Aphrodite, queen of love, inspired love in the heart of Hades because she wished to show her power in the Underworld. He fell in love with Persephone, daughter of Demeter and Zeus, and asked Zeus for her hand. Zeus did not like to deny his brother, nor did he want to cause suffering to Demeter, thus he took the position that he would not interfere in the matter. Hades took this as consent. In his golden chariot, drawn by four black horses, he arose through a cleft in the earth, swooped down on Persephone as she was gathering flowers in a meadow, and carried her back to the Underworld with him. Persephone was a most unwilling bride, and all the time she was in his kingdom she refused to eat. Demeter caused the earth to be barren until her daughter should be restored to her, and Zeus was compelled to send Hermes to Hades with a command to him to restore Persephone to her mother, otherwise the race of men would die and the gods would lose their rich sacrifices. Hades had no choice but to obey. However, before he sent Persephone off with Hermes, he reproached her and reminded her that it was no discreditable thing to be the wife of the lord of the Underworld, and he persuaded her to eat seven pomegranate seeds. For those who have eaten the food of the dead must return to the world of the dead. In this way he brought it about that Persephone was compelled to spend a portion of each year with him, as queen of the Underworld. Persephone bore him no children. She was a careful wife, and transformed the nymph

Minthe, whom Hades would have seduced, into the fragrar[n] mint plant. Again, when Hades was eyeing the nymph Leuc[?] she was transformed into a white poplar tree, and thencefor[?] ward stood beside the Pool of Memory in the Underworl[d] Heracles, come here to seize the dog Cerberus, plucked th[e] leaves of the poplar and made a wreath for his head. Th[e] leaves were black, the color of the Underworld, but th[e] divine sweat of Heracles' brow as he labored with Cerberu[s] bleached the leaves where they touched his skin, which [is] why one side of the leaves of the poplar gleams whitel[y] while the other side is dark. Heracles was one of few wh[o] succeeded in visiting the realm of Hades and escaping fro[m] it. As one of his labors for Eurystheus he was required t[o] drag up the dog Cerberus from Tartarus. When he bold[ly] demanded the dog, the god agreed to let him take it if h[e] could do so without weapons. Heracles succeeded. While h[e] was in Tartarus Heracles freed Theseus, who had gon[e] there with Pirithous with the purpose of abducting Pers[e]phone. Hades had invited them to be seated when the[y] made their arrogant demand for his wife, and as soon as the[y] did so they found themselves bound fast to the Chairs [of] Forgetfulness. Heracles was able to wrench Theseus fro[m] his seat, but Pirithous had to be abandoned. Orpheus s[o] charmed Queen Persephone and the shades of the dead tha[t] Hades agreed to allow him to take Eurydice, his dead wif[e] back to earth with him on condition that he not look bac[k] until he reached the upper air. Orpheus in his anxiet[y] looked back too soon and Eurydice was lost forever. Som[e] say that at the command of Zeus Hades came to earth [to] fetch Sisyphus, the greatest knave that ever lived, to Ta[r]tarus. Sisyphus persuaded Hades to try on a pair of golde[n] handcuffs, once they were on Sisyphus locked them and ke[pt] Hades a prisoner. As long as Hades was a prisoner no on[e] could die, not even the most grievously wounded. Ar[es] came to the rescue and freed Hades. On another occasio[n] when Hades visited the earth he took part in the war b[e]tween Heracles and the Pylians. The god fought again[st] Heracles, was wounded by him and was compelled to wit[h]draw.

As he had no temples, he had very few names. The Gree[ks] preferred not to think of him. The cypress and the narciss[us] were sacred to him. In art he is represented in a form ki[n] dred to that of Zeus and that of Poseidon, and bearing the staff or scepter of authority, sometimes in company with Persephone or the dog Cerberus. The Romans also called him Pluto, and identified him with their Dis or Orcus.

Hades. [More properly, *The House of Hades.*] The lower or subterranean world in which dwelt the spirits of the dead. Sometimes it was said to be situated in the west. The souls in Hades were believed to carry on there a counterpart of their material existence: those of the righteous without discomfort, amid the pale sweet blooms of asphodel, or even in pleasure, in the Elysian Fields; and those of the wicked amid various torments in Tartarus. Hades was surrounded by five rivers, of which the Styx (across which Charon ferried the souls of the buried dead) and Lethe (the river of forgetfulness) are the best known. The gates were guarded by the monstrous three-headed (sometimes 50-headed) dog Cerberus to prevent the shades from escaping to the upper world.

Haemon (hē'mon). In Greek legend, the son of Creon, king of Thebes. He loved Antigone, daughter of Oedipus, but was ordered by his father to bury her alive because she had defied his order and built a pyre for the corpse of her brother Polynices. Haemon, according to some accounts, agreed to slay Antigone but secretly married her and hid her away. She later bore him a son which Creon recognized as her child because it bore the mark of a serpent, as did all the descendants of Cadmus. Creon again ordered her death, as well as that of the child, and when she was killedHaemon killed himself on her tomb. According to Sophocles, Antigone was killed immediately for her defiance of Creon and Haemon committed suicide on her tomb.

Haemus (hē'mus). In Greek mythology, a son of Boreas and Orithyia. He was a king in Thrace and the father, by Rhodope, of Hebrus. Haemus and Rhodope were so happy in their marriage that they assumed the names of Zeus and Hera. For their presumption, the gods transformed them into mountains, the peaks in the Balkans that bear their names. The whole range, now called the Balkan mountains, was once called the Haemus range.

Hagno (hag'nō). In Greek mythology, Arcadian nymph who, according to the Arcadians, was one of the nymphs who took care of the infant Zeus after he was born on Mount Lycaeus

in Arcadia. A never-failing spring on the mountain was give
her name. This spring had the wonderful property of bring
ing rain to a parched land. When there was a prolonge
drought the priest prayed to its waters and made sacrifice
Then he lowered an evergreen oak branch to the surface
the water. When the water was stirred, a mist rose. This mi
formed a cloud, drew other clouds to it, and caused rain
fall on the Arcadians.

Halia (hal'i-ą). A sea-goddess of Rhodes. By Poseidon sh
was the mother of six sons and a daughter, Rhode. Th(
were brought up on the island of Rhodes, which takes i
name from Halia's daughter. Aphrodite, who had been i)
sulted by the six sons of Halia, inspired them with madne;
and they assaulted their mother. Poseidon hid them in tl
earth, where they became demons. Halia hurled herself int
the sea and was deified as the sea-goddess Leucothea, a
cording to some accounts, but this same story is told of In(
the mother of Melicertes, and the same name is given to In
after she became a sea-goddess. In the *Iliad* Halia is name
as a Nereid.

Halitherses (hal-i-thėr'sēz). In the *Odyssey,* an Ithacan se(
who understood the flight of birds. When two eagles fle
over the assembly gathered by Telemachus and sudden
began tearing at each other, Halitherses interpreted this t
mean that Odysseus would return and tear the suitors
Penelope to pieces. For this reason he advised them to g
home and leave the halls and fortunes of Odysseus in goo
state for their master's return.

Hamadryad (ham-ą-drī'ąd). In Greek mythology, a woo(
nymph supposed to live and die with the tree to which sh
was attached. The hamadryad is the presiding deity of th
tree and shares in its joys and sorrows; whatever wounds th
tree wounds the hamadryad.

Harmonia (här-mō'ni-ą). In Greek mythology, a daughter (
Ares and Aphrodite. Zeus gave her to Cadmus when h
became king of Thebes, and all the gods attended the
wedding. Among the gifts to Harmonia was a necklace fasl
ioned by Hephaestus which was said to guarantee beauty t
its possessor. Some say Hephaestus gave it to Cadmus, an
he gave it to Harmonia. Others say this had been a gift (
Zeus to Europa; and still others say it was given by Aphro
dite to Harmonia. Harmonia was also given a *peplus,* or rob(

by Athena, and some say Athena gave her both the necklace and robe. These two gifts, handed down to the descendants of Cadmus, brought great grief to their possessors, and played a part in the Expedition of the Seven against Thebes as well as in the war of the Epigoni. They were at last taken to the temple of Apollo at Delphi, where the god saw to it that they brought no further disasters. There they remained until the 4th century B.C., when they were carried off by a bandit. Harmonia bore Agave, Autonoë, Ino, Semele, and Polydorus to Cadmus. Although Harmonia and Cadmus were turned into serpents by Zeus, their tomb was to be found in the land of the Encheleans in Illyria. See *Cadmus.*

arpies (här′piz). In Greek mythology, winged daughters of Thaumas and Electra, daughter of Oceanus. They were winged monsters, ravenous and filthy, having the face and body of a woman and the wings of a bird of prey, with the feet and fingers armed with sharp claws, and the face pale with hunger. They served as ministers of divine vengeance. Sometimes they punished criminals themselves, as they tormented Phineus for impiety; sometimes they caught criminals and handed them over to the Erinyes for punishment, as in the case of Merope, Cleothera (or Cameiro), and Clytië, who were punished by the Erinyes for the crimes of their father, Pandareus. The Harpies carried off the souls of the dead and defiled the food of their living victims. They were commonly regarded as two (Aello and Ocypete) or three in number (Celaeno), but occasionally several others were mentioned. Homer mentions only one, named Podarge. They were originally personifications of storm-winds sent by the gods to carry off offenders, and were later personified as fair-haired, winged maidens, their features and characteristics being more or less repulsive at different times and places. The Harpies have been to some extent confounded with the Sirens because of their form, being represented as women in the upper parts of their bodies and as birds below.

earth, Goddess of the. See *Hestia.*

ebe (hē′bē). In Greek mythology, the goddess of youth and spring; the personification of eternal and exuberant youth, and, until supplanted in this office by Ganymede, the cupbearer of Olympus. She was a daughter of Zeus and Hera, who gave her as wife to Heracles after his death and deification, as a reward for his achievements. She bore him two sons. Hebe was worshiped as Dia in certain localities, and in this aspect she is associated with Aphrodite. Powers of rejuvenation were ascribed to her. The Romans called her Juventas.

Hecate (hek′ạ-tē). [Also: **Hekate.**] In Greek mythology, a triple goddess combining the concepts of moon-goddess, earth-goddess, and Underworld-goddess. She had powers over the sky, earth, and sea, and was also a giver of riches and good fortune. As moon-goddess, she was identified with Artemis. As Underworld-goddess, she was an attendant of Persephone; and as leader of souls of the dead she was associated with ghosts, magic, and witchcraft. She was invisible to mortals, but dogs could see her pass; and she was often conceived of as tearing through the night followed by a pack of spectral hounds. Hounds were sacred to her. Hecate was also a crossroads-goddess, and as such was represented with triple bodies back to back. In this aspect the Romans named her Trivia. She was also identified variously with Demeter, Rhea, and Persephone.

Hecatonchires (hek-ạ-ton-kī′rēz). Greek name, used collectively, for the 100-handed monsters Briareus (also called Aegaeon), Cottus, and Gyges (or Gyes). The Roman name was *Centimani.*

Hector (hek′tọr). The Trojan hero of the *Iliad.* He was the son of Priam and Hecuba (but some say he was a son of Apollo), the Crown Prince of Troy, and the leader of the Trojans and their allies in the defense of Troy against the Greeks. He did not approve of the war and unsuccessfully tried to stop it by negotiation and by individual combat, as when he suggested the duel between Menelaus and Paris. He scorned his brother, Paris, as a beautiful coward and seducer of women, and often wished him in Hades. Nevertheless, Hector fought valiantly and was the bravest of the Trojans, as his honor compelled him to fight for his family and for his country. His bravery was the greater because he knew he was doomed to die and that Troy would fall. For sheer love of glorious combat he challenged the Greeks to send a champion against him in single combat. Telamonian Ajax won, by lot, the honor of fighting him and they struggled all day, with neither able to achieve victory. At the end of their duel each expressed admiration for the courage and skill of the other. Hector gave Ajax his sword as a gift. Ajax gave Hector his girdle in exchange.

fat, fāte, fär, fåll, åsk, fāre; net, mē, hėr; pin, pīne; not, nōte, mōve, nôr; up, lūte, pull; oi, oil; ou out; (lightened) ẹlect, agọny, ūnite

In what is probably the most touching and tender scene in the *Iliad*, Andromache, his wife, begs Hector to withdraw from the field and to seek safety inside the city walls, for her sake and that of their son, as well as for his own. With understanding and compassion, for he foresees her gloomy future, he convinces her that he must go, for he cannot evade his destiny. He expresses the hope that his baby son, who now shrinks in terror from his father's glittering war helmet, will be proud of his father and will be a better man. Gently he salutes her and leaves to rejoin the fighting. Aided by Apollo, he leads the Trojans against the ramparts protecting the Greek galleys, smashes open the gates, and fires the ships. He slays Patroclus, the intimate friend of Achilles,

RANSOM OF HECTOR'S BODY
Red-figured Attic skyphos, early 5th century B.C. Hector's body lies under the couch on which Achilles rests; aged Priam is at the left.
Vienna

and puts on his armor. The death of Patroclus causes Achilles to renounce the wrath that has kept him inactive during the struggle, and he enters the battle to avenge Patroclus. Achilles drives the Trojans back into the city. Hector is left alone before the walls to face him. Seized by a moment of human fear Hector flees. Three times Achilles pursues him around the walls of Troy. Now Hector masters his fear and stops to face his enemy. And now the gods forsake him. Athena deludes him by appearing in the guise of his brother.

(obscured) errant, ardent, actor; ch, chip; g, go; th, thin; ŦH, then; y, you;
(variable) ḏ as d or j, ṣ as s or sh, ṭ as t or ch, ẓ as z or zh.

Hector hurls his spear at Achilles then turns to his supposed brother for another weapon. He finds no one is there and realizes that the moment has come to meet his inevitable fate. His request to Achilles that his body be restored to Priam for burial is wrathfully scorned; and Achilles, who recognizes the armor that Hector is wearing, knows that there is a chink in the armor at the throat. He plunges his spear through the chink, and Hector falls. Achilles slits the tendons of Hector's heels, and takes the girdle that had been given to Hector by Ajax and passes it through the slits. Then he fastens the girdle to his chariot and drags the body of his fallen enemy through the dust to the Greek camp. Daily thereafter Achilles maltreats Hector's body, but it is preserved from all signs of injury by the gods, who anoint it with nectar and ambrosia. Thus, when Priam comes at last to ransom it, the body is still fresh. Priam returns to Troy with the body of his son and, as all Troy mourns, gives it funeral honors. Even Helen mourns the death of Hector, for he had always been kind to her and protected her from the spite of some of the Trojan women.

Great "shimmering-helmeted" Hector was one of the noblest characters of Greek literature—valiant, honorable, compassionate, reasonable, skillful in arms, and handsome in body. He paid due respect and honor to the gods, especially to Zeus, who in turn protected him often, but could not save him from his appointed fate. Some say that the bones of Hector were later taken to Thebes in Boeotia, and buried beside the fountain of Oedipus there. This was done in obedience to a command of the oracle, which recommended that the Thebans gain possession of the bones of Hector if they desired prosperity for their land. Others say they were moved at the command of Apollo, who ordered the reburial of Hector's body in a city that had taken no part in the Trojan War, in order to lift a plague that struck Greece. Hector was still worshiped at Troy in the time of the Roman Empire; even, in fact, after the state had recognized Christianity. The Emperor Julian was taken to the sanctuary of Hector in the Troad by the bishop. There he saw a bronze statue of Hector in a little shrine, before which embers of sacrificial fire were still glowing on an altar. The Emperor asked in surprise if people still sacrificed to Hector. The bishop replied that Hector was one of their good townsmen, and if people paid their respects to him it was no more than Christians did to their martyrs.

Hecuba (hek′ū̇-ba̧) or **Hecabe** (hek′a̧-bē). In Greek legend, a daughter of Dymas of Phrygia, or, as some say, of Cisseus. She was the second wife of Priam, king of Troy, who bore him 19 of his 50 sons. Her oldest son, Hector, was sometimes said to be the son of Apollo, as was her son Troilus. Among Hecuba's other sons were Paris, Deïphobus, Helenus, Polites, Antiphus, and Polydorus. Her daughters included Cassandra, Creusa, Laodice, and Polyxena. Before Paris was born Hecuba dreamed that she had given birth to a bundle of faggots tied with fiery serpents. She woke screaming that Troy was in flames. This dream was interpreted to mean that the child she was about to bear would bring destruction to Troy if he and his mother were not killed to prevent it. A second pronouncement said that the child born to a royal Trojan that day must be destroyed with his mother or Troy would fall in ruins. Hecuba bore Paris on the day of the later prophecy and Priam spared them both. Later, on the urgent advice of seers, he gave the infant to his herdsman with instructions to kill him. Some say Hecuba bribed the herdsman to spare her child. In any event, Paris was not destroyed and when he appeared in Troy as a young man he was welcomed delightedly by his parents. During the Trojan War Hecuba pled with Hector to keep himself apart from the struggle but to no avail. When he was pursued to the walls by Achilles, she begged him to save himself but he refused; he stood and faced Achilles and met his death before his mother's eyes. For reasons that have never been satisfactorily explained, Hecuba, with Helen, questioned Odysseus, when he crept into Troy to steal the Palladium, and let him go without denouncing him as the spy he was. In this case, Hecuba acted with Helen. Later she beseeched Menelaus to kill Helen as the cause of the disasters which had overcome Troy and the house of Priam. In the sack of Troy Hecuba saw her son Polites and her husband slain by Neoptolemus. Only her children Cassandra, Polyxena, and Polydorus now remained to her. In the division of the spoils Hecuba was awarded to Odysseus, perhaps in fulfillment of some promise he had made to her when he secretly entered Troy, or perhaps to prevent her from revealing that he had appeared in any but a heroic light on that occasion. As the

(obscured) errant, ardent, actor; ch, chip; g, go; th, thin; ŧH, then; y, you;
(variable) ḍ as d or j, ş as s or sh, ţ as t or ch, ẓ as z or zh.

woman who once had been the proud queen of a rich king
dom waited to be carried off as a slave, she was informed
that Cassandra and her daughter-in-law Andromache were
to be the captives of Agamemnon and Neoptolemus respec
tively; and that, on the advice of Odysseus, her grandson
Astyanax must be destroyed lest at some future time he raise
an army and march against the Greeks. The aged, broken
queen left Troy in flames and sailed with her captors across
the Hellespont to Thrace. Here the Greeks were held by
unfavorable winds. To appease Achilles and secure favora
ble winds, Hecuba's last remaining daughter was sacrificed
on the tomb of Achilles. Hecuba wished that she might have
died with her city, and counted Priam lucky that he had not
lived to see his city fall and his children destroyed. In the
midst of these shattering griefs the body of her son Polydo
rus was brought to her. He had been sent with a rich trea
sure to Polymnestor of Thrace for safe-keeping
Polymnestor had betrayed his trust, some say in his greed
for gold, slain the young prince, and cast his body into the
sea. It was washed ashore at Hecuba's feet. In a sudden fury
for revenge Hecuba, with Agamemnon's connivance, lured
Polymnestor and his two young sons into her tent, with a
story that she had concealed a great hoard of Trojan gold
there. Once they were inside Hecuba and other Trojan
women attacked him, put out his eyes, and killed his two
sons. Cassandra's prophecy that Hecuba would never go to
Greece was fulfilled. The Greeks would have stoned her to
death for the blinding of Polymnestor and the murder of his
two sons, but she was transformed into a bitch, Maera, and
ran howling off into the wilderness. Others say that she was
taken to Thrace by Odysseus, but that she so hideously
condemned the Greeks for their barbarity and treachery and
uttered such constant invectives that they put her to death.
Her spirit was transformed into a black bitch that leaped into
the sea and swam off to the Hellespont. Even the gods
agreed that Hecuba had not deserved to meet such an end.

Helen (hel'en). [Also: **Helen of Troy**.] In Greek legend, the
"all-glorious" woman whose divine beauty led to a disastrous war which ended in the complete destruction of Troy
and the empire of King Priam. Various stories are related
concerning her birth, but certain it is that Zeus was her
father. Some say that Zeus pursued Nemesis; that she fled

from him, transforming herself from one animal to another
to escape. At last she took the form of a goose and flew off.
Zeus assumed the form of a swan, overtook her and ravished
her. Nemesis laid a blue and silver egg which was found by
Leda, wife of Tyndareus. She took it home and hid it in a
chest, and from this egg Helen was born. Others say that
Hermes found the egg Nemesis had laid and tossed it between Leda's knees, and it was from this that Leda bore
Helen. The most common account is that Zeus, in the form
of a swan, made love to Leda, and she bore him Helen.
Helen's brothers were the twins, Castor and Polydeuces, of
whom Polydeuces, and sometimes both, are said to be the
sons of Zeus. Her sister was Clytemnestra, the child of Tyndareus. From childhood Helen was famed for her beauty. As
a child, some say at the age of 12, she was kidnaped by
Theseus and Pirithous and taken to Athens. Theseus, having lost his wife, intended to make Helen his bride. However, the Athenians frowned on this exploit of Theseus and,
to avoid their displeasure, he sent her to Aphidna with his
mother for safe-keeping. Helen's loyal brothers swooped
down on Aphidna and rescued her, and carried her back to
Sparta. As she grew to marriageable age the richest and
most powerful princes of Greece sought her hand. Tyndareus, her supposed father, turned none of the suitors
away. On the other hand, he dared not choose any one
among them lest the others turn on him in wrath. Odysseus,
not one of Helen's suitors, suggested a scheme whereby
Tyndareus might award his daughter's hand without incurring the anger of the disappointed suitors. He advised Tyndareus to require each of the suitors to take an oath, on the
joints of a horse, by which each would swear to come to the
aid of the man who became Helen's husband in the event
that any ill should come to him because of his marriage.
Diomedes, Ajax, Teucer, Patroclus, Philoctetes, Idomeneus,
and many others willingly took the oath. Tyndareus gave her
to Menelaus, whom he also made the heir to the throne of
Sparta. Whether Menelaus was also Helen's choice is not
known. Helen bore Menelaus one daughter, Hermione, and,
some say, three sons. However Helen and Menelaus may
have felt about each other, the gods had decreed that their
marriage was doomed. Some say Zeus wanted to make
Helen famous for having embroiled Europe and Asia in a

(obscured) errạnt, ardẹnt, actọr; ch, chip; g, go; th, thin; ꟻн, then; y, you;
(variable) ḍ as d or j, ṣ as s or sh, ṭ as t or ch, ẓ as z or zh.

devastating war, or that he wanted to exalt the demigods. Some say Aphrodite was punishing Tyndareus, who had once overlooked her when he was sacrificing to the gods, by causing his daughters to become notorious adulteresses. Whatever the reason, the gods deliberately caused the war and took an active role in its progress. As Homer pictures Helen, she was the helpless tool of the gods, neither responsible for her beauty nor the disasters it caused.

Aphrodite had promised Paris, son of King Priam of Troy, the fairest woman in the world if he awarded her the golden apple which Eris had tossed among the wedding guests at the marriage of Peleus and Thetis. Paris did award Aphrodite the apple. Helen was the fairest woman in the world and already married. Yet Aphrodite set all in train to carry out her promise. Paris, with the blessing of his father, sailed to Sparta, telling no one the true object of his journey. In Sparta he was courteously welcomed and entertained by Menelaus. Apparently Menelaus felt perfectly secure in the affections of Helen, for though it was obvious to everyone that Paris was madly in love with Helen and making no effort to hide it, at the end of nine days Menelaus sailed off to Crete to attend his grandfather's funeral. He left his kingdom and the task of entertaining his distinguished and handsome Trojan guest in charge of Helen. The night of Menelaus' departure Helen eloped with Paris, taking a son and a great treasure with her. Paris' fleet was delayed by storms sent by Hera, and more time elapsed in side journeys to Cyprus, Phoenicia, and Egypt, before Paris arrived in Troy and formally married Helen. She bore him several children, all of whom perished in infancy. The entire city of Troy fell in love with Helen; old men stood at the walls to watch her pass; Priam vowed he would never let her go. Embassies from the Greeks demanding her return were summarily dismissed. The resolution of Paris and Priam to keep Helen did not weaken even when the Greeks gathered a great fleet of over 1000 ships and raided the coasts of the Troad. This resolution was concurred in by most of the Trojans. Men like Antenor, who advised from the very beginning that she be restored to her husband and reparations made, were regarded as traitors.

After nearly ten years of raids and attacks on the allies and cities of the Troad, the Greek fleet was beached off the plain of Troy and the city was besieged. Violent encounters followed between the Greeks under Agamemnon and the Trojans under Hector. Then Paris and Menelaus, by agreement between the Greek and Trojan chieftains, fought in single combat to decide who should have Helen. This was a sensible solution to avoid further bloodshed by limiting the fighting to the two men most intimately concerned. If the gods had not intervened, the Trojan War would have ended here. Menelaus was about to strangle Paris in this duel when Aphrodite snatched him away in a mist and restored him to Helen. Helen was by no means grateful; she chided both the goddess and Paris. She would have preferred to go back to Menelaus and her homeland, but was compelled to accept the bidding of the goddess. In the *Iliad,* Helen's elopement is the dynamic force which sets off the great struggle between the Greeks and Trojans, but once the struggle is in progress Helen plays a minor role. Homer makes no criticism of Helen. His attitude is one worshipful of her beauty and sympathetic to her plight as a pawn of the gods. Following the interference of Aphrodite in the duel between Menelaus and Paris, full-scale war broke out again. As the Greeks massed on the plain Priam called Helen to him and asked her to identify various outstanding Greeks he could see from the towers of Troy. She named and characterized such heroes as Ajax, Odysseus, and others, and looked for her brothers among the throng, unaware that they had died and been deified. Watching the Greeks and remembering her happy life in Sparta, Helen regretted the trouble she, at Aphrodite's hands, had caused, and longed for her husband and her daughter. She was one of the chief mourners at the death of Hector. He had always been gentle and compassionate with her, and had ever turned aside the anger of others. As she grieved over Hector's death she lamented her years in Troy (20, according to Homer), and wished she had died rather than to have caused so much anguish to so many. Following the death of Paris, Helen feared that she, now without a protector, would suffer the anger of the Trojans for the misery she had caused, but Deïphobus and Helenus, brothers of Paris, quarreled for her hand. She was awarded to Deïphobus, because of his brave deeds. The Trojans disapproved of this marriage by force.

When Odysseus crept into the city in disguise to steal the

Palladium, which the Greeks had learned protected the city as long as it remained in the citadel, Helen recognized him. She took him, cringing and appealing for mercy, to Hecuba. Hecuba and Helen questioned him and let him go free, without telling anyone he had been there. Some say Helen did this to prepare for her return to Menelaus. Others say she succeeded, as she thought, in getting valuable information about the Greeks' plans from Odysseus. But Odysseus returned with Diomedes, and this time the Palladium was stolen from the citadel. Troy's days were numbered. The Greeks sailed away behind the island of Tenedos and left the Wooden Horse on the beach before Troy. The Trojans jubilantly hauled it inside the walls, deluded into the belief that it would please Athena and give them dominion over Europe. Helen, accompanied by Deïphobus, walked around the Wooden Horse. To test whether there were indeed, as Cassandra proclaimed, armed men hidden inside it, Helen imitated the voices of the wives of the Greek warriors and called out their names. So true was her imitation that Anticlus would have replied, and Menelaus and Diomedes wanted to leap out of the horse on hearing her voice, but Odysseus restrained them all. Some say Aphrodite, in disguise, appeared to Helen and told her Menelaus was in the Horse, and that she walked around it to help the Trojans, but Athena came to prevent her from helping the Trojans and caused her to light a signal fire which burned from the roof of her house all night and advised the Greeks it was safe to return. Others say it was Sinon who, after releasing the Greeks from inside the Wooden Horse, lighted the beacon to summon the Greek fleet back. He opened the gates of Troy and the Greeks streamed silently inside the walls and sacked the city. Menelaus made straight for Helen's house. Though he had proclaimed that he would kill her, he was passionately in love with her and could hardly wait to get her back. Deïphobus, with whom Menelaus and Odysseus found Helen, was slain and horribly mangled. Menelaus instantly forgave Helen. He was more than willing to blame the elopement, as she did, on the gods. She feared the anger the Greeks would harbor against her, and went among them in shame, but she was so beautiful everyone "marveled to see the glory of loveliness of that all-flawless woman"; no one reproached her. She accompanied Menelaus to his ship and

fat, fāte, fär, fåll, ȧsk, fãre; net, mē, hėr; pin, pīne; not, nōte, möve, nôr; up, lūte, pull; oi, oil; ou out; (lightened) ĕlect, agŏny, ūnite;

they passed the rest of the night in sweet converse.

Following the destruction of Troy, Menelaus quarreled with Agamemnon and sailed immediately, without offering due sacrifice to the gods. To punish him, Athena drove his fleet off course, and afterward he and Helen were delayed eight years on their journey home. Helen feared the welcome she would get in Greece, but as it turned out, she and Menelaus, who returned to Sparta with rich treasure, lived among their people in great prosperity and harmony. So deep was the affection and understanding between Helen and Menelaus, according to Homer, that she could refer ruefully to the aberration which had caused her to leave her husband and embroil Europe and Asia in a disastrous war. There is a story that the poet Stesichorus wrote a scurrilous account of Helen's elopement. Some time later he went blind and learned that Helen had taken away his sight to punish him for dishonoring her name. He wrote a new account, which he called the true one, and repudiated the former one as spurious. According to his revised version, Helen never went to Troy at all. Zeus sent Hermes to carry her off in a cloud. She was taken to Egypt and left under the protection of the king there. The Helen for whom Menelaus and all the Greeks fought Hector and all the Trojans was a phantom, fashioned from a cloud by Hera. While they fought over this wraith the real Helen, blameless of any infidelity to Menelaus, remained in Egypt, bemoaning the awful fate which had caused her name to be dishonored. Seven years after the end of the Trojan War Menelaus, who had been completely taken in by the phantom Helen, touched at Egypt after a storm had wrecked his fleet. There he found his own true, beautiful, and virtuous wife. They were joyously reunited as the phantom Helen disappeared.

There are as many accounts of Helen's end as there are of her birth. Some say that Helen was threatened by Orestes when she and Menelaus at last landed in Sparta, because he considered her the cause of all his troubles. She was borne off in a cloud to Olympus, at Zeus' command, where she joined her brothers as a goddess who protects mariners. Others record that Menelaus died in Sparta and that Helen, friendless, fled to her former friend Polyxo in Rhodes. Polyxo, the wife of Tlepolemus who was killed in the Trojan War, avenged her husband's death by inciting her servants to hang Helen. But others say that Helen and Menelaus lived happily together; that Menelaus was made immortal as the son-in-law of Zeus, and that he and Helen went to the Elysian Fields together where they wander hand in hand. Still others say that Achilles had fallen in love with her when he saw her on the walls of Troy, and that at the end of her life with Menelaus in Sparta, she went to the island of Leuce, which had been given to Achilles by Poseidon. There she married Achilles and lived happily with him and his companions, Antilochus, Patroclus, and the two Ajaxes. Mariners who sailed near the wooded shores of the island could hear their voices floating over the water as they recited the verses of Homer which recounted their exploits. A special shrine to Helen, as a goddess of beauty, was erected at Therapne and an annual festival was held there in her honor.

Helenus (hel'e̩-nus). In Greek legend, a son of Priam and Hecuba, and the twin of Cassandra. When he was a child the twins were left outside while others celebrated in the temple of Apollo. Sacred serpents came and licked their ears and gave them prophetic powers. When later, Paris proposed to set out for Sparta with the secret intention of abducting Helen, Helenus agreed with Cassandra that Troy would go up in flames if he made the trip, but their prophecies were ignored. In the Trojan War he fought bravely, killing many and wounding Achilles and Menelaus. After the death of Paris, he contended with Deïphobus for Helen's hand. She was awarded to Deïphobus, who forcibly married her, and Helenus withdrew from the city and went to live on Mount Ida. The Greeks learned from Calchas that only Helenus could tell them what protected Troy and determined to seize him. Odysseus captured him in the temple of Apollo and took him to the Greek camp. Helenus agreed to give the required information on condition that he be sent to a land far from Troy at the close of the war. He said Troy could not be taken unless a bone of Pelops was brought to the Greek camp, that Neoptolemus, son of Achilles, must join the fighting, and that the Greeks must steal the Palladium that protected Troy as long as it remained in the city. After the war Helenus advised Neoptolemus to go to Molossia. He also told him to wait two more days before sailing, and prophesied that storms would overtake the others. In gratitude for his advice Neoptolemus took Helenus with him when he left Troy, and bequeathed him Andromache, captive and concubine of Neoptolemus, on his death. Helenus also told Neoptolemus to build a city where he found men living in houses whose foundations were of iron, walls of wood, and roofs of wool. It was because of this advice that Neoptolemus later settled in Epirus, where he came upon a group who were camped under blankets supported by spears. Some say that Neoptolemus also gave Helenus his mother, Deidamia, for a wife. Later, after the death of Neoptolemus, Helenus acquired Andromache (Hector's wife), and a part of Neoptolemus' kingdom in Epirus, thus becoming a ruler over Greeks. He built a miniature Troy, with a copy of the Scaean Gate, near a river which he named Xanthus after the river of Troy. He entertained Aeneas when the latter stopped there on his way from Troy to Italy, and made certain prophecies regarding his fate. He told Aeneas that the voyage and dangers ahead were yet great, that a sow with 30 new-born piglets would mark the site of the city Aeneas was to build, that he should avoid the east coast of Italy because it was peopled by Greeks, that he should sail around Sicily to avoid Scylla and Charybdis, that he should pay particular homage to Hera, and that he should consult the Cumaean Sibyl. He then gave Aeneas a plumed helmet that had once belonged to Neoptolemus and many other presents and guides and sent him on his way.

Heliadae (hē-lī′a-dē). A name given to the seven sons of Helius and Rhode, daughter of Poseidon. They were thought to be especially gifted in knowledge of astrology. For the murder of one of the brothers, the other brothers were scattered through various lands.

Heliades (hē-lī′a-dēz). A name for the daughters of Helius and the nymph Clymene. Their grief for the death of their brother, Phaëthon, was so great that the gods in pity transformed them into poplar trees. There they stand, eternally weeping tears of amber, on the banks of the Eridanus River into which Phaëthon fell when struck by a thunderbolt of Zeus.

Helius (hē′li-us). The sun-god (called Hyperion by Homer). He was the son of the Titan Hyperion and the Titaness Thia, and was the brother of Eos and Selene. By Clymene he was the father of Phaëthon. Aeëtes, Circe, and Pasiphaë were his children by Persa. Helius is also known as a god of herds and flocks, who keeps his own sacred flocks on Trinacria (Sicily) an island which was given to him by Zeus after it was formed in the battle between the gods and Giants, and on the island of Erythea. Helius is represented as a strong and beautiful youth, with heavy waving locks and a crown of rays, driving a four-horse chariot. He keeps his horses in a magnificent stable built for him by Hephaestus, and each morning rises from the ocean on the east and drives across the heavens in his glowing car, descending at evening into the western sea. At night, while asleep, he is borne along the northern edge of the earth in a golden boat or cup, made by Hephaestus, to his rising-place in the east. Because of his passage through the sky nothing escapes the notice of Helius. It was he who warned Hephaestus of the love affair between Ares and Aphrodite, who saw Hades abduct Persephone, who told Artemis that Oeneus of Calydon had forgotten to include her in his sacrifice of first fruits to the gods. Rhodes, the principal seat of his worship, came into Helius' hands in the following manner: when Zeus was parcelling out various cities and islands to the gods he forgot Helius. Helius offered to take as his portion an island which was just then rising out of the sea. This was Rhodes, and Helius made it his own. There he became the father of seven sons and a daughter by the nymph Rhode. His sons became rulers of the island and their descendants built his famous statue, the Colossus of Rhodes. In later times Helius was confused with Apollo because of his association with the sun. The Romans identified him with their Sol.

Helle (hel'ē). In Greek legend, the daughter of Athamas and Nephele, and a sister of Phrixus. The two children flew away on the winged ram with the golden fleece to escape the death plotted for them by their stepmother. Helle fell off and was drowned in the Hellespont, whence its name, meaning "Sea of Helle."

Hellen (hel'en). In Greek legend, a son of Deucalion and Pyrrha. He married Orseïs and settled in Thessaly. Through his sons, Aeolus, Xuthus, and Dorus, he was the eponymous ancestor of the entire Hellenic race. Aeolus was the founder of the Aeolian tribe; the sons of Xuthus, Achaeus and Ion, founded the Achaean and Ionian tribes; and Dorus was the founder of the Dorian tribe.

Hemera (hem′ẻr-ạ). In Greek mythology, a daughter of
Erebus and Nyx (Night). Later she came to be identified with
Eos (Dawn) when, as she accompanied Helius, she changed
from Dawn and became Day.

Hephaestus (hē-fes′tus). One of the 12 Olympian gods, he
was the god of fire and the divine smith. With Athena, he was
the patron of handicrafts, and through his skill as a craftsman he was one of the chief promoters of civilization and of
city life. He was the creator of all that was beautiful and
mechanically wonderful in Olympus, especially arms and
armor for the gods. At the festival of the Apaturia, when
children were enrolled as citizens, Hephaestus was honored
as the god of fire. In general, he was a beneficent god, much
loved by mortals and gods alike for his kindness and his skill
in the peaceful arts.

DIONYSUS CONDUCTING HEPHAESTUS TO OLYMPUS
Red-figured Attic crater, 5th century B.C.
Munich

Some say that Hephaestus was the son of Hera alone, that
he had no father. They say Hera produced him alone after
Athena was born from the head of Zeus to show that she too
could have a child without anyone's help. But others say
Zeus was his father. When he was born, he alone of the
ideally beautiful gods was ugly, and Hera, in disgust, flung

him out of heaven. He fell into the sea and was rescued by
Thetis and Eurynome. The Nereids treated him kindly and
kept him with them in a cavern beneath the sea for nine
years. It was because of her kindness that Hephaestus, in the
Trojan War, made new armor for Achilles, son of Thetis
While living under the sea Hephaestus, "equally skilled in
both hands," made a golden throne to which he attached
golden mesh fetters, so fine they were invisible. This he sent
to Hera, to punish her for hurling him out of heaven. When
she sat on the throne she was immediately held fast by the
invisible fetters. The gods of heaven sought to persuade
Hephaestus to return to Olympus and free her. He refused.
Ares threatened him with force. Hephaestus compelled him
to withdraw by menacing him with molten missiles.
Dionysus came to try his persuasions. Hephaestus trusted
Dionysus and received him. Dionysus got him drunk and led
him to Olympus, where he at last agreed to free Hera. From
then on he took his place among the gods and was greatly
loved by them, and made them beautiful bronze palaces. But
Zeus, angry with Hera because she had caused Heracles to
be shipwrecked on the isle of Cos, punished her by hanging
her out of heaven with anvils attached to each of her feet.
Hephaestus remonstrated with him, and sought to help his
mother. Enraged at his interference, Zeus flung him again
from heaven. Through one whole day he fell, and landed at
last on the island of Lemnos. Half-dead, he was rescued and
cared for by the Lemnians, for which reason Lemnos became one of his favorite haunts. Some say both his legs were
broken in this fall, and that he was ever after lame. But
others say he was born lame. He made himself golden maidens that had the power to move by themselves, and these
helped him to walk and assisted him in his forge. And in his
forge he made golden tripods on wheels, that went of themselves to the gatherings of the gods. He never again inter-
fered in the quarrels of Zeus and Hera. On the contrary, he
tried to persuade his mother to yield to the will of her
husband in the future.

Some say that before he freed Hera from the throne to
which she was bound by invisible chains, he won from her
a promise that Aphrodite would be given to him for a wife.
He paid rich marriage gifts to Zeus for her and she was
married to him. But she was an unwilling wife. She preferred
the straight and handsome Ares, and frequently entertained

him when Hephaestus was absent. Helius, who sees everything in his passage through the skies, saw Aphrodite and Ares together and reported it to Hephaestus. Hephaestus determined to expose the guilty pair. He fashioned a net so fine it was invisible and as strong as it was fine, and placed it over his marriage bed. Then he told his golden wife that he was going on a journey to Lemnos. As soon as he had gone, Ares came joyously to his house and embraced Aphrodite on the marriage bed. Instantly the lovers were caught in the golden mesh and could not escape. Hephaestus returned and called all the gods to witness his dishonor. The gods came and laughed mightily at the plight of Aphrodite and Ares, but the goddesses stayed at home, out of modesty. Hermes was frankly envious of Ares as he viewed the glorious body of Aphrodite, and confessed that he would gladly change places with him. Zeus refused to have anything to do with the matter and rebuked Hephaestus for exposing the dishonor to his name. But Poseidon, fired with love by the sight of Aphrodite, offered, if Ares should default, to make good the marriage gifts Hephaestus had given Zeus for Aphrodite's hand and which he now demanded be returned. Hephaestus accepted his offer and freed the lovers. Aphrodite went to her island of Cyprus and was there purified by her nymphs. Ares went to Thrace. But in a short time all was as before. Hephaestus loved Aphrodite so passionately that he gladly took her back on her terms. Aphrodite bore no children to Hephaestus, but he was the father of Palaemonius the Argonaut, who was lame like his father. He was also the father of Erichthonius. Some say that Poseidon, for a joke, told Hephaestus that Athena would welcome his advances. When she came to his forge for new weapons he attempted to embrace her. She repulsed him, and his seed fell on her leg. The goddess brushed it off with a piece of wool, which she then cast from her. It fell on Mother Earth, and from this accidental union Erichthonius was born. This encounter did not seem to mar the friendly relations between Athena and Hephaestus, for they were often associated in various exploits. Some name Charis, one of the Graces, as a wife of Hephaestus; and some name Aglaia, the youngest of the Graces, as his wife.

In the Trojan War Hera called on him to come to the aid of Achilles. For Achilles had so choked the Scamander River in Troy with the bodies of those he had slain that the river rose up against him to drown him. Hephaestus sent his flames and dried up the river, and the river-god promised to take no further part in the war. Hephaestus used his skill for peaceful purposes usually, and it was greatly against his will and only because he was commanded to do so by Zeus, that he forged fetters and bound Prometheus to a crag in the Caucasus. At the time he mourned that his great art, so often employed for the good of mankind, should be used for such a cruel purpose, even though it was his own fire that Prometheus had stolen and given to man, for which Zeus punished him. Among the marvelous works said to have been created by Hephaestus were bronze palaces for the gods, the fire-breathing bronze-hoofed bulls that Aeëtes required Jason to yoke; Talos, the bronze man who guarded the island of Crete for King Minos; Ariadne's wonderful crown that was afterward set in the heavens; the armor of Achilles; the bronze castanets with which Heracles frightened the Stymphalian birds, and Heracles' golden breastplate; and the necklace of Harmonia that brought sorrow to all who possessed it. It was also Hephaestus who fashioned the figure of Pandora, into which the gods breathed life. But some say the only truly authentic work from the hand of Hephaestus that survived was the scepter he made for Zeus. Zeus sent it to Pelops by Hermes, and ultimately it passed into the hands of Agamemnon. This scepter came to be the most precious possession of the people of Chaeronea, who say they found it on the borders of their land. They worshiped it under the name *Spear*, and offered sacrifices to it daily. It was kept in a house selected by the priest and near it stood a table on which meats and all kinds of cakes were offered. The Lycians also claimed to have one of the works of Hephaestus, a bowl that was dedicated by Telephus in the temple of Apollo.

Lemnos, once a volcanic isle, was of course a favorite place of Hephaestus, and there he had a forge, manned by the Cyclopes. A volcanic island of the Lipari group was said to be the site of another of his forges, and Mount Aetna in Sicily was also said to lie over one of the forges of Hephaestus. In Athens Hephaestus was honored with a splendid marble temple, the Hephaesteum, and an altar. The *Chalkeia*, a feast of the metal workers, honored him and Athena; and at the *Hephaestia* a torch race was run in his honor. He was sometimes known as Mulciber (*Melter*), by the Romans, who identified him with Vulcan. In art he was represented as a bearded man, usually with the short, sleeveless or one-sleeved tunic and the conical cap, and holding the smith's hammer and tongs.

era (hēr'a̧). [Also: *Here.*] One of the 12 Olympian gods, the greatest feminine divinity of Olympus, queen of heaven; daughter of Cronus and Rhea; wife and sister of Zeus, and inferior in power to him only. She was the goddess of women and childbirth, the type of virtuous womanhood, and of the wife and mother. Honored by the Greeks in these capacities, she yet appears in their myths as an extremely unpleasant and rather spiteful goddess, driven to it perhaps by the turmoils of her own married life. She was a sky-goddess, as Zeus was a sky-god. The ancients attributed the storms in the heavens to the quarrels of Zeus and Hera. Aeolus, keeper of the winds, released them at her command.

HEAD OF HERA
From a coin of Cnossus, 4th century B.C.
Museum of Fine Arts, Boston

Like her sisters before her, Hera was swallowed up by Cronus as soon as she was born, and was cast out with them when Zeus duped his father into drinking an emetic. Many places where she was worshiped claimed to be her birth-place. The Samians said she was born on their island. In antiquity they pointed out a tree near the Imbrasus River under which they claimed she was born. At Samos an image

of Hera was annually hidden at the seashore, where it w
annually discovered, as part of her worship. Argos al
claimed to be her birthplace. She contended with Poseid
for control of it; the dispute was submitted to the river-go
Inachus, Cephissus, and Asterion, who decided in favor
the goddess. Samos and Argos were the chief seats of h
worship, although the Arcadians claimed that they were t
first to worship her. According to the *Iliad*, Argos, Mycena
and Sparta were the three cities most loved by her. Ne
Mycenae was the national Argive shrine of the goddess, t
Heraeum, where the great image of her by Polyclitus w
housed. In Argos the years were named according to t
priestesses of Hera who served in the Heraeum. Some s
Hera was brought up by Temenus, son of Pelasgus, in A
cadia, where the Seasons were her nurses. Temenus erect
three shrines of Hera: one of Hera the Child, in commem
ration of her early years under his care; one of Hera t
Bride, in honor of her marriage to Zeus; and a third of He
the Widow, in memory of a time when she quarreled wi
Zeus and left him. Homer says that Hera dwelt at some ti
in her youth with Oceanus and Tethys, for whom she alwa
had a high regard. When she reached marriageable age h
brother, Zeus, courted her, but she repulsed him. He a
sumed the form of a cuckoo and approached her, some s
on Mount Thornax in Argolis, others say it took place
Crete. Deceived, she picked up the bird and nestled it in h
bosom. Zeus at once resumed his own form and ravish
her. Thus was she persuaded to marry him. Almost as ma
places as claimed to be her birthplace also claimed to be t
scene of her marriage, which took place in the spring. T
wedding was attended by all the gods, who brought gi
Gaea presented her with a tree bearing golden apples, whi
was set out in the Garden of the Hesperides and guarded
the daughters of Atlas. The wedding night, which lasted 3
years, was spent on the island of Samos. Each year thereaf
Hera was said to renew her virginity by bathing in the spri
of Canathus in Argos. In all things except the capacity
bestow the power of prophecy, Hera's powers, thou
great, were inferior to those of Zeus. He often confided
her and sometimes even took her advice, but zealou
guarded his right to do as he pleased in any given ca
When the arrogance of Zeus became unbearable to the g
they plotted against him and bound him as he sle

Through the intervention of Thetis he was freed by Briareus. To punish Hera, the ringleader in the plot, Zeus fastened bracelets of gold on her wrists, anvils on her feet, and hung her out of heaven. Only when the gods pleaded with him and promised never again to revolt did he relent and restore her to Olympus. When the Giants waged war on the gods it was Hera who prophesied that they could never be slain by the gods, but only by a mortal who was protected by a magic herb. She took vigorous part in the battles against the Giants. Porphyrion sought to violate her, Zeus sprang to her aid and wounded him, and Heracles, the mortal of her prophecy, slew Porphyrion.

Hera bore Ares, Hephaestus, and Hebe to Zeus. Hephaestus was born lame, and in disgust Hera flung him out of heaven. To punish her, Hephaestus, a master-smith, built a magnificent chair and sent it to her. When she sat in it the arms closed about her and held her fast. The gods tried in vain to free her. At last Dionysus went to Hephaestus, got him drunk, and led him to Olympus where he freed his mother. When she saw what a gifted craftsman he was, Hera became reconciled with Hephaestus and set up a forge for him on Olympus. Hera was also said to be the mother of Ilithyia, the birth-goddess, and of Python, the serpent she sent to pursue Leto throughout the world before she bore Apollo and Artemis, the children of Zeus. And some say that, angry because Zeus bore Athena from his own head without any help from her, she bore the monster Typhon without the help of Zeus and gave him to the serpent at Delphi to rear.

The marriage of Zeus and Hera was the only proper marriage on Mount Olympus, but it was an exceedingly stormy one. Any subject was a cause for argument. Once they disputed as to which sex enjoyed the pleasures of love more. Hera contended the masculine sex did. Zeus assured her that the feminine sex did. The dispute was submitted to Tiresias, who had lived both as a woman and as a man, for decision. His answer was that if the pleasures of love were counted as ten, women enjoyed nine parts and men one. Hera was so infuriated by his judgment, some say, that she struck Tiresias with blindness. The unflagging interest of Zeus in other women, mortals or immortals, was a constant source of anger to Hera. Whenever possible she punished the objects of Zeus' readily bestowed love, even when, as

(cured) errạnt, ardẹnt, actǫr; ch, chip; g, go; th, thin; ŦH, then; y, you; (able) ḍ as d or j, ṣ as s or sh, ṭ as t or ch, ẓ as z or zh.

was often the case, they had submitted reluctantly to
caresses, and she was as vindictive to the children of Ze
by other women as she was to their mothers. She sen
gadfly to pursue Io, whom Zeus had transformed into
heifer when Hera was about to discover him dallying w
her. Echo, a nymph who tried to protect Zeus by chatteri
with Hera and so delaying her that she did not come up
Zeus and Io until he had changed the form of Io, was pu
ished by Hera. She was permitted to go on talking, as s
loved to do, but her conversation was limited to the repe
tion of the last words of whomever had spoken to her. He
transformed Callisto, mother of Zeus' son Arcas, into a be
Zeus placed Callisto's image among the stars. Such an hon
to one of her rivals so infuriated Hera that she induc
Poseidon to forbid the image of the Bear ever to sink in
his waters, which is why the constellation of the Bear nev
sets. By a trick she caused the destruction of Semele, a
later drove Athamas mad, so that he killed his own so
because Athamas sheltered the infant Dionysus, son of Ze
and Semele; or, as some say, because Athamas put aside t
wife Hera had given him and took another in her place.
for Dionysus, some say Hera commanded the Titans to te
him to pieces. He was restored through the agency
Athena, but when he was grown Hera recognized him a
drove him mad.

The two most afflicted objects of Hera's enmity were He
acles and the Trojans. Basic to her hatred of Heracles w
that he was the son of a rival. Even before he was born s
hated him. Zeus boasted before his birth that the king of t
Perseid line was about to be born. Hera tricked Zeus in
giving the most solemn oath that the first child born that d
to the house of Perseus would become master of the lar
Having secured the oath, she hastened to the house
Sthenelus and caused Nicippe, his wife, to produce her ch
before its time. She then kept Ilithyia, the birth-godde
from going to the aid of Alcmene, who was momentar
expecting her child, and delayed the birth of Heracl
Thus, in fulfillment of his oath, Zeus was forced to all
Eurystheus, son of Sthenelus and Nicippe, to be suprer
over Heracles, his own son by Alcmene. But the name Her
cles means "Glory of Hera," and was perhaps given becau
through Hera's enmity he was forced to accomplish migh
deeds. Some say that by a trick Hera was duped into nursi

Heracles, but he nursed so vigorously she turned him over to his own mother, unaware whose child he was. When he was an infant in his cradle she sent huge serpents to attack him. He strangled them. Throughout his life she tormented him. She drove him mad, so that he killed his children by Megara. Some say she was responsible for the poisonous, many-headed Hydra, whose killing was one of the labors imposed on Heracles by Eurystheus. Hera sent an enormous crab to help the Hydra when Heracles attacked it, but to no avail; he killed the Hydra. Hera set the image of the crab in the heavens, as Cancer, one of the signs of the Zodiac, to reward it. As another of his labors, Heracles was sent to fetch the cattle of Geryon. Hera came to Geryon's aid and fought Heracles, but he wounded her in the right breast and she was forced to withdraw. Even so, as he was leading the cattle back to Eurystheus, she sent gadflies to sting them and they scattered in a frenzy, so that he was forced to roam widely in order to recover them. She set the dragon Ladon to guard the Apples of the Hesperides, and set his image among the stars after he was killed by Heracles. Once when he was returning from Troy, Hera bribed Sleep to lull Zeus, and when he had succumbed she ordered up a great storm and caused Heracles to be shipwrecked on the island of Cos. Some say it was on this occasion that Zeus was so angered by her that he hung her out of heaven. In his war against Pylus, Hera took the side of Pylus and engaged in the fighting. Again Heracles wounded her. On only one occasion did she fail to hamper him. This was when he fought against the sons of Hippocoön. He was so grateful for her indifference in this case that he sacrificed goats, the only victims available, to her and built a shrine of "Goat-eating Hera" in Sparta. The Spartans were the only ones to give her this name and to offer goats to her. When Heracles was suffering and begged for death, Philoctetes lighted his funeral pyre to bring his suffering to an end. Some say Hera punished Philoctetes for his compassion by sending the serpent that bit him when he accompanied the Greeks to the Trojan War. But when at last Heracles was burned and made immortal, Zeus persuaded her to go through a ceremony that imitated the birth process and to adopt him as a son, and she gave him her daughter Hebe in marriage.

The reason for her relentless hatred of the Trojans came from the Judgment of Paris. Hera, with Aphrodite and

Athena, contended for the Apple of Discord, the gold
apple that was thrown among the wedding guests at t
marriage of Thetis and Peleus, and was inscribed "To t
Fairest." Zeus refused to rule as to which of the three go
desses was the fairest and recommended them to cons
Paris, son of Priam, who was reputed to be a fine judge
beauty. The goddesses sought Paris and put the problem
him. Each of them offered a handsome bribe if he wou
award the apple to her. Paris, as is well known, accept
Aphrodite's bribe—the most beautiful woman in the wo
for his wife—and gave the apple to her. This brought do
the unending wrath of Hera on Paris and, by extension,
all Trojans. She took an active part in the Trojan War th
resulted when Paris carried off his reward—Helen, wife
King Menelaus of Sparta—and lent her aid to the Greeks
every occasion. When the Trojans had hurled back t
Greeks with ruinous losses, Hera again prevailed on Sle
to lull Zeus, and with the aid of Aphrodite's magic gird
which she borrowed for the occasion, so aroused desire
Zeus that he forgot all about the war and gave himself up
love and sleep. While he was so occupied, the Greeks salli
out against the Trojans and inflicted heavy losses. Aga
Zeus raged when he learned how she had tricked him, a
forbade the gods to take any part in the war for a time.
last, however, fearful that the Trojans would be utterly d
stroyed when Achilles rejoined the fighting, he gave h
permission for the gods to interfere as they wished. He
attacked Artemis and scattered her arrows. She encourag
Athena to attack Aphrodite, and when the Xanthus Riv
rose up to engulf Achilles for glutting its waters with t
bodies of slain Trojans, Hera prevailed on Hephaestus to s
the river afire and forced its withdrawal from the strife.

Pelias felt the wrath of Hera because, in his youth,
dragged Sidero from Hera's altar where she had soug
refuge, and because Pelias withheld honors that were d
the goddess. She favored Jason against Pelias, partly for t
above reason, and partly because, to test Jason, she d
guised herself as a crone and asked him to carry her acro
the swollen Anaurus River. Jason courteously obliged, a
though he found his burden heavy, and won unceasing gra
tude and help from the goddess in his later exploits.

Hera was worshiped throughout the Greek world, esp
cially as a protectress of women. Among the festivals ce

brated in her honor were the *Daedala,* celebrated at Plataea, the *Heraea,* celebrated in Argos, and the Heraean Games, celebrated at Olympia in Elis. There were temples and shrines of Hera in many places, the most famous of which were the Heraeum, near Mycenae in Argolis, the great temple in Samos, and her ancient temple at Olympia. The temple of Hera Prodromia *(Guide)* at Sicyon was said to have been founded by Phalaces, son of Temenus, because Hera guided him on the road to Sicyon. In a sanctuary of Hera Protectress, on the road from Sicyon to Phlius, the men celebrated a festival by themselves. The women's temple there was called the Nymphon. Before the temple of Hera Anthea *(Flowery)* at Argos, was a common grave of women who came to help Dionysus in a war against the Argives. Every spring, a flower festival was celebrated in honor of Hera Anthea by the women of the Peloponnesus. The Spartans had a sanctuary of Hera Hypercheiria *(Protectress),* because she saved the land when the Eurotas River was flooding it. This sanctuary was dedicated in obedience to an oracle. The Spartans also had a temple of Argive Hera, said to have been founded by Eurydice, a daughter of Lacedaemon and the wife of Acrisius. The Eleans poured libations and sang hymns to Hera Ammonia at Olympia once a month; this name for the goddess was given her as the wife of Zeus Ammon, the Libyan name for Zeus. The Argives, and many others, sacrificed cows to Hera. Sacred to her also were the cuckoo, the crow, and, in later times, the peacock. The pomegranate, symbol sometimes of fruitfulness and sometimes of death, was also sacred to her.

Homer describes Hera as "Ox-eyed," "White-armed," and in general as a majestic personage to whom the other gods and goddesses paid homage. He also shows her as passionately punishing the Trojans by whatever means she could contrive. In art the goddess is represented as a majestic woman, fully clad in flowing draperies, characteristically with a crown on her brow, and bearing a scepter. The renowned statue of Hera by Polyclitus in the Heraeum in Argolis remains only in description or, as some scholars think, in the copies, the Farnese and Ludovisi Junos. By the Romans Hera was early identified with their Juno, originally a distinct divinity; and the Latin name is often incorrectly given to the Greek goddess.

Heracles (her′a̞-klēz). [Latin, *Hercules*.] The mightiest ar
most famous of Greek heroes. His deeds were fabulous f
the courage and strength which he displayed in performi
them and his name—Herculean, a Latinized form—has b
come synonymous for prodigious strength, courage, or siz
His sufferings, largely as a result of Hera's antagonism, we
equally heroic and were endured by him with immense for
tude. Beginning with the circumstances of his birth, eve
characteristic and deed of his life was extraordinary. Zeu
having decided to father a hero to end all heroes, cho
Alcmene, wife of Amphitryon of Tiryns, to be the her
mother. She is said to have been the last mortal wom;
whom Zeus embraced. Since she was impeccably chas
Zeus appeared to her in the guise of her husband, ar
caused the sun and stars to halt in their courses so that tl
night the god spent with her was three times as long
usual. When the day arrived on which Heracles was to l
born, Zeus exultantly vowed that the first male child bo
that day would reign over the descendants of Perseus. Hei
as usual inflamed by the infidelities of her husband, hu
riedly arranged to delay the birth of Heracles and to hast
the birth of Eurystheus, son of Sthenelus, king of Mycena
She summoned Ilithyia, the birth-goddess, to sit outsic
Alcmene's door at Thebes with crossed knees and clench
hands. By this magic Alcmene's labor was prolonged un
Galinthias, a handmaiden of Alcmene's, falsely announce
the birth of Heracles, whereupon Ilithyia was so startled th
she jumped up, uncrossing her knees and relaxing h
hands, and allowed Heracles to be born. In a rage at tl
deception, Ilithyia seized Galinthias and changed her into
weasel. But by this time Eurystheus had already been bor
and Zeus, although he was furious, was obliged to honor h
vow. Nevertheless, he persuaded Hera to agree that Eury
theus should be king but that Heracles, after performing t
great labors for Eurystheus, should become immortal. Al
mene, now aware that she had been seduced by a god, aba
doned her child out of fear of the jealousy of Hera. The bal
was found by Athena, the friend and patron of Heracl
throughout his life, who gave him to Hera to rear, preten
ing that she did not know what child it was. Hera took tl
child but the infant sucked so forcefully that Hera refus
to nurse him and, unaware of his parentage, unwitting

fat, fāte, fär, fåll, a̤sk, fāre; net, mē, hėr; pin, pīne; not, nōte, mö
nôr; up, lūte, pu̇ll; oi, oil; ou out; (lightened) ē̞lect, agǫny, ūni

gave him to his own mother to bring up. Alcmene had produced another son, a twin half-brother of Heracles, by Amphitryon. This was Iphicles, younger than Heracles by one night, and the two children were bedded down together. Hera was not long in ignorance of the true origin of Heracles, who at this time was called Alcaeus. She sent two serpents into the cradle where Heracles and Iphicles were sleeping. The infant Heracles grasped the serpents in his bare hands and strangled them.

In his youth Heracles was taught to drive a chariot by Amphitryon, to wrestle by Autolycus or by Harpalycus, son of Hermes, to shoot with the bow and arrow by Eurytus, to fence by Castor. His studies in literature were supervised by Linus, son of the river-god Ismenius, and he was given instruction on the lyre by Eumolpus. It happened that on one occasion Linus attempted to improve his performance on the lyre by boxing his ears. In a rage Heracles flung the lyre at him and killed him. He was acquitted of a murder charge on the ground that he had resisted an aggressor, but Amphitryon sent him to tend his flocks around Mount Cithaeron to keep him out of trouble. While there he went to Thespiae to hunt the Thespian Lion which roamed over Mount Helicon and Mount Cithaeron and was ravaging Amphitryon's flocks. According to some accounts, he killed the lion, skinned it, and wore its pelt as a cloak, using the massive head as a kind of helmet. Others say it was the Nemean Lion's skin he wore, and that Alcathous killed the Thespian Lion. In any event, Heracles so impressed Thespius, founder and king of Thespiae, that he wished to have descendants by Heracles and gave him his 50 daughters to bring about the desired end. All but one of the 50 maidens was delighted with the attentions of Heracles, and between them they produced 51 sons, including two sets of twins. The one who refused his advances was condemned to lifelong virginity as a priestess in his temple. Of these 51 sons, Heracles later sent 40 to colonize the island of Sardinia, as he had been commanded to do by an oracle.

Heracles next followed his foster father Amphitryon to Thebes. He found the city under bondage to Erginus, king of the Minyans, and compelled to pay annual tribute to Erginus. Heracles met the heralds who had come to collect the tribute, cut off their ears and noses, which he threaded

on a string and hung around their necks, tied their han‹
behind their backs, and sent them back to Erginus. As w
to be expected, Erginus raised a force to punish Thebes f‹
this outrage. The Thebans, having been disarmed in pre‹
ous wars with the Minyans, would have surrendered, b
Heracles rallied them and armed them with the shields ar
spears which were hanging in the temples as offerings to t
gods. Under his leadership the Minyans were defeated ar
Erginus was slain, and thenceforth the Minyans were cor
pelled to pay a tribute to the Thebans twice as large as tl
one they had been exacting from Thebes. In gratitude
Heracles, Creon, king of Thebes, gave him his daught‹
Megara in marriage.

The fame of Heracles spread far and wide. Eurysthe‹
now summoned him to perform the ten labors. Heracl‹
deemed it unworthy of him to serve an inferior mortal li‹
Eurystheus, and became so despondent at the idea that
a fit of madness, inspired by Hera, he killed his childre
Restored to sanity, and purified by Thespius, he went to t‹
Oracle at Delphi for instructions. The priestess now ga‹
him the name Heracles *(Glory of Hera)* because he woul
obtain glory as a result of Hera's enmity, and ordered hi
to begin his labors for Eurystheus so that he could becom
immortal.

The first labor was to bring Eurystheus the hide of t‹
Nemean Lion. This animal, which could not be killed t
iron, bronze, or stone, had its lair in a cleft in Mount Tretu
between Mycenae and Nemea. Heracles blocked one e‹
trance of the cleft, which ran through the mountain, so th‹
the lion could not escape, followed the creature in and strar
gled it. He then skinned the lion and ever after used i
shaggy pelt as a cloak. Eurystheus was so terrified at th
sight of Heracles clad in the lion's skin, with its fierce hea‹
serving as a cap, that, some accounts say, he ordered him t
report his successes from outside the city walls in the futur‹

The second labor was to kill the many-headed Hydra th‹
lurked in the Lernaean swamp and wasted the surroundin
area with its noisome breath. According to some accoun
the Hydra had nine heads, one of which was immortal. Otl
ers say there were as many as 100 heads. The difficulty i
killing it was that as fast as one head was cut off, two fir‹
breathing heads grew in its place. As Heracles struggle‹

with the monster Hera sent a huge crab to help the monster
by biting Heracles' feet. Heracles crushed the crab, which
Hera then translated to the heavens as the constellation
Cancer. He now called upon Iolaus, companion of many of
his exploits, and as fast as Heracles sliced off one of the
Hydra's heads Iolaus seared the stump with hot pitch. In this
way it was decapitated of all its heads. Heracles dipped his
arrows in the Hydra's venom, and coated them with such a
lethal poison that whoever was wounded by one of them, no
matter how superficially, was doomed to die. Eurystheus
refused to recognize this labor, on the ground that Heracles
had not performed it alone: Iolaus helped him.

On his way to perform the next labor, the capture of the
Erymanthian Boar, Heracles visited Pholus the centaur, in a
cave on a mountain. Pholus entertained him by opening a
cask of wine which had been given to him by Dionysus. The
other centaurs smelled the wine and were maddened by the
fumes. They attacked Heracles, and were aided in their onslaught by a torrential rain. This gave them a distinct advantage, for with their four feet they could maintain their
footing in the slippery mud of the mountainside, whereas
Heracles was constantly slipping to his knees. Even so, he
killed many of them and drove the rest off. They fled to
Chiron in Malea, whither he pursued them, and there by
accident wounded his friend Chiron with one of his arrows.
The wound could not be healed because of the Hydra's
venom on the arrow which caused it. On the other hand, the
centaur Chiron was immortal and could not die. Later, he
was finally released from his suffering by a generous act of
Prometheus, who offered to assume Chiron's immortality so
that Chiron could die. Pholus also died as a result of this
engagement. In withdrawing an arrow from one of the fallen
centaurs he unfortunately dropped it. It pricked his foot and
he died instantly. Heracles buried him on the mountain and
named it Mount Pholoe in his honor. He now pursued the
Erymanthian Boar, which he was ordered to take alive. He
chased it to the north and finally caught it in a deep snow
drift or, as some say, with a net, and returned to Eurystheus
carrying the Boar on his shoulders. Eurystheus hid in a
specially constructed bronze vessel, buried in the ground,
when he learned that Heracles was approaching with the
Boar. (Some say it was this deed that so terrified Eurystheus

that he ordered Heracles to report his future successes from outside the city walls.)

The fourth labor was to catch the golden-horned Hind which dwelt near the Cerynean river in Arcadia. Since the Hind was sacred to Artemis it had to be taken alive. Heracles pursued it for a year and finally caught it as it drank at the river Ladon. With one perfect shot of his bow he transfixed the forefeet of the Hind and captured it. As he carried it off on his shoulders Artemis reproached him for harming one of her creatures. The goddess forgave him when he pleaded that he was carrying out the command of Zeus in performing the labors for Eurystheus.

The fifth labor was to drive off the bronze-beaked birds that were infesting the Stymphalian marsh. They were huge pestilential birds with iron feathers, and were sacred to Ares. As they flew over the countryside they dropped their feathers and killed many of the countrymen, and their filthy habits were destroying the crops. Athena gave Heracles a bronze rattle which he shook violently and so startled the birds that they rose in flight and he was able to pick off many of them with his arrows. The rest fled to the island of Ares where they were later encountered by the Argonauts.

For his sixth labor Heracles was commanded by Eurystheus to cleanse the stables of Augeas, king in Elis. Augeas was the possessor of large and magnificent herds but his stables had not been cleaned for years. Heracles approached him and offered, without telling him that he had been sent for this purpose, to cleanse the stables before nightfall in return for the payment of one-tenth of the cattle. Augeas agreed, and called his son Phyleus to witness the bargain. He did not expect to have to make the payment as he felt it would be impossible to accomplish the task in the time stipulated. However, Heracles diverted the Alpheus and Peneus Rivers from their courses, washed them through the stables and carried out his end of the bargain as proposed. Augeas refused to pay. He said that the river-gods had helped Heracles, and furthermore, he had learned that Heracles was commanded to carry out this task by Eurystheus. Heracles called on Phyleus to state whether Augeas had promised a payment of one-tenth of his cattle. Phyleus supported Heracles and urged his father to pay. In a rage Augeas banished his son and expelled Heracles. Heracles swore he would get his revenge. He then proceeded to Olenus and killed Eurytion, a centaur who tried to ravish the daughter of the king there. But some say this centaur attacked the daughter of Eurystheus, and that Heracles generously aided his enemy by slaying the centaur.

The seventh labor was to bring back the Cretan Bull beloved by Pasiphaë from Crete. King Minos offered to help in this task but Heracles subdued the bull by himself, and rode on its back as it swam the sea from Crete to Greece. Eurystheus took one look at the bull and turned it loose. It roamed the countryside until it came to Marathon and thereafter became known as the Marathonian Bull.

When he had accomplished this labor Heracles established the Olympic Games, dedicated to Zeus, on the banks of the Alpheus River. He paced off the stadium and won all the contests himself in the first Games. The gods gave him valuable gifts: Athena gave him a robe, Hephaestus a war-club and coat of mail, Poseidon horses, Hermes a sword, Apollo bow and arrows; but on the whole Heracles preferred to fight with a club he cut himself from a wild olive tree, or with his bow and arrows.

For his eighth labor Heracles captured the man-eating mares of Diomedes of Thrace. Diomedes, a son of Ares and Cyrene, fed his animals on human flesh. Heracles tamed them by feeding them the flesh of their master. He founded the city of Abdera, in memory of his servant Abderus who had been killed as he tended the mares while Heracles captured Diomedes. He then returned with the mares to Eurystheus, who consecrated them to Hera.

The news of Jason's expedition to Colchis to recover the Golden Fleece now came to Heracles' ears and he interrupted his labors to join the Argonauts. They unanimously chose him as their leader but he would not take the honor from Jason, who had organized the expedition. It was Heracles who reminded the Argonauts that their goal was Colchis when he thought they lingered overlong enjoying the favors of the women of Lemnos. Heracles took his squire, Hylas, with him on the voyage, and when the Argonauts stopped in Mysia Hylas, who had gone to fetch water at a spring, disappeared. Heracles delayed so long in his search for Hylas that the Argonauts sailed without him. Heracles wandered through Mysia, searching for Hylas and commanding

the Mysians to do likewise. Ever after, once a year the My
sians sacrificed to Hylas, calling his name aloud and pre
tending to search for him.

Heracles returned to Eurystheus and learned that Ad
mete, his daughter, had a fancy for Hippolyte's girdle, and
that his ninth labor was to fetch it. Hippolyte was a quee
of the Amazons, who dwelt near the Thermodon River tha
flows into the Euxine Sea (Black Sea), and her girdle was
belt given to her by her father Ares. On his way to th

HERACLES

Red-figured Greek volute crater, Euphronius, end of the
6th century B.C.

Museo Pubblico, Arezzo

Amazon country Heracles landed on the island of Paros and
carried off two hostages in revenge for the slaying of two of
his crew who had gone to fetch water. In Mysia he was
entertained by Lycus, and helped that king to defeat Myg
don, king of the Bebryces, and gave the land he seized from
the Bebryces to Lycus, who named it Heraclea in his honor

Proceeding then to the port of the Amazons, he was graciously welcomed by Hippolyte, who freely consented to give him her girdle. But Hera stirred up the Amazon women with a rumor that Heracles was attacking their queen. They marched against him and he, thinking he had been tricked, killed Hippolyte, took the girdle, and set out for Hellas, taking Antiope, a sister of Hippolyte, with him as a captive. On his way home he passed Troy and saw a beautiful maiden chained to a rock. On inquiring the reason for this he learned that she was Hesione, the daughter of Laomedon, king of Troy, and that she was being offered as a sacrifice to a sea-monster sent by Poseidon to punish Laomedon. Heracles offered to slay the monster on condition that Laomedon give him the immortal horses of Tros which Zeus had given Tros in compensation for his abduction of Ganymede. Laomedon agreed to the conditions, whereupon Heracles leaped fully armed into the jaws of the monster, hacked about in its belly for three days, and then emerged, victorious but completely bald. Laomedon refused to honor his agreement, now that the danger was passed, and Heracles departed, vowing revenge. He sailed to the island of Thasus, where he subdued the Thracians, and finally arrived at Mycenae, where he presented the girdle to Eurystheus. The captive Antiope was given to Theseus.

His tenth labor, to fetch the cattle of Geryon from the island of Erythea, took him over most of Europe. Heracles went to Crete, gathered a large force, and rid the island once and for all of wild beasts in gratitude to the Cretans for their hospitality. He sailed from Crete to Libya. There he wrestled with Antaeus, a giant whose strength increased as his body came in contact with the earth. Heracles overcame him by holding him aloft and crushing his ribs. He then subdued all Libya and put it under cultivation. Next he went to Egypt and killed Busiris, who was in the habit of sacrificing strangers. Heracles allowed himself to be bound and led to the altar, then he suddenly burst his bonds and killed Busiris. In Egypt he founded the 100-gated city of Hecatompylon, or Thebes. From Egypt he went to Gadira and set up the Pillars of Heracles, one on each continent. According to some accounts, this passage between Calpe (Gibraltar) and Abyla (Ceuta) was very wide and Heracles built each side out so that his Pillars make the passage narrower and thus keep ocean monsters out of the inner sea. Others say that the two

continents were joined and that Heracles cut a passage b
tween them so that the waters of the ocean could ming
with those of the inner sea. In any event, setting up th
Pillars was hot work under the broiling sun. Heracles se
a threatening arrow at the Sun for sending such heat. B
the Sun was amused at his presumption and indulgent
gave him a golden goblet in which to cross the sea. Heracle
apologized and set off in the goblet for Erythea. There h
killed Orthus, the hound that guarded Geryon's cattle, an
Eurytion, the herdsman. He then slew Geryon and took h
cattle. Passing through Liguria on his way home he wa
attacked by two sons of Poseidon and their forces. When h
had used up all his arrows he prayed to Zeus for help. Zeu
sent a shower of stones which Heracles hurled at his attack
ers and so repelled them. The place where this event oc
curred, between Massilia (Marseilles) and the Rhodanu
(Rhone) River is still noted for its many stones about as bi
as a man's fist, and is called the Stony Plain (Plaine de l
Crau). He then crossed the Alps, marched to the Tiber and
pitching his tent where Rome now stands, was hospitabl
received by Evander, a Trojan immigrant who became a kin
in Latium. In Italy he slew the monstrous three-heade
Cacus, who was terrorizing the countryside, and bein
weary from this effort went to rest at Paestum, but cicada
made such a noise he could not sleep. He prayed for relie
and Zeus banished the cicadas from Paestum, where the
have not been heard again from that day to this. One o
Geryon's bulls now escaped and, stepping into the sea a
Rhegium, swam across to Sicily. It wandered to the kingdom
of Eryx and was put into Eryx' own herd. When Heracle
came in search of it Eryx agreed to surrender the bull i
Heracles should defeat him in a wrestling match. Heracle
killed him and turned his kingdom over to the natives
Resuming his journey home, he came to the Ionian Sea
Here Hera sent gadflies to madden the cattle, and many o
them escaped to Thrace. Those which Heracles did no
recover became the forebears of the Thracian cattle.

Eight years and one month had now passed since Heracle
began his labors for Eurystheus. That king, however
refused to count the slaying of the Lernaean Hydra and the
cleansing of the Augean Stables, because in the one case
Heracles had the help of Iolaus and in the other he did it fo
pay. Thus two more labors were laid on him. The eleventh

was to fetch the Golden Apples of the Hesperides, the apples which had been given to Hera as a wedding gift and which were guarded by the Hesperides, daughters of Atlas, and by the 100-headed dragon, Ladon. Heracles did not know where the apples were to be found. He journeyed to the Eridanus River and there, at the prompting of the river-nymphs, seized the sea-god Nereus as he slept. Nereus went through many transformations in an effort to escape but Heracles held him fast and compelled him to give the information he wanted. On the advice of Nereus he went to Rhodes where, being hungry, he took a bullock from a cart, killed it, roasted it, and ate it. Meanwhile the owner of the bullock stood on a hill at a safe distance and cursed helplessly. For this reason it became the custom in that country to curse when sacrificing to Heracles. Next he passed through Arabia, where he slew Emathion, crossed Libya, and again received a golden goblet from the Sun in which he crossed the sea to the Caucasus. He found Prometheus chained to a crag there, while vultures daily gnawed at his liver. Heracles killed the vultures and freed Prometheus, who assumed Chiron's immortality and thus permitted the suffering centaur, accidentally wounded by one of Heracles' poisoned arrows, at last to die. In the land of the Hyperboreans Heracles found the olive tree, which he took home with him, and acting on instructions from Prometheus he approached the Titan Atlas, in whose garden the tree with the golden apples grew. Heracles offered to hold up the heavens while Atlas fetched the apples, as he had been advised not to pluck them himself. Atlas demurred, in fear of the dragon, whereupon Heracles sent an arrow over the garden wall and killed Ladon. He then shouldered the heavens while Atlas went for the apples. When Atlas returned he offered to take the apples to Eurystheus himself as long as Heracles was so obliging as to hold up the heavens. Heracles agreed but asked Altas to relieve him a moment so that he could pad his shoulders and make his burden less uncomfortable. Atlas resumed the burden and Heracles, who had no intention of taking over Atlas' monotonous job, walked off. He gave the apples to Eurystheus, but as it was unlawful to possess them they were restored to the garden through the good offices of Athena.

For his twelfth and last labor Heracles was to fetch Cerberus from Hades. To prepare for the task he went to Eleusis and asked the priest to initiate him into the Eleusinian Mysteries. However, since it was a rule that only Athenians could properly be initiated and he was a foreigner, Demeter established the Lesser Mysteries in his honor, which were celebrated at Agrae on the Ilissus River. Duly purified, he descended to Hades through an opening at Taenarum in Laconia, or as some say, at Heraclea on the Euxine Sea, guided by Athena and Hermes. As he stepped from Charon's boat—he had persuaded the ferryman of the Styx to take him across by assuming a terrifying expression—all the shades fled in fear except Meleager and Medusa, who boldly faced him. He would have run his sword through Meleager but was assured that he had nothing to fear from ghosts, and as they then engaged in friendly conversation, Heracles promised Meleager that he would marry Deianira, Meleager's sister, on his return to earth. In Hades Heracles found Theseus and Pirithous immobilized on Chairs of Forgetfulness. He freed Theseus and took him back to earth with him, but was unable to free Pirithous. He also rolled away the stone with which Demeter had flattened Ascalaphus for talebearing concerning Persephone's food in the Underworld, but Demeter immediately transformed Ascalaphus into a short-eared owl as an alternate punishment. Hades, persuaded by Persephone, allowed him to take Cerberus on condition that he capture him without weapons. This he did by grasping him firmly around the neck and choking him until the hound submitted. He returned to earth with Cerberus by an entrance near Troezen, or some say through a cave in the land of the Mariandyni on the Euxine Sea. When he had shown Cerberus to Eurystheus he returned the hound of Hades to the Underworld.

Now that he had finished his labors for Eurystheus Heracles gave his wife Megara to his faithful friend Iolaus, as he feared to have more children by her, remembering how he had slain her children in his madness. He sought Eurytus in Oechalia and asked for the hand of his daughter Iole. Eurytus, who had learned archery from Apollo and had in turn taught it to the youthful Heracles, had promised his daughter to whoever could defeat him in an archery contest. Heracles defeated him but Eurytus, claiming that Heracles used divine arrows, and fearful because of his former madness, refused to give up his daughter. Heracles departed, and shortly thereafter some of Eurytus' cattle were missing. He was convinced that Heracles had stolen them. His son Iphitus, who had urged his father to carry out his bargain and give Iole to Heracles, claimed Heracles was innocent, and in truth it was the well-known thief Autolycus who had taken them. Iphitus set out to find Heracles and prove his innocence. He met him as he was returning from Pherae. Heracles, having brought Alcestis up from the Underworld, where he wrestled Hades himself, restored her to Admetus. He promised Iphitus assistance in a search for the cattle, but unfortunately, Hera sent another spell of madness, and he hurled Iphitus from the walls of Tiryns and killed him.

Once again in possession of his senses, Heracles was overcome with remorse and asked Neleus of Pylus to purify him. Neleus, with the backing of his sons, refused. Deïphobus of Amyclae purified him for the murder. Even so, he was plagued by disease and went to consult the Oracle at Delphi to learn how he could be cured. The priestess refused to have anything to say to him, whereupon Heracles seized her tripod and threatened to set up his own oracle. Apollo rushed onto the scene to defend his priestess and the dauntless Heracles attacked the god. Zeus separated them by hurling a thunderbolt between them and the priestess hurriedly gave him instructions. She told him to sell himself as a slave and give the purchase price to the sons of Iphitus. Omphale, queen of Maeonia, bought him. For her he seized the Cercopes, deceitful men who had been turned into apes by Zeus, and, hanging them head down from a pole, carried them to Omphale. He killed Syleus for his unpleasant habit of forcing travelers to compete with him in tilling his vineyards. Omphale, impressed with his deeds, freed him and married him and bore him a son, Lamus. It is said that while in Omphale's services, Heracles and the queen sometimes exchanged garments. This is the foundation for the story that Heracles worked for Omphale dressed in women's clothes and that he was so effeminate as to engage in spinning and weaving.

Freed of his service, Heracles returned to the Peloponnesus to carry out his vows of revenge on Laomedon, Augeas, Eurytus, and Neleus. He sailed to Troy in six ships and attacked the city. Telamon of Salamis, who accompanied him, was the first to breach the wall. Angry that anyone had gotten ahead of him in valor, Heracles was about to kill Telamon but paused as he noticed Telamon hastily piling up stones. When he asked the reason for this Telamon said he was building an altar to Heracles the Victor. His ready answer mollified Heracles and saved Telamon from certain death. Heracles sacked Troy and killed Laomedon and all of his sons except Podarces, who had advised Laomedon to pay Heracles as he had promised for destroying the sea monster. He gave Hesione, Laomedon's daughter, to Telamon. She ransomed Podarces with her veil and thus he gained the name Priam, "Ransomed." Heracles turned over Laomedon's ruined kingdom to him. On his way home from Troy Hera sent violent storms that shipwrecked Heracles on the island of Cos. He was then urgently sought out by Athena, who asked his assistance in the war against the Giants which was now raging on the plain of Phlegra. The goddess helped him to find the magic herb that would protect him and they hurried off to the battle. Although the gods had wounded many of the Giants Heracles was required to dispatch them, as an oracle had foretold that only a mortal could kill them.

He next turned his attention to Augeas. He collected an Arcadian army but was repelled by the sons of Actor and Molione. Eurystheus banished him from Tiryns and he attacked and killed Eurytus, the son of Augeas, near Cleonae, where a temple to Heracles was erected, some say by himself. He made a second attack on Augeas in Elis in which he killed Augeas and gave the kingdom to Phyleus because the latter had supported Heracles in the matter of the payment Augeas had promised. He then marched against Neleus, who had refused to purify him for the murder of Iphitus, and slew Neleus and all of his sons except Nestor. According to some accounts, in this battle he also wounded Hades, Hera, and Ares, who fought on the side of Neleus. He fought against the Spartans, to avenge the death of a son of his friend and to punish them for aiding Neleus, and defeated Hippocoön, who had seized the throne from his brother Tyndareus, and restored Tyndareus.

On his way home he stopped in Tegea, where he was entertained by Aleus. He ravished Auge, daughter of Aleus, a priestess in the temple, and she later bore his son, Telephus. Returning then to Pheneüs, he stayed there five years. At the expiration of this time he left for Calydon and fulfilled the promise made to Meleager in the Underworld to marry Deianira, daughter of Oeneus. First however, he had to overcome the river-god Achelous, who was also one of Deianira's suitors. Achelous fought in the shape of a serpent and then in the form of a bull. Neither form helped him. Heracles seized him by a horn and hurled him to the ground with such force that the horn broke off. This horn eventually became the Cornucopia, the "Horn of Plenty."

Heracles marched with the Calydonians against the Thesprotian city of Ephyra, slew the king and ravished his daughter, who subsequently bore him Tlepolemus. At a banquet with Oeneus he impatiently cuffed the lad who poured water over his hands for the libation. The boy died as a result of what Heracles considered a light tap. It was clearly an accident but Heracles, overcome by remorse, insisted on taking the penalty, which was to go into exile. He set off with Deianira for the kingdom of Ceyx, in Trachis. On the way it was necessary to cross the Evenus River. Nessus, a centaur, offered to ferry Deianira across on his back while Heracles, swimming, went ahead. As they neared the shore Nessus attempted to violate Deianira. Her screams drew instant action from Heracles. He sent one of his poisoned arrows into the centaur. Before he died Nessus advised Deianira to preserve his blood as it would be a potent love charm in the event that Heracles' interest in her should waver, as it was constantly doing. She secretly gathered the blood and kept it in a vial.

At Trachis they were hospitably received, and Heracles fought as an ally of Aegimius, king of the Dorians, against the Lapiths. Among other deeds he performed at this time: he killed Cycnus, the son of Ares and Pelopia, who killed strangers and used their polished skulls to build a temple to his father; he slew Amyntor, who had refused to give Heracles his daughter, on the ground that he already had a wife, and took Astydamia, Amyntor's daughter, by force and became the father of Ctesippus by her; he gathered an army with which he attacked Eurytus, father of Iole, slew him and his sons, and took Iole captive. On his way back from this war he went to Cenaeum, the extreme northwestern point of Euboea, and prepared to sacrifice to Zeus. He sent his

obscured) errant, ardent, actor; ch, chip; g, go; th, thin; ᵺ, then; y, you; variable) ḍ as d or j, ṣ as s or sh, ṭ as t or ch, ẓ as z or zh.

herald Lichas to Trachis to get the robe he customarily wore when sacrificing. Deianira learned from Lichas that Iole was with Heracles and decided that the time had come to make use of Nessus' love charm. She rubbed the dried blood of Nessus on the robe and sent it off with Lichas. After the herald left she noticed that the ground on which a drop of the blood had fallen was smoldering, and in terror she tried to recall Lichas, but it was too late. Lichas gave the robe to Heracles, who put it on and prepared his sacrifice. As the heat of his body warmed the robe the blood of the centaur with which it was covered melted, and suddenly it seared Heracles' body as with a sheet of fire. He tried to pull off the robe and his skin came with it. He was in torment, and it was caused by his own arrow which had poisoned Nessus' blood. According to some accounts he leaped into the waters of a stream to cool his burning body, but the only effect of this was to cause the water to bubble and steam, which it has done from that day to this and accounts for its name, Thermopylae, "hot springs." In a frenzy he hurled the innocent Lichas into the sea, and swore to kill Deianira. However, she had learned the effects of Nessus' love charm and hanged herself. On the advice of Apollo, Heracles repaired to Mount Oeta and built a great pyre. He secured a promise from his son Hyllus to marry Iole, and mounted the pyre. No one had the courage to light it for him, in spite of his pleas to be released from his sufferings. Only Philoctetes, in compassion, found the heart to set it alight. In return for this he was given the bow and arrows of Heracles. As the pyre blazed up, a flash of lightning blinded all present; a cloud passed under Heracles' body and bore it away. The pyre was instantly consumed and as no bones were found all took it for granted that Heracles had been carried to Olympus. Zeus took him to Olympus in a four-horse chariot and persuaded Hera to adopt him as a son. This the goddess did, partly because she had no choice, but also partly in gratitude because Heracles had protected her in the war with the Giants when one of the Giants sought to violate her. She even permitted him to marry Hebe and acquiesced when he was made gate-keeper of Olympus.

The Locrians began to sacrifice to Heracles as a hero immediately after his death. They were followed in this by the Thebans, but it was the Athenians who first worshiped him as a god. The general opinion was that Heracles' immortal parts, reft from his blazing pyre, went to Olympus, but his mortal parts went as a shade to the Underworld, and Odysseus saw it when he visited the Underworld.

Heracles was worshiped throughout the Mediterranean world. Each town and city added some act or exploit to the hero's life which would identify him with their own people. The legion of sons he was supposed to have fathered gave many places a direct ancestor who was a son of Heracles. Only Euripides speaks of Heracles as being the father of one daughter, Macaria. The Romans took over Heracles, whom they called Hercules, lock, stock, and barrel, and added some incidents to his life which were exclusively connected with their own history and nation. Every town, village, and city wished to be connected in some way, no matter how slightly, with the great hero. This perhaps accounts for the incredible number of exploits which were added to the list of his accomplishments.

Heracles, Labors of.   According to some accounts, Heracles was obliged to perform only ten labors for Eurystheus, but because Eurystheus refused to count two of them, Heracles performed 12 great labors. The order of the 12 labors differs in the accounts given by different writers, and even the labors themselves differ. Following is a list that includes those labors generally regarded as the 12 great labors of Heracles: 1) the strangling of the Nemean Lion; 2) the killing of the Lernaean Hydra; 3) the capture of the Erymanthian Boar; 4) the capture of the Cerynean Hind; 5) the cleaning of the Augean Stables; 6) the slaughter of the Stymphalian Birds; 7) the capture of the Cretan Bull; 8) the capture of the man-eating mares of Diomedes of Thrace; 9) the securing of the girdle of Hippolyte, queen of the Amazons; 10) the fetching of the red oxen of Geryon; 11) the procuring of the Golden Apples of the Hesperides; 12) the bringing to the upper world the dog Cerberus, guardian of Hades. Labors that are sometimes substituted for some of those on the above list by other writers are: the strangling of the serpents; the battle with the centaurs on Mount Pholoe; the killing of the guest-slayer Cycnus; and the rearing of the Pillars of Heracles to hold up the heavens.

Heracles the Dactyl (dak′til). In Greek mythology, one of the five Dactyls of Crete who, according to some accounts, protected the infant Zeus on Mount Ida in Crete. Afterward he went, with his brothers, to Elis to propitiate Cronus. Some say he engaged in a race with his brothers at Olympia in Elis, and that this was the origin of the Olympic Games, and that they were held every fifth year because there were five brothers. And some say that Heracles the Dactyl had brought back the wild olive from the land of the Hyperboreans and crowned the winner in this first race with a wreath made from its branches, thus establishing the custom of crowning the victor with wreaths of the wild olive. Heracles the Dactyl is also said to have built the first altar to Zeus at Olympia, constructing it from the ashes of the bones of victims he had sacrificed. The image of Heracles found floating on a raft in the sea between Chios and Erythrae and won by the Erythraeans with a rope made of women's hair was said to be of Heracles the Dactyl, not Heracles son of Alcmene.

Heraclidae (her-a̯-klī′dē). Descendants of Heracles; specifically, in Greek legend, certain Achaean chiefs claiming descent from Heracles, who in prehistoric times joined the Dorian migration to the Peloponnesus. The sons of Heracles were said to have been expelled from their heritage in the Peloponnesus by Eurystheus (to whom Hera had given the region) and to have settled in Attica. The most notable of their descendants who joined the Dorians were Temenus, who in the partition of the conquered territories obtained Argos; Procles and Eurysthenes, who obtained Lacedaemon; and Cresphontes, who obtained Messenia. The invasion of the Peloponnesus by the Heraclidae in alliance with the Dorians was commonly referred to as the return of the Heraclidae.

Hercules (her′kū̯-lēz). The Roman name for Heracles (q.v.). (For the Labors of Hercules, see *Heracles, Labors of.*) The Romans adopted the Greek hero Heracles, lock, stock, and barrel, and added to the legends assembled about his name some purely Roman adventures.

Hercyna (her-sī′na̯). In Greek mythology, a fountain-nymph of Lebadia in Boeotia, and a playmate of Persephone. Once as they were playing, a goose she was holding escaped and fled into a cave. Persephone pursued it and lifted the rock in the cave under which it was hiding. A spring immediately gushed forth from the place where the rock had lain, which became the source of the Hercyna River. Near the source of the river in the cave stone images were placed. On the bank of the river was a temple of Hercyna, with an image of the maiden holding a goose in her arms. The bones of Arcesilaus, brought back from Troy by Leïtus, were entombed beside the river. Across the river was a grove sacred to Trophonius, in which there was an image said to have been made by Praxiteles. Those who sought to consult the oracle of Trophonius had first to bathe in the waters of the river Hercyna.

Hermaphroditus (her-maf-rō-dī'tus). In Greek mythology, a son of Hermes and Aphrodite, born on Mount Ida. In his youth he journeyed to Caria, where he came to the fountain in which dwelt the nymph Salmacis. Salmacis fell in love with his beauty, which combined that of Hermes and Aphrodite, but he rejected her advances and begged her to go away. As he bathed in Salmacis' pool the nymph dived into its clear water and clung to him, praying they might be united in one person. Her prayer was answered; the bodies of Hermaphroditus and Salmacis were fused into one being combining both male and female attributes.

Hermes (her'mēz). One of the 12 Olympian gods. He was the messenger of the gods, the bringer of dreams, the god of flocks and herds, and of the market-place; he was god of commerce and trade, of inventions, science, and the arts, and of craft in oratory. As an ancient fertility god, he became also a god of wealth, hence of luck, hence of thieves. He conducted the souls of the dead to Hades, and thus was a link between the worlds of the living and the dead, equally beloved in both. The story of Hermes is that while Hera slept Zeus went to a cave on Mount Cyllene, in Arcadia, and there embraced Maia, the daughter of Atlas. In this same cave his son Hermes was born to Maia one day at dawn. The infant was wrapped in swaddling clothes and laid on a winnowing fan, but he refused to stay in his cradle. On the very first day of his life he crept to the entrance of the cave, and there, on the threshold, he found a tortoise. He greeted the tortoise with joy, took it up, scooped out the flesh from its shell, and bound it with ox hide. To the sounding box he made in this manner he attached horns, which he connected at their free ends with a bridge of reed. From the bridge he strung seven sheep-gut strings to the sounding box. (Some say he strung only three strings, others say it was four, and that it was Apollo who added the strings that make the seven-stringed lyre.) After he invented a plectrum he tried out his new musical instrument; he plucked the strings and sang of the love of Zeus and Maia and of his own birth.

HERMES
Black-figured Attic amphora, 6th century B.C.
Museum of Fine Arts, Boston

Then, being hungry, he set off to the meadows of Pieria, where the cattle of Apollo were grazing. Here he selected 50 head from the herd and prepared to make off with them. But to cover his tracks, he made huge sandals of oak bark, fastened together with woven grasses, and put them on the hoofs of the cattle. But some say he made the cattle walk backward, to disguise their path, and that he put the sandals on his own feet and camouflaged himself with branches as well. All agree that he was the inventor of sandals, and that he made them to help him carry out his theft of Apollo's cattle. As he started off with the cattle for Pylus, on the Alpheus River, he was spotted by an old man who was cultivating his crops in the nearby fields. Hermes promised the old man rich crops if he would say he had not seen him. According to some accounts the old man agreed; but others say he would make no promise. Hermes proceeded with the cattle to the Alpheus River, where he fed them, penned them in a cave, and built a fire by scraping sticks of wood together. He was the first to build a fire in this manner. He killed two of the steers, roasted their flesh, and nailed their hides to the rocks. The flesh of the roasted steers he cut into 12 portions but, though he was hungry, he ate none of it himself, as it was a sacrifice to the gods. Some say he did eat of the flesh, and that this was the first flesh sacrifice made to the gods. He then quenched the fire, threw his sandals into the river, and returned to Cyllene, where he slid through the keyhole into the cave, and was back in his cradle before his absence had been discovered, having, in the first 24 hours of his life, invented sandals, a method of making fire by rubbing sticks together, the first flesh sacrifices to the gods, and the lyre, to say nothing of having stolen his brother Apollo's cattle. Some say his mother saw him as he slid back into his cradle and pulled the covers around his neck; and she chided him, and predicted he would come to a bad end. He at first innocently answered that he was much too young to do anything that merited such a rebuke, then reproached her for talking to him as if he were a "wordless babe," assured her that he would get along all right, and would look after her too. As he had already made up his mind to be a god, he promised her that they would dwell among the immortals. For, he said, if his father Zeus would not make him a god he would make himself one. At dawn the next day Apollo discovered that 50 of his cattle were missing. Some say Apollo searched fruitlessly for them, and finally offered a reward for their return. Silenus and his companions, eager for the reward, set out to track down the missing cattle. They came to the cave in Cyllene and heard strange music issuing from it. They questioned the nymph Cyllene about the music and learned from her that a marvelous child had been born the day before, who had invented a new instrument from ox hides and sheep gut. The Sileni were suspicious, especially when they heard of the ox hide, and charged that this marvelous child had stolen the cattle of Apollo. Cyllene was indignant at this ridiculous charge. Just then Apollo arrived, guided thither by a long-winged bird, some say, but others say he knew by divination that Hermes had stolen his cattle. They say that when Apollo noticed the loss of his cattle he asked the old man working in the fields if he knew what had become of them. The old man answered that many passed by as he worked and he could not know them all, but he did especially notice a child, a mere babe, driving cattle backward. Apollo found the tracks and the strange imprints made by the sandals Hermes had invented, and although he didn't understand the strange tracks, he knew where to look for his lost cattle.

Now he arrives, full of wrath, at the cave on Cyllene and charges Hermes with the theft. Hermes cowers in his cradle as Apollo sweeps through the cave looking for his cattle, in vain. He threatens Hermes. Hermes answers that he is a mere infant, who knows nothing of such things and is interested only in his mother's milk. After all, he says, he was born only yesterday, and scarcely understands the meaning of the word "cattle." Apollo is beguiled by the cheekiness of his infant brother. Nevertheless, as Hermes refuses to say where the cattle are and protests his innocence, Apollo hales him off to Zeus. Zeus, too, is amused by Hermes' lies, but orders him to restore the stolen cattle, and asks Apollo to forgive his baby brother. Hermes submits to the will of Zeus; he leads Apollo to Pylus and brings the cattle from the cave where he had hidden them. Now Apollo notes the two hides nailed to the rock, and resolves to punish Hermes. But the willow bonds he makes to bind him fall to the ground and sprout. Apollo asks what he did with the two steers he killed, and is told that they were sacrificed to the 12 gods. Surprised, Apollo says he knows of only 11 gods; who is the twelfth? Hermes modestly names himself. As Apollo prepares to set his cattle to graze Hermes plucks his lyre, which up to now he has kept hidden under his swaddling clothes, and sings of the creation of the world and of the gods. Apollo is enchanted with the music. He agrees to give Hermes the cattle in exchange for the lyre, and promises to honor him and his mother. Hermes hands the lyre over and in his turn promises never again to steal anything of Apollo's. They become fast friends. As the cattle graze Hermes invents a shepherd's pipe of reeds and pipes on it guilelessly. Apollo, hearing it, demands this instrument too, and offers in exchange the golden wand with which he herds his cattle. But Hermes bargains. He will exchange the pipe for the golden wand *and* instruction in the art of prophecy. Apollo gives him the golden wand, which will make him a warder of cattle and bring him wealth, but will not teach him the art of prophecy. However, he tells Hermes of the three sisters, the Thriae, who dwell on Mount Parnassus and who will teach him the art of divining by pebbles. In addition to learning this, Hermes also invented the art of divining by knucklebones. Apollo names him god of flocks, cattle, and all animals, and tells Zeus of the deeds young Hermes has already performed. Zeus appoints him herald of the gods, gives him a herald's staff wound with white ribbons, which must be respected by friend and foe, and a round hat and winged sandals, and Zeus appoints him protector of travelers, god of treaties and commerce. Thus Hermes is enrolled as one of the gods. Hades appoints him as the god who summons the dying by laying his golden staff gently on their eyes, and Hermes becomes Pterseus *(Destroyer),* because he is the herald of Death, and Psychopompus, because he conducts the dead souls to the Underworld. Sometimes Hermes uses his staff merely to bring sleep to mortals, and as such he is the bringer of dreams and to him libations are poured before bedtime. In time Hermes shared with Apollo the honors given to the god of the *palaestra* (athletic contests), and feasts called *Hermaia* were dedicated to him as the god of athletic skills that make men strong and handsome.

As herald of the gods Hermes performed many errands. After the flood that Zeus sent to destroy wicked men, Hermes was sent to ask Deucalion, who survived it, what he wished for. Deucalion wished for men to repopulate the earth. It was Hermes who sent the ram with the fleece of gold to rescue Phrixus and Helle when their father was about to sacrifice them. At the command of Zeus he killed 100-eyed Argus, set by Hera to guard Io after she had been transformed into a heifer. Because of this Hermes won the epithet Argeiphontes *(Slayer of Argus).* He guided Perseus to the Phorcides when he was on his mission to fetch the head of Medusa, gave him the adamantine sickle to cut off the Gorgon's head, and restored the cap, wallet, and sandals to the nymphs when Perseus was through with them. It was Hermes who led the goddesses——Athena, Aphrodite, and Hera—to Paris to be judged for the prize of beauty that Eris had thrown among the wedding guests at the marriage of Thetis and Peleus. Some say Hermes, at the command of the gods, carried Helen off to Egypt and delivered her into the charge of the king, and that the Helen Paris carried off to Troy, and for whom the Greeks and Trojans fought a disastrous war, was only a phantom, a wraith created by Hera to punish the Trojans. In the Trojan War he aided the Greeks, with the permission of Zeus, but when Hector was killed by Achilles, Hermes, in disguise, led Hector's aged father Priam to the camp of the Greeks and spirited him into Achilles' tent so that he could ransom his son's body. He then conducted the grieving old king, with Hector's corpse, safely back to Troy. By his cunning and his gift for crafty language Hermes often helped the gods. He retrieved the sinews of Zeus that had been cut out and hidden by the monster Typhon and restored them to Zeus, who then conquered Typhon. He helped to rescue Ares when he was imprisoned in a bronze vessel by Otus and Ephialtes. To him was entrusted the infant Dionysus to save him from the wrath of Hera. He took Dionysus to Ino and Athamas and persuaded them to rear him as a girl. When Hera drove Ino and Athamas mad, Zeus transformed Dionysus into a kid, and in that guise Hermes took him to the nymphs of Nysa. In the gods' war with the Giants Hermes wore the cap of invisibility, loaned to him by Hades, and overcame the giant Hippolytus. As a god who had connections with the Underworld he bore a message from Zeus to Hades, demanding the release of the abducted Persephone so that the earth might not become barren because of Demeter's sorrow, and he brought Persephone back to her mother Demeter in his chariot. On the other hand, he forcibly restored Sisyphus to the Underworld, from which he had escaped by a trick. But he fetched up Protesilaus, killed in the Trojan War, to spend a few hours with his wife on earth. It was Hermes who sold Heracles for three talents to Omphale, to purge him of his crime of murdering Iphitus. Hermes was sent by Zeus to help Atreus in his struggle for the throne of Mycenae; and again, he was sent to warn Aegisthus not to seduce Clytemnestra while her husband was off at the Trojan War. He gave the lyre to Amphion and gave the magic herb moly to Odysseus to protect him from the spells of the enchantress Circe. Altogether, Hermes was a most helpful god; a deity of great ingenuity, craft, and, on the whole, good will.

fat, fāte, fär, fâll, ȧsk, fāre; net, mē, hėr; pin, pīne; not, nōte, mȯve, nôr; up, lūte, pŭll; oi, oil; ou out; (lightened) ĕlect, agǫny, ūnite;

Like most of the gods, Hermes had many loves. Apemosyne, daughter of King Catreus of Crete, rebuffed him. However, as she was returning from a spring one day he spread fresh hides in her path, and when she attempted to run from him she slipped and fell: he seized her and ravished her. Some say Hermes was the father of Eros by Aphrodite, and some say he was the father of Pan by Penelope. He also loved Herse, daughter of Cecrops, and she bore him Cephalus, who was carried off by Eos, and Ceryx, the first herald of the Eleusinian Mysteries. Other sons were: Autolycus, the notorious thief; Echion and Eurytus the Argonauts; Daphnis, who invented bucolic poetry; Myrtilus, the charioteer of Oenomaus, for whose murder Pelops erected the first temple of Hermes in the Peloponnesus; Abderus, who accompanied Heracles to Thrace to fetch the man-eating mares of Diomedes and perished there.

In recognition of his role as protector of travelers and wayfarers, square pillars were set up in his honor. They were called *Hermae,* and were to be seen at cross-roads, lanes, byways, and before houses. In addition, there were heaps of stones at the crossroads to which passing travelers added their stones in tribute to Hermes. An image of Hermes of the Gateway stood at the entrance to the Acropolis. As god of the Market-place his image stood near the Painted Portico in Athens. Another image, bearded and made of stone, stood in the market-place at Pharae. Here there was an oracle of Hermes. In front of the image was a hearth to which bronze lamps were fastened. At nightfall, the inquirer at the oracle burned incense on the hearth, filled and lighted the lamps, put them on the altar to the right of an image of a coin called a "copper," then he whispered his question into the ear of the image of Hermes. Having asked his question, the inquirer stopped his ears and left the marketplace, when he unstopped his ears. The first words he overheard thereafter constituted the oracular response. Hermes was called Cyllenian *(Of Cyllene),* for his birthplace; Epimelius *(Keeper of Flocks),* and the god who brought fertility to flocks and fields; Pronaos *(Of the Fore-temple)* and had an image said to have been made by Phidias at the entrance to the Acropolis at Thebes; he was Acacesius *(Of Acacesium)* after Acacus, founder of Acacesium, because, some say, as a child he lived in Acacesium and Acacus was his foster-father; he was

Dolius *(Crafty)*; Champion, especially at Tanagra where he led the youths of the city against invading Eretrians, and where there was a wild strawberry tree under which he was said to have been nourished; he was Spelaites *(Of the Cave)*; and Promachos *(Defender)*. He was the god of luck and of profit; whatever was found by chance was a gift of Hermes. He was born on the fourth of the month and that day and number were sacred to him. His worship, which was particularly strong in Arcadia, its ancient seat, extended throughout Greece. In art he was sometimes represented bearded, but after the archaic period usually as a graceful and vigorous youth, slightly draped, with *caduceus* (staff), *petasus* (round hat), and *talaria* (winged sandals) as attributes. The most noted artists of antiquity executed works in which Hermes was the subject. One of the most beautiful as well as one of the best-known statues of antiquity that have been preserved is the *Hermes Carrying the Infant Dionysus,* found in the ruins at Olympia. The Roman Mercury, their god of commerce, became identified with Hermes.

Hermione (hėr-mī′ọ̄-nē). In Greek legend, the daughter of Helen and Menelaus. She was nine years old when her mother eloped with Paris and left her in Sparta. Menelaus gave her into Clytemnestra's charge while he sought the return of Helen. She was betrothed to Orestes at the command of Apollo, but some say that toward the end of the Trojan War when oracles foretold that Troy could not be taken without the presence of Neoptolemus, Menelaus promised her to Neoptolemus in return for his aid at Troy. Others say she was given to Neoptolemus because Orestes, pursued by the Furies for the murder of his mother, could not marry her. She married Neoptolemus long after he returned from the war accompanied by his captive and concubine Andromache. Hermione bore no children to Neoptolemus and accused Andromache, whom she constantly referred to as a barbarian, of putting a spell on her. Neoptolemus went to Delphi to consult the priestess concerning his wife's childlessness. While he was gone Hermione plotted to kill Andromache and her sons by Neoptolemus. She was prevented from doing so by the timely arrival of Peleus, grandfather of Neoptolemus. In fear of her husband's wrath for what she had tried to do, Hermione attempted to kill herself by hanging, but was saved by her handmaidens. She later married Orestes, who some say had a hand in Neoptolemus' death at Delphi, and bore him a son, Tisamenus.

Hero (hē′rō). In Greek legend, a priestess of Aphrodite at Sestos, on the Hellespont, beloved by Leander, who swam across the Hellespont every night from Abydos to see her. One night Leander was drowned and Hero, heartbroken, drowned herself also.

Heroic Age. One of the five Ages of Man described by Hesiod. It followed the Bronze Age and preceded the Iron Age. Men of the Heroic Age were descended from mortals and fought gloriously and for the joy of combat in the Trojan War. The siege of Thebes and the expedition of the Argonauts were among other glorious exploits of the Heroic Age. At the end of their days, the men of the Heroic Age were transported to the Elysian Fields.

Ierophile (hē-rof′i-lē). A legendary prophetess of Delphi. She is said to have lived before the Trojan War, for she foretold that Helen would be reared in Sparta and would be the ruin of Europe and Asia, and that for her sake the Greeks would capture Troy. She claimed that her mother was immortal, a nymph of Trojan Mount Ida, and that her father was a mortal. She was an attendant at the temple of Apollo Smintheus but spent most of her life in Samos, with occasional visits to the sanctuaries of Apollo at Clarus, Colophon, and Delphi. At Delphi she stood on a high rock and chanted her oracles. She died in the Troad and was buried in the grove of Sminthian Apollo, whom at various times she claimed as a husband and a brother in her oracles.

erse (hėr′sē). In Greek mythology, one of the three daughters of Cecrops, the half-man, half-serpent king of Attica, and Agraulos. Hermes, beholding her in a procession for Athena, fell in love with her and bribed Agraulos the Younger to facilitate a visit to her. Agraulos took the bribe but refused to do anything to help Hermes because she had been inspired by Athena with gnawing envy of her sister's good fortune in being loved by a god. In anger, Hermes turned Agraulos to stone and sought Herse. She bore him two sons, Cephalus and Ceryx. Long before this happened, however, Athena had given Agraulos and her daughters a chest to guard. She cautioned them not to open the chest.

Some time after the death of Agraulos the Younger, Hers͏
and her mother and sister could no longer control thei͏
curiosity. They opened the chest and were horrified to fin͏
therein an infant which was half-child and half-serpent͏
Maddened by this discovery, they leaped from the Acropoli͏
and were killed. Athena was so grieved when she learned o͏
their deaths from her sacred crow that she dropped the hug͏
stone she was carrying to fortify the Acropolis, and it be͏
came Mount Lycabettus. She also changed the crow's feath͏
ers from white to black for bringing her bad news, an͏
forbade all crows from ever again visiting the Acropolis.

Hesione (hē-sī′ō-nē). In Greek legend, a daughter of Laome͏
don, king of Troy, and Leucippe. On the advice of an oracl͏
she was chained to a rock on the shores of Troy as a sacrifice͏
to be killed by a sea-monster sent by Poseidon to devastat͏
the land because Laomedon had refused to pay Poseido͏
and Apollo for their help in building the walls of Troy͏
Passing by Troy, Heracles saw her and when he learned th͏
reason for her pitiful situation he offered to slay the monst͏
and free her. Laomedon promised to pay him with the mar͏
velous horses that Zeus had given to compensate for th͏
abduction of Ganymede. Heracles slew the monster an͏
freed Hesione but once the danger was removed Laomedo͏
refused to honor his promise. Heracles vowed reveng͏
After some time he returned and attacked Troy. He kille͏
Laomedon and all of his sons except Podarces (Priam͏
sacked the city, and took Hesione captive. He gave her t͏
Telamon, who had aided him in his attack, and she bore hi͏
a son, Teucer, the half-brother of Telamonian Ajax. Accord͏
ing to some accounts, when Priam, the new king of Tro͏
had reëstablished his kingdom he sought the return of h͏
sister, and sent his son Paris with a fleet to bring her bac͏
Paris took the occasion to go to Sparta and seduce Hel͏
and bring her back to Troy, thus causing the Trojan Wa͏
Others say that Hesione fled from Telamon to Miletu͏
where King Arion found her and married her. She bore ͏
second son, Trambelus, whom Arion reared as his own so͏
although he was the child of Telamon, and who was afte͏
ward killed at Troy by Achilles.

Hespera (hes′pėr-a̦). In Greek mythology, the daughter ͏
Erebus and Nyx (Night). The name for Eos when, as sh͏

accompanied Helius, she had passed through the heavens to the western shore and had become Evening.

Hesperides (hes-pèr'i-dēz). In Greek mythology, three maidens, Hespere, Erytheïs, and Aegle, who guarded the tree with the golden apples which Gaea (Earth) caused to grow as a marriage gift for Hera. According to Hesiod they were daughters of Nyx and Erebus; in later accounts they are named as the daughters of Atlas and Hesperis. They dwelt in the gardens of the west, or among the Hyperboreans, or in Libya; the location of their garden is variously given. Ladon, a 100-headed dragon, helped them guard the apples, but to no avail. Heracles came and slew Ladon and obtained some of the golden apples to take to Eurystheus. The Hesperides were also visited by the Argonauts, who had been blown to the coasts of Libya by a storm and then lifted in the *Argo* by a mighty wave which washed them into the interior and left them stranded. They carried their ship over the desert to the Tritonian Lake and came to the Hesperides, who first transformed themselves into dust and earth before the Argonauts, and then into trees—Hespere into a poplar, Erytheïs into an elm, and Aegle into a willow. The reason for their fear at sight of the Argonauts was that only the day before Heracles had come and taken the golden apples. When they found the Argonauts were not hostile they told them how to find a spring which Heracles had caused to gush up from the earth in the desert and wished them good luck.

Hesperus (hes'pe̱-rus). Personification of the evening star, in Greek mythology; son of Astraeus and Eos (according to Hesiod): identified with the planet Venus. The Latin name for it was Vesper.

Hestia (hes'ti-a̱). One of the 12 Olympians. She was the eldest daughter of Rhea and Cronus and, like Artemis and Athena, was a virgin goddess. This came about because Apollo and Poseidon were rivals for her love. She settled their quarrel by vowing to remain a virgin forever. For thus preventing strife from breaking out on Olympus Zeus ordered that the first victim of every public sacrifice be dedicated to Hestia. As goddess of the hearth and the hearth fire, Hestia was intimately linked with every Greek family, for the hearth was the center of Greek life. She presided over individual well-being and the duties of hospitality. Hestia, who

remained aloof from the wars and disputes in which th
other gods and goddesses reveled, was worshiped as
beneficent and kindly goddess. Her shrine was a sanctuar
for suppliants, and her fire, both in private and publi
hearths, was sacred. The Romans identified her with thei
Vesta.

Hiera (hī'ẹ-rạ). According to some accounts, the wife o
Telephus, and a leader of the Mysian women, allies of th
Trojans in the war against the Greeks. She was slain in battl
by Nireus. Some say she was a daughter of King Priam o
Troy, and that she surpassed Helen in beauty.

Himeros (hī'mẻr-os). The god of longing or desire, closel
associated with Eros.

Hippocamp or **Hippocampus** (hip'ọ-kamp, -kam'pus). I
Greek and Roman mythology, a sea-horse with two forefee
and a body ending in the tail of a dolphin or other fish. Th
car of Poseidon and those of other deities were drawn b
such sea-horses.

Hippodameia (hi-pod-ạ-mē'ạ, -mī'ạ). See **Briseis.**

Hippodamia (hi-pod-ạ-mī'ạ). In Greek legend, a daughter o
Oenomaus, king of Pisa and Elis, and Sterope. Either be
cause of incestuous love for her or because an oracle ha
declared that he would die at the hands of one of her off
spring, her father refused to give her in marriage. He com
pelled her suitors to run a race with him, from Olympia t
the Isthmus of Corinth. If Oenomaus, who gave the contes
tants a head start, overtook them he flung his spear int
their backs and killed them. When Pelops came wooing Hip
podamia, she fell in love with him and bribed Myrtilus
Oenomaus' charioteer, so that Pelops could win. Pelops als
bribed Myrtilus; he won the race, and Oenomaus was killed
Hippodamia established games to Hera, the Heraea
Games, in gratitude for her marriage to Pelops. She bor
him many children, among them: Pittheus, Atreus
Thyestes, Copreus, and Sciron. She became jealous o
Pelops' affection for his bastard son Chrysippus. Some sa
she murdered Chrysippus but was recognized and fled. Oth
ers say she and her sons Atreus and Thyestes were im
plicated in the murder. However it was, she fled to Argoli
and killed herself. Later her bones were brought back an
buried at Olympia. Annual sacrifices were made by wome
in her sanctuary.

Hippolyte (hi-pol'i-tē) or **Hippolyta** (-ta). In Greek legend, a queen of the Amazons; a daughter of Ares and Harmonia, or, according to other accounts, of Otrera or of Aphrodite and Ares. She dwelt near the Thermodon River on the Euxine Sea, and was the possessor of a famous girdle, a gift to her from Ares, which Heracles was told to fetch as one of his labors for Eurystheus. When Heracles came to her shores she received him graciously and voluntarily agreed to give him the girdle. However, Hera stirred up the Amazon women with a rumor that Heracles was about to abduct their queen. They armed themselves and prepared to attack. Heracles, suspecting treachery, killed Hippolyte and took her girdle. According to other accounts, Heracles got the girdle in exchange for one of Hippolyte's sisters whom he had captured; or by engaging in personal combat with Hippolyte and slaying her; or even from Theseus, who had secured the girdle and gave it to Heracles in exchange for Antiope, a captive Amazon princess.

Hippolyte. Name sometimes given to the Amazon queen who bore Hippolytus to Theseus. See *Antiope.*

Hippolytus (hi-pol'i-tus). In Greek legend, a son of Theseus and the Amazon Antiope. When Theseus had sons by his lawful wife Phaedra, he sent Hippolytus from Athens to Troezen where his grandfather Pittheus made him his heir. Hippolytus was a handsome, athletic, and chaste youth. He built a temple to Artemis in Troezen and devoted himself to the worship of that goddess to the exclusion of others. By this devotion to Artemis he denied the power of Aphrodite, and she resolved to punish him. She caused Phaedra, his stepmother, to fall madly in love with him. Phaedra followed him to Troezen and covertly watched him every day as he exercised on the gymnasium ground, jabbing the pin of her jeweled brooch in the leaves of a nearby myrtle tree in her frustration. After some time, encouraged by her nurse, Phaedra sent Hippolytus a letter in which she confessed her love for him and invited him to share her couch. Hippolytus was horrified. He destroyed the letter, his only evidence that she had made the advances, and reproached Phaedra. She, fearing he might expose her, wrote a letter to Theseus accusing Hippolytus of committing the acts she wished he had committed, and then hanged herself from the lintel. When Theseus read the letter he accused Hippolytus and without

bscured) errant, ardent, actor; ch, chip; g, go; th, thin; ŦH, then; y, you;
ariable) ḍ as d or j, ṣ as s or sh, ṭ as t or ch, ẓ as z or zh.

listening to the protests of his son, who had come to Athens
banished him from the city. Theseus called on Poseidon to
punish Hippolytus. As Hippolytus drove furiously along the
coast road in his chariot, Poseidon sent a huge wave from
the sea. Riding the crest of the wave was a great bull, or
according to some accounts, a sea monster. The horses were
terrified and shied and reared. Hippolytus prevented them
from plunging over the cliffs but they had swerved from the
road. Either the reins caught on a fig tree by the roadside
or the axle of the chariot wheel struck the tree bole. The
chariot overturned and Hippolytus, entangled in the reins
was dragged to his death. Too late Theseus learned that his
son was innocent. Some say the body of Hippolytus was
buried beside that of Phaedra in a tomb in Troezen near the
myrtle tree, the leaves of which still bear the scars of being
jabbed by Phaedra's brooch. The people of Troezen paid
Hippolytus divine honors, brides cut off a lock of their hair
and dedicated it to him. But some say the people of Troezen
did not believe Hippolytus was killed by his horses, and that
he was not buried in Troezen. They say his spirit went to
Tartarus and there Artemis demanded that Asclepius restore him to life. Asclepius, with the aid of an herb, did as
she requested, but since it was against divine law for the
dead to return to life Artemis wrapped him in a cloud, transformed his appearance and rapt him off to Italy. She
changed his name to Virbius and sent him to live in her
sacred grove in Aricia. There, with the permission of the
goddess, he married the nymph Egeria. No horses were
allowed in the sacred grove. Priests of the temple were
drawn from runaway slaves.

Hippomedon (hi-pom'e̜-don). In Greek legend, a son of Aristomachus. He was an Argive and was one of the seven chieftains who marched against Thebes to restore Polynices to
the throne. He perished in the expedition. Some say he was
slain by Ismarus, others say he was overcome by a cloud of
Theban missiles after he had nearly drowned in the Ismenus
River. His body was recovered by Theseus after the Thebans had refused honorable burial to those who fell at
Thebes. He was the father of Polydorus, one of the Epigoni.

Hippomenes (hi-pom'e̜-nēz). In Greek legend, the son of
Megareus and Merope, and the grandson of Poseidon. As a
woman-hater, he went to sneer as he watched Atalanta race

against her suitors, but remained to fall in love with her. With the help of Aphrodite he resolved to race Atalanta and to win her. Aphrodite gave him three golden apples which, during the course of the race, he cunningly threw in front of Atalanta. She, who had at one time vowed to remain a virgin, stooped to pick them up and lost ground. In this way Hippomenes won the race and won Atalanta for his wife. According to some accounts, Atalanta had already fallen in love with Hippomenes at sight, and thus was the more ready to take advantage of any delay which would permit him to win. In his joy at winning Atalanta Hippomenes forgot to give proper thanks to Aphrodite, and the goddess became his enemy. She induced him to commit a sacrilege in the temple of Cybele. Cybele, in her turn punishing, turned him and Atalanta into lions and yoked them to her car. According to other accounts it was Zeus who turned them into lions; Hippomenes is also known as Melanion.

Hoples (hop'lēz). According to tradition, one of the four sons of Ion. One of the four ancient tribes of Athens was named for him. His brothers were Aegicores, Argades, and Geleon.

Horae (hō'rē). In Greek mythology, three nature-goddesses who preside over the changes of the seasons and the accompanying course of natural growth and decay. According to Homer, they are handmaidens of Zeus, who guard the gates of heaven and control the weather; according to Hesiod, they are daughters of Zeus and Themis, named Eunomia ("Good Order"), Dice ("Justice"), and Eirene ("Peace"), guardians of agriculture and also of social and political order. Their number varied from two, as at Athens (Thallo, goddess of spring flowers, and Carpo, goddess of summer fruits), to four. The dance of the Horae was a symbolized representation of the course of the seasons.

Horn of Plenty. In Greek mythology, a horn of the goat Amalthea, or of a goat belonging to the nymph Amalthea, which nursed the infant Zeus. The horn was said to be always full of whatever food and drink one desired. For the Romans, the Horn of Plenty—*Cornu Copiae*—was the horn of Achelous, the river-god who had taken the form of a bull to fight Heracles and lost one of his horns in the struggle. This Horn of Plenty was always full of fruits and flowers.

Hyacinthides (hī-a-sin'thi-dēz). In Greek mythology, the daughters of Hyacinthus the Spartan. They were Aegleis,

Antheis, Lyctaea, and Orthaea, and were sacrificed i
Athens on the advice of the oracle to save the city when i
was attacked by Minos, king of Crete, to avenge the murde
of his son. The city was wracked by plague and earthquake
and it was thought that the sacrifice of the maidens woul
bring relief from these as well as protection from Mino
However, the sacrifice was unavailing, and the Athenian
were compelled to yield to Minos and pay him tribute o
their sons and daughters before the plague and earthquake
stopped.

Hyacinthus (hī-a-sin′thus). [Also: *Hyacinth.*] In Greek myth
ology, a beautiful youth, the son of Amyclas, king of Amy
clae in Laconia. He was loved by Thamyris the poet, b
Apollo, and by Zephyr (the West Wind). Thamyris was de
feated in a musical contest by Apollo, and blinded, whic
removed him as a rival for the affections of Hyacinthus. Bu
one day when Apollo was teaching young Hyacinthus t
throw the discus, or a quoit, Zephyr seized the discus an
blew it back against Hyacinthus with such force that it kille
him. From his blood Apollo caused the hyacinth to spring
and upon the petals of the plant was thought to be marke
the exclamation AI ("woe!"). Hyacinthus represents th
death of young things just as they are approaching the fu
bloom of their beauty, as fruits and flowers that flourish i
the spring but die under the heat of the summer sun. Th
tomb of Hyacinthus was at Amyclae, under the great imag
of Apollo. Sacrifices were offered to him as a hero and hi
festival, the *Hyacinthia,* was observed at Amyclae durin
three days in July. Modern scholarship sees in Hyacinthus a
agricultural or vegetation deity, and in his annual festival
typical resurrection ritual.

Hyades (hī′a-dēz). [Also: *Hyads.*] In Greek mythology,
group of nymphs, the daughters of Aethra and Atlas, an
the sisters of Hyas. They grieved so over the death of thei
brother that they were translated to the heavens as the seve
stars in the head of the constellation Taurus. Others say th
Hyades were the nymphs of Nysa who nurtured the infar
Dionysus, and that they were translated to the heavens b
Zeus as a reward for their care of his son. The rainy seasor
which begins with their rising, is a mark of their continuin

care, for the rain they send nurtures the vine sacred to Dionysus. The Romans, through a mistaken etymology, called the constellation Succulae *(Little Pigs)*.

Hyas (hī′as). In Greek mythology, a son of Aethra, daughter of Oceanus and Tethys, and Atlas. He was a mighty hunter who sought a lioness and her cubs and was killed by a Libyan boar. His sisters grieved so for him they were placed among the stars as the Hyades.

Hydra (hī′dra). In Greek mythology, a monstrous dragon of the Lernaean Spring, in Argolis, represented as having nine heads, each of which, being cut off, was immediately succeeded by two new ones unless the wound was cauterized. The destruction of this monster (by searing each neck as he cut off the head, with firebrands supplied by Iolaus) was one of the 12 labors of Heracles.

Hygea (hī-jē′a). [Also: *Hygieia*.] In Greek mythology the goddess of health. She was the daughter of Asclepius; in later myth, his wife. In later myth also, she became the goddess of mental health.

Hylas (hī′las). In Greek legend, a son of Thiodamas, king of the Dryopians, and the nymph Menodice. Heracles slew Thiodamas and carried off his young son, Hylas, who became his squire and beloved companion. He accompanied Heracles as an Argonaut. When the Argonauts landed in Mysia, Hylas went to the fountain of Pegae to fetch water while Heracles searched for a tree from which to make an oar. Dryope, the nymph of the fountain, fell in love with Hylas as he stopped to draw water, and pulled him into the spring to dwell thereafter with her and her sister nymphs. It was because he stayed to search for Hylas that Heracles was left behind by the Argonauts and did not take part in the recovery of the Golden Fleece.

Hyllus (hil′us). In Greek legend, a son of Deianira and Heracles. He took his dying father to Mount Oeta, built a funeral pyre at his request, and promised to marry Iole, daughter of Eurytus of Oechalia. He learned from Heracles that his death, as a result of Nessus' blood having been rubbed on his sacrificial robe by Deianira, fulfilled an old prophecy that no living mortal would destroy him, but that he would die because of a dead enemy. Hyllus could not bear to carry out his father's last request, which was to light the pyre on which

Heracles was lying. This was done by Philoctetes. After the apotheosis of Heracles, Hyllus joined with the Athenians in a war against Eurystheus, captured him, and, according to some accounts, cut off his head. He then successfully invaded the Peloponnesus, but a plague broke out and he was warned by the oracle at Delphi to withdraw and to await the third crop before he returned. Hyllus took this to mean three years, and at the expiration of this time he returned. In order to avoid bloodshed he offered to engage in single combat with a representative of Mycenae, on the condition that if he was victorious the kingdom of Mycenae would be his, but if he lost the Heraclidae would withdraw for fifty years. Echemus, king of Tegea, accepted his challenge. In the duel Hyllus was slain and was buried in Megara. The Heraclidae honored his agreement and withdrew from the Peloponnesus. The oracle at Delphi explained that the third crop meant the third generation, not the third year, as Hyllus had interpreted it.

Hymen (hī′mẹn) or **Hymenaeus** (hī-mẹ-nē′us). Originally, the marriage song among the Greeks. The names were gradually personified, and Hymen, the marriage song personified, was invoked as the god of marriage. According to legend he was the son of Apollo and one of the Muses, or of Dionysus and Aphrodite, or, in some accounts, a mortal youth who was invoked in hymeneal songs. He is represented as a beautiful youth, more serious than Eros, carrying a bridal torch.

Hyperboreans (hī-pẹr-bō′rē-anz). In early Greek legend, people who were believed to live beyond the north wind and were not exposed to its blasts, but enjoyed a land of perpetual sunshine and abundant fruits. They were free from disease, violence, and war. Their natural life span was said to be 1000 years, and was spent in the worship of Apollo, who was said to pass the winter among them. No one ever actually described their land, and its existence was doubted by some in ancient times, but Abaris, who in legend went around the world on an arrow, claimed to have visited it. According to Herodotus, those who were supposedly neighbors of the Hyperboreans—for example, the Scythians—never mentioned them, but they were named by Hesiod. Again according to Herodotus, those who had the most to say about the Hyperboreans were the people of Delos. The

fat, fāte, fär, fâll, ȧsk, fãre; net, mē, hẽr; pin, pīne; not, nōte, mȯve, nôr; up, lūte, pȧll; oi, oil; ou out; (lightened) ẹlect, agȯny, ūnite,

Delians claimed that two Hyperborean maidens, Hyperoche and Laodice, brought offerings of the first fruits wrapped in wheaten straw to Delos. They were accompanied by five men. When the Hyperboreans found that their envoys to Delos did not return they no longer sent their envoys direct to Delos. They sent their offerings to the Scythians, who passed them on to their neighbors, and eventually the offerings, given in honor of Apollo, reached Delos. Some say Apollo came from their land. It was also claimed that the Hyperboreans sent the birth-goddess Ilithyia to assist Leto on Delos when she was about to bear Apollo. Some said that the wild olive was brought from their land into Greece by Heracles. And some said that it was the Hyperboreans who first established the oracle of Apollo at Delphi where, later, they sent a temple made of bees' wax and feathers. The Hyperboreans Pagasus and Agyieus were said to have established the oracle. When the Gauls attacked Delphi (279 B.C.), Pagasus and Agyieus were said to have appeared in superhuman form and to have driven them away. In later times the Greeks gave the name Hyperboreans to inhabitants of northern countries generally.

Hyperion (hī-pir′i-on). In Greek mythology, a Titan, one of the sons of Gaea and Uranus. By the Titaness Thia he was the father of Eos *(Dawn)*, Helius *(Sun)*, and Selene *(Moon)*. In the *Odyssey* he is identified with Helius, and in late mythology with Apollo.

Hypermnestra (hī-pèrm-nes′tra̱). In Greek mythology, one of the 50 daughters of Danaus. When she and her sisters were about to be married to the 50 sons of Aegyptus, Danaus gave each of them a sharp pin or dagger and ordered them to kill their husbands on the wedding night. Hypermnestra, divinely inspired, looked on her sleeping husband Lynceus and could not bear to kill him. She told him of her father's plot and begged him to flee. To inform her of his safety she asked him to light a beacon when he reached Lyncea, 60 furlongs away, and she promised to answer his signal. Lynceus escaped and made known his safety to her. Danaus was enraged by her disobedience. He imprisoned her and would have killed her but the Argives acquitted her and she dedicated an image to Aphrodite in gratitude. Later Danaus reluctantly reunited her with Lynceus. But some say Lyn-

ceus returned and won her back by force and killed Danau?
Hypermnestra bore Abas, the ancestor of Perseus, to Lyn
ceus.

Hypnos (hip′nos). In Greek mythology, the god of sleep; so
of Erebus and Nyx (Night), and brother and companion c
Thanatos (Death). He is usually represented as a winge
figure accompanying Thanatos. He had three sons, name
Morpheus, Icelus, and Phantasus, regarded as dream-bring
ers. Hypnos is identified with the Roman Somnus.

Hypsipyle (hip-sip′i-lē). In Greek legend, a daughter c
Thoas, king of Lemnos. When the women of Lemnos ros
up and killed all the men because they had abandoned thei
true wives for captive women, Hypsipyle secretly spared he
father and set him afloat on the sea in a chest. She the
became queen. By the time the Argonauts landed in Lemno
on their way to find the Golden Fleece, Polyxo, aged nurs
of Hypsipyle, was easily able to change the attitude of th
Lemnian women toward men. They invited the Argonaut
to stay and share their island. Hypsipyle entertained Jaso
and by him became the mother of twin sons. According t
some accounts, when the Lemnian women later learned tha
Hypsipyle had spared her father they rose against her, kille
her sons and sold her into slavery to Lycurgus, king c
Nemea, under whom she became the nurse of Opheltes, hi
son. According to other accounts, her sons were not kille
but rescued her and returned her to Lemnos, after she ha
carelessly allowed Opheltes to be slain by the bite of a se
pent. Her sons were Euneus and Thoas, and according t
Homer, Euneus supplied the Greeks at Troy with wine fror
Lemnos during the Trojan War.

Hypsipyle was the subject of a play by Euripides, lost fror
the manuscript tradition but fortunately now represented b
extended passages on papyrus recovered from the villag
dumps of Greco-Roman Egypt.

Hyrnetho (hèr-nē′thō). In Greek legend, a daughter of Teme
nus, a son of Aristomachus who won Argos as his share c
the Peloponnesus. He favored his daughter and her hus
band over his sons, and proposed to leave his kingdom t
Hyrnetho and her husband Deiphontes. When they learne
of this, his sons—Agelaus, Eurypylus, and Callias—hire
assassins to murder their father. Hyrnetho accompanied he
husband when he marched to Epidaurus and took over th

land without a struggle. Her brothers tried to persuade her to abandon Deiphontes, and when she refused they carried her off in their chariot and then, pursued by Deiphontes, they killed her. Deiphontes and his sons buried her in a place that came to be known as the Hyrnethium, and established a hero-shrine in her honor. It was the custom to place in her shrine branches and twigs that fell from olive trees.

Iacchus (ī′a̱-kus). In Greek mythology, a divinity peculiar to Athens, and important for his intimate connection with the Eleusinian mysteries. His mother is variously given as Demeter, Persephone, or Semele; his father as Zeus or Dionysus. He is undoubtedly a personification of the ritual cry raised by the worshipers of Dionysus, and the resemblance of his name to Bacchus (Dionysus) easily led to his identification with the latter. His image, crowned with myrtle and bearing a torch, was carried in the famous procession from the Eleusinium at Athens to the *sekos* (sanctuary) at Eleusis, and he presided over the mysterious rites there. He was sometimes called the Phrygian Bacchus, who, as a son of Demeter, was distinct from the older Dionysus.

Iamus (ī′a̱-mus). According to Greek tradition, a son of Evadne and Apollo. His mother abandoned him through shame, and he was nursed by two serpents who fed him honey. From them and from his father Apollo he received the gift of prophecy and founded a family of seers called, after him, Iamidae.

Ianthe (ī-an′thē). According to legend, a beautiful maiden of Phaestus, in Crete. She was the daughter of Telestes. She loved and was loved by Iphis, the daughter of Telethusa. Telethusa had brought Iphis up as a boy, because her husband intended to kill her child if it was a girl. Thus Ianthe supposed that she was in love with a young man. The two young people were betrothed, but Telethusa and Iphis, fearing the revelations marriage would bring, delayed the ceremony. At last, when it could be delayed no longer, Telethusa entered the temple and prayed to Io for aid. Her prayer was answered. As she left the temple Iphis was transformed into a man. The next day Ianthe and Iphis were married.

Iapetus (ī-ap'ę-tus). In Greek mythology, a Titan; son of Uranus (the sky) and Gaea (the earth); father by the nymph Clymene of Prometheus (and therefore ancestor of the human race), Epimetheus, Atlas, and Menoetius. He was thrown by Zeus into Tartarus after the Titans were overthrown.

Iasion (ī-ā'zi-ǫn). In Greek mythology, a Titan, or according to other accounts, a son of Zeus and the Pleiad Electra; the twin of Dardanus and a founder of the Trojan race. Demeter fell in love with him at the marriage of Cadmus and Harmonia and he lay with her in a "thrice-plowed field" and begot Plutus (the wealth-giver, especially the giver of agricultural bounty). For this association with the goddess Zeus struck Iasion dead with a thunderbolt. This myth is probably the rationalization of some very early Greek fertility rite associated with Demeter in her aspect as a grain goddess.

Iaso (ī-ā'sǭ). In Greek mythology, a daughter of Asclepius and the sister of Aigle, Hygea, and Panacea. She was a goddess of healing.

Iason (ę-ā'sǫn). See *Jason.*

Icarius (ī-kär'i-us). In Greek mythology, an Athenian who entertained Dionysus, not knowing he was a god. As a reward for his hospitality, Dionysus taught Icarius the cultivation of the vine and the art of wine-making. Icarius offered some wine to a band of peasants but as they did not mix it with water they got drunk from it. Thinking themselves poisoned, they killed Icarius and buried his body under a pine tree. See *Erigone.*

Icarus (ik'ạ-rus, ī'kạ-). In Greek legend, the son of Daedalus and a Cretan slave, Naucrate. He was imprisoned with his father in the labyrinth that Daedalus had built for King Minos. Freed by Pasiphaë, Daedalus and Icarus escaped from Crete with the aid of wings that Daedalus made by threading feathers together and fastening them with wax. Before they flew off, Daedalus warned his son not to fly too low lest the sea wet his wings and make them heavy, and not to fly too high lest the sun scorch them. Above all he warned Icarus to follow his father closely and not to be diverted by the creatures he would see in the sky. They passed the islands of Delos, Paros, and Samos safely. Icarus then became over-confident as he soared through the air and forgot his father's warnings. In his pleasure at wheeling in flight he flew so near the sun that the wax bindings of his wings melted and he fell into the sea and was drowned. Daedalus rescued his corpse and buried it on an island now known as Icaria in the Icarian Sea. Some say that it was Heracles who buried his body on the island where his body was cast up.

Icelus (īs′ė-lus). The dream-god who sent dreams of birds and beasts. He was the child of Nyx *(Night)* and the brother of Hypnos *(Sleep)* and Thanatos *(Death)*. Men called him Phobetor, "the Terrifier," but the gods named him Icelus.

Ichor (ī′kôr, ī′kėr). An ethereal fluid believed to flow instead of blood in the veins of the gods.

Ichthyocentaur (ik″thi-ō-sen′tôr). In Greek mythology, a fabulous creature of the sea with the body of a man, the legs of a horse, and the tail of a fish. The Ichthyocentaurs were attendants of Triton and other sea-gods.

Idaean Mother, The (ī-dē′an). Another name for Cybele, deriving from her sanctuary on Mount Ida. Other names are Mater Idaea, and the Great Mother of the gods.

Idas (ī′das). In Greek legend, the son of Arene by Poseidon, but brought up as the son of Aphareus, Arene's husband. He was a man of great valor, a skilled bowman, a strong man with the spear, and the devoted brother of Lynceus. The brothers took part in the Calydonian Hunt, and accompanied Jason on the *Argo* in the quest for the Golden Fleece. As an Argonaut, Idas boasted that his own spear was of more help to him than was Zeus, and was chided for blasphemy by Idmon the seer. Orpheus stilled the ensuing quarrel between them by playing his lute. Later Idas slew the boar which had attacked and killed Idmon, and still later, when the Argonauts arrived in Colchis, he objected violently when Jason decided to seek the assistance of Medea. Idas considered it an insult to his manly valor and skill as a warrior to accept help from a woman.

Idas and Lynceus were betrothed to their cousins, the Leucippides, but Castor and Polydeuces carried the Leucippides off and had sons by them, thus earning the enmity of Idas and Lynceus. Idas fell in love with Marpessa, the daughter of Evenus. To win her he had to defeat her father in a

chariot race, and did so with the help of a winged char
given to him by Poseidon. Apollo also loved Marpessa
When he learned that Idas had won her he engaged in a due
with him—Idas was one of very few who dared challenge th
gods—but Zeus intervened and said Marpessa could choos
between Apollo and Idas. She chose Idas, because sh
feared the immortal would too soon tire of her. After th
death of Aphareus, Idas and Lynceus resolved their quarre
with Castor and Polydeuces and made a raid with them fo
some cattle in Arcadia. In the division of the spoils Idas an
Lynceus won the cattle by a trick and drove them off. Late
Castor and Polydeuces stole the cattle from them, and hi
in a hollow tree to waylay Idas and Lynceus. Lynceus, whos
sight was so keen he could see through a tree trunk, spotte
them. He and Idas rushed up and in the fight that broke ou
Lynceus and Castor were killed, and Zeus, to protect his so
Polydeuces, hurled a thunderbolt that killed Idas.

Idmon (id′mon). In Greek legend, an Argonaut, the son o
Apollo and Cyrene, but reared as the son of Abas of Argos
He was a seer (his name means "the knowing one") wh
learned the augury of birds from Apollo. At the start of th
expedition in the *Argo* he predicted that though there woul
be grievous trials, both coming and going, the Argonaut
would bring back the Golden Fleece. He also predicted tha
he would not return with them. This prophecy was fulfille
in the land of the Mariandyni, where he was attacked an
killed by a wild boar.

Idomeneus (ī-dom′e̯-nūs, ī″dō̱-me̯-nē′us). In Greek legend
the son of Deucalion. He was king of Crete, and was re
nowned for his courage, and for his good looks. As a forme
suitor of Helen he commanded a fleet and sailed to join th
Greeks in their expedition against Troy to recapture Hele
from Paris. Although he was no longer young, he fough
with the courage of a wild boar and accounted for man
Trojans with his spear. With others, he volunteered to mee
Hector in single combat but was eliminated in the drawin
of lots. He and the two Ajaxes were the chief defenders o
the Greek fortifications against Hector's attack. On his wa
home after the war his ship was beset by storms. He praye
to Poseidon to abate them, promising to sacrifice the firs
thing he met upon landing. This, to his sorrow, was his so
True to his vow, he prepared the sacrifice, but was inte

rupted by a pestilence which swept Crete. On this occurrence Leucus, who had first become the paramour of Idomeneus' wife Meda and then murdered her and seized the throne, banished Idomeneus from Crete. He went to Bruttii, where he ended his days.

Ilione (il-ī′ō̠-nē̠, -ō′nē̠). [Also: *Iliona*.] In Greek legend, the oldest daughter of Priam and Hecuba. She was the wife of Polymnestor, king of Thrace, and the mother of his son Deïpylus. Entrusted with the care of her young brother, Polydorus, Ilione purposely confused the two children so that if one died the other would succeed to the throne. According to some accounts, Polymnestor, bribed by the Greeks to kill Polydorus, by mistake killed his own son, whereupon Ilione first blinded and then killed him.

Ilioneus (il-ī-ō′nē̠-us, il-ī′ō̠-nūs). In Homeric legend (*Iliad*), a Trojan hero, the only son of Phorbas. Peneleus pierced him through the eye-socket with his lance, then cut off his head and waved it on the end of his lance as he taunted the Trojans. This is one of the few instances of brutality for its own sake in the *Iliad*.

Ilithyia (il-i-thī′ya̠). [Also: *Eileithyia*.] The goddess who presides over childbirth, sometimes called the daughter of Hera. In her role as the goddess who helps women in childbirth she can either hasten or delay delivery. Hera enlisted her aid to delay the birth of Heracles until after Eurystheus, whose arrival was speeded up, was born. On the Hill of Cronus, near the site of the Olympic Games, an infant was transformed into a serpent, and so terrified the Arcadians, who were warring on the Eleans, that they fled with great losses. The spot where the serpent then disappeared into the hill was marked by a shrine to Ilithyia. In it priestesses fed a snake on cakes of honey in memory of this miracle. The Romans identified Ilithyia with Juno, whom they called Lucina in this aspect.

Ilus (ī′lus). In Greek legend, a son of Dardanus and the brother of Erichthonius. According to some, he was the grandnephew of Dardanus and son of Tros. Having been victorious in a wrestling match in Phrygia, he was awarded 50 youths and 50 maidens as a prize. He was also given a spotted cow and told to follow it until it should lie down. On that spot he was to erect a city. Ilus carried out his instructions and followed the cow until it came to rest on a hill in the Trojan plain. There he built Ilium, named for himself. He prayed to Zeus for a sign that he had chosen well, and was answered by finding a wooden image in the ground in front of his tent. This was the Palladium. Apollo told Ilus that as long as the Palladium remained within its walls the city would be safe. Ilus was the father of Laomedon, by Eurydice, daughter of Adrastus, and the grandfather of Priam.

Inachus (in′a̯-kus). In Greek mythology, the god of the river Inachus, son of the Titan Oceanus and his sister Tethys, whose children were the Oceanids and the rivers of the world. He was the first king of Argos and was the father of Io and of Phoroneus by the nymph Melia. When Poseidon contended with Hera for control of Argolis, Zeus asked the river-gods Inachus, Cephissus, and Asterion to mediate the quarrel. The river-gods decided in favor of Hera. Poseidon was enraged that they had awarded Argolis to Hera and to punish them dried up their rivers so that they ceased to flow in the summer.

Ino (ī′nō). In Greek mythology, a daughter of Cadmus and Harmonia, and the sister of Semele, Agave, Autonoë, and Polydorus. She married Athamas, king of Orchomenus, after he had abandoned his first wife, Nephele, by whom he had two children, Helle and Phrixus. Ino also had two children by Athamas, Learchus and Melicertes. She plotted to destroy Phrixus and Helle so that her own children would be the heirs. By some means she parched all the grain seed secretly, so that when it was planted no crops grew and there was a famine. Messengers were sent to consult the oracle and returned with the news, as they had been bribed to do by Ino, that the gods could be propitiated and starvation avoided if Phrixus were sacrificed to them. Athamas took Phrixus and Helle to a mountain top and prepared to sacrifice them. Just as he was about to put the knife to their throats, however, Hermes sent a miraculous winged ram with fleece of gold which rescued them and bore them off on his back. Hera punished Athamas for abandoning Nephele, whom she had arranged for him to marry in the first place, by driving him mad. In his frenzy he killed Learchus and would have killed Ino. She escaped, carrying her son Melicertes in her arms, and leaped into the sea. However, Zeus was grateful to her for sheltering his son Dionysus and transformed her into a sea-goddess who was known thereafter as Leucothea. Melicertes became the sea-god Palaemon. It was in her capacity as sea-goddess that Leucothea saved Odysseus from drowning when his raft was shattered in a storm. She gave him her veil and helped him to reach shore on the island of the Phaeacians.

Io (ī′ō). In Greek mythology, a beautiful daughter of the river-god Inachus. She was a priestess of Hera at Argos. Zeus saw her as she wandered by the river and fell in love with her. He appeared to her in dreams and told her she had inspired his heart with love. One day he overtook her as she returned from the river. She fled from his embrace. He called a dark cloud to cover the earth, seized her, and ravished her. From her seat on Olympus Hera saw the cloud which appeared from nowhere and, ever suspicious of her notoriously unfaithful husband, she hurried down to earth to investigate. Zeus, hearing her approach, transformed Io into a beautiful pure white heifer, so that Hera should not discover his love-affair and heap angry recriminations on his head. Hera was acutely suspicious on finding Zeus in the company of a heifer and inquired where it had come from. He had had no time to think what he would say and improvised a tale that the heifer had sprung from the earth. Hera admired it and asked Zeus to give it to her as a gift. He was most reluctant but dared not risk further questions by refusing this gift to his wife, and turned Io over to Hera. She set the 100-eyed Argus to guard the heifer and went off, if not satisfied with his explanation at least content that she had foiled whatever plan he had in mind for the heifer. Argus, whose 100 eyes were never all asleep at once, guarded Io vigilantly. By day he allowed her to graze; at night he tied her up. Inachus searched in vain for his daughter. At length he came upon Argus and his charge. Io ran up to her father and licked his hand, but he had no idea this was his daughter. In despair that she could not speak to him and tell him of her plight she at last traced her name in the dust with her hoof—the hoofprint of a cow still spells her name. Inachus was desolate when he realized what had happened to his daughter, but he was powerless and Argus soon drove her on to new pastures. At length Zeus, in pity for Io, sent Hermes to slay Argus and set Io free. Hermes lulled all his

100 eyes to sleep and cut off his head. But Io was still no
delivered. The shade of Argus pursued her, and Hera sen
a gadfly to torment her. Half-crazed by the continual sting
of the gadfly, she wandered distractedly through Greece
The Ionian Sea is so-named because she swam across it to
Thrace. There she found Prometheus, bound to a rock. She
pleaded with him to tell her if the future held any hope. He
could not be immediately encouraging. He told her tha
much weary wandering lay ahead of her. Hounded by the
gadfly, she would cross over into Asia—the place where she
crossed, he said, would be known as Bosporus, "Ox-ford"
—then after many years of wandering and suffering she
would arrive at the Nile. Here at last she would regain her
true shape. Zeus would touch her and she would bear him
a son, Epaphus. With a frenzied cry Io left Prometheus and
fled, stung by the gadfly. All turned out as he had predicted
She came at last to the Nile, was retransformed into her own
shape, and bore Epaphus after Zeus touched her. She married Telegonus, king of the Egyptians, and set up images to

HERMES ABOUT TO SLAY ARGUS, THE GUARD OF THE HEIFER
IO
Red-figured hydria, 5th century B.C.
Museum of Fine Arts, Boston

Demeter. The Egyptians called the goddess Isis, and they
also gave Io the name Isis, which may be the reason why
images of the goddess are shown with a cow's horns. The
descendants of Epaphus were Aegyptus, Danaus, Cepheus,

and Phineus, and ultimately, as Prometheus foretold, a male child was born, a mighty archer, who brought about the release of Prometheus; he was Heracles. According to later rationalizations of the Io story, she was not seduced by Zeus at all. Rather, it was a group of Phoenician traders who landed in Argos and carried her off to Egypt. Later the Greeks identified Io with Isis, the Egyptian moon-goddess. The starry skies symbolized the 100-eyed Argus; her transformation into a horned heifer was represented by the crescent moon.

Iobates (i-ob′a-tēz). In Greek legend, a king in Lycia and the father of Antia, wife of Proetus. He received Bellerophon kindly when he came to him with a message from Proetus, and after entertaining him hospitably for nine days he read the message. In it Proetus asked him to kill Bellerophon, charging that he had insulted Antia. Iobates did not want to offend the gods by slaying Bellerophon himself. He sent him, in turn, to kill the Chimaera, to fight the Solymi, and then to fight the Amazon women. As Bellerophon was successful in each case Iobates set an ambush to kill him, but Bellerophon slew the Lycian heroes who sprang on him from ambush and returned to Iobates. He decided that Bellerophon must have divine aid and therefore must be innocent of the crimes charged against him by Proetus. Iobates then gave him his daughter in marriage and a wide domain to rule over in Lycia. The message from Proetus to Iobates is the earliest reference to writing in European literature.

Iocaste (i-ō-kas′tē). *Jocasta.*

Iodama (i-od′a-ma). According to Greek tradition, a daughter of Itonius. Some say she was a priestess in the temple of Athena Itonia in Boeotia, between Alalcomenae and Coronea. She went into the sacred precinct at night and Athena appeared to her. When Iodama saw the Gorgon's head on Athena's aegis she was turned to stone. Fires were lighted daily on the altar, and chants were thrice intoned, saying Iodama lived and desired fire. Others say Athena was a daughter of Itonius and that Iodama was her sister, and that the goddess accidentally turned her to stone by allowing her to see Medusa's head on her aegis.

Iolaus (i-ō-lā′us). In Greek legend, the son of Iphicles. He was the nephew, faithful friend, and companion of Heracles, and accompanied him as he carried out his labors for Eurys-

theus, sometimes acting as Heracles' charioteer and some
times as his armor-bearer, but in all cases giving whateve
aid he could to his beloved uncle. Heracles loved him dearly
but when, in a spell of madness inspired by Hera, he kille
his children, he also attacked Iolaus, but the latter escape
his attacks and comforted Heracles when his senses wer
restored to him. Later Heracles gave Megara, the mother c
his murdered children, to Iolaus as his wife. Iolaus led 40 c
Heracles' sons by the daughters of Thespius to Sardinia an
founded a colony there. He established the city of Olbia an
named the colonists Iolarians after himself. Heracles estab
lished a sanctuary of Iolaus in Sicily. Iolaus returned t
Greece and became the protector of Heracles' children afte
the latter had become immortalized. When the son of The
seus gave the children of Heracles sanctuary in Marathor
causing a war with Eurystheus, Iolaus, by then an old mar
armed himself with weapons which he took from the wall
of the temple. Despite protests that he was too old and wea
to fight, he jumped into a chariot and drove into the battle
first praying to the gods to be given youth and strength fo
one day. Two stars lit on the yoke of his chariot, and cast ;
shadow over him. When the shadow lifted Iolaus was re
vealed as a stalwart youth. He pursued and captured Eurys
theus and took him back to Alcmene, mother of Heracles
to give her the privilege of deciding the fate of her son'
enemy. But some say Iolaus cut off Eurystheus' head and
Alcmene then gouged out his eyes with a spike.

Iole (ī′ō-lē). In Greek legend, a daughter of Eurytus, king o
Oechalia. Heracles sought her for a wife and was promised
her hand if he defeated Eurytus in an archery contest. Wher
Heracles won, her father refused to keep to his bargain
Heracles vowed revenge, and in the meantime he marrie
Deianira. He later slew Iphitus, son of Eurytus, and after
ward gathered an army, attacked and killed Eurytus and hi
sons, and took Iole captive. Deianira, to whom Heracles sen
Iole, had nothing but pity for the youthful captive, but she
was determined to recapture Heracles' affections if possible
She sent him a robe anointed with what she thought was ;
love charm. But it turned out to be a poison that entere
Heracles' blood and ended his mortal life. Hyllus, his son
married Iole, as he had promised his dying father he woul
do, and Deianira hanged herself.

Ion (ī′on, ī′ọn). According to Greek tradition, a son of Creusa, daughter of King Erechtheus of Athens, and Apollo; eponymous ancestor of the Ionians. His mother abandoned him as an infant in the cave where Apollo had ravished her, and when, overcome by remorse and anxiety, she returned to fetch him, no trace of the child was to be found, and she feared he had been carried off by eagles. But Apollo had sent Hermes to rescue his son, and Ion was taken to the temple of Apollo at Delphi, where he was reared by the priestess. By the time he was grown to young manhood he had become a priest in the service of Apollo at Delphi. Meanwhile, Creusa had married Xuthus, an alien from Thessaly who had come to Athens and saved the city in a war with the Euboeans. Creusa and Xuthus ultimately went to Delphi to ask the oracle why they had no children. There Creusa met the young priest. By command of the oracle, he was given to Xuthus as a son. Creusa, driven nearly to madness by grief for her own lost son and jealousy over Xuthus' new son, sought to poison Ion. By the intervention of the gods the poisoned wine which she intended for him was poured on the ground, doves that sipped it died, and her plot was discovered. At this, Ion tried to kill Creusa, but again the gods intervened, and mother and child were made known to each other and reunited. Ion returned to Athens with Creusa and Xuthus, who was not informed that Ion was his wife's own son. Ion married Helice, daughter of King Selinus of Aegialus, and succeeded his father-in-law as king of the Aegialeans. The name of his people was changed to Ionians. They afterward colonized the coast of Asia Minor, which became known as Ionia. Ion gave his assistance to the Athenians in a war against the Eleusinians and, being successful in this, was made king of Athens. The four sons of Ion and Helice—Geleon, Hopletes, Argades, and Aegicores—became the ancestors of the four Ionic tribes.

Iphianassa (if″i-ạ-nas′ạ). Named by Homer (*Iliad*) as a daughter of Agamemnon. She was offered by her father to Achilles as a wife if he would forget his quarrel with Agamemnon and return to fight at the side of the Greeks, in the tenth year of the Trojan War.

Iphicles (if′i-klēz, ī′fi-klēz). In Greek legend, the twin brother of Heracles; son of Amphitryon (a mortal) and Alcmene, Heracles being the son of Zeus and Alcmene. According to some accounts, Amphitryon wanted to find out which of the two boys was his own son. He therefore put two harmless serpents in the cradle where the infants were sleeping. Heracles grasped the serpents firmly and strangled them, laughing as he did so, but Iphicles screamed and tried to hide. Thus Amphitryon knew that Iphicles was his son. But others say that Hera introduced the serpents, which were deadly, into the cradle to destroy Heracles but was frustrated by the fearless strength of Heracles. Iphicles was the father of Iolaus, the faithful companion of Heracles. Iphicles and Heracles were also companions in several adventures before Iphicles was killed in the war which Heracles waged against Augeas, king of Elis.

Iphiclus (if'i-klus, ī'fi-). In Greek legend, the only son of Phylacus, king of Phylace. He was a famous runner, who was reputed to be able to run over a field of standing grain without bending it, and to be able to speed over the sea. Nevertheless, he was beaten by Nestor in a footrace, according to Nestor. According to some accounts, he was one of those who joined Jason on the expedition of the Argonauts. His father was the possessor of famous flocks and herds and Melampus, the seer, tried to steal them for his brother Bias. Being caught, Melampus was imprisoned, but freed when he told Phylacus how Iphiclus could be cured of his childlessness. Melampus said that Iphiclus had been frightened when, as a child, he saw his father approaching him with a bloody knife with which he had been gelding rams. Phylacus stuck the knife into a tree and ran to comfort Iphiclus. Melampus instructed Phylacus to find the knife, scrape rust from it into wine, and give the wine to Iphiclus. After this had been done Iphiclus and his wife Clymene had two sons: Protesilaus, who was the first Greek killed at Troy, and Podarces, who then took command of the Phthians in his place.

Iphigenia (if″i-jē-nī′ạ). In Greek legend, a daughter of Agamemnon and Clytemnestra, and a sister of Orestes and Electra. Her father sacrificed her to Artemis at Aulis, where the Greek fleet was prevented from sailing to Troy by violent storms, to appease the goddess for the death of one of her creatures and to obtain favorable winds. However, as the knife was put to her throat Artemis snatched her up and substituted a hind in her place. Agamemnon thought that she had been taken to live among the gods, but Artemis wafted her to Tauris. There she became a priestess in the temple which contained a sacred image of Artemis. Her duty was to prepare all strangers who inadvertently landed in Tauris as victims to be sacrificed in the temple. After some time, two Greeks were brought before her to be cleansed before they were sacrificed. She gloated over the opportunity thus presented to avenge herself on the people who had been willing to slay her at Aulis, but in the course of talking to the two strangers and of hearing of many whom she had known, her love for her country and her people revived and she resolved to help them escape. First she would give them a message to take to her brother. She handed a scroll to one of the Greeks and, reciting the message contained in it, directed him to give it to Orestes. At that he handed it to his companion. When suitable proof was forthcoming that this was indeed Orestes the three made plans to escape which, with the aid of Athena, they subsequently did, taking the sacred image with them. According to some accounts, Iphigenia ended her days as a priestess in a temple, set up at Brauron, which thereafter housed the sacred image brought from Tauris. Iphigenia is sometimes said to have been the daughter of Theseus and Helen, and to have been adopted and brought up by her aunt, Clytemnestra.

Iphis   (ī'fis). In Greek legend, an Argive, the son of Alector. Polynices sought his advice when he wished to persuade Amphiaraus to join him in the expedition against Thebes. Iphis said that Eriphyle, wife of Amphiaraus, feared she was losing her looks and suggested to Polynices that he bribe her with the necklace of Harmonia (said to make its wearer beautiful), on condition that she persuade her husband to join the expedition. Some accounts list Eteoclus, son of Iphis, as one of the Seven against Thebes.

Iphis.   According to legend, a maiden of Crete who was brought up as a boy. Before she was born her father had ordered her mother, Telethusa, to put the expected child to death if it turned out to be a girl, because he could not afford to bring up a girl. Io appeared to Telethusa in a dream and advised her to deceive her husband if the child was a girl, and to bring it up as a boy, and promised to help Telethusa if necessary. When Iphis was born the deception was carried out and the father, unaware of it all, in due course betrothed his supposed son to a beautiful Cretan maiden, Ianthe. Iphi fell desperately in love with Ianthe, and the love was re turned. Telethusa delayed the marriage as long as she could Whey delay was no longer possible, Telethusa prayed to I and reminded her of her promise of aid. As Telethusa an Iphis left the temple, Io answered her prayers and Iphis wa transformed into a man.

Iphitus (if'i-tus, ī'fi-). In Greek legend, a son of Eurytus, kin of Oechalia; he was the brother of Iole. He and his brother Clytius, joined Jason on the expedition of the Argonauts t Colchis. Iphitus tried to persuade his father to honor th agreement which he had made with Heracles: to give him hi daughter Iole if Heracles defeated him in an archery contest but when Heracles won, Eurytus refused to carry out hi agreement. Later, Eurytus missed some of his cattle, an thought Heracles had taken them for revenge. He sen Iphitus to bring them back. Iphitus thought Heracles wa innocent. Nevertheless he followed him and told him abou the missing cattle. Heracles, inwardly seething because h erroneously thought Iphitus suspected him, took him to a tower in Tiryns, asked him if he could see the cattle, and when Iphitus admitted that he could not, Heracles hurled him to his death. Iphitus was the possessor of a famous bow said by some to have been given to Eurytus by Apollo Iphitus gave the bow to Odysseus, who had gone to Iphitus land in search of some missing cattle, and it was afterward used by Odysseus to slay the suitors of Penelope.

Irene (ī-rē'nē). In Greek mythology, the goddess of peace one of the three daughters of Zeus and Themis known as the Horae (goddesses of order and the seasons). The Roman identified their Pax with Irene.

Iris (ī'ris). The "wind-footed" messenger of the gods, and the goddess of the rainbow—the arc that touches sky and earth. She was the daughter of Thaumas and Electra and wa the sister of the Harpies. She could go to the ends of the earth or even to the Underworld on her golden wings, and traveled along the rainbow, carrying messages to gods as well as to men. In the *Iliad* she is the messenger from Zeus who warns the gods not to help their favorites, or stir up the courage of the Trojans. Later she was considered more

fat, fāte, fär, fåll, åsk, fãre; net, mē, hèr; pin, pīne; not, nōte, mȯve; nôr; up, lūte, p·ull; oi, oil; ou out; (lightened) ēlect, agǫny, ūnite;

especially as the messenger of Hera. She was sent by Hera to tell Peleus to prepare for his marriage to Thetis; to warn the Boreadae not to kill the Harpies; to tell Menelaus that Paris had carried off Helen; to release Dido's soul from her body after she had committed suicide in despair over being abandoned by Aeneas. As a messenger, Iris had no will of her own, but must convey the commands, for good or ill, as she was instructed to do. Some say that as Hera's messenger she carried a jug of water which put perjurers to sleep.

Iron Age.   In classical mythology, a name given to the last (and the worst) of the five ages of mankind or the world, as described by Hesiod and Ovid. It is an age of hard work and agricultural toil, of constant care and trouble, of shame and falsehood, of moral, mental, physical, and spiritual decay; a period in which the only thing that triumphs is Evil. In this age, the land, which was formerly common to all, is divided into private property and becomes a source of conflict. Iron and gold are discovered and find use as material for arms in the wars that continually erupt. The evils of men are so great that Justice leaves the earth and retires to Olympus. It is in marked contrast to the first, and best, age, the Golden Age, when Cronus (Saturn) ruled, and is inferior even to the Silver Age, when people were foolish and arrogant, and to the Bronze (or Brazen) Age, which was an age of war. Hesiod, who described the Ages of Man, and with particular bitterness his own Age of Iron, also wrote of the Age of Heroes, in which men descended from gods fought gloriously and at the end of their days were transported to the Elysian Fields. This Age preceded the Iron Age.

Irus   (ī′rus). In the *Odyssey,* a nickname given to Arnaeus, a beggar of gigantic stature whose size deluded him into thinking he was as strong as he looked. He kept watch over the suitors of Penelope and was employed by them as a messenger, whence his nickname. When Odysseus, disguised as a beggar, returned to his own palace, Irus threatened him and told him to be off. He wanted no other beggars poaching on his territory. Odysseus refused to leave and Irus, egged on by the amused suitors, challenged him to a fight, hoping that his challenge would not be accepted. Odysseus was glad to accept, however, and with one mighty

obscured) errant, ardent, actor; ch, chip; g, go; th, thin; ᴛʜ, then; y, you; variable) ḍ as d or j, ş as s or sh, ṭ as t or ch, ẕ as z or zh.

blow knocked him out of the palace. He never begged in those halls again.

Ischys (is′kis). In Greek mythology, a son of Elatus of Arcadia. Coronis, beloved by Apollo, was unfaithful to the god with Ischys. White crows reported her infidelity to Apollo and were turned black for bringing the bad news (which the all-seeing god already knew), instead of remaining to peck out the eyes of Ischys. Ischys was slain, either by a thunderbolt of Zeus or by an arrow of Apollo

Island of the Sun. An island where the magnificent oxen of the Sun (Helius) lived. Whoever ate of the oxen was doomed to death. It was here that Odysseus lost his entire company because, in spite of warnings given them by Circe and Odysseus, they slew and roasted some of the cattle. The island was Trinacria (Sicily).

Islands of the Blest. Another name for the Elysian Fields, or Elysium, the last home of heroes, sons of the gods, and those whose noble lives or participation in the Mysteries of Demeter earned them the happiness of dwelling there.

Ismene (is-mē′nē). In Greek legend, a daughter of Oedipus and Jocasta, and the sister of Antigone, Eteocles, and Polynices. She dared not join Antigone in her defiance of Creon when he forbade anyone to bury the body of Polynices, who had been slain attacking Thebes. Ismene wanted to share Antigone's punishment when the latter was led away to her death for her defiance, but Antigone scorned her. She told Ismene that since she had cautiously refused to act in defiance of Creon because she desired to live, now she must live.

Itys (ī′tis, it′is). In Greek legend, the son of Tereus and Procne, killed and served as a meal to his father by Procne and her sister Philomela. Tereus had seduced Philomela and torn out her tongue. After the revenge of the sisters, they fled, with Tereus in pursuit. See *Procne.*

Ivory Gate. In classical mythology, the gate of sleep by which false dreams are sent from the lower world.

Ixion (ik-sī′on, ik′si-on). In Greek mythology, a son of Phlegyas, king of the Lapithae. In order to avoid paying the gifts he had promised so that he might marry Dia, daughter of Eioneus, he constructed a hidden pit in front of his palace, in which he placed a red-hot charcoal fire. When Eioneus

fat, fāte, fär, fâll, åsk, fāre; net, me, hėr; pin, pīne; not, nōte, möve, nôr; up, lūte, pùll; oi, oil; ou out; (lightened) ēlect, agŏny, ūnite;

DEATH OF ITYS
Red-figured Attic kylix, early 5th century B.C. Procne
holds her son Itys, as Philomela gesticulates.
Louvre

came to the palace he fell into the pit and was consumed by
the fire. Aeschylus names Ixion as the first murderer. Nevertheless, Zeus purified him and even invited him to dine with
the gods. But Ixion had no gratitude. On the contrary, he
planned to seduce Hera, sister and wife of Zeus. Zeus fore-
stalled him in this by substituting a cloud in the form of Hera
in Ixion's arms. The cloud-born woman, Nephele, eventually bore Centaurus, ancestor of the centaurs, to Ixion but
in the meantime Ixion was punished for his presumption in
daring even to think of embracing Hera. He was fixed to a
fiery wheel and revolves eternally in the deepest reaches of
Tartarus, in the section of Hades reserved for the desperate
men who have sinned against the gods.

Iynx (ī'inks). In Greek mythology, a daughter of Pan and
Echo. According to some accounts, it was she who caused
Zeus to fall in love with Io, by putting a spell on him. She
was transformed by Hera into a wryneck, a kind of woodpecker.

(obscured) errant, ardent, actor; ch, chip; g, go; th, thin; ŦH, then; y, you;
(variable) ḍ as d or j, ṣ as s or sh, ṭ as t or ch, ẓ as z or zh.

J

Jason (jā'sǫn). In Greek legend, a son of Aeson. His mother
is variously named as Perimede, Amphinome, Alcimede,
and Polymede. Pelias, the half-brother of Aeson, seized
Aeson's throne in Iolcus and would have killed Jason but his
mother pretended that he had been born dead and lamented
over him. She then spirited him away to Chiron the centaur
who brought him up on Mount Pelion. When he reached
manhood, Jason returned to Iolcus to claim the throne. On
the way he came to the Anaurus River. It was in flood and
an old hag waiting on the bank asked him to carry her across.
Jason did so, although many others had refused her request.
(The old hag was Hera in disguise, and from then on she
aided and protected Jason.) As he was crossing the river he
lost one of his sandals in the mud. He arrived therefore
before Pelias clad in a leopard skin but wearing only one
sandal. Now Pelias had been warned to beware of a man
wearing one sandal, and when he saw Jason he was frightened. He asked Jason who he was. Jason told him his name
and his errand and the relationship between the two was
revealed. Pelias assured Jason that he would be glad to give
up the throne in his favor, but that he was troubled by the
ghost of Phrixus, which haunted him with the demand that
the Golden Fleece of the ram on which Phrixus had escaped
from Orchomenus, and which now hung in a grove in Colchis, be restored to Hellas. Once the Fleece was brought
back, Pelias assured him, he would be glad to give up the
throne. Jason agreed to go to Colchis to secure the Golden
Fleece. Other accounts say that when Pelias saw Jason shod
with one sandal, he asked him what he would do if he knew
someone threatened his life. Jason replied that he would
send him to Colchis to fetch the Golden Fleece. Hera had
put these words into his mouth, wishing to bring glory to
Jason and to punish Pelias.

However it happened, Jason made ready to go to Colchis.
Many heroes of Greece responded to his call to help him
secure the Fleece, among them Heracles, Iphiclus, Ad

metus, Oileus, Telamon and Peleus, Idmon, Castor and Polydeuces, Mopsus, Augeas, Idas and Lynceus, Meleager, the Boreadae, various sons of Hermes, Poseidon, Apollo, and many others. A ship was built at Pagasae and named the *Argo* after Argus, who built it with Athena's help. Those who sailed in her became known as the Argonauts. Jason was made commander of the expedition. The *Argo* sailed from Pagasae, and after a brief stop on the coast of Magnesia, went to Lemnos. There the Argonauts were beguiled for more than a year by the Lemnian women who, having killed all the males on the island, were delighted to welcome the Argonauts. Jason became the father of two sons, Euneus and Nebrophonus, by Hypsipyle, the Lemnian queen. After more than a year had passed, Heracles, according to some accounts, reminded the Argonauts of their mission and they continued their journey. In the course of the voyage the Argonauts landed among the Doliones, and by a tragic mistake killed their king Cyzicus. In Mysia they lost Heracles, who was separated from his companions while he searched for his squire Hylas. On the island of the Bebryces, Amycus, their king, challenged any member of the crew of the *Argo* to a boxing contest. He was defeated and killed by Polydeuces, and his followers were crushed by the Argonauts. Continuing, the Argonauts landed at Salmydessus in Thrace, where they found Phineus, a son of Agenor or Poseidon. He was living in misery, tormented by Harpies who defiled his food, and blinded by Zeus because of his power to predict the future accurately. The Boreadae banished the Harpies and Phineus gave the Argonauts much valuable advice on how to avoid the pitfalls that lay ahead of them. Leaving Phineus, they passed safely through the Symplegades, the "Clashing Rocks," sailed by the land of the Mariandyni after having been welcomed there by the king, and passed the country of the Amazons and the island of Ares. There they found King Aeëtes' four grandsons who had been shipwrecked, and took them aboard the *Argo* to return them to Colchis.

After many adventures in which Jason was often discouraged, they arrived in Colchis, the kingdom of Aeëtes where hung the Golden Fleece. King Aeëtes was enraged when he learned the errand of the Argonauts, but he planned to avoid giving up the Fleece by making Jason submit to a test which he was sure would destroy him. H agreed to give Jason the Fleece if he could yoke two fire breathing bulls, plow a field, and sow it with the dragon' teeth which Athena had given to Aeëtes. These dragon' teeth had come from Thebes where Cadmus had killed th dragon, sown some of the teeth, and given the rest t Athena. Hera and Athena, anxious for Jason, appealed t Aphrodite to aid him. The goddess of love and beaut bribed her son Eros with a golden ball, and he cause Medea, daughter of Aeëtes, to fall in love with Jason b piercing her with one of his arrows at the instant whe Medea's eyes lighted on Jason. Torn between her filial dut and the great love which had come to her so· suddenly Medea decided to betray her father by telling Jason how h could succeed in the trial of courage which her father ha set for him. She met Jason in a grove at night and offere her help. Jason promised to take her to Iolcus and to marr her in return for her aid. She gave him the Charm of Prome theus which made invulnerable for one day the person an weapons of whoever was anointed with it. This protecte him from the fire-breathing bulls. She told him that when h sowed the dragon's teeth, armed men would spring up. H must cast a stone among them, whereupon they would figh each other to the death. Jason followed her instructions an successfully carried out the test that Aeëtes had set for him

Aeëtes, however, was enraged. He knew that Jason ha succeeded only with the help of Medea, and plotted to seiz and kill him. Medea warned Jason of her father's intentions She lulled the never-sleeping dragon and allowed Jason t steal the Golden Fleece; then they fled to the ship and saile from Colchis, pursued by Aeëtes. Some say Apsyrtus brother of Medea, went with them, and that Medea cut him to pieces and flung the parts of his body into the sea. This delayed Aeëtes in his pursuit, because he stopped to gathe the pieces of his son's body for burial. Others say Apsyrtus pursued Jason with a large fleet, that he was lured into meeting Medea alone, and that Jason sprang out on him from ambush and killed him. The Argonauts then continued their flight. But they were harassed by many ills. At last the sacred oak of Dodona, which had been placed in the hull of the *Argo* by Athena, spoke to Jason and informed him his woes would not cease until he had been purified for the

fat, fāte, fär, fȧll, ȧsk, fāre; net, mē, hėr; pin, pīne; not, nōte, möve, nôr; up, lūte, pull; oi, oil; ou out; (lightened) ĕlect, agǫny, ūnite;

murder of Apsyrtus. He was to go to the island of Circe where the enchantress would sprinkle the blood of a pig on his hands and purify him.

After being purified, Jason and the Argonauts continued their journey. They passed the Sirens successfully, and with the help of Thetis navigated safely by the Wandering Rocks and Scylla and Charybdis. They landed at length on Drepana (also known as Corcyra) and were received by Alcinous, king of the Phaeacians. Here the Colchians caught up with them and would have taken Medea, but Arete, wife of Alcinous, persuaded her husband not to give up Medea if she were already married to Jason. But if they were not married he would hand Medea over to the Colchians. Arete immediately arranged a wedding. When the Argonauts at last returned to Iolcus, Jason learned that his father and mother were dead and that the king Pelias, having heard a false rumor that the Argonauts had all perished, had slain his young brother, Promachus. Jason planned to attack Pelias and seize the throne. However, Medea disposed of Pelias single-handed by means of her magic arts. Jason arranged good marriages for the three daughters of Pelias and out of fear of vengeance resigned the throne of Iolcus to Acastus, the son of Pelias. He then took the Golden Fleece to Orchomenus and hung it in the temple of Zeus. Next he dedicated the *Argo* to Poseidon on the Isthmus of Corinth. Then he and Medea went to Corinth where they lived happily together for ten years and became the parents of several children, some say seven boys and seven girls.

At the end of this time Jason proposed to leave Medea and to marry Glauce (or Creusa), daughter of Creon, the king of Corinth. Medea reminded him of all he owed to her. But Jason persisted in his plan to abandon Medea, although he offered to make suitable provision for her and her children. Medea, inflamed by his ingratitude, sent a robe to Glauce as a wedding gift. It was impregnated with magic and the instant Glauce put it on, it burned her to ashes. Her father also was consumed by the flames which sprang from it. Medea fled in a winged chariot drawn by dragons, after killing some of her children, and Jason too was forced into exile for being false to his oath to Medea. He wandered friendless about Greece and at last came to the Isthmus of Corinth where he had beached the *Argo*. As he sat in the shadow of its hull, remembering his past glorious exploits, the prow of the old ship broke off and fell on him, killing him instantly. To show that the *Argo* was innocent of his death, its image was set among the stars. The legend of Medea's betrayal and revenge spawned many variants. In Euripides' tragedy, for instance, Jason and Medea, with two sons, are living in exile at Corinth when the king offers Jason his daughter's hand in marriage, and with it the right of succession. It is Jason's eagerness to embrace this opportunity to repair his fortune which triggers Medea's insane response.

Jocasta (jō-kas′ta̧) or **Jocaste** (-tē).[CalledinHomer: *Epicaste*] In Greek legend, a daughter of Menoeceus of Thebes and the sister of Creon. She was married to Laius, king of Thebes. When her son was born, Laius had his feet pierced and bound and ordered him exposed on Mount Cithaeron because an oracle had foretold that his son would slay him and marry his mother. But his orders were not carried out. Oedipus, his infant son, fell into the hands of Polybus of Corinth and was brought up by him and his wife Merope as their own son. On reaching manhood, Oedipus fled from Corinth, because he regarded Polybus and Merope as his parents and he had been made aware of the oracle by visiting Delphi. On the road he met Laius and, unaware of his true identity, killed him. He then solved the riddle of the Theban Sphinx, thus causing her death, and went to Thebes where he was made king and given the newly widowed Jocasta for a wife. Jocasta bore him two sons, Eteocles and Polynices, and two daughters, Antigone and Ismene. When dark hints began to gather that Oedipus himself might be the murderer of Laius, for whom all Thebes—led by Oedipus—was seeking in order to lift a plague, Jocasta tried to persuade him to give up his investigations. She also pleaded with him to cease his inquiries into his origin. To his talk of oracles she cited many which, as she thought, had not come true. She said an oracle had told Laius that he would be slain by his son, but that his son had been exposed, and Laius was killed by robbers. But all the reassuring things she told him became hollow as the pieces of Oedipus' story fell into place. When Jocasta learned the horrifying truth that he was actually her son, his father's murderer, and the father of her children, she hanged herself.

Juno (jö′nō). In Roman mythology, the queen of heaven, the highest deity in the Roman pantheon next to Jupiter, of

---

fat, fāte, fär, fâll, ȧsk, fãre; net, mē, hėr; pin, pīne; not, nōte, möve, nôr; up, lūte, pùll; oi, oil; ou out; (lightened) ḝlect, agǫny, ūnit

whom she was both the sister and the wife. As a daughter of Saturn she was identified with the Greek Hera.

Jupiter   (jö'pi-tėr). [Also: **Jove.**] In Roman mythology the supreme deity, predominantly a sky-god. The name *Jupiter* (*Iuppiter*), also found in Latin as *Diespiter*, reveals its original conception as a sky-god by its linguistic connection with *diēs* (Latin: "day"), and *deus* (Latin: "god"). The second element of the name represents the Latin word for "father." It is related to Greek *Zeus.*

Juventas   (jö-ven'tạs). In Roman mythology, the goddess who protected the *iuvenes,* men of military age. She had a shrine in the cella of Minerva in the great temple on the Capitoline, and a temple close to the Circus Maximus. Juventas has been erroneously identified as the Roman counterpart of Hebe (q.v.) and as a goddess of youth.

—K—

Keres   (kē'rēz). In Greek mythology, malign or evil spirits associated with death, sometimes regarded as souls of the dead, or as goddesses dealing death through the medium of disease. In late mythology, they became identified with the Furies.

Kithairon   (kē-the-rôn'). See *Cithaeron.*

Kore   (kō'rẹ). [Also: **Cora.**] In Greek mythology, one of the names of Persephone, daughter of Zeus and Demeter. She was called Kore or Cora especially in her fertility-cult aspects. The meaning of the name is "Maiden."

L

Labors of Heracles   or **Hercules**. See **Heracles, Labors of.**

Labyrinth (lab'i-rinth). "Place of the double ax," from *labry* "double-bladed ax." In Greek legend, a vast maze built a Cnossus by the Athenian artificer Daedalus at the comman of Minos, ruler of Crete. It was built as a place in which t confine the Minotaur, the child with a bull's head and huma body born of the union of Queen Pasiphaë with a handsom bull in the royal stables. On the walls and furnishings o Minos' great palace at Cnossus the double ax appears re peatedly, suggesting that it was a symbol of Minos' rega authority, so that "Hall of the Double Axes" would be a appropriate epithet for this extensive structure. The con cept of a labyrinth as a maze would thus have arisen late in consideration of the Labyrinth's hundreds of rooms an endless corridors, and the difficulty of a stranger in findin his way about it. (JJ)

Lacedaemon (las-ẹ-dē'mọn). In Greek mythology, a son o Zeus and the Pleiad Taÿgete. Some say he married the niec of Taÿgete, also named Taÿgete, who bore him a son, Him erus, and a daughter, Cleodice. But others say he marrie Sparta, the daughter of Eurotas, and inherited her father' kingdom. He named the people of his kingdom (formerl called Leleges) Lacedaemonians after himself, and name the Mountain Taÿgetus after his mother. He founded a cit in Laconia, and named it Sparta after his wife, from whicl the name finally was applied to the entire kingdom. Ther was a hero-shrine of Lacedaemon at Alesiae in Laconia, an the Spartans claimed that it was he who instituted the wor ship of the Graces, of whom there were only two, accordin to the Spartans, named Cleta and Phaenna.

Lachesis (lak'ẹ-sis). In Greek mythology, one of the thre Moerae or Fates. As first explained by Hesiod, Lachesi assigns the lot of life to each person, Clotho spins the threa of it, and their sister Atropos cuts it. (JJ)

adon (lā′dǫn). In Greek mythology, a many-headed dragon or serpent that had the power of human speech and never slept. According to some accounts he was the son of Ceto and Phorcys. Others say he was the son of Typhon and Echidna, or that he was earth-born. He was set to guard the Apples of the Hesperides, either by Hera or by Atlas, and was slain by Heracles when he came to steal the apples. He was then translated to the heavens as the constellation Serpentarius.

aelaps (lē′laps). According to legend, a marvelous hound that was given to Procris, wife of Cephalus, by Artemis. The hound had the power of always catching whatever it pursued. Amphitryon borrowed the hound to catch a vixen that had been sent to plague Thebes. The vixen had the gift of always out-running its pursuers. As Laelaps, the dog that always caught its quarry, chased the vixen that could never be caught, Zeus settled the matter by turning them both into stone. According to some accounts it was Minos who had received Laelaps from Artemis, and gave him to Procris in return for her favors.

aertes (lā-ėr′tēz). In Greek legend, a son of Acrisius the Argive. He was married to Anticlea, daughter of Autolycus. Some say he was one of the Argonauts who went on the expedition to secure the Golden Fleece. In Homer Laertes is represented as the father of Odysseus. Later writers said that Odysseus was the son of Sisyphus, but he passed as the son of Laertes. During the long absence of Odysseus at the Trojan War and after it, Laertes retired to his farm in the country and grieved for his son. He was still living when Odysseus returned, was joyously reunited with him, and helped him confront the fathers of the suitors of Penelope, suitors whom Odysseus had slain on his return.

aestrygones (les-trig′ǫ-nēz). [Also: *Laestrygonians*.] In the *Odyssey*, a race of cannibal giants visited by Odysseus in a remote country, where "the nights are so short that the shepherd driving his flock out meets the shepherd who is driving his flock in," clearly an echo of some traveler's tale of northern latitudes. Eleven of Odysseus' 12 ships moored in their nearly landlocked harbor and went to scout the countryside, while only Odysseus anchored outside. The ships in the harbor were attacked and destroyed by the man-eating Laestrygones, who devoured their crews, only Odys-

seus' ship escaping. Later writers placed the Laestrygones i
Sicily, S of Mount Aetna, and Roman authors blandly trans
ferred them to Formiae (Formia) in Latium. (JJ)

Laius (lā'us, lā'yus). In Greek legend, a son of Labdacus, kin
of Thebes. He succeeded to the throne of Thebes but wa
expelled by Amphion and Zethus. He went to the court o
Pelops at Pisa and was hospitably received. There he fell i
love with Chrysippus, the bastard son of Pelops, and carrie
him off to Thebes. Pelops pursued him to Thebes but whe
he arrived Chrysippus was dead, some say by his own han
and some say his death was engineered by Hippodamia, wif
of Pelops. Pelops forgave Laius and he was restored to th
throne. He married Jocasta, daughter of Menoeceus, bu
time passed and she bore him no children. Laius consulte
the oracle and was told he should not mourn his childless
ness, for the child Jocasta bore him would kill him. Even so
Jocasta did ultimately produce a son to Laius but he, remem
bering the oracle, had the infant's feet pierced and boun
and ordered him exposed on Mount Cithaeron. His order
unknown to him, was not carried out and the child, who wa
named Oedipus, "Swollen-footed," was reared by Polybu
of Corinth as his own child. Hera sent a monster to punis
Thebes because Laius had abducted Chrysippus. This mon
ster, a Sphinx, ravaged Thebes by killing all who could no
answer a riddle she propounded. Laius set out for Delphi t
ask the oracle how he could free Thebes of the Sphinx. O
the way he met Oedipus, neither knowing who the othe
was, and ordered him out of the road. Oedipus refused t
move and angrily struck Laius' charioteer when the latte
treated him violently. When he saw a chance, Laius strucl
the young stranger full on the head with his goad. Oedipus
enraged, set upon him, and killed him and all his compan
ions save one, who escaped. Thus the oracle was fulfilled

Lamia (lā'mi-ạ). In Greek mythology, a daughter of Belus
She was a beautiful Libyan queen who was loved by Zeus
Zeus gave her the power to take out and replace her eyes a
will. Hera, out of jealousy, killed all Lamia's children excep
Scylla; thereafter, because she could not revenge herself or
Hera, Lamia sought to destroy the children of men. She i
usually depicted with a serpent's body and beautifu
woman's head. In later belief she was regarded as a seduce
of young men. Keat's poem *Lamia* treats of this story.

aocoön (lā-ok'ọ̄-on). In Greek legend, a priest of Apollo at Troy who had offended the god by marrying and becoming the father of children, and who had profaned the image of the god. He was chosen by the Trojans to propitiate Poseidon in the last year of the Trojan War, because the Trojans had slain their former priest of Poseidon. When the Wooden Horse was seen on the beach before Troy, Laocoön hurled his spear into its side and urged the Trojans not to take it inside the walls. It was a trap, he declared, as he uttered the words, "I fear the Greeks, especially when they bring gifts." While the Trojans hesitated, a great serpent sent by Apollo to punish Laocoön for his earlier offenses came slithering out of the sea, and grasped Laocoön and his two sons, Antiphas and Thymbraeus, in its coils. The serpent crushed them to death and carried them off to the shrine of Athena. The Trojans erroneously concluded that Laocoön had been punished for doubting the holiness of Athena's gift—as they thought of the Wooden Horse—and for dishonoring it by thrusting his spear into its side. They thereupon resolved to take the Wooden Horse inside the walls to Athena's shrine, with disastrous results.

aodamia (lā-od-ạ-mī'ạ). In classical legend, a daughter of Acastus. She was the wife of Protesilaus, and missed him so when he went to Troy that she made a wax image of him to keep her company. When she learned that he had been slain at Troy by Hector she prayed to the gods to let him revisit her from Hades, if only for three hours. Zeus permitted Hermes to bring the shade of Protesilaus from the Underworld for three hours. While with his wife, Protesilaus exhorted her to follow him when it was time for him to return to the Underworld. At the end of the three hours Laodamia stabbed herself so that she could go with him.

aodice (lā-od'i-sē). In the *Iliad*, a daughter of Priam and Hecuba. According to Homer, she was the fairest of Priam's daughters. She was the wife of Helicaon, son of Antenor. When Acamas journeyed to Troy with Diomedes to demand the return of Helen, Laodice fell in love with him and bore him a son, Munitus. When Troy fell, she prayed that she might be swallowed up by the earth rather than live a life of dishonor as a slave and concubine of the Greeks. The earth parted and she was swallowed up as she had prayed.

Laodice. The name Homer gives to Electra, daughter of Aga memnon and Clytemnestra.

Laomedon (lā-om'ẹ-don). In Greek legend, a son of Ilus an Eurydice, and a descendant of Dardanus. He was a king Troy. To punish Apollo and Poseidon, Zeus sent them work for Laomedon and they built the walls of Troy. B when their year of service was up, he refused to pay then Instead, he threatened to cut off their ears, bind them, an ship them abroad to be sold as slaves. In revenge, Poseido sent a sea-monster to ravage Troy. Heracles rescued Hes one, Laomedon's daughter, who had been chained to a roc to appease the monster, and offered to slay the beast i return for the famous horses of Tros, immortal horses whic had been given to Tros by Zeus to atone for the loss c Ganymede, and which had been handed on to Laomedor Laomedon agreed, but once again refused to honor hi agreement. In a fury, Heracles attacked Troy and kille Laomedon and all his sons except Podarces (Priam).

Lapithae (lap'i-thē) or **Lapiths** (lap'iths). A Thessalian peo ple descended, according to some accounts, from Lapithe a son of Apollo and Stilbe. Others say the Lapithae wer descendants of Ixion. One of their kings was Pirithous. O the occasion of his marriage to Hippodamia the centaurs who as cousins of Pirithous had been invited to the wedding got drunk from drinking wine unmixed with water and at tacked the bride. A fierce struggle broke out between th Lapithae and the centaurs when the Lapithae resisted th attacks of the centaurs on their women. This episode resul ted in the expulsion of the centaurs from Mount Pelion Later the centaurs invaded the territory of the Lapithae and overwhelmed them. Those Lapithae who escaped fled t Mount Pholoe in Elis from which they were also subse quently driven by the centaurs. The remnants of the Lapi thae finally settled in Malea.

Lapithes (lap'i-thēz). According to some accounts, a son o Apollo, and a descendant of Oceanus and Tethys. He rule the region about the Peneus River, the land of his grandfa ther, the river-god Peneus. His sons, Phorbas and Periphas became kings after him and named their subjects Lapiths, o Lapithae, after their father.

Latona (lạ-tō'nạ). In mythology, the mother of Apollo an Diana. A Latin name of Leto.

Leander (lē-an′dèr). In Greek legend, a youth of Abydos, the lover of Hero. Each night he swam the Hellespont to visit her secretly. Marriage was forbidden them because Hero was a priestess of Aphrodite at Sestos. One stormy night the light in the tower, by which his course was guided, was extinguished, and he perished. His body was washed ashore, and on discovering it Hero threw herself into the sea and was drowned.

Leda (lē′da̧). In Greek mythology, a daughter of Thestius, king in Aetolia. Her father gave her in marriage to Tyndareus of Sparta. Some say she found a blue and silver egg, dropped by Nemesis, lying in a marsh. She took it home and hid it. From it Helen was born, the daughter of Zeus. Others say that Hermes threw the egg between Leda's knees and that from this she bore Helen. But the most common account is that Zeus fell in love with Leda, transformed himself into a swan, and in this form embraced her. She subsequently bore an egg from which Helen and Polydeuces, her children by Zeus, were born. By her husband she was the mother of Castor, twin-born with Polydeuces, and Clytemnestra. But the paternity of her twins, Castor and Polydeuces, is disputed. Clytemnestra was the daughter of Leda and Tyndareus, Helen of Leda and Zeus. Homer says that Tyndareus fathered Castor and Polydeuces also, but others make one or both the sons of Zeus. According to some accounts, Leda hanged herself because of her shame over the notorious elopement of Helen with Paris. Odysseus saw her shade when he visited the Underworld on his way home after the Trojan War. Pausanias, traveling in Greece in the 2nd century A.D. says that in the sanctuary of the Leucippides in Sparta there was an egg suspended by a ribbon from the roof-tree, and that this was supposed to be the egg that Leda had brought forth.

Leïtus (lē′i-tus). In Homeric legend (*Iliad*), a captain of Boeotians at the siege of Troy. He was wounded by Hector in the struggle for possession of the body of Patroclus. However, he recovered, and was the only one of the Boeotian chiefs to return home safe from Troy. He brought back with him the bones of Arcesilaus and buried them near the oracle of Trophonius at Lebadia. The tomb of Leïtus was at Plataea.

Lelex (lel′eks). According to Lacedaemonian tradition, he was the first king of the Lacedaemonians, and called his people Leleges after himself. Some say he was a son of Poseidon and Libya, the daughter of Epaphus, and that he came to Megara from Egypt and became king of Megara. This was a Megarian tradition. The son of Lelex was Myles, who succeeded him as king.

Leos (lē′os). According to legend, a herald, who informed Theseus that the sons of Pallas had divided their forces to attack Athens. One of these forces was hidden in ambush. Because of the information Leos gave him Theseus surprised and killed them. Because he had informed on the sons of Pallas, their descendants in Pallene never intermarried with the people of Agnus from which Leos came. They would not permit their heralds to make the customary introduction to their proclamations, *"Akouete leoi!"* (Hearken, ye people!) because the word *leoi* reminded them of the treachery of Leos.

Leos. According to some accounts, a son of Orpheus. During his time Attica was afflicted by a crippling famine. The oracle of Delphi said the famine would be ended if there were a human sacrifice. Leos offered his three daughters—Praxithea, Theope, and Eubule—for the good of the state, and the famine was ended. Some say the three girls gave their lives of their own accord for the public good. In any event, the famine was over, and ever after the three maidens were worshiped at a shrine called the Leocorium in the district of the Ceramicus at Athens. It was beside this shrine that Hipparchus was slain by Harmodius and Aristogiton.

Lepreus (lep′rē-us). According to tradition, a son of Caucon. He founded the city of Lepreum near the Messenian border of Elis. This city, named after him, or as some say because of the leprosy that attacked the earliest settlers of the district, became the chief seat of his father's worship. Lepreus incurred the enmity of Heracles because he advised Augeas to bind Heracles when the latter asked to be paid for cleaning the Augean stables. Later, on learning that Heracles was on his way to the city, Lepreus, at his mother's urging, agreed to receive Heracles and ask his forgiveness. Heracles agreed to do so, but challenged him to three contests: throwing the discus, drinking the greatest quantity of water, and eating an ox. Heracles won the first two, but Lepreus ate his ox the faster. Immediately he challenged Heracles to a duel, in which Lepreus was clubbed to death.

Lethe   (lē′thē). In Greek mythology: 1) The personification of oblivion; a daughter of Eris. 2) The river of oblivion, one of the streams of Hades, the waters of which possessed the property of causing those who drank of them to forget their former existence. The dead drank upon their arrival in Hades; and souls destined for reincarnation had to drink of it to forget everything they had seen before returning to earth. Ariosto places Lethe in the moon; Dante places it in purgatory.

Leto   (lē′tō). [Latin, **Latona**.] In Greek mythology, a daughter of the Titans Coeus and Phoebe. Some say she was the gentle wife of Zeus, before he married Hera, and bore him the twins Apollo and Artemis. But others say Zeus pursued her after he was married to Hera, and that he transformed himself and Leto into quails before he ravished her. Hera was wild with jealousy when she learned Leto was to bear the children of Zeus. She sent the serpent Python to pursue her. She ordered that no place on earth where the sun shone should receive Leto. As the time for the birth of her children approached, Leto was rejected by heaven, earth, and sea; she fled before Python hopelessly. Some say the South Wind bore her to Ortygia, a tiny island near Delos, and that there she bore Artemis without pain; but others say Poseidon sent a dolphin that carried her over the sea on its back. As soon as Artemis was born she helped her mother across the sea to Delos, another tiny island, which was the only spot on earth to offer her hospitality. There, leaning against a palm tree on the side of a mountain and shaded from the sun, or as some say, in a cave, Leto bore Apollo after nine days of labor. Up to this time Delos had been a floating island; it now became anchored or, as some say, four pillars sprang up from the bottom of the sea to hold it in place because of the kindness to Leto. As the birthplace of Apollo it became one of his favorite and most sacred shrines. In a later time no one was permitted to be born there: women near the time of their confinement were removed to a nearby island. And no one was permitted to die there: the very ill were also carried to a nearby island so that they might not pollute the sacred place. Some say both Artemis and Apollo were born on Delos. According to some accounts, Hera continued to harass Leto, and compelled her to flee from Delos shortly after her children were born. She arrived at last in Lycia.

(obscured) errạnt, ardẹnt, actọr; ch, chip; g, go; th, thin; ᴛʜ, then; y, you;
(variable) ḍ as d or j, ṣ as s or sh, ṭ as t or ch, ẓ as z or zh.

Exhausted, she came to a lake in a valley. She knelt to drink of its waters for she was faint from hunger and thirst. Peasants gathering rushes on the brim of the lake tried to prevent her from drinking, and ended by muddying the waters so that she could not drink. To punish them, Leto said they should live forever in this lake of theirs that was so precious to them: she transformed them into frogs. An altar was raised to Leto on that spot. Apollo at length killed the Python and Leto went to Delphi. On her way she stepped into a sacred grove to perform some rites. Tityus, the giant son of Elara and Zeus, attacked her and attempted to violate her. Apollo, hearing her cries, rushed to her defense and with his arrows slew Tityus. Apollo and Artemis were ever devoted protectors of their mother's honor. When Niobe boasted of her lineage, her beauty, her riches—and above all—of her children, and called on the people of Thebes to worship her instead of Leto who had only two children, Leto called on Apollo and Artemis to avenge the insult and the insolence of Niobe. Apollo and Artemis swept down and killed all the seven sons and seven daughters of Niobe. As the mother of the Olympians Apollo and Artemis, Leto went to dwell in Olympus and was worshiped in connection with her children.

Leuce (lö'sē). In Greek mythology, a nymph who was pursued by Hades. To prevent him from violating her, she was transformed into a white poplar tree and stands beside the Pool of Memory in the Underworld.

Leucippe (lö-sip'ē). According to legend, the mother of Teuthras, king in Mysia. When her son was smitten with madness and a violent skin disease for killing a boar that had fled to the temple of Artemis, Leucippe, taking the seer Polyidus with her, appeased the goddess with rich sacrifices. When Teuthras was restored to sanity and his skin disorder was cured, Leucippe built an altar to Artemis. She caused a boar, with the head of a man, to be made of gold. This image, when threatened, sought refuge in the temple of Artemis and cried, "Spare me!", even as did the real boar which Teuthras had impiously slain.

Leucippus (lö-sip'us). In Greek mythology, a son of Oenomaus. He loved the nymph Daphne, but she was a follower of Artemis and scorned men. Leucippus disguised himself as a maiden and was accepted as a companion of

Daphne and her friends in their hunting expeditions. Apollo also loved Daphne, and he advised the maidens to bathe naked to be sure that all were maidens. When the disguise of Leucippus was thus revealed, Daphne and her companions set upon him and tore him to pieces.

Leucothea (lö-koth′ē-ạ). A sea-goddess, formerly the mortal Ino who had been metamorphosed into a goddess when she leaped into the sea to escape from her husband Athamas whom Hera had driven mad. She gave Odysseus a veil to buoy him up when Poseidon in a great storm destroyed the raft on which he had left the island of Calypso. Leucothea advised Odysseus to abandon the fragments of the raft and with the help of the veil to swim to Phaeacia, after which his troubles would be over. See also, *Ino.*

Leukothea (lö-kō-thē′ạ). See *Leucothea.*

Lichas (lī′kạs). In Greek legend, a herald of Heracles. He escorted the captive Iole to Deianira, and tried to protect Deianira from the knowledge that Heracles had transferred his affections to Iole and intended his wife to share her house with his captive. Deianira gave the ceremonial robe which she had anointed with what she thought was a love charm to Lichas to take to Heracles. When Heracles put it on he was soon consumed as by a fire, for the love charm turned out to be a poison. Lichas, although he was innocent of any evil intent—as indeed, was Deianira—hid from his master's fury, but Heracles found him and, condemning him for being the bearer of the fatal robe, flung him into the Euboean Sea. Lichas turned to stone as he whistled through the air, and his stone body formed a small reef onto which sailors feared to step because they did not want to hurt Lichas.

Lichas. According to Greek tradition, a Spartan who was sent to the oracle at Delphi to learn how he could find the bones of Orestes, after the Spartans had learned from the oracle that they would not be victorious in their wars against the Tegeans until they secured the bones of Orestes from Tegea. The priestess told Lichas to go where two winds meet, where stroke meets stroke, and where evil rings upon evil. There he would find the bones he sought buried in the earth. The oracle instructed him to bring them to Sparta and make Sparta the master of Tegea. Lichas went to Tegea and came to a smithy. The smith was forging a sword of iron, instead of the usual bronze. When Lichas commented on this unusual sight, the smith told him stranger things had happened than the forging of an iron sword. He volunteered that he had found an enormous coffin containing an equally enormous skeleton when he was digging a well beneath the smithy floor. Lichas remembered the oracle and deduced that the winds referred to were those that came from the smith's bellows, the strokes were those of the hammer, and the evil upon evil was the iron sword beaten by the iron hammer, as iron was the symbol of the cruel days of the Iron Age. He returned to Sparta with the information he had gathered. The Spartans sent him back to Tegea, disguised as a fleeing slave, and he sought refuge with the smith. During the night he stole the bones from the coffin and escaped with them to Sparta. In this way the Spartans secured the bones of Orestes, and under their protection secured ascendancy over the Tegeans.

Limon (lī'mọn). In Greek legend, a son of Tegeates of Tegea and Maera, and the brother of Scephrus. When Apollo was investigating the rulers who had refused to receive Leto before her children were born, he came to Tegea with his sister Artemis. Scephrus took him aside and talked privately with him. Limon thought Scephrus was accusing him to Apollo, rushed forth and murdered his brother. Artemis pursued Limon and shot him with her arrows. Afterward, at the festival of Apollo Agyieus *(God of the Streets)* the pursuit of Limon by Artemis was commemorated by having the priestess of Artemis pursue a man.

Linus (lī'nus). In Greek mythology, a son of Apollo and Psamathe, daughter of Crotopus of Argos. Psamathe feared the wrath of her father and left her child on a mountain to die, but he was found and brought up by shepherds. Psamathe, learning of this, was relieved to know her son lived, but when he was a youth, he was torn to pieces by dogs that belonged to her father, and Psamathe was unable to disguise her grief. Crotopus realized that the slain youth was his daughter's son and condemned her to death. In grief and anger over the double loss, Apollo sent a monster, Poena, who stole young children from their mothers. This monster brought great sorrow to the land, and at last Coroebus slew it. Argos was then afflicted by a plague. The Argives sent to the oracle at Delphi to learn how they could free themselves from the plague, and were told they must sacrifice to Psamathe and Linus. They did this but the plague continued. At last Coroebus confessed that he had slain Poena. He was commanded by the priestess at Delphi to take a tripod and set forth from Delphi; where the tripod should fall to the ground, he was to raise a temple. Coroebus followed her instructions. The tripod fell to the ground on Mount Gerania; there he raised a temple of Apollo and founded the city of Tripodisci, named for the tripod. The plague now ceased, and thenceforth Linus was honored by a festival, called Arneis *(Feast of Lambs)* because he had been reared by shepherds among lambs, and by the singing of songs of lamentation called "Lini" in his memory.

Linus. According to some accounts, the son of the muse Calliope and Oeagrus, and thus a brother of Orpheus. Others give him different fathers, including Apollo, Hermes, and Amphimarus, a son of Poseidon, and different mothers, including the muses Urania and Clio. In any event, he was regarded as a great poet and as the musician who invented melody and rhythm; and it is said he was slain because of Apollo's jealousy of his talents. This Linus was the teacher of Thamyris and Orpheus. His portrait adorned the walls of a cave on Mount Helicon, and to it sacrifices were offered just before the annual sacrifices to the Muses. The body of Linus is supposed to have been buried at Thebes.

Litae (lī'tē). The daughters of Zeus, personifications of Prayer, especially prayers of repentance. In the *Iliad* they are described as halting of foot and with downcast eyes. They are appointed to follow in the footsteps of Sin, but Sin, being swift of foot, outruns them and causes many to falter and fall. The Litae come to heal the fallen, and if they are welcomed by the sinner, Zeus listens when the Litae intercede; but if they are repelled, they request that Zeus punish the offender.

Lityerses (lit-i-ėr'sēz). In Greek legend, a Phrygian farmer, bastard son of King Midas. He compelled his guests to engage in reaping contests with him in his fields. Whoever reaped less than he did had his head cut off and wrapped in a sheaf. Daphnis, who had come to Lityerses' home in search of Pimplea, was compelled to enter a reaping contest with him, but Heracles took his place, killed Lityerses and hurled his body into the Maeander River.

Lotis (lō′tis). In Greek mythology, a nymph who fled from
pursuer and was turned into a lotus tree. There are sever;
variations on this story, in one of which it was a naiad wh·
fled and was turned into a water lily.

Lotophagi (lō-tof′ạ-jī). "Lotus-Eaters"; in the *Odyssey*, th·
name of a people in whose country storm-driven Odysseu·
lands with his crews. There they are offered a plant calle·
Lotus. Some of Odysseus' men eat of this and lose all desir·
to return to their friends and native land, so that Odysseu·
has to have them brought back by force and shackled to thei·
rowing-benches. The Greeks applied the name *lotus* to ·
number of different plants, none reported to have narcoti·
effect; the ripe seed pod of the opium poppy, however·
somewhat resembles the seed pod of the true lotus, suggest·
ing that possibly back of Homer's allusion lay some travel·
er's encounter with opium. One reading the *Odyssey* passag·
uncritically would conclude that the land of the Lotus-Eater·
was along the North African coast, Cyrenaica or Tripoli·
tania; the geography of Odysseus' adventures defies system·
atic analysis, but later geographers agreed in locating th·
Lotophagi in Cyrenaica. (JJ)

Lyaeus (lī-ē′us). In Greek mythology, the "Loosener," th·
god of wine and song who loosens care; an epithet or sur·
name of Dionysus.

Lycaon (lī-kā′ọn). According to Greek tradition, a son o·
Pelasgus, the first king of Arcadia, who succeeded his fathe·
as king. Some say he founded the city of Lycosura on Moun·
Lycaeus, and that it was he who gave Zeus the name Lycaeus·
and established the Lycaean Games in his honor. The Lycaean Games were older than the Panathenaea but not so old·
as the Olympic Games. Lycaon had 50 sons who became the·
founders of many of the cities of Arcadia. The youngest of·
them, Oenotrus, was said to have sailed to Italy and to have·
colonized Oenotria, of which he became king. This, according to some accounts, was the first expedition from Greece·
to found a colony. Besides his 50 sons, Lycaon was the father·
of one daughter, Callisto, beloved of Zeus. Some say it was·
a deed of Lycaon, typical of the general wickedness of mankind, that caused Zeus to send a flood to punish the race of·
men. Zeus, visiting the world in the guise of a mortal, came·
to the house of Lycaon. He informed Lycaon of his divinity,·
but Lycaon doubted that he was really a god, and decided·

to test him. He cut up and cooked a child (his own son Nyctimus, according to some accounts) and served the flesh to Zeus. For this impiety Zeus destroyed his house and transformed Lycaon into a savage wolf. Some say he also struck all the sons of Lycaon, except Nyctimus whom he restored, with his thunderbolt. But others say the sons of Lycaon were also turned into wolves. And some say, that at the sacrifice to Lycaean Zeus a man was transformed into a wolf. If, after nine years, he had not tasted human flesh, he became a man again. But if he had eaten human flesh, he remained a beast.

Lycaon. In Homeric legend, a son of Priam and Laothoë, and half-brother of Hector and Paris. While cutting shoots from a fig tree in his father's orchard, he was captured by Achilles. Achilles sold him to King Euneus of Lemnos for a mixing bowl. Next he was ransomed by Eëtion of Imbrus and sent to Arisbe, from which he escaped. He returned to Troy but 11 days later he was again captured by Achilles, who this time, in spite of Lycaon's pleas, slew him and hurled his body into the Scamander river. Apollo assumed the form of Lycaon to rally Aeneas against Achilles when the Trojans fled before the latter after the death of Patroclus.

Lycomedes (lī-kọ̄-mē′dēz). In Greek legend, a king of Scyrus. He welcomed Theseus when that hero was blown to his shores by a storm but when Theseus decided to stay in Scyrus, on land that belonged to him, Lycomedes, under the pretext of showing him the land, treacherously led Theseus to a cliff and pushed him over. Afterwards Lycomedes announced that Theseus had fallen off the cliff while under the influence of wine. In another legend, Thetis, who knew that if her son Achilles went to Troy he would never return, tried to prevent Achilles from going to fight against the Trojans by sending him to the court of Lycomedes disguised as a girl. Lycomedes sheltered him but was unable to prevent Odysseus from finding him and carrying him off to Troy. Achilles left behind a son, Neoptolemus, by Lycomedes' daughter, Deidamia, whom Lycomedes brought up. When the oracles declared that Troy could not be taken without the aid of Achilles' son, Lycomedes allowed Neoptolemus to depart for Troy.

Lycurgus (lī-kėr′gus). In Greek mythology, a son of Dryas. He was king of the Edonians in Thrace, and an opponent of the worship of Dionysus. When Dionysus and his attendants landed in his kingdom on their return from Asia, Lycurgus attacked them with an ox goad and scattered the god's followers. Dionysus himself escaped by fleeing under the sea to Thetis for protection. Lycurgus' arrogance in attacking a god aroused the wrath of Zeus who, according to some accounts, struck him blind. According to other accounts, he was driven mad by the gods and killed his own son with an ax under the mistaken impression that he was cutting down a vine. Thrace became barren after this horrible crime and the Thracians learned that their land would become productive again only when Lycurgus was punished. His people then seized and bound him and left him on Mount Pangaeus where he was torn to pieces by wild horses.

Lycus (lī'kus). In Greek legend, a son of Pandion the Younger and Pylia. He was the brother of Aegeus, Pallas, and Nisus. Pandion, king of Athens, was expelled from his kingdom. After his death his four sons marched against Attica and defeated their enemies. They then divided Attica among them. Aegeus, being the eldest, became king of Athens. Lycus became ruler of Euboea. But the brothers were not satisfied. They claimed Aegeus was an adopted son of Pandion and therefore not a true descendant of Erechtheus, with no claim to the throne. Lycus intrigued against Aegeus, and at length became so threatening that Aegeus banished him. He went to Cilicia in Asia Minor where Sarpedon, brother of Minos of Crete, had made himself king. Lycus succeeded Sarpedon on the throne and the country was renamed Lycia after him.

Lycus. According to legend, a king of the Mariandyni in Mysia. He entertained Heracles and won his support in a war against the Bebryces, in which the Bebrycian king Mygdon was slain. He named Heraclea, land in Paphlagonia which was regained in this war, in honor of Heracles. When Heracles left, the Bebryces under the new king, Amycus, attacked again and retook the land. Later, Lycus welcomed the Argonauts when they visited his kingdom on their way to Colchis. He built a shrine to Polydeuces, one of their number because he had killed Amycus in a boxing contest, and sent his son Dascylus to join the Argonauts in gratitude to them for having defeated his ancient enemies, the Bebryces, in war.

Lycus. A legendary ruler of Thebes. He was the husband of Dirce and uncle of Antiope. To carry out his promise to Antiope's father, he attacked Sicyon, whither Antiope had fled, killed the king and took Antiope captive. Much later, he was slain by Antiope's sons, Amphion and Zethus, because of his cruel treatment of their mother. See **Antiope.**

Lycus. In Greek legend, a son of Lycus and Dirce. During the absence of Heracles he killed Creon, the father of Heracles' wife Megara, made himself king of Thebes in Creon's place, and threatened to destroy Megara and the children of Heracles. Lycus dared do this because Heracles was occupied on the labor for Eurystheus of bringing Cerberus from Hades, and he had been gone so long that it was thought he would never return. However, he did return, his task successfully completed. And when he learned of Lycus' deeds, he killed him.

Lynceus (lin′sūs). In Greek mythology, the son of Aegyptus and the husband of Hypermnestra. On the advice of Artemis, Hypermnestra spared her husband on their wedding night. She was the only one of the 50 daughters of Danaus to spare her husband. Danaus had given each of his daughters a slender dagger and had ordered them to kill their bridegrooms. Hypermnestra helped Lynceus to escape to Lyncea, where he lighted a beacon to inform her that he had arrived safely. She also lighted one to show that his message had been received, and this act was commemorated annually by the lighting of signal fires. Lynceus and Hypermnestra were subsequently reunited.

Lynceus. In Greek legend, the son of Aphareus and Arene and the brother of Idas. His sight was so keen he could see through the bole of a tree. See **Idas.**

— M —

Macareus (mak′a̱-rōs). In mythology, a son of Aeolus, keeper of the winds, and Enarete. He and his five brothers and six sisters lived happily on the island where the winds were confined. Unaware that incestuous unions were displeasing

to the gods, the brothers and sisters considered themselves married to each other. When Aeolus discovered this, he threw the child of Macareus and his sister Canace to the dogs, sent Canace a sword, with which she killed herself, and forced four of his other sons to seek homes in other lands.

Macaria (mạ-kar′i-ạ). In Greek legend, the daughter of Heracles and Deianira, the only daughter he ever had. In the war between Theseus (or Demophon, his son) and Eurystheus that followed the persecution of Heracles' children by the latter, an oracle prophesied that the Athenians would win only if one of Heracles' children was offered as a sacrifice. Macaria volunteered to serve as the sacrifice, and when it was suggested that lots should be drawn she scorned the suggestion, saying she wished to offer her life of her own free will, and not to give it up as a result of chance. She was sacrificed and the Athenians, who had given sanctuary to the harassed children of Heracles, won. The Macarian Spring at Marathon, where Macaria died, is named for her.

Machaon (mạ-kā′on). In Homeric legend (*Iliad*) a son of Asclepius and a brother of Podalirius. He was famed as a surgeon and his brother as a physician. Both went from Oechalia with the Greeks to Troy. Machaon, regarded as one of the most valuable of all the Greeks for his skill in healing, was wounded by a three-barbed arrow shot by Paris, and was taken off the field of battle by Nestor. According to some accounts he was finally slain by the Amazon queen Penthesilea; according to others it was Eurypylus, son of Telephus, who killed him. Nestor took his bones back to Pylus where they became the center of a healing sanctuary.

Maenads (mē′nadz). [Known also as *Bacchae* or *Thyiades*.] The female followers of Dionysus; priestesses of Dionysus. Their tradition sprang from those who accompanied the god when he roamed all over the world in a frenzy of madness inspired by Hera. The maenads celebrated the festivals of Dionysus with mad songs and boisterous courses in gay companies amid the crags of Parnassus and Cithaeron, particularly on the occasion of the great triennial festival of Dionysus. During the celebration they donned the *nebri* (fawnskin), chewed laurel leaves, and carried the ivy-twined pine-cone-tipped thyrsus. Their faces and arms were sometimes painted or tattooed as a disguise during their orgies on the mountain tops when they became the lovers of Pan

The maenads, inflamed by wine and Dionysiac ecstasy, helped Agave tear her son Pentheus to pieces under the impression he was a young lion, because he had doubted the divinity of Dionysus. At the instigation of Dionysus, they attacked Orpheus at Dium in Thrace. They first murdered their husbands, who were in a temple where Orpheus was a priest of Apollo, and then tore Orpheus limb from limb, and hurled his head into the Hebrus River. Dionysus saved their lives from the vengeance this provoked by transforming them into oak trees, and ever after the maenads in that region were tattooed by their husbands as a warning against the murder of priests.

MAENAD
Red-figured Greek amphora, Cleophrades Painter, c500
B.C.
Munich

Maeon (mē'on). Named by Homer as the "godlike" son of Haemon. He was a Theban, one of the 50 valiant Theban warriors who were set to ambush Tydeus when he left Thebes after having fruitlessly attempted to persuade the Thebans to restore Polynices to the throne. As Tydeus made his way back to the camp of the Seven against Thebes, these

50 leaped on him from ambush. He slew them all except
Maeon, who was allowed to escape and return to Thebes to
tell what had happened. In the subsequent battle of the
Seven against Thebes it is said that Maeon, in gratitude for
being spared by Tydeus, buried the fallen hero's body with
full funeral honors.

Maera (mē'rạ). In Greek legend, Icarius' faithful hound. He
led Erigone to the spot where peasants had buried her father
after killing him. The hound was later translated to the
heavens and became the Lesser Dog Star.

Maera. According to some accounts, the bitch into which
Hecuba was transformed after she had blinded the Thracian
king, Polymnestor.

Manto (man'tō). In Greek mythology, a daughter of the seer
Tiresias. She also had the gift of prophecy. When Thebes
was taken by the Epigoni, Manto, who had not fled from the
city as her father advised the Thebans to do, was taken
captive by Alcmaeon, the leader of the Epigoni. By Alcmaeon she became the mother of Amphilochus and Tisiphone. Later Manto was sent as part of the booty of Thebes to
the temple of Apollo at Delphi. Apollo sent her to Colophon
in Ionia, where she married Rhacius, king of Caria, and
became the mother of the seer Mopsus, either by Rhacius or
Apollo.

Marathonian Bull. See *Cretan Bull.*

Marmax (mär'maks). Said to have been the first suitor for the
hand of Hippodamia, daughter of Oenomaus. As demanded
by Oenomaus, he engaged in a chariot race with Oenomaus
and he was the first of the many suitors to be killed by
Oenomaus. Oenomaus also butchered Marmax' horses and
buried them in a tomb with their master beside the river
Parthenia in Pisa. The river took its name from one of the
mares. The tomb of Marmax and his mares was still shown
to visitors in the 2nd century A.D.

Marpessa (mär-pes'ạ). In the *Iliad,* known as the "beautiful-
ankled" daughter of Evenus. Her father sought to prevent
her marriage by challenging her suitors to a chariot race
with him. He was invariably the winner and the unlucky
suitors were slain. Idas, with the help of winged horses,
succeeded in defeating Evenus and carried Marpessa off.
Apollo, who also loved her, fought Idas, but Zeus intervened
in the unequal struggle between a mortal and a god. He gave

Marpessa the privilege of choosing between them, and she chose Idas. She feared Apollo would tire of her and preferred to risk her life and love with another mortal like herself. She was the mother of Meleager's wife, Cleopatra.

Mars (märz). In Roman mythology, the god of war. In later mythology, Mars became completely identified with the Greek Ares.

Marsyas (mär'si-as). In Greek mythology, a satyr (or in some accounts a Phrygian or a peasant) follower of Cybele who was defeated by Apollo in a musical contest in the following manner: Athena had made a flute which she played at a banquet of the gods. Although the music was beautiful, Hera and Aphrodite could not stop laughing. Athena then played beside a stream. She saw from the reflection of her face in the water how playing the flute distorted her features, and threw away the flute with a curse on the person who picked it up. Marsyas found it and when he put it to his lips the flute played by itself, remembering the sweet strains Athena had drawn from it. Marsyas was delighted and went about the land entertaining the natives. He became so proud of his music-making that he declared Apollo himself could not do better. This boast came to the ears of Apollo, and the god challenged Marsyas to a contest, with the Muses acting as judges. As the Muses could not choose a victor, Apollo turned his lyre upside down and continued to play sweet hymns to the gods. Marsyas could not draw any sounds at all from his flute in an upside down position and the Muses awarded Apollo the victory. For his presumption in vying with a god Apollo flayed Marsyas alive and fastened his skin to a tree near the river in Phrygia which bears his name. Some even say the river was formed from the tears which the nymphs and satyrs shed over his death.

Medea (mē-dē'a). In mythology, a daughter of Aeëtes, king of Aea in Colchis, and Idyia. She was the granddaughter of Helius, and was noted as a sorceress, skilled in the use of drugs and poisons. To aid Jason, who had come to Colchis to secure the Golden Fleece and restore it to Hellas, Hera and Athena appealed to Aphrodite. Aphrodite bribed her son, Eros, to pierce Medea's heart with one of his arrows at the instant when her eyes fell on Jason as he entered her father's courtyard. Out of loyalty to her father and her country Medea tried to resist the surge of love for Jason which overwhelmed her, but she was powerless, as Hera and Athena had meant her to be; she yielded to her love and betrayed her father. She met Jason at night in the grove of Hecate. On coming face to face with the object of her love she was nearly speechless. But in return for his oath in the name of Hecate to take her away with him and to marry her she told him how he could fulfill the task her father had set for him. She gave him the charm of Prometheus, an ointment which would render him and his weapons invulnerable for one day. This would protect him from the fire-breathing bulls that Aeëtes had commanded him to yoke. Once the bulls were yoked he must plow the field and sow the dragon's teeth in the furrows. Armed men would spring up from the dragon's teeth, she said, and he must hurl a stone among them, whereupon they would set to fighting among themselves until all were dead. The next day Jason followed her instructions to the letter, and all turned out as she had predicted. He performed the task Aeëtes had set for him, on the successful completion of which Aeëtes had promised to give him the Golden Fleece. Aeëtes, however, was in a furious rage. He knew well that Jason could not have accomplished this trial of his courage without Medea's help. He planned to seize and destroy Jason, burn the *Argo*, and attack the Argonauts. Medea learned of her father's intention. She hurriedly sent for Jason, went with him to the orchard of Ares where the Golden Fleece was hanging, lulled the dragon that guarded it while Jason snatched the Fleece, and together they fled to the *Argo* and hurriedly put to sea. According to some accounts, Apsyrtus, the young brother of Medea, accompanied them; Medea slew him and cast the pieces of his dismembered body into the sea. Aeëtes, pursuing the Argonauts with a fleet, stopped to gather up the fragments of his son's body, and was soon outdistanced by the *Argo*. Other accounts say that Apsyrtus did not accompany Medea, but that he commanded a ship in pursuit of her. Jason would have surrendered Medea in violation of his oath to her. She persuaded him to adopt a different course. She sent word to her brother that she wished to return to Colchis with him, and arranged to meet him at a temple in a lonely grove. Apsyrtus met her at the appointed spot and as they talked, Jason leaped out from ambush and killed Apsyrtus. In either case, Medea's passion for Jason led

fat, fāte, fär, fåll, åsk, fāre; net, mē, hèr; pin, pīne; not, nōte, möve, nôr; up, lūte, pùll; oi, oil; ou out; (lightened) ĕlect, agǫny, ūnite,

to her brother's death. After suffering many hardships in their voyage, the Dodonian oak which Athena had placed in the hull of the *Argo* spoke and informed them that their woes would not cease until Jason and Medea had been purified by Circe for the murder of Apsyrtus. Accordingly, they proceeded to Circe's isle and were purified. They next successfully passed the isle of the Sirens as well as Scylla and Charybdis, and came to the island of the Phaeacians. Here they were received by Alcinous, king of the Phaeacians, and here the Colchians, still pursuing Medea, caught up with the Argonauts. Again, Jason would have surrendered Medea. She appealed to Arete, wife of King Alcinous. That worthy queen persuaded her husband to make a decision: if Medea was still a chaste maiden, he would restore her to her father; he would not separate husband and wife. A marriage was hastily arranged. To marriage music supplied by Orpheus, Jason and Medea were married in a cave, which became known as the sacred cave of Medea. The Golden Fleece and flowers decorated the marriage couch. The frustrated Colchians abandoned their pursuit. When the *Argo* at last came in sight of the mainland of Greece a disastrous storm overtook it and lashed the ship for days. It was swept onto the shoals of Syrtis, and then borne on a great wave into the desert near the Tritonian Lake, where it was left high and dry. The Argonauts, encouraged by nymphs, placed their ship on rollers and propelled it over the desert to the Tritonian Lake. From there Triton guided them back to the sea. In the last stage of the journey the *Argo* sailed by Crete where, according to some accounts, Medea slew Talos, the bronze man who guarded the island, by pulling out the pin in his ankle which stoppered the life-giving ichor in his body.

By the time the *Argo* landed at Pagasae, the port from which it had originally sailed, King Pelias, who had sent Jason for the Golden Fleece, thought that he and his companions had all perished on the voyage, as he had hoped they would do. He had forced Aeson, father of Jason, to die by drinking bull's blood, and had killed Jason's young brother. Jason's mother had committed suicide. No one knew of the successful return of the *Argo*, and Jason resolved to take advantage of surprise to kill Pelias and seize the throne, which was rightfully his anyway. Medea offered to get rid of Pelias by her own arts and, as had happened so

many times, Jason was more than willing to let Medea do it
Medea appeared to the daughters of Pelias and informed
them that she would make their father young again. To
prove her powers she transformed an old ram into a skip
ping lamb by cutting up its body and boiling it in a cauldron
with magic herbs. The daughters of Pelias were convinced
by this demonstration and followed Medea's instructions.

MEDEA AND PELIAS
Black-figured Attic vase, 6th century B.C. Pelias sits at the
left while Medea, next to him, works her magic on the
ram; the daughters of Pelias are on the right.
British Museum

They approached their father as he slept under the influence
of one of Medea's drugs, and cut his throat. They then cut
him into pieces which they boiled in the cauldron. But
Medea had put no magic herbs in this cauldron, and Pelias
was irretrievably dead. His daughters, with the most loving
intentions, had become his murderers. According to an
other story, when Jason and Medea returned to Iolcus, they
found Aeson alive, but weak and old. Jason asked Medea to
take some of the years he might expect to live from him, and
give them to his father. Medea assured him she could do
better than this. She swept off in a winged chariot drawn by
dragons and disappeared for nine days. In this time she had
no contact with mortals, but spent her time collecting drugs
and herbs known only to her and Hecate. At the end of the

period she returned, sacrificed to Hecate, and cast Aeson into a deep sleep. She cut his throat, letting all the aged blood drain out, dismembered his body, and boiled the pieces in a cauldron in a liquid prepared from the magic herbs she had gathered. Aeson emerged from the cauldron restored to the physical condition he had enjoyed 40 years before. On seeing the magic restoration of Aeson, the daughters of Pelias begged Medea to do the same for their father. Medea agreed. But as noted before, Medea put no magic herbs into the cauldron with Pelias' body. After the death of Pelias, Jason seized the throne, but fearing vengeance he resigned it to Acastus, son of Pelias, and went with Medea to Corinth, where they lived happily for ten years, and Medea was highly thought of by the Corinthians. At the end of that time Jason decided to abandon Medea and their children, seven boys and seven girls, according to some accounts, and marry Glauce (or Creusa), daughter of King Creon of Corinth. Medea was in a frenzy when she learned of this proposal. She pleaded with Jason not to make a mockery of her love, and not to violate his sacred oath. She reminded him of all she had done for his sake—betrayed her father, killed her brother and Pelias, helped him to win the respect of the Corinthians, to say nothing of having borne him many children. Jason was obdurate. He offered to make some provision for Medea and their children but persisted in his plan to marry Glauce. Medea plotted a horrible revenge that would cause Jason great suffering and discredit him with the Corinthians. Pretending that she finally saw the wisdom of his plan, she sent Glauce a magnificent robe and chaplet as a wedding gift. The instant Glauce donned them, she was consumed to ashes. Creon, attempting to rescue his daughter, was destroyed by the flames which shot out from her body. The people of Corinth, in a raging desire for vengeance, seized the children of Medea from the altar in Hera's temple where they had gone as suppliants, and stoned them to death. For this reason, in expiation, each year thereafter seven boys and girls, with shaven heads and clad in black garments, were sent to spend a year in Hera's temple. Jason was scorned for having broken his oath to Medea, and reviled for the consequences of his broken oath. He wandered forlornly about Greece until his death. Euripides, some say bribed by the Corinthians to hide their own dishonor, wrote that Medea herself killed her children, as the worst possible revenge on Jason. Aegeus, king of Athens, had passed through Corinth, and had promised Medea sanctuary should she ever need it. In return she had promised to give him a son by her magic arts. She now fled from Corinth in a winged chariot drawn by dragons, which was sent to her rescue by Helius. Some say she went first to Thebes, where she cured Heracles of his madness. She then went to Athens, where Aegeus received her kindly, as he had promised, and married her. All went well until Theseus, the son of Aegeus, came to his father's court. Aegeus did not know his son, who had been born and brought up in Troezen. But Medea instantly recognized him, and feared him as a rival of her own son, Medeus. She prepared a wine-cup, poisoned it with aconite and prevailed on Aegeus to give it to the unknown youth. At the last instant Aegeus recognized the sword the young man was carrying as his own, and realized that this young stranger was his son. Medea fled; some say that Aegeus even provided an escort for her in gratitude for giving him the son she had promised. With her she took Medeus, who some say was her son by Aegeus and others say was the only one of her children by Jason to escape the wrath of the Corinthians after the murders of Glauce and Creon. According to some accounts, she went to Italy after leaving Athens, and taught the tribes the art of snake-charming. At last she learned that her uncle Perses had seized her father's kingdom. She went to Colchis, taking Medeus with her, brought about the death of Perses and restored Aeëtes to his throne. Medeus conquered additional territory for the kingdom and gave his name to the Medes. Some say that Medea was made immortal by Hera because she had repulsed the advances of Zeus, and that she went to the Elysian Fields. There she married Achilles and lived as a queen.

Medeus (mē'dē-us). In Greek mythology, a son of Medea by Aegeus, king of Athens, to whom Medea fled after Jason abandoned her. Medea's plot to poison Theseus, the heir of Aegeus, was thwarted and she fled to Asia, taking Medeus with her. Together they killed Perses and restored Aeëtes, Medea's father, to the throne of Colchis. Medeus enlarged the kingdom and gave his own name to his new subjects, the Medes. According to other accounts, Medeus was Medea's oldest son and his father was Jason. He was educated by Chiron. Still others say he was the son of an Asiatic king whom Medea married after she fled from Aegeus and Athens.

Medusa (mẹ-dū′sạ, -zạ). In Greek mythology, one of the three Gorgons, daughters of Ceto and Phorcys, who dwelt in Libya. Medusa, the only one of the three who was mortal, was originally a beautiful maiden who was transformed into a hideous winged monster by Athena because with Poseidon she had violated one of the temples of that goddess. Her hair was changed into writhing serpents and her face was so fearful to look upon that whoever saw it was changed into stone. Accordingly, when Perseus sought her to cut off her head, he attacked her with averted face, seeing only her reflection in the shield of Athena, who also guided his hand. From the decapitated body of Medusa, Pegasus and Chrysaor, the children of Poseidon, sprang full-grown. Perseus later gave the head to Athena, who used it on her aegis. According to some accounts, Athena also flayed Medusa's body and used the skin for her aegis; and drained the blood from the body and divided it with Asclepius. Athena used the blood to bring about war and death. Asclepius used his half to heal, and even to restore life. When Heracles went to the Underworld to fetch Cerberus, all the spirits fled in terror from him except fierce Medusa and valiant Meleager. In Roman mythology Medusa was said to have been, by Vulcan, the mother of the half-human giant Cacus.

Megara (meg′ạ-rạ). In Greek mythology, a daughter of Creon, king of Thebes. She was given in marriage to Heracles by her father, as a reward to him for conquering Erginus and the Minyans, who had been exacting tribute from the Thebans. Hera, ever jealous because Heracles was the son of Zeus, drove him mad, and in his frenzy he killed his children by Megara. Later, he gave Megara to his beloved nephew, Iolaus, for a wife, because he feared to have more children by her himself after his terrible experience. According to some accounts, Heracles killed Megara also during the spell of madness in which he killed his children.

Megareus (mẹ-gar′ẹ-us). In Greek mythology, a son of Oenope and Hippomenes. He was an ally of Nisus, father of Scylla and ruler of Nisa (afterwards Megara), and married Iphinoë, another daughter of Nisus. Megareus had two sons, one of whom, Euippus, was killed by a lion that was ravaging Mount Cithaeron. Megareus promised his throne and his daughter, Euaechme, to whomever should kill the lion, and gave both to Alcathous who accomplished this deed. Nisa then became known as Megara, after Megareus. He was buried near the acropolis of the city.

Melampus (me-lam′pus). In Greek mythology, a son of Amythaon of Pylus and Idomene, and the brother of Bias. The brothers went with Neleus when the latter invaded Messene and captured the city of Pylus. According to some accounts Melampus was the first mortal who enjoyed the power of foretelling the future. In his youth he rescued some young serpents whose parents had been killed by servants who wanted to kill the offspring also. Melampus buried the parent serpents. In return the young serpents licked his ears as he slept; and when he awoke he had the power to understand the language of birds and beasts and thus learned many secret things. Furthermore, Apollo taught him the art of augury by means of the entrails of sacrificial victims. Melampus was also said to have been the first to mix wine with water, to build temples to Dionysus and to establish certain mysteries in his honor, and the first to act as a physician. He was strongly attached to his brother Bias. Bias fell in love with Pero, a daughter of Neleus and the sister of Nestor. Neleus, compelled to choose among the many suitors for Pero's hand, agreed to award her to that one who could steal the prize cattle of Phylacus of Phylace in Thessaly. Melampus agreed to help his brother obtain the cattle and win Pero. By his prophetic powers he learned that whoever tried to steal the cattle would win them as a gift, but only after having served a year in prison. Melampus went to the building where the cattle were housed, prepared to spend a year in prison before he would gain them. The ferocious dog that guarded them gave the alarm and Melampus was captured by the minions of Phylacus and imprisoned. He had been confined exactly a year when he overheard some woodworms talking in the beams of his prison. One of them asked another how much longer they must gnaw at the beams. The other answered that they would have gnawed through the beam by the following morning. Melampus instantly set up a clamor to be removed to another cell, saying the building would collapse before morning. Although his guards scoffed at his story, Phylacus permitted him to be moved. Next day his former prison collapsed as the woodworms finished gnawing through the beams. Phylacus was much impressed by this evidence of Melampus' gift of prophecy. He agreed to free Melampus and give him the cattle if he could cure his son Iphiclus of his childlessness. Melampus undertook to do so. He sacrificed two bulls to Apollo and invited the birds to feast on their carcasses which he left lying on the altars. Two vultures flew down to eat the sacrificial victims. Melampus listened to their speech and learned from it that Iphiclus had been frightened as a child when he watched his father gelding rams and saw him with the bloody knife. Phylacus plunged the knife into the trunk of a tree and ran to comfort his child. Since then Iphiclus had been impotent. The vultures agreed that the only cure for his condition would be to scrape some of the rust from the knife, which remained buried in the tree trunk where Phylacus had thrust it, mix the rust with wine, and give it as a potion to Iphiclus for ten successive days. But the vultures concluded that probably there was no one other than themselves wise enough to employ such a cure. However, Melampus, having overheard them, at once prepared the potion as they had suggested and gave it to Iphiclus. In the course of time he was cured and had a son. Phylacus now willingly gave Melampus his cattle. Melampus gave them to Bias and his grateful brother was able to present them to Neleus and win Pero. Melampus now went to Argos. There the daughters of Proetus, co-king of Argos, were afflicted by madness because they had denied the divinity of Dionysus, and went raging about the countryside. Melampus, at the request of Proetus, offered to cure his daughters in return for one-third of his kingdom. Proetus scorned to accept such a high price. The result was that increasing numbers of the women of Argos were seized with madness and roamed wildly through the mountains. Proetus had no alternative. He went to Melampus, and offered to accept his terms. Melampus, seeing Proetus' need had increased, increased his price. He now demanded another third of the kingdom for his brother Bias as the price of curing the Argive women. Proetus had no choice but to agree. Melampus pursued the Argive women and drove them to a well where he purified them. He then pursued the three daughters of Proetus— Lysippe, Iphianassa, and Iphinoë—across Arcadia and overtook the first two near the river Styx. The third, Iphinoë, had died in flight. Melampus married Lysippe, and Bias, whose wife Pero had died, married Iphianassa. Proetus partitioned his kingdom as he had agreed. Melampus was the father of Antiphates, who was the father of Heracles' companion Oïcles, and he was the father of Mantius, who in his turn fathered Clitus, carried off by Eos. The family of seers founded by Melampus was known as the Melampodidae.

Melanippe (mel-a-nip′ē). In Greek legend, an Amazon queen, a daughter of Ares. She ruled a city near the Thermodon River. According to some accounts, when Heracles came to the land of the Amazons in quest of Hippolyte's girdle, he captured Melanippe, sister of Hippolyte, and held her until Hippolyte ransomed her by giving him the girdle.

Melanippus (mel-a-nip′us). In Greek legend, a Theban who was one of the defenders of the city when it was attacked by the Seven against Thebes. He wounded Tydeus but Amphiaraus cut off Melanippus' head and gave it to Tydeus and told him to gulp Melanippus' brains. Tydeus did this and thus Melanippus, although dead, caused the death of Tydeus.

Melanthius (mē-lan′thi-us). In the *Odyssey,* a goatherd of Odysseus. He was not faithful to his master in the 20 years while Odysseus was away, but instead toadied to the suitors of Penelope. When Odysseus returned disguised as a beggar, Melanthius met him on his way to the palace, and reviled and attacked him. In the fight between Odysseus and the suitors, Melanthius was captured as he tried to slip away and fetch weapons for the suitors. He was strung up to a beam where he could watch the combat. When it was over and all the suitors were dead Melanthius was taken down, his nose, hands, and feet were cut off, he was disembowelled and the severed members were thrown to the dogs.

Meleager (mel-ē-ā′jėr). In Greek legend, the son of Oeneus, king of Calydon, and Althaea. When he was seven days old, the Fates told his mother that he would live until a log of wood then on the fire was completely consumed by the flames. Althaea immediately snatched the burning brand from the fire, quenched it, and hid the charred remains. As a youth, Meleager accompanied Jason on the quest for the Golden Fleece, and was wounded by the Colchians as the Argonauts fled with Medea and the Fleece. He married Cleopatra, daughter of Idas and Marpessa. However, when the hunt for the Calydonian Boar was organized, Atalanta joined it and Meleager fell in love with her. According to some accounts, he had a son, Parthenopaeus, by her. Some of the greatest warriors of Greece joined in the chase for the boar. Atalanta, who hunted at Meleager's side, was the first to wound it; others also drew its blood, and Meleager dealt the death blow. He awarded the boar's hide and tusks to Atalanta as a prize for drawing first blood. Two of his uncles objected to giving Atalanta the prize, and in a rage, Meleager slew them. A war with the Curetes for possession of the boar's hide followed. Meleager refused to defend Calydon because his mother had put a curse on him for the death of his uncles, her brothers. He scorned the rich gifts the Calydonians offered him, withdrew from the battle, and amused himself with his wife. At last, the Curetes being about to scale the walls of Calydon, Meleager yielded to the entreaties of his wife, his mother and his friends. He joined in the battle and repulsed the Curetes, at the same time killing two more of his uncles. Althaea, maddened by the death of all her brothers, took the half-burned brand which she had snatched from the fire so many years ago and hurled it into the flames. As it was consumed, Meleager felt a fiery breath scorch him and he died. He was a celebrated warrior, and when, in after years, Heracles visited Hades and frightened the spirits of the dead into fleeing before his sword, Meleager held his ground. Medusa was the only other spirit who dared face the mighty Heracles in the Underworld.

Meleagrides (mel-ē-ag′rī-dēz). The sisters of Meleager of Calydon. They grieved so at his death that Artemis took pity on them and changed all, save Deianira and Gorge, into guinea hens.

Melete (mel′ē-tē). In older Greek mythology, one of the Muses: the muse of Practice.

Meliad (mē′li-ad). In Greek mythology, a nymph of fruit trees or of flocks.

Meliboea (mel-i-bē′ạ). In Greek mythology, a daughter of Niobe and Amphion. According to some accounts, she was spared when the other daughters of Niobe were slain by Artemis, because she offered up a propitiatory prayer to Leto. According to these accounts she was given the name Chloris, which means "pale," and under this name became the wife of Neleus.

Melicertes (mel-i-sėr′tēz). In classical mythology, a son o Athamas, king of Orchomenus, and Ino, daughter of Cac mus of Thebes. His father, inspired with madness by Her; sought to kill him, but his mother snatched him up in he arms and leaped into the sea with him. The gods tran; formed him into a sea-god and he was henceforth known a Palaemon. As a sea-god he rode on the back of a dolphin t Corinth. His identification with the Phoenician Melkarth i uncertain. He was worshiped on the coast, especially ; Megara and the Isthmus of Corinth, where his mortal bod was cast ashore. His uncle Sisyphus founded in his honor th Isthmian Games, held every four years; whenever they wer neglected, famine struck the locality. By the Romans he wa identified with Portunus, god of harbors.

Melic (mel′ik) *Nymphs.* In Greek mythology, nymphs wh sprang from the blood of Uranus when he was mutilated b Cronus. They were distinguished by the spears of ash the carried, and were also said to be the nymphs of ash tree; With many others, they are sometimes said to have take care of the infant Zeus in a cave on the island of Crete.

Melissa (mẹ-lis′ạ). In Greek mythology, a Cretan nymph wh helped her sister Amalthea care for the infant Zeus by feec ing him on honey, while her sister supplied goat's milk. He name, which means "bee," was also applied to othe nymphs and sometimes to priestesses.

Melpomene (mel-pom′ẹ-nē). In Greek mythology, one of th daughters of Zeus and Mnemosyne. Originally the muse c song and musical harmony, she was looked upon later as th especial patroness of tragedy. She is generally represente as a young woman, bearing the tragic mask and often th club of Heracles, and with her head wreathed with vin leaves in token of her relation with the dramatic deit; Dionysus. According to some accounts, Melpomene was th mother of the Sirens by Achelous. See *Muses.*

Melus (mel′us). In Greek mythology, a companion of Adoni; son of Cinyras of Cyprus. He married Pelia, a kinswoman c Cinyras, but he and his wife grieved so when Adonis wa killed in his youth by a boar, that Aphrodite transforme Melus into an apple tree and Pelia into a dove.

Memnon (mem′non). A mythical Aethiopian king, the son c Eos and Tithonus, who came to the aid of the Trojans. Th Trojans, shattered by the loss of Hector and then of the ally Penthesilea, the Amazon queen, were considering flight or the surrender of Helen. The arrival of Memnon with his Aethiopians inspired them with new courage. In the furious battle Memnon killed Antilochus, son of Nestor, but ordered Nestor to withdraw as he did not wish to fight an old man. For a time Memnon was irresistible, and as he forced the Greeks back to their ships, Nestor called on Achilles to avenge Antilochus. When Achilles and Memnon, both descendants of gods and endowed with great prowess, met face to face, their fates had already been sealed. Memnon's black fate came to his side. Achilles plunged his sword through Memnon's breast and "snapped the chord of life." Myrmidons stripped him of his armor, while the Trojans fled in terror. Grief-stricken Eos veiled her face and the earth was in shadow as her other children slipped down and rescued Memnon's body. Drops of blood which fell from his corpse became a river, the Paphlagonia, whose waters, so it was said, annually flowed with blood on the anniversary of Memnon's death. His Aethiopian soldiers, whom the gods did not desert, were transformed into birds that flew off mourning their lord. The Greeks and Trojans watched in awe as the whole Aethiopian horde vanished. The body of their fallen leader was carried to the banks of the Aesepus River, where his transformed soldiers darted and wheeled with wailing cries about his tomb. From the ashes of his funeral pyre a great flock, the Memnonides, rose in the air and circled the pyre three times. The fourth time the flock divided. The birds of the two groups made fierce attacks on each other until they fell into the ashes of the funeral pyre as offerings to the dead hero. Annually the Memnonides are said to rise, fight, and fall on Memnon's tomb. On the death of her son, Eos vowed she would withdraw her light from the world. The Horae, however, conducted her to Zeus, who commanded her to resume her daily course. This she did, but each morning she weeps tears of dew in memory of her son. The ancients depicted Memnon as a youth of marvelous strength and beauty. His original home was said to be at Susa in Elam, where his temple or monument, the Memnoneum, was situated. The Greeks gave his name to one of the colossi of Amenophis III at Thebes in Egypt, a great stone statue called "the vocal Memnon" because the stone,

when reached by the rays of the rising sun, was said to giv
forth a sound resembling that of a breaking chord.

Memnonides (mem-non′i-dēz). According to legend, th
ashes that rose from the funeral pyre of Memnon were tran
formed into birds that annually rise, fight, and fall on h
tomb. See *Memnon.* Other accounts say the Memnonides ar
maidens, companions of Memnon, who mourned so over h
death that the gods in pity transformed them into birds, an
that they also annually visit the tomb and drop water fro
the Aesepus River on it.

Menelaus (men-ẹ-lā′us). In Greek legend a son of Atreus an
Aërope. He was the brother of Agamemnon and Anaxibi
Following the murder of their father by Aegisthus, Menelau
and Agamemnon were sent, some say as children, to Poly
phides, lord of Sicyon. Next they went to the court c
Oeneus in Calydon. Ultimately they were brought back t
Argos by Tyndareus and expelled Aegisthus, Agamemno
becoming king of Mycenae and Menelaus becoming king c
Sparta. Menelaus was a suitor of Helen, supposedly th
daughter of Tyndareus and Leda, but said to have been
daughter of Zeus, who embraced Leda in the shape of
swan. So many noble and valiant princes of Greece sued fc
the hand of Helen that Tyndareus feared to award her t
anyone lest the disappointed suitors turn on him in wrath
Odysseus advised him to require all the suitors to take a
oath that they would aid the one who succeeded in case an
ill should come to him as a result of his marriage to Heler
The suitors readily took the oath, and Tyndareus then gav
Helen to Menelaus. Whether he was also Helen's choice ha
never been definitely ascertained. She bore Menelaus
daughter, Hermione, and according to some accounts, thre
sons. Menelaus cordially welcomed Paris when he came t
Sparta with the secret intention of carrying off Helen. Afte
entertaining Paris royally for nine days Menelaus, with ap
palling obtuseness, for it was obvious that Paris was madl
in love with Helen, sailed blandly off to Crete to attend th
funeral of his maternal grandfather. The night after h
sailed, Helen eloped with Paris, taking with her a great trea
sure and a son. On learning of the abduction, Menelau
appealed to Agamemnon at Mycenae to raise an army an
sail against Troy. Agamemnon sent messages to the king
and princes of Greece, reminding them of the oath they ha

taken as suitors of Helen and declaring that the abduction
was an insult to all Greece; that if it was not avenged, they
risked losing their own wives. The heroes answered his call.
An army and fleet were mustered which assembled at Aulis.
For the first nine years the Greeks raided the coasts of Asia
Minor at intervals, and for considerable lengths of time were
at home in Greece. Then the fleet reassembled at Aulis, and
after the sacrifice of Iphigenia to appease Artemis, they put
to sea and arrived at the island of Tenedos. Menelaus and
Odysseus were sent as envoys to Troy to demand the return
of Helen. Their mission was unsuccessful. They would, in
fact, have been murdered by the angry Trojans except for
the intervention of Antenor, who sheltered the envoys and
secured safe passage for their return in the name of the laws
of hospitality and of war. The Greek fleet now sailed to Troy
and the city was attacked. A truce was then arranged and,
with the approval of both armies, Menelaus met Paris in
single combat: the winner to have Helen and thus conclude
the war. Menelaus had by far the best of the battle, and
would have slain Paris but for the intervention of Aphrodite,
who spirited him away in a mist and restored him to Helen.
The truce was broken when Athena caused Pandarus to
shoot at Menelaus an arrow which merely grazed him, and
the war was resumed. Menelaus fought bravely, killing many
Trojans. He accepted Hector's challenge to single combat
but was dissuaded by Agamemnon from submitting his
name for the drawing of lots, and Telamonian Ajax fought
Hector. He boldly rescued Odysseus when he was wounded
and cut off by the Trojans. He wounded Helenus, the Trojan
seer and brother of Paris, and, aided by Athena, killed Euphorbus, who had just wounded Patroclus, and protected
the body of Patroclus when he was slain by Hector and
helped to carry it back to the Greek ships. After the deaths
of Achilles and Telamonian Ajax, Menelaus proposed that
the Greeks give up the war and return home. He cared more
for his Greeks, he said, than for Helen. But this suggestion
was put forth purely for psychological reasons. As he expected, the Greeks protested that this would be cowardly
and vowed to fight harder than ever. Calchas the seer encouraged them by recalling that Troy was fated to fall in the
tenth year of the war, which was now passing. When the
Greeks decided to abandon direct siege of the city and to

penetrate it by stratagem, Menelaus was one of those wh
entered it in the Wooden Horse. Remembering the kindnes
of Antenor when he had gone as an envoy to Troy, Menelau
hung a leopard's skin in front of Antenor's house, when th
Greeks stole out of the Wooden Horse, as a sign that th
house and family of Antenor should be spared in the de
struction of the city. During the sack of Troy he searche
for Helen, vowing he would kill her. He found her wit
Deïphobus, to whom she had been forcibly married after th
death of Paris. According to some, it was Menelaus who sle
Deïphobus and horribly mangled his body. He raised hi
sword against Helen in the presence of Agamemnon, bu
was prevented, as he had expected to be, from plunging i
into her breast. For Menelaus, whatever he might have said
still passionately loved Helen and could hardly wait to ge
her back. This was possibly owing to the interference o
Aphrodite. They withdrew to his ship and he completel
forgave her. He was willing to blame her infidelity, as di
she, on the will of the gods. When the city was destroyed
Menelaus wanted to sail immediately. Agamemnon insiste
they first sacrifice to the gods. The brothers quarreled an
parted; Menelaus never saw his brother again. He put to se
but was caught in a great storm and lost all but five of hi
ships. Except for Odysseus, he was the last of the Greeks t
return home. For eight years he was buffeted about th
Mediterranean, sailing to Libya, Phoenicia, Cyprus an
Egypt, and collecting a vast treasure. On the island o
Pharos, in the mouth of the Nile, he was becalmed for man
days. Idothea, a sea-goddess, told him he must catch th
sea-god Proteus and force him to tell why Menelaus wa
prevented from returning home. Idothea helped him to dis
guise himself and some of his companions as seals and hid
them among the seals of Proteus' herd, among which th
sea-god took his midday nap. To prevent them from suffo
cating from the stench of the seal skins in which they wer
wrapped, Idothea filled their nostrils with ambrosia. Pro
teus, unaware that masqueraders had joined his herd, cam
to take his usual nap among them. As he slept, Menelau
seized him, and held him firmly as the sea-god rapidly trans
formed himself into a lion, then to a serpent, to a panther
and even to running water. Proteus was thus compelled t
prophesy. He said the gods were preventing Menelaus from

fat, fāte, fär, fâll, ȧsk, fāre; net, mē, hėr; pin, pīne; not, nōte, mȯve
nôr; up, lūte, pull; oi, oil; ou out; (lightened) ĕlect, agŏny, ūnite

getting home because he had not made proper sacrifices. He must return to Egypt and sacrifice to Zeus, and then favorable winds would permit his return. He also told him that Agamemnon had been murdered by Aegisthus and Clytemnestra, that Ajax the Lesser had perished at sea, and that Odysseus was held on an isle by Calypso. Menelaus returned to Egypt as instructed, offered sacrifices, and then sailed easily to Sparta with Helen. He arrived to find that Orestes had avenged the murder of Agamemnon by slaying Aegisthus and Clytemnestra. He then raised a temple to Zeus in Sparta in honor of Agamemnon. Telemachus, son of Odysseus, later visited Menelaus in search of news of his father, and found him and his beautiful Helen living in perfect harmony in the midst of splendid prosperity. So complete was their understanding that Helen could ruefully refer to the aberration which had caused her to run off with Paris and win an affectionate smile from Menelaus. Hera made Menelaus immortal, because he was a son-in-law of Zeus, and he and Helen ultimately departed this world and went to dwell in the Isles of the Blest.

Menoeceus (mẹ-nē'sūs). In Greek legend, a descendant of one of the Sparti, the men who sprang from the dragon's teeth sown by Cadmus. He was the father of Jocasta and Creon. When a plague broke out in Thebes, some time after the marriage of Oedipus and Jocasta, the seer Tiresias said the plague would be dispelled if one of the descendants of the Sparti would give his life for the city. Menoeceus thereupon leaped to his death from the walls to save the city.

Menoeceus. In Greek legend, the son of Creon, king of Thebes, and a grandson of the Menoeceus named above. In the war of the Seven against Thebes, Tiresias, the seer, again prophesied that Thebes would remain safe only if a descendant of the Sown Men freely gave his life for the city and appeased Ares, who was still angry over the death of the Sown Men brought about by Cadmus. Creon refused to sacrifice his son but Menoeceus, knowing of the prophecy, disobeyed his father's command to flee, and killed himself before the gates of the city. Others say he took part in the fighting, being young and inexperienced and knowing that he would be killed, and was slain in that way.

Menoetes (men-ē'tēz). In Greek mythology, a cowherd who tended Hades' cattle on Erythea. It was he who warned

Geryon that Heracles was stealing his cattle, although Heracles had not touched any of the cattle of Hades. Later, when Heracles went to the Underworld to fetch Cerberus, he slaughtered one of Hades' cows to give blood to the spirit of the dead. Menoetes challenged him for stealing Hades' cattle as he had Geryon's, and in the wrestling match which followed Menoetes would have been crushed to death by Heracles' strong arms had it not been for the intervention of Persephone who rescued him.

Mentor (men′tor). In the *Odyssey,* an Ithacan to whom Odysseus, when about to depart for the Trojan War, entrusted the care of his house and the education of his son Telemachus. His name has become a synonym for a faithful adviser.

Mercury (mėr′kū-ri). In Roman mythology, the god of commerce, who became identified with the Greek Hermes and took on various other attributes of Hermes, such as being messenger of the gods.

Merope (mer′ọ-pē). In Greek mythology, a daughter of Atlas and Pleione, one of the seven Pleiades. She was the wife of Sisyphus, king of Corinth. When Sisyphus was taken to the Underworld for betraying secrets of Zeus he told Merope not to dress him in burial clothes. Thus he was able to convince Persephone that he had not had proper burial, and won her permission to return to earth to see that the proper rites were carried out. However, Sisyphus did not escape for long, and when he returned to the Underworld for good Merope, ashamed because she was the only one of the Pleiades to have a husband who was a prisoner in the Underworld, left her six sisters in the heavens and is now no longer visible. According to another account, her shame is due to the fact that she, alone of the sisters, married a mortal.

Merope. In Greek mythology, a daughter of Oenopion, king of Chios. She was loved by Orion who, for her sake, cleared the island of Chios of wild animals. Oenopion agreed to give Merope to Orion in marriage in return for this service, but kept delaying the fulfillment of his promise. At last Orion, in a drunken state, insulted the maiden. Oenopion called on Dionysus to punish him. While he was in a deep sleep, Oenopion blinded him. Merope is also sometimes called Aero.

Merope. In Greek mythology, a daughter of Pandareus and Harmothoë, and a sister of Cleothera and Aëdon. When

fat, fāte, fär, fåll, ȧsk, fãre; net, mē, hėr; pin, pīne; not, nōte, möve, nôr; up, lūte, pŭll; oi, oil; ou out; (lightened) ẹlect, agǫny, ūnite;

their father was punished by the gods for his part in a theft, the goddesses took charge of his daughters. Aphrodite, Hera, Artemis, and Athena endowed them with beauty, wisdom, strength, and skill. But they were snatched away by the Harpies one day when the goddesses were not attending them, and handed over to the Erinyes, who hounded them for their father's crimes.

Merope. In Greek legend, an Arcadian; she was the wife of Cresphontes, a king in Messenia and a descendant of Heracles. Two of her sons and her husband were killed in a rebellion, and Polyphontes, who succeeded Cresphontes, married her. Her third son, Aepytus, had been hidden in Arcadia to save him, during the rebellion. When he grew up he returned to Messenia and with the help of his mother, who at first did not recognize him, he murdered Polyphontes and assumed the throne.

Merops (mē′rops). In Homeric legend *(Iliad)*, a Percosian who excelled in the art of divining. He tried to prevent his two sons, Adrestus and Amphius, from joining the Trojans, as he knew they would never return from the war, but was unsuccessful in his attempts to help them escape their fate, which was to die at Troy.

Messene (me̞-sē′nē). According to tradition, the daughter of Triopas, son of the Argive Phorbas. She married Polycaon, son of Lelex, and accompanied him, with a band of Argives and Spartans, to the country which came to be named Messenia after her.

Metis (mē′tis). In Greek mythology, a Titaness, the daughter of Oceanus and Tethys. She was the first wife of Zeus. It was she who advised Zeus to mix mustard and salt into the honeyed drink of Cronus in order to make the latter regurgitate the brothers and sisters of Zeus whom Cronus had swallowed as soon as they were born. When Metis became pregnant, Zeus learned from an oracle that her first child would be a girl, and that if she bore a second child, it would be a boy who would dethrone his father. Zeus thereupon swallowed Metis. Some time later he was passing near Lake Triton and was assailed by a frightful headache. Prometheus, or possibly Hephaestus, split his skull with an ax and out leaped fully-armed Athena, the daughter of Zeus and Metis. Metis is also known as the personification of Pru-

dence and Insight, and Zeus claimed that she often gave him
advice from within him.

Midas   (mī′dạs). In Greek mythology, a Phrygian king, the son
of Cybele and a satyr. Some say he was the son of Gordius
who became king of Phrygia, but others say he was adopted
by Gordius, who was childless, and succeeded him as king.
Midas had famous rose gardens in which, it was said, the
sweetest roses in the world grew of themselves. When
Dionysus passed through his lands, Silenus, who was in his
train, fell behind and was captured by peasants. They took
him to King Midas. Silenus amused the king by telling him
fantastic tales of the strange lands he had visited with
Dionysus. Midas treated him kindly and after some days
restored him to Dionysus. The god was grateful to Midas
and offered to grant him the fulfillment of any wish he might
make. Midas asked that whatever he touched might be
turned to gold. Dionysus granted his wish, although he
thought it an unworthy one, and Midas at once tested it. He
touched the pillars of his palace, the grain in his fields, the
very earth itself: all were instantly turned to gold. Midas was
delighted. However, when he was hungry and would eat, or
thirsty and would drink, whatever he put into his mouth was
also turned to gold. Deeply regretting his greedy wish, he
prayed to Dionysus, acknowledging that he had done wrong
to ask such a gift and praying that it might be taken from
him. Dionysus pitied him. He told Midas to go and bathe in
the headwaters of the Pactolus River to free himself of his
ruinous gift. Midas obeyed his instructions. His miraculous
powers were washed off in the river, whose waters and sand
ever after bore grains of gold. Midas promoted the worship
of Dionysus and founded the city of Ancyra. He also sent
gifts to the shrine of Delphi, the first foreigner to do so, and
dedicated his throne there, where it remained a thing worth
to see for a long time. But now Midas made another stupid
mistake. Apollo and Pan engaged in a musical contest with
Tmolus as judge. Tmolus awarded the prize to Apollo, but
Midas disagreed with the award and maintained that Pan
was the winner. For having ears so unfitted to judge the
god's music, Apollo caused long ass-ears to grow from the
head of Midas. In deep humiliation he concealed them under a cap, but he was unable to conceal them from his
barber. Midas warned the barber, on pain of death, not to

---

fat, fāte, fär, fåll, ȧsk, fâre; net, mē, hėr; pin, pīne; not, nōte, möve;
nôr; up, lūte, pùll; oi, oil; ou out; (lightened) ẹlect, agǫny, ūnite.

reveal his secret. The barber was tormented because he could not tell his strange news to a soul. Unable to keep it to himself any longer, he went to the bank of the river, dug a deep hole there, and whispered into it, "King Midas has ass's ears." Then he filled in the hole and went away relieved. But reeds growing on the spot whispered the secret and soon it was known throughout the land. When Midas realized that his disgrace was common knowledge, he ordered the barber to be killed and then drank bull's blood, and so died himself.

Miletus (mī-lē'tus). According to Greek tradition, a son of Apollo and Aria (Deione, according to Ovid), born in Crete. Minos, Rhadamanthys, and Sarpedon, the sons of Europa, quarreled for the love of Miletus. The beautiful youth preferred Sarpedon. Minos went to war against them and Miletus fled with many followers to Caria in Asia Minor. There he killed the giant, Asterius, who had been ruling the land, and whose bones, when they were disinterred, measured ten cubits in length. Miletus founded the city and kingdom of Miletus and married Cyaneë, daughter of the river-god of the Maeander. She bore him the twins Byblis and Caunus.

Minerva (mi-nėr'va̱). In Roman mythology, one of the three chief divinities, the other two being Jupiter and Juno. The chief seat of the cult of all three was the great temple on the Capitoline Hill. In Roman myth, Minerva was the virgin daughter of Jupiter, the supreme god, and hence was identified, as the Romans came more and more under the influence of Hellenic culture, with the Greek Athena.

Minos (mī'nos, -no̱s). In Greek mythology, a son of Europa and Zeus, born on the island of Crete. He was the brother of Rhadamanthys and Sarpedon. Asterius, king of Crete, married Europa and adopted her three sons as his heirs. When they grew up the brothers quarreled over the affections of Miletus, a son of Apollo and Aria and, when Miletus showed a preference for Sarpedon, Minos drove him out of the country and banished Sarpedon. Minos married Pasiphaë, daughter of Helius and Persa. She bore him Acacallis (Acalle), Ariadne, Androgeus, Catreus, Glaucus, and Phaedra, and, some say, Deucalion, the father of Idomeneus. Minos was also the father of sons by the nymph Paria and was, according to some accounts, the lover of Procris, wife of Cephalus. He pursued Britomartis and others. Upon the

death of Asterius, Minos wished to become king of Crete
He declared that he had received the kingdom from the
gods, and in proof of his special favor in their sight he
claimed that whatever he prayed for would be accomplished
As he was sacrificing to Poseidon, he prayed that a bull
might emerge from the sea, which he promised he would
then sacrifice to Poseidon. Poseidon answered his prayer by
sending a magnificent white bull from the sea. Minos was so
enchanted with the handsome specimen that he put the bull
among his own herds and sacrificed another in its place. He
became king of Crete and established laws which it is said
he received from Zeus, who met Minos in a cave and gave
him the laws. But Poseidon punished Minos for his failure
to fulfill his vow of sacrificing the bull which he had sent him
from the sea. He caused Pasiphaë to conceive an unnatural
passion for the bull. With the help of Daedalus, the marvel
ous smith who had fled to Crete and had been welcomed by
Minos, she was able to gratify her passion, and ultimately
bore Asterius, or Asterion, called the Minotaur, a monster
with the head of a bull and the body of a man. Minos, to
conceal this evidence of disgrace to himself and Pasiphaë
commanded Daedalus, on the advice of an oracle, to build
the Labyrinth in which to hide the Minotaur. The bull es
caped from the herds of Minos and ravaged the island until
Heracles came and, as one of his labors, subdued the bull
and rode on its back across the sea to Hellas. The bull was
turned loose in Hellas. It ravaged the plains about Marathon
and became known as the Marathonian Bull. Some say An
drogeus, son of Minos, journeyed to Athens and took part
in the Panathenaea. He was victorious in all his contests and
out of jealousy, King Aegeus of Athens sent him to slay the
bull. Androgeus was himself slain in the attempt. But others
say that it was Theseus who slew the bull and that Aegeus
caused Androgeus to be ambushed while he was on his way
to Thebes, because Aegeus feared that Androgeus was con
spiring in a revolt that was brewing against the rule of
Aegeus. Androgeus bravely fought those who attacked him
from ambush but was slain. Minos had by this time made
himself master of the sea, the first ruler to do so, and when
he learned of the death of Androgeus, he vowed vengeance
on Athens. He won the support of some of the island princes
to his projected war against Athens. He bribed with gold the

fat, fāte, fär, fâll, ȧsk, fãre; net, mē, hėr; pin, pīne; not, nōte, mȯve
nôr; up, lūte, pu̇ll; oi, oil; ou out; (lightened) ẹlect, agǫny, ūnite

princess Arne of Siphnus to become his ally, and sought the help of Aeacus of Aegina, but Aeacus refused to aid him and allied himself to the Athenians. Minos attacked Nisa on the Isthmus of Corinth. Scylla, the daughter of King Nisus, saw Minos as she watched the battle from a tower, and fell in love with him. She resolved to betray her father and to help Minos. In fulfillment of this resolve she crept into her father's bed chamber at night and cut off a magic golden, or some say purple, lock of his hair. This lock of hair protected the life and kingdom of Nisus. Scylla gave it to Minos who willingly accepted it, and the city fell into his hands. But he scorned Scylla for betraying her father and refused to take her with him to Crete. He could not subdue Athens, and prayed to Zeus to avenge his son's death. His prayer was answered: all Hellas was shaken by earthquakes and afflicted by famine. An oracle instructed the leaders of the Greek states to request Aeacus, king of Aegina, to pray to their gods on their behalf. When this was done, the earthquakes ceased everywhere except in Attica. The Athenians now sought advice from the oracle at Delphi. They were informed that they must submit to whatever demands Minos might make if they wished to be spared further earthquakes. Minos demanded that they send a tribute of seven youths and seven maidens to Crete every nine years. The Athenians were compelled to submit; the youths and maidens were sent to Crete and there were devoured by the Minotaur. The third time the Athenian youths and maidens came to Crete, Theseus, son of King Aegeus, was one of their number. With the help of Ariadne, daughter of King Minos, he slew the Minotaur and escaped with Ariadne and his fellow Athenians. Minos, who had welcomed Daedalus the smith when he first came to Crete, and later employed him to build the Labyrinth, now discovered that Daedalus had helped Pasiphaë to indulge her passion for the bull. He imprisoned Daedalus and his son in the Labyrinth. Some say Pasiphaë freed them but they could find no ship to take them from the island, and others say Minos had simply forbidden Daedalus to leave Crete. He escaped with his son by means of wax wings which he constructed. He flew to Italy, having lost his son in the sea on the way, and went to the court of King Cocalus in Sicily. Minos resolved to secure his return. As he did not know where Daedalus had gone he resorted to a

stratagem to find him. He procured a many-chambered shell
and, taking it with him as he sailed about the Mediterranean,
he offered a rich reward to the man who could pass a thread
through it. When he landed in Sicily, he showed the shell to
King Cocalus, who undertook to have the shell threaded as
Minos desired. Cocalus gave the shell to Daedalus, who
succeeded in threading the shell with the aid of an ant and
some honey. When the threaded shell was returned to
Minos, he knew he had found Daedalus, as no one else could
have found such an ingenious solution. He demanded the
surrender of Daedalus. Cocalus did not at once refuse. In
stead he invited Minos to remain as a guest in his palace, and
as Minos was resting in his bath the daughters of Cocalus,
who did not want to lose Daedalus, poured boiling water or
hot pitch on Minos and scalded him to death. Cocalus re
turned his body to his Cretan followers and they buried him
in a fine tomb in Camicus in Sicily. Later his bones were
restored to Crete. Minos was the greatest ruler of his time
and was regarded as a friend of Zeus, who made him a judge
in the Underworld. He divided the good from the bad and
assigned the spirits to their final home in Tartarus. Cases
that were too difficult for Rhadamanthys and Aeacus, the
other judges of Tartarus, were turned over to Minos. Ruins
of a palace at Cnossus in Crete, said to have been the palace
of Minos and occupied in the first half of the second millen-
nium B.C., were excavated by Sir Arthur Evans early in the
20th century, and a maze, distinct from the palace, has been
found which may have been the Labyrinth of Daedalus. Ar
chaeologists generally agree, however, that the Labyrinth
was the Palace of Minos itself (*labyr-inthos,* "Place of the
Double Ax," from *labrys,* "double-ax").

Minotaur (min′ō-tôr). Literally, "Minos-bull." The monstrous offspring of Queen Pasiphaë and the Cretan Bull. He
had a human body and the head of a bull. He was confined
in the Labyrinth at Cnossus and fed with human flesh; he
devoured the seven youths and seven maidens whom Minos
compelled the Athenians to send him periodically as a tribute. The Minotaur was killed by the son of Aegeus, the hero
Theseus, with the assistance of Minos' daughter, the princess Ariadne, who thereupon eloped with Theseus. The
Cretans claimed that there was no such animal, and that
Pasiphaë had an intrigue with one Taurus, a general under

Minos, and that one of her children rather too closely resembled Taurus. Another, and anthropologically very attractive, explanation is that for certain rituals, as in many other primitive contexts, the priest, or priest-king of Cnossus wore an animal-head mask, in this case a mask representing a bull, and that the story of the figure with a human body and bull's head may have reached the Greek mainland with a bronze-age traveler who had happened to observe such a ritual without fully understanding it. (JJ)

Minthe (min'thē) or **Menthe** (men'-). In Greek mythology, a nymph who was transformed into a mint plant by Persephone to prevent her from being seduced by Hades. Or, as others say, she was a nymph transformed by Hades into a mint plant to protect her from the jealousy of Persephone. In either case, she became a mint plant because she had aroused the interest of Hades. Mint was used in funeral rites, and the barley water which Demeter drank at Eleusis when she was searching for Persephone was flavored with mint.

Minyades (min-ī'a-dēz) or **Minyae** (min'i-ē). In Greek legend, the daughters of Minyas, king of Orchomenus. They were Alcithoë, Leucippe, and Arsinoë (or Arsippe, or Aristippe). They scorned to take part in the wild revels of Dionysus, and sat quietly at home, spinning and performing their other household tasks. Dionysus appeared to them as a girl, and invited them to take part in the revels but they refused. He then appeared to them as a bull, a lion, and finally as a panther. He caused wine and milk to flow from their spindles, and followed this by causing their spindles to sprout and put forth ivy leaves. At length he drove them mad to punish them for their sacrilege, and they were overcome by an insatiable desire for human flesh. By lot, they chose Hippasus, the child of Leucippe, tore him to pieces and ate him. This is the basis for the assumption that in Orchomenus the human sacrifice was always chosen from the royal family. The murder of Hippasus was annually commemorated at Orchomenus by a feast of atonement and a ritual of seeking Dionysus. The Minyadae, according to some accounts, were transformed by Dionysus into bats. Others say that Hermes changed them into birds.

Minyans (min'yanz) or **Minyae** (min'yē, min'i-ē). In Greek tradition, a prehistoric people, descendants of Minyas, who founded Orchomenus in Boeotia, and there established his family. Another branch is found at Iolcus in Thessaly and the Argonauts were often called Minyans because they sought to satisfy the ghost of Phrixus, grandson of Minyas, by restoring the Golden Fleece to Hellas. Furthermore, Jason was a descendant of Minyas through his mother, who was the granddaughter of Minyas. One of the early exploits of Heracles was the defeat of the Minyans under their king Erginus.

Minyas (min'i-as). In Greek legend, a king of Orchomenus in Boeotia. He had migrated from Thessaly to Orchomenus and founded the kingdom. He was famous for his great wealth and was the first king ever to build a treasury. His daughters were transformed into bats for refusing to take part in the worship and revels of Dionysus. See *Minyades.*

Mnemon (nē'mon). In Greek epic, a companion of Achilles, given to him by his mother Thetis, to warn Achilles that he should not kill a child of Apollo, or Apollo would bring about his death. Achilles killed Tenes, a son of Apollo, on the island of Tenedos, and then, realizing what he had done, killed Mnemon for not reminding him.

Mnemonides (ne-mon'i-dēz). A name for the Muses, from their mother Mnemosyne.

Mnemosyne (ne-mos'i-nē, -moz'-). In Greek mythology, a Titaness, the daughter of Uranus and Gaea. She was the goddess of memory. Zeus visited her nine nights and she bore him the nine Muses.

Moerae (mē'rē). [Also: *Moirai.*] In Greek mythology, the three birth goddesses, identified with the Fates. Homer uses the name in the singular, as of a single divinity, and also in the plural. He also calls them the "spinners of the thread of life." They are spoken of as the daughters of Night and Darkness, and also as daughters of Zeus and Themis. Hesiod represented them as three: Clotho (the spinner), Lachesis (disposer of lots), and Atropos (the inevitable). The first spins the thread of life, the second fixes its length, and the third severs it. Their attributes were, respectively, a spindle, a scroll, and for Atropos, a scale or scissors. Their duty was to see to it that the fate allotted at birth was duly carried out. They were more powerful than the gods themselves, as Homer frequently states, and whoever attempted to defy the Moerae was certain to be visited by Nemesis.

Moirai (moi'rī). See *Moerae.*

Moliones (mō-lī′ō̯-nēz). In Greek mythology, the twin brothers Eurytus and Cteatus. They were the sons of Molione and
Poseidon, but as they were brought up by Actor, the husband of Molione, they are also called the Actoridae. According to some accounts they were joined together at the waist.
Nestor, relating the heroic exploits of his youth to spur
Patroclus into battle during the Trojan War, tells how he
was about to conquer the Moliones when they were spirited
away in a mist by Poseidon. Later they defeated Nestor in a
chariot race. They repelled Heracles when he attacked their
uncle, Augeas, in Elis, but were later ambushed and slain by
Heracles at Cleonae. The sons of Cteatus and Eurytus sailed
to Troy to take part in the Trojan War. As descendants of
Molione they were also known as Moliones.

Moly (mō′li). A fabulous herb of magic power, represented as
having a black root and a milk-white flower; it is said by
Homer to have been given by Hermes to Odysseus to coun-
teract the spells of Circe.

Momus (mō′mus). [Also: *Momos* (-mos).] According to
Hesiod, the son of Nyx (Night). He is the personification of
mockery, ridicule, and censure. He criticized Hephaestus for
not putting a door in the breast of the man he had made, so
that the inmost secrets of his heart could be revealed. He
found fault with Aphrodite because her sandals made too
much noise, and criticized Zeus for putting the bull's horns
where the bull could not see them.

Mopsus (mop′sus). In Greek mythology, a Lapith. He was the
son of Ampycus and a nymph, and was taught the augury of
birds by Apollo himself. He took part in the battle between
the Lapiths and the Centaurs, and it was he who recognized
as the soul of the Lapith Caeneus the bird that flew out of
the pile of trees and logs under which Caeneus was buried.
Mopsus also took part in the Calydonian Hunt, and later
went from Thessaly to Iolcus to join Jason on the voyage of
the *Argo* to Colchis for the Golden Fleece. On the way back
from Colchis the Argonauts were driven into the shoal waters of Syrtis in Libya, and were carried by a great gale into
the desert. Mopsus wandered about in search of water and
was bitten by a serpent. This serpent was one of those which
sprang up from the drops of blood that fell from the severed
head of Medusa when Perseus was carrying it back to Seriphus, and the bite was therefore fatal to Mopsus. Afterward

he was worshiped as a hero in Libya, and there was an oracle of Mopsus there.

Mopsus. In Greek legend, a son of Rhacius, king of Caria, and Manto, daughter of the famous seer, Tiresias. He was a noted seer also. In a contest with the seer Calchas, at Colophon, after the Trojan War, Mopsus gave the correct number of figs growing on a fig tree, and accurately predicted the time of birth and the number of pigs in the litter that a sow was about to produce. Calchas, who had been mistaken in both cases, died, as it had been foretold he would do when he met a seer wiser than himself. Mopsus was the founder with Amphilochus, of the city of Mallus in Cilicia. When Amphilochus returned to Argos, Mopsus ruled alone. But Amphilochus later returned to Mallus, and wished to share in the rule of the city which he had helped to found. Mopsus and Amphilochus quarreled so violently for control of the throne that it was finally suggested they should engage in a combat to see which should rule. In the duel that followed they killed each other. Afterward a common oracle was set up of Mopsus and Amphilochus, which became as celebrated for accuracy as the oracle at Delphi. Questions were put to it on wax tablets, and the answers were revealed in dreams.

Morpheus (môr′fūs or môr′fē-us). In Greek mythology, one of the sons of Hypnos, or Sleep. Morpheus was the god of dreams who imitated human forms and voices, and was therefore summoned when a dream of human beings was required, as distinct from the bringer of dreams of animals or phantoms. It was Morpheus, for example, who appeared to Alcyone as her husband Ceyx, to inform her that Ceyx had been drowned. He is more prominent in literary allusion than in mythology itself, and hence, by extension, is very commonly referred to as the god of sleep.

Muses (mū′zez). Originally there were three Muses: Melete *(Meditation)*, Mneme *(Memory)* and Aoede *(Song)*. According to the earliest writers, the Muses were goddesses of memory, then inspiring goddesses of song, and later, divinities presiding over poetry, the sciences, and the arts, while at the same time having springs and streams as their special province. According to later tradition, Mnemosyne *(Memory)* bore nine daughters, the Muses, to Zeus, who lay with her nine nights. They were born in Pieria (and hence called

Pierides), and there they frolicked around the sacred Pierian springs; or disported in their sacred grove on Mount Helicon in Boeotia, where the winged horse Pegasus had made the Hippocrene Spring for them by stamping his hoof on the earth; or visited the inspirational Castalian Spring on Mount Parnassus; or went to Olympus where they entertained the gods. As companions of Apollo they learned singing, dancing, and poetry, and shared the mastery of the lyre with him. Because they presided over the musical arts, they were sometimes called on to judge musical contests, as that between Apollo and Marsyas, or challenged to enter them themselves, as by the Sirens, who were defeated and lost their wings, or by the daughters of Pierus, who were also defeated, and changed into magpies. The Muses attended the marriages of Peleus and Thetis and Cadmus and Harmonia, where they entertained the guests at the weddings with music and song. The Muses were the mistresses of healing and prophecy, which they sometimes taught to others, as to Aristaeus, and they had many sanctuaries, sacred groves, and springs throughout the Greek world. Anyone inspired by the "violet-crowned" Muses was blessed and highly venerated, for "Happy is he whom the Muses love, and sweet flows his voice from his lips." The nine Muses and their attributes were: Clio, the muse of history, who wears a wreath and carries a scroll; Euterpe, of music, who carries a double flute; Thalia, of comedy, who has an ivy wreath, a comic mask, and a shepherd's staff; Melpomene, of tragedy, with a tragic mask, an ivy wreath, and sometimes a club or a sword; Terpsichore, of choral dance and song, with a lyre; Erato, of lyric and amorous poetry, with the lyre; Polymnia or Polyhymnia, of the inspired and stately hymn and religious dance, who is usually shown veiled and thoughtful; Urania, of astronomy, who holds a globe; and last of all, Calliope, the chief of the Muses, of heroic or epic poetry, who carries a tablet and stylus. The Muses were intimately associated in legend and in art with Apollo, who as the chief guardian and leader of their company was called Musagetes. The Romans identified their Camenae with the Greek Muses.

Myrmidons (mèr′mi-donz, -donz). A warlike tribe of Phthiotis, Thessaly, that originated on the island of Aegina. According to Greek mythology, Hera sent a pestilence on

Aegina, which was named for one of her rivals for the affections of Zeus. The streams were polluted and a plague of serpents appeared. Men and animals died by the thousand and the island was almost depopulated. Sacrifices to the gods had no effect. At last Aeacus, the king of the island and a son of Zeus, prayed to his father to restore his people by sending him as many men as the ants that were crawling up an oak tree in the sacred grove. Zeus answered with a flash of lightning and the next day the ants had been transformed into magnificent warriors, and the plague had lifted. Aeacus named his new subjects Myrmidons in memory of their origin. Emigrants from Aegina to Thessaly continued to hold the ant sacred in their new land. According to Homer, the Myrmidons were led by Achilles in the Trojan War, and performed their warlike duties as faithfully and tirelessly as the ants for which they were named.

Myrrha (mir′a̱). In Greek mythology, the daughter of Cinyras, king of Paphos. Afflicted by an unnatural love for her father because her mother had boasted that Myrrha was more beautiful than Aphrodite, she tried to hang herself. Her devoted nurse saved her and took her to her father, disguised as a young girl who was in love with him. Ultimately Cinyras discovered that she was his own daughter and in horror sought to kill her. She fled and was transformed by the gods into a twisted tree that ever weeps tears of bitter resin, the myrrh tree. The trunk of the tree split open and delivered Adonis, the child of her incestuous union. Myrrha is also sometimes called Smyrna.

Myrtilus (mêr′ti-lus). In Greek legend, a son of Hermes. Accompanied by Oenomaus, king of Elis, he drove the chariot in the races which Oenomaus demanded of the suitors of his daughter, Hippodamia. As Oenomaus had horses born of the wind, he always won the races and killed the defeated suitor. When Pelops sought Hippodamia's hand, he bribed Myrtilus to let him win the race. Hippodamia, having seen Pelops and fallen in love with him, also bribed Myrtilus. Myrtilus substituted wax pins in the axles of the chariot, and as the race was nearing its end, the wheels spun off, it overturned, and Oenomaus, tangled in the horses' reins, was killed, but before he died he laid a curse on Myrtilus. Pelops then set off with Hippodamia and Myrtilus. Myrtilus now demanded his reward—half of the kingdom of Oenomaus—

and Pelops answered by hurling him into the sea at Geraestus, the southernmost tip of Euboea. This part of the Aegean Sea was thereafter known as the Myrtoan Sea. While drowning, Myrtilus cursed the house of Pelops, a curse which brought many woes on his descendants. Hermes set Myrtilus' image among the stars as the constellation Auriga (the Charioteer). His body was washed ashore and buried behind a temple of Hermes in Arcadia. The ghost of Myrtilus haunted the stadium at Olympia, and charioteers made sacrifices to it so that it would not frighten their horses and bring disaster to them in their races.

Naiads (nā′adz, nī′-). In Greek and Roman mythology, female spirits presiding over springs, rivers, streams, and fountains. The Naiads were represented as beautiful nymphs with their heads crowned with flowers, lighthearted, musical, and beneficent. Their beneficence extends to the life-giving properties of water.

Narcissus (när-sis′us). In mythology, a son of the river-nymph Liriope and the river-god Cephissus. When he was born, the seer Tiresias told his mother that he would live to old age only if he never came to know himself. By the time he was a youth he was so beautiful that he was loved by many young men as well as maidens, but he scorned them all out of pride in his own beauty. The wood-nymph Echo fell in love with him and followed him. Narcissus heard her rustling in the forest and called to learn who was there. She could only repeat his last words, since she had been deprived of the power to speak any but the last few words another had spoken. When, therefore, Narcissus called out to his unseen admirer to come to him, she approached him with delight. But Narcissus scorned her love, as he had that of all others and Echo, yearning for love of him, wasted away until nothing was left of her but her voice, ever repeating the last words spoken by others. At length Aminius, whose love for Narcissus had also been scorned, prayed to the gods that one day Narcissus' love would be cruelly denied him, as he had denied others. Nemesis, or as some say, Artemis, heard the prayer and caused Narcissus, who was weary and hot from hunting, to go to a pool deep in the forest to refresh himself. As he bent to drink, he glimpsed his own image in the still surface of the pool and instantly fell in love with it. Each time he stretched his arms into the spring to clasp the image it disappeared. Nothing could tear him away from the spring and he cried to the gods in despair at the cruelty of the fate which denied him from embracing his love. As he lay day after day by the pool pining, he wasted away, adoring his own image. Dying, he prayed that the object of his love which was so beautiful, would outlive him, and when he breathed his last, his body disappeared. In its place was a lovely flower, with a golden center surrounded by white petals: the narcissus, whose bulb came to be useful as a narcotic. Another flower sometimes called narcissus, but more commonly called the iris, was created by Zeus to help Hades seize Persephone. It was a purple and silver blossom, and when Persephone saw it she wandered off from her attendant maidens in delight to pluck it. When she was alone the earth parted, Hades leaped out in his chariot and carried her off.

Nauplius (nô′pli-us). In Greek legend, a son of the Danaid Amymone and Poseidon. He was a celebrated navigator who discovered the art of steering by the constellation of the Great Bear. He was also the founder of Nauplia, the port of Argos.

Nauplius. In Greek legend, a son of Clytonaeus, and a descendant of Nauplius the navigator. He was a king of Nauplia, and he too was a famous navigator. He was one of the Argonauts who accompanied Jason on the expedition for the Golden Fleece. Aleus, king of Tegea, on discovering that his daughter Auge was about to bear a child whose father she claimed was Heracles, gave Auge to Nauplius with instructions to drown her, but he prudently took her to Nauplia and sold her to traders from Caria. Catreus, king in Crete, believing that he would meet his death at the hands of one of this own children, gave his daughter Clymene to Nauplius with instructions to sell her as a slave. Instead Nauplius married her, and by her became the father of Oeax and Palamedes. The latter joined the Greeks in the Trojan

War but was betrayed and killed by the Greeks at the instigation of Odysseus. Nauplius demanded satisfaction for his son's murder but was refused it. To avenge himself on the Greeks for the murder of his son, he visited the wives of the Greek heroes who were fighting at Troy. He told them that their husbands had taken concubines whom they intended to bring home as wives. Some unhappy women committed suicide as a result of his talk. Others were encouraged to commit adultery. Thus, Nauplius was partly responsible when Clytemnestra, wife of Agamemnon, became the mistress of Aegisthus, when Aegialea, wife of Diomedes, took Cometes as a lover, and when Meda, wife of Idomeneus, abandoned her husband for Leucus. In further revenge for the death of Palamedes, Nauplius decoyed the Greeks, returning home from the war in their ships, by lighting huge beacon fires on the coast of Euboea and causing them to dash their ships against the Capharean Rocks, thinking they were heading for safe harbors. Bold sailor as he was, Nauplius at length met his death by drowning after he himself followed a false beacon and was shipwrecked.

Nausicaä (nô-sik′ā-a̲). In the *Odyssey,* the daughter of Alcinous, king of the Phaeacians. Inspired by a dream, she went with her maidens to wash on the shore near where Odysseus, who had just escaped from the sea, was sleeping. She gave him food and clothes when he appeared before her, naked and bleeding, and directed him to the palace. She discreetly advised him to go to the palace alone, rather than in her company, and told him to address himself to her mother first, rather than to her father, the king. Nausicaä has given her name as a model of discretion and tact.

Nebris (neb′ris). A fawn skin worn as a special attribute by Dionysus and his attendant train (Pan, the satyrs, the maenads, etc.), and assumed on festival occasions by priests and priestesses of Dionysus, and by his worshipers generally.

Nectar (nek′tar). In classical mythology, the drink or wine of the Olympian gods, poured out for them by Hebe and Ganymede, the cup-bearers of Zeus. It was reputed to possess wondrous life-giving properties, to impart a divine bloom, beauty, and vigor to him so fortunate as to obtain it, and to preserve all that it touched from decay and corruption. In the *Iliad,* Thetis preserved the body of Patroclus by dripping

nectar through his nostrils. Although nectar and ambrosi
are usually considered the drink and food respectively of th
gods, in ancient literature nectar is occasionally defined a
the food and ambrosia as the drink of the gods.

Neleus (nē'lūs). In Greek mythology, a son of Tyro and Posei
don, and the twin of Pelias. His mother exposed the twin
on a mountain but they were rescued by shepherds an
Neleus was nursed by a bitch. When the twins grew up, the
avenged the cruel treatment their mother had suffered at th
hands of her stepmother, but later they quarreled. Pelia
seized Iolcus and Neleus went into exile in Messenia. Ther
he captured the city of Pylus. It throve so under his manage
ment that it is sometimes said to have been founded by him
He married Chloris, the only daughter of Niobe who sur
vived when her other daughters were slain by Artemis be
cause of Niobe's arrogance. Chloris bore him 12 sons
Heracles asked Neleus to purify him for the murder o
Iphitus, but Neleus refused, and all his sons, except Nestor
supported their father's refusal and refused to receive Hera
cles. In revenge, Heracles later attacked Pylus, captured i
and burned it, and killed all the sons of Neleus except Nes
tor. Neleus himself escaped and lived to dwell again in th
rebuilt city.

Nemean Lion. In Greek mythology, a huge lion that could no
be killed with any weapon of iron, bronze, or stone. Som
say it was the offspring of Typhon and Echidna; others sa
the two-headed dog Orthrus fathered it. It dwelt in a clef
in Mount Tretus, between Mycenae and Nemea. The firs
labor of Heracles was to slay the Nemean Lion, which ha
been ravaging the countryside. He arrived at Cleonae, nea
Mount Tretus, and stopped at a peasant's hut. The peasant
one Molorchus whose son had been killed by the lion, wa
just on the point of offering a sacrifice to Hera. Heracles tol
him he intended to kill the lion, and instructed Molorchu
to wait 30 days. If at the end of that time Heracles had no
returned, then Molorchus must offer sacrifices to Heracle
the hero, but if Heracles did return, then the sacrifice shoul
be offered to Zeus. Heracles left Molorchus and proceede
to Mount Tretus. He encountered the lion but could mak
no impression on it with either his arrows, sword, or club
The lion withdrew to its lair unharmed. Heracles blocked u
one end of the double-entranced lair and went into the clef

after his prey. He seized the lion with his hands and strangled it. He slung the lion across his shoulders and returned to the house of Molorchus, where they sacrificed to Zeus together. Heracles skinned the lion and ever afterward used its hide as a cloak, with the head of the lion serving as a terrifying helmet.

Nemesis (nem′ę-sis). In Greek mythology, a daughter of Nyx and Erebus. According to some accounts, Zeus pursued Nemesis and at last, in the form of a swan, violated her. She took the egg which was produced from this union and gave it to Leda, wife of Tyndareus of Sparta. From this egg Helen, the cause of the Trojan War, was born. Nemesis is a goddess of law and justice, the personification of divine retribution, especially for human presumption. Sometimes she is represented as winged, holding an apple bough in one hand and a wheel of fortune in the other. She is also represented as being borne in a chariot drawn by griffins. By extension she is popularly regarded as a goddess of the inevitable. In the shrine of Nemesis at Rhamnus in Attica were two temples, the earlier, dating perhaps from the morrow of the first Persian invasion of 490 B.C., a modest distyle-in-antis structure, the other, a hexastyle peripteral temple by the nameless Periclean architect who built the temples of Hephaestus and Ares in Athens and of Poseidon at Sunium, begun about 436 B.C. and, probably in consequence of the Peloponnesian War (431–404 B.C.), never finished. It contained a cult statue of Parian marble by Agoracritus, fragments of which are said still to lie in the vicinity. Marble reliefs from its pedestal have survived, and are in the National Museum, Athens. In Augustus' time the temple was rededicated to the empress Livia. (JJ)

Neoptolemus (nē-op-tol′ę-mus). [Also: **Pyrrhus**.] In Greek legend, the son of Achilles and Deidamia, the daughter of Lycomedes, king of Scyrus. After the death of Achilles in the Trojan War, Helenus, a Trojan seer who was captured by the Greeks, told them that Troy could not be taken without the aid of Neoptolemus. Odysseus and Diomedes were accordingly sent to Scyrus to fetch him. He eagerly consented to accompany them in spite of the tears and entreaties of his mother to remain safe in Scyrus. Some say he was only 12 years old at the time, and his name which was originally Pyrrhus means roughly, "he went to war young." On his

arrival at Troy he went immediately into battle. Odysseu
gave him Achilles' armor, Athena sent him glory, and h
drove back Eurypylus, grandson of Heracles, who woul
surely have fired the Greek ships but for Neoptolemus
Night put an end to the battle. Next day it was resumed wit
increased ferocity. Neoptolemus led the Myrmidons agains
the Greeks and, after a fierce struggle, he killed Eurypylu
Troy would have fallen before the Greek onslaught, bu
Zeus capriciously decided to save it by veiling it in a cloud
while Apollo saved Deïphobus from Neoptolemus by hidin
him in a mist, and Thetis prevented her grandson Neop
tolemus from coming face to face with Aeneas out of respec
for Aphrodite, mother of Aeneas. Though Paris had beer
killed, the Greeks decided, with the assistance of the gods
not to try to take Troy by direct attack. Instead they pro
posed to build a great Wooden Horse and enter the cit
secretly and attack from within. Neoptolemus scorned the
plan as cowardly. He preferred to win by valor. However, he
was the first to volunteer to go in the Wooden Horse onc
the plan was adopted. Inside the city he fought ferociously
He found Priam and Hecuba before the altar of Zeus in the
courtyard of Priam's palace, killed their son Polites and ther
slashed off Priam's head with one stroke of his sword wher
the aged king feebly attacked him. He then dragged the
headless body to Achilles' tomb and left it there to rot
According to some accounts, it was Neoptolemus who
hurled Astyanax, still a "wordless babe," the son of Hector
and Andromache, from the towers of Troy. After the fall o
the city, in which he took Andromache as his captive and
concubine, the shade of Achilles appeared to him in a
dream. Achilles announced that Priam's daughter Polyxena
must be sacrificed on his tomb, or else Achilles' wrath woulc
be even greater than when Briseis was taken from him, anc
he would send disastrous storms to prevent the Greeks from
sailing. Neoptolemus related his dream and, over the pro
tests of Agamemnon who thought there had been enough
bloodshed, the sacrifice was carried out; Neoptolemus
wielded the knife as priest. Odysseus recounted the gloriou
exploits of Neoptolemus to Achilles when he saw him in the
Underworld on his way home from Troy.

Neoptolemus now set sail for Molossia, whither Helenus
had advised him to go. According to some accounts, in a

fat, fāte, fär, fâll, ȧsk, fāre; net, mē, hėr; pin, pīne; not, nōte, möve
nôr; up, lūte, pull; oi, oil; ou out; (lightened) ēlect, agǫny, ūnite

shipwreck on the way he lost the arms of Achilles, which had been awarded to Odysseus over the claims of Telamonian Ajax, and which Odysseus had given to Neoptolemus. Thetis washed the arms ashore at the tomb of Ajax on Cape Rhoeteum. Arrived in Molossia with his captive Andromache, whom, some say, he treated kindly and who bore him sons, he learned that his grandfather Peleus had been banished from his kingdom of Iolcus. He went to Iolcus, drove out the usurpers and regained the throne. Next he went to Epirus and built a city near the Oracle of Dodona. But his father's death still troubled him, and he went to the shrine of Apollo at Delphi and upbraided the god for, as he thought, causing Achilles' death. He plundered and burned the shrine and departed for Sparta, where he claimed Hermione, daughter of Menelaus. Although she had been promised to Orestes, son of Agamemnon, the Spartans gave her to Neoptolemus. But she bore him no children, and was intensely jealous of Andromache. Neoptolemus set off again to Delphi to inquire why Hermione was barren. He was told he must appease Apollo for his earlier action of destroying the shrine. Accounts of his death vary. Some say he was slain at Delphi by Apollo's priests. Others say he took the sacrifices he had offered to appease the god from the altar and was slain by Machaereus. Still others say Orestes was the instigator of his murder. In any case, his body was buried in the precincts of the temple and the Delphians made annual offerings to him as a hero. His shade was borne off to the Elysian Fields by the immortal horses, Balius and Xanthus, which had wept at the death of Patroclus and Achilles and now were united with their master in the Underworld.

Nepenthes (nĕ-pen′thēz). A plant that, mingled with wine, had an exhilarating effect, removing sorrow. In the *Odyssey*, it was an Egyptian drug which lulled sorrow for the day, and was given to Telemachus by Helen when he visited the court of Menelaus seeking information about Odysseus.

Nephele (nef′ĕ-lē). In Greek mythology, a cloud, shaped by Zeus into the form of Hera to protect Hera from the amorous advances of Ixion. By this cloud Ixion became the father of Centaurus, the sire of the centaurs. At Hera's command, Athamas later married this phantom and became the father by her of two sons, Phrixus and Leucon, and one daughter, Helle. But Athamas tired of his phantom wife and fell in love

with Ino, the daughter of Cadmus. Nephele, learning of hi
attachment, and being abandoned by Athamas, complaine
to Hera. The goddess vowed vengeance on Athamas an
carried out her vow by causing Athamas to lose Ino and a
his children.

Neptune (nep'tūn). In Roman mythology, the god of the sea
He was originally a water god and rain giver, and thus as
sociated with the growth of vegetation; but he came to be
identified by the Romans with the Greek Poseidon.

Nereids (ner'ē-idz). In Greek mythology, sea nymphs, the 5
daughters of Nereus (whence the name) and Doris. Th
most famous among them were Amphitrite, Thetis, an
Galatea. The Nereids were beautiful maidens helpful t
voyagers, and constituted the main body of the female, a
the Tritons did of the male, followers of Poseidon. The
were imagined as dancing, singing, playing musical instru
ments, wooed by the Tritons, and passing in long pro
cessions over the sea seated on hippocamps and other se
creatures. They were also held to assist mariners in distres
and were therefore especially worshiped on the islands
along the coasts, and at the mouths of rivers. Works o
ancient art represent them lightly draped or nude, in pose
characterized by undulating lines harmonizing with those o
the ocean, and often riding on sea monsters of fantasti
forms.

Nereus (ner'ūs). In Greek mythology, a sea-god; the son o
Pontus and Gaea. He was the husband of Doris, and th
father of the 50 Nereids. On the whole he was a gentle an
kindly god, but he had the power of changing his shape a
will, and like Proteus, only by holding on to him firml
through all his transformations could one force him to an
swer the questions one asked of him. Heracles caught hin
and forced him to tell him how he could obtain the golde
apples of the Hesperides.

Nerites (ner'i-tēz). In Greek mythology, a son of Nereus an
Doris, and a brother of the Nereids. Aphrodite loved him a
long as she lived in the sea. Because he would not follow he
when she left the sea, she turned him into a mussel.

Nessus (nes'us). In Greek legend, a centaur slain by Heracles
He carried Deianira, Heracles' wife, across the river Evenus
but when he attempted to ravish her, Heracles shot him wit
a poisoned arrow. Dying, Nessus secretly declared t

fat, fāte, fär, fâll, àsk, fāre; net, mē, hèr; pin, pīne; not, nōte, möve
nôr; up, lūte, pùll; oi, oil; ou out; (lightened) ēlect, agǫny, ūnit

Deianira that his blood would preserve her husband's love, and she put it in a vial and took it with her. Later she rubbed the dried blood on a sacrificial robe and sent it to Heracles, hoping thereby to regain his love which he had transferred to his captive, Iole, and to speed his return home. Heracles donned the robe to offer sacrifice; the garment, impregnated with the poisoned blood, clung to his flesh and burned him. The herald, Lichas, who brought the robe, was cast by the raging hero into the sea, and Deianira hanged herself when she learned what had happened. Heracles built and ascended a pyre, had it set on fire, and was carried off from it to Olympus, thus fulfilling a prophecy that no living man would kill him but that he would die as the result of action by a dead enemy.

Nestor (nes'tor). In Greek legend, one of the 12 children of Neleus, king of Pylus, and Chloris, only surviving daughter of Amphion and Niobe. In his youth he took part in the Calydonian Hunt. Nestor was the only one of Neleus' sons to receive Heracles when the latter came to Pylus to ask Neleus to purify him for the murder of Iphitus. Although Nestor urged his father to do it, Neleus refused. Because of his good intentions in this case, when Heracles later attacked Pylus and killed the rest of Neleus' sons, he spared Nestor and gave him the city of Messene. He was the first to swear an oath by Heracles and came to be much loved by him. But some say Nestor was away in Gerenia at the time of Heracles' attack. In Homer he is spoken of as the "Gerenian Horseman." At his father's order Nestor made war on the people of Elis, because they had stolen a chariot that Neleus had sent to compete in the games. He acquitted himself gloriously, taking rich booty, although this was his first experience of war. The Eleans retaliated, and Nestor, on foot because his father thought he was too young to control warhorses, furiously counter-attacked and cut a wide swath through their ranks. He slew an Elean and continued the battle from his dead enemy's chariot. He would have killed the Moliones but Poseidon spiritied them away in a mist. The Eleans fled, and Nestor was given the honors for this victory. A truce was arranged and funeral games were held. Nestor won all the contests except the chariot race, and he lost that only because the Moliones commited a foul. He also fought against the Arcadians and took a valiant part in the battle between the Lapiths and the centaurs. Nestor recalled the glorious deeds of his youth when he rallied the Greeks during the dark days of the Trojan War. He succeeded to the throne of Messenia and lived in Pylus, where remains of his palace have recently been found. He had already governed two generations of men, and was ruling a third, when the Trojan War started. Nevertheless he immediately joined Agamemnon's forces, to which he contributed 90 ships. He accompanied Menelaus on his journey to recruit the Greek princes, former suitors of Helen, for the war against Troy. He also went on the mission to Scyrus to fetch Achilles. He became Agamemnon's most trusted and skillful adviser in the war, his "utterance flowed from his smooth tongue sweeter than honey." His name has become a synonym for a wise old man, an elder statesman. He was a bold fighter in spite of his advanced age, and was a master of cavalry and infantry tactics. Agamemnon cherished him and said if he had but ten Nestors, the war would soon be over. Nestor and Odysseus always agreed on the course which should be followed in the conduct of the war. It was Nestor who advised the Greeks to take advantage of a truce in the fighting for burial of the dead, to dig a moat and to raise a wall as protection for the Greek ships drawn up on the beach before Troy. His sound judgment, firm and kindly character made him respected by all. In rallying or advising the Greeks he made many long speeches—the privilege of an old man—citing the magnificent exploits of his own career as a spur to the Greeks. He tried to prevent the quarrel between Agamemnon and Achilles over the captive Briseis. He told them Priam and the Trojans would rejoice if they knew how the Greek chiefs were quarreling among themselves. In this he was unsuccessful. Later he advised Agamemnon to try to resolve the quarrel by restoring Briseis to Achilles and sending him rich gifts. But Achilles refused to accept this peace offer. Nestor, however, did persuade Patroclus, the great friend of Achilles who had withdrawn from the war with him, to don Achilles' armor and lead his Myrmidons against the Trojans. Nestor took full part in the fighting. At one point when his chariot horses were wounded and became unmanageable, Nestor was in danger of his life. Antilochus, his youngest son, came to his rescue. He saved Nestor but lost his own life when Memnon at tacked and killed him. Nestor rushed to attack Memnon, but the Aethiopian told him to withdraw; he did not wish, he said, to wage war on an old man. Nestor grieved for his lost youth, and lamented that his brave heart had been "tamed by time." When, following the death of Achilles, Thetis offered his armor to the bravest of the Argives who had rescued his body, Telamonian Ajax and Odysseus both claimed Achilles' arms. Ajax suggested that Idomeneus, Nestor, and Agamemnon should decide between them. Nestor was filled with foreboding. The careless gods, he said, had laid a great woe on them, because whoever lost in the choice would be lost to the Greeks. He suggested that they should let the Trojan captives decide which one, Ajax or Odysseus, had done them the most harm. In that way the loser's wrath would be turned against the Trojans, and not against his fellow Greeks. This was done, but Nestor proved right in predicting that whoever lost would be lost to the Greeks, for Ajax commited suicide. Nestor was one of the few who had a prosperous voyage home after the war. He took the bones of the physician Machaon back to Pylus with him, and placed them in a sanctuary; many came to be healed there. Odysseus' son Telemachus, in search of news of his father, visited Pylus ten years after the Trojan War had ended. He found Nestor, now at a very advanced age, governing a prosperous kingdom, surrounded by bold, intelligent sons, and blessed by the gods; for he had always been just, courteous, valiant, and one who paid due honor to the gods. By his wife Anaxibia (or Eurydice, as Homer names her), he had two daughters and seven sons. He lived out his days peacefully and died at a very old age. Some say he lived 300 years, after Apollo added to his life span all the years that were denied his uncles, the sons of Niobe and Amphion slain by Apollo. The substantial bronze-age palace, discovered and excavated by a University of Cincinnati expedition directed by Carl W. Blegen, several miles inland from Pylus in Messenia, is plausibly believed to be Nestor's palace. The large numbers of clay tablets found there, inscribed in the syllabic script known as Linear B, essential to Ventris' decipherment of the language as an early form of Greek, are no doubt from the archives of one of Nestor's successors.

Nike (nī′kē, nē′kā). [Latin, *Victoria.*] In Greek mythology, the goddess of victory, especially victory in war. According to

Hesiod she was a daughter of Styx, whom she accompanie
to aid Zeus in his war against the Titans. After the victor
of Zeus in this struggle, Nike remained on Olympus. She wa
identified often with Athena, and by the Romans with thei
Victoria. She was regularly represented as a winged maider
usually as alighting from flight, her most frequent attribute
being a palm branch in one hand and a garland in the othe
or a fillet outstretched in both hands; sometimes she hold
a herald's staff.

Niobe. (nī'ọ-bẹ). In Greek mythology, the daughter of Tar
talus, and thus a sister of Pelops. She was the wife of Ampl
ion, king of Thebes, and the mother of seven sons and seve
daughters, and extremely proud of this fact. (Other ac
counts give various numbers for her children, ranging from
four to 20.) The Theban women, inspired by a seeress, wer
making offerings to Leto when Niobe appeared amon
them. In her arrogance she mentioned her ancestors, Tar
talus, Atlas, even Zeus, who was her father-in-law as well a
her ancestor. She spoke of the wealth and power of he
husband, her own beauty, and above all, of her sons an
daughters. She reminded the worshipers of Leto that Let
had only two children, and that both earth and sea ha
refused her a place to bear them until the tiny island c
Delos sheltered her. For these reasons she considered tha
the Thebans should worship her instead of Leto, and finall
prevailed on them to do so. Apollo and Artemis, Leto'
children, took instant revenge for their mother. Apollo sle
Niobe's sons, and Artemis killed her daughters. (Some sa
one son and one daughter were spared.) Zeus prevented th
burial of the children by turning the Thebans into ston
After nine days, the gods themselves performed the buria
rites. Niobe, distracted by grief, wandered to Mount Sipylus
where she was changed by Zeus into a marble statue whos
face is continually wet with tears.

Nisus (nī'sus). According to Greek tradition, a son of Pan
dion. He and his three brothers conquered Attica and di
vided it between them by lot. Nisus drew Nisa, afterward
called Megara, and his claim to it was confirmed by Aeacus
He founded and gave his name to the port of Nisaea. Nisu
had one purple (or golden) lock of hair, on which his lif
depended. The prophecy was that if it was cut off he woul
die. When Nisus was attacked by King Minos of Crete, hi

fat, fāte, fär, fåll, åsk, fãre; net, mē, hėr; pin, pīne; not, nōte, möv
nôr; up, lūte, pull; oi, oil; ou out; (lightened) ẹlect, agọny, ụnit

daughter Scylla fell in love with Minos, and cut the lock. Nisus died and Minos was successful, but Minos refused to take Scylla to Crete with him, as she had expected him to do, and sailed without her. She leaped into the sea and swam after his ship, pursued by her father who had been transformed into an osprey or sparrow-hawk. The body of Nisus was buried in Athens, in a tomb behind the Lyceum.

Notus (nō′tus). In Greek mythology, the south or southwest wind. Notus was the son of Astraeus or Aeolus and Eos, and the brother of Zephyrus, Boreas, and Eurus. He was the wind of fog and mists, dangerous to shepherds on the mountain tops or to mariners at sea, but a friend of thieves.

Nyctimus (nik′ti-mus). The youngest, according to Greek legend, of the 50 sons of Lycaon of Arcadia. Some say that Lycaon was a pious king, who warned his sons that the gods were ever visiting the earth in disguise to observe mortals. His proud and arrogant sons decided to test whether a visitor who claimed to be Zeus was indeed that god. They cut up their young brother Nyctimus, boiled his flesh and served it to Zeus. Zeus, instantly aware of the nature of the meat set before him, in anger turned the sons of Lycaon into wolves; or as some say, struck them dead with his thunderbolt. He restored Nyctimus to life. Others say Lycaon was as impious as his sons and took part in this means of testing Zeus and was turned into a wolf. It was because of the lawlessness and impiety of Lycaon and his sons, according to some, that Zeus determined to punish mankind by sending a great flood.

Nymphs (nimfs). Inferior divinities, imagined as beautiful maidens, eternally young, who were considered as guardian spirits of certain localities and objects, or of certain races and families, and whose existence depended upon that of the things with which they were identified. They were generally in the train or company of some other divinity of higher rank, especially with Apollo, Artemis, Dionysus, Hermes, and Pan, and were believed to be possessed of the gift of prophecy and of poetical inspiration. Nymphs of rivers, brooks, and springs were called naiads; those of mountains, oreads; those of woods and trees, dryads and hamadryads; those of the sea, Nereids. The nymphs aided humans upon occasion, and guarded the places—tree, spring, mountain, and so on—they themselves inhabited. The nymphs were

wooed and won by gods and mortals alike and from ther
sprang many heroes. They also played a part in many of th
activities of the gods and in general were a protective influ
ence. Groves and grottoes sacred to the nymphs throughou
Greece received offerings of lambs, milk, oil, and wine.

Nysa (nī′sạ). The spot to which the infant Dionysus was ser
by Zeus to protect him from the wrath of Hera. Accordin
to Greek mythology, the young god was nurtured in a cav
in Nysa by nymphs who fed him on honey. The sacred plac
has never been definitely located and is probably mythica
but it was claimed by many areas where the vine is cultivatec
It has been variously named as a mountain in Thrace, a cit
on a mountain in India, a city in Caria about 45 miles E c
Ephesus, Mount Helicon in Greece, and a remote place i
Aethiopia. Nysa was also the name of one of the nymph
who cared for Dionysus.

Nysaean Nymphs or *Nyseides* (nī-sē′ạn, nī-sē′i-dēz). Th
nymphs who cared for the infant Dionysus on Mount Nys;
after Ino, his mother's sister who had first cared for him
died. To hide him from Hera, who was jealous because h
was the child of Zeus by Semele, the nymphs covered hir
with ivy leaves. This plant was ever afterward associated wit
Dionysus. The Nysaean nymphs, Bromie, Cisseis, Erato
Eriphia, Macris, Nysa, and Polyhymno, were rewarded b
being placed among the stars by Zeus, after which the
became known as the Hyades.

Nyx (niks). In Greek mythology, the daughter of Chaos. Sh
was the goddess of night, a very ancient cosmological pei
sonification. By Erebus, her brother, she was the mother o
Hypnos (Sleep), Thanatos (Death), Moros (Doom), Ce
(Fate), Dreams, Momus (Blame or Mockery), Oïzys (Misery)
the Hesperides who guarded the Golden Apples, the thre
Fates (Lachesis, Atropos, and Clotho), Nemesis, Decei
Friendship, Old Age, and Strife. Nyx, riding in a chariot an
accompanied by stars, led forth the brothers Sleep an
Death at the close of day, and was a force for both good an
evil for man, as she brought sleep and rest or darkness an
death. Nyx was even reverenced and feared by Zeus, whon
she instructed. When Sleep, bribed by Hera, lulled Zeus s
that Hera could rouse a great storm and shipwreck Heracle
on the isle of Cos, Zeus on awaking threatened to hurl Slee|
down to Erebus. But Nyx intervened, and Zeus bowed to he

fat, fāte, fär, fâll, ȧsk, fāre; net, mē, hėr; pin, pīne; not, nōte, möv
nôr; up, lūte, pùll; oi, oil; ou out; (lightened) ẹlect, agǫny, ūnit

will and spared Sleep. Nyx had little or no cult worship, but was revered for her oracular powers, which were made known from a cave.

Oceanids (ō-sē′a̯-nidz). In Greek mythology, 3000 ocean-nymphs, daughters of the sea-god Oceanus, and his consort Tethys.

Oceanus (ō-sē′a̯-nus). In Greek mythology, a Titan, the son of Gaea and Uranus. He lived with his wife Tethys in the farthest west, and never attended the meetings of the gods on Olympus, or took part in their quarrels. He and Tethys were the parents of 3000 sons, who were the river-gods of all the rivers of the world, and of 3000 daughters, the sea- and river-nymphs. Oceanus was the oldest of the Titans, and on the fall of Cronus submitted to the sovereignty of Zeus. Oceanus and Tethys brought up Hera, and to them she fled during the war between the Titans and the gods, in which Oceanus took no part. In art Oceanus was represented as an aged, bearded man, sometimes with bull's horns on his head or with a garland of crab's claws, and surrounded by creatures of the deep.

Ocnus (ok′nus). In Greek mythology, the droll of the Underworld and personification of delay or futile effort. He is described as forever plaiting a straw rope, which his ass devours as fast as he makes it; or sometimes he is shown loading the ass with sticks which keep falling off.

Ocyrrhoë (ō-sir′ō-ē). In Greek mythology, a daughter of Chiron and the nymph Chariclo. She was named for the river on whose banks she was born. She had learned the healing and hunting arts of her father, and was also endowed with the gift of prophecy. When Asclepius, the infant son of Apollo, was brought to be reared by Chiron, Ocyrrhoë prophesied that he would bring healing and health to all the world; that he would even be able to restore the dead to life; that by so doing he would rouse the envy of the gods, who would cause Zeus to strike him dead with his thunderbolt;

obscured) errant, ardent, actor; ch, chip; g, go; th, thin; ŦH, then; y, you;
variable) ḍ as d or j, ṣ as s or sh, ṭ as t or ch, ẓ as z or zh.

and that after being a lifeless corpse he would be immortalized and thus twice fulfill his destiny. She also foretold the sufferings that would befall Chiron as a result of an accidental wound from one of Heracles' arrows. Ocyrrhoë bewailed her ability to know the future, for by her own gift she knew that she incurred the wrath of heaven and would be punished by the gods. Her foreknowledge was correct. The gods, angered because she correctly predicted the future, transformed her into a mare and gave her the name Hippo

Odysseus (ō-dis′ūs, ō-dis′ē-us). [Latin: *Ulixes, Ulysses.*] One of the leading Greek heroes in the Trojan War. He not only survived the war but eventually, after ten years of wandering, returned safely to his home in Ithaca. He has many epithets; "wily," "crafty," "Odysseus of many devices," are a few of them. In Homer he is represented as a brave man of great wisdom and ingenuity, always ready with a stratagem to save the day and never wanting in sage counsel or valor. But Pindar thinks that Odysseus owes his reputation to Homer, and that he was, in fact, merely "a supple liar." In later literature Odysseus often appears as unscrupulous, shrewd, and deceitful. Ordinarily in Homer the heroes are described as "glorious," "man-slayer," "flawless," or in other abstract terms, but Odysseus receives some physical description. He had red hair and, though he had broad shoulders so that when he was seated he looked as mighty as any man, he had short legs and showed when he stood up that he was somewhat under the expected height. Odysseus passed as the son of Laertes and Anticlea, but some say that Sisyphus was his father. His name, which means "the angry one," was given to him by his grandfather Autolycus, father of Anticlea. Autolycus so named his grandson because he himself had made many enemies in his lifetime and expected Odysseus to be a target for some of them. In his boyhood Odysseus visited Autolycus on Mount Parnassus and received rich gifts from him. During a boar hunt on this visit he was wounded in the leg and bore the scar the rest of his life. Odysseus went, as did many of the heroes and princes of Greece, to the court of Tyndareus at Sparta. Unlike the others, he was not a candidate for the hand of Tyndareus' daughter Helen. He wanted to marry Penelope, the daughter of Icarius. Tyndareus feared to choose from among the many suitors for Helen's hand, lest in selecting one he

fat, fāte, fär, fâll, ȧsk, fãre; net, mē, hėr; pin, pīne; not, nōte, mōve; nôr; up, lūte, pùll; oi, oil; ou out; (lightened) ēlect, agọny, ūnite,

offend the others and make powerful enemies. Odysseus
proposed a way for him to choose one suitor without an-
tagonizing the others. It was to make them all swear, on the
joints of a dismembered horse, that they would come to the
aid of the man who became Helen's husband in the event
that any ill should come to him as a result of his marriage
to her. Tyndareus adopted his suggestion, the suitors took
the oath, and Helen was given to Menelaus. In return for
this good advice Tyndareus agreed to help Odysseus win
Penelope. Some say he won her as the result of a foot race
that Tyndareus arranged for him to win. In any event, he
married Penelope and took her with him to his home in
Ithaca. There he ruled wisely and won the devotion of his
subjects. Penelope bore him a son, Telemachus. While his
son was still an infant Paris abducted Helen, her former
suitors were called upon to honor their oath, and all was set
in motion for a great expedition to Troy to recover her.
Agamemnon, brother of Menelaus and the commander of
the expedition, learned that it could not succeed without
Odysseus. He and Menelaus, accompanied by Palamedes,
went to Ithaca to secure his services. Odysseus had been
warned by an oracle that if he went to Troy, he would be
gone 20 years and would return alone and destitute. When
the envoys arrived, they found Odysseus plowing with an ox
and an ass yoked together, and flinging salt over his shoulders into the furrows. On his head was a Phrygian peasant
cap. He pretended not to recognize his visitors and gave
every sign that he had taken leave of his senses. But Palamedes suspected him of trickery. He seized the infant
Telemachus and flung him in front of Odysseus' advancing
plow. Odysseus immediately turned out to avoid injuring his
son, and confessed that he had feigned madness to escape
going to Troy. He was now compelled to join the Greeks in
their expedition, but he never forgave Palamedes for unmasking him, and when the Greeks were later gathered
before Troy, he succeeded in having Palamedes accused of
treachery and brought about his death.

Calchas the seer foretold that Troy could not be taken
without Achilles. Odysseus was one of the ambassadors who
went to Scyrus to fetch him. Some say Achilles had been
hidden away among the women of Lycomedes' court by his
mother Thetis to prevent him from going to the war. Odys-

seus appeared at the court and asked for him. Lycomedes le
him search the palace but Achilles was not to be found
Odysseus now asked if he might make presents to th
women of the court. He displayed girdles, jewels, and suc
ornaments as would appeal to women. As the wome
crowded around to look at his gifts Odysseus caused a trum
pet blast and a clatter of arms to be heard from the court
yard. Instantly one of the young women seized the swor
and shield which Odysseus had cunningly included in th
gifts he was displaying, and made ready to fight. Thus wa
Achilles unmasked and brought to join the Greeks. But oth
ers say Odysseus and Nestor found Achilles not at Lyco
medes' court, but at his father's court, that Peleus readil
consented to let his son join the Greek expedition and sen
Achilles off with good advice and the company of his tuto
Phoenix and his dear friend Patroclus. When the Greek flee
was wind-bound at Aulis and Agamemnon learned that onl
the sacrifice of his daughter Iphigenia could appease Arte
mis and cause favorable winds, it was Odysseus, according
to some, who devised the scheme of sending for Iphigeni
on the pretext that she was to be married to Achilles, an
so persuaded Clytemnestra to let her come to the Gree
camp, where she was sacrificed. The Greeks then had favora
ble winds and put to sea. They stopped at the island o
Lesbos where Odysseus wrestled the king, Philomelides
and overcame him. Then they went to Tenedos. At some
point before the actual siege of Troy Odysseus accompanie
Menelaus to Troy as an evoy to seek the voluntary return o
Helen. This mission failed. In the conduct of the war before
the walls of Troy Odysseus and Nestor were Agamemnon's
most trusted advisers. No matter how hopeless the Greek
situation appeared, Odysseus would not hear of giving up
and returning home. On his advice a rampart was built to
protect the Greek ships on the beach. He was a member of
the embassy which tried to patch up the disastrous quarrel
between Agamemnon and Achilles, as a result of which
Achilles had withdrawn from the fighting. This embassy was
unsuccessful, and the Greeks suffered catastrophic losses
without the aid of Achilles. With Diomedes, Odysseus made
a scouting raid on the Trojan camp. He killed the Thracian
Rhesus, who had just come up to the aid of the Trojans, and
seized his marvelous horses, because there was a prophecy

that if the horses of Rhesus grazed on Trojan pastures and drank the waters of the Scamander River, Troy could not be taken. In furious fighting the next day Odysseus was wounded and cut off by the Trojans, but was rescued by Menelaus. In this engagement many of the leading Greek heroes were wounded and the Trojans breached the wall protecting the ships. Agamemnon proposed that the Greeks give up the struggle, put to sea in their galleys, and return to Greece. Odysseus scorned this proposal and successfully urged the continuance of the war. After the death of Achilles, Thetis decreed that her son's armor, made by Hephaestus, be awarded to the bravest of the Greeks. Only Odysseus and Telamonian Ajax dared claim them. Ajax was always the enemy of Odysseus. He said Odysseus fought with words, but when swords were flying Odysseus disappeared. He reminded Odysseus that he had sought to avoid coming to Troy in the first place. For his part, Ajax wished that he had not come, for it was on the advice of Odysseus that wounded Philoctetes, possessor of the bows and arrows of Heracles, had been abandoned alone on the island of Lemnos, and it was due to the machinations of Odysseus that Palamedes had been destroyed. He accused Odysseus of cowardice for keeping his ships in the center of the line, where there was less danger, while Ajax had his ships on the exposed flank. But Ajax despaired of winning by speech, for in that field Odysseus clearly dominated; therefore, he challenged Odysseus to duel with him for the armor of Achilles. Odysseus replied that wisdom increases strength. He listed his contributions to the war and declined to duel with Ajax on the ground that he was still suffering from his wound. Agamemnon did not know how to choose between these two valiant and valuable warriors. Nestor mourned that the careless gods had sent them a great evil by making them choose between two such great men, as whoever lost in the choice would be lost to the Greeks. According to some accounts, Nestor suggested that the Greeks allow the captured Trojans to decide which of the two had done them the most injury, for perhaps thus the wrath of the loser would be turned against the Trojans rather than against his fellow Greeks. The decision of the captive Trojans caused the arms of Achilles to be awarded to Odysseus. Others say the arms were awarded as a result of a secret vote of the Greek leaders. Ajax was infuriated with the decision, and sought to kill Odysseus, but Athena inspired him with madness and he captured a ram under the impression that it was Odysseus, and flogged it unmercifully. Restored to his senses, Ajax was so appalled and humiliated by what he had done that he committed suicide. According to some accounts, Agamemnon refused burial to the body of Ajax, and ordered it exposed as prey for the birds, but he was persuaded by Odysseus to allow the burial on the ground that Ajax had made valiant contributions to the Greeks, and with the warning on the part of Odysseus that yesterday's enemy might become tomorrow's friend. He offered to help in the burial rites for Ajax, and said he would never have claimed the armor of Achilles if he had realized how much it meant to Ajax. Later Odysseus gave the armor to Neoptolemus, the son of Achilles.

When it was learned that Troy could not be taken without the bows and arrows of Heracles, Odysseus went with Diomedes to Lemnos to fetch Philoctetes, the possessor of the bow and arrows. Philoctetes had been abandoned on Lemnos at the suggestion of Odysseus when the Greeks were on their way to Troy, because he had suffered a noisome wound. Now when Odysseus appeared to ask him to go to Troy, Philoctetes' first impulse was to shoot him. But such were the persuasive powers of Odysseus, and the influence of the gods, that Philoctetes agreed to accompany him to Troy. Again with Diomedes, Odysseus went to Scyrus to fetch Neoptolemus, son of Achilles, to Troy, because an oracle said Troy could not be taken without him. On learning that only Helenus knew the oracles that protected Troy, Odysseus captured him and brought him to the Greek camp. Some say Odysseus secretly entered Troy with Diomedes to steal the Palladium, a sacred image which Helenus said protected the city as long as it remained in the citadel. Some say Diomedes climbed on Odysseus' shoulders to scale the wall of the city and got the Palladium himself, and that as the two were returning to the Greek camp Odysseus thought to kill Diomedes and gain the credit for securing the Palladium for himself. He stepped behind Diomedes, but Diomedes saw the glint of his naked sword in the moonlight as he lifted it to strike him, whirled around and disarmed Odysseus, and drove him with the flat of his sword back to the Greek camp.

fat, fāte, fär, fȧll, ȧsk, fãre; net, mē, hėr; pin, pīne; not, nōte, mȯve nôr; up, lūte, pu̇ll; oi, oil; ou out; (lightened) ĕlect, agǫny, ūnite

And some say Odysseus, disguised in rags and matted with blood, entered Troy secretly and alone on another occasion, was recognized by Helen and Hecuba, questioned by them, and allowed to return unharmed to the Greek camp. Again, some say that the idea for the stratagem of the Wooden Horse by which Troy was finally taken came from Odysseus, but others say he merely took the credit for it, us usual. All agree that he was one of those who entered Troy in the Wooden Horse. In the sack of Troy he accompanied Menelaus to the house of Deïphobus, where Helen was, and had a part in the slaying of Deïphobus. According to some accounts, it was Odysseus who persuaded Agamemnon, against his will, to sacrifice Polyxena on the tomb of Achilles, and to dash Astyanax, the young son of Hector, to his death from the walls of Troy. Odysseus took Hecuba as his share in the spoils of the city, some say to prevent her from revealing his craven attitude when he secretly entered Troy and was discovered by her and Helen.

After the sack of Troy Odysseus departed with his ships for his home in Ithaca. At the outset of his voyage he was driven by a storm to the coast of Thrace, north of the island of Lemnos. He plundered the town of Ismarus, belonging to the Cicones, where he lost a number of his followers. Next he was driven to the country of the Lotophagi (the Lotus-Eaters) on the coast of Libya; then to the goat island, which lay a day's voyage to the north of the Lotophagi. Leaving behind all his ships except one, he sailed to the neighboring island of the Cyclopes (which some locate on the W coast of Sicily), where with 12 companions he entered the cave of the one-eyed Cyclops, Polyphemus, a son of Poseidon. Polyphemus devoured six of the intruders, and kept Odysseus and the others prisoners. Odysseus made Polyphemus drunk with wine, put out his one eye with a burning pole, and escaped with the remnant of his companions by concealing himself and them under the bellies of the sheep which the blinded Cyclops let out of his cave (he ran his hands over their backs, but forgot that his enemies might be clinging to their bellies). Thenceforth, however, Odysseus was pursued by the anger of Poseidon, who sought to avenge the injury inflicted on his son. After further adventures, in which he lost all his ships except one, he arrived at the island of Aeaea, inhabited by the sorceress Circe. He remained with her a year and she bore him, according to some accounts, three sons—Agrius, Latinus, and Telegonus. At her insistence he made a journey to Hades, where he consulted the shade of the seer Tiresias. He then sailed by the island of the Sirens (which some locate near the W coast of Italy), passed between Scylla and Charybdis, and arrived at Trinacria, the island of Apollo, or of the Sun. Here his companions killed some of the sacred oxen belonging to the god with the result that they were all drowned in a shipwreck after leaving the island. Odysseus escaped with his life to the island of Ogygia, inhabited by the nymph Calypso, with whom he lived eight years. She bore him twin sons, Nausithous and Nausinous. Leaving Ogygia on a raft built with the assistance of the nymph, he was again shipwrecked, but reached the island of the Phaeacians, where he was discovered naked by Nausicaä, the daughter of their king Alcinous. Clothed, and presented at court, he hold his story. He was carried to Ithaca by the hospitable Phaeacians, and after slaying the suitors of his wife Penelope who had been wasting his property during his long absence, was welcomed by his wife and subjects. He now sacrificed to Hades, Persephone, and Tiresias, and on the advice which Tiresias had given him when he visited him in Hades, he set out to appease Poseidon. He went on foot, carrying an oar, until he came to a people who had never seen the sea. They asked him why he was carrying a winnowing fan. Here he set up the oar and sacrificed to Poseidon. Some say he married Callidice, the queen of this land, which was Thesprotia, and became its king and had a son by his new wife. When she died he gave the kingdom to his son, Polypoetes, and returned to Ithaca, which Penelope had been ruling in his second absence in the name of their young son, Poliporthis. An oracle had foretold that Odysseus would meet his death at the hands of his son. For this reason he banished Telemachus. Tiresias had added to this prophecy that Odysseus' death would come from the sea. Now Telegonus, his son by Circe, came searching for his father. He landed on Ithaca, unaware that it was his father's island home. Odysseus, equally unaware that the apparent raider was his son, rushed to the shore to repel him. Telegonus killed him with his spear, which was tipped with the spine of a sting ray, and thus the prophecies were fulfilled.

fat, fāte, fär, fâll, àsk, fāre; net, mē, hèr; pin, pīne; not, nōte, möve, nôr; up, lūte, pùll; oi, oil; ou out; (lightened) ȩ̄lect, agȯny, ūnite;

Oeax (ē'aks). In Greek legend, a son of Nauplius and Clymene, and the brother of Palamedes, the inventor. The brothers joined the Greek army which attacked Troy. When Palamedes was killed, through the machinations of Odysseus, Oeax informed his father of the murder by writing the message on oars, which he dropped into the sea. He and his father became the implacable enemies of Agamemnon, because he had refused satisfaction for the death of Palamedes. In his scheme for revenge, Oeax told Clytemnestra that Agamemnon was bringing home Cassandra, and provoked her to murder Agamemnon. His enmity extended to Agamemnon's children, Orestes and Electra.

Oedipus (ed'i-pus, ē'di-). In Greek legend, the son of Laius, king of Thebes, and Jocasta, and a descendant of Cadmus. Because of an unfavorable oracle, Laius caused his son's feet to be pierced with a spike and bound when he was born (this accounts for his name, which means "swollen-footed"), and ordered him to be exposed on Mount Cithaeron. However, the shepherd into whose hands he gave the infant was too tender-hearted to leave him to die on the mountainside. Instead, he gave him to a shepherd from another district. The second shepherd gave him to Polybus, king of Corinth. Polybus and his wife Merope (or Periboea), being childless, brought Oedipus up as their own son. When he was grown to manhood, Oedipus was taunted about his origin. Hints were thrown out that he was not the true son of his father. Oedipus questioned Polybus. The king protested and sought to punish those who had made the accusations but, still uneasy in his mind, Oedipus secretly set out to consult the oracle at Delphi. To his horror the priestess told him that he would slay his father and sire children on his mother. Determined to prevent the fulfillment of this awful prophecy Oedipus did not return to Corinth but made his way to a new land. On his way from Delphi, where three roads crossed, Oedipus met an older man in a chariot, who ordered him out of the road. Oedipus refused to move and a quarrel arose. Oedipus was struck and defended himself. The stranger, angry in his turn, lashed out at Oedipus with his goad. Enraged, Oedipus set on him and killed him and all his train, save one who escaped. He then proceeded on his way. On the outskirts of the city of Thebes he was stopped by a Sphinx. This monster had been terrorizing Thebes by stop-

ping passers-by and compelling them to answer a riddle:
What goes on four legs in the morning, two legs at noon,
and three legs in the evening? Whoever failed to give the
correct answer, and all had failed, was slain by the Sphinx.
Oedipus, when the riddle was put to him, answered that it

OEDIPUS AND THE SPHINX
Red-figured Attic amphora, late 5th century B.C.
Museum of Fine Arts, Boston

was man: In infancy he crawls on all fours, in youth he walks
upright on his two legs, and in the evening of his life he
needs the aid of a staff. On hearing the correct answer the
Sphinx killed herself and Thebes was freed of her ravages.
When Oedipus arrived in the city, he learned that the king
had recently been murdered, and that his successor, his
brother-in-law Creon, had proclaimed that whoever vanquished the Sphinx should become king of Thebes and
marry the former king's widow, Jocasta. Oedipus was accordingly made king and married Jocasta. By her he became
the father of two sons, Eteocles and Polynices, and of two
daughters, Antigone and Ismene. Oedipus and Jocasta
dwelt in perfect harmony and Thebes prospered. Then a
plague struck the city. Cattle and men died, no young were
born, the sound of weeping filled the streets. Oedipus sent
Creon to the oracle at Delphi to learn the cause of the
plague. On his return Creon reported that the plague would
be lifted when the murderer of Laius was found and punished. Oedipus now issued a proclamation decreeing that

fat, fāte, fär, fäll, ȧsk, fãre; net, mē, hėr; pin, pīne; not, nōte, möve,
nôr; up, lūte, pu̇ll; oi, oil; ou out; (lightened) e̯lect, agǫny, ūnite;

whoever had knowledge of the murderer and sheltered him would be shunned by all Thebans and subject to banishment. He called down all sorts of terrible punishments on the murderer and on those who knew of him and concealed their knowledge. After some time the seer Tiresias was brought to the city on the advice of Creon. Tiresias at first refused to do more than hint at the identity of the murderer but, goaded by the anger of Oedipus, at last revealed that it was Oedipus himself who had murdered Laius. The tragic story gradually unfolded. The shepherd who supposedly had exposed Oedipus as an infant was found and confessed that he had given the child to a shepherd of Corinth. News came from Corinth of the death of Polybus, and at the same time, the fact that he was not the real father of Oedipus was revealed. All of the pieces of the story fell into place and it became horrifyingly clear that the prophecy the priestess at Delphi had made to Oedipus had come true: He had slain his father and become the father of his own sisters and brothers by his mother. Jocasta hanged herself when she learned the truth. Oedipus despairingly blinded himself and as a consequence of his own order, was shunned by all the people of Thebes. With his daughter Antigone to guide him, he left Thebes and wandered about Greece, endlessly pursued by the Furies. He came at last to Colonus in Attica. There he was befriended by Theseus and at last found peace in death. He was buried and mourned by Theseus and the faithful Antigone. Some say that Oedipus continued to rule Thebes after he learned of the crimes he had unwittingly committed, that he married again, that it was this second wife who bore his four children, and that he finally fell in battle and was honored with funeral games. Others say that once, after his misfortunes, his sons gave him the slave's portion of a sacrificial victim–the haunch, rather than the shoulder. To punish them for their scorn, he laid on them a curse that they should divide their inheritance by the sword. Oedipus was worshiped as a hero after his death. According to some accounts, his bones were treasured as the guardians of the country's safety. Some say the resting-place of his bones was a secret. Others say his grave was in the sanctuary of Demeter at Eteonus, and still others say his bones were taken to Athens.

(obscured) errạnt, ardẹnt, actọr; ch, chip; g, go; th, thin; ᵺH, then; y, you;
(variable) ḍ as d or j, ṣ as s or sh, ṭ as t or ch, ẓ as z or zh.

Oeneus (ē′nūs). In Greek legend, a son of Portheus. He was king of Calydon in Aetolia. He married Althaea and was the father of Toxeus, Meleager, Tydeus, Deianira, and Gorge, although some accounts say Ares was the father of Meleager and Dionysus the father of Deianira. Dionysus gave him a vine plant and he is said to have been the first to cultivate grapes. Bellerophon visited Oeneus at his court and they exchanged guest gifts of lasting friendship, a fact that assumed great significance for their respective grandsons, Glaucus and Diomedes, in the Trojan War. Agamemnon and Menelaus were sheltered by Oeneus for a time after their father's death. Because he neglected to offer first fruits to Artemis when he made offerings to the other gods and goddesses, the goddess sent a savage boar to lay waste his land. The boar was slain by Meleager in a hunt in which many great heroes took part. Afterward Artemis inspired a war over possession of the boar's hide to harass the Calydonians. In his later days Oeneus was driven from his throne by rebels and restored to it by his grandson Diomedes.

Oenomaus (ē-nọ-mā′us). In Greek legend, a son of Ares and a nymph, or of Ares and the Pleiad, Sterope. He was a king of Pisa and Elis. His wife Sterope, a daughter of Acrisius, bore him three sons, Leucippus, Hippodamus, and Dysponteus, and one daughter, Hippodamia. Either because he was in love with her himself or because he feared one of her offspring would cause his death, he determined not to let her marry. However, he did not say this was the case. He said he would wed Hippodamia to the suitor who could beat him in a chariot race from Olympia to the Isthmus of Corinth. If Oenomaus, who gave each suitor a head start while he sacrificed at Olympia, overtook the suitor in the race, he flung his spear into the suitor's back. But if a suitor won, Oenomaus would have to die and Hippodamia would be given to the victor. However, since Oenomaus' horses were given to him by Ares and were the swiftest in Greece, Oenomaus always won. He had already defeated 12 or 13 suitors and nailed their heads to the door of his palace when Pelops, son of Tantalus, came to race for Hippodamia's hand. Pelops' horses and winged chariot had been given him by Poseidon, but to make absolutely sure of winning, he bribed Oenomaus' charioteer Myrtilus, a son of Hermes.

Myrtilus substituted wax pins in the axles of Oenomaus' chariot. As the racers neared the goal on the Isthmus, Pelops, with Hippodamia in the chariot beside him, was in the lead. Oenomaus in a furious attempt to overtake him was suddenly cast out of his chariot. The wheels had flown off. He was dragged along, tangled in the reins, to his death. But some say Pelops won and Oenomaus killed himself, or that Pelops, on winning, killed him. But before Oenomaus died, he put a curse on Myrtilus for betraying him and prayed that Myrtilus would die at the hands of Pelops.

Oenone (ē-nō'nē). In Greek legend, a nymph of Mount Ida. A daughter of the river-god Oeneus, she was versed in the arts of healing, which had been taught her by Apollo, and in the arts of divination, which she learned from Rhea. She was loved by Paris when he lived as a simple shepherd on Mount Ida, and bore him a son, Corythus. When Paris returned to his father's palace and later decided to sail to Sparta, Oenone begged him not to leave her, but her pleas were unavailing. As she said goodby to him, she told him to return to her if he was ever wounded, as she alone could heal him. Toward the end of the Trojan War he did return, grievously wounded. Oenone, jealous of Helen and maddened by Paris' desertion, scornfully told him to get Helen to heal him. She knew Helen could not do this, and in the night Oenone ran through the forest to find Paris. Some say her love for him compelled her to seek him out to cure him. But she arrived too late. Paris was already dead and lying on his funeral pyre. Muffling her face in grief, Oenone flung herself on the lighted pyre, clasped Paris in her arms, and died in the flames with him. Their ashes were mixed in one urn and buried beneath a huge mound. Two pillars were erected on it, facing in opposite directions, for the ancient jealousy persisted in the marble.

Oenopion (ē-nō'pi-on). In Greek mythology, a son of Dionysus and Ariadne, and a king of Chios, which he had inherited from Rhadamanthys of Crete. He was the father, by the nymph Helice, of Merope. He promised his daughter to Orion in return for killing the wild beasts of Chios, but kept delaying the marriage. Orion assaulted Merope, while under the spell of too much wine, and Oenopion punished him by blinding him as he slept. When Orion returned from the East with his sight restored Oenopion hid from him in

(obscured) errạnt, ardẹnt, actọr; ch, chip; g, go; th, thin; ꜰʜ, then; y, you;
(variable) ḏ as d or j, ṣ as s or sh, ṭ as t or ch, ẓ as z or zh.

a palace under the earth built for him by Hephaestus. Oenopion had been taught how to make wine by his father
Dionysus, and it was he who first realized that it was wise to
mix the wine with water for drinking purposes.

Old Man of the Sea. In Greek mythology, a name for Nereus,
the god who came to be thought of as the god of the Mediterranean, as distinct from Oceanus, the personification of
the outer sea. This title or name is also given to Phorcys.

Olen (ō'len). A mythical poet of Lycia. He was reputed to be
the first to sing hymns to the gods in connection with the
worship of Apollo at Delphi. To him was attributed the
legend of Apollo's visit to the Hyperboreans.

Olympians (ọ-lim'pi-ạnz). The 12 high gods of Greek mythology, so named because they dwelt on Mount Olympus.
They are usually counted as follows: Zeus, the supreme god
who ruled over all; Hera, his consort and sister; Hestia,
another sister; Poseidon, his brother; the four daughters of
Zeus, Athena, Hebe, Artemis, and Aphrodite; his four sons,
Hermes, Ares, Apollo, and Hephaestus. Demeter and
Dionysus are sometimes added to the original 12, and sometimes also Heracles.

Omphale (om'fạ-lē). In Greek legend, a daughter of Iardanus.
She was the wife of Tmolus, king in Lydia, and some say she
was the mother of Tantalus by Tmolus. On the death of her
husband, Omphale became ruler of Lydia. It was she who
bought Heracles as a slave when he was ordered to sell
himself to expiate the murder of Iphitus. He performed
many services for her, in the course of which he captured the
Cercopes, and killed Syleus, Lityerses, and a serpent that
was ravaging the countryside. In gratitude, Omphale, who
had now learned his real identity, freed him and became his
mistress. She bore him several sons, among them Lamus.
When Heracles had completed his service, some say at the
end of a year, others say at the end of three years, Omphale
gave him rich gifts and he returned to Tiryns. Some say that
Omphale forced Heracles to dress in women's clothes and
to perform women's work. This was a story spread by Pan.
Heracles and Omphale did sometimes exchange their
clothes, as it amused the queen to behold the brawny Heracles in her delicate garments. On one occasion when they
were dressed in each other's clothes, Pan sought to ravish
Omphale as she slept in a cave with Heracles. Feeling the

fat, fāte, fär, fåll, ȧsk, fāre; net, mē, hėr; pin, pīne; not, nōte, möve,
nôr; up, lūte, pùll; oi, oil; ou out; (lightened) ẹlect, agọny, ụnite;

silken garments in the dark, he mistakenly attacked Heracles and was kicked across the cave for his pains.

Omphalos (om′fạ-los). A sacred stone in the temple of Apollo at Delphi, believed by the Greeks to mark the "navel" or exact centerpoint of the earth. This point was located by Zeus. He released two eagles in opposite directions. They flew until they met, at Delphi, and thus determined the center of the earth. The stone set up to mark the spot was the one Rhea gave to Cronus to swallow in the place of her new-born son, Zeus; for it was the custom of Cronus to swallow his children as soon as they were born. When Zeus

APOLLO SEATED ON THE OMPHALOS
Red-figured Greek vase

grew up, he forced Cronus to disgorge his sisters and brothers and the stone. It was then set up at Delphi and daily anointed with oil. Extant representations show it as a stone of a conical shape, often covered with a kind of network called *agrenon,* similar in character to the sacred garment so called, or wreathed with votive fillets. The Delphic or Pythian Apollo is often represented as seated on the omphalos, in his chief sanctuary, and statues have been found, the feet of which rest on a truncated omphalos.

Oneiros or **Oniros** (ọ-nī′ros). The personification of dreams. He was a winged god who dwelt in the land of the sunset.

Opheltes (ọ-fel′tēz). In Greek mythology, a son of Lycurgus, king of Nemea. He was left alone by his nurse Hypsipyle, former queen of Lemnos, while she went to get water for the Seven against Thebes, who had stopped in Nemea on their way to Thebes. While she was gone, Opheltes was bitten by a serpent and died. The Nemean Games were celebrated in his honor.

Ophion (ọ-fī′on). In Greek mythology, a great serpent who was created, some say, by Eurynome, and with her was the first lord of creation. They created the Titans, according to some accounts, and ruled them from Olympus until they were forced to yield to Cronus and Rhea; after this they disappeared into the sea.

Oreads (ō′rē̠-ạdz). Nymphs of the mountains. They were especially associated with Artemis because they dwelt on the mountains where she hunted, and were her companions in hunting, dancing and frolicking. Because of their association with Artemis they were particularly honored by hunters. They were also connected with the worship of Pan and as such were honored by shepherds.

Orestes (ọ-res′tēz). In Greek legend, a son of Agamemnon and Clytemnestra, and the brother of Electra and Iphigenia. Before Agamemnon returned victorious from Troy and was slain by Clytemnestra and her lover Aegisthus, Orestes had been spirited away to Strophius, king of Phocis. In the eighth year following the murder of Agamemnon he returned in secret to Mycenae, accompanied by his friend Pylades, to avenge his father's death. He went to his father's grave, left offerings on it of locks of his hair, and prayed to his father's spirit for his sanction in the deed he was about to commit. Electra, who had been kept in a state of misery by Clytemnestra and Aegisthus, and who constantly accused her mother of adultery and murder, publicly longed for the return of Orestes to avenge their father's death. Orestes revealed himself to his sister and told her he had come at the command of Apollo to kill Clytemnestra and Aegisthus. He was greatly troubled by the deed he was planning, as to slay one's own kin was the most heinous crime in the sight of gods and men. He found that Electra had no such doubts about it, as the gods also laid an obligation on sons to avenge their fathers. Caught in the dilemma of angering the gods if he failed to avenge his father's death, and of incurring the wrath of the Furies if he killed his mother, Orestes wavered. Electra and Pylades stiffened his will to carry out the command of Apollo and to shed blood for the blood that had been shed. By a ruse he secured entrance to the palace and came face to face with his mother. She did not recognize him at first but when he made himself known to her, she understood what was about to happen. Despite her pleas to spare the mother who had given him life and despite his own doubts, he killed her, calling the gods to witness that he was obeying a command of Apollo and reminding them of the horrible crimes she had committed. He also killed her para- mour, as Hermes had told Aegisthus he would do many

ORESTES SLAYING AEGISTHUS
Red-figured Attic pelike, early 5th century B.C.
Vienna

years before, if Aegisthus persisted in his plan to seduce Clytemnestra and destroy Agamemnon. The murder of Aegisthus could readily be justified as a proper fate for an adulterer. But there was no escape from the avenging Furies who immediately began hounding Orestes for the murder of his mother. After great pain and suffering, and spells of madness, in one of which he bit off his own finger to appease the Furies, he felt that he had been purified of his guilt by his sufferings. He had been purified many times in this pe- riod but to no avail, for the Furies still pursued him. He now made his way to Athens to stand trial before the Areopagus.

Apollo was his advocate. The chief of the Furies was h
prosecutor. Athena was present as an impartial judge to s
that justice was done. The jury was evenly divided as to th
verdict, whereupon Athena cast a vote to break the tie. Sh
decided on the side of Orestes, on the ground that he ha
suffered for his guilt and been purified. She persuaded th
avenging Furies to accept her verdict on the side of merc
and from then on they took up their residence in a grott
on the side of the Acropolis and became known as the Eumen
ides, the "kindly ones," who protected suppliants. The a
quittal of Orestes lifted the curse which had tormented thre
generations of the House of Atreus. Some say that this ve
dict did not render Orestes immune to suffering because n
all of the Furies accepted it; those that did not continued t
harass him. He went to the shrine of Delphi and asked Apo
lo's aid. The priestess told him he must go to Tauris an
secure a wooden image of Artemis from a temple there an
restore it to Attica. Orestes and the faithful Pylades set ou
for Tauris, although it was well known that the Tauria
sacrificed strangers who landed on their shores. The tw
friends landed, were captured, and brought before th
priestess to be prepared for sacrifice. At first the prieste
gloated over the two Greeks who had fallen into her hand
She was Iphigenia, daughter of Agamemnon, and she wa
glad to sacrifice Greeks, as the Greeks so many years befor
would have sacrificed her when they were windbound
Aulis. Only the intervention of Artemis had saved her. A
she talked to the two men, one of whom seemed mad, sh
felt drawn to them and decided to help them escape. In th
course of her conversation with them she told her own hi
tory. Orestes then declared that he was her brother. Afte
joyous reunion they made plans to escape and, aided b
Athena, succeeded in leaving Tauris and returning t
Greece with the image. Some say that they went to Sminth
where they were overtaken by the king of the Taurians, bu
escaped again. Others say they were driven to Rhodes by
storm and set up the image there. Still others say the imag
was taken back to Attica, as commanded by the priestess o
Delphi, and set up in a temple at Brauron, where Iphigeni
became a priestess. But many places claimed the image: i
was said to have been taken to Italy, Susa, Cappadocia, an
Sparta, and all claimed they had the original sacred image

Finally cured of his madness and freed from the persecu-
tions of the Furies, Orestes went to Delphi and there was
reunited with his sister Electra. He then returned to Mycenae and slew Aletes, descendant of Thyestes who had seized
the throne, and became ruler of Mycenae. His next project
was to bring about the murder of Neoptolemus, son of
Achilles, at the shrine of Delphi, and to marry Hermione,
daughter of Menelaus. He had been betrothed to Hermione
but Menelaus had given her to Neoptolemus, some say in
return for the latter's help at Troy, but others claim that
Orestes' madness had caused Menelaus to give her to Neoptolemus. When Menelaus died, Orestes was invited by the
Spartans to become their king. By conquest he added a large
part of Arcadia to his kingdom, and he would have taken
Achaea also, but the oracle at Delphi warned him against it.
In the end he left Mycenae and went to Arcadia, where he
founded the city of Orestia. There, in his old age, he was
bitten by a serpent and died. He was buried at Tegea. Later
the Spartans, informed by an oracle that they would continue to lose their battles with the Tegeans as long as the
bones of Orestes remained in Tegea, sent Lichas to Tegea
to locate the whereabouts of Orestes' grave. He learned that
Orestes' bones had been discovered under the forge of a
Tegean smith; he stole them and returned with them to
Sparta, where they were reïnterred. After that the Spartans
were victorious over the Tegeans. Orestes' son Tisamenus
succeeded him as king. The tragedy of Orestes, caught between the necessity to avenge his father and the crime of
killing his mother if he did so, is treated in *The Choëphoroe* of
Aeschylus, the *Electra* of Sophocles, and the *Electra* and
Orestes of Euripides. The expiation of his crime and his release from suffering are treated in *The Eumenides* of Aeschylus, and *Iphigenia in Tauris* by Euripides.

Orion   (ọ-rī′ọn). In Greek mythology, a giant hunter, the son
of Poseidon and Euryale. He visited Chios and fell in love
with Merope, daughter of King Oenopion. For her sake he
cleared the island of wild beasts. But Oenopion, who had
promised her in marriage to Orion, kept postponing the
wedding day. Frenzied by wine, Orion attacked Merope and
was punished by Oenopion with the aid of Dionysus, by
having his eyes put out while he lay in a drunken sleep.
Orion learned from an oracle that if he went to the East and

turned his eyes to Helius as he rises from the ocean stream
his sight would be restored. He kidnaped a young worke
from Hephaestus' workshop on Lemnos and with him for
guide set off for the East, and had his sight restored. Eos fe
in love with him and accompanied him on his return jour
ney. He was dissuaded from pursuing Oenopion for reveng
by Artemis, whom he met on his way to Crete and whos
passion for hunting he shared. Together they pursued th
pleasures of the hunt and caused Apollo to become uneasy
for he feared that his virgin sister might become enamore
of Orion as Eos had been. Apollo sent a giant scorpion t
attack Orion, and when he found he could not overcome th
scorpion, Orion leaped into the sea to escape. When hi
head was but a distant speck on the sea, Apollo tricke
Artemis, who was unaware that it was Orion, into transfixin
it with an arrow. She was stricken with grief when sh
learned that she had killed her hunting companion, an
sought Asclepius to restore him to life, but Asclepius ha
been killed by a thunderbolt of Zeus. Artemis then place
the image of Orion in the heavens as the constellatio
Orion, the mighty hunter, eternally pursued by the scor
pion. His spirit went to the Asphodel Fields and Odysseu
saw him hunting there when he visited the Underworld
According to another account, Artemis slew Orion becaus
he pursued her chaste companions, the Pleiades, but as th
Pleiades were far from chaste, this version seems unreasona
ble. Still others say Orion was killed by the scorpion, whos
image was also translated to the stars.

Orpheus (ôr′fūs, ôr′fē̇-us). In Greek legend, a son of Oeagrus
king of Thrace, and the muse Calliope and, some say, th
brother of that Linus who was slain by Heracles. But accord
ing to some accounts, Orpheus was the son of Apollo. Who
ever his father was, Orpheus was the most famous poet and
musician in Greek legend. Apollo gave him the lyre and the
Muses taught him to play it so beautifully that trees and
stones danced to his music and wild beasts were tamed by
it. He was taught the Mysteries of Rhea by the female Dactyl
in Samothrace and on a visit to Egypt he saw the Mysterie
of Osiris. In imitation of these latter he invented the Myster
ies of Dionysus and instituted them in Thrace. He taught the
Mysteries of Dionysus to Midas, the Phrygian king, among
others. Orpheus accompanied Jason and the Argonauts o

the expedition to Colchis for the Golden Fleece. With his music he soothed quarrels that sprang up among the Argonauts, made the arduous labor of rowing seem lighter, and drowned out the songs of the Sirens, thus enabling the Argonauts to pass their island in safety on the return voyage. Only Butes succumbed to the charms of the Sirens and leaped overboard. According to some accounts, the Sirens were so chagrined at being out-charmed by Orpheus that they committed suicide, but in Homeric legend they were still on their island when Odysseus passed by a generation later. On the island of the Phaeacians Orpheus sang the marriage song at the wedding of Jason and Medea. When he returned from the voyage of the *Argo*, Orpheus married Eurydice and went to dwell among the Cicones of Thrace. One day as Eurydice was walking in the meadows, Aristaeus saw her and tried to ravish her. As she fled from him she stepped on a viper which bit her ankle, and she died of the poisoned sting. Orpheus was inconsolable and resolved to bring her back from the Underworld. He descended to Tartarus, some say through an entrance in Thesprotia, and so charmed Charon that the ferryman freely carried him over the Styx. Cerberus, the watch-dog of Tartarus was also charmed by his music, and the judges of the Underworld interrupted their task to listen, and the tortures of the wicked were temporarily suspended. Even Hades' heart was softened, and he agreed to let Eurydice return to earth on condition that Orpheus was not to look back as she followed him until she reached the light of the sun. Orpheus gladly accepted this condition and led the way, playing upon his lyre. Eurydice followed, guided by the music. When he reached the light of the sun, he could wait no longer; he looked back eagerly to see Eurydice. But she had not yet stepped into the sunlight and so he lost her forever. After this second loss he retired to Thrace and kept apart from all women. Many maidens sought to win his love but he scorned them and gave his attention to lads in the first bloom and beauty of youth. When he played his lyre, the trees and rocks gathered to listen. One day as he was thus playing, he was set upon by the Ciconian women. Some say Dionysus inspired them with madness because Orpheus had neglected the worship of the god and now honored the sun above all. Orpheus protested against human sacrifice and objected to

the orgies of the maenads. Others say the women set upo
him in revenge for his scorn. While their husbands wer
worshiping in the temple the women rushed at Orpheu
One hurled a stone at him, but the stone, charmed by h
music, dropped harmlessly at his feet. Then the clamor o
the women was so great the music was drowned out. Th
women fell upon him and tore him limb from limb. The
flung his head and lyre into the Hebrus River. From ther
they floated, still singing, across the sea to the island o
Lesbos. As the head lay on the shore of Lesbos a serper
approached to bite, but Apollo appeared and turned th
serpent to stone. The head was placed in the cave at Antissa
where it prophesied continually until Apollo, fearful lest
become more famous than his oracle at Delphi, commande
it to cease prophesying. The lyre was first placed in th
temple of Apollo at Lesbos and its image was placed in th
heavens as a constellation. The Muses, grieving over the los
of the poet, gathered his limbs and buried them at the foo
of Mount Olympus, and ever since, the nightingales of thi
region sing more sweetly than anywhere else in the worlc
The Ciconian women sought to wash the blood of Orpheu
from their hands in the Helicon River, but the river-god, nc
willing to be an accessory in any way in the murder of Or
pheus, dived underground and did not reappear for severa
miles. The women were transformed where they stood int
oak trees as a punishment for the murder of Orpheus, an
there they stood throughout time. In Zone in Thrace wa
another ring of oak trees left standing in the midst of a danc
they had been performing as Orpheus played for them. A
religious sect arose, perhaps in the 5th century B.C., calle
the Orphics. They claimed Orpheus as their founder an
adopted some Oriental and Egyptian ideas of purificatio
and expiation. According to the Orphics, Orpheus was
more ancient poet than Homer and they attributed man
poems, hymns, and prayers to him, some of which survive

Orthrus (ôrth′rus). In Greek mythology, the son of Echidn
and Typhon, and the brother of Cerberus. He was a two
headed monster who guarded the cattle of Geryon. B
Echidna, his mother, he was the father of the Sphinx, th
bane of the Thebans until it was slain by Oedipus. Some sa
that he was the father by the Chimaera of the Nemean Lior
that ravaged the vale of Nemea until it was slain by Heracles

fat, fāte, fär, fåll, ȧsk, fāre; net, mē, hėr; pin, pīne; not, nōte, mŏve
nôr; up, lūte, pùll; oi, oil; ou out; (lightened) ĕlect, agǫny, ūnite

When Heracles came to fetch the cattle of Geryon, Orthrus rushed against him barking furiously. Heracles attacked him with his club and killed him.

)tus (ō′tus). In Greek mythology, a son of Poseidon and the brother of Ephialtes. See *Aloidae.*

—— P ——

•aean, Paeeon, or *Paeon* (pē′an, -on). According to Homer, the physician of the gods. He healed Hades when the latter was wounded by Heracles, and cured Ares when he was wounded by Diomedes during the Trojan War.

•aeon (pē′on). According to tradition, a son of Endymion. His father organized a running race at Olympia, the winner of which was to succeed him on the throne of the region later known as Elis. Paeon raced against his brothers Epeus and Aetolus and lost. Angry at his defeat, Paeon went into exile in the region beyond the Axius River and founded the race that bore his name, the Paeonians.

•alaemon (pa-lē′mon). In classical mythology, a sea-divinity into which Melicertes was metamorphosed when Ino, his mother, fleeing from her frenzied husband Athamas, leaped into the sea bearing him in her arms. See *Melicertes.*

•alamedes (pal-a-mē′dēz). In Greek legend, a son of Nauplius and Clymene, and the brother of Oeax. He was one of Agamemnon's chief lieutenants and went with Agamemnon and Menelaus to Ithaca to secure the services of Odysseus in the war against Troy for the recapture of Helen. Now Odysseus had been warned by an oracle that if he went to Troy he would be gone 20 years and would return alone and destitute. When, therefore, Palamedes, Agamemnon, and Menelaus arrived in Ithaca he pretended to be mad. Palamedes realized that this madness was feigned. According to some accounts, he snatched up Telemachus, the infant son of Odysseus, and made as if to put him to the sword. Other accounts say the envoys found Odysseus plowing with an ox and an ass and sowing salt, and that Palamedes flung Telemachus in front of the plow. In either case, Odysseus

showed by his instant reaction to protect his son that he wa
not mad at all. Thus Palamedes won the valuable services c
Odysseus for the Greeks. But Odysseus never forgave hir
for unmasking his feigned madness and plotted to destro
him. When the Greeks were encamped before Troy he cor
trived to make Palamedes appear as a traitor. He compelle
a Trojan prisoner to write a letter, supposedly set t by Priar
to Palamedes, in which a sum of gold sent as a reward fo
Palamedes' treachery was mentioned. Odysseus then kille
the prisoner and buried gold near Palamedes' tent. H
caused the letter to be found and read by Agamemnon an
gave sufficiently broad hints so that the gold was also found
This was evidence for the Greeks, and they stoned Pala
medes to death as a traitor. Some say Agamemnon was priv
to this plot and encouraged it because he feared Palamedes
Others say Odysseus and Diomedes induced Palamedes t
descend into a well, with the claim of a great treasure there
and then buried him under a shower of stones. For th
murder of Palamedes, Nauplius became a burning enemy c
Agamemnon and other Greek heroes, and avenged himsel
on them in his own way. Palamedes, noted as an inventor
was said to have added letters to the alphabet, to have in
vented weights and measures, dice, the discus, and the ligh
house. He was worshiped as a hero on the island of Lemno

Palladium (pạ-lā′di-um). A wooden image of a maiden, sup
posed to have been sent from heaven as a gift to the Trojan
as a pledge of the safety of Troy so long as it should b
preserved within the city. According to one account, whe
Ilus had marked out the limits of Troy, he prayed to Zeu
for a sign that he had chosen an auspicious site for his cit
and that his efforts would be successful. The next mornin;
he found a legless image of a maiden half buried in th
ground in front of his tent. She was three cubits high (abou
five feet), and in her right hand she held a spear, in her lef
a distaff and spindle (or a shield), and she was wearing th
aegis. Athena had made the image in memory of her dea
playmate, Pallas, and set it up on Olympus, but when Elec
tra, the Pleiad who had been violated by Zeus, accidentall
touched it, Athena hurled it out of Olympus. On discovering
the image Ilus was told by Apollo to guard it, as the city i
which it was kept could not be taken. Another account say
that the image came from heaven while Ilus was building

temple, and that it fell through an opening in the still un-completed roof and landed on the spot where it afterward remained. However it came to Troy, it brought marvelous protective powers with it. It was for this reason that Diomedes and Odysseus entered Troy secretly toward the end of the Trojan War and carried it off, after which Troy fell to the Greeks. In Roman legend, Aeneas rescued the sacred image from the burning city of Troy, took it to Italy, and it became established at Rome. It is said to have saved Rome from the sack of the Gauls in 390 B.C. Many cities in both Greece and Italy claimed and disputed the possession of the original.

allas (pal′as). In Greek mythology, one of the Giants, a son of Gaea and the blood of Uranus, who waged war against the gods. In the battle Athena crushed him with a stone and Heracles killed him. Athena then stripped him of his skin and afterward wore it as a garment.

allas. In Greek legend, one of the four sons of Pandion and Pylia, born at Megara. He and his brothers, Aegeus, Lycus, and Nisus, divided Attica between them, and Pallas received the southern part as his portion. He was the father of 50 giant sons. He and his sons attacked Aegeus, king of Athens, claiming that he was not a true descendant of Erechtheus, but a bastard. They were, however, betrayed by the herald Leos and defeated by Theseus, son of Aegeus. When Theseus later became king of Athens, he killed Pallas and those of his sons who had survived previous battles.

allas. In Greek mythology, a daughter of Triton, in Libya. She was a youthful playmate of Athena who was accidentally killed by the goddess. In grief, Athena put the name of Pallas before her own name. The goddess also made a wooden image of Pallas which later was flung out of heaven and landed before the tent of Ilus, founder of Troy. This image was placed in the temple, and as the Palladium, became the guardian of the safety of Troy as long as it remained within the city. Scholars agree that the name Pallas was originally a title of the goddess Athena, who is often called Pallas Athena.

an (pan). A woodland god and god of pastures and of flocks. According to most accounts, he was a son of Hermes. It has even been claimed that he was a son of Penelope, wife of Odysseus, by her suitors, or of Amalthea, the goat who

obscured) errant, ardent, actor; ch, chip; g, go; th, thin; ᴛн, then; y, you; variable) d̦ as d or j, ş as s or sh, ţ as t or ch, z̧ as z or zh.

nursed Zeus, but others say he was a very ancient god, and was the son of Cronus and Rhea, or of Zeus. He was born with horns, a beard, tail, and goat legs. Pan never lived in Olympus, but dwelt in Arcadia where he guarded his flocks and herds, played with the mountain-nymphs, and aided hunters. Although he did not dwell with the gods he was associated with Cybele, Dionysus, and Aphrodite. Early in the 5th century B.C. his worship, which was native to Arcadia, spread over the rest of Greece and was strongest in country areas. He passed his days in comparative idleness

APHRODITE AND PAN PLAYING FIVE-STONES
Engraved Greek bronze mirror, 4th century B.C.
British Museum

playing on his pipes and resting. It was his custom to frighten any who distrubed his noonday rest with a sudden shout, and this was the reason shepherds did not play on their pipes at midday. Sudden terror (panic) without reasonable or visible cause was attributed to his influence. It was Pan's sudden shout, in the long war between the gods and Titans, which finally caused the precipitous retreat of the Titans. Another shout so frightened the monster Delphyne who was guarding Zeus, disabled by Typhon, that Hermes was able to free Zeus. Some say Pan stopped Phidippides the messenger whom the Athenians sent to ask Sparta for aid on the eve of the Battle of Marathon, as he ran to Sparta. The god asked him why the Athenians neglected him, when he was so friendly to them and would aid them in the future as he had in the past. The Athenians believed that Pan caused the panic which helped them to rout the Persians later at Marathon (490 B.C.). Afterward, the Athenians erected a cave-shrine to Pan on the Acropolis and established annual sacrifices and torch-races in his honor. Pan taught Apollo the art of prophecy and taught Daphnis to play the pipes. He considered himself a fine musician and, on boasting of his skill, was challenged to a contest by Apollo. Midas and Tmolus, the god of the mountain, were the judges. Tmolus decided in favor of Apollo; Midas obstinately favored Pan, but as everyone else agreed with Tmolus, Apollo was the victor. By the nymph Echo, Pan was the father of Iynx; by Eupheme, the father of Crotus; and he boasted that he was the lover of all of Dionysus' maenads at the time of their wild orgies on the mountain tops. Pitys escaped his amorous advances by becoming transformed into a fir tree, and ever afterward Pan wore a wreath of pine about his head. Syrinx escaped him by turning into reeds along the Ladon River. Pan cut the reeds and, as they made a gentle singing sound, bound them together and invented the Pan-pipes. Of all the gods, Pan was the only one whose death was announced. A sailor, Thamus, on a ship voyaging to Italy, heard a voice shout across the waves telling him to proclaim that "the great god Pan is dead." When he reached Italy Thamus did as he was bid and the land mourned. The story of Pan's death was described by Plutarch in the 1st century A.D. but shrines, altars, mountains, old oaks, pine trees, and caves sacred to Pan were still honored and much frequented over a century later. The tortoise was sacred to Pan. The Romans identified Pan with their god Inuus, and sometimes also with Faunus.

Pandareus (pan-dār'ē-us). In Greek mythology, a son of Merops. He was a native of Miletus in Crete, and was the father, by Harmothoë, of Aëdon, Cleothera, and Merope. He stole the golden dog which Hephaestus had made to guard the infant Zeus from the temple of Zeus at Dicte, and gave it to Tantalus to keep for him. When he later asked Tantalus to return it to him Tantalus denied that it had ever been in his possession. Hermes discovered the whereabouts of the dog, on Mount Sipylus, and restored it to the temple. Tantalus was buried under Mount Sipylus for his lies and

Pandareus fled to Sicily. There he was slain by Zeus. H
daughters were brought up by Aphrodite, with the assis
ance of Artemis, Athena, and Hera. According to other a
counts, it was Tantalus who stole the dog, and Pandare
who received it for safe-keeping, and for his part in the the
Pandareus was slain by Zeus or turned into stone.

Pandarus (pan'da̱-rus). In Homeric legend *(Iliad)*, a Troja
the son of Lycaon. A renowned archer, being the possess
of a bow given to him by Apollo, he came from Zeleia, at th
foot of Mount Ida, to aid the Trojans in the war against th
Greeks. The Greeks and Trojans, both tired of the wa
exchanged oaths of friendship and agreed that the winne
of a duel between Paris and Menelaus should have Hele
and all her possessions. This duel was inconclusive becaus
when it appeared that Paris might lose Aphrodite snatche
him away in a cloud. Following this, Athena, in the guise
Laodocus, appeared to Pandarus and urged him to shoot
Menelaus and win fame for himself. Beguiled by the goc
dess, Pandarus treacherously aimed an arrow at Menelau
Athena deflected it so that Menelaus was only wounded, bu
the truce had been broken by the Trojans, and the war wa
resumed. Pandarus, "peer of immortals," wounded D
omedes and, encouraged by Aeneas, sought to kill hin
although by that time he was convinced that the gods wer
protecting Diomedes, as indeed they were. In their secon
encounter, Pandarus wounded Diomedes with his spear an
then was slain by Diomedes.

Pandion (pan'di-on). In Greek legend, a king of Athens, fa
ther of the twins Butes and Erechtheus, and of Procne an
Philomela. He died of grief following the transformation c
his daughters into a nightingale and a sparrow, respectively
See *Procne.*

Pandora (pan-dō'ra̱). According to Greek mythology, Prome
theus defied Zeus, stole fire from heaven and gave it to men
Zeus punished Prometheus for loving mankind too well, an
took his revenge on men by sending an evil which counter
balanced the benefits of the gift of fire. He commande
Hephaestus, the master smith, to create a maiden. She wa
a most beautiful creation. Athena taught her woman's work
Aphrodite endowed her with beauty, Hermes gave her
deceitful nature, the Charites and the Horae adorned he

with delicate raiment, flowers, and a crown of gold. She was
called Pandora because all the gods of Olympus gave her
gifts. Zeus ordered Hermes to take her to Epimetheus as a
gift. Prometheus, still loving mankind, shut up in a casket all
the evils which might plague the world. This was given to
Pandora as a dowry. Prometheus warned Epimetheus not to
accept any gift from Zeus but Epimetheus forgot the warning, and only remembered it when it was too late. He married Pandora, and forbade her to open her box, as
Prometheus had instructed him to do. But as Pandora had
been created as a scourge to mankind, she one day yielded
to her curiosity and opened the box. All the evils which
Prometheus had imprisoned therein flew out and from that
time on brought misfortune to men. Only hope remained.
Some say this was at the order of Zeus. Others say it was
Prometheus who gave wild hope to men. At all events, until
the arrival of woman, in the shape of Pandora, men lived
without evil and hardship, but with her coming, the world
became a dangerous and unhappy place.

anopeus   (pan′ọ-pūs). In Greek legend, a son of Phocus (son
of Ornytion) and Asteria. He was the twin of Crisus, with
whom he struggled in his mother's womb. The hatred thus
begun persisted throughout their lives. Panopeus took the
part of Aegisthus and Clytemnestra, while Crisus and his
family sided with Orestes. He took part in the Calydonian
Boar Hunt and also allied himself with Amphitryon, foster
father of Heracles, in the war against the Taphians and
Teleboans. Before going into battle he swore in the name
of Athena, as did the other allies, that he would not hide any
of the spoils which might be taken in the war. He was the
only one to break his oath and was punished for so doing
by becoming the father of a cowardly son, Epeus, who, nevertheless, accompanied the Greeks to Troy and built the
Wooden Horse. Panopeus was also the father of Aegle, for
whom, some say, Theseus abandoned Ariadne on the island
of Naxos.

aphian Goddess   (pā′fi-ạn). In ancient Greek religion, Aphrodite, as goddess of sexual love. The term arose from the
worship paid her at her cult center at the city of Paphos, in
Cyprus.

Paphos or ***Paphus*** (pā'fos, -fus). In Greek legend, a son o
Pygmalion and Galatea. He succeeded his father as king o
Cyprus. The city on Cyprus, which bears his name and wa
one of Aphrodite's favorite cities, was founded by his so
and successor Cinyras, according to Greek tradition.

Paraebius (pạ-rē'bi-us). In Greek legend, a friend of Phineu
in Salmydessus in Thrace. His father had cut down a hama
dryad's tree, despite the pleas of the nymph to be spared
As a result he and his children were cursed. Phineus tol
Paraebius how he could lift the curse on himself by prope
sacrifices to a nymph. Ever after, Paraebius loyally tended t
the needs of the blinded and Harpy-harried Phineus. Whe
the Argonauts visited Phineus on their way to Colchis, it wa
Paraebius who prepared the altar and sacrifices which the
required.

Paria (pär'i-ạ). In Greek mythology, a nymph. She was love
by Minos, king of Crete, and bore him four sons: Euryn
edon, Nephalion, Chryses, and Philolaus. Her sons colo
nized the island of Paros in the Cyclades and named it fo
their mother. Heracles, on his way to fetch the Apples of th
Hesperides, stopped at Paros for water. Two of his me
were killed. In retaliation he killed the sons of Minos an
Paria.

Paris (par'is). [Also: ***Alexander.***] In Greek legend, a son o
Priam and Hecuba. Before he was born his mother dreame
that she had given birth to fiery serpents and awoke scream
ing that Troy was in flames. Her dream was interpreted t
mean that the child she would bear would bring disaster t
Troy. On the day Paris was born another prophecy wa
made: that the child born to a royal Trojan that day woul
cause the ruin of Troy and that therefore he and his mothe
should be destroyed. Priam, despite the pleas of priests an
seers to kill Paris, who was born late that day, could no
destroy his wife and child, and gave the child to a herdsma
with instructions to kill him. The herdsman exposed Par
on Mount Ida, but when he returned after a few days h
found the infant alive and well, having been suckled by
she-bear. He carried him home and brought him up with h
own son. Paris became a shepherd on Mount Ida and live
happily with Oenone, a nymph, the daughter of the rive
god Oeneus. He was disporting with Oenone and innocentl

tending his flocks on Mount Ida when Hermes approached and told him he had been selected to judge a contest between goddesses: Eris had thrown a golden apple, marked "To the Fairest," among the wedding guests at the marriage of Peleus and Thetis. Athena, Aphrodite, and Hera each claimed the prize. Zeus had refused to settle the dispute and had advised the goddesses to consult Paris. They agreed to accept his decision. Hera promised to make him ruler of all Asia if he awarded the apple to her; Athena promised him victory in all his battles, as well as wisdom and beauty; Aphrodite promised him the fairest woman in the world as his wife. Paris awarded the apple to Aphrodite, and thus won the eternal hatred of Athena and Hera for himself and for all Trojans. The fairest woman in the world was Helen, wife of Menelaus, king of Sparta. Before she married Menelaus, her foster father made all her suitors swear an oath that they would take up arms for the man she married if any evil ever came to him because of his wife. By chance, Paris shortly after the contest returned to Troy and was discovered to be the supposedly lost son of Priam and Hecuba. (Some say Hecuba had bribed the herdsman not to destroy her infant.) The priests immediately urged that he be put to death before he could cause the destruction of Troy, as the oracles had foretold, but Priam would not consent and welcomed his handsome son warmly. Without divulging his true purpose, which was to go after Helen, Paris asked Phereclus to build him a fleet in which he could sail to Sparta, and when it was ready he sailed off, in spite of the burning admonitions and prophecies of Cassandra, his prophetic sister, that his voyage would bring ruin to Troy. Helenus, a seer and a brother, added his warnings, but Priam ignored them and permitted Paris to sail. Oenone, his nymph, also tried to dissuade him from his journey, but her tears were unavailing. As she bade him farewell she told him to return to her if he was ever wounded, because only she could heal him. Arrived in Sparta, Menelaus welcomed him courteously, entertained him for some days, and then, oblivious of the apparent fact that Paris was headlong in love with Helen, Menelaus left for Crete to attend his grandfather's funeral. That same night Helen, swept on by the fate which Aphrodite had spun for her, eloped with Paris, taking one of her

sons and a great treasure with her. On the way to Troy the
were driven to Cyprus by storms, and later spent som
months in Egypt, fearing pursuit by Menelaus. When the
finally arrived at Troy they were married, and all Troy fe
in love with Helen's glorious beauty. No one blamed Pari

HELEN, PARIS, ANDROMACHE, HECTOR
Black-figured Attic vase, 6th century B.C.
Wurzburg

According to some accounts, Helen bore Paris several chil
dren, all of whom died as a result of an accident in thei
childhood. In spite of envoys and threats Paris refused, with
the full consent and approval of the Trojans, to give u
Helen. The Trojan War, in which all the Greek suitors o
Helen who had taken the oath took part, followed. Afte
nearly ten years of war Menelaus and Paris arranged, with
the approval of both the Greek and Trojan armies, to figh
in single combat, the winner to have Helen and end the war
In the duel, Paris was about to be overcome by Menelau
when Aphrodite spirited him away and restored him t
Helen. Hector, brother of Paris, frequently accused him o
being a coward and a wife-stealer, but in truth Paris fough
bravely. He wounded Diomedes, Machaon, and Eurypylus

and led a group at the attack on the Greek fortifications. But each time that it was proposed that he restore Helen to Menelaus, as after the death of Hector and later the deaths of Penthesilea and Memnon who had come to aid the Trojans, he refused and accused those who made the proposals of cowardice, or what was worse, treachery. According to most accounts Paris, with the help of Apollo, mortally wounded Achilles by shooting an arrow into his vulnerable heel. He attacked Telamonian Ajax, who was defending the body of Achilles, and was flattened by a huge stone flung by Ajax. Again, he fearlessly attacked Philoctetes, who had been brought from Lemnos with the arrows he had inherited from Heracles. This attack was Paris' downfall. His arrow missed Philoctetes, but he was wounded by one of the poisoned arrows Philoctetes aimed at him. He withdrew from the battle in great pain, as the poison invaded his body. No one could cure his wound. In his desperate need he sought out Oenone, his deserted nymph, who alone could heal him. He implored her to free him of his pain, declared that it was fate which had made him desert her, and asked her forgiveness. But Oenone had also been wounded, by desertion and jealousy. She scornfully advised Paris to go to Helen to be cured. Deserted in his turn by Oenone, Paris died of his wound. The Trojans did not mourn him, for he was the cause of all their woes. His death frightened Helen, for she did not know what the Trojans would do with her now that Paris was dead. But Oenone's deep love for Paris reasserted itself. Her heart was pierced with grief. She left her home in the night and ran through the woods to the pyre on which Paris was lying. Muffling her face, she leaped into the flames and died in the fire, with Paris clasped in her arms. Their ashes were mingled in one urn and a common burial mound heaped over it. Two pillars were erected at the burial mound, facing in opposite directions because the jealousy which Oenone harbored for Helen still lived in the marble pillars.

Parthenopaeus (pär″thē-nō-pē′us). In Greek legend, a son of Atalanta. According to some accounts, he was the son of Melanion (or, as some say, Hippomenes), who had won the race with Atalanta by means of the golden apples provided by Aphrodite. Some say he was a son of Ares. Still others say he was the son of Meleager, who had fallen in love with

Atalanta when she joined the Calydonian Boar Hunt, and that she exposed the child when he was born, on Mount Parthenius. A she-bear found him and suckled him until he was found by shepherds and taken to Corythus, their master. At the same time, Telephus, son of Heracles, who had been abandaoned by his mother Auge, was found and the two children were brought up together. According to some accounts, Parthenopaeus accompanied Telephus to Mysia when the latter went in search of his mother, and acted as his spokesman, and also helped him defeat the enemies of the king of Mysia. Later, against the advice of Atalanta, he was one of the Seven who marched against Thebes under the command of Adrastus. In the attack he was slain by Periclymenus. Before he died, he asked that his head be shorn and his hair sent back to his mother. His body was one of those reclaimed by Theseus and the Athenians, after the Thebans had refused burial to those who were slain, and was returned to Athens for burial.

Parthenope (pär-then′ō-pē). In Greek mythology, a siren who threw herself into the sea because her singing could not beguile the hero Odysseus. She drowned, and her body was cast up on the shore of Naples, for which reason her name is sometimes given for Naples.

Pasiphaë (pạ-sif′ā-ē). In Greek legend, a daughter of Helius and Persa, and the sister of Aeëtes and Circe; like her sister she was a mistress of the black arts. She married Minos, king of Crete, and was the mother of Acacallis, Ariadne, Androgeus, Glaucus, Catreus, and Phaedra, among others. Poseidon had sent a magnificent white bull to Minos, which the latter had promised to sacrifice to the god. But Minos hated to slay the handsome creature and sacrificed another bull in its place. Poseidon punished Minos for this breach of his oath by causing Pasiphaë to fall in love with the bull. Pasiphaë confessed her bizarre passion to Daedalus, the marvelous smith and builder who was living in Crete at that time. He built her a wooden image in the shape of a cow and made it possible for her to enter the structure and consort with the white bull. As a result of this union she produced the monstrous Minotaur, half-man and half-bull. To hide the disgraceful story of his wife's passion Minos asked Daedalus to construct a labyrinth, and in it the Minotaur and, some say, Pasiphaë as well, were hidden. When Minos later

fat, fāte, fär, fâll, àsk, fãre; net, mē, hėr; pin, pīne; not, nōte, möve, nôr; up, lūte, pùll; oi, oil; ou out; (lightened) ĕlect, agǫny, ūnite;

learned that Daedalus had helped Pasiphaë to gratify her unnatural lust he locked Daedalus up in the labyrinth also, but Pasiphaë freed him and, some say, helped him to escape from Crete. There was an oracle of Pasiphaë at Thalamae in Laconia, where answers were given in dreams.

Patroclus (pạ-trō'klus). In Greek legend, a native of Opus in Locris. His father was Menoetius. His mother is variously named as Sthenele, daughter of Acastus; Polymele, daughter of Peleus; Periapis, daughter of Pheres; or Philomele, daughter of Actor. As a youth he had accidentally slain a friend in a childish argument over jackstones, and had fled to the court of his uncle Peleus. There he became the intimate friend and inseparable companion of Achilles. He was a suitor of Helen and had sworn to defend and assist whomever she chose as her husband in the event that any ill came to him as a result of his marriage. Thus, he accompanied Achilles and his Myrmidons to Troy when the Greeks sailed to recapture Helen from Paris. On the way to Troy their ships landed in Mysia and the Myrmidons ravaged the country, under the impression that it was a part of the Troad. The king, Telephus, drove them back to their ships but was in his turn repelled and wounded by Achilles, with the staunch assistance of Patroclus. In the years of the war before the actual siege of Troy Patroclus took part with Achilles in raids and captures of many cities that were allied to Troy. In the tenth year of the war Achilles withdrew his ships and men from the Greek camp and threatened to sail home, because of his anger at Agamemnon. Patroclus withdrew from the fighting with him. However, they both kept close watch of the battle, and after a furious struggle in which Hector drove the Greeks back to their ships, they saw a chariot racing toward the ships bearing a wounded man. Patroclus was sent to find out who it was. "This for Patroclus was the beginning of evil." He learned that it was Machaon, the surgeon, and that the Greeks had just barely prevented Hector from setting fire to their ships. Nestor pleaded with Patroclus to urge Achilles to come to the aid of his beleaguered friends or, if he refused that, at least to send him Myrmidons under Patroclus' command to their aid. Patroclus started back to Achilles with the message. On the way he met Eurypylus, who had been wounded by Paris, and learned that Ajax, Diomedes, and Odysseus had also been wounded, and that

(obscured) errạnt, ardẹnt, actọr; ch, chip; g, go; th, thin; ᴛʜ, then; y, you;
(variable) ḍ as d or j, ṣ as s or sh, ṭ as t or ch, ẓ as z or zh.

Eurypylus thought nothing could now stop Hector from destroying the Greek host. Patroclus attended to his wound and sped back to Achilles with the news. In spite of his plea to give up his anger Achilles refused to join the battle, but he did yield to Patroclus' request to borrow his armor and his Myrmidons so that Patroclus could lead them into battle. Achilles helped him into the armor and cautioned him to drive the Greeks away from the ships but not to go onto the plain, lest a victory by Patroclus tarnish the glory of Achilles. Patroclus entered the fray with a furious onslaught. Aided by Zeus, he drove the Trojans back to the plain and, in defiance of Achilles' command, pursued them to the walls of the city. There Apollo came to the Trojans' rescue. Patroclus slew Cebriones, Hector's brother and charioteer, and struggled with Hector over his body. Three times he attacked the walls, each time killing nine Trojans. The fourth time he attacked, Apollo smote him and stunned him, his helmet fell off and his armor was loosened. Euphorbus wounded him with his spear and Hector dealt him the death blow. With his dying breath Patroclus defied Hector, saying it was the gods who had slain him, not Hector. Hector stripped off Achilles' armor and donned it himself. A furious struggle then broke out for possession of Patroclus' body but Achilles, who had learned of his dear friend's death from Antilochus, appeared on the Greek fortifications and so terrified the Trojans that Menelaus and Meriones, protected by the two Ajaxes, were able to carry his corpse to the Greek camp. Achilles was wild with grief over the death of his comrade, and Briseis, Achilles' captive princess, expressed his epitaph as she mourned him by remembering that he was ever gentle. Thetis preserved Patroclus' body from corruption, and made it whole of its wounds by dripping nectar through his nostrils, as Achilles, mourning, refused to bury the body. The ghost of Patroclus at last appeared to Achilles in a dream and asked him to bury the body so that the soul of Patroclus could rest. Prophesying the death of Achilles before Troy, the ghost of Patroclus asked that his ashes be placed in the same urn with those of Achilles. And so, when Achilles died, it was done.

Pegasus (peg′a̱-sus). In Greek mythology, the winged horse that sprang from the blood of Medusa when she was slain by Perseus. His father was Poseidon. Athena gave him to the

Muses and with a stroke of his hoof he caused the poetically inspiring fountain Hippocrene to well forth, on Mount Helicon in Boeotia. Bellerophon, on the advice of a seer, sought Pegasus when he undertook to slay the Chimaera for Iobates, king of Lycia. Some say the seer told Bellerophon to go and sleep in the temple of Athena, if he would find the winged horse. Bellerophon followed his advice, and dreamed that the goddess appeared and spoke to him. When he woke he found a golden bridle at his feet. Carrying this, he found Pegasus drinking at the Pirene spring in Corinth. He threw the bridle over the horse's neck. Thus Pegasus was tamed and willingly carried Bellerophon to hunt the Chimaera. Because he could fly above it on the back of Pegasus, Bellerophon was able to kill the Chimaera. Later Bellerophon sought to fly to the heavens. Zeus sent a gadfly that stung Pegasus. He reared in pain and Bellerophon was hurled to earth. Pegasus went to Olympus and was stabled with the steeds of Zeus. Ultimately his image was placed among the stars as a constellation.

Peirene (pī-rē′nē). See *Pirene.*

Peirithous (pī-rith′ọ-us). See *Pirithous.*

Peitho (pī′thō). In Greek mythology, a cult title of Aphrodite, and also a separate, lesser deity, attendant on Aphrodite, interpreted as a personification of persuasion, especially to love.

Pelasgus (pẹ-laz′gus). In Greek mythology, according to some accounts, the first man, a son of Earth who sprang from the soil of Arcadia and taught those who followed him to build huts and sew tunics of pigskin. He was the father of that Lycaon whose impieties caused Zeus to send the flood. Others say Pelasgus was the son of Zeus and Niobe, and the founder of the Pelasgian race. Still others, that he was the son of Phoroneus, and thus the grandson of the river-god Inachus, and that he was the founder of the Pelasgian division of the Greeks.

Peleus (pē′lūs, pē′lẹ-us). In Greek legend, a king of the Myrmidons in Thessaly. He was a son of Aeacus and Endeïs, and the brother of Telamon and the half-brother of Phocus. He was born on the island of Aegina. Peleus and Telamon were jealous of Phocus because he was their father's favorite and excelled at athletic games. Acting on the advice and encouragement of their mother, they challenged Phocus to an ath-

letic contest in the course of which Phocus was killed. Some
say he was struck by a discus and then beheaded with an ax.
The brothers were accused of the murder and fled. Peleus
went to Phthia, where he was purified by Eurytion, the
adopted son of King Actor. He married Polymela, Actor's
daughter, and received one-third of the kingdom. But he
was again forced to flee for having accidentally killed Eurytion in the Calydonian Hunt, of which they were both partici-
pants. He went to Iolcus and was again purified; this time it
was Acastus, a son of Pelias, who performed the rite. In
Iolcus, Cretheïs, wife of Acastus, falsely accused Peleus of
making improper advances to her, and when Polymela
learned of the charges she hanged herself. Acastus, who
believed his wife's accusations against Peleus, challenged
him to a hunting contest. Peleus had a magic sword made
by Daedalus, and with it he soon killed many beasts. Acastus
claimed that they were his victims but Peleus proved that he
had slain the animals by producing their tongues, which he
had had the forethought to cut out and keep to one side.
During the night Acastus stole and hid Peleus' sword, and
left with his followers, but the sword was restored to Peleus
by Chiron, the centaur, who also protected him from other
centaurs who were minded to murder Peleus. Peleus then
departed to Chiron's cave. Here a messenger from Hera
came to him to tell him that he was to marry Thetis, the
sea-goddess who had scorned the amorous advances of
Zeus. Zeus had given up his pursuit of Thetis when he
learned that she would bear a son who would be greater
than his father, but to punish her for rejecting him he vowed
that she would not marry a god but would be yoked to a
mortal. Chiron warned Peleus that Thetis would be a reluctant bride, and advised Peleus to seize her as she took her
midday nap in a cave on the shores of a small island off
Thessaly. Peleus hid behind a myrtle bush near the cave, and
watched as the naked goddess rode on the back of a dolphin
to the island. When she had entered the cave and fallen
asleep he followed Chiron's advice, seized the sleeping goddess and held on to her manfully as she changed herself into
fire, water, a lion, and a serpent in her attempt to escape. At
last she yielded. Peleus and Thetis were married near Chiron's cave on Mount Pelion as the gods, seated on their
twelve thrones, looked on approvingly, the Muses sang, and

the 50 Nereids who accompanied Thetis danced. The gods gave wedding gifts: an ashen spear, golden armor, and a pair of immortal horses, Balius and Xanthus. The only one of the immortals who was not invited to the wedding was Eris, goddess of discord, and this deliberate slight led to the interminable struggle and disaster of the Trojan War, for Eris hurled the Apple of Discord among the wedding guests which led to the Judgment of Paris and the Trojan War. Peleus and Thetis passed through Trachis, where Peleus' herds were attacked by a wolf sent by the mother of Phocus to avenge her son's murder, but Thetis turned the wolf to stone with a glance. They next proceeded to Iolcus, which Peleus captured, and where he killed Acastus and his lying wife, Cretheïs, and hacked her body to pieces. He then led an army of his Myrmidons into the city. Some say the Myrmidons had fled with him from Aegina, others say they sprang from an army of ants supplied by Zeus. Thetis bore seven sons to Peleus. Each of the first six she held in the flames to burn away their mortal parts and sent the immortal remainder to Olympus. Peleus happened to see her as she was performing this rite on their seventh son, Achilles. He screamed in fright. Thetis dropped the child, left Peleus and returned to her home in the sea. (The best known tale is that Thetis plunged the infant Achilles into the Styx and made every part of him invulnerable except his heel.) Peleus never saw her again, although she permitted him to hear her voice from time to time. Peleus accompanied Heracles on his voyage to fetch the girdle of the Amazon queen, and again when Heracles attacked and sacked Troy to punish Laomedon. He also accompanied Jason on the voyage of the *Argo* to Colchis. He was too old to fight at Troy, but he gave his ashen spear, golden armor, and immortal horses to his son Achilles when the latter set off for the war. Peleus outlived his famous son, who was mightier than his father as had been prophesied, and he outlived his grandson, Neoptolemus. According to some accounts, although old and weak he protected and preserved the life of Neoptolemus' bastard son by Andromache, after the Trojan War, when Menelaus and his daughter Hermione would have killed Andromache and her child out of jealousy. In his old age, and after he had been expelled from Iolcus by the sons of Acastus, Thetis spoke to Peleus, advised him to return to the cave where he had first mastered her, and await her there. She promised that she would come and confer immortality on him, and carry him away to live with her under the sea. But, according to some accounts, Peleus, although he went to the island as instructed, became impatient. In quest of news of Neoptolemus, he set out across the sea, was caught and shipwrecked in a great storm, died and was buried on an island near Euboea before Thetis had a chance to make him immortal.

Pelias (pē′li-ạs). In Greek legend, a son of Tyro and Poseidon, twin-born with Neleus. The twins were exposed on a mountain to die but were rescued. A horse belonging to the rescuer kicked Pelias and bruised his face, whence his name, which means "livid" or "black and blue." When the twins grew up they learned that Tyro was their real mother, and proceeded to avenge her for the mistreatment she had received at the hands of Sidero, her stepmother. They found her before the altar of Hera, where she had gone for sanctuary, and Pelias slew her. For this act in the temple of Hera, Pelias incurred the anger of Hera and later suffered from the goddess' displeasure. It is also said that Pelias withheld sacrifices to Hera, which made her the more resolved to punish him. Tyro married Cretheus, founder and king of Iolcus, and he adopted Pelias and Neleus. After the death of Cretheus, Pelias and Neleus quarreled. Pelias forced Neleus into exile. But when he was warned by an oracle that a descendant of Aeolus would cause his death, Pelias killed all the descendants of Aeolus he could find except his half-brother Aeson, a son of Cretheus and Tyro and the rightful heir to the throne. He kept Aeson as a prisoner. Pelias married Anaxibia, a daughter of Bias, or Phylomache, a daughter of Amphion, and became the father of Acastus and several daughters. Among the latter was Alcestis, who had many suitors. According to some accounts, Pelias gave her to Admetus of Pherae, because he alone of the suitors met the conditions set up by Pelias: to yoke a lion and a wild boar to his chariot and drive them around a race-course. But others say Jason arranged the marriage of Alcestis and Admetus. A second oracle warned Pelias to beware of a man wearing one sandal. When, therefore, a youth clad in a leopard's skin and wearing but one sandal appeared before him, Pelias resolved to destroy him. On learning that the youth was Jason, his nephew, he agreed to resign the throne to him, but said he was troubled by the ghost of Phrixus, which demanded proper burial and the return of the Golden Fleece, now in Colchis, to Hellas. He assured Jason he would give up the throne once these things were accomplished. He did this in the expectation that Jason would never return from the dangerous errand. Jason accepted his proposal and departed with a band of heroes and demigods to fetch the Fleece. After some time had passed Pelias was sure that Jason had perished. He was about to kill Aeson, father of Jason, but allowed him to commit suicide by drinking bull's blood. Aeson's wife thereupon uttered a curse on Pelias and hanged herself. (According to other accounts, aged Aeson was still living when Jason and Medea returned, and was restored to youthful vigor by Medea's magic.) Pelias murdered the young son of Aeson. Jason, however, returned to Iolcus with Medea and the Fleece. Medea tricked the daughters of Pelias into murdering their father. She appeared to Pelias and told him Hecate had empowered her to rejuvenate him. She transformed an old ram into a skipping lamb to demonstrate her powers. Pelias was convinced and allowed himself to be drugged into a deep sleep. His daughters, instructed by Medea, cut his throat, dismembered his body, and cast the pieces into a cauldron. But Medea added no magic herbs to the brew as she had done with the ram, and the daughters of Pelias unwittingly brought about his miserable end.

Pelopia (pe̯-lō̯-pī′a̯) or *Pelopea* (-pē′a̯). In Greek legend, a daughter of Thyestes, and the niece of Atreus. She was separated from her father in the quarrels between Thyestes and Atreus, and went to Sicyon where she became a priestess. Thyestes had been advised by the oracle at Delphi to father a son by his own daughter, in order to get revenge on Atreus (who had killed three of Thyestes' sons and served them to Thyestes at a banquet). He found Pelopia sacrificing to Athena, at night, attacked and ravished her. She did not know who her attacker was in the darkness, but she managed to steal his sword, and hid it in the temple of Athena. Thyestes fled. Shortly afterward, Atreus came to Sicyon in search of Thyestes, because the oracle had ordered him to bring Thyestes back from exile. Atreus saw Pelopia, fell in love with her, and asked the king, thinking she was the king's daughter, for her hand in marriage. The king, Thesprotus, was anxious to have Atreus for an ally, and did not tell him that Pelopia was not his own daughter, but gladly gave his consent to the marriage. Pelopia later bore a son, the child of Thyestes, and exposed him on the mountain to die, but he was found by shepherds and brought to Atreus. Atreus thought Pelopia had temporarily taken leave of her senses after giving birth to her son, and brought up the child, Aegisthus, under the impression that it was his own son. A few years later, Aegisthus was ordered by Atreus to kill Thyestes, who had fallen into his hands again. Thyestes escaped the young boy's attack (some say Aegisthus was only seven years old at this time), but recognized the sword in his hand as the one which had been taken from him the night he attacked Pelopia. When he learned from Aegisthus that the sword had been given him by his mother he asked Aegisthus to bring Pelopia to him. She came, and recognized her father joyfully, but on learning that the sword she had stolen from her ravisher was her own father's, and that he was the father of her son, she plunged the infamous sword into her breast and died.

Pelopidae (pẹ-lop'i-dẹ). A name for the descendants of Pelops, applied especially to Atreus, Thyestes, Agamemnon, Menelaus, and Orestes.

Pelops (pē'lops). In Greek legend, a son of Tantalus and a grandson of Zeus. His sister was Niobe. Tantalus was on terms of great intimacy with the gods and dined at their table, but he betrayed their friendship by stealing the nectar and ambrosia upon which they fed, and gave it to his mortal friends so that they could enjoy the immortality it conferred. He also, in his pride, invited the gods to dine, and served them his son Pelops, whom he had cut up and cooked to test whether the gods would recognize human flesh. All the gods except Demeter refused to touch the repast, being quite well aware what had been set before them. But Demeter, mourning for her lost daughter, inadvertently ate a piece of Pelops' left shoulder. Tantalus was horribly punished by the gods for his crimes. They then ordered Hermes to restore Pelops by cooking his flesh in the same cauldron, after which Rhea breathed life into the reformed body, and an ivory shoulder was substituted for the one Demeter had eaten. (Pindar was aghast at this revolting story. He claimed that Poseidon had fallen in love with the beauty of Pelops and had stolen him away. Pindar said the other story was a lie, and a reflection on gods and mortals alike.) Restored, Pelops was so beautiful that Poseidon carried him away to Olympus and fed him on ambrosia. He returned to his father's kingdom in Paphlagonia, but was driven out and went to Elis, where he sued for the hand of Hippodamia, daughter of Oenomaus. He won her, with the aid of winged horses and a golden chariot that could skim across the waves given to him by Poseidon, by defeating her father in a chariot race. Myrtilus, a son of Hermes and a charioteer of Oenomaus, accepted a bribe from Pelops to help Pelops win the race, and he removed a pin from the axle of Oenomaus' chariot and caused the death of Oenomaus. Afterward, Pelops hurled Myrtilus into the sea when he tried to collect his payment. As he fell, Myrtilus laid a curse on the House of Pelops which brought disaster to many of his descendants. The murder of Myrtilus also aroused the wrath of Hermes. Hephaestus purified Pelops for the murder and he built a temple to Hermes to appease that god. He then succeeded to the throne of Oenomaus and, "smiter of horses" as he was termed by Homer, made himself master of the whole region which he renamed Peloponnesus after himself. He was rich and powerful, and envied by all the princes of Greece. A sanctuary of Pelops, containing his bones, was dedicated to him at Olympia by his descendant, Heracles, and annually a black ram, roasted on a fire of white poplar-wood, was offered to him. His chariot, his golden sword, and the spear-shaped scepter made by Hephaestus, were preserved long after his death in various sanctuaries in Greece, and he was regarded by the Achaeans as their ancestor. The spear-shaped scepter was awarded to the people of Chaeronea who worshiped it as their most important deity, offering victims and a rich variety of food to it daily. Towards the end of the Trojan War, Helenus told the Greeks they must fetch the shoulder of Pelops, among other things, if they expected to defeat the Trojans. Agamemnon accordingly sent envoys to Pisa to secure the ivory shoulder. This ivory shoulder was first revealed to Pelops himself when he mourned the death of his sister Niobe by baring his breast. Incidentally, he was the only one to mourn that arrogant woman. According to Pausanias, the ship carrying the shoulder back to Greece, after

(obscured) errant, ardent, actor; ch, chip; g, go; th, thin; ᴛʜ, then; y, you;
(variable) ḍ as d or j, ş as s or sh, ṭ as t or ch, ẓ as z or zh.

the Trojan War, was sunk in a storm. Years later, when a plague was ravaging Elis, a fisherman pulled up the huge bone in his net and, according to instructions from the oracle at Delphi, gave it to envoys from Elis. The envoys returned with it to Elis and the plague was lifted. The fisherman was honored by being made custodian of the sacred bone. Among the many children of Pelops were Atreus, Thyestes, Alcathous, Pittheus, the bastard Chrysippus, who was his favorite and aroused the jealousy of Hippodamia, Copreus the herald, Sciron the bandit, and Astydamia, said to have been the mother of Amphitryon.

Penelope (pē-nel'ō-pē). In Greek legend, the daughter of Icarius of Sparta and the naiad Periboea. According to some accounts, at her father's command she was hurled into the sea, but purple ducks bore her up and conveyed her to shore, hence her name, which means "duck." Odysseus was one of her many suitors. He advised Tyndareus, foster father of Helen, how to choose a husband for his daughter without making enemies of Helen's disappointed suitors. In return for his advice, Tyndareus helped Odysseus to win a suitor's foot-race for Penelope in Sparta. Icarius protested when Odysseus set out with his bride for Ithaca, but Penelope signified her desire to go with her husband by drawing her veil over her face, and they proceeded to Ithaca. Telemachus, the son of Penelope and Odysseus, was only an infant when Odysseus left for the Trojan War. The war lasted ten years. Many more years elapsed after it was over and Odysseus did not return. Consequently, he was presumed dead by many in his kingdom and Penelope was besieged by suitors. She was described by Homer as a beautiful woman, with great charm and intelligence, and enormous character. Besides, she was the mistress of rich estates. Over 100 suitors, princes of the kingdom, sought to win her. They plotted to murder Telemachus, just coming to manhood, and seize the throne. Penelope, hoping Odysseus would return, refused to choose a husband from among her suitors. She said she must first finish a shroud she was weaving for her father-in-law, Laertes. Each day she worked at her loom; and each night she secretly unraveled what she had done. This went on for three years before her ruse was discovered. In the meantime, the suitors daily made themselves at home in the palace of Odysseus, eating up his flocks and herds, drinking his wine, seducing his servants, and wasting his substance. At the end of nearly 20 years, Penelope was hard-pressed by the wooers. Telemachus was not strong enough to expel them, and she did not know which way to turn, although Athena visited her frequently in one guise or another to encourage her. When she learned that Telemachus had secretly left for Sparta to seek news of his father and that the suitors planned to ambush and kill him on his return, she hid her fears and boldly chided the wooers for their evil designs. She reminded Antinous, the most insolent of them, that Odysseus had protected his father when he was harassed by enemies. The suitors replied with soothing words and increased their clamor for her decision as to which of them she would take as her husband. Telemachus, aided by Athena, escaped their ambush and returned safely. At the same time Odysseus at last came home. He appeared disguised as a beggar, and so complete was the disguise Athena had given him that no one recognized him. (He did reveal his true identity to Telemachus, and later, to two faithful servants.) Penelope heard that a stranger had come to the palace. She sent for the beggar, who had already observed her demanding bridal gifts from the suitors in the great hall and secretly applauded her prudence in getting what she could from them. She was immediately drawn to the beggar, and questioned him closely. He assured her that Odysseus lived, that he had seen him, and promised his immediate return. Penelope, hopeful but not convinced, ordered a servant to bathe and refresh the beggar. She told him a dream she had had, in which 20 geese, feeding in the yard, were attacked and destroyed by an eagle. The beggar said the geese represented the suitors, and the eagle represented Odysseus, who would come home and destroy them. In a state of sorrow and great uneasiness, Penelope told him she was being compelled to choose from among the suitors, and that she had decided to accept the one who could string her husband's great bow and shoot an arrow through the eye holes of 12 axes set up in a row, as her husband could do. The beggar urged her to carry out her plan at once, and the next day Penelope announced the contest. None of the suitors could even bend the bow to string it. Odysseus seized it and, as the suitors reviled him for his arrogance, Penelope left the hall. He strung the bow easily and turning on the suitors killed every one of them, aided by Athena, Telemachus, and his two faithful servants, Eumaeus and Philoetius. Euryclea brought the news that Odysseus had returned and destroyed the suitors, but Penelope was dubious. Odysseus had been gone so long, and she had grieved so much and had so many troubles, that her hope of good fortune was nearly killed. But Odysseus was not worried, and calmed his son, who was rebuking Penelope for her coldness. He told Telemachus there were certain signs, known only to the two of them, by which they would know each other. To test him, Penelope gave an order to have his bed moved. Odysseus was exasperated. No one could move his bed, he said, because he himself had carved it from a living olive tree that grew through the palace. Thus he proved that he was not an impostor and Penelope welcomed him warmly, apologizing for her previous coolness and doubts. Penelope is regarded as the model of the chaste and faithful wife, who bore her sufferings during the absence of her husband with great nobility and fortitude. She is pictured as a tender mother and a paragon of the domestic virtues. According to later accounts, Odysseus left her again to appease Poseidon, and Penelope ruled Ithaca in his place. Odysseus was mistakenly killed by his son Telegonus, the child of Circe, and Penelope then married Telegonus. Other accounts say that Penelope was not faithful to Odysseus, that she became the mother of Pan by Hermes, or as the result of consorting with all her suitors; as Pan was a very ancient god, long before the time of Penelope, these stories are obviously later embroideries.

Penthesilea (pen″the-si-lē′a̤). In Greek legend, an Amazon queen. She left her home in Thermodon, fleeing the reproaches which followed the accidental killing of her sister Hippolyte, and came to the aid of the Trojans in the last year of the war, after Hector had been killed. Her arrival put new hope into the Trojans, and the flashing beauty which glowed in her face as she vowed to slay Achilles convinced them that she would do even as she said. Only Andromache, who had lost her husband to Achilles' spear, questioned the wisdom of such a boast. Clad in armor given her by Ares, Penthesilea led her 12 Amazon princesses into battle, but as Priam prayed for her success, an eagle clutching a dove in its talons flew screaming over his head; it was a gloomy omen. Penthesilea slashed about her mightily and the Greeks fled in panic. Achilles, mourning for Patroclus, at last heard the din of the fray and hurriedly joined the struggle. Penthesilea, whose path to death was strewn with the glory of killing many Greeks, leaped like a leopard to meet him. But her hour of glory was over. Her lance splintered on Achilles' magic armor. He wounded her in the breast with his sword, and as she debated whether to ask for mercy he impaled her and her horse with his spear. When she fell he gloated over her but when he removed her helmet and saw the wonder of her beauty, "like a child of Zeus sleeping," he fell wildly in love with her and was filled with remorse. Ares was so enraged by the death of his daughter that he would have killed Achilles, but was prevented from doing so by Zeus. Thersites mocked Achilles, who remained sorrowfully at Penthesilea's side, and roused the hero's wrath. Achilles dashed him to the ground. He permitted Agamemnon and Menelaus to restore Penthesilea's body to Priam and she was given funeral honors as a beloved daughter by the Trojans. She, and the Amazon princesses, were buried beside the bones of Laomedon.

'entheus (pen'thūs). In Greek legend, a son of Agave and Echion and a grandson of Cadmus. He succeeded his grandfather as king of Thebes. When Dionysus arrived in Thebes and invited the Thebans to join in his revels Pentheus, who disapproved the extravagances of the new religion, forbade his people to take part. He seized and imprisoned the maenads who had come with Dionysus from Asia. However, the fetters which bound them dropped from their limbs, the doors of prisons opened of their own accord, and the prisoners were freed. Pentheus resolved to capture and imprison Dionysus himself, against the advice of Cadmus. The latter warned him not to despise the gods or resist their will. But Pentheus scorned the claim that Dionysus was a god. And he mocked the prophecy of the seer Tiresias that he would be torn limb from limb if he denied the divinity of the god. Dionysus allowed himself to be taken before Pentheus, and tried to persuade him to accept the new god. As Pentheus refused, and added his doubting comments on the divinity of Dionysus, the god resolved to punish him. He inspired Pentheus with madness, and under the pretext of sending him to spy on the revels of the women on Mount

Cithaeron, he induced him to disguise himself as a woman. Pentheus then went to the mountain and climbed a tree from which he could view the revels. The women, among them his mother Agave, spied him in the tree. Frenzied with religious ecstasy, they mistook him for a wild beast. They shook the tree and finally tore it up by the roots. They then set upon Pentheus and, with Agave as leader, tore him limb from limb. Agave, still under a spell of madness, bore his head proudly back to the palace and exhibited it as the head of a young lion which she had overcome. The fate of Pentheus is often cited as an example, in ancient writing, of the swift fate which overtakes those who question, defy, or resist the gods.

Perdix (pėr′diks). In Greek mythology, the sister of Daedalus and the mother of Talos, who was also sometimes called Perdix. When Daedalus killed Talos, jealous because he rivaled him as a smith, Perdix hanged herself and was changed into a partridge. The name "Perdix" means partridge. She was also known as Polycaste (q.v.).

Pergamos (pėr′ga̱-mo̱s). [Also: *Pergamum.*] Name given in the *Iliad* to the citadel or walls of Troy. Also, the Trojan citadel of Helenus in Epirus, which was made to resemble that of Troy.

Pergamus (pėr′ga̱-mus). According to Greek tradition, a son of Neoptolemus and Andromache. After the death of Neoptolemus, Andromache married Helenus and went with him to the new city he founded. When he died she went to Asia, according to some accounts, and took Pergamus with her. There he conquered the king of Teuthrania, in Asia Minor, and won the city, which he renamed Pergamum, after himself.

Periclymenus (per-i-klī′me̱-nus). In Greek mythology, the oldest son of Neleus and Chloris (or Meliboea, daughter of Amphion and Niobe). Poseidon gave him boundless strength and the power to assume whatever shape he wanted. Some time after the journey in the *Argo*, in which he took part, he attempted to defend Pylus, his father's kingdom, against Heracles. In combat with Heracles he changed himself into a lion, a serpent and a bee. Lastly he transformed himself into an eagle and tried to peck out Heracles' eyes, but as he flew away to dodge Heracles' club, the hero seized a bow and shot him.

Perigune (per-i-gū′nę). In Greek legend, a daughter of Sinis the "Pine-bender." When Theseus encountered Sinis and struggled, successfully, to overpower him, Perigune, in terror of Theseus, ran and hid from him. He found her cowering among wild asparagus and rushes, appealing to the shrubs to hide her, and promising them that she would never burn or destroy them if they would protect her from Theseus. Theseus assured her that he meant her no harm, and so convinced her that she fell in love with him. He embraced her and in due time she bore him Melanippus. Theseus later gave her to Deioneus of Oechalia. The descendants of Perigune in Caria, who were called Ioxids because Ioxus, grandson of Perigune, led a colony to Caria, made it a practice not to burn the wild asparagus and rushes. Instead they revered these plants for their service to Perigune.

Perimele (per-i-mē′lę). In mythology, a daughter of Hippodamas. The river-god Achelous fell in love with her and ravished her. Hippodamas was enraged with his daughter and hurled her into the sea, but as she was falling Achelous caught her and held her up. He prayed to Poseidon that she might be given a resting place or become a place, herself. His prayer was answered: Perimele was transformed into an island off the mouth of the Achelous River. She became one of the Echinades Islands.

Periphas (per′i-fas). According to some accounts, an ancient king of Attica, before the time of Cecrops. He was renowned for his justice and piety, and was called "Zeus" by men. For this presumption Zeus wanted to destroy him, but was persuaded by Apollo to change him into an eagle instead, and he became king of the birds.

Periphetes (per-i-fē′tēz). In Greek legend, a Giant. Some say he was a son of Poseidon, but others say he was a son of Hephaestus and Anticlea, and like Hephaestus, he was lame. He lived at Epidaurus, and was in the habit of attacking travelers with a huge iron club (he was sometimes called Corynetes, "Cudgel-bearer"). When he attacked Theseus, who was passing that way, Theseus seized the club from his hands and battered Periphetes to death with his own club. Ever after, Theseus carried the huge club and used it to good effect.

Pero (pē′rō). In Greek legend, a daughter of Neleus, king of Pylus, and Chloris, daughter of Amphion and Niobe. She was the sister of Nestor. She had many suitors and her father promised her to the one who could bring him the cattle of Phylacus (or his son, Iphiclus). She was finally won by Bias, who with the help of his brother Melampus, a seer, got possession of the cattle. She was said by some to be the mother of the river-god Asopus, by Poseidon. She died young and Odysseus saw her shade when he visited the Underworld on his way home from the Trojan War.

Persephone (pėr-sef′ō-nē). [Also: *Core, Kore,* meaning "the Maiden."] In Greek mythology, the daughter of Zeus and Demeter. Hades fell in love with her and sought permission from Zeus to make her his wife. Zeus neither gave his consent, for he knew Demeter would not want to lose her daughter in the Underworld, nor withheld it, for fear of offending Hades. One day as Persephone was gathering flowers in a meadow with her companions, Hades suddenly appeared in his chariot drawn by four black horses and seized her. As she struggled to escape, the earth opened and the chariot disappeared into the chasm, bearing Hades and the unhappy maiden in it. Demeter was wild with grief over the loss of her daughter. She wandered tirelessly over the world searching for her. Some say Enna, in Sicily, was the place where Hades carried off Persephone; others say Colonus in Attica, Hermione or Lerna in Argolis, Pheneus in Arcadia, Nysa in Boeotia, a place in Crete, and various other places visited by Demeter in her search for her daughter were the scene of the abduction. But the priests of Demeter said she was carried off from Eleusis in Attica. Demeter learned from Hecate that Hades had abducted her daughter with the tacit consent of Zeus and carried her off to his realm to be his wife. In her wrath, Demeter withdrew her gifts of fertility from the earth; fields and vineyards ceased to bear. Zeus, fearing the destruction of mankind, sent Hermes to Hades with a command to restore Persephone to her mother, on condition that she had eaten nothing while in his kingdom. Persephone had eaten some seeds of a pomegranate—one, three, six, or seven—and for that reason was compelled to spend part of each year as Hades' wife in his kingdom, where she lived with him in a palace, had a grove of black poplars sacred to her, and exercised great powers.

fat, fāte, fär, fåll, åsk, fãre; net, mē, hėr; pin, pīne; not, nōte, möve, nôr; up, lūte, pùll; oi, oil; ou out; (lightened) ĕlect, agŏny, ūnite;

She allowed Heracles to restore Alcestis to earth when she had given her life that her husband might live; deceived by Sisyphus, she gave him permission to return to earth to make arrangements for his own burial, which he said had not been properly performed; and she accepted a myrtle bough from Dionysus in return for permitting him to take his mother Semele from Hades' kingdom to Olympus. Occasionally she was compelled to deal with a rival. She transformed the nymph Minthe into a mint plant when she observed Hades dallying with her. For the same reason, the nymph Leuce was transformed into a white poplar that stood beside the Pool of Memory in Hades. Variations on the story of Persephone were that she was the daughter of Zeus and the nymph of the river Styx in Hades; that she was the mother of Zagreus and Dionysus by Zeus. The annual disappearance from the earth of Persephone brought death to vegetation. When she appeared to spend the rest of the year with her mother the earth flowered in rebirth. Persephone and Demeter were worshiped as the Great Goddesses, the central figures of the Eleusinian Mysteries, from which a concept of immortality evolved. Persephone was also worshiped as "the Maid," whose name it was unwise to utter. Symbolically, Demeter and Persephone were interpreted as two aspects of the grain goddess, Persephone representing the new young grain, Demeter the ripened harvest. Persephone is also associated with the mother-goddess Aphrodite in the fertility myth regarding the vegetation-god Adonis. Adonis dwelt with Persephone under the earth for one-third of the year, and spent the other eight months with Aphrodite in the world. Persephone's cult name was Core, or Kore, "the Maiden," and in this aspect she figured in the Eleusinian mysteries. She was associated with Dionysus in the Eleusinian mysteries when, under the name Iacchus, he represented her brother, her son, or her bridegroom. In the Peloponnesus she was honored with a festival of flowers, the Anthesphoria. In later times Persephone came to be identified with Hecate, a dread goddess of darkness and of spirits. As a virgin who dwelt with her mother, Persephone was represented as a beautiful maiden, and had a flowing cornucopia, a sheaf of wheat, and the cock as her attributes. As the stern queen of the Underworld, she held a torch or a pomegranate, symbolizing death and

rebirth. The Romans called her Proserpina and made littl
or no change in the myth or its interpretation. She wa
especially worshiped in Sicily, which was sacred to Demete
and Persephone and where many festivals were held in thei
honor.

Perseus (pėr′sūs, -sē-us). In Greek mythology, a son of Zeu
and Danaë. He was born in a bronze underground chambe
in which Acrisius had imprisoned Danaë to prevent her from
having any traffic with men. He did this because he had been
warned by an oracle that his grandson would kill him. Bu
Zeus visited Danaë in a shower of gold and she bore hin
Perseus. Acrisius was reluctant to kill his own grandson, fo
fear of the wrath of the gods. He therefore placed mothe
and child in a chest and cast it into the sea. The chest floate●
to the island of Seriphus. There it was recovered by Dictys
a fisherman. He took Danaë and her son to his house an●
sheltered them; Perseus grew up under his care to be ●
fisherman. Polydectes, brother of Dictys and king of th●
island, saw Danaë and fell in love with her. By this tim●
Perseus had grown to be a strong and handsome youth
Some say Perseus objected to the marriage which Polydecte
tried to force on his mother. Others say Polydectes simpl
wanted to get rid of Perseus. At any rate, Polydectes sum
moned his friends to his palace and asked them to mak●
contributions to him for a wedding present to Hippodamia
daughter of Pelops, whom he pretended he was going t●
marry. He asked his friends to give him horses. Perseus, ●
poor fisherman, could give no such gift. Instead he agreed
to fetch the head of the Gorgon Medusa as his contribution
Some say he idly promised he would even fetch the head o
Medusa to prevent Polydectes from marrying Danaë, and
that Polydectes immediately accepted his offer. Others sa▼
Perseus, humiliated by his inability to give a horse as the
others were promising to do, proudly offered to fetch th●
head of Medusa instead. This then was his mission, and
Polydectes thought he had seen the last of him, for he ex
pected him to be killed on this dangerous errand. Perseus
sailed to Greece, without telling his mother of his daring
plan, to consult the oracle at Delphi and learn where the
Gorgons might be found. The oracle directed him to a land
where the people eat only acorns. Perseus took this to mean
Dodona, the site of the oracle of the talking oak trees. The
priests of Dodona, however, could not tell him where to find

fat, fāte, fär, fåll, àsk, fâre; net, mē, hėr; pin, pīne; not, nōte, möve
nôr; up, lūte, pùll; oi, oil; ou out; (lightened) ēlect, agǫny, ūnite

the Gorgons. They did tell him that Athena and Hermes would help him. As he wandered about searching for information, Perseus met Hermes and learned from him that only the nymphs of the North could tell him where the Gorgons dwelt, and that only the Graeae, who lived at the foot of Mount Atlas in Libya, could direct him to the nymphs.

PERSEUS FLEEING FROM A GORGON
Red-figured Greek amphora, c490 B.C.
Munich

Hermes accompanied him on his journey to the Graeae. These shadowy old women shared one eye and one tooth between them and lived in a land that knew no sunlight. They were sisters of the Gorgons. As they came to the sisters, Hermes advised Perseus to steal their eye and their tooth as these were passing from hand to hand, and to keep them until the Graeae revealed the home of the nymphs. Perseus followed his instructions. The Graeae, compelled by their need for the eye which Perseus had snatched from them, told him how to find the nymphs of the North. He then set off with Hermes to find the nymphs, who lived in the far northern land of the Hyperboreans. The nymphs treated him kindly and gave him a wallet, winged sandals, and a cap of darkness. They also told him where to find the Gorgons. Hermes gave him an unbreakable sickle. Athena

gave him a polished shield. She told him not to look directly
at the Gorgons, for they were so revolting and frightening
with their snaky locks that whoever looked on them was
instantly turned to stone. She showed him how to use the
shield as a mirror so that he need not look directly at the
Gorgons, and told him how he would recognize Medusa, the
only one of the Gorgons who was not immortal. Perseus flew
over the ocean on his winged sandals until beneath him he
saw the Gorgons reflected in the polished shield. He
swooped down and, using the shield as Athena had directed,
cut off Medusa's head with one sweep of Hermes' sickle and
put it into the wallet the nymphs had given him for this
purpose. From the blood of Medusa sprang Pegasus, the
winged horse, and Chrysaor. Her sisters woke up and pursued Perseus, but as he was wearing the cap of darkness he
was invisible and they soon gave up the chase. Hermes and
Athena now left him and he flew off, carrying the head in the
wallet. Drops of Medusa's blood that fell on the land as he
flew over it turned into serpents, and thenceforth this land
was infested with poisonous snakes. Some say that Perseus,
on his way to find the Gorgons, visited Atlas and asked his
hospitality. Atlas, remembering a prophecy given him by
Themis that the golden apples would one day be stripped
by a son of Zeus from the trees which he guarded, refused
to entertain him. As Perseus returned with the head of
Medusa, he again stopped at the house of Atlas, exhibited
the head of Medusa and turned Atlas to stone to punish him
for his inhospitality. There Atlas stands to this day, a mighty
mountain called by his name. Continuing his journey, Perseus flew to Chemmis, the home of his ancestor Danaus in
Egypt. He stopped there briefly to refresh himself. The
Egyptians honored him with an image in the sacred precinct
of the temple of Chemmis; they said that a huge sandal
belonging to Perseus frequently is found, and that on the
occasions when the sandal comes to light all Egypt prospers.
The Egyptians worshiped Perseus with games in the Greek
manner. Perseus next flew over the coasts of Aethiopia and
saw a beautiful maiden chained to a rock on the shore. He
fell in love with her at sight, and flew down to inquire the
reason for her unhappy state. She told him she was Andromeda, daughter of Cepheus, king of Aethiopia. She was
chained to the rock as a sacrifice to a sea-monster that Poseidon had sent to ravage the land. Perseus offered to slay the

monster if in return Cepheus would give him Andromeda in marriage. Cepheus was delighted to agree. Perseus took the head of Medusa from the wallet and laid it on some seaweed, which instantly turned to coral, in case he should need it to kill the monster. But it was not necessary. As the beast emerged from the sea Perseus flew above it, swooped down and cut off its head with a single blow. He then raised altars and sacrificed to Hermes, Athena, and Zeus, and claimed his bride. At the wedding festivities Phineus, who some say was the brother of Cepheus and some say was a son of Agenor, burst into the hall and claimed the bride. Andromeda had been betrothed to him before the monster was sent by Poseidon, but when she was chained to the rock as a sacrifice Phineus had given up his interest in her. Now that all was safe, he reasserted his claim to her. Perseus refused to give up Andromeda. He fought off Phineus and his companions, killing many, but he was seriously outnumbered and must surely have perished if he had not exposed the head of Medusa and turned Phineus and his followers to stone. After this he departed with Andromeda for Seriphus. Arrived there, he learned that his mother and the kindly Dictys, whose wife had long since died, had been forced to flee because of the violent importunities of Polydectes. They had taken refuge in a temple. Perseus set off for the palace, where Polydectes and his friends were gathered at a great banquet. As he entered the banquet hall all eyes turned to him. He held up the head of Medusa and Polydectes and all his companions who had been unfriendly to Danaë were instantly turned to stone. A circle of lifeless boulders on Seriphus marks the site of this event. Now Perseus sought his mother and Dictys. He made Dictys king of the island, and with his mother and his wife he set out for Argos to find his grandfather. Acrisius, who had heard all about his glorious exploits, rememberd the oracle that warned he would be killed by his grandson and fled to Larissa. Thither Perseus followed him. Some say he took part in funeral games at Larissa unaware that Acrisius was among the spectators. However that may be, in the discus throwing contest Perseus' discus was caught by the wind, struck Acrisius and killed him. Thus the oracle was fulfilled, as oracles invariably are. Perseus was reluctant to return to Argos after he had killed his grandfather, even though it was an accident. He exchanged his kingdom of Argos with his cousin Megapen-

obscured) err**a**nt, ard**e**nt, act**o**r; ch, chip; g, go; th, thin; ŦH, then; y, you;
variable) **d** as d or j, **s** as s or sh, **t** as t or ch, **z** as z or zh.

thes for the kingdom of Tiryns. In his new kingdom he fortified Midea and Mycenae. Some say indeed, that Perseus founded Mycenae; that one day when he was thirsty a mushroom sprang up and provided water. He founded the city on this spot and named it Mycenae in honor of the mushroom (*mykos*). Perseus gave the sandals, wallet, and cap of darkness to Hermes, who restored them to the nymphs. He gave the head of Medusa to Athena. The goddess placed the head in the center of her shield, or aegis. Andromeda bore Perseus six sons: Perses, from whom the kings of Persia were said to have sprung, Alcaeus, Sthenelus, Heleus (or Aelius), Mestor, and Electryon, and one daughter, Gorgophone. As far as is known, Andromeda rejoiced in the undiluted affection of her lord, a rare occurrence for the wives of Greek heroes. Perseus was worshiped as a hero in Athens and Seriphus, and had a shrine on the road between Argos and Mycenae.

Phaeacians (fē-ā'sḫanz). A legendary seafaring people who inhabited the island of Corcyra, or as some say, Scheria. According to some accounts they considered themselves to be of the blood of Uranus, because the sickle with which Cronus mutilated his father was flung into the sea by Cronus, either near their island or to form it, and its people were sprung from the drops of Uranus' blood on the sickle. Others say they were descendants of Phaeax, a son of Poseidon. And some say they emigrated to their island to get away from their noisy neighbors, the Cyclopes. As descendants of Poseidon, the Phaeacians were extraordinary navigators and mariners. Their ships traveled the seas without the aid of steersman or helm, knowing of themselves the course they must take. Muffled in misty clouds and darkness, they flew over the waters like birds. On their island the Phaeacians lived in the midst of splendid prosperity and happiness, remote from wars and often enjoying visits from the gods themselves. Traditionally they were extremely hospitable to other seafarers and never refused their aid in danger and shipwreck. The women, thanks to Athena, were as skilled in weaving as the men were in seamanship. Jason and Medea stopped among the Phaeacians, during the reign of Alcinous, and were hospitably received. Odysseus was cast ashore on their island when the raft on which he sailed from Calypso's shores was broken up in a great storm. Nausicaä, the daughter of Alcinous, encountered him on the beach and directed him to her father's magnificent palace of bronze, gold, and silver. There the Phaeacians clothed and fed him and after hearing his story promised to convey him to Ithaca in one of their ships. They gave him rich gifts and put him aboard a ship at night. While he slept the ship skimmed over the sea to Ithaca, and the sleeping Odysseus was gently put ashore. On the return to Phaeacia, Poseidon, enraged that the Phaeacians who were of his own blood had given aid, comfort, and rich treasure to his enemy, sought permission from Zeus to punish the Phaeacians. Zeus advised him to turn the ship into stone and to raise a mountain which would overshadow their island. Just as the ship was in sight of the harbor, on its way back from Ithaca, Poseidon turned it to stone, and there it can be seen to this day. On seeing this disaster Alcinous remembered that an oracle had foretold Poseidon's anger because they convoyed mortals. The Phaeacians therefore sacrificed to Poseidon, to appease him and to plead with him not to raise up a mountain over their city. Withdrawing into their battlemented island they resolved that henceforth they would no longer give safe escort to mortals who came to them from the sea.

Phaeax (fē'aks). In Greek mythology, a son of Corcyra and Poseidon. He was born on the island named for Corcyra and became the ancestor of the Phaeacians. Some say he piloted the Athenian fleet which carried Theseus and the other Athenian youths and maidens who were going to Crete as tribute to King Minos, because the Phaeacians were skilled pilots. And it was Phaeax who steered them away to safety after Theseus killed the Minotaur and the Athenians escaped to the ships. Theseus afterward established the Pilots' Festival in his honor.

Phaedra (fē'drȧ). In Greek legend, a daughter of Minos, king of Crete, and Pasiphaë. She was the sister of Ariadne. After the death of Minos, her brother Deucalion became king of Crete, and made an alliance with Theseus of Athens. To bind the alliance he gave Theseus Phaedra for wife. She bore him two sons, Acamas and Demophon. By Antiope the Amazon Theseus was the father of Hippolytus. He was a chaste and handsome youth. Theseus sent him to Troezen where he raised a temple to Artemis. Phaedra fell in love with him and followed him to Troezen. She built a temple

to Aphrodite which overlooked the gymnasium where Hip
polytus daily exercised. It is said that in her frustration a
watching the unobtainable youth, Phaedra pierced th
leaves of a nearby myrtle tree with the pin of her jewele
brooch, and that the leaves still bear the marks of her jab
bings. Although she confided her feelings for Hippolytus t
no one, her nurse, seeing that she ate little and slept les:
soon guessed the truth. She encouraged Phaedra to send
letter to Hippolytus, confessing her love. Hippolytu:
shocked to read such a letter, destroyed it and went to Phae
dra to reproach her. She, fearing he might expose her, wrot
a letter to Theseus in which she accused Hippolytus of actu
ally committing the deeds she only wished he had done, an
then hanged herself. Some say it was Aphrodite who cause
Phaedra to fall in love with Hippolytus, because he ha
dedicated himself to Artemis, thus denying the power o
Aphrodite, and Phaedra was the innocent victim implicate
in the punishment of Hippolytus by Aphrodite.

Phaëthon (fā′ẹ-thǫn). In Greek mythology, a son of Heliu
and Clymene. When his boasts that he was a son of Heliu
were jeered by his companions, he asked his mother to giv
him some proof of his paternity. Clymene advised him to g
to his father's palace and question him in person. Phaëthor
joyfully set out for the palace, which some say was in Col
chis. On appearing before Helius he was assured that he wa
indeed his son, Helius even offering to grant him any boor
he demanded as proof. Phaëthon immediately asked permis
sion to drive his father's chariot (the sun) across the heav
ens. Helius, regretting his promise, tried to persuade
Phaëthon to choose some other boon. He knew that Phaë
thon would not be able to control the fiery horses that drew
the chariot, and that such an expedition would end in disas
ter. But Phaëthon insisted and as Helius had given his oath
he now sorrowfully fulfilled it. As Helius had foreseen, Phaë
thon had not the strength to control the horses, nor was he
familiar with the path the chariot must take across the heav
ens. Moreover he was frightened by the monsters—the
Scorpion, Crab, Serpent, and others—that menaced the
path. The horses, missing the firm hand that usually reined
them in, charged about the heavens in a frenzy of freedom.
They soared so high that the heat of the chariot did not
reach the earth and earth shivered, but the North Star be-

came warm. Then they swooped down, setting fire to the clouds and coming so close to earth that it burst into flames. Some say the brown people of Ethiopia got their color when the chariot came too close and scorched them. The heat of the chariot, skimming so close to the earth, dried up rivers and set the land afire. Zeus, to preserve the earth and to protect Olympus from burning, hurled a thunderbolt and struck Phaëthon. He fell, blazing, into the Eridanus River. The horses broke from the yoke and scattered across the heavens. Helius kept the earth dark for a day in his grief for his son, after which he corralled his horses and resumed his daily course through the heavens. Nymphs of the Eridanus buried Phaëthon and erected his tomb. His mother and sisters came weeping to the river bank. The sisters lamented so grievously that the gods in pity turned them into poplar trees which stand on the river bank, weeping tears of amber.

Phaëthon.   In Greek mythology, a son of Eos. His father was Cephalus, whom Eos had loved at sight and carried away from his rightful wife, Procris. Aphrodite stole Phaëthon and carried him off to be an attendant in one of her most sacred temples. He was called Adymnus by the Cretans; the name meant the morning and the evening star to them.

Phalanthus   (fạ-lan′thus). According to tradition, a Spartan hero who founded Tarentum in Italy (traditional date, 707 B.C.). Before he set out he was told by the oracle at Delphi that when he felt rain under a cloudless sky *(aethra)* he would win both a territory and a city. He didn't give much thought to the oracle and set out for Italy in his ships. On the way he was shipwrecked, but rescued and borne to shore by a dolphin. As he won many victories over the barbarians of Italy but took no cities, he remembered the oracle. He thought it was impossible for rain ever to fall from a cloudless sky and that therefore the oracle meant he would never take a city. He thus despaired. His wife sought to comfort him. She took his head between her knees and began to pick lice out of his hair. Seeing him so unhappy she wept for him, and covered his head with her tears. Then Phalanthus realized the meaning of the oracle, for his wife's name was Aethra. On that very night he seized the city on the Taras river from the barbarians. This city was named Tarentum, after Taras, a son of Poseidon. Coins of Tarentum showed

Phalanthus riding on the dolphin's back in memory of th
divine protection that brought him to Italy.

Phanes (fā'nēz). An Orphic deity. According to some ac
counts, Phanes was born from a silver egg laid by Nyx, and
afterward created the earth, sky, sun, and moon. Other ac
counts have him born from an egg fashioned by Cronus in
the Aether. He is also called Eros, Ericapaeus, Metis, and
Protogonus (First-born).

Phantasus (fan'tạ-sus). According to some accounts, a chilc
of Nyx *(Night),* and the brother of Hypnos *(Sleep)* and
Thanatos *(Death).* Others say he was a son of Hypnos (Latin
Somnus). Phantasus is the god of dreams who causes
dreams of inanimate objects. His brothers are Morpheus
Icelus, and Phobetor.

Phegeus (fē'jūs). In Greek legend, a son of Alpheus. He was
a king of Psophis. He purified Alcmaeon for the murder or
his mother, Eriphyle, and gave his daughter Arsinoë to Alcmaeon for a wife. Alcmaeon betrayed Arsinoë and married
Callirrhoë, without letting either Phegeus or Arsinoë know
of his new attachment. When Phegeus learned of it he ordered his sons to kill Alcmaeon, and they did so before
Arsinoë's eyes. She was still unaware of Alcmaeon's treachery, and would not listen to her father's explanation of it.
She prayed that her father and her brothers would die
before the new moon, to avenge the death of Alcmaeon.
Phegeus gave her away as a slave. Meantime, Callirrhoë
learned of the murder of Alcmaeon and prayed that her
infant sons by him would grow up overnight and avenge
their father's death. Her prayer was answered; her sons
found the sons of Phegeus, killed them and Phegeus too,
before the appearance of the new moon in the heavens.
Thus the prayers of both betrayed wives of Alcmaeon were
answered.

Phemius (fē'mi-us). In the *Odyssey,* a minstrel and bard, who
entertained the suitors of Penelope during the absence of
Odysseus. Odysseus spared him when he returned and destroyed the suitors, because Phemius had sung for them
against his will, and because the person of a poet and singer
was sacred.

Philemon (fi-lē'mọn, fī-). See **Baucis and Philemon.**

Philoctetes (fil-ok-tē′tēz). In Greek legend, a son of Poeas,
king of Meliboea in Thessaly. He was the only one who had
the compassion and courage to set the funeral pyre of Heracles alight when that hero laid himself down and begged to
be released from his suffering. As a reward, Heracles gave
him his bow and arrows. Some say Heracles also made Philoctetes promise not to reveal his grave. When the Greeks
assembled to sail against Troy to recover Helen, Philoctetes,
as one of her former suitors, commanded seven ships. After
the second mustering at Aulis the Greeks sailed to Tenedos.
There, as they were sacrificing to Apollo, Philoctetes was
bitten by a water-snake; some say Hera punished him in this
manner for helping her enemy, Heracles. His wound did not
heal, and became so repulsive that the Greeks put him
ashore on the island of Lemnos and abandoned him. Some
say however, that he was bitten on the small island of
Chryse, near Lemnos, where for centuries an altar of Philoctetes, a bronze serpent, bow, and breastplate could be seen.
The island had disappeared beneath the sea by the 2nd
century A.D. Still others say Philoctetes was not bitten by a
snake at all, but accidentally stepped on one of Heracles'
poisoned arrows, and that this was a punishment for revealing Heracles' grave, by stamping on it meaningfully when he
was questioned. In any event, on the advice of Odysseus he
was abandoned on Lemnos and lived there in misery, cloth-
ing himself with the feathers of birds, eating what he could
catch, and suffering horribly from his festering wound. After
the death of Achilles the Greeks learned that Troy could not
be taken without the arrows of Heracles and hurriedly sent
Odysseus and Diomedes to fetch Philoctetes from Lemnos.
He would have slain them in his anger at their heartless
desertion but, aided by Athena and the shade of Heracles,
Odysseus persuaded him to accompany them to Troy.
There he was healed by Podalirius (or as some say, by Machaon), and seemed like one reborn. He went immediately
into battle, and one of his arrows killed Paris. He disapproved of the proposal to take Troy by the stratagem of the
Wooden Horse, as he preferred to fight bravely in the open,
but yielded and was one of those who entered the city by this
means. At the end of the war Philoctetes returned to his
home but was forced to flee from it by rebels. He went to
the Campanians in Italy, and founded the cities of Petelia

and Crimissa. Nearby he founded a sanctuary of Apollo th
Wanderer, in which he dedicated the bow and arrows c
Heracles. When he died he was buried beside the Sybar
River.

Philomela (fil-ọ-mē′lạ). In Greek legend, a daughter of Par
dion, king of Athens. She was the sister of Procne, and wa
transformed into a swallow by the gods. See *Procne.*

Philyra (fil′i-rạ). In Greek mythology, a daughter of Oceanu:
She lived on an island named for her. Cronus, in the infanc
of Zeus, lay with Philyra, deceiving Rhea. When he wa
discovered by Rhea, Cronus changed himself into a stallior
Philyra gave birth to Chiron, half-horse and half-god (c
man), as the result of Cronus' transformation. She prayed t
be relieved of her burden of nursing her unnatural child an
was metamorphosed into a linden tree, the flowers of whic
came to be frequently used in medicine, and the bark c
which was used in foretelling the future.

Phineus (fī′nūs, fin′ẹ-us). In Greek mythology, a son c
Agenor and Telephassa and the brother of Cadmus and
Europa. After searching vainly for his sister Europa whe:
she was abducted by Zeus, he settled down and became kin
of Salmydessus in Thrace. He married Cleopatra, daughte
of Boreas, and had two sons. Then he abandoned Cleopatr
and married Idaea, daughter of Dardanus. According to on
account, he was blinded by Zeus because of his unerrin;
prophecies—Zeus wanted the gods alone to know the se
crets of the future—and was tormented by the Harpies whe
defiled his food so that he was perpetually on the verge o
starvation. When the Argonauts, accompanied by Cleopa
tra's brothers Calais and Zetes, landed on Phineus' shore
they promised to help him. As winged sons of Boreas (the
North Wind), Calais and Zetes swiftly overtook the horribl
creatures and would have slain them, but Iris was sent tc
forbid them to kill "the hounds of Zeus" and to promise tha
they would no longer torment Phineus. In return, Phineu:
gave them valuable advice for their journey. He told then
how they could safely pass the Symplegades, or Clashing
Rocks, how to drive away the birds of Ares so that they coulc
land on the island of Ares, and predicted that Aphrodite
would assist them when they arrived in Colchis. According
to some accounts, Phineus was blinded by Zeus because he
had blinded his own sons on receipt of false accusation:

fat, fāte, fär, fâll, ȧsk, fãre; net, mē, hėr; pin, pīne; not, nōte, mǒve
nôr; up, lūte, pủll; oi, oil; ou out; (lightened) ẹlect, agǫny, ūnite

against them from Idaea. As a punishment, he could choose between death or blindness. When he chose blindness, Helius sent the Harpies to torment him because of his impiety in choosing never to look upon the sun again. In this version, Phineus was killed by his sons, whose sight had been restored, and they became rulers of his kingdom.

Phineus. In classical mythology, a brother of Cepheus, king of Ethiopia, and the uncle of Andromeda, to whom he was betrothed. When Andromeda was chained to a rock as a sacrifice to a sea monster, to punish her mother for boastfulness, Phineus lacked the courage or ability to slay the monster and rescue the maiden. Perseus, on his way home from killing Medusa, slew the monster and won Andromeda for his bride. But Phineus, since the monster was safely dead, invaded the palace during the wedding feast with a mob and claimed Andromeda, saying she had been promised to him. With his followers he attacked Perseus. A fierce struggle broke out, in which many were killed, but Perseus won the battle and retained his bride by exhibiting the head of Medusa and so turning Phineus and his remaining companions to stone. In other accounts the man who claimed Andromeda and was turned to stone by Perseus was named as Agenor of Tyre.

Phlegethon (fleg′e̱-thon). In Greek mythology, one of the five rivers surrounding Hades. It was a river of fire which flowed into the Acheron.

Phlegyas (flej′ya̱s). In mythology, a son of Ares and Chryse. He was king of the Lapithae and lived near Orchomenus in Boeotia. He was the father of Ixion and Coronis. When he learned that his daughter had born Asclepius to the god Apollo he violated Apollo's shrine at Delphi and was slain by the god. As further punishment he was condemned to Tartarus, the region of Hades reserved for the worst criminals—those who had sinned against the gods. There he stood beneath a rock which was forever on the verge of falling and was continually hungry because his food was contaminated by one of the Furies.

Phobetor (fō-bē′tôr). The name men gave to Icelus, the god who brought dreams of animals and birds. The name means "the Terrifier."

Phobus (fō′bus). In late Greek mythology, a son of Aphrodite and Ares, and an attendant of Ares, the god of war. He personifies the fear which terrifies whole armies and causes rout.

Phoebe (fē'bē). In Greek mythology, a Titaness, the daughter of Uranus and Gaea. According to some accounts, Eurynome gave her dominion over the Moon. By Coeus she was the mother of Leto, and thus the grandmother of Artemis and Apollo. The name Phoebe became synonymous with the moon in later writings, and hence with both Artemis and the Roman Diana, as identified with the moon.

Phoebus (fē'bus). In late Greek mythology, Apollo in his aspect of sun god and dispenser of light.

Phoenix (fē'niks). According to some accounts, a son of Agenor of Canaan (afterwards Phoenicia) and Telephassa. He was the brother of Cadmus, Cilix, Thasus, Phineus, and Europa. When Europa was carried off by Zeus in the form of a bull, Phoenix, with his brothers, was sent by Agenor to find her. He journeyed beyond Libya to what afterwards became Carthage in his search for her. After his father died he returned to his own country and became king there. It was renamed Phoenicia in his honor, and he came to be regarded as the ancestor of the Phoenicians.

Phoenix. In Greek legend, a son of Amyntor and Cleobule. At his mother's request he seduced his father's mistress, and was denounced by her to Amyntor. To punish him, Amyntor blinded him and put a curse on him: that he should never have a son of his own. Phoenix fled to the court of Peleus, where he was kindly received. Peleus persuaded Chiron to restore his sight, and then made him ruler of the Dolopians. He became the preceptor and foster father of Achilles, son of Peleus, and thus the curse of childlessness was to some extent overcome. He accompanied Achilles to the Trojan War. Phoenix tried, unsuccessfully, to persuade Achilles to give up his wrath at Agamemnon over the captive Briseis. Later he, as one whom Achilles loved and respected, was one of the ambassadors to offer him rich gifts and the restoration of Briseis if he would give up his quarrel and come to the aid of the Greeks. When Achilles rejected this attempt to settle the quarrel, Phoenix elected to remain with him. He commanded a group of the Myrmidons under Patroclus when that hero prevailed on Achilles to loan him his armor and his men so that he, at least, could go to the aid of his countrymen. After the death of Achilles he was one of the

fat, fāte, fär, fåll, åsk, fãre; net, mē, hèr; pin, pīne; not, nōte, mŏve, nôr; up, lūte, pùll; oi, oil; ou out; (lightened) ĕlect, agŏny, ūnite;

envoys to Scyrus to fetch Neoptolemus, son of Achilles, to the war. At the end of the war he left Troy with Neoptolemus but died on the way home to Greece.

Phoenix.   [Also: ***Phenix.***] Greek name for the ancient Egyptian mythological bird, the *bennu,* a bird of great beauty which, after living 500 or 600 years in the Arabian wilderness, the only one of its kind, built for itself a funeral pyre of spices and aromatic gums, lighted the pile with the fanning of its wings, was burned upon it, but from its ashes rose new and young. The Phoenix was the Egyptian symbol for the rising sun and the hieroglyph for the sun. In Christian symbolism the Phoenix represents resurrection and immortality. The story exists in Arabia, Persia, and India. It is mentioned in the Old Testament (Job, xxix. 18). In heraldic symbolism the Phoenix is always represented in the midst of flames.

Pholus   (fō′lus). In Greek legend, a centaur who lived in a cave on Mount Pholoë and guarded the wine given to the centaurs by Dionysus. Heracles visited him and, in accordance with the oracles, Pholus opened the wine of Dionysus to serve to him. The other centaurs were attracted by the aroma of the wine and maddened by its fumes. They attacked Heracles. Their mother sent a torrential rain to help them—as they were four-footed they could fight in the mud whereas Heracles, with only two feet, was continually slipping and falling. Nevertheless, Heracles killed many of the centaurs and drove the rest away. Pholus, his friend, in extracting an arrow from a fallen centaur marveled that such a slender weapon could be so deadly. It fell from his hand and pierced his foot slightly. Heracles tried to save him from succumbing to the poisoned arrow, but since it had been dipped in the venom of the Lernaean Hydra its effect, even in the slightest wound, was deadly and Pholus died. Heracles buried him on the mountain and named it after him, Mount Pholoë.

Phorbas   (fôr′băs). In Greek legend, a son of Lapithes. He freed the Rhodians from a plague of serpents, and was honored by them as a hero. He was placed in the heavens as the constellation Ophiuchus (the Serpent-holder). Another Phorbas was a famous boxer, who challenged pilgrims en route to Delphi to contend with him, killed them, and eventually was slain by Apollo.

Phorcids (fôr′sidz). [Also: **Phorcides, Phorcyads, Phorkyads.**] In Greek mythology, the children of Phorcys and Ceto: Ladon, Echidna, the Gorgons, the Graeae, and according to some accounts, the Hesperides.

Phorcys (fôr′sis). [Also: **Phorcus, Phorkys.**] In Greek mythology, a son of Gaea and Pontus (Outsea) or Nereus. He was a sea-deity, a leader of the Tritons, and was the brother and consort of Ceto (a sea-goddess) and father of the Phorcids (especially the Graeae) and the Gorgons, and in some accounts of the Sirens and Scylla also.

Phormion (fôr′mi-ọn). According to Greek tradition, a Spartan who acquired the house once lived in by the Dioscuri. When they came to him as strangers he regretfully denied their request to sleep in their old room, because his daughter was occupying it. Next day the maiden and everything belonging to her had vanished. Only images of the Dioscuri and a table on which was some silphion (a medicinal herb) remained in the room.

Phoroneus (fôr-ō′nē-us). In Greek mythology, a son of Inachus and the ash nymph Melia, and the brother of Io. He was the first to found a market town; its original name, Phoronicum, was later changed to Argos, and he is regarded as the founder of Argos. In the contest between Hera and Poseidon over Argos, Phoroneus was a judge. According to some accounts, he was the first man, and the one who discovered the use of fire, after Prometheus had stolen it. He established the worship of Hera, who had won in the contest for Argos, and is generally credited with being the originator of civilization in the Peloponnesus. According to some accounts, he married the nymph Cerdo and was the father of Iasus, Agenor, and Pelasgus, who divided the Peloponnesus between them. Others say his wife was Teledice, and his children were Apis and Niobe.

Phosphorus (fos′fọ-rus). In Greek mythology, the morning star; a son of Astraeus and Eos. It is also the name of the planet Venus when seen in the early dawn. Phosphorus is sometimes depicted as a youth carrying a blazing torch.

Phrixus (frik′sus). In Greek legend, a son of Athamas, king of Orchomenus in Boeotia, and Nephele, a cloud-born woman whom Athamas married at Hera's command. Phrixus was falsely accused by his aunt of making amorous advances to her. Actually, he had honorably scorned her approaches to him. In addition, Athamas' new wife, Ino, wished to remove him as an heir of Athamas so that her own children could inherit the kingdom. She therefore arranged a famine in the land and bribed messengers to bring word from the oracle at Delphi that only the sacrifice of Phrixus to the gods would lift the famine. As Athamas was about to put the knife to his throat a winged, golden-fleeced ram, sent by Hermes, arrived at the altar. Phrixus and his sister Helle leaped on the ram's back and were borne away through the skies. Helle fell off over the strait which now bears her name, Hellespont. Phrixus was carried safely to Colchis. There he was kindly received by the king, despite the the Colchians' reputation for unfriendliness, and sacrificed the ram as he had been instructed to do. Its golden fleece, guarded by a dragon, was fastened to an oak tree in a grove sacred to Ares. In Colchis, Phrixus married Chalciope, daughter of King Aeëtes. On his death he was denied proper burial. His ghost haunted Pelias, who had seized the throne of Iolcus, demanding proper burial rites and the return of the Golden Fleece to Hellas. This provided a ready pretext when Pelias sought to get rid of his unwelcome nephew Jason. See *Argonauts, Jason, Medea.*

Phyleus   (fī'lē̱-us, -lūs). In Greek legend, a son of Augeas, king of Elis. He witnessed Heracles' oath to cleanse the Augean stables in one day and his father's oath to pay Heracles one-tenth of his cattle if the task was performed on time. When Augeas refused to fulfill his part of the bargain, claiming he had never made it, Phyleus reminded him that he had been a witness to his oath. Augeas angrily banished his son and he went to Dulichium. Phyleus, father of Meges, was a famous horseman beloved of Zeus.

Phyllis   (fil'is). In Greek mythology, a princess of Bisaltia in Thrace. On his return from the Trojan War, Demophon, son of Theseus, landed at Thrace. Phyllis fell in love with him and married him, and he became king. After a time Demophon wished to return to Athens and, after promising Phyllis that he would return within a year, he made ready to leave. Phyllis gave him a casket which she said contained a charm, and told him not to open it until he had decided he would never return to her. At the end of the year Demophon had not returned. Phyllis invoked Rhea to curse his name, took poison, and died. At the same time, Demophon decided to open the casket. The sight of its contents (which remained forever unknown) is said to have driven him mad and caused his death. Another Thracian Phyllis fell in love with Demophon's brother Acamas, who had stopped in Thrace on his way to the Trojan War. When she learned of the fall of Troy she made eager visits to the shore to welcome him on his return, but as days passed and he did not come (storms had delayed him), she died of grief and was transformed into an almond tree by Athena. The next day Acamas arrived. He embraced the trunk of the almond tree, whereupon it instantly burst into flower. The Athenians performed dances annually in honor of Phyllis and Acamas.

Phylonome or *Philonome* (phil-on'ọ̄-mē). In Greek legend, the second wife of Cycnus of Colonae. She falsely accused Tenes, her stepson, of making advances to her and produced witnesses to attest to her lies. Cycnus banished his son. When Cycnus later learned that she had lied about Tenes he buried Phylonome alive.

Phytalus (fit'ạ-lus). In Greek mythology, one of the inhabitants of Eleusis who received Demeter when she was searching for Persephone. As a reward for his kindness to her Demeter gave him the fig tree and taught him how to cultivate it. His sons later purified Theseus for the murders he had committed on his way to Athens.

Phyteus (fit'ẹ-us). In Greek mythology, Apollo as the Pythian god, i.e., as killer of the dragon, Python, and specifically as god of the Delphic oracle.

Pielus (pī'ẹ-lus). According to Greek tradition, a son of Andromache and Neoptolemus, son of Achilles. Alexander the Great traced his descent from Neoptolemus and Andromache through this Pielus, one of whose descendants, they say, was Olympias, mother of Alexander and sister of King Neoptolemus of Epirus.

Pierides (pī-ir'i-dēz). In Greek mythology, the Muses. They were so named from Pieria in Thessaly, their reputed birthplace.

Pierides. In Greek legend, nine maidens of Pieria, in N Thessaly. They were so proud of their numbers and of their voices that they challenged the Muses to a contest on Mount Helicon. River-nymphs were selected to be the judges. When, not unexpectedly, the Muses were adjudged the winners, the Pierides hurled abuse on them. It was for this reason, not because of their arrogance in challenging the Muses, that they were turned into magpies with endless power to chatter and scold. The Pierides were so named and the incident thus reported by Nicander of Colophon, a poet of the 3rd century B.C. They are also said to be the daughters of Pierus, a king of Macedonia.

Pirene (pī-rē′nē). A daughter of the river-god Achelous, or of the river-god Asopus and Metope. Her son by Poseidon, Cenchrias, was accidentally slain by Artemis. Pirene wept so copiously that she was metamorphosed into a fountain, which was located at Corinth.

Pirithous (pī-rith′ọ̄-us). [Also: *Peirithous*.] In Greek legend, a Lapith prince, the son of Ixion and Dia, daughter of Eioneus, or, as some say, a son of Zeus and Dia. He heard of the great exploits of Theseus and resolved to find out whether he could live up to his reputation for strength and courage. To carry out his resolve he invaded Attica and made a raid on a herd of cattle near Marathon. Theseus pursued him, whereupon Pirithous turned in his tracks to confront him and test his mettle. But when he saw Theseus, who showed every sign of his reputed valor, he had a change of heart. Instead of fighting him he admitted his wrong and put himself in Theseus' hands, to ask of him whatever recompense he desired. Theseus answered that the only recompense he wanted was the friendship of Pirithous. They then swore an oath of friendship which both kept until death. Pirithous married Hippodamia, daughter of Butes. He invited Theseus and many noted guests to the wedding, at which the centaurs were also present, but he did not invite Eris and Ares, and they determined to punish him for the slight. The centaurs became unruly as the result of taking too much wine, which in their ignorance they had failed to dilute with water, and attacked the bride. Pirithous, with the ready assistance of Theseus, fought them off and drove them from the wedding festivities. Pirithous was a member of the hunt for the Calydonian Boar and some say he accompanied Theseus on his expedition to the land of the Amazons. He had a son, Polypoetes, by Hippodamia, who later fought in the Trojan War. When Hippodamia subsequently died, Pirithous determined to seek a daughter of Zeus for a wife. He made a compact with Theseus by which they agreed to abduct Helen, the supposed daughter of Tyndareus, and draw lots to see which would win her. They bound themselves by oath that the winner would assist the loser to gain the bride he might seek. On the successful abduction of Helen, Pirithous lost in the drawing of the lots. He chose Persephone as the wife he would seek, and in spite of the efforts of Theseus to dissuade him he insisted that no other woman would suit him. Theseus, bound by his oath, descended to Tartarus with him and demanded Persephone from Hades. Hades, who received them courteously, invited them to be seated. Unwittingly, they took seats on Chairs of Forgetfulness, and instantly the chairs grew about them. They were unable to move. They sat there for years. Heracles, on a mission to fetch Cerberus from Tartarus, found them and answered their pleas for help. He wrenched Theseus from his chair but Pirithous, whose impious idea it was to invade the world of the dead and steal Persephone, remains fast to his chair, and there he sits through eternity.

Pittheus (pit'thūs). In Greek legend, a son of Pelops and Hippodamia. He was king in Troezen, a city which he named after his brother and which he dedicated to Athena and Poseidon, and was said to have been the wisest man of his time. He founded an oracle of Apollo in Troezen, dedicated an altar to Themis, and was a teacher of oratory and rhetoric. He gave his daughter Aethra to King Aegeus, who was paying him a visit, and reared and instructed their son Theseus, in Troezen. Later he adopted Hippolytus, son of Theseus and Antiope, and made him heir to the throne of Troezen.

Pitys (pi'tis). In Greek mythology, a nymph who fled from Pan and was changed into a fir tree. Pan used the branches of the tree for a garland for his head.

Pleiades (plē'a̯-dēz, plī). [Also: *Pleiads*.] In Greek mythology, the daughters of Atlas and Pleione. They were born on Mount Cyllene in Arcadia, and their names are: Alcyone, Celaeno, Electra, Maia, Merope, Sterope (or Asterope), and Taÿgete. According to some accounts they were transformed into doves by the gods to protect them from Orion who had been pursuing them for five years, and their images were set among the stars. Others say they killed themselves in grief for their sisters, the Hyades, and were placed among the stars by the gods. Only six of them are visible in the cluster because Merope, ashamed that she was the only one of the sisters to have married a mortal, withdrew. Other accounts say it is Electra who is missing, and that she withdrew so that she would not be compelled to witness the fall of Troy, founded by her son. Literally, Pleiades means "The Weepers;" they are also called the Seven Sisters. Their rising is the signal that the time for the spring sowing is at hand, and their setting marks the time of harvest.

Pluto (plö'tō). In Greek mythology, a cult name of Hades, god of the infernal regions. The word means "rich one" or "wealth-giver," and thus he is associated with Plutus. Pluto is commonly the name used for him in the Persephone abduction myth. The Romans called him Dis.

Plutus (plö'tus). In Greek mythology, a personification of wealth; a son of Iasion and Demeter, and intimately associated with Irene, goddess of peace, who is often represented in art holding the infant Plutus. Zeus is said to have blinded him in order that he might not bestow his favors exclusively on good men, but should distribute his gifts without regard to merit (however, by some accounts he was later cured and gave wealth only to those whom he could see were honest).

Podalirius (pod-a-lī'ri-us). In Greek legend, a son of Asclepius. He and his brother Machaon, both "excellent leeches," accompanied the Greeks to the Trojan War as physicians. According to some accounts, Podalirius healed Philoctetes of his noisome wound when he was brought from Lemnos to Troy in the last year of the war. Others say it was Machaon who cured him. Podalirius tended the wounds the Greeks received at the hands of the Trojans as well as the wounds they gave each other, as at the funeral games for Achilles. When Machaon was killed Podalirius was wild with grief and was only prevented from taking his own life on his brother's grave by the persuasion of Nestor. Later he was among those who entered Troy in the Wooden Horse. He did not sail for Greece at the close of the war, but went overland to Colophon in Caria and then, searching for a place to settle, he chose Syrnos, in Caria, a spot ringed by mountains. He selected this site to fulfill instructions given by the oracle to go where he would be safe, even if the skies should fall. He shrewdly considered that the mountains surrounding his new home would hold up the skies if they should temporarily slip from their moorings.

Podarces (pō-där'sēz). The original name of Priam. When Heracles attacked Troy to punish Laomedon for reneging

on his promise, he killed Laomedon and all of his sons
except Podarces. He took Hesione captive and awarded her
to Telamon. Hesione was given the chance to ransom any
of the prisoners she chose and she chose her brother Podarces, after which he took the name Priam.

Podarge (pō-där′jē). In Greek mythology, a Harpy. She was
the mother, by Zephyr (the West Wind) of the immortal
horses Balius and Xanthus, which Poseidon gave to Peleus
at his marriage to Thetis. The horses afterward went to the
Trojan War with Achilles.

Poeas (pē′as). In Greek legend, a king of Meliboea, in Thessaly. He was an Argonaut and, according to some accounts,
as the Argonauts passed Crete on their way home Poeas
killed Talos, the bronze man of Crete, by shooting him in
his vulnerable heel with a poisoned arrow. When Heracles,
in agony as the result of the burns of a poisoned robe,
begged that someone would light the funeral pyre on which
he was lying, only Poeas had the courage and sympathy to
cast the brand which set the pyre afire. In return Heracles
gave him his bow and arrows, which Poeas later gave to his
own son Philoctetes to take to Troy. Others say it was Philoctetes, at the command of Poeas, who set fire to the pyre
and received the bow and arrows.

Poena (pē′na). [Also: *Poine*.] A goddess of punishment and a
companion of Nemesis. Poena is also pictured as a monster
who robbed mothers of their children. She was sent by
Apollo to ravage Argos to punish Argos for the deaths of
Linus and Psamathe. The depredations of Poena ceased
when the Argives raised a temple to Apollo and established
a festival in honor of Linus and Psamathe.

Pollux (pol′uks). Latin name of Polydeuces. See *Dioscuri.*

Polybus (pol′i-bus). In Greek legend, the king of Corinth,
husband of Periboea, or Merope, to whom Oedipus was
brought as an infant after shepherds had found him on the
mountain with his ankles pierced. Polybus brought Oedipus
up to believe he was his own son, and it was to avoid fulfillment of the prophecy that he would kill his father that
Oedipus left Corinth and went to Thebes. Polybus died
peacefully of old age.

Polybotes (pol-i-bō′tēz). In Greek mythology, one of the
Giants, a son of Gaea and the blood of Uranus, who waged
war on the gods. In the battle he fled to Cos. Poseidon

pursued him there and broke off a chunk of the island, hurled it at Polybotes and buried him under it. The new island thus formed became known as Nisyrus.

Polycaste (pol-i-kas′tē). In Greek mythology, the sister of Daedalus. She was the mother of Talos, a gifted smith. Daedalus, jealous of the boy's skill, hurled him from the top of the Acropolis. Polycaste was so grief-stricken over her son's death that she hanged herself and was metamorphosed into a bird. Some say the bird that chattered and laughed while the sorrowing Daedalus later buried the body of his own son Icarus, was Polycaste, delighted to see Daedalus suffer as she had suffered. The Athenians built a sanctuary in honor of Polycaste beside the Acropolis. Polycaste is also sometimes called Perdix.

Polydamas (pō-lid′a-mas). In Greek legend, a son of Panthous and Phrontis. He was the brother of Euphorbus and Hyperenor, and was a close friend of Hector. In the Trojan War he showed himself as a daring and courageous fighter, but as an even more courageous and skillful strategist who dared argue with Hector about the conduct of the war. In the attack on the Greek fortifications he advised Hector not to take his horses and chariots through the Greek moat lest the Greeks, in a counterattack, force them back into the narrow moat where there would be no room to maneuver and they would become easy targets for the Greeks. Instead, he advised that they attack on foot. Hector was pleased to follow this advice and the attack was successful. But as they prepared to breach the wall an eagle, clutching a serpent in its talons, flew over. The serpent, still alive and writhing, bit the eagle and the eagle screamed and dropped it to the ground. Polydamas interpreted this to mean that the Trojans, if they attacked the wall now, would miss the prize and many would fail to return, even as the eagle had failed to return with its prey to its nest. He therefore urged Hector to withdraw and regroup his forces. Hector scorned his advice, and accused him of being frightened by the confusion of battle. Polydamas smarted under this rebuke but continued to advise what he thought was sensible and possible. When Achilles had driven the Trojans back simply by appearing unarmed at the ships, Polydamas again advised withdrawal. He said they should withdraw into the city and fight from there, but again his advice was scorned. Later, as

Hector stood alone outside the walls he remembered what Polydamas had advised and regretted that he had not followed his counsel. He felt that the approaching defeat was his fault for ignoring Polydamas. After the death of Hector, and later that of Penthesilea, the Trojans withdrew to the city in terror. Polydamas now counseled that they neither flee, as some urged, nor wait the arrival of other help, as others suggested. Rather he advised they should restore Helen with rich gifts to Menelaus. To the accusation of Paris that this was cowardice, Polydamas replied that he preferred wise discretion to foolish valor. His interest was in protecting the city, whereas Paris was bringing ruin to Troy. But the proposal to restore Helen which he had made many times was never carried out. Nor was his final plea to retire and fight from the walls and towers of the city heeded, for each time aid came to the Trojans they sallied out of the city and fought on the plain. Polydamas was probably right in all his advice, but the end result had already been determined by the gods.

Polydectes (pol-i-dek′tēz). In Greek legend, a son of Magnes and a nymph. He was the brother of that Dictys who rescued Perseus and Danaë when they were washed ashore on Seriphus. Polydectes was king of Seriphus. He wanted to marry Danaë, but was prevented from doing so by Perseus. In order to get rid of Perseus, Polydectes sent him to get the head of Medusa, on the pretext that this would be a suitable gift for him to give for his supposed plan to marry Hippodamia, daughter of Oenomaus. Polydectes was convinced that Perseus would be killed on this errand. While Perseus was away, Polydectes sought Danaë but she fled with Dictys and hid in a temple. When Perseus returned he searched for and found his mother and learned of the treachery of Polydectes. He went to the court and turned Polydectes and his followers to stone by revealing to them the head of Medusa.

Polydeuces (pol-i-dū′sēz). The twin brother of Castor. See **Dioscuri**.

Polydorus (pol-i-dō′rus). In Greek legend, the youngest son of Priam and Hecuba. During the Trojan War he was sent to Polymnestor, a king in Thrace, for safe-keeping, along with a great store of treasure. Polymnestor betrayed the Trojan allies and went over to Agamemnon. He murdered Polydorus and stole the treasure he had brought with him.

---

fat, fāte, fär, fåll, àsk, fāre; net, mē, hėr; pin, pīne; not, nōte, mõve, nôr; up, lūte, pùll; oi, oil; ou out; (lightened) ĕlect, agǫny, ūnite;

After the war, when Aeneas landed in Thrace and attempted to found a city, the blood of Polydorus gushed black from the ground and the voice of Polydorus warned Aeneas not to settle there. The voice further told of Polydorus' murder by Polymnestor and of his anguish because he had not been given honorable burial. Aeneas performed funeral honors for Polydorus, and then, in accordance with his advice, sailed away.

Polyhymnia (pol-i-him'ni-ạ), or *Polymnia* (po-lim'ni-ạ). One of the nine daughters of Zeus and Mnemosyne. She is the muse of the sublime hymn and also of pantomime and the religious dance. In art she is usually represented in a meditative attitude, heavily draped, and without any attribute. See *Muses.*

Polyidus (pol-i-ī'dus). In Greek mythology, a seer of Corinth, and a descendant of Melampus. He advised Bellerophon to capture the winged horse Pegasus in order to kill the Chimaera. He was visiting in Crete when Glaucus, young son of King Minos, disappeared and could not be found. On likening a heifer—which changed color from white to red to black —to a mulberry which changes color in the same order as it ripens, Polyidus was informed that, in accordance with instructions from an oracle, he must find Glaucus. He found Glaucus drowned in a vat of honey, and was then told he must restore the drowned child to life. Polyidus, watching by the dead child, saw a serpent glide near the body. He killed it. Presently another serpent approached, and finding its mate dead it slid off and returned with an herb which it laid on the dead serpent's body, whereupon the dead serpent was slowly revived and glided away. Polyidus took the herb and applied it to the corpse of Glaucus. The child too, was restored to life. Polyidus was given rich gifts by Minos, who commanded him to teach the arts of divination to Glaucus. Polyidus did so, but before he left Crete he commanded Glaucus to spit into his open mouth. As soon as Glaucus did so he forgot all Polyidus had taught him. Polyidus prophesied that his own son Euchenor, who was longing to join the Greeks in the Trojan War, would either die in his home, worn out by affliction, or fall at Troy if he accompanied the Greeks. Knowing the alternatives, his son went to Troy, where he perished from one of Paris' arrows.

Polymnestor (pol-im-nes′tọr). In Greek legend, a king in Thrace and the husband of Ilione, oldest daughter of Priam. Polydorus, the youngest son of Priam and Hecuba, was sent to Polymnestor with great treasure for safe-keeping during the Trojan War. Polymnestor changed sides and went over to Agamemnon. He murdered Polydorus and stole the treasure. When Hecuba, brought as a captive to Thrace after the war, learned of Polydorus' death—according to some accounts, his body was washed ashore at her feet—she, with other captive Trojan women, blinded Polymnestor and killed his children.

Polynices or *Polyneices* (pol-i-nī′sēz). In Greek legend, a son of Oedipus and Jocasta. After the withdrawal of Oedipus from Thebes, Polynices and his brother Eteocles agreed to share the throne of Thebes by ruling alternately. Eteocles, the elder, ruled first, but when his term came to an end he refused to relinquish the throne on the grounds of Polynices' violent character, and banished Polynices. He fled to Argos, to the court of King Adrastus. There he fell into a quarrel with Tydeus of Calydon, who had also fled to Argos. Adrastus separated them and, remembering an oracle which told him to yoke his daughters in marriage to a boar and a lion, he gave his daughter Aegia (or Argia) to Polynices, who bore the device of a lion on his shield, and promised to restore him to his lands. Aegia bore Polynices a son, Thersander. Adrastus now proposed to march on Thebes and began to assemble the leaders of the expedition of the Seven against Thebes. Polynices bribed Eriphyle, wife of the seer Amphiaraus, to persuade her husband to accompany the expedition by giving her the necklace of Harmonia which he had brought with him from Thebes. This necklace had been given to Harmonia as a wedding gift by Aphrodite, and had a history of bringing disaster to its possessor. In the war on Thebes, Polynices met Eteocles face to face and in single combat to decide who should have the throne, the brothers killed each other. All the other Argive leaders were slain except Adrastus, who fled on his winged horse Arion. Creon, uncle of Polynices and Eteocles, succeeded to the throne of Thebes. He gave orders that the bodies of the Argive dead should remain unburied. Polynices' body was cast out of the city to become the prey of scavenger birds because he had treacherously attacked his own city. But

Antigone, the sister of Polynices, defied Creon's order and gave her brother's body a ritual burial. Creon sentenced her to death for disobeying his order.

Polyphemus (pol-i-fē′mus). In Greek mythology, a one-eyed giant, the chief of the Cyclopes. He was a son of Poseidon and the owner of great flocks and bountiful gardens. He loved Galatea, the daughter of Nereus and Doris, and for love of her tried to tame his wild appearance and gave up his savage ways. But Galatea loved Acis and paid no attention to the songs of love that Polyphemus played to her on his shepherd's pipe, nor to his promises of gifts and honors. When Polyphemus, sighing of love for Galatea, came upon her lying in the arms of Acis, he was enraged. Galatea escaped his wrath, but Acis was crushed under a huge rock hurled at him by Polyphemus.

Telemus, a seer, had warned Polyphemus that one day Odysseus would come and put out his single eye, but Polyphemus scorned the prophecy. When Odysseus, with some of his companions, appeared in his cave, Polyphemus rolled a great stone before the entrance and imprisoned them. Each day thereafter he devoured some of them when he returned from the fields with his sheep, until the wily Odysseus made him drunk and put out his eye with a wooden stake especially sharpened for that purpose. Polyphemus screamed in pain and rage, but when his brothers gathered outside the cave and asked who was wounding him he replied, "Noman," for that was the name Odysseus had given him, and his brothers went away. The Greeks escaped the next day by clinging to the bellies of the sheep which Polyphemus let out of the cave to graze. As they fled to the shore and their ship Odysseus could not resist shouting back to Polyphemus and telling him who he really was. Polyphemus recalled the prophecy of Telemus and was chagrined, because he had expected Odysseus, if he ever came, to be a bigger man. As the mocking Greeks sailed off Polyphemus called on his father Poseidon to avenge him; and this was the reason that Poseidon prevented Odysseus from returning to his homeland for such a long time.

Polyphontes (po-li-fon′tēz). According to tradition, a brother of Cresphontes, king of Messenia. He murdered Cresphontes and two of his sons in a rebellion, and married Merope, Cresphontes' widow. A third son of Cresphontes

(obscured) errạnt, ardẹnt, actọr; ch, chip; g, go; th, thin; ᵵʜ, then; y, you; (variable) ḍ as d or j, ṣ as s or sh, ṭ as t or ch, ẓ as z or zh.

and Merope had been sent away for safety during the rebellion, and survived, unknown to Polyphontes. He secretly returned to Messenia and announced to Polyphontes that he was the murderer of Cresphontes' third son, Aepytus. When Merope heard of his coming, and learned that Aepytus was no longer in the place where she had sent him for safe-keeping, she resolved to kill this self-confessed murderer. But when she went to do so he was revealed to her as her own son Aepytus, come in disguise to kill Polyphontes. Thereupon Merope and Aepytus resolved to kill Polyphontes and did so. Others say that Polyphontes was not the brother but the uncle of Cresphontes, and that it was Cresphontes who slew him.

Polyxena (pō-lik′sē-na̯). In Greek legend, a daughter of Priam and Hecuba. Achilles saw her, either in the temple of Apollo or on the walls of Troy at the time of the ransoming of Hector's body, and fell in love with her. He tried by secret negotiations to persuade either Hector or Priam to give her to him, but the price demanded was too high and involved either treachery (Hector), or abandoning Helen to the Trojans (Priam). As he was dying from Paris' wound Achilles is said to have requested that Polyxena be sacrificed on his barrow, and after the fall of Troy the shade of Achilles appeared to Neoptolemus, his son, in a dream, and warned that he would send high winds to prevent the Greeks from sailing for home if Polyxena was not sacrificed to appease his shade. Calchas, the seer, confirmed that only the death of Polyxena would bring favorable winds. Agamemnon was unwilling to shed more blood but he was ultimately persuaded by Odysseus to agree to the sacrifice, and a herald was sent to fetch Polyxena from her mother's side. She accompanied the herald willingly as she had, she said, nothing to live for except dishonor and slavery. She bared her throat to the sacrificial knife with such courage that even the Greeks were overawed and gave her honorable burial. After her death, the storm winds were stilled and a favorable breeze permitted the Greeks to sail. Some say the sacrifice of Polyxena occurred at Troy. Others say it took place after the Greeks and their captives had already left Troy and landed in Thrace. Other accounts say that Polyxena had fallen in love with Achilles, and had run away from Troy to join him in the Greek camp, and killed herself at his death.

She was the subject of a lost tragedy by Sophocles, and of the tragedies *Hecuba* by Euripides and *Troades* by Seneca, but she is not mentioned by Homer.

Pontus (pon'tus). In Greek religion, a personification of the sea. He is variously mentioned as both son and consort of Gaea, the earth goddess, and as the father of Nereus, Ceto, Phorcys, and others.

Poseidon (pō-sī'dọn). One of the 12 Olympian gods, son of Cronus and Rhea, brother of Zeus and Hades. He was lord of the sea and navigation. The Arcadians say that when Rhea bore Poseidon she laid him in a flock of lambs in Arcadia to save him from Cronus, and gave Cronus a foal to swallow in his stead. A spring near Mantinea called "the Lamb" was named by the Arcadians as the place near which Poseidon was hidden. Some say he was brought up by the Telchines of Rhodes, who forged the trident with which he cleft rocks, caused fountains and springs to gush forth, and raked the sea into mighty storms. But the general account is that Poseidon, like his brothers and sisters before him, was swallowed up by his father Cronus as soon as he was born. Zeus tricked Cronus into disgorging the children he had swallowed, and the brothers immediately plotted to dethrone their father. The Cyclopes provided them with weapons, giving the trident to Poseidon, and they waged war on the Titans, of whom Atlas was the leader since Cronus had become too feeble for the role. The Titans were defeated; Cronus was overthrown and fled. Zeus, Hades, and Poseidon cast lots in a helmet to divide up the universe among them. Poseidon drew the sea as his realm. Zeus drew the heavens, and Hades drew the underworld; earth and Olympus were shared by all. Poseidon built an underwater palace for himself near Aegae, in Euboea. In its stables he kept his white chariot horses with bronze hoofs and golden manes, and a golden chariot. Clad in a robe of gold he rode the sea in this equipage, accompanied by sporting dolphins, tritons, and other sea creatures. At his approach storms were dispelled, the waves flattened, and the sea smiled. At first Zeus, Hades, and Poseidon were equal in power, but gradually Zeus came to be the acknowledged master of them all. He was so overbearing that the gods and goddesses on Olympus revolted and bound him as he slept. Through the intervention of the Nereid Thetis, Zeus was freed by Briareus.

Enraged at their rebellion, Zeus punished the gods. He sent Poseidon and Apollo as servants to King Laomedon of Troy, who commanded them to build a wall about his city. Some say Poseidon and Apollo were assisted in their task by Aeacus, a son of Zeus, because if the wall were built by the gods alone it would be invulnerable. When the wall was

POSEIDON
Red-figured Greek amphora, Nikoxenus Painter

finished, Laomedon refused to pay Poseidon and Apollo as he had promised. On the contrary, he threatened to cut off their ears and send them off in chains. Poseidon sent a sea-monster to scourge Laomedon's country, and would not recall it until Laomedon agreed to sacrifice his daughter Hesione to it. Laomedon exposed Hesione on a rock for the monster, but Heracles came along and slew it, and gave Hesione to his friend Telamon.

Poseidon was ever seeking to increase his realm, trying as he could to encroach on the land and add it to his sea kingdom. He contended with Athena for control of Athens. He struck the rock of the Acropolis with his trident and caused a fountain of sea water to gush forth. Athena planted an olive tree as her gift to the city and claimed the city for herself. Poseidon challenged her to single combat, and she accepted. However, Zeus forbade them to fight, and ordered their dispute submitted to the gods and goddesses for settlement. All the gods voted in favor of Poseidon and the goddesses voted in favor of Athena, and since Zeus had refused to take part, Athena won by one vote and claimed the city. Poseidon was so enraged he sent a flood over the Thriasian plain. In the end he was reconciled to Athena, and shared her temple, the Erechtheum, on the Acropolis. In his part of the temple the well of sea water he had caused to spring forth was housed, and whenever the south wind blew a sound of the sea could be heard coming from it. He contended with Hera for control of Argolis. Their dispute was submitted to the river-gods Cephissus, Inachus, and Asterion. The river-gods awarded the land to Hera. This time Poseidon, since, some say, he had promised to send no more floods, dried up the rivers, so that ever after their beds were dry in summer. Danaus came into the land with his 50 daughters and urged them to find some way to propitiate Poseidon. Amymone, one of his daughters, was seized by a satyr one day while hunting. Poseidon, hearing her cries, came to her rescue and hurled his trident at the satyr. The satyr dodged and the trident pierced a rock from which a spring immediately gushed forth. Poseidon fell in love with Amymone and embraced her. She bore him a son, Nauplius, and Poseidon promised that the spring his trident had brought forth would never fail. As the fountain of Amymone, it is the source of the Lerna River, which does not dry up in the summer. But some say Poseidon, in this contest with Hera for Argolis, inundated Argos, and was finally persuaded by Hera to withdraw the waters, and that because of the flooding he was called Prosclystius (*Flooder*). The Argives raised a sanctuary to Poseidon Prosclystius at the point in Argos where the flood ebbed. And some say he sent brine to kill the roots and seeds in the land about Hermione, but when he was propitiated by sacrifices and prayers he stopped sending the brine and the plants grew and the land prospered. For this reason he was called Phytalmios (*Nourishing*). Poseidon vied with Helius for control of Corinthia, and was awarded the isthmus by Briareus. The land became sacred to him and altars of Isthmian Poseidon were raised.

(obscured) errant, ardent, actor; ch, chip; g, go; th, thin; ŦH, then; y, you;
(variable) ḍ as d or j, ṣ as s or sh, ṭ as t or ch, ẓ as z or zh.

In a second contest with Athena, he claimed Troezen. Zeus ordered them to share control, and the Troezenians worshiped him as "King." He even claimed Aegina, an island belonging to Zeus, and Naxos, the island of Dionysus, but his claim in each case was useless.

Poseidon and Zeus were rivals for the love of the Nereid Thetis, but when they learned from an oracle that she would bear a son greater than his father, they both lost interest in her. Poseidon then courted Amphitrite, another Nereid. She fled, and he sent Delphinus as ambassador to plead his cause. Delphinus was successful and Amphitrite agreed to marry Poseidon. As a reward, Poseidon set the image of Delphinus among the stars as the constellation of the Dolphin. Amphitrite bore Triton, Rhode, and Benthesicyme to Poseidon. He was a very inconstant husband and had nearly as many love affairs as Zeus. When Amphitrite learned of his love for the sea-nymph Scylla, she transformed the unfortunate nymph into a monster with six hideous dogs' heads and 12 long arms. Poseidon also wooed Medusa, once a beautiful maiden, but because he made love to her in one of Athena's temples the goddess transformed her into a hideous snaky-haired Gorgon. When Perseus cut off Medusa's head, the monster Chrysaor and the winged horse Pegasus sprang from her spilled blood; these were her children by Poseidon. He carried off Tyro, daughter of Salmoneus and, hidden by a huge violet sea wave, ravished her. She bore him Pelias and Neleus. By Libya, a daughter of Epaphus and a granddaughter of Zeus, he was the father of the Phoenician kings Agenor and Belus. He seduced Alope, daughter of King Cercyon of Arcadia. She bore him a son Hippothous. When Alope died he transformed her into a spring. The nymph Caenis was seized and embraced by him, and he promised to fulfill whatever wish she might ask. She asked to be transformed into an invulnerable man. He carried out his promise, and as a man she was named Caeneus. Aethra, daughter of King Pittheus of Troezen, having been embraced by Aegeus, king of Athens, was ordered in a dream to wade across to the island of Sphaeria and make an offering in the temple there. While she was there Poseidon came upon her and ravished her. For this reason, some say that he was the father of Theseus. Most say Aegeus was his father, but Poseidon many times came to his aid, and prom

fat, fāte, fär, fåll, ȧsk, fãre; net, mē, hėr; pin, pīne; not, nōte, mȯve, nôr; up, lūte, pu̇ll; oi, oil; ou out; (lightened) ēlect, agȯny, ūnite

ised to fulfill any three wishes Theseus might ask of him. Theseus used one of his wishes to request the destruction of his own son Hippolytus, who he thought had betrayed him with his wife Phaedra. Poseidon sent a great sea-monster, riding the crest of a huge wave, to frighten the horses drawing the chariot of Hippolytus. The horses bolted, overturned the chariot, and dragged Hippolytus to his death. By Gaea Poseidon was the father of Antaeus, king in Libya, whose strength increased as his body had contact with the earth. Antaeus forced strangers to wrestle with him, and when he had slain them he used their skulls to build a temple to his father Poseidon. Antaeus was slain by Heracles. Amycus, king of the Bebryces; Cycnus who was transformed into a swan; Busiris, king of Egypt; Orion whose image was placed among the stars; the Argonauts Ancaeus and Euphemus; Halirrhothius, slain by Ares, and Eumolpus, priest of Eleusis slain by Erechtheus, were among his many sons. He won Aphrodite's gratitude by offering to pay off her marriage gifts to Hephaestus when she had been discovered with Ares. She bore him Rhodus and Herophilus. He pursued Demeter who was desperately searching for her lost daughter Persephone. Demeter sought to escape by transforming herself into a mare. Poseidon changed himself to a stallion and ravished her. She bore him the marvelous horse Arion and Despoena, a nymph. Some say it was because he transformed himself into a stallion on this occasion that he had the epithet Hippios *(Horse)*. At the foot of Mount Alesium in Arcadia, Agamedes and Trophonius built a sanctuary of Poseidon Hippios from oak logs. Some say that a sea wave rose up in the sanctuary. Odysseus dedicated an image of Poseidon Hippios at Pheneüs in Arcadia, and there was an altar of Poseidon Hippios at Olympia. He was especially worshiped by this name in Attica, perhaps because, as some say, he created the horse by striking the rock of the Acropolis with his trident. Some say Poseidon was the father of Athena, and a blue-eyed statue of the goddess in Athens was taken as evidence of his paternity.

In the Trojan War, Poseidon aided the Greeks whenever possible. At one time he disguised himself as the seer Calchas in order to talk to the Greeks and inspire them with renewed courage for the fight, but he was recognized as a god by his well-formed legs. He aided the Greeks because he had never forgotten that Laomedon cheated him when l built the walls of Troy. But when the Greeks took advantag of a truce for burial of the dead to build a great wall abov their ships, Poseidon complained to Zeus that the Greek wa might rival the wall he himself had built about Troy with th aid of Apollo. Zeus soothed him by assuring him that as lor of the sea he could break down the Greek wall whenever h wished, and after the war was over Poseidon diverted th courses of several rivers, washed them against the Gree wall and destroyed it. Though he favored the Greeks in th war, he once rescued Aeneas when he was wounded, out pity for the Trojan hero. After the war, he joined wit Athena to harass the Greeks on their return from Troy sending great storms at sea. The change of heart of the god toward the Greeks was occasioned in part by the suppose arrogance of Ajax the Lesser. Poseidon's greatest anger wa reserved for Odysseus. On the way home Odysseus stoppe at the island of Polyphemus the Cyclops, a son of Poseido To escape from him Odysseus blinded Polyphemus. Th latter called on Poseidon for vengeance. To avenge his soi Poseidon harried Odysseus unmercifully, and prevente him from returning home for ten years.

In earliest times Poseidon was a god of the depths of th earth. In this aspect he was thought to cause earthquake whence his title "Earth-shaker," and was especially wo shiped in regions subject to earthquake, as Sparta and The saly. It was Poseidon, for example, who cleft the earth wit one of his earthquakes and created the Vale of Tempe i Thessaly. In most ancient times he shared the oracle a Delphi with Gaea. When Apollo slew the Python tha guarded the oracle and seized it for himself, he gave th island of Calauria, off the coast of Troezen, to Poseidon i exchange for his half of the oracle. Poseidon came increas ingly to be worshiped solely as a god of the sea, who ha sovereignty over all its waters, everything in them, and nav gation on them. He raised storms and caused shipwreck o calmed the waters at his pleasure; he also gave victory at se and because he could send favorable winds or victory he wa called Soter (*Giver of Safety*). His temples were usually to b found on promontories and headlands jutting into the se typical were those at Taenarum and Sunium, where in th latter place ruins of his temple may still be seen. As god o the sea he was the "Earth-girdler," for the sea was thought to be a vast band surrounding the earth. He was particularly worshiped by seafaring peoples, who claimed descent from him. The island of Chios, for example, was named for a son of Poseidon; Nauplia, the port on the Gulf of Argolis, was founded by his son, Nauplius; the Phaeacians, greatest sailors of legend, were said to be his descendants. Away from the sea, Poseidon was worshiped as the donor of the life-giving waters of springs and fountains. He was also worshiped as a god of horses. His worship was very ancient and extended throughout the Greek world. The Ionians of Helice in Achaea had a very holy sanctuary of Heliconian Poseidon. When they were expelled from Helice they went to Athens, where they continued to worship Heliconian Poseidon. Afterward, the descendants of these Ionians emigrated to the coasts of Asia Minor and colonized the region that came to be known as Ionia. They carried Heliconian Poseidon with them and spread his cult in the expanding Greek world. They raised altars to him near Miletus and in Teos, and in their chief sanctuary on the promontory of Mycale, the Ionians celebrated their great festival in honor of Heliconian Poseidon called the Panionia. As for the original site of the cult of Heliconian Poseidon, Helice in Achaea, Poseidon caused it to be swallowed up by an earthquake and drowned in a flood, because the Achaeans dragged some suppliants from his altar in the shrine there.

The horse, dolphin, and pine tree were sacred to Poseidon. Bulls, especially black ones, were sacrificed to him, and sometimes flung alive into rivers to propitiate him. In Ionia and Thessaly bull-fights were held in his honor. His chief festival was the Isthmian Games, which were held every other year on the Isthmus of Corinth. In these games, of which he was the patron, the victors were crowned with wreaths of his sacred pine. After the victory of the Greeks over the Persians at Plataea (479 B.C.) the Greeks used part of the Persian booty to erect a bronze statue of Isthmian Poseidon ten feet high. Other great statues of Poseidon stood at harbors and on promontories. In art Poseidon is represented as a majestic figure; his most common attributes are the trident, the dolphin, and the horse. The original Roman or Italic Neptune became assimilated to him.

Pothos (pō'thos). The personification of desire and longing
A companion of Aphrodite, along with Eros, Himeros, an
the Graces.

Praxidicae (prak-sid'i-sē). In Greek religion, three goddesse
of justice, especially of retribution. They were often so
emnly sworn by, but always in the open air (even their tem
ple had no roof). The singular form of the name was a
epithet of Persephone.

Priam (prī'am). In Greek legend, a son of Laomedon, king o
Troy, and Strymo; and a descendant of Dardanus and Tro
He was originally named Podarces, "swift-footed." Whe
Heracles sacked Troy to punish Laomedon for reneging o
his agreement to pay Heracles for the destruction of a sea
monster, Podarces and his sister, Hesione, were taken cap
tive. Laomedon and his other sons were slain. Hesione wa
awarded to Telamon and was allowed to ransom any one o
the captives. She ransomed Podarces with her veil. Hence
forth he was called Priam, meaning, according to popula
etymology, "redeemed." Heracles gave Laomedon's ruine
kingdom to Priam, because he had urged Laomedon to pa
Heracles as promised. Priam rebuilt the city on the old sit
and restored the kingdom to a state of great wealth an
prosperity. He first married Arisbe, the daughter of Merops
the seer. By her he had one son, Aesacus. After the birth o
this son Priam gave Arisbe to Hyrtacus for a wife, and h
married Hecuba. Priam was said to have fathered 50 sons
19 of them by Hecuba, and 12 daughters. They all live
about the palace courtyard with their wives and husbands
Among Priam's children were Hector, Paris, the twins—
Helenus and Cassandra—Deïphobus, Polites, Polydorus
Antiphus, and Troilus; and among his daughters there wer
Creusa, Laodice, and Polyxena. According to some, Hecto
and Troilus were Hecuba's sons by Apollo. Ominous por
tents before the birth of Paris caused Priam to order him t
be exposed at birth, but he was saved, and restored as
young man, although seers and prophets urged that he b
destroyed or he would bring ruin to Troy. Priam gave hi
approval when Paris asked for a fleet to sail to Sparta, possi
bly under the impression that Paris would demand satisfac
tion for the abduction of Hesione. And when Paris returned
after many months, with Helen of the flawless beauty, Priam
like all Troy, fell in love with her, vowed he would never le

her go, and did not chide Paris at all for his flagrant breach of hospitality. He refused all requests by Greek envoys for the return of Helen, and as he was too old to fight himself he entrusted the command of the Trojans to his son Hector. One after another he saw his sons fall before the ferocious onslaughts of the Greeks. When Achilles rejoined the Greeks in their siege against Troy, Priam watched from the towers as Achilles drove Hector to the walls of the city. He pleaded with his son to come inside the walls, but Hector remained to face Achilles and death. The Trojans saw Achilles' barbarous treatment of Hector's body before he dragged it away to the Greek camp behind his chariot. Iris appeared to Priam with a message from Zeus which advised Priam to go to Achilles alone and ransom Hector's body. With one frail companion the aged king set out, carrying great treasure. Hermes came to guide him and spirited him into the tent of Achilles. Some say Achilles was sleeping and that Priam might easily have murdered him and avenged the death of his son. But Priam is always pictured as a man of honor, grave, courteous, and humane, with an abiding interest and love for his children. He appealed to Achilles on his knees for the return of Hector's body. The old king pointed out that few had done what he was doing, kissing the hands that had killed his son. Achilles and Priam wept together— the one for his dead friend, the other for his son. Achilles was touched by the dignity and frailty of the bereaved king who reminded him of his father. He promised to give him Hector's body and to allow the Trojans a truce of as many days as they required to perform funeral honors for Hector. In pride and grief Priam then conveyed his son's body back to Troy and the whole city mourned. In succeeding days Priam was encouraged by the arrival of Penthesilea, Memnon, and Eurypylus, only to see them all fall before the enemy. He also lost Paris, the cause of all the disaster. Now the Greeks resorted to stratagem; they left the Wooden Horse before the walls of Troy. Over the flaming protests of his prophetic daughter Cassandra, and in spite of numerous portents of doom, Priam agreed that the Horse should be drawn inside the city. The sack of Troy followed. The king prepared to join the fighting in defense of his city but was dissuaded, on the grounds of his age and weakness, by Hecuba. He mourned the loss of his sons and wished he had died rather than see the destruction of Troy. With Hecuba he was seated before the altar of Zeus in the courtyard of his palace when his young son Polites rushed in. He was followed by Neoptolemus, and was slain before his father's eyes. In a last glow of wrath Priam attacked the slayer of his son, but Neoptolemus swung on him and slashed off his head with one sweep of his sword. He then dragged the decapitated body to Achilles' tomb and left it there to rot.

Priamid (prī'a̯-mid). A name applied to any one of the 50 sons of Priam, king of Troy.

Priapus (prī-ā'pus). In Greek mythology, a god, a son of Dionysus and Aphrodite, the promoter of fertility in crops, cattle, and women. A statue of him was set up in vineyards and gardens to promote fertility, and he was honored in the city as well as in the country. Sometimes also known as Ithyphallus, he is depicted as a faunlike deity with penis always erect. In Rome he was identified with Mutinuus (or Mutunus), another fertility god. The first fruits of garden and field were sacrificed to him. Poems composed in his honor were called Priapea. In the Middle Ages he became the protector of cattle, herds, shepherds, farmers, and fishermen, and of women in childbirth.

Procne (prok'nē). In Greek legend, a daughter of Pandion, king of Athens. She was the sister of the twins Butes and Erechtheus, and of Philomela. Her father gave her to Tereus, king in Thrace, in marriage, as a reward to Tereus for his aid in defeating the enemies of Pandion. Their wedding was not blessed by the Graces nor by Hera, but the people of Thrace rejoiced at the marriage of their king, and were delighted when a son, Itys, was born to the royal couple. After five years, Procne longed to see her sister and Tereus went to Athens to fetch Philomela for a visit. Pandion yielded to the pleas of Philomela and to the even more ardent ones of Tereus, who had fallen in love with his wife's sister on sight but did not betray himself, and consented to let Philomela go to Thrace with her brother-in-law. The voyage went well, but when they landed Tereus, true to the violence for which the Thracians were noted, could no longer restrain his feelings. He ravished Philomela. She begged him to slay her, as she could not bear to face her sister after such a double betrayal, and when Tereus refused, she vowed vengeance. To silence her, Tereus cut out her tongue and imprisoned her. He returned to Procne and told her that Philomela had died on the voyage. In her prison Philomela wove a tapestry on which was pictured the whole story of her ravishment, maiming, and imprisonment by Tereus. She sent the tapestry by a servant as a gift to the queen, her sister. Procne examined the tapestry and read in it the story of the wrongs that had been done her sister and herself. In secret she went to the house where Philomela was imprisoned and was reunited to her. The sisters returned to the palace secretly and planned their revenge on Tereus. Equally maddened by the faithlessness and crimes of Tereus, the two sisters murdered the child Itys, Procne's son, cut up his flesh, cooked it and served it to Tereus. After he had eaten Procne told him of what his banquet had consisted, and at the same moment confronted him with Philomela. The grief and horror which Tereus knew at the fearsome death of his son temporarily stunned him and the sisters fled. Tereus was then consumed by a bloodthirsty rage. He pursued Procne and Philomela, and was about to kill them near Daulis, when suddenly the gods transformed Procne into a nightingale, whose song is eternally of grief for her son. Philomela was changed into a swallow, and Tereus became a hoopoe, forever pursuing her. In some Latin versions of the myth, the roles of the sisters, or of the birds into which they were transformed, were reversed.

Procris (prō'kris). In Greek legend, a daughter of Erechtheus, king of Athens, and the sister of Orithyia. She was married to Cephalus and loved him deeply. He was carried off by Eos, the goddess of Dawn, and returned to Procris in disguise to test her fidelity. After many protestations of love and the offerings of rich gifts, Procris, who had been grieving for her husband, yielded. Cephalus immediately denounced her, revealed himself, and deserted her. According to some accounts, she fled from Athens and forswore the company of men, devoted herself to hunting as a companion of Artemis. Artemis gave her a marvelous hound, Laelaps, that could not fail to catch his quarry, and a spear that always hit its target. Others say Procris fled to Crete after Cephalus deserted her, and there she was seduced by King Minos, and that it was he who gave her the hound and the spear, which he had received from Artemis. She later joined Cephalus on a hunting expedition, disguised as a beautiful youth, Pterelas, and agreed to give him the hound and the spear, bu only for love. Cephalus accepted this proposal and she the revealed herself as his wife. The couple was happily reunite and spent some years in devotion to each other. But Artemi was displeased by the manner in which her gifts were bein handed around. She caused Procris to suspect that Cephalu was still meeting a lover in secret. She had overheard hir calling on a breeze to cool him, and thinking it was a love he summoned, she jealously followed him on one of hi hunting trips. As she spied on him from a thicket the bushe which hid her moved; Cephalus, thinking the movement wa caused by a wild beast, hurled his spear and transfixed her Her spirit fled to the Underworld, where Odysseus saw he when he visited there on his way home from the Trojan Wai

Procrustes (prǭ-krus'tēz). In Greek legend, an outlaw whe lived near the road to Athens, in Attica. It was his custon to offer hospitality to travelers. He had a bed (named for hin the Procrustean bed) which he insisted his guests use. Those who were too short he stretched on a rack to fit it, and those who were too long had their legs sawed off to the prope length. Some say he had two beds; one short which he of fered to tall travelers, then cut off their legs to fit it; and one long on which he stretched short travelers. Theseus, whe passed his house on his way to Athens, killed him. He wa: also known under the names of Damastes, Polypemon, anc Procoptas. He was the father of Sinis, the "Pine-bender."

Proetus (prǭ-ē'tus). In Greek legend, a son of Abas, king o Tiryns in Argolis. He and his twin Acrisius fought in thei mother's womb and continued the struggle ever afterwards Proetus violated Acrisius' daughter, Danaë, lost control o the throne to his brother, and fled to Iobates, king of Lycia Iobates gave him his daughter Antia in marriage and helpec him to win back Tiryns from Acrisius, which Proetus ther turned into a fortress with the aid of the Gasterocheires Proetus and Antia had three daughters: Iphianassa, Iphinoë and Lysippe, who were driven mad for offending eithe Dionysus or Hera. Melampus offered to cure them but Pro etus thought the price—a part of his kingdom—too high Then all the women of Tiryns went mad and Proetus was forced to use, and pay for, Melampus' services to cure them Bellerophon fled to the court of Proetus and was hospitabl) received by him. However, Antia fell in love with Bellerophon and when he spurned her advances she accused him falsely of making love to her against her will and demanded his death. Proetus feared to offend the gods by killing one to whom he had offered hospitality so he sent Bellerophon to Antia's father, Iobates, with a secret message instructing Iobates to kill Bellerophon. Proetus had a son, Megapenthes, who succeeded him as ruler of Tiryns.

Promachus (prom'ạ-kus) or **Promachos** (prom'-ạ-kos). A deity, as Athena or Apollo, who fights before some person, army, or state, as a protector or guardian. In art and archaeology the type is distinguished by the attitude of combat, often with upraised shield and the spear or other weapon extended threateningly. Also, an epithet of Athena, meaning, "the Defender."

Prometheus (prọ-mē'thẹ-us). In Greek mythology, a Titan, the son of Iapetus and the nymph Clymene, or as some say, the son of Themis, who revealed the secrets of the future to him. His brothers were Epimetheus, Atlas, and Menoetius, all of whom suffered at the hands of Zeus. He was the father of Deucalion, king of Phthia, and warned him that Zeus was going to send a flood to destroy mankind; he advised Deucalion to build an ark to save himself and his wife. When the Titans waged war on the Olympian gods, Prometheus, who knew what the outcome would be, took the side of Zeus, after the Titans had scorned his advice, and helped him to defeat the Titans and make himself king. According to some accounts it was Prometheus who split the skull of Zeus so that Athena, fully armed, could spring from his head. She taught Prometheus many arts and these he passed on to man. Some say Prometheus created man by forming an image from the clay and water of Phocis, into which Athena then breathed life. He caused man, alone of the animals, to walk erect and lift his head to the sun and the stars. He taught men the use of numbers and letters, how to build ships and sail the seas, how to cultivate the fields and tame beasts to work for them; all human arts come from Prometheus. When Zeus was firmly in power he took no thought for mankind and would have blotted out the race of men altogether. Only Prometheus interceded for man and Zeus relented. Prometheus was once called upon to judge which parts of a sacrificial animal should be reserved to the gods and which to men. He cut up a bull and placed all the flesh

obscured) errạnt, ardẹnt, actọr; ch, chip; g, go; th, thin; ŦH, then; y, you; variable) ḍ as d or j, ş as s or sh, ṭ as t or ch, ẓ as z or zh.

into one bag, made of the bull's hide. But on top of the goo●
flesh he laid the stomach of the bull, the least appetizing pa●
of the animal. In a second bag he placed all the picked bone●
of the animal, but disguised the fact that there were onl●
bones in the bag by covering them with a layer of rich fa●
He asked Zeus to choose one of the two bags. The on●
chosen would contain the parts reserved for the gods in
sacrifice. Zeus, either because he was duped, or because h●
wished an excuse to punish men, chose the bag containin●
the bare bones, and henceforth bones wrapped in fat wer●
offered the gods in sacrifices. But Zeus was angered by thi●
successful deception and decreed that though men woul●
have the flesh of the animals they would have to eat it raw●
as he would now withhold the gift of fire from mankind●
Prometheus, ever pitying mankind's vulnerable state, stol●
fire from heaven and, carrying it in a fennel reed, gave it t●
man. Zeus counterbalanced this great benefit by sendin●
Pandora, the first mortal woman, to Prometheus' brother
Epimetheus, for a wife. Prometheus warned his brother no●
to accept any gift from Zeus, but Epimetheus married he●
anyway. Zeus punished Prometheus for stealing the divin●
fire by ordering Hephaestus to bind him in fetters to a roc●
in the Caucasus forever. Prometheus, bound to his lonel●
rock, proclaimed that Destiny had declared his ultimate de●
liverance and that Zeus would one day be dethroned be●
cause of a foolish marriage, even as he himself ha●
dethroned his father Cronus. Prometheus said he knew al●
these things from his mother. (His name means "fore●
thought".) Zeus sent Hermes to learn from Prometheu●
what marriage would cause his downfall, so that he coul●
avoid it, but Prometheus, defiant even in chains, refused t●
reveal his secret. To add to his torment Zeus hurled the rock●
to which he was chained into Tartarus and sent an eagle●
which daily tore at Prometheus' liver (which was nightl●
restored). For 1000 years, or as some say, 30, Prometheus●
hung on his rock in torment. Heracles came to the Caucasus●
where the rock had now emerged, after one of his labors●
and begged Zeus to free Prometheus. Zeus was willing to d●
so because Prometheus had warned Zeus in time not t●
marry the Nereid Thetis, as she would bear a son greater
than his father. But Prometheus could not be freed until●
some other immortal would go to Tartarus in his place.

Chiron, doomed to eternal suffering because he had been accidentally wounded by one of Heracles' poisoned arrows, gladly gave up his immortality to end his own and Prometheus' sufferings. Zeus consented to this exchange but decreed that Prometheus must eternally wear a ring, containing a stone of the rock to which he had been chained, to show that he had been a prisoner. This was the first instance of a ring being worn. Heracles shot the eagle which had tormented Prometheus, and he was set free. To honor Prometheus, men began to wear rings, as he was compelled to do, and wreaths, because he was ordered to crown himself with a willow wreath when he was freed. Zeus set the arrow with which Heracles killed the eagle among the stars as the constellation Sagitta. Prometheus went back to Olympus and resumed his role as adviser to the gods. He was honored with an altar, shared by Hephaestus, and an annual torch race in Athens.

Prometheus, Charm of.   According to Greek legend, a plant or flower that rose from the ground where the drops of ichor fell from Prometheus as the eagle gnawed at his liver. This herb conferred invulnerability on the person and weapons that were anointed with it. The invulnerability lasted for one day. Medea gave an ointment of it to Jason to protect him from the fire-breathing bulls which her father required him to yoke.

Propoetides (prọ-pọ-ē′ti-dēz).   In mythology, maidens of Amathus, in Cyprus. They flagrantly denied the divinity of Aphrodite. To punish them Aphrodite caused them to become wantons, and later they were turned into stone. Some say it was the sight of these women and their immoral lives that made Pygmalion decide to remain a bachelor, and to carve a statue of a woman who would be free from their faults.

Proserpina (prọ-sėr′pi-na).   Latin form of **Persephone.**

Protesilaus (prọ-tes-i-lā′us).   In Greek legend, a son of Iphiclus (whose impotence was cured by Melampus), and an uncle of Philoctetes. He and his brother Podarces came from Phylace to join the Greeks in the war against Troy. According to a prophecy, the first man to set foot on Trojan ground was destined to be killed. Protesilaus, who some say knew of the prophecy, was the first to leap ashore and was killed, either by Hector or by Euphorbus. He was buried in Thracian Chersonese and was awarded divine honors. Nymphs planted a grove about his barrow, and it is said that the leaves of the trees which faced Troy withered rapidly and fell to the ground, whereas the leaves on the trees away from Troy stayed green all winter. Protesilaus was married to Laodamia, daughter of Acastus (others say his wife was Polydora, daughter of Meleager), and when she learned of his death she grieved so that the gods permitted him to return from the Underworld for three hours to visit her. He used this time to urge her to follow him to the Underworld, and when the time came for his departure she committed suicide.

Proteus (prō'tē-us, prō'tūs). In classical mythology, an oracular sea-god, the son of Oceanus and Tethys, who had the power of assuming different shapes. If caught, however, and held fast through all his many changes until he reassumed his own shape, he was compelled to answer questions. With the help of Idothea, daughter of Proteus, Menelaus disguised himself in a seal skin and caught Proteus when he took his daily nap among his seals on the island of Pharos in the Nile Delta. He forced Proteus to tell him how he could escape from Pharos, where he was becalmed on his way home from Troy, and to tell him what had happened to the Ajaxes, Agamemnon, and Odysseus. Aristaeus also overcame Proteus on his island home, and forced him to tell him why his bees sickened and died.

Protogenia (prō″tō-je-nī'a̲) or *Protogenea* (-ē'a̲). According to some accounts, the daughter of Deucalion and Pyrrha. She was the first woman to be born after the great flood that Zeus sent on the world and from which only Deucalion and Pyrrha survived. Her name means "First-born." Some say she was the mother, by Zeus, of Aëthlius, the first king of the land that came to be known as Elis.

Psyche (sī'kē). In Greek mythology, a mortal maiden, beloved by Eros, the god of love, who after long tribulation and suffering was accorded her place among the gods as the equal of her god consort. Psyche as personification of the soul came into Greek mythology in the 4th–5th centuries B.C. Psyche as soul symbolized by a butterfly first appeared in the 5th century B.C. Before this the soul was conceived of and depicted either as a bird or as the spirit-double of the individual.

---

fat, fāte, fär, fâll, àsk, fãre; net, mē, hèr; pin, pīne; not, nōte, mõve, nôr; up, lūte, pùll; oi, oil; ou out; (lightened) ē̲lect, agǫny, ū̲nite

Pterelas (ter'e-las). Name that Procris assumed when she appeared to Cephalus, disguised as a beautiful youth, to try and regain his love. It is said that when Cephalus leaped into the sea, he called the name "Pterelas," because it was under that name that his wife won back his love.

Pterelaus (ter-e-lā'us). In Greek legend, a son or grandson of Poseidon, who had provided him with one gold lock of hair which conferred immortality on Pterelaus. He was king of the Teleboans. With the Taphians he attacked Electryon's kingdom, killed his eight sons, and stole his cattle. Electryon's daughter Alcmene had been promised to Amphitryon, but she would not allow the marriage to be consummated until her brothers were avenged. Amphitryon therefore made war on Pterelaus. Comaetho, daughter of Pterelaus, saw Amphitryon and fell in love with him. To help him she plucked the golden lock from her father's head. Pterelaus died and Amphitryon achieved a crushing victory over the Taphians and Teleboans.

Pygmalion (pig-mā'li-on). In Greek legend, a son of Belus, a marvelous sculptor, and a king of Cyprus. According to some, he was disgusted by the evil lives he saw some women leading, and withdrew from the society of women, resolved to remain a bachelor. He made an exquisite ivory statue of an ideal maiden, more beautiful than any he had ever known, and as he gazed upon its loveliness he fell in love with the statue. At a festival in honor of Aphrodite he prayed the goddess to send him a maiden like the statue. As he prayed the flames of the altar leaped up to show that the goddess had heard him. When Pygmalion returned to his house he kissed and caressed the statue and was overjoyed to find that Aphrodite had indeed endowed it with life. The maiden, Galatea, and Pygmalion were married in the presence of Aphrodite and afterward had a son, Paphus, whose name was sometimes given to the island of Cyprus. Other accounts say Pygmalion fell in love with Aphrodite herself, and made his wonderful statue when his love was rejected. But the goddess was pleased with his homage, and breathed life into the statue.

Pygmies (pig'mēz). In Greek legend, a race of men whose height equalled one *pygme,* that is, the distance from the elbow to the knuckles, or about 13½ inches. Homer represents the Pygmies as dwelling on the southern shores of Ocean, and as being warred upon by the cranes in their annual migrations. The battle with the cranes started because once a beautiful Pygmy, Gerana, considered herself more beautiful than Hera and Artemis. As a punishment for her pride Hera changed her into a crane and caused her to be hated by her people. Heracles, as he was sleeping, was once attacked by Pygmies, but he laughed at them, gathered a few up in his lion's skin and took them to Eurystheus (or to Omphale). The African Pygmies described by Herodotus, and once supposed to be equally fabulous, were apparently the same as the remarkable race or races of dwarfs found by explorers in various parts of equatorial Africa.

Pylades (pil′ạ-dēz). In Greek legend, a son of Strophius, king in Phocis, and of Agamemnon's sister. When Orestes was brought to Strophius' court to protect him from the evil designs of Aegisthus, Pylades became his intimate and faithful friend. He accompanied Orestes when he returned in secret to Mycenae, and reminded him of the command of Apollo when Orestes wavered in his decision to kill his mother· to avenge his father's murder. After the murder of Clytemnestra by Orestes the Furies pursued him. Pylades, disowned by his father for his part in the murder, refused to desert Orestes and accompanied him in his wanderings. He also went with him to Tauris to secure the sacred image of Artemis, although it was well-known that the Taurians sacrificed any strangers they caught landing on their shores. On his return from Tauris, Pylades married Electra, sister of Orestes. She bore him two sons, Medon and Strophius.

Pyramus and Thisbe (pir′ạ-mus, thiz′bē). In classical legend, two Babylonian lovers. They were forbidden to see each other by their parents, and talked together through a crack in the garden wall. They finally planned to defy their parents and to meet under a mulberry tree that grew beside the tomb of Ninus, outside the city walls. Their rendezvous was set for the hours of darkness. Thisbe was the first to arrive at the trysting place. As she waited for her lover she was frightened away when a lion, whose jaws were dripping with blood from a recent kill, came to drink at the spring nearby.

fat, fāte, fär, fâll, ȧsk, fãre; net, mē, hėr; pin, pīne; not, nōte, mõve, nôr; up, lūte, pùll; oi, oil; ou out; (lightened) ẹlect, agǫny, ụnite;

She fled into a cave, dropping her veil as she ran off. The lion seized the veil and mauled it about so that it was daubed with blood and then loped off. Pyramus, who now arrived, saw the blood-stained veil and instantly concluded that Thisbe had been killed. In despair, because he had asked Thisbe to undertake the secret meeting and now felt himself responsible for the death of his love, he killed himself under the mulberry tree that was to have been the meeting place. After a time Thisbe dared return. She found Pyramus dying, and resolved that death should not separate them. She seized the sword with which Pyramus had slain himself and plunged it into her own breast. Ever after, the berries of the mulberry tree, which were originally white, ripened to a dark purple, in memory of the blood of Pyramus and Thisbe which was shed because of their love for each other, under its boughs.

Pyrene (pī-rē′nē). In Greek legend, a daughter of Bebrys, a king in the Pyrenees. Heracles ravished her when he visited her father's kingdom on his labor to fetch the cattle of Geryon. According to some accounts, she gave birth to a serpent. She fled from her father's anger and was killed by wild beasts. Heracles found her body and buried it. Some say that this princess gave her name to the range of mountains in which her father's kingdom was located: the Pyrenees.

Pyreneus or *Pyrenaeus* (pī-rē-nē′us). According to legend, a Thracian warrior who seized the lands of Daulis and Phocis and made himself king. He saw the Muses on their way to their temple on Mount Parnassus and invited them to take shelter in his palace from a sudden storm. When the weather cleared and the Muses prepared to depart, Pyreneus barred their way and attempted to assault them. The Muses escaped from him by flying off. Pyreneus, maddened for his arrogance, sought to pursue them. In his madness he leaped from a tower and fell to his death.

Pyriphlegethon (pir-i-fleg′e-thon). Another name for Phlegethon, the river of fire in the Underworld.

Pyrrha (pir′a). In Greek mythology, a daughter of Epimetheus. With her husband Deucalion she survived the flood which Zeus sent to destroy the wicked race of man. In fulfillment of the instructions of an oracle, after the flood she helped to found a new race to repeople the earth. See *Deucalion.*

Pyrrhus (pir′us). Another name for Neoptolemus, son of Achilles.

Pythia (pith′i-a̱). The priestess who was said to hold communion with Apollo and receive his oracles in the inner sanctuary of the great temple at Delphi, throughout historic antiquity.

Python (pī′thon). In Greek mythology, a huge female dragon or serpent born from the mud of the Flood. She guarded the cave and chasm at Delphi and there was killed by Apollo, who thus became henceforth the possessor and motivating deity of the oracle at Delphi. A ritual drama representing the killing of the dragon by the god was annually reënacted there. Also, in classical antiquities and in the New Testament, a soothsaying spirit or demon; hence, also, a person possessed by such a spirit; especially a ventriloquist. Some ancient writers speak of the serpent Python as having delivered oracles at Delphi before the coming of Apollo, and during the Roman imperial period we find the name often given to soothsayers. The spirit was supposed to speak from the belly of the soothsayer, who was accordingly called a ventriloquist.

R

Raven. In Greek mythology, a bird sacred to Apollo. Originally its plumage was pure white, but in anger with the raven for bringing him the message that Coronis, one of Apollo's loves, had been unfaithful to him, Apollo changed the raven's feathers to black.

Rhadamanthys (rad-a̱-man′this). In Greek mythology, a son of Europa and Zeus, and the brother of Minos and Sarpedon. When Europa married Asterius, king of Crete, he adopted her sons and made them his heirs. The brothers quarreled over the youth Miletus. Minos drove the youth from Crete, Sarpedon fled, and Rhadamanthys made his peace with Minos, and on the death of Asterius received one-third of his kingdom. He was renowned for his wise and just rule, and established laws which were followed in Crete and in the Ionian islands. He obtained the laws from Zeus, who received him in a cave every ninth year. Rhadamanthys divided his kingdom among his sons and nephews. He fled from Crete to Boeotia, some say because he had killed a kinsman. There, according to some accounts, he married Alcmene, the mother of Heracles, after the death of Amphitryon. They lived in Ocalea and their tomb was shown in Haliartus. But some say he married Alcmene in the Elysian Fields. Zeus was devoted to Rhadamanthys and would have liked to spare him the burdens of old age. However, if he gave this blessing to one of his sons, the other gods might justifiably claim the same boon for their children, so he wisely gave up the idea. But he appointed Rhadamanthys as one of the three judges in the Underworld, where one of his special duties is to bring to justice those whose crimes have gone undetected on earth.

Rhadine (rad′i-nē). According to legend, a maiden of Samos who was compelled to marry a tyrant of Corinth, although she loved another. Her lover, Leontichus, followed her to Corinth in a cart; the tyrant seized him and killed him and Rhadine, and threw their bodies into the cart. Later he took pity on them and buried their bodies, so that their souls would not have to wander homeless for 100 years, as they would have done if they had not received proper burial.

Rhea (rē′a). The great mother goddess; she was a Titaness, the daughter of Gaea and Uranus. She was the sister and wife of Cronus, and bore him Hestia, Demeter, Hera, Hades, and Poseidon, for which reason she is often called the mother of the gods. Cronus seized each of his new-born children and swallowed them, because it had been prophesied that he would be dethroned by one of his sons. When it was time for Zeus to be born, Rhea fled to Mount Lycaeus, according to some accounts, and there in a spot where no shadow is cast gave birth to Zeus. She entrusted her infant to Gaea, who gave him to the nymphs of Crete. But some say Rhea bore Zeus in Crete, either in a cave on Mount Ida or on Mount Dirce. And some say that when she was bearing Zeus she pressed her fingers into the earth of the Cretan cave and that the Dactyls were generated by her fingers, five females from her left hand and five males from her right hand. Rhea wrapped a stone in swaddling clothes and presented it to Cronus, who swallowed it. According to some accounts, Rhea was also the mother of the Curetes, who guarded the infant Zeus in Crete. She assisted Zeus, when he was grown, to compel Cronus to disgorge his other children. Rhea purified Dionysus of the murders he had committed during his madness, and initiated him into her mysteries. As an emissary from Zeus she persuaded Demeter to make the earth fruitful again when that goddess, in despair over the loss of her daughter Persephone, had withdrawn her life-giving blessings and caused the earth to become barren. She also used her influence to persuade her son Hades to allow Persephone, whom he had carried off to the Underworld, to spend part of her time on earth. The cult of Rhea was associated with fertility rites. One of the oldest places of her worship was in Crete, where she hid the infant Zeus from Cronus. She was often associated with the great Asian mother goddess Cybele. The Romans identified her with their Magna Mater, or with Ops.

Rhesus (rē'sus). According to some accounts, the son of Strymon, the river-god, and the Muse Calliope. Homer names him as the son of Eioneus. He was a Thracian king who came as an ally of Troy in the tenth year of the Trojan War. He arrived at a time when Hector had driven the Greeks back to their ships and Hector received him somewhat bitterly, accusing him of coming only when the Trojans were successful. Rhesus defended his delayed arrival on the ground that he had been fighting off his own enemies in Thrace. He promised to beat the Greeks once and for all the next day. On the night of his arrival he and his followers, who were encamped at some distance from the Trojans, were attacked by Diomedes and Odysseus. Those two Greeks had come as spies from the Greek camp. On the way they encountered Dolon, a Trojan spy, learned from him of Rhesus' arrival with his wonderful horses, and where he had pitched his tents. Diomedes and Odysseus then killed Dolon and proceeded to find Rhesus. They killed him and 12 of his followers as they slept, and captured his horses. It was important to the Greeks to capture the horses, as it had been prophesied that if they fed on Trojan fodder or drank the waters of the Scamander before Troy—which they had not yet done—the city could not be overthrown.

Rhesus. In Homeric legend *(Iliad)*, a river near Troy which Poseidon and Apollo diverted from its course, after the Trojan War, and caused to turn against the wall which the Greeks had built to protect their ships. It raged nine days against the wall, with other rivers diverted for the same purpose, and washed the wall into the sea. Poseidon had complained to Zeus about the wall, saying that the Greeks had offered no hecatombs to the gods when they built it, and fearing that the great wall which he and Apollo had built for Laomedon would suffer by comparison with this man-made wall. It was then that Zeus promised him that the Greek wall would be destroyed. Zeus helped to destroy it by sending torrential rains during the nine days that the rivers were raging out of their courses against it. The other rivers that helped destroy the Greek wall were the Aesepus, Caresus, Granicus, Heptaporus, Rhodius, Scamander, and Simois.

Rhodius (rō′di-us). Named by Homer as one of the rivers of the Troad. The Rhodius, after the Trojan War had ended, was diverted from its course by Apollo and Poseidon and sent against the wall the Greeks had erected to protect their ships. The rivers so diverted from their courses, with the aid of Zeus, washed the wall into the sea. See ***Rhesus,*** river.

Rhodope (rod′ọ̄-pē). In Greek legend, a beautiful maiden skilled in hunting; she was a companion of Artemis. She incurred the wrath of Aphrodite by taking an oath to Artemis that she would eschew the society of men. To punish her for denying her power, Aphrodite caused her to fall in love with a hunter she met in a cave. Artemis, enraged in her turn at this violation of an oath, changed Rhodope into a spring in the cave. This spring came to be used as a test for virginity. A maiden whose virtue was in question was required to write that she was a virgin on a tablet and then, holding the tablet in her arms, to step into the spring. If her tablet expressed a lie the spring rose up to her neck and covered the tablet. If her tablet expressed the truth the water did not touch it.

Rhoecus (rē′kus). In mythology, a Greek youth who noticed that an oak tree was about to fall and propped it up. In so doing he saved the life of the dryad that inhabited the tree and won her gratitude. She promised to give Rhoecus whatever he asked as a reward. He asked for her love and she consented to give him this gift, telling him that she would send him a bee as a messenger with instructions. When Rhoecus departed he fell in with some companions and forgot all about the bee, so that when it came he impatiently brushed it away and injured it. In anger at Rhoecus for so quickly forgetting her and for injuring her messenger, the dryad blinded Rhoecus.

Ruinous Dream. In the *Iliad,* a dream sent by Zeus to Agamemnon which led the latter to believe that the opportunity had come to seize Troy at last, after nearly ten years of besieging it. The dream was sent by Zeus in fulfillment of his promise to Thetis to punish Agamemnon for his arrogant seizure of Achilles' captive Briseis. For in the struggle that followed as Agamemnon led his forces against Troy, Achilles refused to take part.

Salamis (sal′ạ-mis). In mythology, a daughter of the river-god Asopus and Metope. Poseidon fell in love with her and carried her off to an island in the Saronic Gulf. She bore Poseidon a son, Cychreus, who became king of the island, which was subsequently named Salamis in honor of his mother.

Salmoneus (sal-mō′nẹ-us). In Greek mythology, one of the sons of Aeolus and Enarete. He left Thessaly and went to Elis, where he founded the city of Salmonia on the Enipeus River. His wife Alcidice died in giving birth to Tyro, a maiden of surpassing beauty. He next married Sidero, who ill-treated his daughter Tyro. Salmoneus was an arrogant and violent ruler, who considered himself godlike. In his insolence he imitated Zeus to such an extent that he confused himself with the god. He had a chariot so constructed, with bronze drums covered with hides, that there was a clangor as of thunder when he drove through the streets. On the festival day of Zeus he dashed through the streets in his thundering chariot hurling firebrands in imitation of the lightning, and calling on the people to worship him as Zeus the Thunderer. The vengeance of Zeus was swift. Real thunder roared and a bolt of lightning struck him dead and put the city in flames. He was hurled down into Tartarus, where Aeneas saw him when he visited Anchises in the Underworld on his way to Italy.

Saon (sā'ọn). In Greek legend, a Boeotian who went to Apollo's shrine at Delphi to seek advice in a time of drought. He was advised by the priestess to go to Lebadia. There a swarm of bees led him to a cave which had opened up to swallow Trophonius after he had slain his brother Agamedes. At the cave, which had become an oracle of Trophonius, Saon got instructions from the oracle for ending the drought, and afterward established the worship of Trophonius.

Sarpedon (sär-pē'dọn). In Greek legend, a son of Zeus and Laodamia. He became ruler of the Lycians when his uncles withdrew their claim to the kingdom, and with his close friend and cousin, Glaucus, led the Lycians to the defense of Troy in the Trojan War. In the last year of the war, when the city was directly attacked by the Greeks, Sarpedon chided Hector, claiming that he was leaving the hardest fighting to the allies. He, he said, had no reason to fight, no quarrel with the Greeks, yet as a faithful ally he would do his best. When the Trojans and their allies attacked the fortifications around the Greek ships Sarpedon was in the forefront of the battle. Addressing his friend Glaucus, he said that as they had been honored the most as kings now they must fight the most to repay their loyal subjects for that honor, and prove themselves worthy of being honored. Charging into the battle, he exhorted Glaucus: together they would go on to glory; if successful it would be their own; if not, it would add to the glory of whoever stopped them. He breached the Greek wall and was the first into the Greek encampment. Although he was assailed by Telamonian Ajax and Teucer, Zeus protected him. Zeus grieved that his son was fated to die at the hands of Patroclus, who entered the struggle after the Greek ships had been set afire, and for a time considered saving him from his fate. However, Hera reminded him that the sons of other gods were fighting before Troy. If Zeus saved his son from his fate as a mortal, another god might wish to do the same. With sorrow Zeus accepted her point. As Patroclus and Sarpedon struggled, Zeus sent a shower of bloody raindrops on the Trojan plain to express his grief at his son's approaching death. Sarpedon fell, mortally wounded. Dying, he called on Glaucus to rescue his body and his arms. Glaucus, wild with grief, withdrew the spear which Patroclus had imbedded in his friend's body, and as it left Sarpedon's side his spirit fled with it. A violent struggle then broke out for possession of his body. The Greeks succeeded in gaining his armor—later it was given as a prize in the funeral games for Patroclus—but Zeus sent Apollo to rescue the corpse and bear it away from the range of weapons. Apollo wafted it away, cleansed it in a stream of pure water, and anointed it with ambrosia to erase the marks of battle. He then delivered it into the hands of Slumber and Death and it was borne back to Lycia for funeral honors.

But some say Sarpedon was the son of Zeus and Europa, and the brother of Minos and Rhadamanthys, and that he fled from Crete following a quarrel with Minos. He went to Cilicia, which was named Lycia after his successor, made himself king there, and it was because Zeus gave him the boon of living for three generations that he was among those who went to Troy.

Satyr (sā′tėr). A sylvan deity, representing the luxuriant forces of Nature, and closely connected with the worship of Bacchus. Satyrs are represented with a somewhat bestial cast of countenance, often with small horns upon the forehead, and a tail like that of a horse or a goat, and they frequently hold a thyrsus or wine-cup. Late Roman writers confused the satyrs with their own fauns, and gave them the lower half of the body of a goat. Satyrs were common attendants on Bacchus, and were distinguished for lasciviousness and riot.

Scaean Gate (sē′ạn). The northwest gate of the city of Troy. When the Scaean Gate was opened it signified war. It was by this gate that the Trojans departed from the city when they fought the Greeks and by which they entered it when fleeing before Achilles. As had been prophesied, Achilles was slain by an arrow, some say of Apollo, before the Scaean Gate.

Scamander (skạ-man′dėr). In the *Iliad*, a plain where the Greeks assembled for the assault on Troy. It was the plain of a river of the same name which rose near Mount Ida and emptied into the Hellespont near Troy. It was believed that the waters of the river made the hair a beautiful color, and for this reason Aphrodite, Athena, and Hera bathed in it in preparation for the contest before Paris for the golden apple. The river was honored as a god by the Trojans and had its own priests. It was one of the rivers in the Troad which Poseidon, with the aid of Apollo, diverted from its course for nine days in order to wash down the wall which the Greeks had built to defend their ships. The destruction of the wall, because Poseidon feared that this man-made structure would overshadow the wall he and Apollo had built for Laomedon, took place after the Trojan War was over. The gods called the river and the river-god Xanthus, but men called it the Scamander. As a river-god, Xanthus was the son of Oceanus and Tethys, and the father of Teucer, the first king of the Trojans. See **Xanthus,** river-god.

Scamandrius (ska-man′dri-us). Another name for Astyanax, son of Andromache and Hector.

Scheria (skir′i-a). In the *Odyssey,* the island of the Phaeacians where Odysseus landed after shipwreck and was welcomed by Nausicaä and her father, the king. The people of the island were wonderful navigators, and conducted Odysseus to Ithaca overnight. The actual place most commonly suggested as identical with Scheria is Corfu, but this identification is highly questionable.

Sciron (sī′ron). In Greek legend, a son of Pylas, and as such the uncle of Theseus; but some say he was a son of Poseidon or of Pelops. He was a robber who frequented the Molurian Rocks overlooking the sea near Megara, and forced strangers passing by to wash his feet. While they were doing so he would kick them off the rocks into the sea, where they were devoured by a turtle. When Theseus passed by on his journey from Troezen to Athens, he hurled Sciron himself into the sea, and his bones are said to form the high cliffs which still exist in the region. But some say that Sciron quarreled with Nisus over control of Megara and, in accordance with a judgment of Aeacus, was given command of the armies while Nisus retained the throne. And they say that he was an upright man, whose daughter Endeïs married Aeacus and was the mother of Peleus and Telamon. And that Theseus killed him when he captured Eleusis many years after he had become king or ruler of Athens. Later Theseus instituted the daytime Isthmian Games, formerly mysterious nocturnal rites in honor of Melicertes, in honor of Sciron.

Scylaceus (sil-a-sē′us). In Greek legend, a Lycian companion of Glaucus and Sarpedon, allies of the Trojans. In the clos-

(obscured) errant, ardent, actor; ch, chip; g, go; th, thin; ŦH, then; y, you;
(variable) ḍ as d or j, ṣ as s or sh, ṭ as t or ch, ẓ as z or zh.

ing days of the war he was wounded by Ajax the Lesser but escaped death, as it was his fate to die beside the wall of his own city. He fled alone to his home city and was met at the walls by the Lycian women. They questioned him about their husbands and sons who had gone to fight at Troy, and when he told them they had all been slain, in grief and rage the women stoned Scylaceus to death as the bearer of the evil news. His tomb was built of the stones that killed him, and stood beside Bellerophon's tomb. Afterward, at Apollo's command, Scylaceus was worshiped as a god.

Scylla (sil′a). In classical mythology, a sea nymph. Some say she was a daughter of Phorcys and Crataeis. Others say Zeus and Lamia were her parents. Echidna, Typhon and Triton are also mentioned as the parents of Scylla. Glaucus, the sea-god, fell in love with her and wooed her with promises and prayers, but she scorned him. He asked Circe's aid to win the love of Scylla. Circe, however, notoriously susceptible, fell in love with Glaucus herself, and when she realized that his love for Scylla was unswerving she resolved to avenge herself on Scylla, whom Glaucus preferred to her. She concocted a mixture of magic herbs and sprinkled them on the pool in an arm of the sea where Scylla was wont to bathe, uttering a magic spell at the same time. When Scylla went into the pool she was transformed. The upper part of her trunk and her head, which had not been immersed in the pool, remained that of a beautiful maiden. But her waist was girdled with the necks and heads of six hideous dogs. Her lower limbs were changed into a dolphin's tail. There she stands, rooted in the sea, and whenever a ship passes near the dogs' heads reach out and grasp six seamen and devour them. Some say Scylla was transformed by Amphitrite, who was jealous because Poseidon was enamored of her, and that she had 12 arms and six terrible heads with three rows of teeth in each head. She barks like a young dog and no longer bears any resemblance to the lovely maiden she was. The lower part of her body rests in a cave in the middle of a smooth, mountainous rock in the sea which none can ascend. She eats marine animals and any seamen who are unfortunate enough to come within her reach. Odysseus lost six of his best men when he sailed too near Scylla in order to avoid Charybdis on his way home from the Trojan War. Some say Scylla seized one of Geryon's cattle from Heracles when he passed her way, and that Heracles wrathfully slew her, but Phorcys burned her corpse and she rose anew from the ashes.

Scythes (sith'es). According to Herodotus, Heracles, returning with the cattle he had stolen from Geryon, came to the land later known as Scythia. There, overcome with cold and weariness, he drew his lion's skin around him and went to sleep. When he woke up his mares, that he had loosed for grazing, had disappeared. He looked for them and came upon a curious serpent-tailed maiden. She admitted she had his mares but would not release them until he became her lover, and she kept him with her, although he was longing to be on his way. When she finally permitted him to depart she told him she would bear him three sons, and asked him what she should do with them. Heracles instructed her to watch them, if she saw any one of them bend the bow as he now bent it, or girdle himself as he now demonstrated, she should make this one stay in the land with her where she was ruler. Any who failed to perform these acts as Heracles performed them she should send away out of the land. In due time the woman bore triplets, Agathyrsus, Gelonus, and Scythes. When they were grown their mother tested them as Heracles had ordered. Only Scythes performed the tasks as Heracles had done. His mother sent his brothers out of the land, but Scythes she kept with her. He became the ruler of the people who took their name, Scyths, and the name of their country, Scythia, from him.

Selene (se̦-lē'nē). In Greek mythology, a daughter of the Titans Hyperion and Thia, and the sister of Eos and Helius. Some say Pan, in disguise, persuaded her to ride off on his back and then seduced her. She is also said to have borne a daughter to Zeus who was worshiped in Athens with her father. One night she came upon Endymion sleeping in a cave on Mount Latmus in Caria. She instantly fell in love with him and kissed his closed eyelids. By Endymion she became the mother of 50 daughters. Some say that when he later returned to the same cave he fell into a deep sleep from which he has never awakened, and that nightly Selene gently kisses him as she adores his unchanging youth and beauty. Some say Endymion himself asked Zeus to put him into an eternal sleep because he did not want to grow old. But others say it was Selene who caused him to sleep forever, so that his beauty would not fade and so that she alone could embrace him. Selene was the goddess of the moon, a beautiful winged maiden whose golden diadem casts a soft light on the earth. Her chariot was drawn by white cows, whose horns symbolized the crescent moon. She was worshiped at the time of the new and the full moon. Later Selene was identified with Artemis and with the Roman Diana.

Semele (sem′ẹ-lē). In Greek mythology, a beautiful daughter of Cadmus and Harmonia, and the sister of Ino, Autonoë, Agave, and Polydorus. She was loved by Zeus. Hera learned that she was about to bear Zeus' child and, jealous as always of her rivals for the affections of Zeus, appeared to Semele in the guise of her old nurse. She hinted to Semele that her lover was not really divine, and suggested to Semele that she ask him to prove his divinity by appearing to her in the same majesty as he appeared to Hera. When next he visited her Semele asked that he grant her a request. Zeus swore by the Styx that he would grant her whatever she asked. However, when he learned her request he urged her to change it, but she persisted and Zeus, bound by his oath, appeared to her with his thunderbolts and the lightning. His blazing majesty burned Semele to ashes. Zeus seized her unborn child and sewed it up in his thigh until the time for its birth should arrive. This child was the god Dionysus. When Dionysus was grown he descended to Tartarus at Lerna and bribed Persephone with a gift of myrtle to release his mother. He ascended with her at Troezen, changed her name to Thyone, in order to delude the other shades who might be jealous of her good fortune, and took her to Olympus. Semele was worshiped at Athens during the Lenaea with singing, dancing, and the sacrifice of a young bull.

Seven against Thebes (thēbz), **Expedition of the.** Polynices and Eteocles, the sons of Oedipus, agreed to rule Thebes alternately, each to rule a year and then give way to the other. Eteocles, the elder, ruled first, but when his term was ended he refused to give up the throne and banished Polynices. Polynices went to Argos. There King Adrastus gave him his daughter Aegia (or Argia) in marriage and promised to restore him to the throne of Thebes. Adrastus sought the help of six chieftains for his expedition against Thebes. He first called on his brother-in-law Amphiaraus. Now Amphiaraus was a seer and he knew that if the expedition were undertaken it would end in disaster and that Adrastus alone would survive it. He was therefore reluctant to go and tried to discourage others. But in an earlier time Adrastus and Amphiaraus had quarreled and would have attacked each other. They were prevented from so doing by Eriphyle, the wife of Amphiaraus and the sister of Adrastus. She composed their quarrel and extracted a promise from them that in future she should have the deciding word in any dispute which arose between them. Polynices learned of this agreement and acted on a suggestion that he bribe Eriphyle to persuade Amphiaraus to join Adrastus in the expedition. He gave her the necklace of Harmonia which he had brought with him from Thebes and begged her to compel Amphiaraus to join the expedition. Eriphyle succumbed to the bribe although she had been forbidden by Amphiaraus to accept any gifts from Polynices. She reminded him of his promise to let her settle any disputes between him and Adrastus and thus forced him to take part in the war on Thebes. Amphiaraus agreed to go but left instructions for his sons to kill their mother and march on Thebes when they grew up. The other leaders of the Seven against Thebes were Capaneus and Hippomedon, both Argives, and Parthenopaeus, the Arcadian son of Atalanta, Tydeus of Calydon, and Polynices of Thebes. Some writers don't count Tydeus and Polynices as leaders but name Eteoclus and Mecisteus, brother of Adrastus, in their places. The leaders set out at the head of their forces and proceeded to Nemea. There they sought water. They approached Hypsipyle, a former Lemnian queen who had been sold as a slave to Lycurgus, king of Nemea, and who was now acting as nurse to his son Opheltes. Hysipyle temporarily abandoned her young charge to lead the Argives to a spring. While Opheltes was alone a serpent attacked him. The Argives returned and slew the serpent but the child was already dead. They buried his body and founded the Nemean games in his honor. Ever after this the judges at the games wore dark robes in mourning for Opheltes, and the victors were crowned with parsley, a symbol of mourning. Opheltes' grave was in a sacred enclosure in Nemea, in which altars were set up. Amphiaraus said the death of Opheltes was a bad omen for the expedition, and renamed the child Archemorus, which means "Bringer" or "Beginner of Doom."

The Seven then went on to Cithaeron. Here they paused and sent Tydeus ahead to Thebes as an envoy to demand the restoration of Polynices. The Thebans refused. Now the Argives approached the walls of Thebes. One champion was assigned to each of the seven gates of the city. Within the walls Eteocles assembled his forces. He assigned one Theban chieftain to each gate to match those of his enemies. Eteocles then consulted the seer Tiresias and was told that Thebes would be victorious if a son of Creon voluntarily sacrificed himself to Ares. In spite of his father's protests, Menoeceus, son of Creon, slew himself before the gates. The Argives attacked. Capaneus, boasting that not even Zeus could stop him, set about to scale the wall on a ladder and was struck dead by a thunderbolt of Zeus. Hippomedon was slain by Ismarus, or as some say, he was overcome by a cloud of missiles hurled by the Thebans after he had nearly drowned in the Ismenus River. Parthenopaeus was slain by Poseidon's son Periclymenus. Tydeus was wounded by Melanippus and died of his wound. Amphiaraus fled in his chariot. He was pursued by Periclymenus but Zeus made this virtuous man immortal. Before Periclymenus could hurl his spear into Amphiaraus' back Zeus cleft the ground with his thunderbolt and Amphiaraus, his chariot and his charioteer vanished into the chasm. Polynices and Eteocles met in single combat to decide who should have the throne and killed each other. Only Adrastus of the attacking force survived the disaster. He fled on the winged horse Arion which, some say, was the offspring of Demeter and Poseidon. Following the death of Eteocles, his uncle, Creon, succeeded to the throne of Thebes. He cast out the Argive dead and gave orders that their bodies were to remain unburied and at the mercy of scavenger birds. Antigone defied his order, recovered the body of her brother Polynices, and buried it. Adrastus fled to Athens, or as some say, to Eleusis, and laid an olive branch on the altar of the god as a sign that he was seeking divine protection. He appealed to Theseus and the Athenians to compel Creon to return the dead for burial. Theseus recovered the bodies and they were given funeral honors. But some say it was the wives of the fallen heroes who came as suppliants praying for the return of their husbands' corpses, and some say that Theseus made a successful war on Thebes to recover the bodies.

Sibyls (sib′ilz). In ancient mythology, certain old women or young maidens reputed to possess special powers of prophecy or divination and intercession with the gods in behalf of those who resorted to them. They dwelt in caves or by springs, and under the influence of a frenzy supposedly inspired by a god, they uttered prophecies, often in equivocal language. Heraclitus, in the 6th century B.C., mentioned one prophetess named Sibyl, whose legend spread to various localities; by c350 B.C. she was mentioned as many. Different writers mention from one to ten Sibyls, enumerated as the Persian, Libyan, Delphian, Cimmerian, Erythraean, Samian, Cumaean, Hellespontine or Trojan, Phrygian, and Tiburtine. Of these the most celebrated was the Cumaean Sibyl (of Cumae in Italy) whose story is that she appeared before Tarquin the Proud and offered him nine books for sale. He refused to buy them, whereupon she burned three, and offered the remaining six at the original price. He again refused them; she destroyed three more, and offered the remaining three at the price she had asked for the nine. Tarquin, astonished, bought the books, which were found to contain directions as to the worship of the gods and the policy of the Romans. As the earliest Sibyl was thought to have dwelt on Mount Ida in the Troad this accounts for the introduction of foreign gods into Rome. These Sibylline Books, or books professing to have this origin, written in Greek hexameters, were kept with great care at Rome, and consulted only by the direction of the Senate. They were destroyed at the burning of the Temple of Jupiter in 83 B.C. Fresh collections were made, which were finally destroyed soon after 400 A.D. The 14 or 15 Sibylline Oracles referred to by the Christian fathers, and still extant, have no connection with the Sibyls of mythology. They belong to early ecclesiastical literature, and are a mixture of Jewish, Hellenistic, and later Christian material. In composition they seem to date from the 2nd century B.C. to the 3rd century A.D.

Silenus (sī-lē′nus). In Greek mythology, a forest-god, depicted as a shaggy, full-bearded old man, with horse ears, and sometimes horse legs, usually drunk, and often riding on an ass or on a wine-vessel. He was reported to be extraordinarily wise, and if caught could be made to reveal his wisdom and give answers to questions. The Phrygian king

Midas is said to have plied Silenus with wine and question and received astounding answers; but nobody learned wha Silenus told Midas, except that it would be better never to be born. In the 6th century B.C. Silenus became associated with Dionysus and thereafter appeared in the Dionysian frolics and processions attended by troops of satyrs. He became credited with being the foster father and boon companion of Dionysus. The term *sileni* (plural) is applied to a group of woodland spirits or semideities, who were much confused with the satyrs, whom they resembled, except that the sileni were old and were differentiated from the goatlike satyrs by their horselike characteristics. They, too, were characterized as wise, drunk, and prophetic. They were credited with being wonderful musicians, and with having taught Dionysus the secrets of the vine and wine-making. Socrates was compared to Silenus in wisdom, irony, and appearance.

Silver Age. This was the second age of man created by the gods. It followed the Golden Age and was less glorious. The time of childhood and helplessness was long. The duration of manly strength was short, owing to the tendency of men to war against each other. Man in the Silver Age was less devout, and failed to make sacrifices to the gods. It was not an entirely bad age, however; there were men of honor, and after mortal life was over men were thought to live on as spirits.

Simois (sim'ō-is). In Homeric legend *(Iliad)*, the god of the river of the same name near Troy. It was at the mouth of this river that Protesilaus leaped ashore from the Greek ships and became the first Greek to be slain in the Trojan War. Toward the end of the war Xanthus, also a river-god, called on Simois to help stop Achilles when he was murderously attacking the Trojans. Simois flooded his banks and washed stones and tree trunks against Achilles in a raging torrent, but all to no avail. Hephaestus, at Hera's request, came to the aid of Achilles and set the rivers afire. After the war was over Simois was one of the rivers which Poseidon, with the aid of Apollo, diverted from its course for nine days in order to wash down the wall that the Greeks had built to defend their ships. The wall was destroyed because Poseidon feared that this man-made structure would overshadow the wall he and Apollo had built for Laomedon, if it were left standing.

fat, fāte, fär, fâll, àsk, fāre; net, mē, hėr; pin, pīne; not, nōte, möve, nôr; up, lūte, pùll; oi, oil; ou out; (lightened) ĕlect, agǫny, ūnite;

Simois the river-god was one of the many sons of Oceanus and Tethys.

Sinis (sī′nis). In Greek legend, a son of Polypemon and Sylea. He was a thug who lived on the Isthmus of Corinth. He was given the name of Pityocamptes (*Pine-bender*) because it was his custom to require travelers who came his way to help him bend down tall pine trees until their tops touched the ground. Sinis would then let go his hold and the tree, freed from his restraining hold, would spring upright, hurling the unlucky traveler into the air as from a catapult; when he fell to the ground he was dashed to pieces. Or as some say, Sinis bent two pines to the ground and tied his victim between them. When he released the arched trees they sprang upright, tearing the victim in two. Theseus, on his way to Athens, encountered Sinis. He overpowered him and treated Sinis as Sinis had treated others.

Sinon (sī′non). In Greek legend, a cousin of Odysseus. He accompanied the Greeks to Troy and volunteered to remain behind and allow himself to be captured when the Greeks resorted to the stratagem of the Wooden Horse in the tenth year of the Trojan War. The Greeks built the Horse and left it on the beach before Troy. They then put out their camp-fires and sailed away behind the island of Tenedos. As the Trojans swarmed out of the city to inspect the huge image, Sinon arranged for himself to be captured. He was brought before Priam in chains and cast himself on the mercy of his former enemy. He said he had been a squire of that Palamedes whose death was brought about by Odysseus, and because he knew the secret of Palamedes' death Odysseus wanted to destroy him. The Greeks, he said, resolved to secure favorable winds so that they could return to their homeland, proposed to propitiate Athena with a blood sacrifice as they had formerly sacrificed Iphigenia at Aulis. Calchas, inspired by Odysseus, had chosen Sinon for the victim, but at that moment a breeze sprang up and the rush to sail permitted Sinon to make his escape. Priam listened courteously to his tale, and as he finished it ordered the fetters removed from his limbs and promised him asylum. The king then inquired the meaning of the Wooden Horse. Sinon, well coached by Odysseus, explained that it was an offering to propitiate Athena for the theft of the Palladium from Troy; that it had purposely been made huge so that the

(obscured) errạnt, ardẹnt, actọr; ch, chip; g, go; th, thin; ŦH, then; y, you; (variable) ḍ as d or j, ṣ as s or sh, ṭ as t or ch, ẓ as z or zh.

Trojans could not take it into their city, for if they succeeded in doing that Troy would become the master of Europe. In spite of the warnings of Cassandra and Laocoön, all worked as Odysseus had foreseen: the Trojans feverishly breached their walls and took the Wooden Horse inside the city. During the night Sinon gave the signal to the warriors concealed in the Horse to come out and signaled to the fleet to return from Tenedos. He opened the gates to the city and Troy, which for years had resisted frontal assaults, at last fell through the treacherous stratagem of the Wooden Horse.

Sinope (si-nō′pē). In Greek mythology, a daughter of the river-god Asopus and Metope. According to some accounts, Apollo fell in love with her and carried her off to a peninsula in the Euxine Sea to a city which later bore her name. Some say she bore Apollo a son, Syrus, who became king of the Syrians and named his people after himself. Zeus also fell in love with Sinope, and sought to gain her affections by promising to give her whatever she asked for. She craftily demanded that he assure her of lifelong virginity. He was compelled by his oath to grant her wish and Sinope thenceforth enjoyed a solitary couch. It is said that she frustrated the intentions of the river-god Halys in the same fashion.

Sirens (sī′renz). In Greek mythology, a group of sea-nymphs who by their singing fascinated those who sailed past their island, and lured them to their deaths. According to some accounts they were the daughters of Terpsichore and the river-god Achelous. Half birds and half maidens, they had once been sweet-singing maidens, companions of Persephone. When the latter was snatched away by Hades the Sirens searched in vain for her, and at last prayed that they might be given wings so that they could search the seas. The gods gave them wings, but to preserve their sweet songs the upper half of their bodies remained those of maidens. Later, the Sirens lost their wing feathers and their power to fly after being defeated by the Muses in a singing contest. In art they are often represented as hideous, malevolent, and monstrous, with the head, arms, and breasts of young women, and the wings and lower body, or only the feet, of birds. Homer mentions two Sirens; three are often depicted; but they are usually thought of as a large group. Odysseus passed them safely by sealing the ears of his companions

fat, fāte, fär, fâll, ȧsk, fãre; net, mē, hèr; pin, pīne; not, nōte, möve, nôr; up, lūte, pùll; oi, oil; ou out; (lightened) ēlect, agōny, ūnite;

with wax and lashing himself to the mast. Orpheus saved the
Argonauts from their enchantment by singing even more
enchantingly. The Sirens were doomed to die when mortals
could resist them (they leaped into the sea and became
rocks). In early belief they were thought of as accompanying
the souls of the dead from earth to Hades.

SIRENS
Greek funeral marble of Chios

Sirius (sir′i-us). [Also: *Dog Star.*] According to legend,
Orion's dog, who accompanied him wherever he went, and
was placed with him in the heavens, forever following at his
master's heels, as the constellation Canis Major. As a star,
Sirius is a brilliant one, the brightest in the heavens.

Sisyphus (sis′i-fus). In Greek mythology, a son of Aeolus, and
a brother of Salmoneus and Athamas. He lived on the Isthmus of Corinth and was married to Merope, one of the
Pleiades, who bore him Glaucus (father of Bellerophon),
Ornytion, and Sinon. According to some accounts, he was
the founder of Ephyra (later Corinth), where he promoted
the trade and navigation of the city and founded the Isthmian Games in honor of Melicertes. Others say Medea bequeathed him the kingdom of Corinth when she fled from
there. Homer names Sisyphus as the craftiest of mortals. At
one time Sisyphus noticed that his fine cattle were disap-

pearing, and suspected his neighbor Autolycus, a noted thief. But he could not prove anything because Autolycus had the ability to change the color of the cattle or add to or subtract horns from them at will. Sisyphus put a secret mark on the hoofs of his animals, and next day traced them to Autolycus. When he went to reclaim them he took the opportunity to ravish Anticlea, daughter of Autolycus, who subsequently bore him Odysseus (as Anticlea was the wife of Laertes, Odysseus was brought up as Laertes' son). Later Sisyphus seduced Tyro, daughter of his brother Salmoneus, in the execution of an oracular pronouncement that he should have sons by his niece if he wished to regain Thessaly, which Salmoneus had seized from him. However, Tyro killed the children she bore him. In exchange for a permanent spring, with which Asopus the river-god supplied Corinth, Sisyphus informed Asopus that Zeus had abducted his daughter Aegina. Zeus punished him for talebearing by commanding Hades to take him away to the Underworld, but when Hades came for him Sisyphus tricked him so that he was powerless. As long as Hades was compelled by Sisyphus to remain on earth no one could die. After a few days of this horrible state Ares rescued Hades and Sisyphus was led off to the Underworld. Before he went, however, Sisyphus instructed his wife not to perform burial rites for him. Arrived in the Underworld, he appealed to Persephone, saying he had not been properly buried, and requesting the privilege of returning to earth to arrange for his burial, after which he promised to return. Persephone granted his request, and of course Sisyphus broke his promise as soon as he saw the light of day. Hermes was commanded to pursue him and to carry him back to the Underworld. For his various crimes and deceptions Sisyphus was given the punishment of being compelled to push a huge stone up a slope. As fast as he got it to the top the stone slipped away from him and rolled down again. Thus he is eternally pushing a stone which eternally escapes just when he is on the point of completing his labor. Odysseus saw him toiling away at this task when he visited the Underworld. As one of the great sinners, Sisyphus is confined to Tartarus.

Sleep. [Greek, **Hypnos;** Latin, **Somnus.**] In classical mythology, the brother of Death (Thanatos) and the child of Night

fat, fāte, fär, fåll, àsk, fāre; net, mē, hèr; pin, pīne; not, nōte, möve, nôr; up, lūte, pùll; oi, oil; ou out; (lightened) ĕlect, agǫny, ūnite;

(Nyx). Sleep dwelt in the Underworld, in a cave near the misty land of Cimmeria where the rays of the sun never reached. No birds or beasts lived in the land, and the only sound came from the murmuring of the river Lethe as it washed over the pebbles in its bed. Poppies and other drugs grew in profusion before the cave of Sleep. Inside the cave, he rested on a sable-draped couch, surrounded by empty dreams. Sleep was often called on by the gods to deliver dreams to mortals or for other reasons. In the *Iliad,* Sleep was bribed by Hera to lull Zeus so that he would neglect the Trojans and give the Greeks a chance to win. Sleep was not anxious to do Hera's bidding in this case, because he remembered the anger of Zeus when he had lulled him to sleep before so that Hera could shipwreck Heracles on the isle of Cos. Sleep escaped that time only with the help of Night and by changing himself into a bird. Hera overcame his reluctance and he once again lulled Zeus to sleep.

Smyrna (smẽr′na̤). A daughter of Cinyras. See **Myrrha.**

Solymi (sol′i-mī). In Greek legend, famed warriors of Asia Minor. Proetus, desiring to get rid of Bellerophon but not willing to slay him because he had come as a guest, sent Bellerophon to fight the Solymi with the idea that he would surely be killed. Contrary to his expectations, Bellerophon conquered them.

Sown Men. See **Sparti.**

Sparti (spär′tī). In Greek mythology, a race of fully-armed men that sprang from the soil when Cadmus sowed the dragon's teeth. The name means "the Sown Men." Cadmus hurled stones into their midst when they sprang from the earth and they fell upon each other and fought until only five survived. These five: Chthonius, Echion, Hyperenor, Pelorus, and Udaeus, became the ancestors of the noble families of Thebes.

Sphinx (sfingks). In Greek mythology, the monstrous daughter of Echidna and Orthrus, or as some say, of Echidna and Typhon. She had the head of a woman, the body of a lion, the tail of a serpent, and eagle's wings. The Sphinx was sent by Hera or Apollo to punish Thebes for the crimes of Laius, king of Thebes. She frequented a high rock near the gate of Thebes and waylaid passers-by, asking them: "What creature with one voice walks on four legs in the morning, on two at noon, and on three in the evening?" She hurled those who could not answer the riddle to their deaths from her rock, or as some say, she devoured them. When Oedipus came to Thebes, he answered correctly: "Man, who crawls on all fours as a babe, walks upright in his prime, and needs a staff in old age." The Sphinx thereupon perished (or killed herself), and Oedipus entered Thebes as deliverer of the people from the monster.

Stentor (sten'tôr). In Greek legend, a Greek herald before Troy, who, in Homer's *Iliad*, had a voice as loud as those of 50 men together. The adjective "stentorian" is derived from his name.

Sthenelus (sthen'ẹ-lus). In Greek legend, a son of Actor. He was a comrade of Heracles in the war against the Amazons, and was struck by an arrow and wounded. On his return to Paphlagonia he died of his wound and passed to the Underworld. When the Argonauts passed his burial mound on their way to Colchis, Persephone yielded to his request to go from the world of the dead to the world of the living so that he could see once more heroes such as he used to be. The Argonauts stopped when they saw his spirit looking at their ship, and at the urging of Mopsus sacrificed to his spirit, after which his spirit returned to the world of the dead.

Stone People. In Greek mythology, the race of men that sprang up after the flood which only Deucalion and Pyrrha survived. To repopulate the earth, Deucalion and Pyrrha hurled the stones of earth, their mother, behind them. The stones thrown by Deucalion became men; those hurled by Pyrrha became women.

Stymphalides (stim-fā'li-dēz). In Greek legend, a flock of fierce man-eating birds near Lake Stymphalus. They had bronze claws, beaks, and wings, and could discharge their own feathers like arrows. To kill them was the sixth labor of Heracles.

Stymphalus (stim-fā'lus). In Greek legend, a son of Elatus and Laodice, daughter of Cinyras. He was a king in Arcadia. When Pelops came into the Peloponnesus he waged war on Stymphalus, but could not defeat him by force of arms. He invited Stymphalus to meet with him for discussion under truce, and when Stymphalus came to his camp, he murdered him, dismembered his body, and cast his limbs to the four winds. This treacherous murder by Pelops brought a terrible drought on all Greece, which was lifted only when, on the advice of the oracle at Delphi, Aeacus prayed to Zeus for relief. Stymphalus in Arcadia is named for him.

Styx (stiks). In Greek mythology, a nymph, the daughter of Oceanus and Tethys. Because she was the first of the deities to go to the aid of Zeus when the Titans attacked him, Zeus took her children, among them Nike, to Olympus. He also made her the goddess by whom the most inviolable oaths were sworn. Styx dwelt on the western shore of the river Styx, near the edge of night, in a house with silver pillars. She guarded the Aloidae, who were tied to pillars with living serpents as a punishment for having attacked Olympus. Some say Styx was the mother of Persephone by Zeus.

Styx. In Greek mythology, one of the five rivers surrounding Hades, over which the ghosts of the dead who have been properly buried must pass. The river is so sacred that the gods swear by it. When one of the gods takes an oath by the Styx, Iris brings water from the river in a golden cup. Punishment for breaking an oath taken by the Styx consists in banishment from the councils of the gods for nine years. In ancient geography Styx was also the name of a river that flowed by the city of Nonacris in Arcadia. The water trickles down from a high cliff and flows into the Crathis River, or, as some say, it flows to Tartarus. The waters of the Styx were believed to bring death to all who drank them. Among the wonderful properties of the water it was claimed that it broke all things of glass, crystal, stone, and pottery, and corroded all metals. The only material that could withstand it was a horse's hoof. The Arcadians swore their most binding oaths by their river Styx. Hither the daughters of Proetus fled when they were struck by madness, and near here Melampus overtook them and cured them.

Symplegades (sim-pleg'a-dēz). In Greek legend, two rocky cliffs at the entrance to the Euxine Sea. The ancients believed that they clashed together in order to crush any vessel that tried to pass between them. Legend has it that Jason's ship, the *Argo*, got safely through by sending a dove first, and slipping through quickly while the rocks were opening for the bird.

Syrinx (sir'ingks). In Greek mythology, a mountain-nymph of Arcadia. She was a huntress, like the goddess Artemis, and

(obscured) errant, ardent, actor; ch, chip; g, go; th, thin; ᴛʜ, then; y, you;
(variable) ḍ as d or j, ṣ as s or sh, ṭ as t or ch, ẓ as z or zh.

like her wished to remain chaste. Pan caught sight of her on
day on Mount Lycaeus and pursued her. The nymph fle
through the forests until she came to the river Ladon. Ther
she prayed to the nymphs of the stream to rescue her. Jus
as Pan grasped her she was transformed into reeds, and a
the wind blew through them they gave off a gentle singing
sound. Pan cut the reeds into unequal lengths and fastened
them together into a Pan's pipe, or Syrinx.

Talaria (ta̱-lā′ri-a̱). In classical mythology and archaeology,
the sandals, bearing small wings, worn characteristically by
Hermes or Mercury and often by Iris and Eos, and by other
divinities, as Eros and the Furies and Harpies. In late or
summary representations of the deity the sandals are sometimes omitted, so that the wings appear as if growing from
the ankles, one on each side of the foot. Sometimes, especially in archaic examples, the talaria have the form of a sort
of greaves bearing the wings much higher in the leg. They
symbolize the faculty of swift and unimpeded passage
through space.

Talos (tā′los). [Also: **Perdix, Talus.**] In Greek mythology, a
son of Polycaste, or Perdix, sister of Daedalus. He was an
even more marvelous smith than Daedalus, to whom he had
been apprenticed when he was ten years old. It is said that
he invented the saw: using the spine of a fish as a model he
cut teeth in an iron blade. He was also said to have invented
the potter's wheel and the compass for describing circles.
Daedalus was intensely jealous of his nephew's skill. His
desire to destroy Talos was spurred, some say, by a rumor
that Talos had incestuous relations with his mother. He
lured Talos to the top of a tower and pushed him over. He
then gathered up the corpse but was discovered before he
could bury it. The soul of Talos was transformed into a
partridge, a bird which does not soar on the heights, as
Talos remembered his fall, but flutters near the earth and

lays its eggs on or near the ground. His body was buried in Athens.

Talos. In Greek mythology, a man of bronze. Some say he was created by Hephaestus. Others say he was sprung from ash trees and that he was the last one left of the sons of the gods. He was entirely of bronze. In his ankle was a pin which stoppered the ichor that ran through his body in a single vein and sustained his life. Zeus gave him to Europa to be the guardian of Crete. Three times a day he marched around the shore of Crete, inspecting for invaders. These he repelled by hurling great rocks at them or, if they came too close, he heated himself red-hot and burned them by clasping them in his arms. When Jason and Medea, returning to Iolcus from Colchis, sailed near the shores of Crete in the *Argo,* Talos prevented them from landing by hurling stones at them. Medea called to him and induced him to let them land by promising him a magic potion. Instead she gave him a sleeping draught, and while he slept she pulled out the pin in his ankle. All the life-giving ichor in Talos' single vein flowed out and he died. But others say Talos scraped his ankle against a rock and, the pin being loosened, he bled to death. Still others say he met his death when he was shot in the ankle by an arrow.

Talthybius (tal-thib′i-us). In Greek legend, Agamemnon's herald. He accompanied Menelaus and Odysseus to Cyprus to seek the aid of King Cinyras in the Trojan War. As Agamemnon's herald throughout the Trojan War he had many unpleasant missions to perform. It was he who went to bring Iphigenia to be sacrificed at Aulis. He fetched Briseis when she was taken from Achilles and given to Agamemnon to make up for the loss of Chryseis. He had to tell Hecuba, after the fall of Troy, that she was to be Odysseus' captive, that Cassandra would be taken by Agamemnon, and that Andromache would go to Neoptolemus. Talthybius, for all his gruesome message-bearing, seems to have been a compassionate man. He pitied the fallen queen, Hecuba. When it was his sad duty to tell her that Astyanax, her young grandson, must die, and that her daughter Polyxena must be sacrificed on Achilles' tomb, he shuddered for her sorrows and hoped he would die rather than fall so low as the once great queen had done. When Agamemnon was slain by Clytemnestra after the war, Talthybius, according to some ac-

counts, took care of his young son Orestes and hid him from
Aegisthus. According to some accounts, he emigrated to
Crete and founded Tegea there. He died either at Mycenae
or in Sparta. There was a shrine to him in Sparta and a
family, said to have been descended from him, had the
hereditary function of state heraldry there.

Tantalus (tan'ta-lus). In Greek mythology, some say Tantalus
was a son of Zeus, or of Tmolus, the god of Mount Tmolus
in Libya. Others say he was a king of Argos or of Corinth
or of Sipylus in Libya. He was the father of Pelops, Niobe,
and Broteas. Tantalus was most fortunate in being on intimate terms with the gods and dined often at their table. But
he abused the confidence of the gods. He stole the nectar
and ambrosia on which they fed, and which confers immortality on those who partake of it, and gave it to his mortal
friends. He also, according to some accounts, committed a
horrible crime. When the gods were invited to dine with
him, he cut up his son Pelops and boiled the pieces in a
cauldron. Some say he served the gods this gruesome meal
to test their omniscience. The gods were instantly aware of
the contents of the dish set before them and all, except
Demeter, refused to eat of it. She was so preoccupied with
her grief over the disappearance of her daughter Persephone that she distractedly ate part of the left shoulder. Pindar,
on the other hand, says that Poseidon had fallen in love with
Pelops and stolen him away. Zeus punished Tantalus for his
ingratitude for the favors bestowed on him by the gods by
destroying his kingdom. Tantalus then committed a third
crime. Zeus had been guarded in his infancy by a golden dog
made by Hephaestus. It was stolen by Pandareus and given
into Tantalus' hands for safe-keeping. When Pandareus
came to claim the dog, Tantalus swore by Zeus that he knew
nothing about it. Zeus heard that Tantalus had taken an oath
in his name and sent Hermes to investigate. On learning that
the oath was false, he crushed Tantalus under a huge stone
on Mount Sipylus. Some say, however, that Tantalus stole
the golden dog himself and that Pandareus was the receiver.
But the fact remains that Tantalus swore falsely in the name
of Zeus that he knew nothing of the matter. Zeus continues
to torment Tantalus in Tartarus, the Underworld. For his
first two crimes he is condemned to stand forever in water
up to his neck, but whenever he stoops to drink of it, the

fat, fāte, fär, fåll, àsk, fāre; net, mē, hèr; pin, pīne; not, nōte, möve,
nôr; up, lūte, pùll; oi, oil; ou out; (lightened) ēlect, agōny, ūnite;

water recedes. Around him grow trees bearing luscious fruits, but when he stretches a hand to eat one of them, they sway beyond his reach. For his third crime, a huge stone perches constantly over his head, ever on the verge of falling and crushing him. It is from Tantalus, and his fate of ever having food and drink just beyond his grasp, that the word "tantalize" is derived.

Tantalus.   In Greek legend, a son of Broteas. He was a king of Pisa. He was married to Clytemnestra, daughter of Tyndareus of Sparta, and had one son by her. Agamemnon attacked Pisa, killed Tantalus and his infant son, and forced Clytemnestra to marry him. The bones of Tantalus were buried in a large bronze vessel at Argos.

Taraxippus   (ta-rak-sip'us). Said by some to be the ghost of Glaucus, the owner of mares that he refused to allow to breed and by which he was torn to pieces. It was said to haunt the Isthmus of Corinth and frighten horses at the Isthmian Games, causing the death of many charioteers. Others said Taraxippus was a dwarf-like spirit that rode behind men on horseback and frightened their horses. It was thought to be the spirit of a rider or driver who had been killed, and sacrifices were offered to propitiate it.

Tartarus   (tär'ta̧-rus). In Greek mythology, an earth-god; some say he came into being after Gaea, but others say he was the child of Gaea and Aether (Air). By Gaea he was the father of the monster Typhon.

Tartarus.   Deep and sunless abyss, according to Homer and also to earlier Greek mythology, situated in the lowest region of the Underworld. Here Zeus imprisoned the rebel Titans. Later poets described Tartarus as the place in which the wicked were punished. Sometimes the name is synonymous with the lower world in general.

Taÿgete   (tā-ij'ȩ-tē). In Greek mythology, a daughter of Pleione and Atlas; one of the Pleiades. She was transformed into a hind by Artemis so that she could escape the pursuit of Zeus. In gratitude, she dedicated a hind to Artemis, which some say was the Cerynean Hind captured by Heracles. Zeus discovered Taÿgete's disguise and ravished her. She became the mother of Lacedaemon and then hanged herself on the mountain which thereafter bore her name, Mount Taÿgetus. With her sisters', her image was placed among the stars. See **Pleiades.**

(obscured) errạnt, ardẹnt, actọr; ch, chip; g, go; th, thin; ŦH, then; y, you; (variable) ḑ as d or j, ş as s or sh, ţ as t or ch, ẕ as z or zh.

Tegeates (te-jē'ạ-tēz). In Greek tradition, the son of Lycaon
for whom the region around the city of Tegea, founded later
by Aleus, was named. Some say it was in the time of Tegeates that Apollo and Artemis visited Tegea to punish the
persecutors of Leto. Tegeates sacrificed to them and appeased them. The tomb of Tegeates and his wife Maera was
in Tegea. The sons of Tegeates were Cydon, Gortys, and
Archedius. Some say they migrated to Crete and founded
the cities of Cydonia, Gortyna, and Catreus there. But the
Cretans denied this. They said Cydon, a son of Hermes and
Acacallis, founded Cydonia; Catreus, son of Minos, founded
Catreus; and Gortys, son of Rhadamanthys, founded Gortyna.

Teiresias (tī-rē'si-ạs). See *Tiresias*.

Telamon (tel'ạ-mon). In Greek legend, a son of Aeacus, king
of Aegina, and Endeïs. He was the brother of Peleus and the
half-brother of Phocus. Telamon and Peleus were jealous of
Phocus because of his skill as an athlete and because he was
their father's favorite. Encouraged by their mother, they
schemed to kill him. In the course of an athletic contest to
which they had challenged him, Phocus was struck by a
discus, as if accidentally, and then slain with an ax. Which
one of the brothers administered the fatal blow is not certain, but together they buried Phocus' body and fled. Telamon went to Salamis and sent back messengers to his father
claiming he had no part in the murder. Aeacus forbade him
to set foot on Aegina. In order to discuss the matter with
Aeacus, Telamon secretly caused a mole to be built out into
the sea from Aegina. He then stood on the end of the mole
and shouted his plea of innocence to Aeacus. But Aeacus
refused to believe him and Telamon returned to Salamis.
There he married Glauce, daughter·of King Cychreus, and
succeeded Cychreus to the throne. When Glauce died, Telamon married Periboea. She was about to bear a child when
Heracles visited at their court on his way to attack Troy. He
prayed that Telamon's wife would bear a son as tough and
brave as a lion. An eagle at once swooped down and Heracles declared this to be a sign that his prayer had been heard.
Almost immediately thereafter Periboea was delivered of
Telamonian Ajax. Telamon accompanied Heracles on his
voyage against Troy and was the first to break through the
wall and enter the city. Heracles was instantly enraged that

Telamon had exceeded him in bravery and prepared to strike Telamon dead. But Telamon realized that he had aroused Heracles' wrath by his impetuous valor. With great presence of mind he began to collect stones. Heracles paused in the act of hurling his spear at Telamon to ask what he was doing. The quick-witted Telamon answered that he was building an altar to Heracles the Victor. Heracles was mollified and the attack proceeded. In the capture of Troy by Heracles, Telamon was awarded Hesione, a daughter of Laomedon and the sister of Priam. He took her back to Greece and she bore him Teucer, a noted archer. Priam sought repeatedly for the restoration of his sister but was denied satisfaction each time. Partly on this account Priam later felt completely justified in refusing to restore Helen to Menelaus after she had been abducted by Paris. Both of Telamon's sons took a valiant part in the second war against Troy, for the recapture of Helen. Thus the oracle which prophesied that the descendants of Aeacus would twice take Troy was fulfilled. Apollo had proclaimed this oracle at the time when the walls of Troy were built by him and Poseidon, with the help of the mortal Aeacus. At the end of the Trojan War Teucer returned to Salamis with the news that Ajax had committed suicide. Telamon banished him, even as he had been banished in his youth, claiming that he had not protected his brother's interests and blaming Teucer because he had not prevented his brother's death. Telamon took part in the Calydonian Hunt. He accompanied Jason and the Argonauts on the expedition to Colchis in quest of the Golden Fleece. He was a friend of Heracles and went with him to Thermodon when Heracles went there to fetch the girdle of the Amazon queen.

Telchines (tel-kī′nēz). In Greek mythology, nine children of the Sea (Thalassa). According to some accounts they had dogs' heads and flippers for hands. They were the first inhabitants of Rhodes and founded the cities of Lindus, Camirus, and Ialysus, which they named for three of the Danaids. With Caphira, a daughter of Oceanus, they nurtured the infant Poseidon who had been entrusted to them by Rhea, and made his trident. Later he fell in love with one of their number, Halia, and by her became the father of six sons and one daughter. The Telchines were renowned as smiths, and made the sickle with which Cronus castrated his father

Uranus. They possessed the evil eye, could change thei shape at will, could summon rain, clouds, snow, and hail and were the first to make images of the gods. Zeus wanted to destroy them because of their magic powers and because of the unhealthy mists they caused, but Artemis warned them and they fled. Those who settled in Boeotia were destroyed in a flood. Those who went to Lycia were destroyed by Apollo.

Telegonus (tē-leg′ō̜-nus). In Greek legend, a son of Circe and Odysseus, born when Odysseus, on his way home from the Trojan War, stopped and lingered some time with Circe. Years later Circe sent Telegonus to find his father. He landed on the shores of Ithaca, under the impression that it was Corcyra, and set about to raid the island. Odysseus came to repel the invader. Each was ignorant of the other's identity and in the struggle Telegonus came face to face with Odysseus and killed him with his spear, which was tipped with the spine of a sting ray. Thus the prophecy which Tiresias had made to Odysseus in the Underworld—that his death would come from the sea—was fulfilled. Telegonus returned to Circe's isle with Telemachus and Penelope, and married Penelope. He was said to have been the founder of Tusculum and Praeneste in Latium, according to some accounts. Circe made Telegonus and Penelope immortal and they eventually went to dwell in the Isles of the Blest.

Telemachus (tē-lem′a̜-kus). In Greek legend, a son of Odysseus and Penelope. While he was still an infant, his father left Ithaca to go to the Trojan War. In the long absence of Odysseus Telemachus grew up. Although he was manly, straightforward, and intelligent, he was not able to exercise authority over the numerous suitors who came to woo his mother and who wasted the property of his father in eating and drinking at his expense. In the twentieth year of Odysseus' absence Athena appeared to Telemachus in the form of Mentes, a captain of the Taphians, and encouraged him to call a council of the Ithacans to ask the wooers to go home. The suitors refused to leave and mocked the youthful Telemachus. Athena advised him to seek information about Odysseus. She provided a ship for him in which he sailed to Pylus to question Nestor. Nestor sent him on to Menelaus in Sparta. In neither place did he hear any recent news of his father and Athena again appeared to him and told him to go home. She warned him that his mother's suitors were lying in wait to kill him, told him how to avoid them, and instructed him to go to the house of the faithful swineherd Eumaeus. Telemachus followed her instructions. At the house of Eumaeus he was reunited with his father, who had at last landed in his own country and had gone to Eumaeus, to whom he appeared in the guise of a beggar. Together, Odysseus and Telemachus planned to expel the suitors. They went to the palace of Odysseus and in due course attacked and killed the arrogant suitors. After Odysseus was reunited with Penelope and resumed control of his estates, he learned from an oracle that he would meet his death at the hands of his son. Thinking that this meant Telemachus, he banished him to the island of Cephallenia. But it was another son, Telegonus, who caused the death of Odysseus. Unaware of his father's identity, Telegonus, the son of Circe and Odysseus, landed on the shores of Ithaca and killed Odysseus. When he realized he had killed his father, he took the body of Odysseus back to the land of Circe. Telemachus and Penelope went with him. Circe made them all immortal and married Telemachus.

Telemus   (tē′le̯-mus). In Greek mythology, a noted seer who journeyed to Sicily and there encountered Polyphemus the Cyclops. He warned Polyphemus that his single eye in the middle of his forehead would one day be gouged out by Odysseus. Polyphemus laughed at the prophecy. He remembered it only after Odysseus, having blinded him, was sailing safely away.

Telephus   (tel′e̯-fus). In Greek legend, a son of Heracles and Auge, a priestess of Athena. He was abandoned on Mount Parthenius by his mother but was nursed by a doe and found by herdsmen who took him to King Corythus. On reaching manhood he was told by the oracle of Delphi to sail to Mysia for news of his parents. There he learned from King Teuthras, now married to his mother, of his parentage. He married Teuthras' daughter, Argiope, and later became king of Mysia. According to other accounts, Telephus, speechless, went to Mysia accompanied by Parthenopaeus, son of Atalanta, who acted as his spokesman. In Mysia he defeated the enemies of Teuthras and was rewarded by being given Auge, the king's adopted daughter, as his wife. On the wedding night Auge attempted to kill him, as she was faithful to

Heracles, but a serpent slithered into the room and pre
vented it. Thereupon Auge cried out to the spirit of Hera
cles, and Telephus was miraculously informed that she wa
his mother and Heracles was his father. In the early years o
the Trojan War the Greeks landed in Mysia and ravaged i
under the impression that it was part of the Troad. Telephu
had driven them back to their ships when Achilles and Patro
clus appeared. He turned to run from them but tripped o
a vine and was wounded by Achilles' spear. The Greeks ther
sailed away. Telephus' wound did not heal. He was told by
Apollo that only he who caused it could cure it. Having gone
in disguise to Mycenae, at Clytemnestra's suggestion he
snatched up the infant Orestes and told Agamemnon he
would kill the child unless he healed his wound. Because
there was a prophecy that the Greeks could not take Troy
without the aid of Telephus, Agamemnon sent for Achilles,
who cured the wound by scraping rust from his spear onto
it. Telephus had agreed to pilot the Greeks to Troy but
afterward refused to carry out his promise, claiming that his
wife was Priam's daughter. However, he charted the course
that the Greeks successfully followed to get to Troy.

Telesphorus (tĕ-lĕs'fôr-us). A deity attendant on Asclepius,
who appeared in dreams and healed the sick or wounded. In
ancient art he is represented as a child, often with Asclepius.

Telphusa (tĕl-fū'så). In Greek mythology, a nymph of a spring
in Boeotia. According to some accounts, she persuaded
Apollo not to erect a temple and oracle at her spring but
advised him to go to Delphi where, since she was a prophetess, she knew he would have to overcome the Python.
Apollo punished her by hiding her spring under rocks near
which he built an altar.

Tenes (tēn'ēs). In Greek legend, a son of Apollo, or as some
say, of Cycnus, and Proclea. His stepmother Phylonome fell
in love with him but he honorably rejected her amorous
advances. She then denounced him to Cycnus, accused him
of seeking to ravish her, and called Eumolpus, a flute-player,
as her witness. Cycnus believed her, and to punish Tenes,
he put him and his sister Hemithea in a chest and set them
adrift on the sea. The chest went aground on an island near
the coast of Asia Minor. Tenes became king of the island and
named it Tenedos after himself. Cycnus later learned that
Tenes had been blameless in the affair with Phylonome. He

fat, fāte, fär, fåll, åsk, fāre; net, mē, hėr; pin, pīne; not, nōte, möve,
nôr; up, lūte, pùll; oi, oil; ou out; (lightened) ḝlect, agǫny, ūnite;

had the flute-player who had born false witness stoned to death, and buried Phylonome alive. Cycnus then sailed to Tenedos to ask forgiveness of his son. Tenes at first refused to allow him to moor his ship in the waters of Tenedos. Afterward, however, he forgave his father and Cycnus settled near him on Tenedos. When the Greeks sailed from Aulis the second time on their way to Troy, they coasted by Tenedos and sought to land. Tenes tried to prevent them from landing by hurling rocks at them from a cliff. Achilles swam ashore and killed Tenes. The Greeks landed and ravaged the island. But some say the Greeks were allowed to land peaceably but that Achilles seduced Hemithea, sister of Tenes, and in the resulting quarrel killed Tenes. In killing Tenes Achilles had carelessly forgotten his mother's warning that if he killed a son of Apollo, he would die by Apollo's hand. Thetis, mother of Achilles, had even sent a servant, Mnemon, whose sole duty was to remind Achilles not to slay a son of Apollo. When Achilles realized that he had forgotten his mother's warning, he killed Mnemon for failing in his duty. Tenes was buried on Tenedos and a shrine was erected to him. He was worshiped as a god after his death. No flute-player could enter the sacred precincts of his shrine because a flute-player had borne false witness against him, and it was forbidden to utter the name Achilles in these precincts.

Tereus (tē′rös). In mythology, a king of Thrace, who went to the aid of Pandion, king of Athens, when the latter was beset by enemies. Pandion showed his appreciation by giving Tereus his daughter Procne in marriage. Tereus was transformed into a hoopoe for the outrage he committed on Philomela, the sister of Procne. See *Procne.*

Terpsichore (tèrp-sik′ō̱-rē). One of the nine daughters of Zeus and Mnemosyne. She is the muse of the dance, the patroness of lyric poetry, the choral dance, and the dramatic chorus developed from it. In the last days of the Greek religion her province was restricted to lyric poetry. In art she is usually represented as bearing a lyre. According to some accounts, Terpsichore was the mother of the Sirens. See **Muses.**

Tethys (tē′this). In Greek mythology, a Titaness, the daughter of Gaea and Uranus. She was "the lovely queen of the sea," the wife of Oceanus, and the mother of all the river[s] and 3000 Oceanids.

Teucer (tū'ser). In Greek legend, a son of the Cretan princ[e] Scamander and the nymph Idaea. He was born in Phrygia[,] whither Scamander had come to escape a famine in Crete[.] Teucer succeeded his father and became the first king o[f] Troy, for which reason the Trojans are sometimes calle[d] Teucrians. According to some accounts, Aeneas and hi[s] companions were told to seek the home of their ancestor[s] after they fled from Troy. Thinking the oracle referred t[o] Scamander, or Teucer, they mistakenly went to Crete. Teu-cer's daughter Batia married Dardanus, a Thracian prince[,] who succeeded to the throne on Teucer's death. But some say it was Teucer who emigrated to Phrygia from Crete, and that he found Dardanus there and was welcomed by him. Still others say Teucer emigrated from Attica, founded Troy, and received Dardanus when he landed in Phrygia.

Teucer. In Greek legend, a bastard son of Telamon and Hesi-one, and adoring half-brother of Telamonian Ajax. He was a master of archery. He had been one of Helen's suitors before she married Menelaus, and as such was compelled to live up to his oath to aid Menelaus in any difficulty arising from his marriage. Therefore he joined the Greeks who went to Troy to recapture Helen. In the war he fought bravely at Ajax' side, at times using his brother's shield as a protection. He darted out from behind the enormous shield carried by Ajax, shot his lethal arrow, and then retired behind the shield. With his arrows he killed many, and tried several times to kill Hector. The first time, he struck Gor-gythion instead; the second time, Apollo deflected his arrow and he killed Archeptolemus, Hector's charioteer. On his third try, Hector wounded him by hurling a great stone that struck him in the shoulder just as he was about to shoot. When he fell, Ajax again protected him with his shield. He wounded Glaucus, Sarpedon's comrade, when the Trojans breached the Greek wall, and assailed Sarpedon himself, but Zeus protected the latter. Again, Zeus caused his bowstring to snap as he once more aimed at Hector. The death of Ajax by suicide caused him bitter grief. As he stood over his fallen body, he recognized the sword Ajax had used to kill himself as the one Hector had given him, and recalled that Hector had been tied to the back of Achilles' chariot by the girdle

Ajax had given him. He defied Menelaus' order not to bury Ajax, and with the wife and young son of Ajax as witnesses, buried him in the sands of Troy. When he returned to Salamis, Telamon forbade him to land and banished him because he had not brought back Ajax' bones, nor his wife, nor his son. He then went to Sidon, where he was hospitably received by Belus, father of Dido, and got help from him to conquer Cyprus. He married the daughter of the king who had given the island his name, built a city there which he named Salamis after his home in Greece, became king of Cyprus, and founded a dynasty of kings which traced their descent from him.

Teucrians   (tū'kri-ạnz). Another name for the Trojans, from their ancestor Teucer.

Teuthis   (tū'this). [Also, known as **Ornytus**.] In Greek legend, a leader of Arcadians from the village of Teuthis. When the Greeks were windbound at Aulis, Teuthis quarreled with Agamemnon and threatened to withdraw with his Arcadians. Athena came to persuade him not to withdraw, but he was so angry he struck the goddess with his spear and wounded her in the thigh. Teuthis then led his army back to Arcadia. Once at home, he was struck by a wasting disease and famine fell on his village, alone of the Arcadian villages. The oracle of Dodona told the inhabitants how they might appease the goddess. In addition, they made an image of Athena, showing the wound in her thigh, and dedicated it in the temple. The image, with its thigh wrapped in a purple bandage, was seen by the traveler Pausanias in the 2nd century A.D.

Teuthras   (tū'thrạs). In Greek legend, a king in Mysia. Once while hunting, he raised a great boar and pursued it. The boar fled to the temple of Artemis and as Teuthras overtook it there, it cried out in a human voice to be spared as one of Artemis' creatures. Teuthras ignored the plea for mercy and ruthlessly killed it. This so enraged Artemis that she restored the boar to life and punished Teuthras with madness and disease. His mother at length appeased Artemis with rich sacrifices and Teuthras was cleansed of his disease and purified of his madness. This Teuthras gave refuge to Auge when she fled to his kingdom. According to some accounts, he married Auge. When her son Telephus later arrived in Mysia in search of news of his parents, Teuthras welcomed him. Telephus helped Teuthras to rout his ene-mies, and as a reward was given the daughter of Teuthras for a wife and made heir to his kingdom. Others say Teu-thras adopted Auge as his daughter when she fled to him, and that when Telephus appeared, Teuthras offered him Auge in return for his aid in driving off his enemies. But on the wedding night the relationship between Auge and Tele-phus was revealed and Teuthras, learning of it, sent them both back to their homeland with his blessing.

Thalassa (thạ-las′ạ) or *Thalatta* (-lat′ạ). In later Greek myth-ology, the personification of the sea. She was a goddess of the sea who was sometimes thought of as the mother of Aphrodite by Zeus, but this was not the traditional version of the origin of Aphrodite. In other accounts she was the wife of Pontus and the mother by him of fish children. Again, she was said to be the mother of the Telchines.

Thalia (thạ-lī′ạ). One of the nine daughters of Zeus and Mnemosyne, she is the muse of comedy. By Apollo, accord-ing to some accounts, Thalia was the mother of the Cory-bantes. In later art she is generally represented with a comic mask, a shepherd's crook, and a wreath of ivy. See *Muses.*

Thamus (thā′mus). An Egyptian sailor who, according to tra-dition, was in a ship bound for Italy when he heard a shout across the water. A voice called his name and told him when he reached Italy to proclaim that "the great god Pan is dead." Thamus did as he was bid and all the people mourned.

Thamyris (tham′i-ris). A legendary Thracian poet and musi-cian who fell in love with the handsome youth Hyacinthus. Apollo was his rival for the affections of Hyacinthus, and when he overheard Thamyris boast that he could vie with the Muses in singing, he reported this boast to the Muses. They pursued Thamyris and overtook him at Dorium. To punish him for his boasting they blinded him, took away his voice, and caused him to forget his skill on the lyre.

Thanatos (than′ạ-tos). Ancient Greek personification of death. He was not worshiped as a god. In ancient Greece as elsewhere in the world, death personified was a folk concept. Later he became prominent in literary allusion. He was re-garded as a healer and remover of pain; he was inexorable in his purpose, and unbribable. Hesiod said he was even hated by the gods. In the *Iliad* he is the son of Nyx (Night) and the brother of Hypnos (Sleep).

Thaumas (thou'mạs). In Greek mythology, a son of Pontus and Gaea. He was the husband of Electra, daughter of Oceanus. Their children were the Harpies, Aello and Ocypete, and Iris of the "fast-flying feet" who became the messenger of the gods.

Thea (thē'ạ). In Greek mythology, a daughter of Chiron the centaur. She was a chaste companion of Artemis but was ravished by Aeolus, king of Magnesia in Thessaly. She feared her father's wrath if he should learn that she was about to bear a child. To protect her, Poseidon transformed her into a mare, Euippe, until after her child was born. When her foal Melanippe was born, Poseidon set the image of the mare among the stars as the constellation of the Horse, and transformed the foal into a baby girl.

Theano (thē-ā'nō). In Greek mythology, the wife of Metapontus, king of Icaria in Attica. She had no children and feared that her husband would abandon her if she remained childless. She tricked him by adopting twin boys who had been exposed to die and presenting them to Metapontus as her own children. The twins were the sons of Poseidon and Arne: Boeotus, founder of the Boeotians, and Aeolus, who became guardian of the winds. They had been ordered exposed by Desmontes, foster father of Arne, who had blinded and imprisoned their mother. Later Theano produced twin sons of her own. When they grew up, she became jealous because Metapontus, thinking that all four were his children, preferred Aeolus and Boeotus. She engineered a plot against them, advising her own sons to take advantage of a hunting expedition to kill Boeotus and Aeolus. They attempted to do so but, with the aid of Poseidon, Aeolus and Boeotus killed the sons of Theano and carried their dead bodies back to the palace. When Theano learned how her plot had miscarried, she committed suicide.

Theano. In Greek legend, a daughter of Cisseus, king of Thrace, and Teleclia. She was the wife of the Trojan Antenor, and among her sons were Acamas, Agenor, Archelochus, Helicaon, Iphidamas, and Polybus. She also tenderly reared Antenor's bastard son Pedaeus. Antenor and Theano believed that Helen and her possessions should be returned to Menelaus, and according to some accounts, they enter-

(obscured) errạnt, ardẹnt, actọr; ch, chip; g, go; th, thin; ŦH, then; y, you;
(variable) ḍ as d or j, ṣ as s or sh, ṭ as t or ch, ẓ as z or zh.

tained Odysseus and Menelaus when they came on a mission to Troy to secure Helen's return. Theano was a priestess of Athena and, according to some accounts, it was she who gave the sacred Palladium to Odysseus and Diomedes when they entered the city in secret some time after the death of Hector. For these reasons the Greeks spared Antenor and Theano after the fall of Troy, and they crossed to Thrace and from there went to the northern part of Italy where, according to tradition, they eventually founded the city of Patavium (Padua).

Thebe (thē′bē). In Greek mythology, a daughter of the river-god Asopus and Metope. She was the twin sister of Aegina, and like her was carried off by Zeus. She was known as the nymph of Thebes and, according to some accounts, married Zethus, one of the brothers who built the lower city. The name of the city, formerly Cadmea, was changed to Thebes in her honor.

Themis (thē′mis). In Greek mythology, a Titaness, the daughter of Gaea and Uranus. She was the mother by Zeus of the Moerae (Fates)—Atropos, Clotho, and Lachesis; of the Horae (Seasons); and of Prometheus. Early mythology says that she received the oracle of Delphi from Gaea, and the prophetic gift remained one of her attributes, for she warned her son Prometheus of what was in store for him. Later Themis, no longer the wife of Zeus, is the "fair-faced divinity," the handmaiden of the gods who presides with Zeus over justice and order, and sits on the throne beside him as his trusted counselor. She is the patron goddess of the rights of hospitality and a protector of the oppressed. It was Themis who told Deucalion and Pyrrha how to repopulate the earth after the disastrous flood which had swept away all mankind save these two. Themis, with the power of foretelling the future, told Poseidon, and after him Zeus, that Thetis the Nereid whom both were pursuing, would bear a son greater than his father. Because of this Zeus abandoned his designs on Thetis and wed her to Peleus. Themis, who became the personification of law, custom, and justice, was worshiped especially in Athens, Delphi, Olympia, Thebes, and Troezen.

Themisto (thē-mis′tō). In Greek legend, a wife of Athamas. According to some accounts, Athamas married her after he had settled in Thessaly, having been banished from Boeotia after the death of Ino and his sons, and raised a new family. But others say that Ino, the wife of Athamas and the mother of his sons Learchus and Melicertes, went out hunting one day and did not return. A blood-stained robe that was found convinced Athamas that Ino had been killed by wild beasts. After a brief period of mourning he married Themisto. But Ino had only gone to Mount Parnassus for a prolonged revel with the maenads and by the time Athamas learned that she was still alive Themisto had borne him twin sons. Athamas tried to conceal Ino as a nurse for his young children but Themisto learned her true identity, although she pretended not to know who Ino was. She went to the nursery and told the new nurse to prepare mourning garments for the two sons of the former wife of Athamas, and told the new nurse (Ino) that the garments were to be used on the next day. The next day Themisto ordered her servants to break into the nursery and kill the two children who were dressed in mourning garments. The servants obeyed her orders but Ino, suspecting foul play by Themisto, had dressed the children of Themisto in mourning garments rather than her own children. Thus it was the children of Themisto that were killed. When Athamas learned of their deaths he went mad, killed his son Learchus and would have killed Ino and Melicertes, but she took her son in her arms and leaped into the sea. Themisto, learning of the death of her children by her own orders, killed herself.

Theoclymenus   (thē″ō-klī′mē-nus). According to Euripides, a son of Psamathe and Proteus, king of Egypt. He succeeded his father. Having determined to marry Helen, who had been transported to Egypt while a phantom Helen went to Troy, he became a fierce enemy of the Greeks and killed any who chanced to land in his country. He was about to kill his sister Theonoë because she had not told him that Menelaus had landed in Egypt, and as a result Menelaus succeeded in escaping with Helen, but the Dioscuri (Helen's brothers) appeared in the heavens and told him to spare her; that all had been done at the will of the gods.

Theonoë   (thē-on′ō-ē). In Greek legend, a daughter of Thestor, and the sister of Calchas who accompanied the Greeks to Troy, and of Leucippe. While at play on the seashore near Troy she was captured by pirates and sold to King Icarus of Caria, whose mistress she became. Some time later a handsome priest of Apollo arrived in Caria. Theonoë fell in love with him but he scorned her advances. Theonoë, enraged, resolved to have the priest slain, but did not want to ask her slaves to commit the sacrilege of killing a priest, so she ordered that one of the foreign slaves must slay him. The foreign slave went to the room where the priest was confined and announced that he had been ordered to kill him but that he refused to do so; rather, he would kill himself, but first he wanted to tell how he came to be in such a sad plight. The slave announced that he was Thestor, the father of Theonoë and Leucippe, and that he had fallen into the hands of the king's concubine while searching for his lost daughter Theonoë; then, as he made ready to kill himself, the priest of Apollo revealed that he was really Leucippe, Thestor's own daughter, disguised as a priest at the command of the oracle of Delphi and engaged on the same errand as Thestor, namely, a search for Theonoë. Father and daughter wept in each other's arms and then resolved to kill the king's wicked mistress. They entered Theonoë's apartments and Leucippe announced to her that for lusting after the young priest, she must prepare to die at the hands of Thestor, son of Idmon. Hereupon Theonoë revealed that she was the daughter of Thestor who had been carried away by pirates years before and had not recognized her father and sister. Now all three rejoiced and gave thanks to Apollo. King Icarus, being informed of their history, gave Theonoë her freedom and sent them all home together.

Theophane (thē-of'a-nē). In Greek mythology, a beautiful maiden, the cousin of Phrixus and Helle. She had many suitors, among them Poseidon. To get her away from the other suitors he carried her off to the island of Crumissa. When her other suitors followed, he transformed her into a ewe and himself into a ram and the inhabitants of the island into cattle. The suitors, arriving and finding no people, slew the cattle and began to eat them. Poseidon changed them into wolves. In his form of a ram he married Theophane and she bore him the ram with the golden fleece that bore Phrixus to safety in Colchis and whose fleece was the object of the expedition of the Argonauts.

Therapne (thē-rap'nē). In Greek legend, a daughter of Lelex, who gave her name to a town in Laconia between Amyclae and Sparta, near the Eurotas River. Some say Helen and

Menelaus were buried here, and sacrifices were offered to both as to a goddess and a god, and festivals were held for them. There was a sanctuary there which some thought was a sanctuary of Helen but others say it was a temple of Menelaus. At Therapne, according to some accounts, there was a burial place of the Dioscuri.

Thersites (thêr-sī'tēz). In the *Iliad*, a son of Agrius of Aetolia. He was bowlegged, lame, and deformed in the shoulders. Homer says that he was the ugliest Greek at Troy. He roused the wrath of Odysseus by accusing Agamemnon of greed and Achilles of cowardice. Odysseus beat him and threatened to drive him off in dishonor if he again heard him assail the name of Agamemnon. His impudent, quarrelsome, abusive nature made him disliked by his fellow Greeks. No one mourned when Achilles, enraged because Thersites had mocked him for his grief over the death of Penthesilea, smote him so hard that his teeth fell out, accompanied by his gushing blood, and he fell to earth dead.

Theseus (thē'sōs, thē'sē-us). In Greek legend, an Athenian hero, the Athenian counterpart of Heracles, who traced his descent from Erechtheus and Pelops. Aegeus, king of Athens, being childless, consulted the oracle at Delphi. He could not interpret the answer the priestess gave him and later, when visiting Pittheus, son of Pelops, in Troezen, he told Pittheus the oracular pronouncement and asked what it meant. Pittheus, renowned for his wisdom, did not interpret the response. He entertained Aegeus lavishly and when he was flushed with wine, he sent his own daughter Aethra in to him. Aegeus embraced her. The same night Aethra, in obedience to a dream, waded across the sea to a nearby island and was ravished by Poseidon. For this reason Poseidon is sometimes called the father of Theseus, and indeed many times he came to the hero's aid, but generally Theseus is called the son of Aegeus. Before Aegeus left Troezen, he placed a sword and a pair of sandals under a huge stone. He told Aethra if she should bear a son, to rear him in secret in Troezen, lest the 50 sons of Pallas should seek to destroy him. When she thought he was strong enough, she was to take him to the rock. If he could lift it and recover the sword and sandals, Aegeus said, she was to send him to Athens. Aegeus then departed. In due course Aethra bore a son and named him Theseus, because of the tokens Aegeus had "deposited" under the rock, but some say he took this name later. He was reared in Troezen by his grandfather Pittheus. When he grew to young manhood, Theseus journeyed to Delphi to offer the first clippings of his hair to Apollo, as was the custom. He was a strong, spirited, intelligent youth. On his return, Aethra told him the story of his birth and led him to the rock under which the tokens lay. Theseus easily lifted it and recovered the sword and sandals. Then, following the instructions of Aegeus, he set out for Athens. Aethra and Pittheus urged him to go by sea, as the land route was made dangerous by brigands, monsters, and terrorists. But Theseus, in the hope of emulating his greatly admired relative Heracles, determined to follow the more hazardous overland route. He wished, he said, to present his father with a sword that had been blessed by use. He promised to wrong no man but to punish any who attacked him.

Near Epidaurus he met Periphetes, the "Club-bearer," who attacked travelers with his bronze club and beat them to death. Theseus seized the club and used it against Periphetes, slaying him. He was then so pleased with the huge club that he kept it as his own and carried it with him ever after, as Heracles had done with his club of olive wood. At the Isthmus of Corinth he came upon Sinis, the "Pine-bender," who compelled travelers to help him bend down pine trees. When, by main strength, Sinis and the traveler were holding the top of the arched tree to the ground, Sinis would let go. Without his strength the tree snapped upright, flinging the traveler into the air and then dashing him to his death on the ground. But some say Sinis bent two trees to the ground, tied his victim to the two trees, then released them. As the trees sprang upright, the victim was torn apart. Theseus slew Sinis by the same means. He found Perigune, daughter of Sinis, hiding in the rushes in terror of him. He persuaded her that he would do her no harm and won her love. She bore him Melanippus. Theseus later gave her to Deioneus of Oechalia. Theseus next slew the Crommyonian Sow, a savage beast said by some to be the offspring of Echidna and Typhon. The animal had been roaming the countryside, terrorizing the inhabitants. This sow, also called Phaea, was said by some not to have been an animal at all, but an evil female robber, whose greed and habits won her the name of sow. Theseus dispatched her and pro-

ceeded on his way. At the Megarian cliffs he came upon
Sciron, whose custom it was to compel travelers to wash his
feet as he sat near the edge of the cliff. As they squatted to
carry out his bidding, he kicked them into the sea. Theseus
refused to obey him. Instead he hurled Sciron into the sea.
But some say it was not on the journey to Athens that he
killed Sciron, whom they call an upright man, but later,
when he captured Eleusis from the Megarians. Proceeding
to Eleusis, he met Cercyon the wrestler and overcame him,
not by strength but by skill, as Theseus was the first to
understand the principles of wrestling. Next he encountered
Damastes, called Procrustes, "Stretcher." He had two beds
in his lodging, one short and one long. It was his evil practice to lure travelers to spend the night in his house. Short
travelers he place on the long bed, and stretched them out
until they fitted the bed. Tall travelers were given the short
bed, and had as much of their limbs lopped off as was necessary to fit them to the bed. But some say Procrustes had only
one bed which he used in both manners. Theseus killed him.
At the Cephissus River Theseus came to the home of the
Phytalidae, the sons of Phytalus. They purified him of the
murders he had committed and treated him with courtesy.
These were the first on his journey to receive him in a
friendly manner. He later rewarded them by making them
priests of a temple of Artemis which he raised in Troezen.
Proceeding to Athens, Theseus passed an uncompleted
temple of Apollo on the outskirts of the city. Masons working on the roof of the temple spied him and jeered his
youthful appearance. They pretended they thought he was
a girl and coarsely wondered that he should be walking
about alone. Theseus made no reply to their taunts. Instead
he unyoked an ox from the masons' cart and hurled the
animal high into the air above the roof of the temple. Without more ado he went on to find his father's house.

   In the years since he had visited Pittheus in Troezen and
embraced Aethra, Aegeus had married Medea, the sorceress
whom Jason brought back with him from Colchis. She bore
him a son, Medeus, and feared that Theseus, whom by her
arts she recognized the instant he came to Athens, would
displace her son in the affections of Aegeus and as heir to
his throne. She plotted to kill Theseus. Aegeus did not know
that the youth who appeared before him, and whom he had

never seen before, was his own son. Some say that at Medea's suggestion he sent Theseus to capture the Marathonian Bull. This bull had been brought over the sea from Crete by Heracles and was ravaging the countryside. Theseus subdued the bull and dragged it by its horns through Athens and sacrificed it to Apollo. But some say he did this later, after he had been recognized as the son of Aegeus. Medea persuaded Aegeus, who still had not learned that this was his son, that the young stranger was a threat to him. She induced Aegeus to offer him a cup of wine that she had poisoned with aconite. This occurred at a banquet held in the temple on the Acropolis where Aegeus lived. As Theseus lifted the cup to his lips, Aegeus caught sight of the hilt of the sword the young man was wearing. By the serpents twined about the hilt he recognized it as his own sword and realized that this must be his son. He dashed the cup from Theseus' hand. The spot where it fell was afterward barred off in the temple. Aegeus was overcome with joy at this meeting with his valiant son, and all Athens celebrated. Medea, for her plots, was expelled from Athens, and her child with her. The sons of Pallas, brother of Aegeus, claimed that Aegeus was not a true descendant of Erechtheus, and they had been plotting to seize the throne. The arrival of Theseus put their plans out of joint and they resolved to divide their forces and attack the city from two sides. But Theseus was warned of their intentions by the herald Leos. He fell upon one of the forces of the Pallantids and slew them. Those in the other force scattered.

When he had been in Athens but a little while, the time came for the Athenians to send the tribute which King Minos of Crete exacted every nine years with the sanction of the gods, because the Athenians had caused the death of his son Androgeus. This tribute consisted of seven youths and seven maidens who were selected by lot and sent to Crete, there to be devoured by the Minotaur, the monstrous son of Pasiphaë, who was kept concealed in a winding labyrinth. The most common account is that Theseus won the hearts of the Athenians by volunteering to be one of the seven youths. Some say, however, that his lot was drawn; and others say that Minos came from Crete to select the young Athenians himself, and that he instantly chose Theseus. The custom was to send the youths and maidens to

fat, fāte, fär, fâll, ȧsk, fāre; net, mē, hėr; pin, pīne; not, nōte, mȯve, nôr; up, lūte, pu̇ll; oi, oil; ou out; (lightened) ĕlect, agǫny, ūnite;

Crete in a ship fitted with a black sail as a sign of mourning for the loss Athens suffered. Theseus assured Aegeus that he meant to slay the Minotaur and return. Aegeus gave him a white sail, or as some say, a scarlet one, and instructed him to replace the black sail with it if he was successful in escaping from Crete. Before his departure Theseus made vows and prayers to Apollo at Delphi, and was told by the priestess to take Aphrodite as his guide. When the youths and maidens of the tribute were gathered at the shore, he sacrificed to Aphrodite, and his victim, a she-goat, was transformed into a he-goat as it died. With this favorable omen the Athenians departed. At that time the Athenians were not so skilled at navigation as they were to become later. Theseus took as his pilots for the voyage to Crete Nausithous of Salamis and Phaeax, who some say was the ancestor of the Phaeacians. The *Cyberneria*, or Pilots' Festival, was afterward celebrated at Phalerum in their honor. When the Athenians arrived in Crete, Minos came down to the shore to look them over. He was favorably impressed by one of the maidens in the group and would have seized her. Theseus sprang forward in anger and forbade him to touch any of the maidens who had been sent as tribute. He said that as a son of Poseidon he would protect the virgins who had come with him to Crete. Minos mocked his claim to be a son of Poseidon. He took a ring from his finger and, hurling it into the sea, commanded Theseus to prove he was a son of Poseidon by retrieving the ring. "First," said Theseus, "prove that you are, as you claim, a son of Zeus." Minos prayed to Zeus for a sign and immediately there was a loud clap of thunder and a flash of lightning. Theseus acknowledged this proof. He leaped into the sea to prove his own claim. A school of dolphins escorted him to the underwater palace of Thetis the Nereid. She, or as some say, Amphitrite, gave him a jeweled crown and sent out the Nereids to find the ring. When they recovered it, they gave it to Theseus, who then emerged from the sea carrying the ring, which he restored to Minos, and the jeweled crown, which he later gave to Ariadne as a wedding gift. For among those who had witnessed his defiance of Minos over the maiden, and had seen him subsequently leap into the sea and recover the ring, was Ariadne, the daughter of Minos. She fell in love with Theseus on the spot. This was the work of Aphrodite, whom

Theseus, as advised, had taken as his guide. Ariadne resolved to save him from death in the labyrinth. She had a ball of magic thread from Daedalus, the builder of the labyrinth, which had the property, as it was unwound, of leading whoever held it to the heart of the labyrinth. By rewinding it one could follow it out of the labyrinth. Ariadne offered to help Theseus in exchange for his promise to take her away from Crete with him as his wife. She gave him the ball of thread, told him to fasten one end of it to the lintel of the labyrinth as he entered and unwind the ball until he came to the Minotaur. To escape from the labyrinth he had only to rewind the thread. He followed her instructions, found and slew the Minotaur, which he offered as a sacrifice to Poseidon, and returned to the entrance where Ariadne awaited him. Together with the Athenians who had accompanied him to Crete, they fled to their ship and escaped. Theseus took the precaution of knocking holes in the hulls of the Cretan ships before he left, and thus the Cretans were not immediately able to pursue them.

The Cretans did not accept this story of the Minotaur, offspring of Pasiphaë and a bull. They claimed there was no such animal, and said that the labyrinth was simply a dungeon where the Athenians were kept until they were either offered as sacrifices at the funeral games for Androgeus, or given as prizes. They said that the most powerful general under Minos was one Taurus (bull). He was a great athlete and bully. According to the Cretans, they held funeral games for Androgeus, at which the prizes were Athenian youths and maidens given to the winners as slaves. Taurus always won. The Cretans resented his prowess and his arrogance. Theseus, coming as part of the tribute, asked permission to take part in the games. Minos, in the hope that he might defeat Taurus and also because he suspected Taurus of carrying on an intrigue with Pasiphaë, gave his consent. Theseus wrestled Taurus and, to the delight of Minos and the watching Ariadne, three times hurled him flat and pinned his shoulders to the ground. Minos was so pleased by the humiliation of Taurus that he released the Athenians, sent them back to Athens with Theseus, and gave him his daughter Ariadne for wife. So much for the Cretan story.

After leaving Crete, carrying Ariadne with him, Theseus put in at the island of Naxos. There, as she slept, he abandoned her. Some say Dionysus appeared to him in a dream and demanded her; others that Athena appeared to him in a dream and warned him to leave her; others that his ship, with him in it, was driven to sea by a storm, and when he returned Ariadne had disappeared. Still others say he abandoned her out of love for a daughter of Panopeus. In any event, he did not take Ariadne to Athens with him. He sailed from Naxos to the island of Delos and dedicated an image of Aphrodite in the temple of Apollo there. Around an altar made of horns taken entirely from the left side of the head he danced the so-called Crane Dance, which in its weavings and circlings imitated the winding passages of the labyrinth. (The Delians continued to perform this dance at least as late as the first century of the Christian era.) In Delos he also instituted athletic contests and established the custom, the first to do so, of awarding the palm to the victor. He then sailed for Attica. Some say it was grief over the loss of Ariadne that caused him to forget to change the black sail. Others say it was jubilation at escaping from Crete and joy at beholding the shores of Attica that made him forget. In any event, Aegeus, anxiously looking out to sea, scanning the horizon for a glimpse of a sail, saw a black sail and read in it a message that his son was dead. In his despair he hurled himself from the Acropolis and was killed, or, as some say, he flung himself into the sea which thereafter was called Aegean in his honor. Theseus landed and sent heralds with the good news to the city. The ship in which he was said to have voyaged to Crete, a 30-oared galley, was preserved by the Athenians to the end of the 4th century B.C.

Aegeus being dead, Theseus now became king. He destroyed his enemies and the sons of Pallas, and strengthened the kingdom by incorporating the 12 independent demes into which Attica had formerly been divided into one municipal unit, to which some say he gave the name Athens. He established an orderly democracy in which he was the leader, and divided the citizens into classes, each of which had its own duties and privileges. He was said, incorrectly as it happens, to have coined money, stamped with the image of an ox, to have established the Panathenaic Festival, which was open to all of Attica, and to have added Megara to the control of Athens. When he had done these things he gave up the throne and gave Athens a constitution, for the

Dephic oracle now prophesied that Athens could sail the stormy seas with the security of an inflated pig's bladder. Some say the Isthmian Games, previously mysterious rites held at night in honor of Melicertes, came to be held as athletic and other contests in the daytime and in honor of Sciron at the instigation of Theseus. He secured a promise from the Corinthians, where the games were held, that the Athenians should occupy a place of honor equal in area to the space which could be covered by the sail of the ship in which they sailed to the games.

According to some accounts, Theseus accompanied Heracles on his mission to the Euxine Sea to fetch the Amazon's girdle. Heracles gave him the Amazon Antiope as a reward and he returned with her to Athens. But some say Theseus went to the Amazon country after the expedition of Heracles, and captured Antiope himself. At all events, the Amazons marched from the Euxine Sea against Athens to avenge the attack Theseus made on them. The war lasted three months and ended in a treaty. Some say Antiope, who bore Hippolytus to Theseus, was killed in this war, fighting at his side. Others say she was killed later, when Theseus made an alliance with Deucalion, who had succeeded his father Minos as king of Crete. He gave Theseus his sister Phaedra for wife. Antiope, infuriated at being cast aside, burst into the hall where the wedding ceremonies were in progress and threatened to kill Theseus. The doors were hastily closed and Antiope, with her attendant maidens, was killed. Phaedra bore Acamas and Demophon, who took part in the Trojan War, to Theseus. She later fell in love with her stepson Hippolytus and when he repulsed her advances she hanged herself.

Theseus was said to have ravished the daughters of Sinis and Cercyon—his love adventures paralleled those of Heracles; to have married Periboea, who later married Telamon and bore Ajax; to have sailed with Jason in the *Argo;* to have taken part in the Calydonian Hunt; to have aided the Lapiths in their war with the centaurs; to have recovered the corpses of those who fell at Thebes in the Expedition of the Seven against Thebes; and to have settled a boundary dispute between the Peloponnesians and the Ionians. Indeed, so many were the deeds of Theseus that the expression "Not without Theseus" came into use.

fat, fāte, fär, fåll, åsk, fãre; net, mē, hèr; pin, pīne; not, nōte, möve, nôr; up, lūte, pùll; oi, oil; ou out; (lightened) ḛlect, agǫny, ūnite;

Pirithous, king of the Lapiths, heard such tales of the valor and spirit of Theseus he resolved to test whether he could live up to his reputation. He made a raid on Attica and drove off some of the cattle. Theseus pursued him. Pirithous stopped in his tracks and turned to confront Theseus. He was so impressed by him that he confessed he had done wrong and offered to do whatever Theseus commanded of him. Theseus, equally impressed, asked of him only that he be his friend. At the wedding of Pirithous Theseus helped to subdue the unruly centaurs who attacked the bride. The wife of Pirithous subsequently died. As Theseus was also a widower, he and Pirithous resolved to seek daughters of Zeus as wives. They decided first to abduct Helen, the beautiful ward of Tyndareus of Sparta, although she was but a child (some say ten years old) at the time. They carried out their plan, seizing the youthful Helen as she was sacrificing in a temple, and drew lots to see which would win her for his wife, on the understanding that the winner should then help the loser to find a bride. Theseus won, but as he feared the disapproval of the Athenians, for his act might cause a war with Sparta, he sent Helen away to Aphidna in the care of his mother. Pirithous later reminded Theseus of his bargain, and informed him that he meant to take Persephone from Hades for his bride. Theseus tried to dissuade him from the perilous enterprise of descending to Tartarus to steal Persephone, but Pirithous insisted and Theseus was bound by his oath to help him in the undertaking. They descended to Tartarus through an entrance at Taenarus and demanded Persephone from Hades. He asked them to be seated. The chairs on which they sat were the Chairs of Forgetfulness and at once became part of their bodies. They could not move, and stayed where they were for four years. Then Heracles, in Tartarus to fetch Cerberus, found them and answered their appeal for help. He succeeded in wrenching Theseus off his chair, but he left a good deal of his flesh stuck to the chair, for which reason the descendants of Theseus were noted for their thinly covered buttocks. Heracles, however, could not free Pirithous, and he and Theseus returned to earth without him. Some say this Persephone sought by Pirithous was the wife of one Aidoneus, a king in Thesprotia, and he captured Pirithous and Theseus when they came to steal his wife. He threw Pirithous to the dogs and locked Theseus up in a dungeon, from which Heracles ultimately freed him.

When he returned to Athens after his long stay in Tartarus, Theseus found that the Dioscuri had recovered their sister Helen, and carried her and Theseus' mother off to Sparta, and that Menestheus had seized the throne of Athens. In his absence the people had become corrupt and they did not welcome him on his return. In sadness he went to the island of Scyrus, where he owned estates. Lycomedes, the king, welcomed him and pretended friendship. Under the pretext of pointing out to Theseus where his estates were located, he led him to a cliff, and while his back was turned, he pushed Theseus off the cliff to his death. According to tradition, at the Battle of Marathon (490 B.C.) an image of Theseus in full armor rose up and rushed at the head of the Athenians against the Persians. Afterward the oracle of Delphi ordered the bones of Theseus restored to Athens; Cimon, the Athenian general, went to Scyrus to find them, but the islanders refused to tell him where Theseus was buried. He was led to his grave by an eagle which he saw tearing the earth with its talons. On that spot Cimon dug and found a coffin containing huge bones which he took to be the bones of Theseus. He restored them to Athens, where they were buried in a tomb in the heart of the city. This tomb became a sanctuary for runaway slaves and the oppressed, whom Theseus had always championed. The Athenians worshiped Theseus as the founder of their city and as a hero, but they never succeeded in having him declared a god.

Thespian (thes′pi-ạn) *Lion.* In Greek legend, a lion that roamed the forests of Cithaeron and the glades of Mount Helicon, and preyed on the flocks of Amphitryon, foster father of Heracles. Heracles, as a young man, sought and found the lion. He killed it and wore its skin as a cloak. According to other accounts, it was the skin of the Nemean Lion that Heracles wore, and Alcathous was the man who slew the Thespian Lion.

Thespian Maids. The Greek Muses. They were so called because their games were performed at Thespiae, at the foot of Mount Helicon.

Thespius (thes′pi-us). In Greek legend, a son or descendant of Erechtheus, king of Athens. He was the founder and king of Thespiae in Boeotia, and the father of 50 daughters by his wife Megamede. Being anxious to have descendants by Heracles, he welcomed the hero when he came to Thespiae to hunt the Thespian Lion, and gave him all his 50 daughters. All except one were delighted with Heracles' attentions, and among them produced 51 male children, including two sets of twins. The one daughter who refused Heracles' favors was forced to become a priestess in his temple and was thus condemned to lifelong virginity. Thespius' admiration and friendly relations with Heracles endured. He purified Heracles after the latter, in a fit of madness, had murdered his own sons. Later, at Heracles' order, he sent 40 of his 51 grandsons to colonize the island of Sardinia.

Thessalus (thes′a-lus). In Greek legend, a son of Jason and Medea. Some say he was stoned to death, along with his sisters and brothers, by the Corinthians to avenge the death of Glauce and Creon, and that he was buried in the sacred precinct of Hera in Corinth. Others say he escaped and went to Iolcus, where he found that Acastus, son of Pelias, had died. Thessalus took over the throne of Iolcus and named the people of the land Thessalians after himself.

Thestor (thes′tor). In mythology, a son of Apollo, according to some accounts; or a son of Apollo's son, Idmon the Argonaut. He was the father of Calchas, to whom he taught the art of prophecy. In later versions of his story he was said to have been the father also of two daughters: Leucippe and Theonoë. Theonoë was kidnapped by pirates, who took her to Caria where she became the mistress of King Icarus. Thestor set out to search for his daughter but was overtaken by a storm and shipwrecked on the coast of Caria. He fell into the hands of King Icarus, who did not know of his relationship to Theonoë, and he was made a slave. Leucippe later sought for news of her father and sister, whom she had not seen since she had been a child. The oracle at Delphi told her to go to Caria, disguised as a priest of Apollo, to search for them. In Caria Theonoë fell in love with the beautiful young priest, but her advances were rejected. Enraged, Theonoë then ordered that one of the slaves should put the young priest to death. Thestor was the slave chosen for the purpose. Thestor confronted the young priest, but instead of killing him, he recited his own name and history and prepared to plunge the sword into his own breast in his misery. Leucippe recognized that this was her father and revealed her true identity to him. Together they then planned to kill the king's mistress. They found her alone in her room and told her to prepare to die. However, before they killed her, they wanted her to know what noble persons she had persecuted. On hearing their names, it was Theonoë's turn to recognize her father, and the family was happily reunited. King Icarus nobly shared their joy. He gave them rich gifts and sent them all home to Greece.

THETIS RECEIVING THE ARMOR OF ACHILLES FROM
HEPHAESTUS
Red-figured Attic cup.
Berlin

Thetis (thē'tis). In Greek mythology, a sea-goddess, attended by fifty Nereids, the daughters of Nereus and Doris. Zeus fell in love with her and pursued her, but Thetis eluded him, thus earning the gratitude of Hera. Zeus gave up his pursuit, as Poseidon had also done, when he learned from Prometheus that Thetis would bear a son more powerful than his father. He promised her to Peleus, son of Aeacus. Thetis had no desire to marry Peleus, and since she had the power to transform herself at will she endeavored to escape him when he had caught her as she slept in a cave by the sea, by turning herself successively into fire, water, a lion, a serpent, and a fish. Peleus, as he had been warned to do by Chiron, maintained his grasp through these changes and she consented to marry him. All the gods and goddesses were present at their wedding except Eris, who had not been invited because of her disruptive influence, and who threw the Apple of Discord among the wedding guests in revenge. Thetis bore several sons to Peleus. One after the other she immersed them in flames to burn away their mortal parts and sent them to Olympus. Peleus happened in one night while she was performing this rite on Achilles. He screamed at the sight. Thetis dropped Achilles and fled to the sea. Peleus never saw her again, although she sometimes spoke to him and told him what to do while keeping herself invisible. According to some accounts, Thetis dipped Achilles into the River Styx and thus made him invulnerable except for the one place on his ankle where she held him.

On the whole, Thetis was a kindly goddess and rendered service to many of the gods. When Hera, Poseidon, and Athena bound Zeus in 100 fetters, Thetis summoned Briareus, who used his 100 hands to free him instantly. She gave Dionysus asylum beneath the sea when Lycurgus pursued him. She sheltered Hephaestus for nine years when Hera hurled him from heaven because of his lameness. At Hera's request, she lifted the *Argo* over the dangerous Clashing Rocks and then, with her Nereids, propelled it safely past Scylla and Charybdis. Because of her previous aid, Zeus granted her request to favor the Trojans to punish the Greeks for Agamemnon's insult to her son Achilles in the tenth year of the Trojan War, and Hephaestus willingly made armor for Achilles to replace that which he had loaned to Patroclus and which had been captured by Hector. After the death of Achilles it was Thetis who decreed that this magic armor should be awarded to the bravest of the Greeks. She prophesied accurately that if Achilles went to Troy he would die young; that if Achilles killed a son of Apollo he would die by Apollo's hand; that the first man to go ashore at Troy would be the first to die there.

Thiodamas (thī-od'a-mas). A legendary king of the Dryopians. Heracles, passing through his land, found the king plowing with a yoke of oxen. Since he was hungry Heracles asked for one of the oxen. Thiodamas refused him, whereupon Heracles slew him and took his son Hylas as his squire.

He killed and roasted the ox and ate it. Then he drove the Dryopians out of their city on Mount Parnassus and sent the leading citizens as slaves to Delphi. But some say this Thiodamas was a native of Rhodes, and that it was when Heracles was in Rhodes that he seized one of his oxen. Thiodamas fled to a nearby hilltop and from this safe position hurled curses on Heracles. Heracles was unimpressed and ate of the ox, which he had meantime roasted, to his satisfaction. But some say it was from this incident that the custom arose in Rhodes of uttering curses when sacrifices were made to Heracles.

Thisbe (thiz'bē). See under *Pyramus and Thisbe*.

Thoas (thō'as). In classical mythology, a son of Ariadne and Dionysus, or according to some accounts, of Theseus. Rhadamanthys of Crete gave him the island of Lemnos for his kingdom. However, the Lemnian women rose against the men of the island and killed all the males. Thoas was saved by his daughter Hypsipyle, who concealed him in a chest and set him adrift on the sea. The chest landed safely on the island of Oenoë and there Thoas became the father of Sicinus by the nymph of the island. Thoas was the king of the Taurians when Iphigenia was brought to Tauris, having been saved by the gods from being sacrificed at Aulis. He made her priestess of Artemis in Tauris. When her brother came to steal the statue of the goddess and discovered that the priestess was his own sister, he suggested that they should kill Thoas and escape with the statue. Iphigenia would not agree to the slaying of Thoas because he had been kind to her. They did escape by a trick and Thoas, in anger, would have pursued and killed them but Athena appeared to him and told him it was the will of the gods that they should go free.

Thrasymedes (thras-i-mē'dēz). In Greek legend, a son of Nestor who accompanied his father to Troy and was chief to the Greek sentries. He furnished his sword, shield, and bullhide helmet to Diomedes when the latter went as a spy against the Trojan camp. With his father he battled against Memnon for possession of the body of Antilochus, his brother, but both were forced to withdraw. He fought bravely throughout the war and at its close returned safely to Pylus with his father. Telamachus met him there when he visited Nestor in search of news of his father.

fat, fāte, fär, fåll, åsk, fāre; net, mē, hèr; pin, pīne; not, nōte, möve, nôr; up, lūte, pùll; oi, oil; ou out; (lightened) ęlect, agǫny, ūnite;

Three Graces, The. See *Graces, The Three.*

Thriae (thrī′ī). In Greek mythology, three nymphs of Parnassus who nursed Apollo. They were seeresses who foretold the future by casting pebbles in water. At the request of Apollo they taught Hermes how to foretell the future by this method.

Thyestes (thī-es′tēz). In Greek legend, a son of Pelops and Hippodamia, and the brother and arch-rival of Atreus. Thyestes and Atreus fled from their home in the Peloponnesus because they were implicated in the murder of their half-brother Chrysippus. They were invited to Mycenae by Sthenelus, who had seized the throne there. When Sthenelus and his son Eurystheus were dead, an oracle proclaimed that Mycenae should be governed by a Pelopid. The question was whether it should be Atreus or Thyestes. In the rivalry between the brothers Zeus took the part of Atreus; Artemis favored Thyestes. Thyestes, who had become the lover of Aërope, wife of Atreus, now induced her to steal a golden-fleeced, horned lamb that Atreus possessed. It had been sent to him by Hermes, to increase the enmity between the brothers and thus to punish the Pelopids for the murder of Myrtilus by their father Pelops. Atreus had sacrificed the flesh of the lamb to Artemis in accordance with a vow, but had kept the fleece, stuffed it, and kept it hidden away in a chest. Once Thyestes had it in his possession, he claimed that the throne of Mycenae should go to whoever held the golden-fleeced lamb. Atreus, under the impression that the lamb was safely in his possession, was agreeable. It then developed that Thyestes, thanks to Aërope's treachery, had acquired the lamb. He would immediately have been made king but for the intervention of Zeus. The god sent Hermes to ask if Thyestes would withdraw in favor of Atreus if the sun reversed its course through the heavens. Thyestes agreed, and Zeus for one day caused the sun to go backwards across the sky. Atreus became king and Thyestes was banished. According to some accounts, Thyestes avenged himself by causing Atreus to kill Plisthenes, his own son by his first wife, under the impression that Plisthenes, who had been brought up by Thyestes, was the latter's son. When Atreus learned of Aërope's adultery with Thyestes, he sent for Thyestes on the pretext that he was willing to share his kingdom with him. When he arrived, Atreus seized his three sons—Aglaus, Orchomenus, and Callileon—from the altar of Zeus where they had fled for refuge. He cut off their limbs and boiled their bodies in a cauldron. He then invited Thyestes to a feast. Only when the banquet was over did Atreus order the bloody limbs of Thyestes' sons brought in to reveal to their father that he had eaten of his own sons' flesh. Sickened with horror, Thyestes pronounced a fearful curse on the house of Atreus, which brought disaster to his sons, and fled to Sicyon. There, in accordance with instructions from an oracle, he ravished his daughter Pelopia. She did not know his true identity, and in her struggle to escape seized his sword. Atreus came to Sicyon looking for Thyestes. He saw Pelopia and fell in love with her. Since he had killed Aërope for her infidelity, he asked the king of Sicyon, who he thought was Pelopia's father, for permission to marry her. The king did not enlighten him as to her parentage, but gladly gave his permission. Later Pelopia bore Thyestes' son, Aegisthus. Atreus thought this was his own child, and rescued him when Pelopia left him on a mountain to die. Some years later, famine afflicted Mycenae. Atreus sent his sons, Agamemnon and Menelaus, to fetch Thyestes. They found him and brought him to Mycenae. Atreus imprisoned him and ordered young Aegisthus to kill him as he slept. But Thyestes awoke, recognized the sword which Aegisthus held unsteadily over him, and asked where he had found it. Aegisthus said his mother had given it to him, and Thyestes realized that this was his own son. He sent for Pelopia, who plunged the sword into her breast on learning that the father of her child was her own father. Aegisthus took the bloody sword to Atreus as proof that Thyestes was dead and, as Atreus thankfully sacrificed near the sea, Aegisthus and Thyestes set upon him and killed him. Thyestes at last became king of Mycenae. When he died, he was buried near the shrine of Perseus outside Mycenae, and a ram was placed over his tomb. None of this complicated horror story for control of Mycenae appears in Homer. In the *Iliad,* the scepter, made by Hephaestus, was given by Zeus to Pelops; Pelops bequeathed it to Atreus, who in turn passed it to Thyestes, and he handed it over to Agamemnon.

Thyia (thī′ä). In Greek mythology, a daughter of the river-god Cephissus according to some accounts. Others say Cas-

fat, fāte, fär, fâll, ȧsk, fāre; net, mē, hèr; pin, pīne; not, nōte, möve, nôr; up, lūte, púll; oi, oil; ou out; (lightened) ēlect, agǫny, ūnite;

talius, a mortal, was her father. She was the mother by
Apollo of Delphus, who gave his name to Delphi. Since she
first sacrificed to Dionysus at Delphi and celebrated revels
in his honor, her name was given to the followers of
Dionysus, who were called Thyiades. The Delphians raised
an altar in the sacred precinct of Thyia in gratitude to the
winds that helped them in the Persian Wars by causing great
storms that scattered the Persian fleet at Artemisium.

Thyiades (thī'yạ-dēz). A name for the maenads or bacchantes.
See *Thyia.*

Thymoetes (thī-mē'tēz). In Greek legend, an elder of Troy
and a counselor of Priam. His son Munippus, by Cilla, sister
of Priam, was born earlier on the same day that Hecuba bore
Paris to Priam. According to a prophecy, the royal Trojan
who bore a son that day must be destroyed, along with her
child; otherwise the child would bring ruin to Troy. Priam
took the prophecy to apply to Cilla and her son, and had
them both killed. Many years later, after the death of Hector
and Penthesilea at the hands of Achilles, Thymoetes advised
the Trojans to flee their doomed city, as Achilles was irresistible. His advice in this instance was disregarded. However, when the Wooden Horse was discovered before the
gates of Troy, Thymoetes advised, either from treachery in
revenge for the death of Munippus, or because Troy's fate
was already sealed, that the Trojans bring it inside the walls.
This time his advice was heeded and brought disaster to
Troy.

Thyone (thī'ọ-nē). The name that was given to Semele when
she was translated to Olympus from Tartarus. Dionysus
gave his mother this name so that the ghosts who were left
in Tartarus would not be jealous that she had escaped.

Thyrsus (thèr'sus). One of the most common emblems of
Dionysus and his thiasus and votaries. It was a staff tipped
with an ornament like a pine-cone and sometimes wrapped
round with ivy and vine branches, and appears in various
modifications in ancient representations. The bacchantes
carried thyrsi in their hands when they celebrated their orgies.

Tiresias or *Teiresias* (tī-rē'si-ạs). In Greek mythology, a son of
Everes and the nymph Chariclo. He was a blind Theban
seer, whose very long life was three times as long as that of
an ordinary man's, or, as some say, lasted for seven genera-

(obscured) errạnt, ardẹnt, actọr; ch, chip; g, go; th, thin; ₮ʜ, then; y, you;
(variable) ḍ as d or j, ṣ as s or sh, ṭ as t or ch, ẓ as z or zh.

tions. His mother was the intimate companion of Athena. According to some accounts, when Tiresias was a child he was roaming the forests one day and chanced to go to the Hippocrene Spring on Mount Helicon to drink. At the moment when he arrived there, Athena and Chariclo were bathing in the pool. Athena laid her hand across his eyes, or some say splashed water into them, and blinded him because he had seen her in her bath. Chariclo chided the goddess for blinding her son. Athena answered that it was not by her will but by the law of the gods that whoever saw them without their permission would be blinded. To atone somewhat for the loss of sight Athena gave him the gift of prophecy and divination, a long life, and the power to retain his mental accomplishments in the Underworld. Or as some say, she caused serpents to cleanse his ears so that he could understand the talk of prophetic birds. Quite another account of how Tiresias became blind has to do with the anger of Hera. According to this account, Tiresias once saw two snakes coupling on Mount Cyllene in Arcadia. He wounded them or, as some say, killed the female, and instantly he was transformed from a man to a woman. For seven years he lived as a woman and was notorious for his love affairs. At the end of that time he again saw two snakes coupling and, as some say, killed the male and was transformed once more into a man. Hera and Zeus, being engaged in an argument about which sex enjoys the physical aspects of love more, decided to consult Tiresias, who had experienced these aspects as both a man and a woman. Hera maintained that the male derived the most pleasure from love-making, and contended that this was why Zeus was so often unfaithful to her. Zeus mocked her and claimed that it was the female who enjoyed it most. On being appealed to, Tiresias agreed with Zeus. If the parts of the pleasure of love were counted as ten, he said, women got nine parts and men only one. This infuriated Hera and she struck Tiresias blind. Zeus, to make up for this, gave him long life and the art of soothsaying. But some say he was blinded because he revealed things to men that only the gods should know. In the reign of Oedipus and Jocasta a plague struck Thebes. Tiresias said it would cease only when the murderer of Laius, Jocasta's former husband, was found and punished. As no one knew who that murderer was Tiresias was at length compelled to inform them that it was Oedipus himself, who had unwittingly murdered his father and sired children on his mother. In the war of the Seven against Thebes, Tiresias predicted to Eteocles, a son of Oedipus who now ruled in his father's place, that Thebes would be victorious if a son of the royal house voluntarily sacrificed himself to Ares. Menoeceus, son of Creon, killed himself and the Seven were routed. Of the seven attacking leaders only Adrastus survived. Ten years later the Epigoni (sons of the Seven against Thebes) attacked the city to avenge their fathers. This time Tiresias advised the Thebans to negotiate with the Argives and to flee the city, for, he said, Thebes would fall when the last of the original seven died, and Adrastus was even now dying of grief over the death of his son Aegialeus who had fallen before Thebes. The Thebans fled and the city fell, as Tiresias had predicted. But Tiresias did not escape with the Thebans. He knew he was fated to die when Thebes fell into the hands of the Argives. As he drew water to drink from a spring, he suddenly died. Tiresias was the father of Manto, a prophetic daughter who was taken by Alcmaeon in the war of the Epigoni and later was sent to Delphi. Some say he had another daughter, Daphne, who became a Sibyl. Tiresias predicted that Narcissus would have a long life, if he never knew himself. According to some, he foretold the heroic exploits of Heracles to Alcmene when Heracles, as an infant, strangled the serpents Hera had sent to kill him. Odysseus, long prevented from returning home after the Trojan War, was instructed by Circe to go to Hades and consult Tiresias to learn the fate that awaited him when he reached his homeland of Ithaca. Tiresias told him Poseidon was angry over the blinding of Polyphemus and would cause him much trouble. He warned Odysseus not to eat the cattle of the sun on Trinacria, told him of the wooers who were besieging Penelope in Ithaca, and said he would avenge their insolence. He also instructed him to seek a land where the men knew not the sea, and told him how he would recognize this land. There he must make sacrifices to Poseidon, after which he could dwell in Ithaca in peace. He also told Odysseus that death would come to him from the sea. All that he predicted came to pass.

Tisamenus   (ti-sam′ẹ-nus). In Greek legend, a son of Orestes and Hermione, daughter of Helen. He was ruler of Sparta and was slain by the descendants of Heracles when they

---

(obscured) errạnt, ardẹnt, actǫr; ch, chip; g, go; th, thin; ᵺн, then; y, you;
(variable) ḍ as d or j, ṣ as s or sh, ṭ as t or ch, ẓ as z or zh.

attacked his country. According to other accounts, he was
not killed by the Heraclidae but lost his life when he was
driven out of Sparta and sought to conquer regions in the
northern part of the Peloponnesus.

Titans (tī'tanz). In Greek mythology, the sons of Gaea and
Uranus. They were Oceanus, Coeus, Hyperion, Crius, Iapetus, and Cronus. Their sisters, the Titanesses, were Tethys,
Rhea, Themis, Mnemosyne, Phoebe, and Thia. Their descendants were also called Titans. Gaea incited them to
make war on Uranus. They dethroned him and made
Cronus ruler in his place. When Zeus succeeded Cronus, the
sons of Iapetus, led by Atlas, made war on Zeus. After a long
struggle, during which the Titans fought from Mount Othrys and the gods fought from Mount Olympus, Zeus secured
the aid of Cyclopes and put the Titans to rout. He hurled
them all except Atlas into Tartarus and set the Hecatonchires to guard them. But some say they were banished and
at length joined Cronus in the Isles of the Blest.

Tithonus (ti-thō'nus). In Greek mythology, a son of Laomedon, and a brother of Priam, king of Troy. Eos fell in love
with his youthful beauty and carried him off. He became the
father of two of her sons, Memnon and Emathion, and settled in the east. Toward the end of the Trojan War Priam
bribed Tithonus with a golden vine to send his son Memnon
to the aid of the Trojans. This led to Memnon's death. Eos
beseeched Zeus to grant immortality to Tithonus. Zeus
granted her request, but as she had forgotten to ask for
perpetual youth for him, Tithonus grew older and older,
and finally shriveled up so that there was not much more left
of him but a chirping voice. Eos shut him up in a chamber
and he was transformed into a grasshopper.

Tityus (tit'i-us). In Greek mythology, the giant son of Zeus
and Elara. Zeus hid Elara in a cave to protect her from the
wrath of Hera, and there her son was born. A cave in Euboea
was named the Elarium in her honor. When Tityus grew up
Hera incited him to attack Leto. As she was on her way to
Delphi, she withdrew to perform some private rite and
Tityus assaulted her. As he seized her veil she cried out, and
her children, Artemis and Apollo, instantly came to her aid
and killed Tityus with their arrows. Because he had had the
presumption to attack one of the immortals Tityus was sent
to the farthest reaches of Tartarus. There he was stretched

out (his body covered nine acres) and pegged down, and vultures were sent to peck at his heart continually. Aeneas saw the awful punishment of Tityus when he visited the Underworld, and the distinguished painter Polygnotus depicted it in his painting of *Odysseus in the Underworld,* in the hall of the Cnidians at Delphi. The tomb of Tityus, a rounded barrow, was shown in Phocis, and in Euboea he was worshiped as a hero and had a shrine.

Tlepolemus   (tle-pol′e̦-mus). In Greek legend, a son of Heracles and Astyocheia, and a grandson of Zeus. As a youth he accidentally killed his father's maternal uncle Licymnius, whom he loved dearly, and was forced by the other sons and grandsons of Heracles to flee. He built a fleet and, after many hardships, landed with his followers in Rhodes, where he founded cities and married Polyxo. As an ally of the Greeks he captained nine ships in the Trojan War. In the war he encountered Sarpedon, son of Zeus, and taunted him with a lack of courage, saying he could not really be the son of Zeus. He then attacked him and although he succeeded in wounding Sarpedon he was slain by the latter.

Tmolus   (tmō′lus). In Greek mythology, a son of Ares. He was a king in Lydia, the husband of Omphale, and, according to some accounts, the father of Tantalus. While out hunting on a mountain Tmolus saw and fell in love with one of the chaste companions of Artemis. He pursued her to the temple of Artemis where she sought refuge before the altar. There Tmolus found her and violated the sanctity of the temple by ravishing her. The maiden hanged herself, but before she died she called on Artemis to avenge her. Artemis sent a wild bull that attacked Tmolus, tossed him in the air with his horns, and caused him to fall on sharp stakes and stones. Tmolus perished as the result of his injuries. His son Theociymenus buried him on the mountain where he died and named it Tmolus after him. As the deity of the forest-covered mountain, Tmolus wore a wreath of oak leaves on his head. He acted as judge in the musical contest between Pan and Apollo and proclaimed Apollo the victor.

Triptolemus   (trip-tol′e̦-mus). In Greek mythology, a favorite of Demeter. His symbol was an ear of wheat. He was everywhere honored as the one who taught the arts of agriculture to mankind. The Eleusinians said he was a son of Celeus and Metanira of Eleusis, or a brother or fellow townsman of

(obscured) errȧnt, ardȩnt, actọr; ch, chip; g, go; th, thin; ᴛʜ, then; y, you;
(variable) ḏ as d or j, ṣ as s or sh, ṭ as t or ch, ẕ as z or zh.

Celeus. The Argives said he was a son of Trochilus, a priest of the mysteries in Argos, who fled to Attica and married a woman of Eleusis who bore him Triptolemus and another son Eubuleus. The Athenians claimed he was the son of Celeus but others said Oceanus was his father and Gaea his mother, or that Dysaules was his father, or even Poseidon. The truth is that many were anxious to claim him because of his great gifts to mankind. Some say he was the only one to recognize the goddess Demeter when she sought shelter in the house of Celeus during her search for Persephone. Triptolemus was able to tell her that the earth had parted and a chariot drawn by black horses and bearing Persephone had disappeared into the chasm. He became a favorite of Demeter and she taught him her sacred rites and mysteries. She also gave him seed wheat, instructed him in the use of the plow, and sent him a chariot drawn by winged serpents in which to travel throughout the world instructing mankind in the arts of agriculture. He went through Europe and Asia spreading the knowledge of agriculture and, some say, he came at last to the land of Scythia. There he revealed his name and his mission to the king, Lyncus. Lyncus pretended to welcome him but, out of jealousy, resolved to kill him. As Triptolemus slept he attacked him with a sword. His effort was in vain; before he could harm Triptolemus, Demeter transformed Lyncus into a lynx. Triptolemus continued his journeying. According to some accounts, he was the founder of Eleusis and established the worship of Demeter there, as well as the festival called the Thesmophoria. He was honored in Eleusis with a temple dedicated to him, and was honored throughout as the patron of agriculture. Some say that when Demeter came to the house of Celeus in Eleusis, she acted as nurse for his son Demophoön, and would have made him immortal had she not been interrupted by the child's mother. In her anger at the interruption she dropped the child in the fire in which she had been burning away his mortal parts, and he perished. The goddess promised to bring great honor to his brother Triptolemus to atone for his loss.

Triton   (trī′ton). In Greek mythology, a gigantic son of Poseidon and the Nereid Amphitrite. He was the brother of Rhode and Benthesicyme and dwelt at the bottom of the sea; he was also thought to frequent the Lake Tritonis in Libya.

---

fat, fāte, fàr, fåll, àsk, fãre; net, mē, hèr; pin, pīne; not, nōte, möve, nôr; up, lūte, pùll; oi, oil; ou out; (lightened) ēlect, agǫny, ūnite;

When the Argonauts voyaging home from Colchis were driven into the desert of Libya by a great storm, Jason propitiated the deities of the land by offering two bronze tripods that had been given to him by the priestess of Delphi before he set out for Colchis. Triton appeared and seized the tripods. In response to requests of the Argonauts he towed the *Argo* back to the sea. He gave Euphemus a clod of Libyan earth that made Euphemus and his descendants masters of Libya. In the later mythology Tritons appear as a class of minor sea-deities, figuring with Nereids in the train of the greater sea-gods. They were conceived as having human figures from the waist up combined with those of fish from the waist down. A common attribute of the Tritons is a shell-trumpet, which they blow to raise or calm storms.

Troilus (trō'i-lus, troi'lus). In Greek legend, a younger son of Hecuba. He was acknowledged as a son of Priam but some say Apollo was his father. According to a prophecy, Troy would not fall to the Greeks in the Trojan War if Troilus reached the age of twenty. Some say Achilles saw Troilus and pursued him to the sanctuary of the temple of Thymbraean Apollo and killed him there, where, according to some accounts, Achilles himself was fated to die. Others say Achilles came upon him while he was exercising his horses near the sea and killed him, or that Troilus dared meet Achilles in face-to-face combat and, having fallen wounded, was dragged to his death by his own horses. In any case, it was certainly Achilles who killed or caused the death of Troilus. The story of Troilus' tragic love for Cressida (or Criseyede or Criseida) comes not from ancient sources but from a poem by a 12th century troubadour. It relates that Troilus was in love with Cressida, a daughter of Calchas, who remained in Troy and was loyal to the Trojans. On the demand of Agamemnon she was restored to her father by Priam, and went to the Greek camp. She betrayed the undying love which she had sworn for Troilus by falling in love and yielding to the caresses of Diomedes.

Trojan (trō'jan) *Horse.*   In Greek legend, the huge wooden horse which the Greeks constructed and left on the beach before Troy in the last days of the Trojan War. The Trojans, believing it to be a sacrifice to Athena, hauled it into the city. But inside the horse were armed warriors. They descended from it in the night, opened the city gates to their comrades,

---

(obscured) errant, ardent, actor; ch, chip; g, go; th, thin; ŦH, then; y, you;
(variable) ḏ as d or j, ş as s or sh, ṭ as t or ch, ẓ as z or zh.

and brought about the fall of Troy. Thus the Greeks, who could not overcome the Trojans by direct assault, penetrated their city by stratagem and brought about its ruin from within. The phrase has come to mean a stratagem or method that appears innocent, or that is carried out in secret, which is used by a foe to penetrate his opponent's camp, literally or figuratively, and weaken it from within. See also, **Wooden Horse.**

Trojan (trō'jạn) **War.** A war between the Greeks and the Trojans, celebrated by ancient writers, notably by Homer in the *Iliad,* which is now thought to have taken place about 1200 B.C. The actual causes of the war have been obscured under layers of myth and legend in which brilliantly imaginative writers recorded the actual event. Trade routes sought by the vigorous and expanding Greek cities may have occasioned the struggle. An unfriendly or uncoöperative power in Troy, which commanded the entrance to the Hellespont, had to be subdued or, as it happened, to be utterly destroyed, to permit the expansion of the peoples of Hellas into the area about the Euxine (Black) Sea. Some of the figures named in the epics had historical prototypes, as Agamemnon and Nestor. Others were added as the creative invention of ancient writers demanded.

As developed in myth and legend, the cause of the Trojan War goes back to the marriage of Peleus and Thetis and was the result of a deliberate plan on the part of Zeus and Themis, for reasons never satisfactorily explained. All the gods and goddesses except Eris were invited to the wedding of Peleus and Thetis. Eris, goddess of discord, took her revenge for being left out by hurling a golden apple inscribed "To the Fairest" at the feet of the goddesses Athena, Hera, and Aphrodite as they stood talking together among the guests. Each of the three goddesses claimed that the apple was intended for her. They appealed to Zeus to settle the dispute, but he wisely refused to make a choice and referred them to a young shepherd on Mount Ida in the Troad who was reputed to be a great and fair judge of beauty. The young shepherd was Paris, son of Priam, king of Troy, and to him the goddesses repaired. Athena offered him wisdom and victory in all his wars if he awarded the apple to her. Hera promised to make him rich and the lord of all Asia. Aphrodite offered him the most beautiful woman

fat, fāte, fär, fåll, åsk, fãre; net, mē, hèr; pin, pīne; not, nōte, mōve, nôr; up, lūte, půll; oi, oil; ou out; (lightened) ẹlect, agọny, ūnite;

in the world for a bride. Paris awarded (the "Judgment of Paris") the apple to Aphrodite. From that time the Trojans, as the race of Paris, suffered the implacable hatred of Hera and Athena. Most of the Olympian deities freely took sides, playing active and decisive roles in the war that resulted from this judgment of Paris.

The fairest woman in the world was Helen, wife of Menelaus, king of Sparta. Paris, although married to the nymph Oenone, went to his father's palace in Troy, and was recognized as that son of Priam and Hecuba who had been left on the mountain to die in his infancy because of prophecies that he would cause the destruction of Troy. He had been saved and brought up by a shepherd. Delighted with his beauty and courage, Priam and Hecuba welcomed their new-found son despite the urgent warnings of Cassandra, Helenus, and other seers that he would bring ruin to Troy. Secretly thinking of Helen, the bride promised him by Aphrodite, Paris offered to go on a mission to Greece to discuss the return of Hesione, sister of King Priam, who had been carried off by Telamon some years before and whom the Greeks had refused to return. If he was unsuccessful in this mission, he volunteered that he might bring back some Greek princess as a hostage. Priam, again disregarding the warnings of his prophetic daughter Cassandra, provided a fleet and Paris set out. Menelaus received him kindly in Sparta and entertained him royally for nine days. At the end of that time, ignoring a fact obvious to all—that Paris was madly in love with Helen —Menelaus blandly sailed off to Crete to his grandfather's funeral, leaving his kingdom and the entertainment of his guest in Helen's charge. Helen eloped with Paris that same night, taking with her her young son and a great treasure, but leaving her only daughter Hermione behind in Sparta. Hera sent great storms that drove Paris' fleet off its course. Furthermore, to avoid pursuit by Menelaus, Paris sailed to Cyprus, Sidon, Phoenicia, and Egypt, so that it was some time before he returned to Troy with Helen.

In the meantime Menelaus had learned of the abduction of Helen. He immediately went to Agamemnon in Mycenae and demanded that an expedition be assembled to sail against Troy and recover her. Agamemnon agreed to do this if peaceful means failed. He sent envoys to Troy to demand the restoration of Helen, but the Trojans refused. According to some accounts, they knew nothing of the matter because Paris had not yet landed in Troy with Helen. But once he did bring her to Troy, all Troy fell in love with her and Priam vowed he would never let her go. As a result, each of several embassies that demanded her return was rejected, and those Trojan advisers who on divers occasions throughout the war counseled that she be restored to her husband were scorned. As peaceful means of regaining Helen failed, Agamemnon called on the Greek princes to fulfill their oath. This oath had been taken under the following circumstances. Helen was so beautiful and had so many suitors that Tyndareus, her supposed father, feared to give her hand to any one of them lest the disappointed suitors turn against him. Odysseus suggested to Tyndareus that he require all the suitors to swear on the joints of a dismembered horse that they would go to the aid of whichever suitor won Helen's hand, in the event that any ill should come to him as a result of his marriage to Helen. Tyndareus adopted this course and all the suitors took the oath. The mightiest and richest princes of Greece had been suitors of Helen; all were now commanded to fulfill their oath and come to the aid of Menelaus. Moreover, Agamemnon added, if the Trojans were not punished for the theft of Helen, no Greek husband could be sure of his wife's safety. Odysseus, although not one of the suitors, was needed for his widom and skill. Reluctantly he came from Ithaca. Achilles, accompanied by his intimate friend Patroclus and leading his Myrmidons, came from Scyrus. Diomedes, fresh from his victory at Thebes, came with his friends Sthenelus and Euryalus. Idomeneus, king of Crete, brought his squire Meriones and 80 ships. Aged Nestor, noted for his wisdom, arrived from Pylus with his sons Thrasymedes and Antilochus. Telamonian Ajax and his half-brother Teucer commanded a fleet from Salamis. Oïlean, or Lesser Ajax, and his half-brother Medon commanded the men of Locris. King Cinyras of Cyprus promised to send 50 ships but defaulted. Tlepolemus, son of Heracles, brought nine ships from Rhodes. Many other heroes and demigods joined Agamemnon's expedition. The Greek fleet, over 1000 ships strong, assembled at Aulis. There, while Agamemnon was sacrificing, a blue serpent with crimson markings on its back darted out, coiled its way up a plane tree and devoured eight nestlings and a mother sparrow in their nest. The serpent was then turned to stone. Calchas, the seer who advised Agamemnon throughout the war, said this was an omen that nine years would be swallowed up and that in the tenth year Troy would fall. Others made the same prophecy about the duration of the war. But some say the war lasted twenty years. Homer has Helen say it is now the twentieth year since she left Sparta.

The Greeks sailed from Aulis and raided the coasts of Asia Minor. Some say they did not know the course to Troy, and that they landed in Mysia and ravaged it under the impression that they were in the Troad. For some time they cruised along the coast, attacking and sacking cities. At length the fleet was scattered by violent storms and the ships returned to their homeland. After nine years, according to some accounts, the fleet again assembled at Aulis. This time unfavorable winds delayed their sailing. In accordance with a prophecy by Calchas, Agamemnon sacrificed his daughter Iphigenia and thus secured favorable winds. Telephus, a king of Mysia who had been wounded in the raids on his shores, had come to Greece to be cured of his wound. He marked out the course the Greeks should take to Troy, and the correctness of his course was confirmed by divination. The fleet sailed once more. They touched at Lesbos and then at the island of Tenedos, within sight of Troy. There Achilles attacked and killed Tenes, who tried to prevent the Greeks from landing on his shores. This Tenes was reputed to be a son of Apollo, and Thetis, among other warnings to her son Achilles, had told him if he killed a son of Apollo, he would die by Apollo's hand. The death of Tenes by Achilles was only one of many signs and portents that foretold to Achilles that he would not survive the Trojan War. On Tenedos also, according to some accounts, Philoctetes, possessor of the bow and arrows of Heracles, was bitten by a snake with such disastrous results that the Greeks were at length compelled to abandon him on Lemnos. According to some accounts, Agamemnon sent Menelaus, Odysseus, and Palamedes to Troy from Tenedos to make a final demand for the return of Helen. They were unsuccessful, and would have been killed by the indignant Trojans if Antenor had not prevented such an outrage against the laws of war and of hospitality. The Greeks now sailed past Sigeum, the headland of Troy, and beached their ships within sight of the city. Protesilaus was the first to leap ashore and, in accordance with a prophecy that the first ashore at Troy would die, was killed; some say, by Hector. The siege of Troy itself which now began, the disastrous quarrel between Agamemnon and Achilles, the death of Patroclus, and the death and burial of Hector, noblest of the Trojans, comprise the *Iliad:* The Trojans were not without allies: heroes and demigods, such as Aeneas, Sarpedon, and Glaucus, had joined them, and, after the death of Hector, Penthesilea the Amazon and Memnon the Ethiopian son of Eos came to the aid of Troy. After inflicting great damage on the Greeks and so discouraging them that Agamemnon considered withdrawal, each was in turn killed by Achilles, who drove the Trojans back into the city each time. But Achilles had run his course. Apollo, some say, directed an arrow from Paris' bow that pierced Achilles' ankle or heel, his one vulnerable spot. Achilles pulled out the arrow and flung it away; it was wafted back to Apollo. Enraged with his wound and blaming Apollo, Achilles with his last strength hurled his spear and killed a Trojan; then he expired. Telamonian Ajax bore his body back to the Greek ships through a raging press of Trojans who were trying to gain possession of their fallen enemy's corpse. The death of Achilles brought about the death of Telamonian Ajax. At the command of Thetis, the armor of Achilles was to be awarded to the bravest of the Greeks. Odysseus was given the honor and the armor. Ajax, who had great ground for thinking he deserved it, was inspired with madness by Athena. In his frenzy he slaughtered innocent cattle under the impression that they were Greeks who had been unfriendly to him. When Athena decided to restore him to sanity, he was appalled at what he had done. In despair at the humiliation he had brought on himself he committed suicide.

The loss of Achilles and Ajax discouraged the Greeks and, as had happened before, they talked of giving up the struggle and sailing for home. Calchas reminded them of the omen of the serpent and the sparrows, and that this was now the tenth year, when victory was prophesied. He informed them that Troy could not be taken without the bow and arrows of Heracles. Their possessor Philoctetes was accordingly fetched from Lemnos and was healed of his wound by

Machaon the physician; then with the arrows of Heracles he
shot Paris. After the death of Paris, Deïphobus and Helenus,
his brothers, struggled for Helen's hand. She was awarded
to Deïphobus, who forcibly married her, and Helenus left
the city. He was captured by the Greeks and told them that
Troy could not be taken without the presence of a bone of
Pelops, nor without Neoptolemus, son of Achilles, nor could
it be taken as long as the Palladium remained in the citadel.
Agamemnon immediately sent for the bone of Pelops, and
to Scyrus for Neoptolemus. Eurypylus, descendant of Heracles, now came to the aid of the Trojans. He fought valiantly
and again drove the Greeks back to their ships. But the gods
intervened, as they had done from the beginning, and
caused Neoptolemus to slay Eurypylus. Odysseus and Diomedes disguised themselves and entered Troy. Some say
Odysseus was recognized by Helen and brought before
Hecuba, that he told them the Greeks' plans and was allowed to go free. Another account is that this mission of
Odysseus was a different one from the raid made with Diomedes, and was in the nature of a scouting sortie. When
Odysseus and Diomedes made their raid Diomedes scaled
the wall of Troy from the shoulders of Odysseus, gained the
Palladium, and returned with it to the Greek camp. In any
event, it seems agreed that Odysseus at some time entered
Troy secretly, was recognized by Helen and Hecuba, and
was allowed to return to the Greek ships.

   In all the years of the war there had been some in Troy
who advised that Helen be restored to Menelaus, with all the
treasure she had brought with her. This advice had always
been scorned, and those who gave it were regarded almost
as traitors. Now, after the disasters following the deaths of
Hector, Penthesilea, Memnon, Eurypylus, and Paris, there
were some in Troy who advised flight from the city, rather
than be caught like rats in a trap. Others said the war should
be carried on from the walls and towers of Troy rather than
on the plain where the great battles had cost so many lives.
But this advice, as militarily sound as the other was politi-
cally sound, was rejected.

   The Greeks too had their hours of doubt and despair. It
was now proposed to take the city by stratagem rather than
by direct assault. The idea of the Wooden Horse was put
forth, some say by Odysseus, who in any case took credit for

(obscured) errạnt, ardẹnt, actọr; ch, chip; g, go; th, thin; ᵺн, then; y, you;
(variable) ḍ as d or j, ṣ as s or sh, ṭ as t or ch, ẓ as z or zh.

the idea. This proposal was enthusiastically adopted, except by Neoptolemus and Philoctetes who protested that it was cowardly. Epeus, aided by Athena, built the Wooden Horse in three days. Odysseus now proposed that the Greeks leave it on the beach before Troy with the most valiant warriors concealed inside it. The fleet would sail away behind the island of Tenedos, the camp fires would be doused, and the Trojans would happily conclude that the Greeks had sailed for home. In addition, Odysseus proposed that some one be left behind with a tale to account for his presence, who would persuade the Trojans to draw the Wooden Horse with its deadly freight inside the walls of Troy. Sinon volunteered to carry out this part of the plan. When the Trojans saw that the Greeks had apparently departed, they swarmed out onto the beach to examine the great horse. As they wondered about it and heard Laocoön and Cassandra plead with them to destroy it or it would destroy Troy, Sinon, who had arranged to be captured, was dragged forward. He said he had just escaped being sacrificed by the Greeks, who had sailed for home in despair, and that the Wooden Horse was an offering to Athena, to propitiate the goddess for the theft of the Palladium. The offering had purposely been made huge so that it could not be taken inside the walls of Troy, for the city that possessed it would conquer Europe. On hearing this the Trojans, deaf to the warnings of Cassandra and Laocoön, resolved to take the enormous offering into the city. The fact that a serpent slithered from the sea and crushed Laocoön and his two sons in its coils, indicated to them that the gods had punished Laocoön for his doubts and confirmed them in their resolve to take the offering into the city. They breached the walls to make way for the horse and rolled it inside the walls, decorated it with flowers and performed ritual dances about it. Then the Trojans went wearily to bed. In the night Sinon gave the signal to the men in the Wooden Horse, lighted a beacon to advise the Greek fleet to return from Tenedos, and opened the gates of Troy. The Greeks streamed in and sacked the city. Priam was slain by Neoptolemus before the altar of Zeus in his courtyard. Deïphobus, Helen's new husband, was killed and horribly mangled. The Greeks protected the family of Antenor by hanging a leopard's skin over the door of his house, because he had protected early envoys from the Greeks and had consistently advised the restoration of Helen. Aeneas escaped with his father and son from the burning city, carrying the gods of Troy with him. Astyanax, young son of Hector, was hurled to his death from the towers of Troy. Polyxena, daughter of Priam, was sacrificed on Achilles' tomb. In the division of the captives, Odysseus took Hecuba, Agamemnon claimed Cassandra, and Neoptolemus took Andromache. When the Greeks departed with their captives, Troy was in flames. The city, which had been an important bastion guarding the Hellespont and thus the entry into the Euxine Sea, never regained its important role. In fact, for centuries, even the site was lost.

Trophonius (trō-fō'ni-us). In Greek mythology, a son of Erginus the Argonaut, of Orchomenus, or, according to some accounts, a son of Apollo. He was the brother of Agamedes. He and his brother, born in their father's old age, were famous builders. According to legend, they built the temple at Delphi on foundations laid by Apollo, the temple of Poseidon at Mantinea, the chamber of Alcmene in Thebes, and the treasuries of Augeas in Elis and of Hyrieus in Boeotia. To reward them for their labors on his temple Apollo told them to feast and be merry for six days, and on the seventh day they would receive the greatest gift in his power. They feasted and enjoyed themselves for six days. On the seventh they went to bed and died peacefully in their sleep. An easy death was Apollo's best gift. According to another account, when the brothers built the treasury for Hyrieus, king of Boeotia, they so constructed it that one stone could be removed, allowing them to rob the treasury at will. Agamedes was caught in the act by a trap set by Hyrieus, and Trophonius cut off his brother's head and removed it so that no one would know who the thief was and he would not be implicated. Trophonius was at once swallowed up by the earth. He had an oracle in a cavern at Lebadia in Phocis, which enjoyed great repute for centuries. Croesus and many leading Greeks and Romans consulted it down to historical times. The ritual for consulting the oracle was most intricate, and of such solemnity that suppliants lost their ability to laugh for some time after consulting it; and it came to be said of unusually sober persons that they must have visited Trophonius. Suppliants at the oracle were addressed, once they had penetrated to an inner cavern, by the ghost of

---

(obscured) errạnt, ardẹnt, actọr; ch, chip; g, go; th, thin; ŦH, then; y, you;
(variable) ḍ as d or j, ş as s or sh, ṭ as t or ch, ẓ as z or zh.

Trophonius in the form of a serpent. The payment to the oracle was made in the form of honey cakes.

Tros (trōs). Named by Homer as a son of Erichthonius and a grandson of Dardanus. He gave his name to the Trojans, and the region about Troy, the Troad, is named in honor of him. By his wife Callirrhoë, daughter of the river-god Scamander, he had three sons, Assaracus, Ganymede, and Ilus, and one daughter, Cleopatra. Ganymede, most beautiful of mortals, was taken up into heaven by Zeus to become his cupbearer. To atone for the loss of his son, Zeus gave Tros his immortal horses. Boreas fell in love with these mares and they bore swift fillies that bounded over the sea. The horses were ultimately inherited by Laomedon, grandson of Tros, who promised them to Heracles but failed to deliver them.

Tyche (tī′kē). In Greek mythology, the goddess of fortune. Some say she was the daughter of Zeus, by whom she was given the power to decide the lot of individual mortals. She could assure prosperity, wealth, and good luck, but she might capriciously deprive one of all good fortune for no reason at all, or because the beneficiary of her gifts failed to make proper sacrifices to her. The overwhelming aspect of Tyche was her uncertainty. She became identified with the Roman Fortuna and, like her, is depicted with the cornucopia of plenty and the wheel of fortune.

Tydeus (tī′dūs, tid′ē-us). In Greek legend, a son of Oeneus of Calydon. Some say he killed his brother, others say he killed his cousins, and still others say any deaths that he caused were accidental. In any case, he was banished from Calydon and went to the court of Adrastus, king of Argos. There he quarreled with Polynices, son of Oedipus, who had been banished from Thebes. Adrastus separated them and was reminded of an oracle which advised him to yoke his daughters in marriage to a boar and a lion. He gave his daughter Deïpyle to Tydeus, who had the device of a boar painted on his shield, and promised to restore Tydeus to his lands. Deïpyle bore Diomedes to Tydeus. Adrastus first proposed to restore Polynices, who bore the device of a lion on his shield and to whom he gave his daughter Aegia (or Argia), to the throne of Thebes. Tydeus, in the expectation that he would be restored on the successful completion of the expedition, was eager to march against Thebes and was one of the Seven who made up the leaders of the expedition. He

fat, fāte, fär, fåll, àsk, fãre; net, mē, hèr; pin, pīne; not, nōte, möve, nôr; up, lūte, pull; oi, oil; ou out; (lightened) ēlect, agǫny, ūnite;

was sent as an envoy to Thebes to demand the restoration of Polynices. The Thebans refused. Tydeus then challenged the leading Theban warriors to single combat, and over-came each of his opponents until no more dared to meet him. On his way to rejoin the Argives where they had stopped at Cithaeron, he was set upon by 50 Theban warri-ors who attacked him from ambush. He killed them all ex-cept Maeon, whom he allowed to escape. In the attack on Thebes Tydeus was wounded by Melanippus. But as Tydeus was a favorite of Athena, the goddess came hurrying up with a drug she had procured from Zeus that would cure him and make him immortal. But Amphiaraus, who hated Tydeus because he was one of the causes of the war against Thebes, cut off Melanippus' head (some say Tydeus, though wounded, had killed Melanippus, others say it was Am-phiaraus), and gave it to Tydeus, pretending it would cure him. Tydeus split the skull and gulped down the brains of Melanippus. Athena, arriving on the scene at that moment, was so revolted by this sight that she refrained from giving Tydeus the magic drug that would have immortalized him, and he died of his wound. Some say Maeon, in gratitude for being spared by Tydeus, buried his body.

Tyndareus   (tin-dār'i-us). In Greek legend, a son of Gorgoph-one, daughter of Perseus, and Oebalus, king of Sparta. His brothers were Icarius and Hippocoön. He succeeded his father to the throne but was driven out by Hippocoön and his sons, and fled to Thestius, king of Aetolia. There he married Leda, daughter of Thestius, who bore Helen, Cas-tor and Polydeuces, and Clytemnestra. Some say Castor and Clytemnestra were the children of Tyndareus, the others having been fathered by Zeus. Others say only Clytemnestra was his child. But he passed as the father of them all. Once when sacrificing to the gods, Tyndareus carelessly forgot Aphrodite. To punish him, Aphrodite caused his daughters to become notorious adulteresses. Tyndareus was restored to the throne of Sparta by Heracles. Helen had so many powerful suitors that he feared to give her to any one of them lest the others turn on him in wrath. In return for his promise to help Odysseus win Penelope, daughter of Icarius, Odysseus advised him to require the suitors to take an oath that they would come to the aid of the man who married Helen if any ill should come to him as a result of his marriage. Tyndareus followed this advice and, all the suitors having taken the oath, awarded his beautiful daughter to Menelaus, who also became his heir on the death of Castor and Polydeuces. Tyndareus also compelled Thyestes to relinquish the throne of Mycenae to Agamemnon, and forgave Agamemnon for slaying Clytemnestra's husband and making her his wife by force. Some say that Tyndareus and Leda reared their grandson Orestes following the death of Agamemnon, but when Orestes later killed Clytemnestra and her lover, Tyndareus caused him to be brought to trial for matricide. Tyndareus, whose tomb was at Sparta, was one of those said to have been raised from the dead by Asclepius.

Tyndaridae (tin-dãr′i-dē). A name applied to Castor and Polydeuces as the children of Tyndareus, their supposed father.

ZEUS AND TYPHON
Black-figured Greek hydria, 6th century B.C.
Munich

Typhon (tī′fọn). [Also: *Typhoeus.*] In Greek mythology, the son of Gaea, who in anger over the defeat of her sons the Titans, by Zeus, lay with Tartarus and produced Typhon in a cave in Cilicia. He was a tremendous monster, whose body consisted of snakes from the hips down. On his long arms he had serpents heads in place of hands. By Echidna, Typhon was the father of many monsters: Cerberus, the Hydra, the Chimaera, Orthrus, the Sphinx of Thebes, the dragon that guarded the Golden Fleece, and some say he was also the father of the Nemean Lion and of the eagle that daily gnawed at the liver of Prometheus. Incited thereto by Gaea, Typhon attacked Zeus and the Olympian gods. They fled, taking the form of various animals to escape him. Zeus hurled a thunderbolt and a sickle at him and burned and wounded him. Typhon fled, but when Zeus overtook him he overcame Zeus and cut the sinews of his hands and feet. He took Zeus to the cave in Cilicia, set a dragon to guard him, and hid the sinews. Hermes and Pan came to the cave and succeeded in stealing the sinews and restoring them to the god. Now that he could move again Zeus pursued Typhon with his thunderbolts. Typhon fled to Thrace and hurled mountains at Zeus, but Zeus struck him over and over again, and Typhon, wounded, made off. Some say he wandered to Egypt and lies beneath a lake there. Others say he went to Sicily and that there Zeus buried him under Mount Aetna. As Typhoeus, Typhon was the personification of violent, hot windstorms.

Tyro (tī'rō). In Greek mythology, the beautiful daughter of Salmoneus and Alcidice. She was seduced by Sisyphus, her uncle, and bore him two sons, whom she destroyed. Her stepmother Sidero treated her cruelly. In Elis, to which Salmoneus had gone from Thessaly, Tyro fell in love with the river-god Enipeus, and spent many lonely hours on the banks of his river wooing him. But Enipeus did not respond to her overtures. Instead Poseidon took advantage of the situation. He disguised himself as Enipeus and invited Tyro to join him at the river. After casting her into a deep sleep he raised up a great wave to hide him and ravished Tyro. She bore him twin sons, Pelias and Neleus, but exposed them on the mountain rather than subject herself to the anger of her stepmother by acknowledging her children. Some say she put the children in a chest and set them afloat on the Enipeus River, but in either case, they were saved, and when they grew up they avenged their mother for the cruel treatment she had suffered at Sidero's hands by killing the latter. Tyro married Cretheus, who founded Iolcus and was another of her uncles, and by him was the mother of Aeson, Amythaon, and Pheres.

(obscured) errạnt, ardẹnt, actọr; ch, chip; g, go; th, thin; ᴛʜ, then; y, you; (variable) ḍ as d or j, ṣ as s or sh, ṭ as t or ch, ᶎ as z or zh.

Ulysses (ū-lis′ēz). Latin name of **Odysseus.**

Upis (ö′pis). Ancient pre-Hellenic goddess of childbirth, whose name was later given to Artemis in reference to her function as birth goddess.

Urania (ū-rā′ni-ạ). One of the nine daughters of Zeus and Mnemosyne. She is the muse of astronomy and celestial forces, and the arbitress of fate, second only to Calliope in the company of the Muses. Her usual attributes are a globe, which she often holds in her hand, and a little staff or a compass for indicating the course of the stars. According to some accounts, Urania was the mother of the poet Linus by Apollo. See **Muses.**

Uranus (ū′rạ-nus, ū-rā′nus). In Greek mythology, the god and personification of the sky. Some say he was the first ruler of the world, and that he received his scepter from Nyx (Night). According to others he was the first child of Gaea, born while she slept. The gentle, fertile rains he sent on her caused trees and verdure to grow, and brought forth the mountains as well. His children by Gaea were: the Hecatonchires, Briareus, Cottus, and Gyges, who each had 100 hands and were the most terrible of the sons of Uranus and Gaea; the Cyclopes, Arges, Steropes, and Brontes, tyrannous-souled giants who had one eye in the middle of their foreheads, and who gave the thunderbolts to Zeus; the Titans, Oceanus, Coeus, Hyperion, Crius, Iapetus, and Cronus who hated his father; the Titanesses, Tethys, Rhea, Themis, Mnemosyne, Phoebe, and Thia. Uranus hated the Cyclopes and hid them in Tartarus. This so aroused the fury of Gaea that she plotted with the Titans to destroy Uranus. While he slept, all the Titans except Oceanus attacked him. Cronus used a sickle that had been forged by the Telchines and given to him by Gaea to cut off his father's genitals. He flung them and the sickle into the sea. Drops of blood falling on Gaea (Earth) from the dismembered parts of Uranus caused Gaea to produce the Erinyes (Furies), the Melic

fat, fāte, fär, fåll, ȧsk, fāre; net, mē, hėr; pin, pīne; not, nōte, möve, nôr; up, lūte, pull; oi, oil; ou out; (lightened) ēlect, agǫny, ūnite;

nymphs, and some say Aphrodite was born from the foam which was caused when Uranus' genitals fell into the sea. Some say the sickle that Cronus hurled from him fell into the sea near Drepanum in Sicily. After the mutilation of Uranus the Titans released their brothers, the Cyclopes, and made Cronus their ruler, but as Uranus was dying he prophesied that Cronus would also be dethroned by one of his own children.

Venus   (vē'nus). In Roman mythology, the goddess of grace and love. Originally she was an Italic goddess of gardens and growth, and only at a comparatively late period became identified with the Greek goddess of love, Aphrodite. In medieval times her name became synonymous with earthly love as contrasted with spiritual love.

Vesta   (ves'ta). Hearth-goddess of the ancient Romans, equivalent to the Greek Hestia.

Vulcan   (vul'kan). In Roman mythology, the god of fire, especially volcanic fire. Originally an independent, and not benevolent, deity, he became completely identified with the Greek Hephaestus, and as such patron of metallurgy and handicrafts.

Vuvos   (vö'vôs). See *Cocytus.*

Wooden Horse, The   or   *Trojan Horse.* An immense figure of a horse, built by Epeus, with which the Greeks tricked the Trojans and so took Troy, according to Greek legend. As described by the epic poet Tryphiodorus (5th century A.D.), it was built of wood from the plain of Ida, which had also provided wood for the fleet in which Paris sailed when he abducted Helen. It was white, had a purple mane fringed with gold, eyes of sea-green beryl and red amethyst, and had rows of ivory teeth in its jaws. The harness was purple, inlaid with ivory and bronze. Under the hoofs were wheels for propelling it. It was left on the beach before the walls of Troy. Inside many Greeks were hidden. Included among them was Epeus, although he was quaking with fear, because he was the only one who knew how to operate the lock on the trapdoor by which the Greeks had entered the horse. Sinon, a Greek left behind for the purpose, persuaded the Trojans that the horse was an offering to Athena, and they hauled it inside the walls in spite of the warnings of Cassandra and Laocoön. Cassandra, prophesying the evil it would bring, foretold the deaths of Priam, Polyxena, and Agamemnon, but no one believed her. Laocoön hurled his spear into its side and uttered the warning (as recorded in the *Aeneid*), "Timeo Danaos et dona ferentes." (I fear the Greeks even when they bring gifts.) Laocoön was destroyed by a sea monster and the Trojans mistakenly interpreted this as a punishment for his doubts. Once inside the walls, the Trojans decked it with flowers and performed the Crane dance around it. This was a dance which Theseus did before the altars of Delos, and its winding movements imitated his path as he escaped from the labyrinth of the Minotaur. With joy and relief the Trojans offered sacrifices to the gods, but the fires on the altars fizzled out, the victims didn't burn, the smoke rose blood red from the fires, and statues of the gods wept. Nevertheless the Trojans refused to be warned and went wearily to bed. During the night the Greeks let themselves out of the horse, opened the gates of Troy to their comrades who had returned from behind the island of Tenedos at their signal, and from within the city the Greeks laid waste the Trojan citadel.

Xanthus (zan'thus). In Homeric legend *(Iliad)*, one of a pair of immortal horses. His mate was Balius. They were the children of Podarge the Harpy, and Zephyrus the West Wind. Poseidon gave them to Peleus the father of Achilles. Achilles loaned them to Patroclus and they wept when he was slain by Hector. Temporarily endowed with speech by Hera when Achilles in his turn yoked them for war, Xanthus

fat, fāte, fär, fåll, àsk, fãre; net, mē, hėr; pin, pīne; not, nōte, mȯve, nôr; up, lūte, pùll; oi, oil; ou out; (lightened) ẹlect, agǫny, ūnite;

promised him a safe return from this battle but foretold that soon thereafter he would be slain by a god and a hero.

Xanthus. In Homeric legend, the name given by the gods to the river-god of the Scamander River in the Troad. When Zeus at last gave permission to the gods to interfere in the Trojan War as they chose, Xanthus at first took no part. Then, horrified by the slaughter Achilles was wreaking, Xanthus asked him to kill on the plain and not to clog up his waters with Trojan corpses. Achilles scornfully rejected his plea. Then Xanthus rose up in anger, flooded his banks and pursued Achilles with tree trunks and boulders tumbling in his swollen waters and sought to drown Achilles. As the river raged after Achilles, Hera, alarmed for him, called on her son Hephaestus to set the river afire. He did so, and Xanthus surrendered before the holocaust, promised to withdraw from the battle and never to reënter it, no matter what happened. Xanthus had only entered the fray in the first place to protect his clear flowing streams from the pollution of Achilles' victims, which in their great numbers were strangling the river.

Xuthus (zö´thus). According to Greek tradition, a son of Hellen and the nymph Orseïs, and the brother of Dorus and Aeolus. He fled to Athens from Thessaly and there married Creusa, daughter of King Erechtheus, unaware that she had born a son to Apollo. At the shrine of Apollo in Delphi, whither he and Creusa had gone to seek the god's help because they had no children, Xuthus was told that the first person he met would be his son. As he left the sanctuary he met Ion, a young priest of Apollo, and claimed him as his son. Creusa learned, with the assistance of Apollo's priestess, that this was the son she had borne to the god and abandoned, but it was commanded that Xuthus should never know this. Xuthus was to consider Ion as a gift from the oracle at Delphi. Later, Xuthus and Creusa had two sons, Achaeus and Dorus. After the death of Erechtheus, Xuthus, with the consent of the chief claimants to the throne, appointed Cecrops to succeed Erechtheus. His decision was unpopular and he was banished from Athens and died in exile. Through his sons, Xuthus was the ancestor of the Achaeans and the Ionians.

Zagreus (zā'grẹ-us). Divine child of Orphic mythology, later identified with Dionysus. The story is that Zeus, in serpent form, begat Zagreus on Persephone, and intended to bestow on him unlimited power. He set the Curetes to guard his cradle in a cave on Crete, and they clashed their weapons about him even as they had done for Zeus in his infancy. Hera, out of jealousy, induced the Titans to do away with the boy. They daubed their faces with gypsum to disguise themselves and came to Zagreus in the night. First they beguiled him to them with such toys as golden apples, a bull-roarer, dice, and tufts of wool, then they set upon him to kill him. Zagreus attempted to save himself by a series of rapid transformations. He changed himself into a lion, serpent, tiger, and bull, but the Titans grasped him firmly in this last transformation, tore him apart, and devoured him. Athena managed to save the child's heart. Some say she put it into a gypsum figure and breathed life into it, thus making Zagreus immortal; others say Zeus swallowed the heart of Zagreus and thus was enabled to rebeget Zagreus in the new Dionysus, son of Semele.

Zephyrus (zef'i-rus). [Also: ***Zephyr.***] In Greek mythology, a personification of the west wind, poetically regarded as the mildest and gentlest of all the winds. He was the son of Eos and Astraeus, or of Aeolus. By the Harpy Podarge he was the father of the two marvelous horses, Balius and Xanthus, that Achilles took with him to the Trojan War. Zephyrus married the nymph Chloris, who bore him a son, Carpus. The Romans identified Favonius, their west wind, with Zephyrus.

Zetes (zē'tẹs). An Argonaut, the winged son of Boreas and Orithyia, and the twin of Calais. See ***Boreadae.***

Zethus (zē'thus). In Greek legend, a son of Antiope and Zeus and twin brother of Amphion. When the twins built the walls of Thebes Zethus boasted of his great strength in placing the huge stones, but Amphion, with his lyre, played so beautifully that the stones slid into place by themselves. According to some accounts, Zethus married Aëdon and was the father of Itylus. According to others, he married Thebe, from whom the city of Thebes took its name. See *Amphion.*

Zeus (zös). The chief of the Olympian gods, whose power is greater than that of all the other gods together. The dual attitude of the Greeks toward their gods is brilliantly illuminated by their contradictory concepts of Zeus. He is "The Father of gods and men," the supreme ruler who grasped kingly power and from whom the power of mortal kings is derived, as he gave the golden scepter fashioned by Hephaestus to Pelops as a sign of kingship. He is Cosmetas

ZEUS
Red-figured Greek psykter, Pan Painter, c490 B.C.
Munich

(*Orderer*), who presides over the state as well as over the family unit. He punishes crime, avenges wrongs, protects suppliants. All the good or evil that falls to the lot of man is distributed by the impartial hand of Zeus, who draws the lot of man from two urns placed at his side and weighs out man's fate on golden scales. He is a god of the sky (his name is derived from a word meaning "bright sky"), who is considered to dwell on all mountain tops, but whose special home is Olympus. Thus he is "Olympian Zeus," the lord of heaven, in whose honor the Olympic Games were celebrated at Olympia in Elis. He wields the thunderbolt and the lightning, he sends the sudden storm. He is "The Cloud-gatherer" who drops the beneficent rain, brightens the skies, or breathes favorable winds as needed. He is the founder and patron of all the institutions of civilization and religion, and the maintainer of justice, law, and order. He is the giver of oracles, with an ancient and revered shrine at Dodona, at Olympia, and other places. Because his will is not always properly understood by mortals he is called "Lord of the crooked counsel." In contrast to the great civilizing and ethical force exerted by the worship of Zeus that pervaded every phase of life, is the Zeus of the Greek myths, abundantly endowed with the frailties and appetites of mortals, and immortally capable of indulging them. It is probable that the legends grew up locally to connect specific local gods or heroes or families with the great god Zeus. As the stories were accepted throughout Greece they were woven into the bewildering complex series of relationships, with incidents to explain them, that present Zeus in two violently contrasting aspects—the god to whom all honor and devotion was owed and given as the supreme ruler of gods and men, and the supermortal who could perform, on a lavish scale, all that imperfect mortal men would like to do.

Zeus was the son of Cronus and Rhea, hence his surname Cronides (*Son of Cronus*). An oracle of Gaea had foretold that Cronus would be overthrown by one of his children, even as he had overthrown his father Uranus. To prevent the fulfillment of the oracle, Cronus swallowed his children as soon as they were born, first Hestia, then Demeter, Hera, Hades, and Poseidon in succession. When the time neared for Zeus to be born Rhea resolved to forestall Cronus. The Arcadians say Rhea went to Mount Lycaeus, in Arcadia, and there at a place called Cretea, where no living creature casts a shadow, she gave birth to Zeus. The infant god was washed in the Neda River and then conveyed by Gaea to the nymphs of Crete. The Messenians claim his birthplace was on Mount Ithome in their land. Thebes, Aegium in Achaea, Olenus in

Aetolia, Mount Ida in the Troad, and so many others that, as Pausanias justly says, it would be impossible to name them all, also claimed to be the birthplace of the god. The generally accepted account is that he was born in a cave on Mount Ida, in Crete, or in the cave of Dicte there. When Cronus demanded his last child, Rhea gave him a stone wrapped in swaddling clothes, which he promptly swallowed. The infant Zeus was handed over to the nymphs Adrastea and Ida, daughters of Melisseus. They fed him on honey and the milk of the goat Amalthea, and the Curetes crashed their shields to drown out the infant's cries so that Cronus would not discover how he had been tricked. When Zeus grew up he sought the Titaness Metis who, according to some accounts, was his first wife. She advised him of a potion by which he could compel Cronus to disgorge his brothers and sisters. Zeus disguised himself as the cupbearer of Cronus and gave him the potion. Hestia, Demeter, Hera, Hades, and Poseidon were cast up, as was the stone Rhea had given Cronus in place of Zeus. The stone was set up at Delphi, and was called Omphalos *(Navel),* as being the center of the earth. Zeus, with his brothers as allies, made war on Cronus and the Titans. After the war had dragged on for ten years without a decision, Gaea told Zeus he would defeat Cronus and the Titans if he released the Cyclopes and the Hecatonchires (Briareus, Cottus, Gyges) whom Cronus had locked up in Tartarus. Zeus went to Tartarus and killed Campe the jaileress. He took her keys and freed the Cyclopes and the Hecatonchires. The Cyclopes forged the thunderbolt for him, gave a cap of invisibility to Hades, and a trident to Poseidon. With their help Cronus and the Titans were overcome, and all save Atlas were hurled into Tartarus, where the Hecatonchires were set to guard them. Having made themselves masters, Zeus, Hades, and Poseidon cast lots into a helmet to divide the rule of the universe. In the lot-drawing Zeus drew dominion over the heavens, Poseidon over the sea, and Hades over the Underworld. The earth and Olympus were to remain common to all. Because of superior divine endowment, Zeus became chief of the three rulers. He decreed that the oaths of the gods must be sworn by the waters of the Styx, because Styx and her children had voluntarily come to his aid in the war with the Titans. Some say Zeus was harsh in establishing himself as supreme ruler, and that his harshness extended to mankind. He denied them the gift of fire lest they make themselves the equal of the gods, and punished Prometheus, who in his pity for vulnerable and weak man stole fire from heaven and gave it to him. Zeus commanded Hephaestus to bind Prometheus to a crag in the Caucasus, where an eagle daily gnawed at his liver, which was renewed each night. Hera, Poseidon, Apollo, and the other gods, except peaceful Hestia, conspired against Zeus. They overcame him as he slept and bound him with thongs tied with a hundred knots. Thetis the Nereid called the hundred-handed Briareus to untie the knots and secured his release. As leader in the conspiracy, Zeus scourged Hera, and he punished Apollo and Poseidon by sending them to serve Laomedon, king of Troy. The other gods were forgiven on their promise never again to rebel against Zeus.

Some say Gaea, who had helped Zeus overthrow Cronus and the Titans with her advice, was enraged at the punishment Zeus meted out to them and brought forth a race of Giants to war against him. Others say the Giants waged war on Zeus because they were angered at his harsh treatment of their brothers the Titans. Because of an oracle that none of the Giants would perish at the hands of the gods, Zeus sent Athena to find Heracles and bring him to the aid of the gods. He ordered Helius, Selene, and Eos to dim their light, and so stop the battle, while Athena and Heracles searched for a magic herb that would render Heracles invulnerable. When they found it, Athena led Heracles to the Phlegraean Plain, which some say was in Chalcidice and some say was in Italy, where he did valiant service in routing the Giants. Gaea was more enraged than ever, and brought forth Typhon in the Corycian Cave in Cilicia. Typhon attacked the gods in heaven and they fled in terror to Egypt, transforming themselves into various animals to escape his fiery breath; Zeus took the form of a ram, but when Athena accused him of cowardice he assumed his own shape, hurled his thunderbolts at Typhon and struck him with an adamantine sickle. He struggled with Typhon on Mount Casius in Syria and was overcome. Typhon wrested the sickle from him and cut the sinews of the hands and feet of Zeus. In a helpless condition, Zeus was carried off to the cave in Cilicia by Typhon, who gave him to the dragon Delphyne to guard, and who hid the sinews of Zeus in a bearskin. Hermes and Pan stole into the cave, found the sinews of Zeus, and replaced them on his limbs. With renewed strength he sought out and attacked Typhon. He pursued him to Mount Nysa, where the Fates aided Zeus by deceiving Typhon into stopping to eat some fruits, under the pretense that they would restore his strength. Zeus came up, hurling thunderbolts. Typhon fled to Thrace and made a stand there. He flung whole mountains at Zeus, who parried them with his thunderbolts. They fell on Typhon and so crushed him that the stream ran red with his blood and was henceforth called Haemus (*Bloody*). As with failing strength Typhon fled through the sea, Zeus hurled Mount Aetna on him and crushed him beneath it forever. There was now no power, god or demigod, to question the authority of Zeus.

Zeus desired the Titaness Metis, and sought to ravish her. She transformed herself into various shapes to escape him, but he seized and violated her. An oracle of Gaea foretold that the child she would bear him would be a girl, and that if she bore him another child it would be a son who would overcome his father. On learning of this oracle, Zeus took a leaf from his father's book and straightway swallowed Metis and her unborn child. He maintained that Metis continued to give him good counsel from inside his belly. After some time had passed, Zeus was afflicted with a violent headache as he walked on the shores of the Lake Tritonis. Prometheus, or as some say, Hephaestus, took up a double-edged ax and smote his brow. Athena, child of Zeus and Metis, sprang fully-armed from his cloven skull. The Titaness Themis bore him the Horae, making him the father of the seasons, and the Moerae. Themis continued to sit by the side of Zeus and give him good counsel, and some call her his wife, but do not explain why she retired from this position. The acknowledged wife of Zeus was his sister Hera. When Zeus first wooed her she rejected his advances. He transformed himself into a cuckoo and approached her in this guise. Hera took up the bird and nestled it in her bosom, whereupon Zeus resumed his own shape and ravished her. The incident was supposed by some to have taken place on Mount Thornax in Argolis, and because of it Zeus was given the surname Coccygius (*Cuckoo*), and the mountain was renamed Cuckoo. The marriage of Zeus and Hera was cele-

(obscured) errạnt, ardẹnt, actọr; ch, chip; g, go; th, thin; ᴛʜ, then; y, you; (variable) ḏ as d or j, ş as s or sh, ṭ as t or ch, ẕ as z or zh.

brated, some say, at Cnossus in Crete. In the temple that was raised on the spot sacrifices were annually offered, and a ceremony was held that reënacted the marriage. Zeus and Hera spent their wedding night, said to have lasted 300 years, on the island of Samos. Hera bore Ares, Ilithyia, and Hebe to Zeus. Their marriage, the only proper marriage on Olympus, was stormy, and marked by continual quarrels. With her spying and her constant recriminations Hera often brought humiliation on Zeus. There was always material at hand for a dispute. On one occasion they argued about which sex enjoyed love-making more. Zeus maintained that the female gets the most pleasure from making love. Hera insisted that women were mere instruments of masculine pleasure. They submitted their dispute to the Theban Tiresias for judgment. He was an authority because he had spent part of his life as a woman. Tiresias declared that if the parts of the pleasures of love-making counted as ten, the female enjoyed nine and the male one. Some say Hera was so vexed by his opinion that she blinded Tiresias. Zeus awarded him long life and prophetic powers. As the wife of Zeus, Hera had great powers and shared his confidence in many respects, but she could not control his interest in and intrigues with other women—goddesses and mortal maidens—despite the jealous watch she kept over his activities. He was the master, and made it plain that he would brook no interference. When Hera incurred his displeasure, as when she caused Heracles to be shipwrecked on the island of Cos, Zeus attached golden bracelets to her wrists and hung her out of heaven, with anvils attached to each of her feet. He had always the thunderbolt at his command to punish any impertinence or rebelliousness, and he had the power to cast out of heaven any who roused his anger, as he hurled Hephaestus to earth for interfering in one of his quarrels with Hera, and as he cast Ate, goddess of folly, out of heaven because she betrayed him into making a rash oath before the birth of Heracles.

Zeus was the father of many famous children—gods, demigods, and heroes. Some say Aphrodite was his daughter by the Oceanid Dione. Leto, daughter of the Titans Coeus and Phoebe, bore him the twin gods Apollo and Artemis. Maia, daughter of Atlas, was the mother of his son Hermes, whom he made the patron of travelers, commerce, and of treaty-making, as well as messenger of the gods. The god Dionysus, whose nurses he transferred to the heavens as the Hyades, was his son by Semele. Eurynome, a daughter of Oceanus, bore him the Charities (Aglaia, Euphrosyne, Thalia). Mnemosyne, with whom he lay for nine nights, bore him the Muses. He was the father of Demeter's daughter Persephone, and looked the other way when Hades carried her off, but later ordered Hades to restore her to her mother. He transferred the Pleiades to the heavens to save them, some say, from the unwelcome attentions of Orion. Of the Pleiades, Taÿgete was the mother of his son Lacedaemon, and Electra of his sons Iasion and Dardanus, the former of whom Zeus slew with a thunderbolt for lying with Demeter in a "thrice-plowed field." Some say he was the father of Pan by Hybris. Elara bore him Tityus. The first mortal woman Zeus embraced was Niobe, daughter (or wife) of Phoroneus; she bore him Argus and, some say, Pelasgus. In a celebrated incident, he pursued Io, daughter of the river-god Inachus, and when about to be discovered by Hera, he transformed Io into a white heifer. After long, tortured wanderings in this form, Io reached the Nile. There she assumed her own shape, Zeus "touched" her, and she bore him Epaphus. Among his other famous children (see separate entries) were Helen and Polydeuces, the children of Leda; Minos, Rhadamanthys, and Sarpedon (allowed by Zeus to live for three generations), sons of Europa; Perseus, son of Danaë, whom he visited in a shower of gold; Amphion and Zethus, sons of Antiope; Arcas, son of Callisto whom he transformed into a bear to save her from the wrath of Hera and whose image he placed among the stars as the Great Bear; Aeacus, for whom he transformed ants into men, son of Aegina; and Heracles whom he made immortal, the son of Alcmene, the last mortal woman Zeus embraced. And some say he was the father of Endymion, who chose to remain ageless in eternal sleep; of Hellen, the ancestor of the Hellenes; and of many others. He vied with Poseidon for the favors of the Nereid Thetis, but when informed by an oracle of Gaea that her son would be greater than his father he gave her to a mortal, Peleus, in marriage.

As a god who punished wickedness and avenged wrongs, Zeus sent a great flood to destroy the men of the Bronze Age for their evil ways. From the flood Deucalion and Pyrrha

(obscured) errạnt, ardẹnt, actọr; ch, chip; g, go; th, thin; ᵺн, then; y, you; (variable) ḍ as d or j, ṣ as s or sh, ṭ as t or ch, ẓ as z or zh.

were spared because of their piety, and in answer to their
prayers Zeus instructed them how to repeople the earth.
Some say he sent the flood because of the wickedness of
Lycaon and his sons. For from time to time Zeus visited the
earth in disguise to test the hearts of men. When he came
to Lycaon's house he was served with human flesh. In disgust at such wickedness Zeus overturned the banquet table
and resolved to wipe out mankind with a flood. Others say
he first turned Lycaon and his sons into wolves and then sent
the flood. But when he visited the humble house of Baucis
and Philemon, and was hospitably welcomed and entertained by the poor and devoted couple, he rewarded them
by granting them their wish that they might die together.
Salmoneus, who in his arrogance imitated the lightning and
thunder of Zeus, who took away the sacrifices of the god and
ordered them made to himself, was struck down by a thunderbolt. Alcyone and Ceyx in their pride likened themselves
unto Hera and Zeus. Zeus transformed them into a
kingfisher and a gannet respectively. In anger at the murder
of Apsyrtus by Jason and the Argonauts, Zeus sent great
storms to blow the Argonauts off their course as they sailed
for home. Some say that in the war of the Seven against
Thebes, Zeus struck the Argive Capaneus with the thunderbolt for his boast, as he scaled the walls of Thebes, that not
even the gods could stop him. He caused Tantalus to suffer
fearful torments in Tartarus for abusing the friendship of
the gods, and he fixed Ixion to a fiery wheel that whirls in
the wind for boasting that he had lain with Hera. In fact,
Ixion had embraced a cloud, made by Zeus in the shape of
Hera to trick him and test him.

Many times Zeus acted as mediator in quarrels. When
Apollo and Idas were fighting for Marpessa, he parted them
and granted Marpessa the right to choose between the
god and the mortal. On another occasion he came upon
Apollo and Heracles fighting over the tripod at Delphi. He
parted them with a thunderbolt and made them agree to
become friends. When Laelaps, the hound fated to catch
whatever he pursued, hunted the Teumessian vixen, fated
never to be caught, Zeus solved the dilemma by turning
both to stone. In the dispute between Athena and Poseidon
for control of Athens, he appointed the gods and goddesses
as judges. When they vied for Troezen he decreed that they

must share it. Some say that he arbitrated the dispute between Aphrodite and Persephone for the love of Adonis, but others say he was disgusted by their sordid quarrel over the handsome youth and appointed Calliope to settle it. And he wisely refused to say for whom the golden apple was intended. It was inscribed "For the Fairest," and was flung among the wedding guests, at the marriage of Thetis and Peleus, by Eris, goddess of Discord. He referred Athena, Hera, and Aphrodite, the chief contenders for the apple, to Paris for a decision.

Mount Ida in the Troad was especially sacred to Zeus. In the *Iliad,* Homer represents that Zeus observed the Trojan War from his place on this mountain. The connection of Zeus with Troy was particularly close. Dardanus, the ancestor of the Trojans, was his son. Ganymede, son of Tros, king of Troy, was carried off by an eagle of Zeus to be his cupbearer on Olympus. This was an insult to Hera, whose daughter Hebe had hitherto filled this function, and was an additional reason for Hera's hatred of Troy and an extra cause of dissension with Zeus. When Ilus had built Troy, he asked Zeus for a sign that his city found favor in the sight of Zeus. In answer to his prayer the Palladium fell from heaven. Some say it landed before the tent of Ilus. Others say it fell into the temple of the Citadel, which was still unroofed, and landed on the place where it ever after stood. Apollo and Poseidon with, some say, the help of Aeacus, built the walls of Troy when they were compelled by Zeus to serve Laomedon. Some say that Zeus and Themis planned the Trojan War to glorify his daughter, Helen, by embroiling Europe and Asia for her sake, or to exalt the race of the demigods. In the war, Zeus promised Thetis that he would allow Hector and the Trojans to harass the Greeks until Agamemnon had atoned for the dishonor he had brought her son Achilles. He did this knowing that it would be a cause of bitterness to Hera, who favored the Greeks, and because he owed something to Thetis for having brought Briareus to his aid when he was bound by Hera, Apollo, and Poseidon. During the last year of the Trojan War he warned the gods and goddesses not to interfere on either side, and went off to Mount Ida to weigh the scales in favor of Hector, in fulfillment of his promise to Thetis. He sent Iris to forbid Athena and Hera to aid the Greeks against

Hector, and foretold that Hector would not cease from battle until Achilles rejoined the war to avenge the death of Patroclus. In this, Zeus said that so Fate had ordained and that he was powerless to interfere with Fate. As the Trojans drove the Greeks back with heavy losses, Hera borrowed Aphrodite's magic girdle and so charmed Zeus that he forgot the battle for a while, and then was lulled by Sleep, who had been bribed by Hera. When he awoke and realized what had happened he threatened Hera, and ordered her to secure the withdrawal of Poseidon from the battle. After the death of Patroclus, Achilles reëntered the war to avenge him, and Zeus now gave permission to the gods to take sides as they liked, for he feared lest the fury of Achilles bring immediate destruction on the Trojans if the gods did not take part. And, according to Homer, Zeus laughed in Olympus when he saw the tumult stirred up by Achilles against the Trojans and by the gods as they struggled among themselves. Zeus pitied Hector and would have saved him, but when he weighed his fate in the scales against the fate of Achilles, "down sank the doomful day of great Hector," and Zeus knew that the time had come for Hector to meet his black fate. But when Achilles killed Hector and abused his body, Zeus was angry. He sent Priam to ransom Hector's body and commanded Achilles to treat the old man kindly and to restore to him the body of his son. In the end, as Fate decreed, Troy was destroyed.

The countless epithets of Zeus, describing his special powers, incidents connected with his worship, protection, divine intervention, places of worship, etc., are too numerous to describe individually. The following is an incomplete list: Aegiochus *(Aegis-bearing)*; Anchesmius *(Of Anchesmus)*; Apesantius *(Of Apesas)*; Aphesius *(Releaser)*; Atabyrian; Cappotas *(Reliever)*; Catharsius *(Purifier)*; Cenaean; Chthonius *(Of the Lower World)*; Cithaeronian; Clarius *(Of Lots)*; Croceatas *(Of Croceae)*; Ctesius *(God of Gain)*; Dodonian; Eleutherius *(God of Freedom)*; Herceius *(Of the Courtyard)*; Homagyrius *(Assembler)*; Ithomatas *(Of Ithome)*; Laphystius; Lecheates *(In Childbed)*; Leucaeus *(Of the White Poplar)*; Lycaeus *(Wolfish)*; Mechaneus *(Contriver)*; Megistus *(Almighty)*; Meilichius *(Gracious)*; Moeragetes *(Guide of Fate)*; Hypsistus *(Most High)*; Nemean; Panhellenius *(God of all the Greeks)*; Patrous *(Paternal)*; Philius *(Friendly)*; Phyxius *(God of Flight)*; Polieus *(Ur-*

ban); Semaleus *(Sign-giving)*; Soter *(Savior)*; Sthenius *(Strong)*; Teleius *(Full-grown)*; and Tropaean *(He who turns to flight)*.

The eagle and the oak were sacred to Zeus. His worship was universal throughout Greece by the time of Homer, who describes him with due honor as "the father of gods and men," the god of grace and mercy, the protector of oaths, and of the rights and privileges of hosts and guests. He is the mightiest of the gods, "the Thunderer," "the Cloud-gatherer," the "Olympian lord of the lightnings," and the counselor who by a nod of his immortal head grants the prayer of the suppliant. He is the avenger of wrongs and the giver of victory. All the institutions of civilization and religion derive from Zeus, as do the powers of the other gods. The Romans identified their Jupiter with Zeus, and added the Zeus myths to the ancient Jupiter mythology. In art, the most famous statue of Zeus was the huge ivory and gold image made by Phidias for the temple at Olympia.